Wireless Application
Protocol Programming

Wireless Application Protocol Programming

Hamad Rashid

M&T Books
An imprint of Hungry Minds, Inc.

Best-Selling Books • Digital Downloads • e-Books
Answer Networks • e-Newsletters • Branded Web Sites • e-Learning

New York, NY • Cleveland, OH • Indianapolis, IN

Wireless Application Protocol Programming
Published by
M&T Books
An imprint of Hungry Minds, Inc.
909 Third Avenue
New York, NY 10022
www.hungryminds.com

Copyright © 2002 Hungry Minds, Inc. All rights reserved. No part of this book, including interior design, cover design, and icons, may be reproduced or transmitted in any form, by any means (electronic, photocopying, recording, or otherwise) without the prior written permission of the publisher.

Library of Congress Catalog Card Number: 2001089326

ISBN: 0-7645-3536-6

Printed in the United States of America

10 9 8 7 6 5 4 3 2 1

1O/RQ/RS/QR/IN

Distributed in the United States by Hungry Minds, Inc.

Distributed by CDG Books Canada Inc. for Canada; by Transworld Publishers Limited in the United Kingdom; by IDG Norge Books for Norway; by IDG Sweden Books for Sweden; by IDG Books Australia Publishing Corporation Pty. Ltd. for Australia and New Zealand; by TransQuest Publishers Pte Ltd. for Singapore, Malaysia, Thailand, Indonesia, and Hong Kong; by Gotop Information Inc. for Taiwan; by ICG Muse, Inc. for Japan; by Intersoft for South Africa; by Eyrolles for France; by International Thomson Publishing for Germany, Austria, and Switzerland; by Distribuidora Cuspide for Argentina; by LR International for Brazil; by Galileo Libros for Chile; by Ediciones ZETA S.C.R. Ltda. for Peru; by WS Computer Publishing Corporation, Inc., for the Philippines; by Contemporanea de Ediciones for Venezuela; by Express Computer Distributors for the Caribbean and West Indies; by Micronesia Media Distributor, Inc. for Micronesia; by Chips Computadoras S.A. de C.V. for Mexico; by Editorial Norma de Panama S.A. for Panama; by American Bookshops for Finland.

For general information on Hungry Minds' products and services please contact our Customer Care department within the U.S. at 800-762-2974, outside the U.S. at 317-572-3993 or fax 317-572-4002.

For sales inquiries and reseller information, including discounts, premium and bulk quantity sales, and foreign-language translations, please contact our Customer Care department at 800-434-3422, fax 317-572-4002 or write to Hungry Minds, Inc., Attn: Customer Care Department, 10475 Crosspoint Boulevard, Indianapolis, IN 46256.

For information on licensing foreign or domestic rights, please contact our Sub-Rights Customer Care department at 212-884-5000.

For information on using Hungry Minds' products and services in the classroom or for ordering examination copies, please contact our Educational Sales department at 800-434-2086 or fax 317-572-4005.

For press review copies, author interviews, or other publicity information, please contact our Public Relations department at 317-572-3168 or fax 317-572-4168.

For authorization to photocopy items for corporate, personal, or educational use, please contact Copyright Clearance Center, 222 Rosewood Drive, Danvers, MA 01923, or fax 978-750-4470.

LIMIT OF LIABILITY/DISCLAIMER OF WARRANTY: THE PUBLISHER AND AUTHOR HAVE USED THEIR BEST EFFORTS IN PREPARING THIS BOOK. THE PUBLISHER AND AUTHOR MAKE NO REPRESENTATIONS OR WARRANTIES WITH RESPECT TO THE ACCURACY OR COMPLETENESS OF THE CONTENTS OF THIS BOOK AND SPECIFICALLY DISCLAIM ANY IMPLIED WARRANTIES OF MERCHANTABILITY OR FITNESS FOR A PARTICULAR PURPOSE. THERE ARE NO WARRANTIES WHICH EXTEND BEYOND THE DESCRIPTIONS CONTAINED IN THIS PARAGRAPH. NO WARRANTY MAY BE CREATED OR EXTENDED BY SALES REPRESENTATIVES OR WRITTEN SALES MATERIALS. THE ACCURACY AND COMPLETENESS OF THE INFORMATION PROVIDED HEREIN AND THE OPINIONS STATED HEREIN ARE NOT GUARANTEED OR WARRANTED TO PRODUCE ANY PARTICULAR RESULTS, AND THE ADVICE AND STRATEGIES CONTAINED HEREIN MAY NOT BE SUITABLE FOR EVERY INDIVIDUAL. NEITHER THE PUBLISHER NOR AUTHOR SHALL BE LIABLE FOR ANY LOSS OF PROFIT OR ANY OTHER COMMERCIAL DAMAGES, INCLUDING BUT NOT LIMITED TO SPECIAL, INCIDENTAL, CONSEQUENTIAL, OR OTHER DAMAGES.

Trademarks: Professional Mindware is a trademark or registered trademark of Hungry Minds, Inc. Openwave, the Openwave logo, Openwave SDK, Openwave SDK, Universal Edition, Openwave SDK, WAP Edition are trademarks of Openwave Systems Inc. All rights reserved. All other trademarks are the property of their respective owners. Hungry Minds, Inc., is not associated with any product or vendor mentioned in this book.

Images of Ericsson products used with permission of Telefonaktiebolaget LM Ericsson.

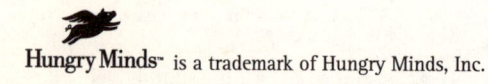

Hungry Minds™ is a trademark of Hungry Minds, Inc.

M&T Books™ is a trademark of Hungry Minds, Inc.

Credits

ACQUISITIONS EDITOR
Grace Buechlein

PROJECT EDITORS
Susan Christophersen
Eric Newman

TECHNICAL EDITORS
Michael Cimilyan
Dale Bulbrook

DEVELOPMENT EDITORS
Susan Christophersen
Kezia Endsley

COPY EDITORS
S. B. Kleinman
Kezia Endsley

EDITORIAL MANAGER
Colleen Totz

SENIOR VICE PRESIDENT, TECHNICAL PUBLISHING
Richard Swadley

VICE PRESIDENT AND PUBLISHER
Joseph B. Wikert

PROJECT COORDINATOR
Nancee Reeves

GRAPHICS AND PRODUCTION SPECIALISTS
Sean Decker, Gabriele McCann,
Kristin McMullan, Laurie Petrone,
Betty Schulte

QUALITY CONTROL TECHNICIANS
Laura Albert, David Faust,
Carl Pirece, TECHBOOKS Production Services

PROOFREADING AND INDEXING
TECHBOOKS Production Services

COVER IMAGE
© Noma/Images.com

About the Author

Hamad Rashid received a B.S. degree in mathematics from Minnesota State University and an M.S. degree in mechanical engineering from the University of Michigan. As a professional trainer for Zsigo Wireless Training, he has in the past five years trained more than 5,000 students in wireless data and related technologies.

Since 1995, he has been Director of Information Technology, Director of Software Engineering, Director of Technical Education, and now Director of Training for the U.S. operations of Zsigo Wireless Training. He has supported and taught WAP and other wireless data technologies around the world and given presentations at conferences in the United States. He is the author of several articles and books, including a Motorola Wireless Java tutorial published by WirelessDeveloper.com and its engineering counterpart published by Zsigo Wireless Training.

for my Mom and Dad, who made it all possible

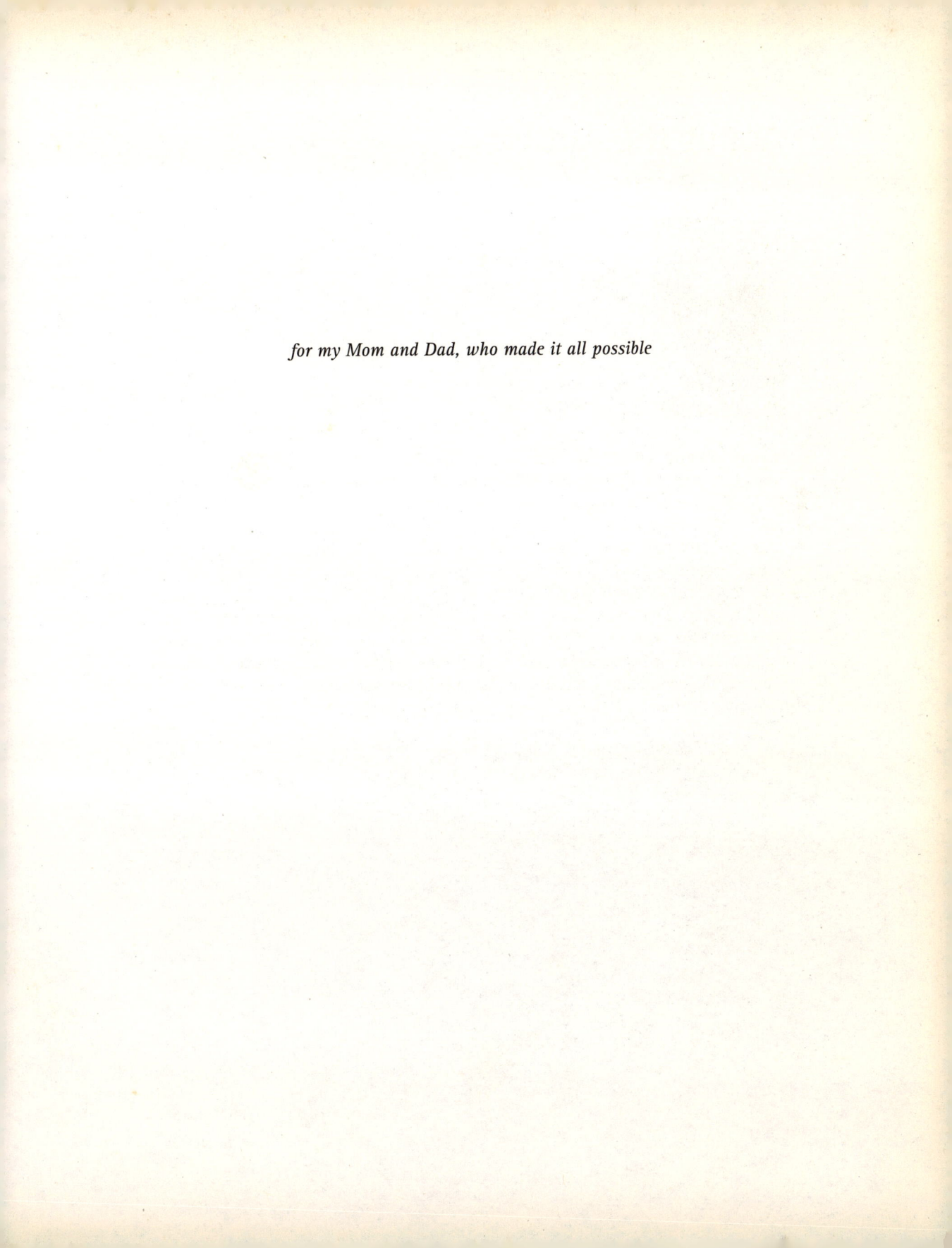

Preface

As has been noted by many, including Isaac Newton with his famous quote "If I have been able to see further, it was only because I stood on the shoulders of giants," humans have the remarkable ability to create tomes upon tomes of knowledge out of anything, be it physics, ice skating, golf, chess, the Internet, or even WAP. Such things can be delightful to witness, as in someone's ordering a pizza from a WAP-enabled phone, but some of us know that thousands of pages have been written to explore their functionality. WAP is a relative newcomer to wireless data, having been around only since 1995, but already a vast amount of information is accumulating on technologies that could be brought into and integrated with the architecture.

Many developers of technology attempt to study this large collection of information on a new language or new system "economically," to achieve an easy success as quickly as possible. In doing this, they commonly copy and paste from similar-looking code and especially look for applications that resemble theirs. Such methods will never help anyone to become a strong coder. Although quickly understanding others' coding ideas is indispensable, it is a well-known fact that the background of any system must be clearly understood and all pieces of the technology must be handled with equal skill if one is to become an appreciable master.

In this book, I have tried to summarize the absolute minimum understanding required of any developer necessary to master the precision of WAP development and prepare developers for any changes by making general recommendations for how to deal with practical situations. The aim is for developers to get a grasp of the principles behind the elements of WAP and not expect them simply to copy and paste or accept certain items on pure faith.

It is also known that the creation of code depends on individual style. For this reason, no author of a work on development can escape criticism that the work has included personal opinion and approach to the work. The work can then be made objective only if the book shows material that is based on the author's own development work and the advice represents the views of various outstanding WAP developers in the industry.

There is also no doubt that the theory of WAP development is vastly different from that of HTML and the Web. The latter has been studied much more in detail, with experts ready to provide the latest ready-made solutions to problems. With WAP, the general development community is only now starting to grasp the issues and unique problems that their ideas face. WAP is continuing to grow in different ways as it begins to meet new challenges in the marketplace and new competition from technologies like i-mode and Wireless Java.

I hope that this book is helpful to you in your quest for knowledge.

What You Already Know

Is this book for you? To help you decide, I make the following assumptions about you, the reader:

- You have knowledge of how to surf the Web. You are familiar with what a Web site is, how to use search engines, and shop for items on the Web by filling out forms and knowing what security measures are available to protect you.

- You know what an operating system is. You know how to edit a document, start a program on the computer, copy a file, find a folder, and perform other general computer maintenance tasks.

- You have experience creating Web pages. You know what Microsoft FrontPage is and are familiar with Microsoft Word's "Save as Web Page" feature and Netscape Composer. You may have also gone so far as to create a Web page from scratch, writing your own HTML code in a text editor.

- You have experience using a variety of browsers and some basic understanding of what goes on when you browse.

- You can think logically and have been involved in writing computer programs, maybe even having used Visual Basic, C, C++, COBOL, FORTRAN, or Java. You know how to formulate a solution to a problem as a reliable, precise sequence of steps.

- You have experience with at least one dynamic scripting server-side language such as ASP, CFML, JSP, Java, CGI, or PHP. You have set up a Web server and used the specific dynamic language to solve a problem, maybe even having used a database environment, such as Access, SQL Server, Oracle, or Sybase.

How This Book Is Organized

There were many ways to organize this material, but I've settled on a scheme that divides the book into five main parts. In addition, I've included a few appendixes that provide supplemental information that you might find helpful.

Part 1: Foundations

The chapters in this part look at the fundamental technologies on which WAP is based. It is important to know how the various aspects of browsing, the Internet, HTML, XML, and TCP/IP work before delving into WAP. This includes the architecture

Part II: Development of Services

The focus of this part is on the nuts and bolts of building WAP services. There is enough information included in the chapters in this part to get even the most novice person able to develop a WAP deck. Covered in these chapters are descriptions of the most important WML elements, WMLScript language pieces, and extensive examples of services.

Part III: Services on Advanced AB Architecture

With this part, this book goes beyond the standard WAP architectures and investigates new components emerging for WAP that allow developers to create better services. Technologies such as WTAI and Push are investigated in this section along with security issues.

Part IV: Designing Usable WAP Services

In Part IV, the focus is on taking a look at some of the development challenges and tradeoffs one faces when developing applications for wireless phones. The chapters examine usability and session management and identification problems.

Part V: Real-World Issues and WAP

In Part V, the focus is on showing how the theory outlined in the specifications and the documentation from the various vendors finally looks when it hits the road. This is a critical part as it gives an honest introduction to the problems veteran WAP developers face as they try to deploy their applications in today's wireless networks. Finally, at the end of this part you get a glimpse beyond the current releases of WAP at things that are coming in the future. There is a description of WAP 2.0 and a discussion of elements even beyond that such as the new UI elements for the creation of standard Weblike displays on wireless handsets.

Appendixes

Finally, the appendixes present additional information on topics covered in the book. They contain detailed listings of the WML language and its variants and tables that specifically point out differences between variants. The appendixes also offer a complete listing of WMLScript data types and function libraries. Also, there is additional reference information concerning images and icons.

Conventions Used in This Book

Each chapter in this book begins with a heads-up of the topics covered in the chapter and ends with a summary of what you should have learned by reading the chapter.

Throughout this book, you will find icons in the margins that highlight special or important information. Keep an eye out for the following icons:

This icon means that the text that follows is an aside to the main point.

This icon indicates tidbits that I picked up along the way and want to share with you.

This icon indicates where in the book you can find more information on the topic at hand.

In addition to the preceding icons, the following formatting and typographical conventions appear throughout the book:

- Code examples appear in a `fixed width font`.
- Other code elements, such as data structures and variable names, appear in `fixed width`.
- File, function, and macro names as well as World Wide Web addresses (URLs) appear in `fixed width`.

Contacting the Author

I invite any and all of your feedback, whether it be negative or positive. I have tried to ensure that the material is accurate and up to date to the best of my ability, but feel free to point out any errors on my part.

Feel free also to send me specific questions about any of the material I've covered. I'll do my best to answer your questions. Please keep in mind that I do have a full-time job, so I cannot guarantee an immediate reply. You can e-mail me at:

hamad_rashid@yahoo.com

Also, I invite you to visit www.hungryminds.com/extras/ on the Web. There, you'll find updates to the relevant sections within the book along with corrections to any errors that may have accidentally found their way into the material. I hope you enjoy the book and find it useful.

Acknowledgments

There are so many people whom I want thank for all their support. I primarily thank all of the folks at Hungry Minds for their commitment and patience with me during this project. I know it was painful at times, but we finally did it. Special thanks to Grace Buechlein and Susan Christophersen for helping to keep me on track and focused during all the changes throughout the project. Many thanks also go to the technical editors, Michael Cimilyan and Dale Bulbrook, for helping keep my explanations straight and making sure that all the code and descriptions were correct.

Thanks to Lev Weinstock for contributing ColdFusion code examples.

To everyone at Zsigo Wireless Training (and to those no longer there after the split), I want to say thanks for your patience and for putting up with me — particularly after those late-night writing sessions. Thank you especially to Emily Anderson, for keeping my life at work in order, and Travis Conti, Mark Bowen, and Lindsey Skaife for giving me pointers on how to present graphical items.

A special honorable mention goes to the master trainer Don Schuerholz and marketing guru Ben Linder of Openwave, without whom I would never have started down the long road of learning and teaching WAP.

And another honorable mention goes to Konny Zsigo of WirelessDeveloper.com, without whose guidance I would never have become involved in wireless data.

Finally, and most important, I have to give a *huge* thank you to my wife, Breen, and sons, Mitch, Gabe, Nate, Mike, Raph, and Zeke. We've been through a lot during this past year, and many times I was really unsure about whether there would be an end to the amount of work required to write this book. Thanks for standing by me and helping me make sure the book was created. I know there were times when you thought this book would never be done — and sometimes I wondered myself — but thank you for standing by me and helping make this book a reality.

And someone please tell the kids that Dad is finally coming home on time tonight.

Contents at a Glance

Preface ix

Acknowledgments xv

Part I	Foundations
Chapter 1	Introduction to the Wireless Internet 3
Chapter 2	Wireless and WAP 11
Chapter 3	WAP Foundations 35
Chapter 4	Introduction to WAP 69
Chapter 5	Introducing WML 93

Part II	Development of Services
Chapter 6	Doing More with WML 145
Chapter 7	Programming with WMLScript 195
Chapter 8	Using the WMLScript Libraries 227
Chapter 9	Dynamic WAP Services 279

Part III	Services on Advanced AB Architecture
Chapter 10	Building Active Applications Using Push Technology 339
Chapter 11	WTA 369
Chapter 12	Caching and Cache Operations 403

Part IV	Designing Usable WAP Services
Chapter 13	Session Management and Identification 423
Chapter 14	Targeted Development 443
Chapter 15	Designing User-Friendly Interfaces 459

Part V	Real-World Issues and WAP
Chapter 16	Implementing WAP Security 477
Chapter 17	Localization and Internationalization 505
Chapter 18	Location-Based Services 515
Chapter 19	Deploying WAP Services 533
Chapter 20	The Future of WAP 545
Chapter 21	Future of WAP Competitors 561

Appendix A: WML Elements and Attributes 575

Appendix B: WMLScript Operators 595

Appendix C: WMLScript Libraries 609

Appendix D: WTAI Libraries and Events 629

Appendix E: WBMP Image Format 641

Appendix F : WML 1.3 DTD Listing 645

Appendix G: Installing, Downloading, and
Configuring WAP SDKs 655

Appendix H: Openwave Icons 659

Index................................. 667

Contents

Preface ix

Acknowledgments xv

Part 1	Foundations

Chapter 1	**Introduction to the Wireless Internet** 3
	Introducing the Wireless Internet 3
	Technology and Society 4
	Technology, Innovation, and Business 5
	Summary 8
Chapter 2	**Wireless and WAP** 11
	What Is Wireless Technology? 11
	Information types: analog versus digital 15
	Using radio waves to transmit and receive information 16
	Cellular networks and 1G 17
	Multiple access 18
	2G Cellular Voice and Data 21
	Global System for Mobile communications (GSM) 22
	High Speed Circuit Switched Data (HSCSD) 23
	General Packet Radio Service (GPRS) 23
	Digital Advanced Mobile Phone System (D-AMPS) or US TDMA ... 24
	Personal Digital Cellular (PDC) 24
	D-AMPS+ 24
	cdmaOne 25
	Integrated Dispatch Enhanced Network (iDEN) 26
	2G packet-data systems 26
	2.5G Technology 27
	3G Technology 27
	IMT-2000 3G upgrade path 28
	W-CDMA (Wideband CDMA) 29
	Understanding the Core Network 31
	GPRS infrastructure 33
	Summary 34
Chapter 3	**WAP Foundations** 35
	TCP/IP 35
	History 36
	Stacks and protocols 37
	The OSI model 38

TCP versus UDP 41
The transport problem 41
HTTP 42
The structure of HTTP requests 47
The structure of HTTP responses 49
The GET method 50
The POST method 51
XML 53
XML concepts 55
Well-formed XML 55
Validated XML 58
MIME 65
Summary 67

Chapter 4 Introduction to WAP 69
Examining Some Examples of WAP Services 72
Understanding WAP Layers 77
The WAE layer 78
WSP 82
WTP 86
WTLS 88
WDP 90
Summary 91

Chapter 5 Introducing WML 93
A Brief Overview of XML 94
XML parsing 95
Element definitions 96
Working with WML Structure 97
A simple example of a WML deck 101
The body of the code 102
Common WML attributes 104
Understanding Text Display 105
Using the ISO-10646 method for character display 109
Using the named-equivalent method for character display 110
Navigating between Cards in WML 112
Navigation principles 114
Navigation using anchors 116
Navigation using soft keys 118
Backward navigation 122
Labeling and other attributes 127
The template element 130
Displaying Text with Tables 133
Displaying Images 137
Summary 141

Part II — Development of Services

Chapter 6 — Doing More with WML 145
Understanding Intrinsic Events 145
Working with Variables 156
Using the setvar Element 160
   Refreshing the display 162
   Escaping variables 164
Obtaining User Input 166
Using the input Element to Obtain User Input
  and Set Variables 177
   Setting an input mask 181
   Posting input data 185
Making Use of Timers 189
Summary 193

Chapter 7 — Programming with WMLScript 195
Why WMLScript? 196
Storing and Calling WMLScript 197
Introducing WMLScript 200
   Variables and data types 200
   Variable declaration, initialization, and scope 204
   Emulated array support 205
   Operators and built-in functions 206
   Comparisons, commas, and typeof 211
   Operator precedence 214
   Control statements 214
   Functions and passing parameters 219
Building a Sine Function 221
Summary 225

Chapter 8 — Using the WMLScript Libraries 227
Introducing Advanced WMLScript Concepts 227
   Using functions 227
   Using pragmas 230
   Using the WMLScript virtual machine 231
Standard WMLScript Libraries 233
   Lang library 234
   String library 239
   URL library 252
   WMLBrowser library 257
   Dialogs library 260
   Float library 263
   Crypto library 268

	Proprietary Libraries 269
	The Nokia Debug library 269
	The Openwave Console library 270
	Building a WMLScript Credit-Card Verifier 271
	Summary 277
Chapter 9	**Dynamic WAP Services** **279**
	Active Server Pages 280
	ASP request object 282
	Response object 283
	Processing user input with ASP 286
	Using the variables to initiate a query 288
	Adding additional headers and cookies 290
	Java Servlets 291
	Processing user input 293
	Using the variables to initiate a query 299
	Creating additional headers and cookies 302
	About the Java servlet process 302
	Java Server Pages (JSPs) 303
	Processing user input 306
	Using the variables to initiate a query 310
	Adding headers and cookies in JSP 312
	Personal Home Page Hypertext Processor 312
	Processing user input 313
	Using the variables to initiate a query 317
	Adding headers and cookies in PHP 319
	Perl CGI 319
	Processing user input 320
	Using the variables to initiate a query 324
	Adding headers and cookies in Perl 326
	ColdFusion Markup Language 327
	ColdFusion architecture 327
	The CFCONTENT tag 328
	Processing user input 329
	Using the variables to initiate a query 332
	Using the HomeSite editor 334
	Summary 335
Part III	**Services on Advanced AB Architecture**
Chapter 10	**Building Active Applications Using Push Technology** **339**
	Introducing Push 339
	Understanding Push Systems 340
	Dealing with Mechanisms Outside WAP: Openwave 343
	Push notification 343
	Pull notifications 345

	Cache operations 345
	UP.Link server queuing 346
	Sending notifications 347
	Using the COM Notification Library 348
	Working with WAP Push 348
	Push architecture 348
	Push access protocol 349
	Service indications, service loadings, and cache operations 361
	PPG 365
	Push OTA 366
	Summary 367
Chapter 11	**WTA** **369**
	A Brief Introduction to WTA 370
	An Overview of the WTA Architecture 372
	WTA user agent 375
	Device-specific features 375
	Repository 375
	WTA server 375
	WTA services 375
	The WTA Security Model 377
	The WTAI Libraries 378
	WTAI syntax 379
	Public WTAI 380
	Network common WTAI 383
	Network-specific libraries 391
	Network Common Events 391
	WTA Repository and Channels 394
	WTA repository 395
	The channel DTD 396
	WTA Event Handling 400
	Example WTA Applications 400
	WTA incoming-call selection 400
	WTA voicemail server 401
	Summary 402
Chapter 12	**Caching and Cache Operations** **403**
	Introducing HTTP Caching 405
	Caching and desktop browsers 405
	HTTP caching and headers 407
	The WAP Caching Model 410
	Intra-resource navigation 411
	WAP gateway responsibilities 411
	Caching Resources for Periods of Time 411
	The Cache-Control: no-cache header 412
	The Expires: and max-age headers 413

Contents

HTTP Headers and Meta Elements 415
WAP Cache Operations 415
Proprietary Techniques 417
Summary 418

Part IV Designing Usable WAP Services

Chapter 13 Session Management and Identification 423
Solving the Identification Problem 424
   Using manual identification schemes 425
   Using proprietary client headers 431
Session Handling 434
   Using cookies 435
   Using hidden postfields 438
   Manipulating URLs 441
The Future of WAP Session Management
  and Identification 441
Summary 442

Chapter 14 Targeted Development 443
What Is Targeted Development? 444
Detecting Device Types 445
Building and Using Device Tables 447
Making Use of Header Information 450
Introducing UAProf 451
Summary 457

Chapter 15 Designing User-Friendly Interfaces 459
Building a Foundation of UI Design 460
   Facing the challenges of UI design 460
   Solving the UI design problem 461
Creating a Consistent User Interface 462
   Developing and maintaining user trust 462
   Evaluating the effectiveness of a WAP UI:
     Three basic questions 464
Building a Site Structure 466
Braving the Browser Wars 467
Designing with Speed in Mind 471
Summary 474

Part V Real-World Issues and WAP

Chapter 16 Implementing WAP Security 477
Understanding Security and Cryptographic Algorithms ... 478
   Security and relativity 479
   Providing security solutions 480
   Key management 487

Understanding the WAP Security Architecture 489
    WTLS (Wireless Transport Layer Security) 490
    SSL and Internet 491
    WIM (Wireless Identity Module) 492
    The Crypto library signText function 492
    WPKI (Wireless Public-Key Infrastructure) 492
    Transport Layer End-to-End Security (TLe2e) 496
    Application-level security 500
Summary 504

Chapter 17 Localization and Internationalization 505
Making WAP Services Usable Internationally 505
    What is localization? 506
    The goal of internationalization 506
    Character sets 507
    Transfer systems 508
    Rendering issues 509
    Languages 510
Application Server Language Detection 510
Transcoding 512
    Charsets and postfields 513
Summary 514

Chapter 18 Location-Based Services 515
Understanding Location Issues 516
    Pinpointing place and time 516
    Establishing proximity 517
    Determining the uses of the service 517
Obtaining the Location 517
    FCC requirements and other market proponents 518
    Other location-services sponsors 519
Location-Based Technologies 519
    TDOA (Time Difference of Arrival) 520
    E-OTD (Enhanced Observed Time Difference) 521
    Assisted GPS methods 522
    Other systems 523
When Will Services Be Available? 523
The Openwave/SignalSoft System 524
WAP Location-Based Services 528
Summary 532

Chapter 19 Deploying WAP Services 533
Understanding Deployment Issues 533
    Choosing your tool: WAP software development kits (SDKs) ... 534
    Choosing your browser 534
    Choosing your gateway 535
    Choosing your architecture 536
    Conversion, compiling, and encoding/decoding overheads 540

		Latency considerations 540
		Choosing bandwidth 540
		Security issues 541
		Working with WAP Application Servers 541
		Using a phased development approach 542
		Controlling a Web server 543
		Working with a gateway 543
		Moving to a Mobile Device 544
		Summary 544
	Chapter 20	**The Future of WAP** **545**
		The Network as a Source of Innovation 546
		Wireless profiled TCP 547
		Convergence with Internet protocols 551
		The Mobile Device as a Source of Innovation 552
		External Functional Interface (EFI) 554
		Bluetooth WAP profile 556
		Persistent storage 557
		SyncML 558
		Summary 560
	Chapter 21	**Future of WAP Competitors** **561**
		M-Services GUI Improvements 563
		Standard GUI improvements 563
		GUI Improvements that require additional code ... 567
		M-Services Download Protocol 572
		Summary 574
		Appendix A: WML Elements and Attributes 575
		Appendix B: WMLScript Operators 595
		Appendix C: WMLScript Libraries 609
		Appendix D: WTAI Libraries and Events 629
		Appendix E: WBMP Image Format 641
		Appendix F: WML 1.3 DTD Listing 645
		Appendix G: Installing, Downloading, and Configuring WAP SDKs 655
		Appendix H: Openwave Icons 659
		Index 667

Part I

Foundations

CHAPTER 1
Introduction to the Wireless Internet

CHAPTER 2
Wireless and WAP

CHAPTER 3
WAP Foundations

CHAPTER 4
Introduction to WAP

CHAPTER 5
Introducing WML

Chapter 1

Introduction to the Wireless Internet

IN THIS CHAPTER

- Introducing the wireless Internet
- Understanding technology and society
- Considering technology, innovation, and business

MUCH CONFUSION ABOUNDS in the wireless industry about the future of WAP (Wireless Application Protocol) and its goals. This chapter focuses on previous technologies and innovations and their respective successes or failures. Frequently, a technological innovation goes unrecognized for a long time. For example, RISC chips were invented in 1979 by IBM and shelved until the late 1980s, when they were promoted by academic professors. WAP, or wireless Internet, is clearly an innovation; however, making this innovation into a real product by commercializing it is still a big challenge. This chapter introduces how society looks at technology and then investigates the triumvirate of technology, innovation, and business and what it may mean for the future of WAP.

Introducing the Wireless Internet

Much debate exists concerning the true potential of WAP in today's marketplace and whether competitors, such as the wireless Java technology or iMode, will quickly displace it. This chapter introduces you to the technological and societal mechanisms that will decide whether WAP succeeds or fails in the marketplace. You must grasp these ideas to truly understand the potential of WAP and wireless Internet in general. New technologies are being created daily in the mobile telecommunications market; however, as in all industries, not all technologies succeed. Many early technologies represented attempts to introduce the Internet to the wireless market in the form of a bit pipe. They gave consumers an Internet connection on the phone and expected consumers to figure out what to do with it. This Internet connection on the phone essentially treated the wireless phone as a modem that customers were expected to plug into their PCs or laptops.

This concept suffered from multiple defects that prevented its acceptance by the mainstream. The first was the overhead of having a mobile computer. Other problems were associated with the service's complexity and difficulty in setup and overall maintenance. These earlier solutions have given way to the more sophisticated concept of a Web browser in a phone. Because this latter concept works more effectively in the mass market, it is a leap forward; however, its poorer performance when compared to accessing the Internet on the desktop PC has challenged its continued existence. New products or applications of the technology must therefore be developed to sustain the concept of a Web browser in a phone.

This is where you as a software developer fit in: It is to your advantage to create new applications of the various methods of wireless Internet access in order to obtain a firstmover advantage in technological understanding and building the necessary partnerships. It is also important that the applications developed are capable of sustaining profits within a long mobile-Internet value chain. This book introduces you to tools that will help you along the way. But first you'll need some information about the sources of the technological revolution.

Technology and Society

Technology is defined by the *Encyclopedia Britannica* as the development over time of systematic techniques for making and doing things. Originally, the term referred only to discussions of applied arts, but eventually it covered a growing range of ideas and processes. By this century, the term has expanded to define any activity by which humankind seeks to manipulate the environment. This has resulted in problems with distinguishing between science and technology.

Other animals are capable of manipulating the environment. For example, the structure of a beehive rivals the complexity of an Internet router. But there is a critical difference: the beehive was created as a result of instinctive forces, whereas human beings consciously invented the Internet router by thinking systematically and creatively. This puts humans in a class by themselves, and therefore a description of technology becomes a discussion of humankind's innovations.

Frequently, technological problems seem to be tackled only because their application may produce more wealth. However, technology can also be used for survival or to improve quality of life. There are other incentives to create technology that are not so prevalent, such as gains in terms of social class, prestige, honor, and so on. And yet other examples of technology incentives are ritual creativity and the arts. Examples of ritual creativity are the creation of complex processes surrounding the Inca sacrifices, the creation of the pyramids, and the development of Moslem, Christian, and Jewish religious proceedings. These fields have produced many technological innovations but are not critical to human survival.

Today, the successful development of a given technology is strongly linked to several societal factors: need, resources, and a receptive public. Without all three of these things, the technology in question will have a difficult time succeeding.

Without a societal need, people are unprepared to devote resources such as their time and energy to innovation. The introduction of a time-saving device or process within a company, for example, will motivate people because the invention stands to benefit them. Military needs, such as a better weapon or process, have always been strong motivators for new technological innovation. Consider the case, during World War I, of the Haber Process, which was developed by a German chemist to create nitrogen using only organic plants. Using the Haber Process, instead of using expensive naturally occurring nitrogen, the military could now create its own. Nitrogen was a critical component of all high-powered explosives and significantly prolonged WWI because the Germans had found a simpler method to produce it even after their supply routes to abundant natural resources were destroyed. The military provided the impetus to solve the problem.

The existence of societal resources, such as capital, skilled employees, and material, comprise another basic requirement for the advancement of a technology. Lacking these resources, many inventions have stalled at the idea phase. Consider the remarkable ideas presented in the fifteenth-century sketches of Leonardo da Vinci. Many of them, such as helicopters, submarines, and airplanes, have only comparatively recently come into being; in da Vinci's time, the resources were not available.

Capital resources are necessary to fund innovative technology and make it a reality. Materials may be required to create certain inventions: the miniaturization of electric circuits, for example, required advances in metallurgical techniques, plastic, chemistry, and physics. Skilled employees are needed to construct the new equipment and devise new processes to create the invention. Sometimes an individual firm has to supply the resources to promote a technological advance, but often it is a certain segment of society that bears the responsibility. For example, in a business environment, businesses promote the creation of new services and goods, which likewise promote an educational system to produce more skilled workers of a new type; consequently, this puts the burden of guiding technological advances in society on businesses.

The third of the key components needed for a technological advance is a receptive society; one that will give the new idea serious consideration. In today's business environment, it is the consumer who is partially responsible for accepting new ideas. Consumers must be willing to use the wireless Internet for their needs and accept it as a solution for their problems before it can become a popular service.

All these social factors will strongly influence the success of this new WAP service and wireless Internet services that follow.

Technology, Innovation, and Business

A firm makes its profits either by offering consumers products that cost less than its competitors or by offering differentiated products whose differentiation is made up by premium prices. One of the critical questions to consider is how these low-cost or differentiated products come about. According to Allan Afuah in *Innovation*

Management, Oxford University Press, 1998, firms use *competencies* and *endowments*. A firm's competencies are the skills it uses to produce a good or service, such as locating opportunities in markets that did not exist before or finding new ways to integrate existing electrical components. Endowments are attributes other than skills, such as a company's size, access to patents, copyrights, location, skilled scientists, reputation, powerful sponsors, or licenses. All of these things can enable a firm to offer better or cheaper products than its competitors.

Consider the case of Ericsson telecommunication switches. The firm's competencies in providing switches to the Scandinavian Nordic Mobile Telephone (NMT) market enabled it to invent new software-management techniques in its switches to handle mobile clients. As it invented and commercialized its switches, the company made incremental innovations that gave it patents, copyrights, a huge installed base of switches, and a reputation for providing good switches. Furthermore, the installed base continues to give it an edge over new competitors. It is very difficult for new firms to imitate an Ericsson switch.

The competencies of a firm and its endowments reinforce each other to provide greater profits. But they do not just appear; they require innovation, either incremental or architectural, and these are the result of a firm's strategy, its structure, its systems, its employees, and chance. For example, when Omnipoint Technologies chose to enter the U.S. carrier market, it was offered an opportunity to enter by securing a license position in the U. S. Court of Appeals, based on an innovative entry. The decision to propose a carrier solution for the U.S. market was made by the firm's strategists, but the opportunity was provided by chance.

Finally, a firm needs a strong organizational structure that turns research results into real products. It needs to reward its employees in order to encourage the right kinds of individual capabilities. The class of people a firm hires, the culture it cultivates, and the leaders it supports all perpetuate the reward system. The arguments have given you a vague notion of what innovation is, but to get a more concrete idea of what I mean, examine the profit equation. Very simply, revenues are the result of products or services sold in a given quantity. The cost of the product or service depends on its quantity and quality. A firm wants to offer superior products or services for which it can charge high prices while keeping its own costs low and keeping competitors out.

Innovation enables a firm to improve its technological or marketing knowledge to offer a new product or service to customers. This product or service may be totally new, or it may have features that previous versions of the product didn't have. For example, the introduction of WAP services on phones represents an innovation because phones have never been able to offer a service like it before. Sometimes the product or service is in itself the innovation. Consider the case of Nokia's 9000 line of data phones. The product created a super-phone by combining a series of business services it recognized as important to business customers. Still in use in Europe as the 9110 series, this line of phones continues to provide complex services at a premium price.

However, a firm cannot stop at developing a new product or service; it must market the product or service so that customers want it. For example, AT&T

Wireless Services was the first to introduce wireless Internet access in the United States, but failed to market the product to consumers at a premium price. Although a commercial failure, the product was repositioned as an anchor service, one that became a necessity to demonstrate to consumers that a carrier was capable enough to provide it if required. This then furthered the carrier brand.

Innovations can be graded in terms of their impact on a firm's capabilities: one type is radical or competence-destroying, and the other is incremental or competence-enhancing. With radical innovations, entire sets of existing knowledge are rendered obsolete and the firm cannot rely on them to provide new products or services. With incremental innovations, the new product or service improves on an existing one and therefore improves the abilities of the organization based on a previous investment.

The effect of the new products on the market can also be either radical or incremental. If the new product makes all existing products noncompetitive then the innovation is radical. If the product allows existing products to remain competitive then the product is incremental or non-drastic. Consider the introduction of wireless Internet services. Existing ISPs don't need to worry about being driven out of business; however, incremental advances in wireless Internet service may eventually make it the dominant product in the market.

Innovations, especially radical innovations, are not always recognized as such. Often the radical innovation does not perform well initially and is bypassed by firms as a result. For example, Pacific Communication Sciences, Inc. (PCSI), together with Unwired Planet, first pioneered what is essentially a WAP second-generation phone back in 1995. However, because PCSI could not compete effectively in the miniaturization of newer digital phones, it was forced out of mobile-phone manufacturing completely. The company had not built up its competencies in diversifying its handset modulation schemes, instead focusing its attention on Advanced Mobile Phone Service (AMPS) and Cellular Digital Packet Data (CDPD), essentially an analog technology and its digital overlay.

In order to properly recognize an innovation you must understand the rationale behind the invention and what it will take to make it commercial, and recognize the potential uses for the new product or service.

Understanding the rationale behind an invention means asking what the components are and how they fit together. For example, when the idea came about to use extensions to the older AMPS technology to handle more users in a cell, the question was: Can a firm actually build a phone with this new digital AMPS component, instead of with the older system? How does the new system work? What are the linkings that result in the same voice services being processed through the system? Will the new digital AMPS service provide a better system? What will it take to build the new system and deliver it to customers? Is this the kind of service that customers actually want?

The next step in recognizing an innovation is determining the applications for the new product. Will the new product perform a job more efficiently than an older one? For example, when word processors were first being compared to typewriters, independent judges examined the work of secretaries producing documents. The documents were assessed for neatness and accuracy. The judges gave the documents the same score. In this case, the innovation has largely replaced the existing technology because it is generally more efficient and offers many more features. The word processor enables you to store, distribute, merge, and edit documents. In fact, an organization can have difficulty exploiting this kind of innovative product, simply because it does not fully recognize the product's potential.

Finally, the innovation can have a completely new application, one that has not been thought of yet. In cases like this it can be very difficult to apply the skills a firm already has to selling a new product or service. Sometimes an innovation is even discarded because the existing customer base and organization do not understand what it is. For example, when IBM developed the first PCs, they were dismissed because they did not have enough storage capability or processing power when compared to the demands of IBM mainframe customers.

The jury is still out on WAP and wireless Internet. Today, browsing the Web on the phone and browsing it on a computer are two very different experiences. The dimensions of a phone screen, its lack of color display, low processing power, and no mouse or keyboard severely hamper any chance of an experience identical to desktop browsing. It is conceivable that it may fall into the third category. Many firms have already dismissed it because the technology has not solved the existing problem well. For example, they feel that the speed is too slow or the screen is too small.

However, carriers have realized that wireless Internet has potential. They are working feverishly to discover new applications for it and to understand the new markets that these applications could bring.

One of the most successful services for wireless Internet has been in the dispatch industry: wireless Internet has made it more efficient for a driver to communicate with a central base station. Such communication generally takes a long time and costs are driven up by the necessity for accurate transfer. With wireless Internet the information transfer is much faster, because reading a message takes a shorter time than listening to someone speak it. Other vertical services have found that wireless Internet offers them improved service in the form of reduced user time.

However, carriers want the general consumer market to sustain the new WAP service – not by finding small niches, because they do not justify their entry costs – but by encouraging WAP development and improvement to the point where it becomes a viable wireless data offering almost as necessary as voicemail. We may look back on this many years from now and ask ourselves what we ever did without it.

Summary

In this chapter, I introduced you to some of the obstacles to the placement of WAP as a technology. We looked at some of the forces that will determine whether WAP succeeds in the long term or not. Many in the market question its ability to provide services to consumers given that it does not meet existing standards for Internet browsing. Why have a phone do Internet browsing when a desktop PC is so much faster? Why browse the Internet using a small display, when 15-inch monitors on the desktop do much better? WAP's advantage here is its mobility. But can this mobility translate into better products? Time alone will tell where these products or services will be created and what markets they position themselves in.

In the next chapter, I cover the wireless technologies currently offering these WAP services. I also look at some technologies that may assist in showing how wireless Internet may achieve performance on a par with existing Internet services.

Chapter 2

Wireless and WAP

IN THIS CHAPTER

- Defining "wireless" technology
- Understanding information types: analog versus digital
- Distinguishing the different generations of cellular data
- Understanding the core network

ONE OF THE MYSTERIES OF THE WAP STACK is the bearer. The bearer is commonly referred to in the specifications and in technical discussions as the subject. The discussion usually ends with someone saying, "Well, that's taken care of by the bearer, and it doesn't need to be discussed." Here, however, I describe the bearers. Although an understanding of the bearer is not absolutely necessary for an understanding of WAP, this chapter reduces the mystery behind how the type of bearer can affect your application. In a perfect world, bearers are equal; in reality that is certainly not the case, even in the case of two equivalent bearers implemented by operators with different architectures.

The story of the bearer begins in a world in which no WAP existed. WAP is a relative newcomer to the scene of wireless data. In fact, wireless data itself has not been around for very long. Our journey starts with an explanation of what wireless is and goes on to explain the architectures of the networks of the past, present, and future.

What Is Wireless Technology?

Electromagnetic waves are all around us. Some are made by people; others emanate from outer space. Every time an electrical charge accelerates, an electromagnetic wave is created. When these electrical charges oscillate continuously, they radiate electromagnetic waves whose frequency equals the rate of oscillation. Examples of these waves are light, radio waves, gamma waves, and X-rays.

Waves transport energy and momentum over a distance. Sound waves move through the air by compressing and expanding the surrounding air. They are referred to as longitudinal waves, in which the disturbance is parallel to the direction in which the wave is moving. Other waves, like electromagnetic waves, still move energy and momentum over a distance but do so by being carried over electric and magnetic fields that propagate through a vacuum. Electromagnetic waves are examples of transverse waves, whose disturbance is perpendicular to the direction of wave movement.

All waves have two basic properties: frequency and amplitude (see Figure 2-1). The frequency of an ocean wave, for example, tells us how often it hits the beach, and the amplitude tells us how high it will be at any point on its journey to the beach. Electromagnetic waves have similar properties but many of these kinds of waves are not visible. The frequency of a wave is a property that is measured in cycles per second, or Hertz (Hz), named for Heinrich Hertz, a physicist who was the first person to generate electromagnetic waves.

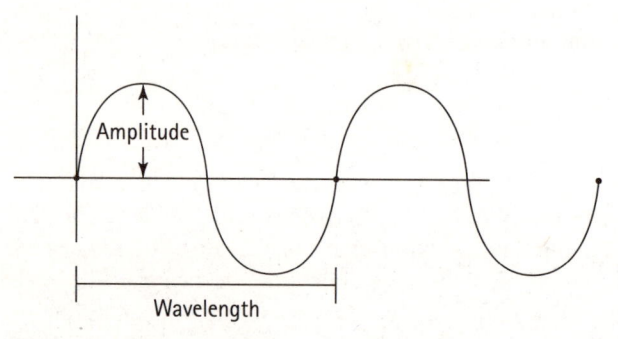

Figure 2-1: Wave properties

Electromagnetic waves all travel at the speed of light. The frequency and wavelength of a wave are related by the equation $c=f\lambda$ where λ (lambda) is the wavelength and f is the frequency. The c in this equation represents the speed of light (about 3×10^8 m/s). All electromagnetic waves travel at this speed in empty space. Obstacles, such as clouds or air, can slow them down, but to a negligible degree. Because the speed of light is a constant, we can uniquely identify each wave using either its wavelength or its frequency. (Either one of them can be calculated from the other.) A frequency chart showing the common waves is shown in Figure 2-2.

Figure 2-2: Frequency chart

Chapter 2: Wireless and WAP

The previous chart is sometimes called the electromagnetic spectrum; it shows the full range of waves. Scientists have given various sections of the spectrum special names showing what waves in a certain frequency or wavelength can be used for. Humans can see electromagnetic waves at around 400 to 700 nanometers. This is visible light. Wavelengths just a little shorter than visible light are called UV rays; wavelengths just a little bit longer are called infrared waves. X-rays are waves that penetrate a lot of materials because of their very short wavelengths and high frequencies. Microwaves have frequencies that match the resonant frequency of natural solids and liquids and can therefore heat foods in microwave ovens.

Radio waves are the electromagnetic waves with frequencies ranging from 10^{10}Hz to 10^{2}Hz. Like other electromagnetic waves, they are generated by an electric charge moving in a circuit. A radio is a circuit connected to an antenna, which transmits this electromagnetic wave. The oscillating frequency of the electrical circuit equals the frequency of the wave. A radio receiver then listens for these waves and duplicates the oscillation it hears. It creates the same oscillation on its end. This is the basic principle behind wireless and radio.

Radio waves are special sections of the spectrum that can carry information for communication purposes. The modern classification uses frequencies to identify particular radio waves. Microwaves, the three highest frequencies of waves, are especially suited for transmitting information. All waves have an attenuation characteristic, which means that the energy they carry dies out after a certain distance because of the wave's collision with obstacles, even air molecules. The higher the frequency of a wave, the greater its rate of attenuation. As the frequency gets higher, the wavelength becomes smaller. A wave is able to go around obstacles only if its wavelength is larger than the size of the obstacle: therefore high-frequency waves, with their small wavelengths (such as one centimeter) couldn't get around my office desk. Light waves have wavelengths of around 500 nm, so they cannot go through objects; radio AM waves, on the other hand, have wavelengths of around one kilometer and are therefore able to go through and around buildings.

The following table shows the relevant radio waves.

TABLE 2-1 RADIO WAVES

Frequency	Name and Abbreviation	Usage
<3kHz	ELF (extremely low frequency)	Military submarines
3–30kHz	VLF (very low frequency)	Merchant marines and maritime communications
20–300kHz	LF (low frequency)	AM radio
300–3000kHz	MF (medium frequency)	AM radio

Continued

Part 1: Foundations

TABLE 2-1 RADIO WAVES *(Continued)*

Frequency	Name and Abbreviation	Usage
3–30MHz	HF (high frequency)	AM radio, amateur radio
30–300MHz	VHF (very high frequency)	FM radio
300–3000MHz	UHF (ultra high frequency)	TV, cellular
3–30GHz	SHF (super high frequency)	Fixed wireless, satellites
30–300GHz	EHF (extra high frequency)	Satellites, radar

Microwaves have small wavelengths and high frequencies, which help in sending communication information. The high frequencies give them a short reach, and their small wavelengths make it difficult for them to get around obstacles. However, microwave bands are good for information transmission because of the large bandwidths possible. The following table shows some microwave-band regions.

TABLE 2-2 SPECIAL MICROWAVE BANDS

Frequency	Main Use	Band Name
0.39–1.55GHz	Cellular	L
1.55–3.9GHz	Cellular	S
3.9–6.2GHz	Satellites	C
6.2–10.9GHz	Satellites, fixed wireless	X
10.9–18GHz	Satellites, fixed wireless	Ku
18–26.5GHz	Satellites, fixed wireless	K
26.5–40GHz	Satellites, fixed wireless	Ka
33–50GHz	Fixed wireless	Q
50–75GHz	Satellites	V
75–110GHz	Future cellular	W

So, up to this point, you know how electromagnetic waves are generated and which frequencies are used to transmit information. The next two important questions are as follows: What is this information that is being transmitted, and how can it be sent over a radio wave?

Information types: analog versus digital

Many phenomena in nature are easily represented by a continuous variation in data. They are referred to as analog. For example, the temperature of the room you are sitting in varies over a range, maybe somewhere between 20 and 38 degrees Centigrade. The exact temperature may be 20.234243, or 20.2423512. You can't know the exact temperature; however, you can get a close approximation of it using a digital format. To measure the temperature of the room, you could use a standard thermometer, a glass tube filled with mercury. As the temperature increases, the mercury expands and rises in the tube. As the temperature decreases, the mercury contracts and falls in the tube. The temperature measurement is tied to the rise and fall of the mercury: it's an analog system.

Sound is another type of information. It varies continuously and is best represented as a wave. Video signals are another type of information that vary continuously. The video or sound signals are converted into radio waves and then back into video or sound through the TV or radio.

Information sent by computers is digital. It consists of series of ones and zeros sent as voltage levels. Because a lot of natural phenomena are easier to represent in analog form than in digital form, digital encoding costs more money and requires more intensive electronics. These sophisticated electronics have only recently become available, which is why a lot of older phones, TVs, and radios are analog rather than digital.

Digital has the following advantages over analog systems:

- Digital systems have better noise-cancellation and noise-reduction techniques. This is true because if an analog signal is somehow distorted, the information is lost forever, whereas if a digital signal is distorted, mathematical techniques can regenerate the lost portions. Remember that all that is being regenerated is a string of ones and zeros.

- Digital systems are more reliable. Many error-correction routes can enhance a system's redundancy. For example, I could duplicate all my information three times before transmitting and then decide on the value of the information at the receiving end by taking a quick 2 out of 3 wins poll of the 3 pieces of repeated information. More sophisticated techniques provide better trade-offs between redundancy and reliability than the simplistic measures introduced here.

- Digital systems enable compression of data and can generally store or transmit more information in the same amount of space than an analog system.

- Digital systems can be made more secure from malicious hackers because of encryption techniques and the availability of mathematical algorithms that make the information tough to decipher. In analog systems the information is difficult to hide and can be obtained with rudimentary equipment.

- Digital systems enable storage of information in some temporary or permanent memory-storage area. This type of storage is difficult to create for analog information. The analog information's representation cannot be quantified easily and stored. Digital systems also enable the use of advanced-delay techniques, which manipulate the order in which information is transmitted and received. These advantages result in better use of the physical media used to send information.

Using radio waves to transmit and receive information

As I mentioned earlier, an electrical circuit can generate electromagnetic waves to carry information. This information can be either analog or digital. Sound, for example, can be represented quite well as a wave form. A sound wave form representation can be imposed on top of a carrier or standard electromagnetic wave in a known pattern. An analog wave can be added to a carrier using four basic techniques:

- **Amplitude modulation (AM):** With amplitude modulation, the resultant wave has an amplitude that varies with the information level. This form of modulation is very inefficient because many cycles of signal are required to send a small amount of information. The only application that still uses amplitude modulation today is AM broadcast radio.

- **Frequency modulation (FM):** With frequency modulation, the wave's amplitude is kept the same while the frequency of the carrier wave varies to represent changes in the information being transmitted. FM uses available radio spectrum better than AM and is known for its use in radio FM broadcasts. It is used in both analog networks and many 2G networks.

- **Phase modulation (PM):** Phase modulation is yet another way that information can be transmitted using radio waves. The PM carrier is modified by moving very quickly between different points in a wave cycle. The different points on the wave cycle represent different bit values. The farther apart the points on the wave are, the less complex the modulation. Standard phase modulation has very sharp breaks between the two cycles and some smoothing techniques are often used to minimize the abruptness of the breaks. One such modulation technique is Gaussian Minimum Shift Keying (GMSK), which smoothes the information signal by passing it through a variety of special filters. This modulation scheme is used in GSM, a 2G network technology.

- **Polarization:** Polarization uses the fact that radio waves that travel at different angles can be distinguished and different information can be sent over them. In reality, this has not yet been implemented, but it is theoretically possible to initially distinguish between at least horizontal and vertical waves. This may be something we see in 4G networks of the future.

Cellular networks and 1G

Because of technical and political reasons, certain regions of radio spectrum were chosen to transmit and receive sound wirelessly. The most popular region of radio spectrum in terms of mass-market usage is called *cellular* and commonly refers to the first generation of mobile-phone technology, although it is not usually referred to as 1G.

Like all wireless signals, after a set distance cellular signals fade to such an extent that information cannot be transmitted on them reliably. Microwave frequencies have a limit of around 30km of usefulness in rural areas. Large obstacles, such as those found in urban areas, decrease this distance to around 15km or less.

A typical design for a cellular system is a radio transmitter on a tower transmitting 30km in all directions. This design forms a circular coverage area around the tower. The radio transmitter in the center of this circle is called the base station. Some stations (or cells) have many buildings in some directions, or a large number of trees in others, so the coverage area of the transmitter is never a perfect circle due to the obstacles. Because the coverage area is good only for 30km or so, additional cells are needed to cover adjacent areas. The combination of all these cells forms a cellular-network coverage area.

Calls established in one cell somehow continue uninterrupted in another cell. In 1G systems this is a noisy process in which the call actually blanks out for a period of time. Moving from one cellular network coverage area to another is called roaming. When one cell transfers a call to another, it is called a handoff (or handover). It is possible, of course, for a call that doesn't make it through the handoff process to be dropped. Cellular systems can have soft handoffs, for example where two calls are in progress, one with the old cell and the other with the new. This capability is part of all 3G systems, and one 2G technology, cdmaOne. The other type of handoff is the hard handoff. In this case, an explicit break with the old call occurs before the new one is established. The hard handoff is less reliable than the soft handoff. Systems before 1G and the older 1G systems sometimes had no handoffs, which meant that a call had to be reestablished when the user changed cells.

> **NOTE** The grouping of any cellular or radio system into 1G, 2G, 3G, or 4G is largely a marketing phenomena and is not based on any one specific feature or group of features of wireless networks. General principles could however be

used to categorize a technology into one of the generational types. The overarching trend is that as electronics becomes more miniaturized, the wireless devices and networks become more capable. The network companies, the carriers, do not jump on this advanced electronics right away because they wait until their older systems have paid themselves off and earned some profit. The carriers and industry pick a time when major advances have been made in technology and sufficient demand exists for faster services, and then a leap is made to the next generation. Of course, this is just a rule of thumb, as some firms may take the leap sooner or ignore the trends.

First generation systems can be thought of as analog cellular, the second generation moved the networks into digital by and improved voice quality, security, and network efficiency. The third generation will allow for seamless voice and data and improve the data rates. The fourth generation is thought to be able to improve the data rates further and add better antenna technology.

In cellular systems, designing radios that are able to transmit *and* receive simultaneously is difficult. The power of transmitted signals is so much greater that they tend to overpower any signals coming in. Also, simultaneous transmission and reception leads to battery drain. To circumvent this problem, two techniques are used. The first is to separate the transmitted and received signals into two different channels, a process known as Frequency Division Duplexing (FDD). The duplexing means that the communication has become two-way, with transmissions being made on the uplink and reception on the downlink. FDD requires pairs that should be separated by some broad range to allay interference. This use of pairs is known as paired spectrum. The pairs can be symmetric or asymmetric, depending on whether an equal distance exists between the pairs. The downlink frequency is always higher because it has a shorter range, which the high transmission power of a base station is able to counter.

The other way to separate uplink and downlink is to use one channel but decide when to perform transmission or reception on a time basis. This technique is known as Time Division Duplexing (TDD). It does not require a paired spectrum and therefore does not require as much bandwidth as FDD.

Multiple access

Given the cellular architecture, a system becomes necessary that enables multiple users to talk to a single base station. This system can be achieved in five ways. 1G systems use only the first of these, which is Frequency Division Multiple Access (FDMA). The others are Time Division Multiple Access (TDMA), Space Division Multiple Access (SDMA), Code Division Multiple Access (CDMA), and Orthogonal

Division Multiple Access (ODMA), all of which are discussed in the following sections.

FREQUENCY DIVISION MULTIPLE ACCESS (FDMA)

FDMA is a very basic method for separating a spectrum into sections so that a single user has access only to a certain frequency and a little section above and below that with which to transmit or receive. FDMA is still used in some 2G systems but is combined with the other multiple-access systems mentioned in this chapter.

The most widely used FDMA system in use today is Advanced Mobile Phone Service (AMPS), which divides the spectrum into two 25MHz chunks: one for downlink, the other for uplink. These are then sliced into 30kHz channels. Each channel can then be used by a single user. If you do the math, you'll find that about 832 channels result, with 416 for uplink and 416 for downlink. Twenty-one channels out of each set are used for control purposes, leaving 395 for uplink and downlink that a carrier/operator can use.

As previously noted, a cell has a powerful transmitter in the center and the limit of the cell is approximately at the edge of the circle where the signal is weak. The signal does not conveniently die out at the edge of this circle; it keeps on going. So, if a transmitter/receiver (transceiver) were to use all 395 channels, it would cause interference with other cells surrounding it, such that none of the channels could be used. In practice, to keep the interference low, the cells are repeated in a three-cluster pattern, and each cell is assigned only about 130 channels. The three-cluster pattern is the bare minimum; seven-cluster patterns are more common. In the case of a seven-cluster pattern, a single base station would transmit/receive at most on about 55 channels.

AMPS is not the only pure FDMA system. Others that have been used in the past are Total Access Communication System (TACS) in the UK, J-TACS in Japan, and NMT in Scandinavia.

TIME DIVISION MULTIPLE ACCESS (TDMA)

Many 2G systems use TDMA. Regardless of what the name sounds like, it is not tied to any specific operator; it does actually represent a generic methodology for allowing multiple access. TDMA is used in GSM, iDEN, PDC, and IS-136 TDMA, to name a few 2G technologies. TDMA still divides a band into different frequencies, but rather than assign that division to a single user it further divides that channel on the basis of time. This means that a user is allowed to use that channel only for a short period of time. These periods are known as time slots. The cell phone remains silent for the period of time that it is not allowed to talk. For example, a GSM time slot is 577 microseconds long. There are eight total time slots for GSM, which means that the radio waits 4039 microseconds to retransmit or receive information.

CODE DIVISION MULTIPLE ACCESS (CDMA)

CDMA is a radically different approach to dividing up the available spectrum. In this case, the entire bandwidth is split as before into uplink and downlink. But then the entire uplink or downlink section is used to either transmit or receive. Each transmission or reception by a unique user is coded differently.

CDMA was originally used in military communications because it is indistinguishable from noise in communication. This prevents enemy units from jamming or listening to a signal. The CDMA system is known as a spread-spectrum system because it spreads the information signal across the available bandwidth.

Two types of CDMA systems exist: FHSS and DSSS. FHSS stands for Frequency Hopping Spread Spectrum and works by using FM signals, such as FDMA, but rapidly switches the specific frequency being used. Therefore, it's difficult for an eavesdropper to predict when and where exactly the conversation will next occur. The transmitter and receiver, however, both know where on the spectrum the next piece of the transmission/reception will occur. Today, this type of CDMA is mostly used in unlicensed bands, such as 900MHz cordless phones, for which the ability to find an unused channel quickly is important.

The next type of CDMA is DSSS (Direct Sequence Spread Spectrum). The required bandwidth is in the order of MHz rather than kHz. This extra bandwidth is used to send multiple copies of the same signal. The more bandwidth available, the more copies of the signal can be sent. All these extra copies are known as *gain*. A higher gain is advantageous because the system is more secure from outside disturbance.

All the cellular systems deployed today use CDMA and are of the DSSS type. Because every radio can use all available channels, there is no concern about reusing frequencies in adjacent cells as there is with TDMA. The ability to reuse frequencies allows CDMA to use spectrum more efficiently. Also, because of this ability to reuse frequencies, a CDMA radio can actually be connected to more than one base station at a time, enabling soft handoffs.

CDMA has been around since WWII; however, because all the radios in the spectrum are transmitting and receiving simultaneously, the electronics necessary to manage CDMA in a handset form factor have only recently become available. Although having all radios transmitting with pure randomness, for example, is possible, a real chance exists that some signals will overpower others. Therefore, the signals must be designed to cancel each other out as little as possible. This situation is often compared to a cocktail party at which everyone is speaking a different language. One of the participants might drown out everyone else if the conversation volume is not kept in check. Also, it is not possible to understand another conversation without knowing the language or, in the case of CDMA, the code to decipher it.

ORTHOGONAL DIVISION MULTIPLE ACCESS (OFDM)

The name OFDM (Orthogonal Frequency Division Multiplexing) refers to the way waves bouncing off surfaces can cancel other waves of similar frequency that bounce off those surfaces at a later time. This canceling out is known as the multipath problem. Multipath is a big problem for high-bit rate signals because of shorter modulation symbols that are overwhelmed by reflections.

OFDM separates user data over several frequencies, but the thing it does differently from all the other technologies introduced so far is that it uses orthogonal carrier waves. This means that the waves are sent at right angles to prevent them from canceling each other out. Because of the special way in which the waves have to be sent, OFDM requires very precise antennae at both the transmitting and receiving ends. The technology will probably not be popular until 4G systems roll around.

SPACE DIVISION MULTIPLE ACCESS (SDMA)
SDMA (Space Division Multiple Access) uses directional transceivers to focus the radio waves so that they are transmitted and received in a very specific direction. In the simplest case, a transmitter may be set up to transmit in a quarter circle rather than a full circle at the center of a cell. The beams from SDMA are more focused than for all other cellular systems, which allows for more precise control of the shapes of the coverage areas.

In the future, SDMA technologies may actually allow for base stations to talk directly to specific radios in a cell, focusing the beam very precisely and therefore increasing the signal strength and bit rates to that radio. Again, such advanced antenna systems may not be big until 4G. Rudimentary SDMA is applied in urban areas today, or at cell boundaries to reduce transmission into unneeded areas.

2G Cellular Voice and Data

2G is often synonymous with the term *PCS*, which stands for Personal Communication Services. These services were planned as an upgrade to the analog systems because the older services had many problems. They required large batteries, and provided poor voice quality and poor coverage. As a result, they saw low usage among average consumers. They also could not carry digital data. To improve the situation, the industry leaders proposed digital services. In the U.S. these are referred to generally as PCS.

The most popular 2G systems use TDMA/FDMA hybrids and CDMA for their multiple-access technologies. It is within these groups of technologies that WAP becomes feasible. Table 2-3 shows the 2G technologies that support WAP.

TABLE 2-3 WAP BEARERS

2G Technology	WAP Supported Bearer Types
GSM	Circuit Switched Data (CSD), Packet (Packet Switched), Unstructured Supplementary Services Data (USSD), SMS (Short Message Service)
CDMA	CSD, Packet, SMS

Continued

TABLE 2-3 WAP BEARERS *(Continued)*

2G Technology	WAP Supported Bearer Types
iDEN	CSD, Packet, SMS
DataTAC	Packet
PDC	CSD, Packet
US TDMA	GUTS, GHOST, CSD, Packet
Motorola Paging	FLEX, ReFLEX
PHS	CSD
TETRA	SMS, Packet
DECT	CSD, Packet, SMS

Although the preceding list features a lot of cellular systems, there are some technologies that consist solely of data-only networks. The most widely deployed 2G technologies are given a closer look in this section.

Global System for Mobile communications (GSM)

Because Europe was a giant mess of individual analog technologies in the first generation of cellular, the major manufacturers and representatives from the European countries decided that all countries should come together and decide on a standard cellular system for the second generation. After several years of discussions among representatives from the major European cellular businesses and countries, the result was GSM. Owing to its immense popularity, it now operates on at least four frequencies around the world. Originally, it started at 900MHz in Europe but was later upbanded to 1800MHz in the U.K., and then again to 1900MHz in the U.S. The 1800MHz is sometimes called DCS1800 (Digital Cordless Standard), and the 1900MHz is sometimes called PCS1900 (Personal Communication Services—confusing!), but they are all GSM. There is a new variant now at 450MHz for the Scandinavian countries.

GSM encodes information on the airlink using a modulation known as GMSK (Gaussian Minimum Shift Keying). This modulation scheme allows for a binary-symbol rate and data rate of 271kbps in a single 200kHz channel. Each 200kHz channel is actually further divided into eight time slots. This split results in individual user rates of about 32kbps. Much of this raw data rate is further used up for error correction, resulting in an overall effective data rate of about 13kbps per time slot.

High Speed Circuit Switched Data (HSCSD)

GSM can carry more than just voice data. GSM can also establish data calls. In this case, a user can use a single time slot like a circuit-switched modem. The data-rate coder within the handset can support up to 14.4kbps of data. Four of these can be tied together to make up to about 57.6kbps. Two and three slots can also be used. The four-time-slot limit is to allow for the handset not to have to transmit and receive simultaneously. GSM is designed so that the uplink time slot is three slots away from the downlink time slot.

Although it is possible to implement HSCSD, handset manufacturers are encountering problems in designing the phones, and the technology takes up too much in time slots that is not easily recouped by billing customers. However, the system can coexist with some of the other data technologies being proposed by GSM.

General Packet Radio Service (GPRS)

This is another data technology for GSM networks. It is more popular than HSCSD or standard GSM-CSD because it has a packet-data format very similar to the Internet. Because it is a packet-data system, time slots are used when needed, giving carriers more flexibility in designing their networks. In CSD and standard GSM, a time slot is kept in use for the duration of the call. In GPRS, time slots are allocated as needed.

Like HSCSD, GPRS is asymmetric and keeps transmission and reception separated by at least three time slots because of design problems with getting handsets to transmit and receive at the same time.

GPRS will probably be added gradually to GSM networks, which means that it will coexist with GSM voice, GSM CSD, and possibly GSM HSCSD. Handsets, therefore, are classified into three grades:

- ◆ Grade C: Can use either packet or CSD but not both simultaneously
- ◆ Grade B: Can only be in standby packet mode when CSD is active
- ◆ Grade A: Can do simultaneous CSD and packet

Even more classes are defined for 29 possible handsets. These classes are mainly needed to differentiate between how many time slots are used on the uplink and downlink and how many slots are simultaneous. It is unlikely that the first set of GPRS handsets will be able to transmit and receive at the same time. GPRS also requires more additions to the back-end architecture. I explain these issues in a later in the Core Network section.

Digital Advanced Mobile Phone System (D-AMPS) or US TDMA

Although the GSM approach was acceptable in Europe, the largest carriers/operators in the U.S. decided that they needed a system that addressed the backward-compatibility issues such as the coexistence with AMPS. The system proposed by them was D-AMPS or TDMA. Like GSM, it divides a frequency band into splices; each splice is then divided using a similar time-slotting technique as GSM. But this time, 30kHz bands are used to be compatible with AMPS bands. The technologies don't actually interoperate; it is much easier to manage bundles of the same type of frequency. The D-AMPS system divides the band into three time slots.

D-AMPS uses a modulation scheme of DQPSK (Differential Quadrature Phase Shift Keying), which is a more complex scheme than GSM's GMSK. It can carry about two times more information than GMSK for GSM. The raw data rates for D-AMPS are about 48kbps, and because these rates are further divided into three time slots per channel, D-AMPS gives each user about 16kbps. The time slots for TDMA are about 6.7 milliseconds (ms), as opposed to GSM's .577 ms, giving the TDMA network some room to add extended signaling information.

Personal Digital Cellular (PDC)

The Japanese have their own version of D-AMPS, called PDC. It is backward-compatible with their older analog system, called J-TACS. This is the system that everyone is talking about these days because it runs the popular Japanese NTT DoCoMo I-mode wireless Web service.

PDC has channels with a size of 25kHz. This channel size is smaller than for D-AMPS and means that the system has lower data rates. In practice, PDC forgoes some error correction to achieve the same data rates as standard D-AMPS. This makes the resulting system less reliable, but the cells are made smaller to counteract that problem. The smaller cell size is less of a problem than it seems because the networks in Japan are extremely dense when compared to other countries. The data rates that can be achieved on PDC are about 9.6kbps – possibly 14.4kbps with no error correction. The I-mode service runs on PDC at 9.6kbps.

D-AMPS+

I discuss D-AMPS+ here only because it will be relevant in later discussions on 3G. The D-AMPS+ system enables carriers to get GPRS onto the smaller bandwidth channels of D-AMPS. With three slots of D-AMPS giving their maximum rate of 9.6kbps, the total comes to 28.8kbps. This rate is possible only if the terminal is transmitting and receiving simultaneously. So, to simplify the radio hardware, the handset could transmit for two slots, receive for one slot, and repeat or transmit for one slot and receive for two slots. Limited as it may be, D-AMPS+ is being implemented by D-AMPS carriers in the U.S.

cdmaOne

cdmaOne is the only system to have initially chosen CDMA as its core technology. This puts it ahead of the pack in terms of upgrades to any of the 3G systems. Most of the original patents for implementing IS-95 came from a company out of San Diego called Qualcomm.

On the surface, it seems that CDMA is much simpler to implement than AMPS or GSM. None of the advanced frequency cell-planning techniques are required for CDMA. All the handsets simply transmit or receive at the same time, all on the entire available bandwidth. Technically, a signal is duplicated many times to achieve a gain.

cdmaOne uses a set of Walsh codes, which is a set of 64 numbers of which each is 64 bits in length. These are special orthogonal codes that cancel each other out. Each bit sent out over the air is effectively sent 64 times as it is encoded with a Walsh code. The cdmaOne transmission takes place using QPSK (Quadrature Phase Shift Keying) on the downlink and OQPSDK (Offset Quadrate Phase Shift Keying) on the uplink.

In theory, using 64 sets of numbers allows for 64 users to be on a single channel. In practice, the best that can be achieved with today's electronics is about 15 or so users on a single channel. Even so, the system still makes a very good use of spectrum.

> **NOTE** cdmaOne achieves raw data rates of about 19.2kbps downlink and 28.8kbps on the uplink.

Base stations in cdmaOne synchronize their transmissions so that every cell uses the same frequency. GPS satellites give an accurate position using a very good time clock. These GPS receivers at the base station keep time so precisely that the exact distance between the stations can be calculated. This distance is then used to maintain power levels with the radios. So, the radio power level is set low when it is close to the base station and the power level is set higher when the radio is far from the base station.

Two versions of cdmaOne exist. They operate at different frequencies and have different cell sizes. Because of the timing requirements, changing something like cell size is a very big deal in a CDMA system. The two versions are IS-95A and ANSI J-STD-008. IS-95A works in 824–894MHz and has larger cell sizes than STD-008, which works from 1850–1990MHz.

There is also a system called cdmaTwo. This is Qualcomm's plan allowing for a single user to use four codes to obtain an aggregate data rate. This system is also sometimes referred to as IS-95B.

Integrated Dispatch Enhanced Network (iDEN)

iDEN is a proprietary system, developed by Motorola, which is based on TDMA. It was intended to be a digital technology, backward-compatible with the Public Mobile Radio networks (push to talk networks). The iDEN channels are 25kHz, the same as PDC in Japan. But the TDMA slot length is 15 ms long, with six time slots to a single channel. The main modulation scheme is Quadratic Amplitude Modulation (QAM), which results in a maximum data rate of about 64kbps per channel.

iDEN supports a packet-data system, based on the Mobile IP standard, that achieves data rates on the order of 19.2kbps. WAP services are deployed on iDEN in the U.S. by carriers such as Nextel.

2G packet-data systems

Many systems exist that have been developed as data-only systems. They were not designed to carry voice data. An example of such a system is a paging network. The most popular system is Flex by Motorola. Motorola has recently extended the Flex system to create ReFlex, a two-way system that supports WAP.

Another packet-data system is CDPD. This is an overlay system over AMPS or D-AMPS that uses a single channel for data. The maximum data rates over CDPD are similar to those over D-AMPS+, using 19.2kbps downlink and about 9.6kbps on the uplink. CDPD is cheaper than AMPS Circuit-Switched for bursty applications, ones with sporadic bandwidth needs, especially like that used for browsing services such as WAP.

> The two other packet-only networks are Mobitex and DataTAC.

Mobitex, developed by Ericsson, was to be used for telemetry, or long-distance monitoring. The maximum data rate is around 8kbps. The network infrastructure uses a lot of time to think about the data sent through it, but it has reasonably good coverage in the U.S. and internationally.

Mobitex networks are actually run today by BellSouth and are used by all Palm VII devices. The Palm VII works only in the U.S. because different countries' Mobitex networks use different frequencies.

The other significant packet-data network is DataTAC. The old name for this network was Ardis. It was developed jointly by Motorola and IBM for IBM field agents. It uses a connection-oriented architecture, giving the system longer connect times. Two versions of DataTAC exist. One is MDC4800, which supports data speeds of up to 4.8kbps; the other is RD-LAP, which supports data speeds up to 19.2kbps. Only the latter supports any kind of WAP service.

2.5G Technology

2.5G describes any intermediate technology implemented by a carrier that is on its way to becoming 3G-compatible. Some of the technologies discussed so far in the context of 2G networks, such as HSCSD and GPRS and even WAP services themselves, are referred to as 2.5G technologies. Figure 2-3 shows the upgrade paths that the different network technologies would take. Any intermediate system can be referred to as 2.5G.

3G Technology

Originally, 3G was intended as a term that would encompass any standard providing data rates of 144kbps or faster to mobile consumers. Providing these rates technically can be done using 2.5G systems such as GPRS or HSCSD, but 3G was supposed to have this high speed even for the lowest-grade handsets in less than optimal conditions. The increased speeds can be achieved with more advanced modulation techniques over the air than any 2G system, and the systems tend to be based on CDMA rather than TDMA.

The accepted standard for 3G in Europe is W-CDMA, which may not be compatible with the Japanese system, depending on the hardware used. Qualcomm has proposed a number of alternative systems, referred to collectively as cdma2000. And a group of large D-AMPS, TDMA, and GSM operators in the U.S. wants to deploy something more compatible with TDMA. The result is about six standards — a giant mess known as 3G. Figure 2-3 shows the competing systems and possible upgrade options.

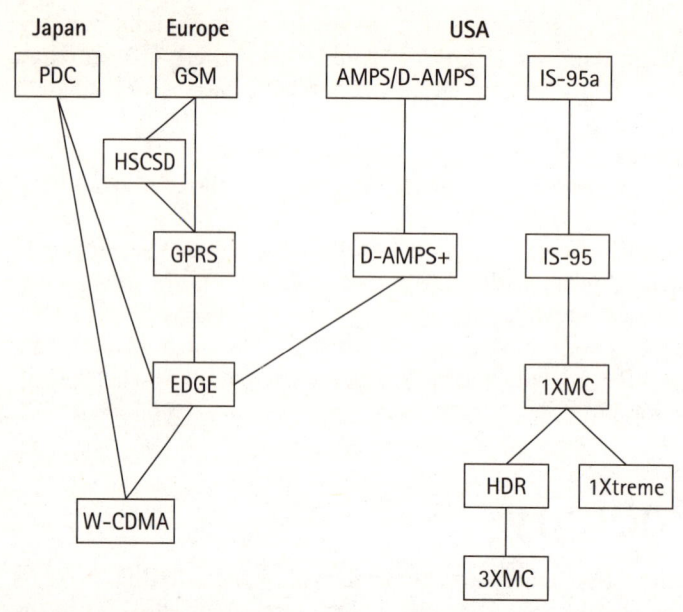

Figure 2-3: 3G upgrade paths

IMT-2000 3G upgrade path

The requirements for 3G were laid down long ago, back in 1992, when the mobile industry thought that a single global standard would exist in the future. The newly invented system was called FPLMTS (Future Land Mobile Telecommunications System), a weird acronym that never stuck and was finally renamed IMT-2000. IMT stands for International Mobile Telecommunications; the 2000 meant three things:

- The 3G network would be deployed around the year 2000.
- The frequency of 2000MHz would be used globally.
- The data rates would be at least 2000kbps.

Although phones were built in 2000, they were the size of a large van. Real deployments are expected, with cautious optimism, sometime in 2005. The U.S. has yet to announce where it plans to make spectrum available for 3G, and it certainly won't be at 2000MHz, because the lower range is taken up by PCS. More than likely, the existing PCS carriers will attempt to shuffle out the older 2G systems and put in 3G systems. And data rates of 2000kbps will be possible only under optimal conditions.

Before it was renamed IMT-2000, the 3G definition was less ambitious. It suggested only that a 3G system be capable of three data rates. These rates were the following:

- 144kbps as the bare minimum, corresponding to a single B-rate ISDN line
- 384kbps as the recommended capacity, corresponding to a single H-rate ISDN line
- 2Mbps as the highest achievable in a small picocell, corresponding to a single P-rate ISDN line

When FPLMTS was renamed to IMT-2000, the Internet was becoming much more popular than it was in 1992, and additional requirements stated that any 3G standard should also support Internet protocols and have a packet-switched back-end network.

Even though one single global standard was supposed to exist, three groups of standards have been proposed to address the issues of roaming, upgradability, and handovers. Two of these standards are based on CDMA and the third has roots in TDMA.

> **NOTE** A mobile device can support airlink protocols and move among different networks worldwide. If the 3G standard were agreed upon everywhere, a mobile device would have to support only one airlink.

Mobile networks without any new 3G spectrum need a way of deploying 3G services without having to rip out too much of their existing design and methodology. This means keeping their existing cells and channel sizes. Because many 2G systems were TDMA based, these requirements limit the options to using a TDMA-based 3G technology.

3G systems will coexist for some time with 2G systems, so 3G networks should be able to hand off a voice call to a 2G network and vice versa. This places some design requirements on the 3G systems. In some cases, designing a 3G system that hands off a call seamlessly between 2G systems such as both a GSM and a cdmaOne network is nearly impossible.

W-CDMA (Wideband CDMA)

W-CDMA was proposed by European carriers who had access to a new spectrum. It is compatible with GSM, allowing for calls placed in GSM to be handed over to W-CDMA networks. A GSM network cannot upgrade to W-CDMA, but some of the GPRS components can be reused for W-CDMA.

> **TIP** *Wideband* refers to the channel bandwidth of 5MHz, as opposed to the 2G bandwidth of 200kHz. This bandwidth is 25 times larger, with the benefit of higher data rates.

W-CDMA adjusts the bit replication amount for data to somewhere between four and 128 times, as opposed to standard CDMA's 64-bit repetition. This adjustment results in conservation of resources on the airlink.

Also, W-CDMA was designed to avoid the need for time synchronization using GPS clocks, resorting instead to gold codes to code information. This new code design was then combined with the same standard CDMA modulation, which was QPSK.

UMTS then defines the European take on all this, and is the planned successor to GSM. Although the Europeans developed the original plan, the first implementers were the Japanese NTT DoCoMo, who wanted a new 3G system deployed fast.

The system has been deployed; the Japanese, however, do not have the same GSM handover requirements as the Europeans and the resulting hardware may introduce incompatibilities.

CDMA2000

This is Qualcomm's direct upgrade path from cdmaOne. The final result of this upgrade path will be a system known as 3XMC. The 3 stands for three channels that, when combined, give each user much higher data rates with a wider band than cdmaOne.

The cdma2000 system is not compatible with GSM, mostly because of the use of a different chip rate in the transceiver. This chip rate is set to a multiple of cdmaOne's rate rather than GSM's.

The standard has been accepted by the ITU as a way to implement a 3G system. Its specifications are almost exactly the same as those for W-CDMA. The two biggest differences have to do with the chip rate and the need for GPS synchronization. Remember that W-CDMA did away with GPS synchronization by using the gold codes. cdma2000 retains the GPS synchronization to be backward-compatible with cdmaOne.

Although 3XMC has been accepted as a 3G standard by the ITU, Qualcomm will make available a technology called High Data Rate (HDR) before 3XMC is finalized. HDR is meant to be an intermediate system for sending and receiving data only, *not* voice.

HDR uses the same channel size as cdmaOne, which is 1.25MHz. The modulation scheme for HDR is 8PSK or 16 QAM, depending on the quality of the airlink.

The maximum data rate with 16 QAM is about 2.4Mbps on the downlink, with 307.2kbps on the uplink. The downlink is shared by about 29 users; that is, 32 minus 3 channels for signaling. The uplink can then be divided into 240 pieces, with each piece or multiples of thereof being given to users.

The HDR system cannot be used to push data, because any data sent must be tied to a request by a handset.

Not wanting to be left in the cold, Nokia and Motorola have proposed their own upgrade paths to cdmaOne. Their system is known as 1xtreme and may be used in place of HDR and 3x Multi-Carrier (3XMC). The system uses only one channel, not three as in 3XMC, but Nokia and Motorola claim that it will provide the same data rates. Also, it uses a system similar to HDR to do both voice and data.

ENHANCED DATA RATES FOR GSM EVOLUTION (EDGE)
EDGE is the only 3G system based on TDMA rather than CDMA. It is being promoted by large U.S. carriers. Originally, it was proposed as a means of extending the lifetime of GSM systems, along with GPRS and HSCSD.

The TDMA carriers in the U.S. picked up the standard and decided that they were going to use it to migrate from the D-AMPS systems.

Because EDGE was a planned upgrade to GSM, it has a channel size of 200kHz. Unlike CDMA systems, EDGE cannot reuse frequencies in neighboring cells. The required bandwidth is only 600kHz for the three channels, making the deployment less intensive for TDMA systems. EDGE has been accepted as an official 3G technology; its standards-based name is UWC-136.

EDGE has the same features as GSM: the eight-time-slot TDMA interface and even the 0.577-millisecond time-slot length. The difference is in the modulation scheme, which is now 8PSK rather than GSM's GMSK. GMSK is binary and 8-PSK supports moving 8 bits per symbol; that is, three times as many bits. So the overall raw slot rate is 64.2kbps rather than 21.4kbps.

Even though this new modulation is supported, it is much more sensitive to problems in connection quality than less sophisticated modulation schemes. As a result, the link can degrade to GMSK if needed.

> **Note:** Owing to the high cost of implementing EDGE, it will probably be combined with GPRS to form a packet-switched 3G technology.

Because the channel width of AMPS channel is 30kHz rather than 200kHz, TDMA proponents devised EDGE Compact as a way to squeeze EDGE into a smaller channel width by eliminating many of the control channels. In discussions of EDGE Compact, the full system is referred to as EDGE Classic. EDGE Compact is used only for data because many voice-control channels have been taken out. EDGE Compact, then, is a temporary system for data service; eventually it will be replaced by a migration to the full EDGE Classic.

Understanding the Core Network

A typical network involves more than just the handset and the cellular base station. The other components involved are shown in Figure 2-4. This first diagram shows voice services and the network components required to enable the voice capability.

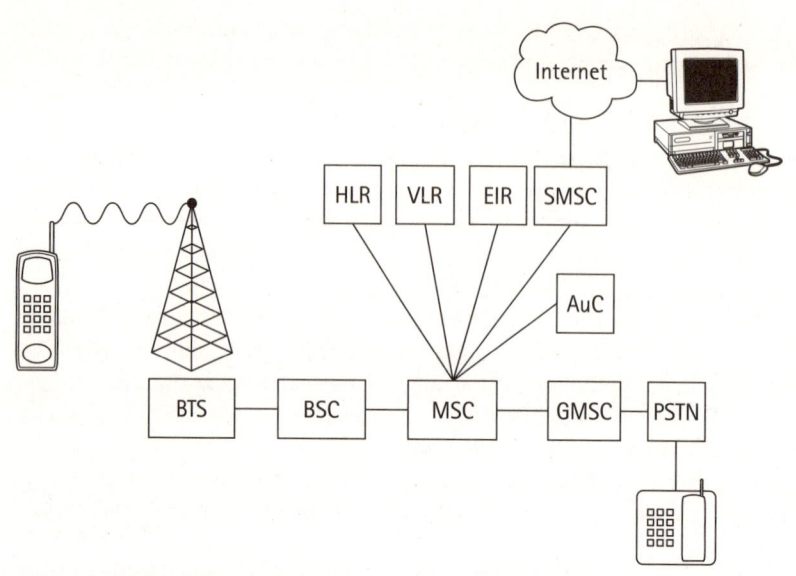

Figure 2-4: A typical voice network

The portion between the handset and the base station is called the airlink. The airlink requires two radios, one at the handset and the other at the base station. The handset is sometimes referred to as the MS (mobile station) or SU (subscriber unit) or even MT (mobile terminal).

The base-station system is called the BTS (Base Transceiver Station) and is a very powerful radio located at the center of a cell. The BTS is a rectangular box attached to several antennas and hoisted far above the ground to avoid obstacles close by.

The next component in the diagram is the BSC (Base Station Controller). This unit manages multiple cells to keep the load on the main center low. These controllers are located several miles away from the actual cells themselves and are stored in a cool, secure environment.

The main component in a voice network is an MSC (Mobile Switching Center), which is responsible for tracking all calls either placed or received by the network. A network can have many of these switches, and each MSC is responsible for a large cluster of cells. The MSC is linked to some important databases. These are the HLR (Home Location Register), VLR (Visitor Location Register), and the EIR (Equipment Identity Register).

The HLR stores information about each user in the system. It stores information about where a user is if that user is within the MSC coverage area; otherwise, it keeps a pointer to the other MSC.

The VLR (Visitor Location Register) temporarily stores the location of all handsets in an MSC's coverage area. A call made to a user in an MSC coverage area will prompt an entry in this database. The user's home HLR still has to be contacted to ensure that the home HLR has a valid pointer to the handset location information.

The EIR is a database that keeps track of handsets that cannot be used, either because they have been stolen or are somehow broken in a way that causes spurious RF activity.

The AuC (Authentication Center) stores security information so that information over the air can be encrypted between the handset and the base station. A user can also be authenticated on the airlink.

The SMSC (Short Message Service Center) is a short-message service center used to send short messages from handsets either to other handsets or to Internet-based hosts.

Another component of the fixed network is the GMSC (Gateway Mobile Switching Center). This special MSCsits on the mobile network and connects the mobile-network switches to those of the standard landline-telephony network.

GPRS infrastructure

The GPRS network is an example of what is in store for all future data networks. Because it is completely packet-switched, it needs components different from those of the standard voice side to make it work. Figure 2-5 shows how a GPRS network could look.

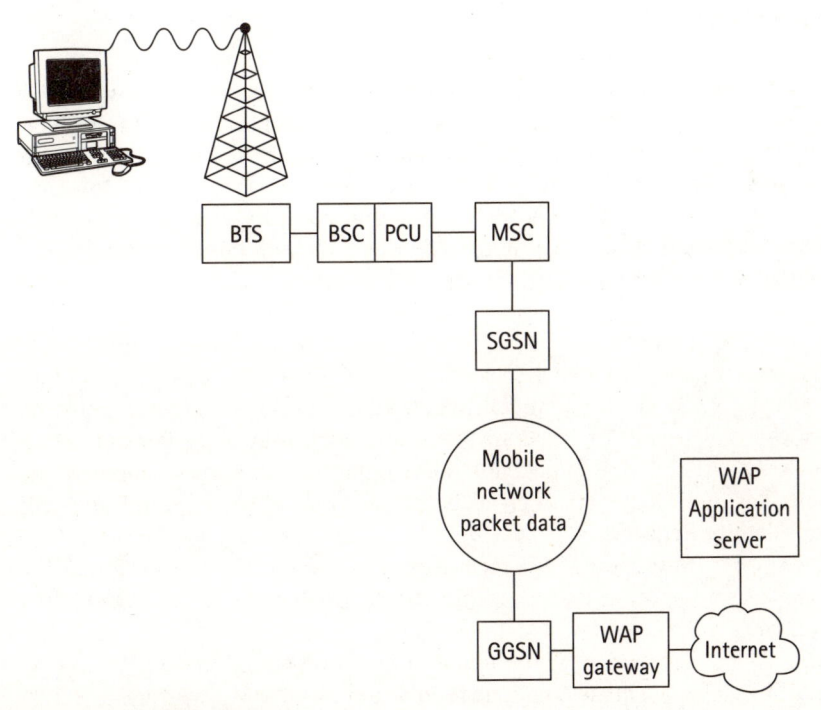

Figure 2-5: A GPRS network

The GPRS network requires a major software upgrade at the base station or close by at the BSC. This major software upgrade is known as the PCU (Packet Control Unit). The PCU is responsible for allowing packet data to travel to the remaining GPRS network pieces.

The next component of the architecture is the SGSN (Serving GPRS Support Node), which is a central switch as far as packet-data processing is concerned. In the future, the SGSN will be connected directly to the PCU. In current practice, though, spare capacity on the voice backhaul may be used up to carry the packet-data information.

Connected to the SGSN is the GGSN, which allows GPRS units access to outside networks. The GGSN (Gateway GPRS Support Node) converts data packets from GTP into TCP or X.25. The first conversion allows GGSNs to be connected directly to Internet-capable routers.

Other components of GPRS are the PTMSC (Point to Multipoint Service Center), which maintains quality-of-service issues, the BG (Border Gateway), a special firewall that monitors connections to external GPRS networks, and the GCG (GPRS Charging Gateway), a charging gateway used for culling billing information from packet data sent over the network.

Summary

In this chapter, I have introduced you to some basic radio concepts. Although these concepts operate very much behind the scenes, understanding this information, even superficially, is important because it will help you to grasp the implications of some of the limited WAP bearers. The next time you have to wait so long for a CDMA CSD connection to start before you can do WAP browsing, you will know why.

Now that you have looked at the WAP bearers, you'll look next at some important prerequisites to understanding the WAP architecture.

Chapter 3

WAP Foundations

IN THIS CHAPTER

- TCP/IP
- HTTP
- XML
- MIME

IN THIS CHAPTER, I discuss some of the core Internet technologies that have been borrowed from or are used in the WAP protocols. It is important that you understand these before investigating the WAP protocols, for two reasons: first, understanding the founding technologies results in a better grasp of WAP concepts; and second, the technologies used in WAP are at times a complex mix of WAP technologies and Internet technologies. The technologies covered in this chapter are TCP/IP, HTTP, XML, and MIME. Even if you are very familiar with these technologies, you may want to refer to the appropriate RFCs (Request For Comments) and references for details about particular aspects exploited by the WAP specifications.

TCP/IP

When discussing the Internet protocols, you can't avoid the basic TCP/IP (Transmission Control Protocol/Internet Protocol) stack. The TCP network or stack has a place in history, as it created the first national network that was completely packet-switched. These packets were self-contained pieces of overhead combined with real data that the intermediate nodes in the network used to determine how the packets got to their destinations.

History

During the Cold War, the United States was faced with the threat of a nuclear attack on its centralized control centers. This threat was the catalyst for the creation of a decentralized network with multiple redundant connections. This new type of network would function even in the event that large sections of it were to be destroyed. The Advanced Research Projects Agency (ARPA), an agency associated with the Department of Defense, funded the research to create this special network. The network started out as a few computers, one at Stanford Research Institute and the others at UCLA and New Mexico. This initial network was known as ARPAnet.

The network was designed such that if a path to a computer was destroyed, other paths could still be used to deliver information to a computer. There was no central control center for the network. In the 70s, many universities joined the network along with many research institutes and some defense companies. At some point in the early 80s, the National Science Foundation (NSF) assumed the responsibility for providing services to haul data among the computers in the network. As the number of commercial entities in the network increased, private telecommunication companies stepped in to provide data services, which they sold or rented. Private companies today own a large part of what has become the Internet. The government agencies have moved to creating other networks for private use.

Most of the traffic on the early Internet was generated by four basic applications (as they were known) sponsored by the Department of Defense. These were electronic mail (e-mail), File Transfer Protocol (FTP), telnet, and news. The most popular of these was e-mail. This service allowed a user on a computer to write a message that could be retrieved and read by a user at another computer on the network. The e-mail application led to the creation of the Network News Transfer Protocol (NNTP), which was used to create discussion lists that computer users could read and post to.

FTP was a popular application at the research institutions, as it allowed users to transfer files quickly among computers. FTP was much faster than the existing mechanisms for transferring research data. The telnet protocol enabled users to log in to a remote computer and send commands to it as if they were sitting right at the local terminal.

These four applications (e-mail, FTP, telnet, and news) drove the Internet for a number of years. The network allowed for quick, easy access to information anywhere. One of the critical problems in the early days was finding the information. Users had to specify the precise location of the information, which made searching for information tedious and too difficult for users without advanced computer skills.

In late 1990, a computer scientist named Tim Berners-Lee from CERN (Conseil Europeen pour le Recherche Nucleaire), otherwise known as the European Laboratory for Particle Physics), together with Robert Cailliau, wrote the first WWW client and the first WWW server along with most of the communications software, defining URLs, HTTP and HTML. They solved the problem of exchanging multiple sets of incompatible data by developing a hypertext storage mechanism. The protocols that they developed enabled users to create links among different computers and display graphics linked to files as well. These links and the related information eventually became known as the World Wide Web. CERN gave the first browser and content-server source code away to programmers for free, which further promoted HTML and HTTP.

Stacks and protocols

The core of the Internet uses a set of protocols to move information from computer to computer. A set of protocols meant to address a particular problem is known as a *protocol stack*. The key protocol in all stacks for Internet use is the Internet Protocol (IP). This protocol provides the address space, routing, and an interface to underlying network technologies. Above the IP protocol rests either TCP or UDP (User Datagram Protocol). A higher layer application is usually designed with the idea that it predominantly uses either TCP or UDP. The four main applications that initially drove the Internet were all based on TCP.

Below the Internet Protocol is an array of physical networks, each with its own characteristics. IP masks this detail so that the higher protocols do not need to be aware of it.

So far I have used the terms *above* and *below* to signify the hierarchy of protocols. Protocols that solve a particular problem come in a stack, wherein the lowest portion of is the physical problem. In this lowest layer, a decision is made about which network to use and how to establish its physical characteristics. Above this layer is the network problem, which determines how computers are addressed on the network and how data are routed among intermediate hosts to a destination. The next layer solves the transport problem: it addresses how data can be sent reliably and what algorithms to use to control how the actual data are stored and read among computers and intermediate routers. The last of the problems lies in creating an application, which achieves the goal of the stack by building upon the lower layers.

In Internet stacks, the physical layer is not usually specified. The network layer is always IP. Above that, the transport layer can be TCP or UDP. TCP is a more reliable protocol but costs more in terms of time, space, and processing requirements. UDP is unreliable and does not ensure that data are actually received in their intended forms. Figure 3-1 shows the four main applications along with their Internet stacks.

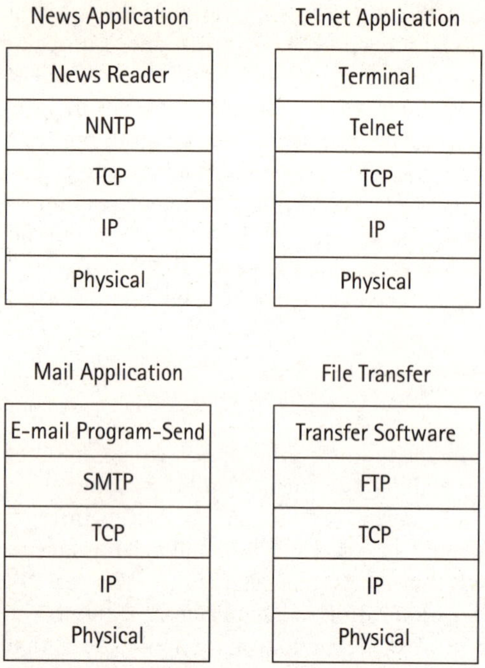

News Application

| News Reader |
| TCP |
| NNTP |
| IP |
| Physical |

(stack order on page: News Reader / NNTP / TCP / IP / Physical)

Telnet Application

| Terminal |
| Telnet |
| TCP |
| IP |
| Physical |

Mail Application

| E-mail Program-Send |
| SMTP |
| TCP |
| IP |
| Physical |

File Transfer

| Transfer Software |
| FTP |
| TCP |
| IP |
| Physical |

Figure 3-1: Stack diagrams for original Internet protocols

The OSI model

The Open Systems Interworking (OSI) model is a newer model, and is more often discussed in academic terms than actually used. I mention it here because I will later compare it to the WAP model.

The OSI model contains seven layers for defining how a computer-networking problem should be solved: Physical, Data Link, Network, Transport, Session, Presentation, and Application. The model takes three layers to define the application rather than just one, and two layers to describe the physical layer rather than just one. Figure 3-2 shows how OSI compares to the Internet.

| Application |
| Transport |
| Network |
| Physical |

| NNTP/FTP/SMTP/Telnet |
| TCP/UDP |
| IP |
| Ethernet & twisted pair |

OSI 7 layer model, its evolution and an example

| Application |
| Transport |
| Network |
| Physical |

| Application |
| Presentation |
| Session |
| Transport |
| Network |
| Data Link |
| Physical |

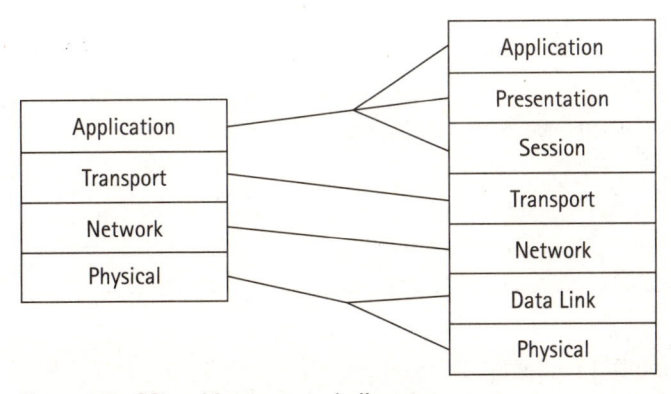

Figure 3-2: OSI and Internet stack diagrams

Table 3-1 describes the components of the OSI stack.

TABLE 3-1 OSI COMPONENTS

Component	Description
Physical	The physical cables and connectors associated with network connection.
Data Link	The data-link layer that controls the transmission of binary frames from one computer to another.
Network	The layer that routes packets and takes care of fragmentation, reassembly, and flow control.
Transport	The layer that actually transmits messages to processes on connected computers.
Session	The layer used to establish and maintain a connection between two computers.
Presentation	The layer that encodes and decodes user data so that different machines can read the data.
Application	The program that serves the user. The users interact with this program to use the communication network.

I show later on how the OSI model applies to the WAP protocols, but Figure 3-3 shows how to analyze HTTP using the OSI model.

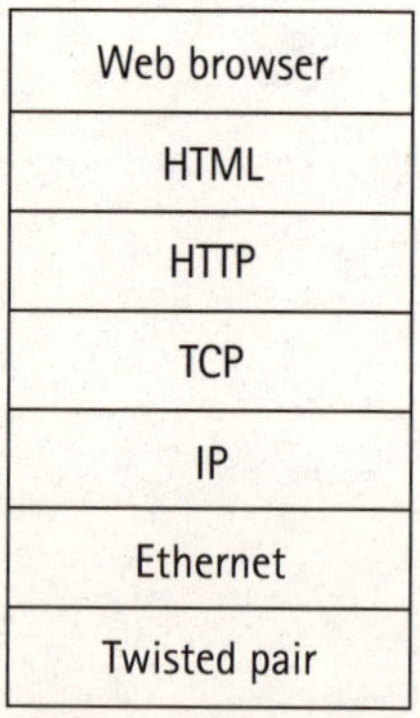

Web browser
HTML
HTTP
TCP
IP
Ethernet
Twisted pair

Figure 3-3: The HTTP stack

TCP versus UDP

The Internet stack defines two transport stacks. I would like to make it very clear what the differences are between the two and which applications work better with each. Both of these protocols compose the data from applications into messages and deliver them to the IP layer. The only address that the IP protocol defines is a computer address, so the transport layer must specify a service address, which it does by using a port number. The transport protocols also provide varying degrees of flow control and end-to-end reliability. UDP offers no flow control or end-to-end reliability guarantee, whereas TCP offers both.

A TCP connection is like a UNIX bit pipe, except that it supports a reliable bi-directional byte stream. Both processes that see the stream do not see any of the individual packets needed to send the messages between computers. All they see is a byte stream that can be read or written to. TCP is a fairly complicated protocol because it ensures end-to-end reliability and ordered sequencing of the byte stream. It also tries to optimize the network bandwidth by managing data flow.

UDP is a lot like TCP; it also uses port numbers to identify computer processes. It encapsulates messages using IP and contains a rudimentary checksum of the data. But unlike TCP, UDP is packet-oriented. Applications that use UDP see the packets delivered to them exactly as they were carried across the network. The protocol has no acknowledgement of received packets and provides no guarantee of reliable delivery.

UDP is an unreliable protocol: messages can arrive out of sequence or be lost, and it becomes the application's responsibility to handle the problem. Although this sounds like a serious liability, the UDP protocol actually does fine under normal network conditions. For those cases where 100% reliability is not required it is the more efficient protocol to use. UDP can also be effective in those cases where applications take care of their own reliability needs. Examples of applications that use UDP are DNS (Domain Name System), voice and video over IP, and RIP (Routing Information Protocol). DNS is the protocol that converts names to numbers for addressing purposes; if 100% reliability is not required, it uses UDP. Voice and video services normally use UDP because it is much more efficient and errors in the stream may not even need to be corrected in time, for example, the viewer may not even notice that pixel 6 out of a 1000 was blue instead of green for $1/100^{th}$ of a second. Routing information on the Internet is also disseminated using the UDP protocol with RIP. One example of the application protocol becoming stronger because of the problems with UDP is NFS.

The transport problem

Now that you have seen some stacks and layers and protocols, it is important that you understand that I provide this academic analysis in order to solve a computer-networking problem. Networking involves at least two processes, communicating either over a long distance or on the same computer. These two processes usually follow a client/server methodology, where one process is listening and the other is sending information. Generally, clients initiate a session, whereas servers sit and wait for clients to connect to retrieve information.

Because at least two processes are involved, it is prudent to include at least two stack diagrams when discussing computer communication. The first stack is for the client and the other for the server. Furthermore, many more computers are involved in facilitating a communication channel. These computers can be included or excluded depending on the area of current focus.

Consider, for example, a Web browser, the client, communicating with a Web server. The browser is an HTTP client. The server is an HTTP server. Imagine that two routers exist between the two. Figure 3-4 shows what the complete stack picture would look like in this scenario.

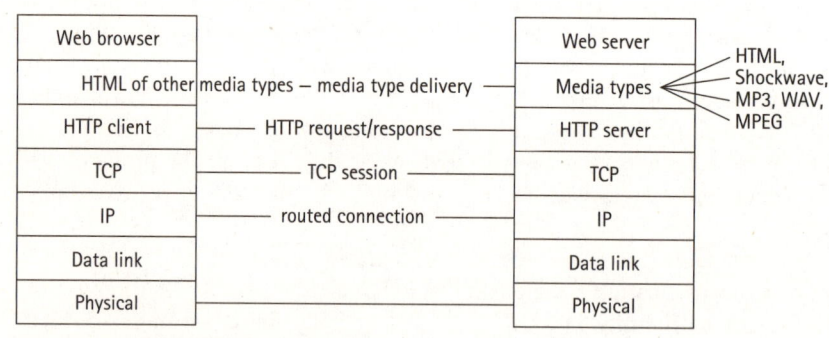

Web browser		Web server	HTML,
HTML of other media types	— media type delivery —	Media types	Shockwave, MP3, WAV,
HTTP client	— HTTP request/response —	HTTP server	MPEG
TCP	— TCP session —	TCP	
IP	— routed connection —	IP	
Data link		Data link	
Physical		Physical	

Figure 3-4: Stacks in communication

In studying wireless Internet, you will see many more diagrams like this to help you understand how computer-networking problems are solved.

HTTP

HTTP is the HyperText Transfer Protocol, which defines a specification for sending and receiving data on the World Wide Web. Clients, known as Web browsers, use this protocol to retrieve data from servers known as Web servers. The protocol solves a specific problem: it allows access to multiple forms of data in remote locations by defining a set of standard exchanges between the remote locations. It also solves the problem by assuming that users are willing to sit in front of machine searching for these data. As you know, this form of protocol is not suitable for all applications. This is why different protocols exist for things such as sending and receiving mail or browsing newsgroups.

> **NOTE:** HTTP as a protocol is a client/server request/response protocol focused on allowing clients to retrieve information on network servers. However, the protocol is focused on providing this exchange linked to a users interaction. Therefore, the request for information is tied to a user's request for it. Because it is not expected that a user will issue 100 requests per second or expect a response to a hundred requests in a second, that performance criteria is not built into the protocol. The protocol is also designed such that the client or browser user is always the initiator of the transaction. Because of this, the server cannot independently push information to the browser. These limitations surface frequently whenever the user browser is substituted with a computer or when the server is required to initiate transactions. So, to summarize, the protocol is designed for a very specific purpose, client searches for information.

As with all Internet session layer protocols, the HTTP protocol is text-based. It uses text-based commands to allow for interaction between a Web browser (or HTTP client) and a Web server (or HTTP server). The actual HTTP session is carried over the TCP protocol. The TCP session is controlled to some extent by the commands and exchanges in the HTTP sessions. The preceding is a simplified view; a more advanced case is that of proxy servers, for which multiple intermediaries between the Web browser and Web server are required to pass the requests and responses between the two end points (Web browser and Web server).

HTTP transactions can be divided into two main types: HTTP requests and HTTP responses. The Web client initiates HTTP requests and must indicate where it wants to go. It does this by using a Uniform Resource Locator (URL). Here is an example URL:

```
http://www.zsigo.com:80/
```

The first portion of this is the protocol name, which is simply `http://`. The browser uses this prefix to go into HTTP mode, as opposed to those of other protocols it may support. TCP/IP hosts are associated with names: `www.zsigo.com` is the name of the host, `www`, and the name of the domain the host resides in, `zsigo.com`. The next part is a number, which identifies the port number to which the browser connects. The standard port number for Web servers is `80`; if no number is specified this is the number the Web browser will use. This number specifies the port on which the Web server is listening for requests. All these parameters are used by the browser to connect to the Web server using TCP/IP. The last portion of the URL is the slash (/). Anything after the hostname and port number is called the document path. The document path defines where the resource is located on the remote Web server.

Once the TCP session is up, the Web browser initiates the HTTP session. The format of the session looks a lot like this:

```
GET / HTTP/1.1
Accept: text/html, image/jpeg, */*
Accept-Language: en-us
Accept-Encoding: gzip, deflate
User-Agent: Mozilla/4.01 Compatible
Host: www.zsigo.com
Connection: Keep-Alive
```

This is an example of a simple HTTP session request. A user types a URL like the one I mentioned earlier, `http://www.zsigo.com:80/`. The browser then picks out the parameters it needs to begin a TCP/IP session and initiates a request using the syntax shown in the preceding code. The first line of the request is `GET / HTTP/1.1`. The first word refers to the `GET` method of HTTP. The next part is the document path, which in this case is quite simple: it is a slash (/). The Web server on the other side will have to determine what a slash means. Many Web servers tie the slash to index.htm or index.html. The next part of the request specifies the version of HTTP protocol being used. Only three versions exist: 0.9, 1.0, and 1.1. Only HTTP 1.1 is supported by WAP gateways, so that is the version I discuss here.

The second line of the request tells the Web server what types of content the browser is willing to accept. In this case, the browser supports the jpeg and html formats and will attempt to display any other types that are sent to it.

The third line tells the server the preferred language of the browser. In this case it is U.S. English. Multiple languages can be specified here in a comma-delimited list. The order in which they appear indicates the order of preference.

The fourth line tells the server what compression algorithms the Web browser supports, so that the server can compress content using those formats and the browser will still be able to read it.

The fifth line shows the user agent (UA), which tells the server what type of browser is connecting to it. The content author, in deciding what format to present to clients, can query this field. For example, if a content author wants to make use of a feature such as hover text in Internet Explorer (IE) he or she can query this field to decide when to use it.

The sixth line tells the Web server what the client perceives to be the hostname. This is important in cases where a single server may have multiple hostnames associated with it. The Web server can use this argument to distinguish between requests and to map requests to the right content tree.

The seventh line is the connection header, which tells the server to keep the TCP/IP connection between the browser and the server open. In older browsers the connection is disconnected immediately after the Web server sends out a single response. For HTTP 1.1, the session is kept open until the Web browser explicitly makes the request. A keep-alive packet ensures that the connection is kept alive until the Web browser makes a request to shut it down.

Taken together, these seven lines comprise an HTTP request. The next important part of the HTTP request is the HTTP response. Everything after the first line is called a request header.

If you were to use the preceding request, and the server were online and accepted the TCP/IP session, it would then look for the resource you mentioned in the document path, and then return a response to the browser. That resource could be a static file or it could be dynamically generated in real time by a server-side script. Here is an example of the type of response that would result.

```
HTTP/1.1 200 OK
Date: Thu, 02 Nov 2000 23:50:03 GMT
Server: Microsoft-IIS/4.0
Content-Type: text/html
Accept-Ranges: bytes
Last-Modified: Wed, 27 Aug 1997 12:44:24 GMT
Etag: "0847cf2e6b2bc1:e28"
Content-length: 33 bytes
Connection: close

<HTML>
    <p>
        A test page in HTML
    </p>
</HTML>
```

In this response, you will see a set of lines in plain text. Each one of the lines contains information about what the browser should do with the response.

The first line contains the control code of the HTTP protocol. The 200-status code tells the browser that the file requested was located on the Web server and can be found in the content of the response. The version of the HTTP protocol that the server uses is also listed here.

The second line shows the current date and time on the server. Browsers may use this property to determine whether the information received is stale.

The third line shows the server software. In this example, the Web server is running version 4.0 of Microsoft Internet Information Server.

The fourth line shows a content type. In this case, the root document path resulted in the return of an HTML document.

The fifth line indicates that the server is able to send documents to the browser byte by byte instead of all at once. This feature becomes important in cases where generating the document all at once may take longer than a user is willing to wait.

The sixth line shows the most recent modification date for the document. This time is used to determine whether content can be reused from the cache or whether a fresh copy is required. This is a complex determination by both the Web browser and Web server; you can find a detailed discussion in Chapter 12.

The seventh line contains an entity tag, which gives the Web browser a unique reference to the document returned in the response. It is used for documents modified more frequently than the date header can show.

Part 1: Foundations

The eighth line tells the Web browser the size of the document packaged in the response. It is important for the browser to know this, because it has to read the data and display them. The entity or response data is 33 bytes long in this example.

The last line tells the browser that the connection will now close. This means that the Web browser opens another TCP/IP session to obtain more data.

After the initial lines is a blank line followed by the actual response data.

Notice how the Web server's only job is to send the right documents back or indicate that some problem prevented it from doing so. All of the grunt work of parsing the response data and packaging them together in a form for the user display is up to the browser. The diagram in Figure 3-5 depicts the entire request-response cycle.

HTTP Browser

```
GET /wireless/index.html HTTP/1.1
Host: test.web.com
Connection: close
User-Agent: Mozilla/3.0
Accept-Language: en
Accept: */*
Accept-Encoding: gzip
```

Web server

```
HTTP/1.1  200 OK
Date: Wed,14 Feb 2001 08:30:44 GMT
Server: Microsoft IIS 4.0
Last modified: Tue,13 Feb 2001 05:43:12 GMT
Content-length: 487
Connection: close
Content-type: text/html

<HTML>
...
<HTML>
```

Web server

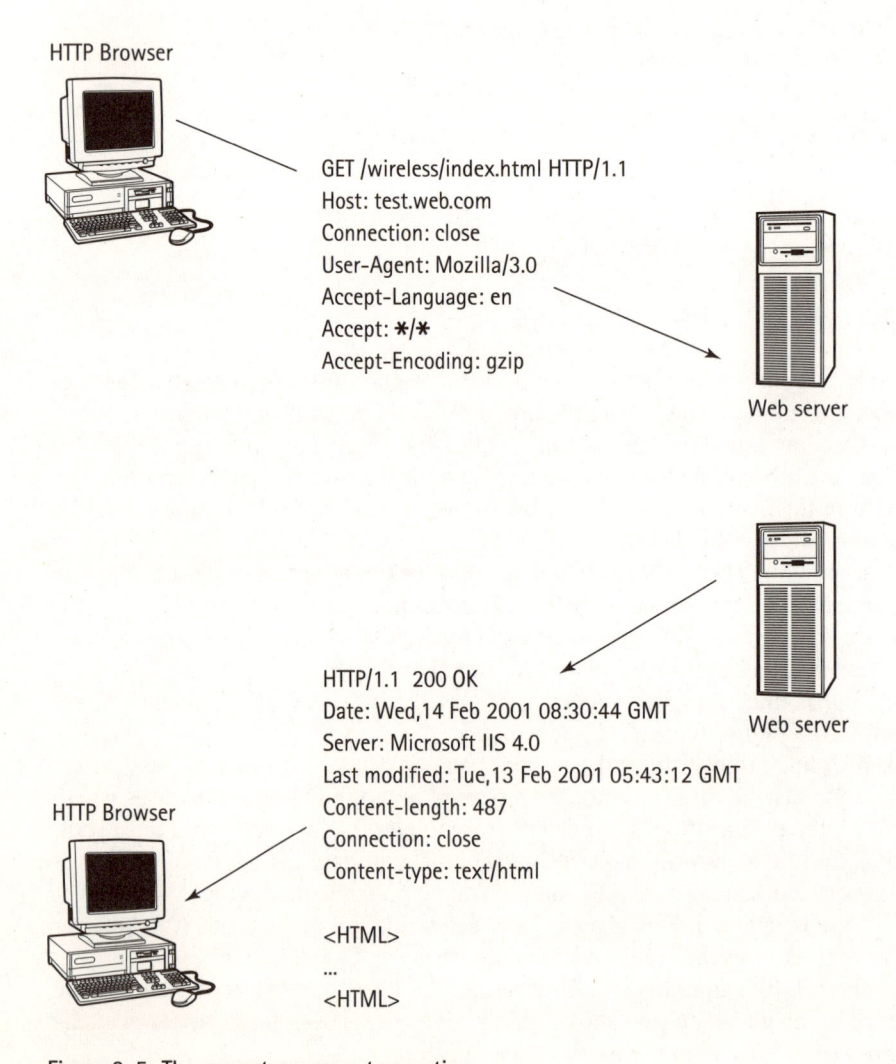

HTTP Browser

Figure 3-5: The request-response transaction

The structure of HTTP requests

In the most general cases, not all HTTP headers are required. In fact, the HTTP version 0.9 required only the method, as in the following example:

```
GET /
```

HTTP version 1.0 therefore required a version number:

```
GET / HTTP/1.0
```

In the case of HTTP 1.1 the minimal amount of information needed to send a request would be the following:

```
GET / HTTP/1.1
Host: www.zsigo.com
```

However, let us examine what the general headers look like. HTTP requests have several general components, as shown in Figure 3-6.

HTTP Client Request Structure

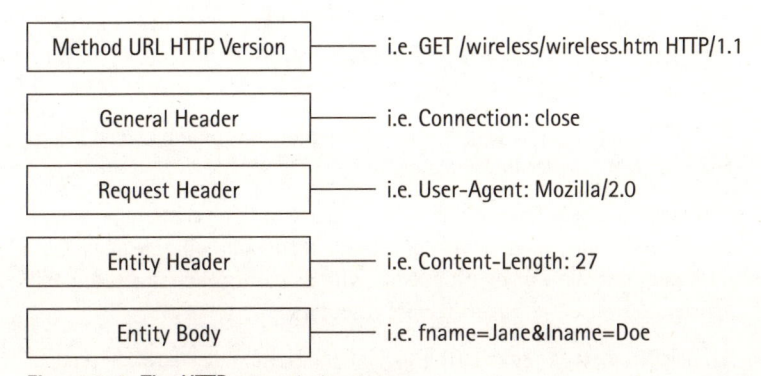

Method URL HTTP Version	— i.e. GET /wireless/wireless.htm HTTP/1.1
General Header	— i.e. Connection: close
Request Header	— i.e. User-Agent: Mozilla/2.0
Entity Header	— i.e. Content-Length: 27
Entity Body	— i.e. fname=Jane&lname=Doe

Figure 3-6: The HTTP request structure

The first of the components is the method. `HTTP/1.1` allows the methods GET, POST, HEAD, PUT, LINK, UNLINK, DELETE, OPTIONS, and TRACE. A Web server from an older version of HTTP will not support some of these methods. For example, an HTTP 1.0 server will not support TRACE or OPTIONS. Table 3-2 lists the various HTTP client methods.

TABLE 3-2 HTTP METHODS

Method	Description
GET	This method simply obtains a resource from a location on the Web server. GET was the only method in HTTP 0.9 and is used in almost all regular Web transactions.
HEAD	This method requests only the return headers in a response. The entity is not packaged with the response.
POST	This method tells the server that besides making a request for a resource, it contains information inside the entity portion of the request. This is the second most common header in all Web traffic.
PUT	This method puts resources onto the server. It can either put a new resource on the server or replace an old one.
DELETE	This method deletes a resource from the Web server.
TRACE	This method asks Web proxies to declare their information to the originating client. It can be a useful debugging tool in cases where proxies are adding information to or deleting information from your original request.
OPTIONS	A Web browser uses this method to find out what methods can be used for a server. Servers may have proprietary methods or documents may have special methods associated with them.
CONNECT	A Web browser uses this method when it needs to communicate with an HTTPS-capable server through a proxy.
LINK, UNLINK (RFC 2068 only)	This method allows for a special link relationship to be created between the document identified by a Request-URI header and other resources. LINK does not allow any entities to be sent as part of the request and is efficient because it does not require resources. An UNLINK method removes the special link created by a LINK method, if one exists. Both of these methods have been deprecated in RFC 2616, the latest version of the HTTP 1.1, because of lack of implementation.
PATCH (RFC 2068 only)	A Web browser uses this method, which is very similar to a PUT method, to put information onto the server; the information sent to the server is a list of differences from the original version of the document that is stored on the server. This method has been deprecated in RFC 2616, the latest version of HTTP 1.1, because of lack of implementation.

This first method's component also contains a URL that points to a location on the server. Different Web servers parse the URL in their own proprietary ways, but at some point they translate the URL into a resource stored on the content server. URLs do not have to map to an actual resource; instead they can point to a dynamic program whose output is then sent to the Web browser.

The last line of this component contains the HTTP version number in use by the browser.

The second component on the list is a general message header. Message headers are optional, as I mentioned in the beginning of this section. They give information about the request that applies to the session in general. The time or connection headers are examples of headers that fall into this category.

The third component of the HTTP request is the request header. The request header gives the server information about the browser. Headers that fall into this category are the user agent, accept, and accept language headers, all of which are example headers that give information about the capabilities of the client.

The fourth component of the HTTP request is the entity header. An entity refers to data, other than the method line or header lines, that are contained in a request. An entity header is rarely sent in a request for information. However, in several WAP examples you will deal with the POST method, which will require an entity header.

The existence of an entity header means that there is another component, the entity body, which is separated from the headers by a blank line.

The structure of HTTP responses

A general structure can also be applied to server responses. The diagram in Figure 3-7 shows what a general response looks like. Many of the same headers that apply to requests are also used in HTTP responses.

HTTP Server Response Structure

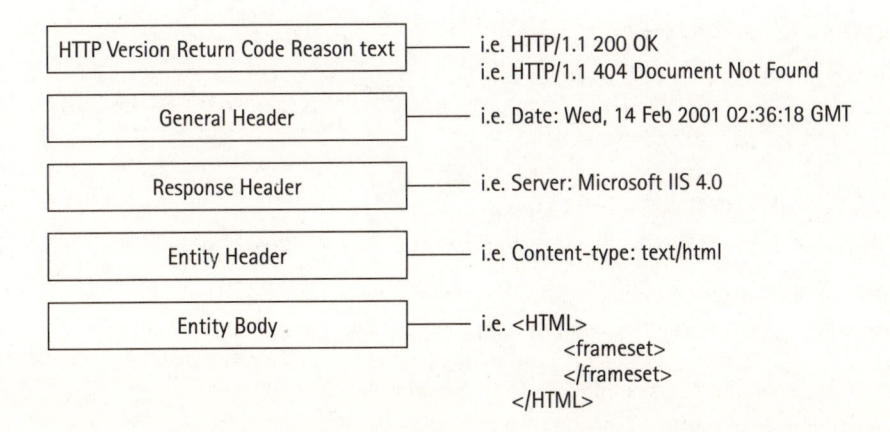

HTTP Version Return Code Reason text	i.e. HTTP/1.1 200 OK
	i.e. HTTP/1.1 404 Document Not Found
General Header	i.e. Date: Wed, 14 Feb 2001 02:36:18 GMT
Response Header	i.e. Server: Microsoft IIS 4.0
Entity Header	i.e. Content-type: text/html
Entity Body	i.e. <HTML>
	<frameset>
	</frameset>
	</HTML>

Figure 3-7: The HTTP response structure

The first component of the HTTP response is the status-code line. This line begins with the HTTP version number in use by the server and is followed by a status code and a reason phrase. This reason phrase is simply the English-language version of what the status code means.

The second component of the HTTP response is the general header. These general header components follow the same format as the request general header. The general header contains general information about the HTTP session.

The third component of the HTTP response is the response header, which tells the Web browser how the server is configured. For example, the server name is a response header. Another example of a response header is one that tells the browser whether basic authentication is supported.

The fourth component of the response is the entity header, which gives the Web browser information about the entity that is to follow. For example, the type of media and the size of the content are examples of specific entity headers.

The last component is separated from the others by a blank line and contains a media entity, which is some representation of the resource that was requested.

The two methods used throughout this book and the WAP specifications are the GET method and the POST method. The following sections delve a little bit into the details behind them and their usage.

The GET method

The GET method is the main method used by Web browsers when data are requested from a Web server. The response to a GET can come from myriad real sources, whose true form can be masked by the Web server. For example, a GET request sent from a Web browser can request a Web server, which in turn makes a request of yet another server for an image that is being collected in real time from an imaging satellite. After the request is made, the server attempts to locate and return the resource along with the related headers.

Listing 3-1 shows how a GET request and its response are packaged.

Listing 3-1: The GET Request and Response

```
GET /logos/background.gif HTTP/1.1
Accept: */*
Referer: http://localhost:8080/
Accept-Language: en-us
Accept-Encoding: gzip, deflate
User-Agent: Mozilla/4.0 (compatible; MSIE 5.01; Windows 98)
Host: localhost:8080
Connection: Keep-Alive
Cookie: ASPSESSIONIDFFEVVSL=PMGBKGGBEKJGJJHKFMEGAMNMD

HTTP/1.1 200 OK
Date: Wed, 14 Feb 2001 23:00:14 GMT
```

```
Server: Apache/1.3.6 (Unix) mod_ssl/2.2.7 SSLeay/0.9.0b
Last-Modified: Thu, 09 Sep 1999 05:19:35 GMT
Etag: "18df3-8ce-37d74367"
Accept-Ranges: bytes
Content-Length: 2254
Keep-Alive: timeout=15, max=99
Connection: Keep-Alive
Content-Type: image/gif

GIF89ad d Äÿ ÿÿÿJ E @ < 7 3 . ) % !

   ...
```

The POST method

The POST method is the most popular for sending data to a program on the server while issuing a request for information. For example, if I wanted to obtain a satellite image for a particular area of the world, I might want that image to be centered on a certain latitude and longitude. The best way to send this information to the server would be to use a POST method along with a request for a resource location.

Today the POST method usually refers to a dynamic script, which turns around and interfaces with other hardware or software. In the future the POST method may expand in capability to directly access the hardware or software.

The POST method is special because the data sent to the server are packaged in the entity body of the request. After the Web server reads the headers it sends the entity data to the dynamic script for processing. POST requests should include a content-type for the entity to be included. The most popular form of content-type in which to package variables for dynamic scripts on the server is URL-Encoding. This enables you to send data collected in HTML forms to a program on the Web server. For example, the following HTML code would display a form for the user:

```
<form method="post" action="/scripts/checkname.pl">
<b>
Enter your name: <input name="nickname" maxlength="15" size="20">
And your favorite color: <input name="favcolor" maxlength="15" size="20">
</b>
<input type="submit" value="Check Name">
<input type="reset" value="Clear Entry">
</form>
```

A user could then fill out the form. After the user clicked on the submit button, an HTTP request that looks like the following code would be issued by the browser:

```
POST /scripts/checkname.pl
Host: www.zsigo.com
Referer: http:/www.zsigo.com/accountsetup.html
Accept: */*
Content-type: application/x-www-form-urlencoded
Content-length: 30

nickname=elvis&favcolor=yellow
```

Notice how the request contains an entity, which contains the variables that were entered in the form. You will see later how these variables could just have well been placed in a GET URL string. However, the use of the POST method is recommended in almost all instances.

The Web server sees the POST method and first processes the headers and the URL. Then it extracts the entity body and sends it the dynamic script referenced by the URL. Usually the path in the URL is a pseudopath, meaning that it is further dereferenced to a secure directory that is allowed to run dynamic scripts.

Here is what the output of the dynamic script for the preceding POST request might look like:

```
HTTP/1.1 200 OK
Date: Thu, 02 Nov 2000 23:50:06 GMT
Server: Apache/ 1.3.7
MIME-Version: 1.0
Content-type: text/html
Last-modified: Thu, 07 Aug 1997 20:10:06 GMT
Content-length: 45

<h1> Your user checks out!  Welcome in.<h1>
```

The encoded parameters shown in the previous example are URL-Encoded. This format is used when the Web browser is sending variables to the server. Variables are packaged as an entity and separated from each other by an ampersand (&). The variable value is separated from the variable name by an equals sign (=). Any characters other than letters and numbers are considered special and must be encoded as their hexadecimal ASCII value preceded by a percent sign (%). For example, $ becomes %24. The only exception is the space character, for which either a plus sign (+) or its hexadecimal representation (2B) is allowed.

The POST method does not only support the URL-Encoded format. You can use other forms, such as multipart/formdata, to send entire files to programs on the Web server. In these cases the data are actually sent with a MIME extension. I will cover MIME in the MIME section of this chapter.

Looking back at Figure 3-4, you will see that HTTP can create a session wherein data can be transferred between clients called Web browsers and servers called Web servers or content servers. The actual data to be transferred is shown to the user and constructed in the presentation layer of a seven-layer stack. The presentation formats in the examples in this section use HTML. However, other presentations such as XML also exist, and WAP defines many of its own presentation formats such as WML. I discuss the presentation formats in greater detail in the next section.

XML

XML (EXtensible Markup Language) is a special presentation markup language extendable enough to enable the creation of other presentation languages. The language allows for the definition of a structure for data such that the data can be transferred between programs, stored, or simply inputted or outputted between processes.

Normally programs store data in text files or binary files. A binary file is a stream of bits created by specialized programs and constructed for other specialized programs. Consider the case of a computer strategy game. It needs to store codes representing the current status of the game, your position, the enemy position, the number of units you and your enemy own, what types of units they are, and so on. When you retrieve a saved game, the game program interprets stored binary codes to display the current game status. Another computer strategy game may use different codes to distinguish the different military units, and it may store the codes differently even if it involves the same type of strategy scenarios. The codes used in these examples are considered metadata; they can be used to create yet other games. A strategy code saved with one type of game in a proprietary format cannot be read by the other game, because the two have incompatible file formats and use different metadata.

> **NOTE**
> Meta is common prefix used in the computer industry that means "about." So for example, a meta tag contains information about other tags. Metafile means a file containing information about files. In this same vein, XML is considered a meta language because it can be used to create other languages.
>
> Metadata is data about data, or in simpler terms, it is data that describes how a set of other data is formatted and collected together.

Binary data are extremely fast for programs to process, so designers of programs are much more likely to use proprietary formats than textual ones. It is hard to disassemble a binary format to find out what the bits mean, making it difficult to obtain a quick, human-readable form.

The other common type of file-storage format is a text file. Text files also store streams of bits, but this time the streams use a known encoding, such as ASCII text. Groups of bits read together form characters that can then be displayed inside a reader. Text files are formatted using a known standard that all programs are aware of, and so they can be read by many applications. The disadvantage of text files is that they cannot easily store coded information or properties; they can only contain textual information. For example, it would be difficult and cumbersome for a strategy game to use textual form because a large number of special codes would be required.

XML is intended to take advantage of the universality of text files and add to them an efficiency of reading comparable to that of binary files. This idea was first developed and standardized by ISO in 1986 with a technology called SGML (Standard Generalized Markup Language). SGML was designed as a language that would allow data to be marked up or coded for any purpose. SGML is used today in large document-management systems, but because of its complexity it has not seen more use. The best-known markup language is HTML, which was created to display and link information. HTML is an example of a specialized SGML application. A lot of the complexity of SGML was removed to create the more compact HTML language.

HTML is a text-based language that contains hyperlinks and other useful display codes. Browsers format the screen by using these display codes, and the hyperlinks enable users to navigate among the different documents.

Although HTML was a very successful language it could not be used as an efficient mechanism for the storage, structure, or transfer of preformatted data because it was highly specialized. SGML was too complicated for the task. XML was then developed by the W3C to meet this need. XML is still a subset of SGML and it was constructed in such a way that SGML readers can still read all XML documents but XML readers cannot still read all SGML documents.

XML's primary function is to create documents that describe information. XML data contains information not just about the data being stored but also about their relative association with other data components. The following code is an example showing a simple XML document that stores a customer name and address:

```
<customer>
  <name>
    <first type="English">Jane</first>
    <middle/>
    <last>Doe</last>
  </name>
  <address>
    <street1>27 North Street</street1>
    <street2/>
    <city>Dallas</city>
    <state>TX</state>
    <zip>27005</zip>
  </address>
</customer>
```

The examples show a sample XML document that has formatted textual information using special text codes. The first code is <customer> and the last code is

</customer>, and these codes act as a container for the rest of the document. These codes taken together are called an XML element. Everything between the angle brackets (< and >) is known as a tag. The tags constitute the markup of the document. The rest of the data is information. The tags can be start tags, which are simply text surrounded by angle brackets, or end tags, which start with </ and end with >. In the preceding example code, the elements adhere to a hierarchy, which is preserved by the XML format. The customer's name and address are independent elements that are both associated with a customer. The first name, middle name, and last name are then associated with a customer name and not a customer address, as you might expect.

You may also notice in the previous XML code listing that some of the tags appear in a shortened form, for example, <middle/> in the first name element. You can use this special form when the element contains no content inside its beginning and ending tags. So the same element could also be written as <middle></middle>. A similar abbreviated form appears in the previous XML code listing for the second street line in the address element.

The text type ="English" in the tag is an example of an element attribute. It provides information about the tag that may be useful to an application. The entire XML document is packaged inside a beginning tag called customer and a similar ending tag. These two tags and everything between them make up what is known as the root element. The root element is a container for all the other tags.

XML concepts

After XML documents have been created, programs called parsers read them. These programs come in two types, non-validating and validating. Non-validating parsers check to see whether the XML information is well formed. Validating parsers check to see whether the information is well formed but also validate the information against a document type definition (DTD). Later in this book, you will learn how the WAP specifications use DTDs to define new data types for a lot of WAP media. But before we discuss DTDs, let's delve into what being well formed means.

Well-formed XML

A well-formed XML document must do the following:

1. Comply with the rules for elements
2. Comply with the rules for attributes
3. Have a valid declaration
4. Respect the rules for white space

A document that meets these requirements is considered well formed. In order to comply with the first requirement on the preceding list, rules for XML elements, a document must comply with the following set of rules:

- Tags must have an end tag
- Tags cannot overlap
- XML documents can only have one root element
- Element names must obey XML naming characteristics
- XML documents must observe case sensitivity
- White space must be preserved in text

Every XML tag must have an end tag. This requirement seems very straightforward when you look at a system like HTML wherein tags do not have to be closed with ending tags. In those cases, the HTML browser has to check whether a single tag or two tags are required in any given context. This increases the complexity of the software needed to write an HTML browser.

XML is a strictly hierarchical language, which means that no tags can overlap. A tag must be completely associated with a single other tag, which is its parent. Therefore, children of parents must be nested completely inside the parents. Generally, this means that information inside an XML document can be formatted into a tree, which can be traced back to a single root element. XML documents can have only one root. All elements are then descendants of this one root element.

In order to follow the rules of elements, the names of the elements can only start with letters or an underscore (_). After the first character, numbers are allowed as well as the period (.) and hyphen (-). The names of XML elements cannot contain any spaces or colons (:). Names can start with letters in uppercase or lowercase and contain letters with both. No spaces are allowed after the initial bracket in a tag, but there can be a space before the ending bracket.

> **CAUTION:** XML tags are case-sensitive. Therefore, even though mixed mode is allowed in the naming of elements, `<tag></tag>` is different from `<TaG></TaG>`. This case-sensitivity can result in confusion and you will find that tags are not usually coded with such potentially confusing names.

White space between the two tags is given a special name, PCDATA. The only limitation on PCDATA is that it cannot include XML syntactical characters such as angle brackets (< or >). If the user does not specify otherwise, this is the default format for all data in XML documents. In HTML, all spaces are usually reduced to one space; however, with XML the spaces are kept in their original form, and it is only in the case of line feeds and carriage returns that a new line is represented as a single line feed. If extraneous space exists between the tags, the parser has to decide what to do with it.

XML attributes also have rules to determine whether a document is well formed. XML attributes must do the following:

- ◆ Have name and value pairs associated with an element
- ◆ Be attached only to the starting tag and not to the ending tag
- ◆ Have values in quotes that match, either single or double
- ◆ Follow the same naming rules as elements
- ◆ Have unique names for an element

It can be argued that attributes are not required in an XML document. For example, this code:

```
<name first="Jane" middle="Ann" last="Doe">
</name>
```

is equivalent to this code:

```
<name>
  <first>Jane<first/>
  <middle>Ann<middle/>
  <last>Doe<last/>
</name>
```

However, in practice, attributes are actually used and reserved for information that is not relevant to all applications reading the XML information. With regard to the storage of names, the first, middle, and last name can be expected to be relevant to all applications: therefore, you would expect them to appear in separate elements. Systems constructed by in-house design teams may conform to different standards.

As shown in a previous example, elements containing no data can be simplified from `<tag></tag>` to simply `<tag/>`. This shorthand form is normally used for elements that have only attributes and no child elements. Sometimes, also, an element is enough to describe the behavior required — as with the `<br/>` for a new line in markup code.

The third rule for XML documents is that if they contain an XML declaration it should appear at the top of the document. The XML declaration declares the version number of XML in use. Only one version of XML is recommended: 1.0. The declaration begins with `<?xml` and ends with `?>` The full declaration looks like this:

```
<?xml version="1.0"?>
```

The XML declaration must contain the version attribute. Other optional attributes are the encoding and standalone attributes and must be used in the XML declaration in that specific order after the version attribute. The encoding attribute contains information about character encodings that are allowed in the text of the XML. The default encoding used by XML and WAP documents is UTF-8, as explained in Chapter 17. The standalone setting is not used by WAP coders but is a legal XML declaration attribute, which refers to where DTD information is located. In WAP media types, the DTD information is usually stored elsewhere, therefore complying with the default setting of standalone, which is no.

Finally, the first characters of the XML declaration must be the first characters of the document. For example, this code:

```
<?xml version="1.0"?>
```

is different from this code:

```
    <?xml version="1.0"?>
```

XML is a strict language when compared to HTML and many parsers will not accept the second form of the XML declaration with extra spaces before it.

You should understand that XML documents use PCDATA as the default format for text data between the tags. This format is limited in that some characters cannot be used, but this is not as bad as it sounds, because only five characters are off limits. These are the ampersand (&), angle brackets (< and >), and single and double quotation marks (' and "). These and other troublesome characters are added to PCDATA using the decimal or hexadecimal notation. The special five disallowed characters are substituted using entity references or special shortcuts that exist in a DTD. I'll discuss the process of substitution in a following section.

Another format for text entry in between tags exists. It is known as CDATA. The advantage of this format is that all characters are acceptable and will be used literally without prejudice. This may be more useful to you than PCDATA, depending on the application you are using. WAP media types are well defined by DTDs, which show whether a given element can contain CDATA or PCDATA.

Validated XML

Validated XML is an XML that is not only well formed but that also conforms to a Document Type Definition (DTD). This is the location of a description about how the XML document is supposed to look. The DTD can be used to create specific instances of XML and to constrain XML documents. If you look over the XML rules for well-formed documents, you'll see that a lot of documents are able to conform to those standards. DTDs are used to tighten those rules as much as the author of the DTD wants. Each XML document is restricted to only one DTD.

A DTD can be internal or external, or a combination of internal and external components. WAP stores all the DTD data in a separate location. All the DTDs for WAP media types are available from the WAP Forum at www.wapforum.org.

DTDs are referenced within an XML document by placing a document type declaration at the beginning of the document. (Yes, document type declaration does happen to have the same acronym as Document Type Definition, but it is never abbreviated as such. It is often called a DOCTYPE declaration.) For a document to be validated, a parser must check its conformance to the DTD stated in the DOCTYPE declaration.

The DOCTYPE declaration must appear only once in a document and must follow the XML declaration. The basic structure for a DOCTYPE is as follows:

```
<!DOCTYPE document_element source loc1 loc2 [internal subset]>
```

The angle brackets delimit the entire DOCTYPE. The exclamation point (!) is a special keyword that begins this declaration. The DOCTYPE is the keyword that differentiates this declaration from other declarations that may be implemented in the future. The next piece is the document element, which is the root element in use by the XML document. Right away, you can see how some control is now instantiated. The root element is fixed by the DTD. The next part is the source. The source can be one of two words, PUBLIC or SYSTEM. (I explain these shortly.) Next in the DOCTYPE are either one or two locations, depending on which source keyword was used. Then there are some additional keywords for an internal subset of references, which is not used by WAP.

As I mentioned earlier, the source keyword can be either SYSTEM or PUBLIC. The SYSTEM keyword is the simpler of the two and refers to single location for the DTD using a URL or more generalized URI format. The PUBLIC keyword can also be used for a source, but with it two locations must be specified. The first location becomes an application-specific means of locating the DTD and the second maintains the same meaning it has with the SYSTEM keyword.

The PUBLIC keyword is often used when the DTD may be posted to some Internet site, but relying on the site to validate your documents is a pain considering that Internet access may be down. In those cases wherein the DTD cannot be located by using loc 2 (location 2), the parser then turns to an internal representation of the DTD. This may be as simple as turning to a cached copy, but is not stated as such in the specification.

BASIC DTD MARKUP

A full tutorial of DTD markup is beyond the scope of this book; in this section I will discuss in detail only those DTD markup concepts pertinent to WAP.

The bulk of the work involved in constraining XML document elements and attributes is done by the special codes inside the DTD. The DTD codes do not themselves comply with XML but use their own special format. All DTD special formats take the following form:

```
<!keyword parameter1 parameter2 ... parameterN>
```

The four basic keywords are ELEMENT, ATTLIST, ENTITY, and NOTATION. They are described in Table 3-3.

TABLE 3-3 BASIC DTD KEYWORDS

XML DTD Keyword	Description
ELEMENT	Declares an XML element type name and any permissible children it has.
ATTLIST	Declares all the valid XML element attribute names and the permissible and default attribute values.
ENTITY	Declares special character references or other repetitive content used in the DTD.
NOTATION	Declares non-XML content external to the DTD.

Elements are the basic building blocks of XML data. In fact they are the only required component of XML and therefore are important in the DTD. An element is declared in DTD markup using the following syntax:

```
<!ELEMENT name category>
```

or

```
<!ELEMENT name (content_model)>
```

The name must be a valid XML name. Table 3-4 describes the categories or content models for XML elements.

TABLE 3-4 XML CATEGORIES AND CONTENT MODELS

XML Category or Content Model	Description
ANY	Indicates that the element can contain any XML data.
EMPTY	Indicates that the element type cannot include any text or child elements, only element attributes.

XML Category or Content Model	Description
element (content model)	Indicates that the element can contain child elements but that no text is allowed.
mixed (content model)	Indicates that the element can contain text and/or child elements.
PCDATA (content model)	Indicates that the element can contain text only.

The following is an example of one use of the EMPTY category:

```
<!ELEMENT access EMPTY>
```

This specifies an access element that does not contain any text or child elements.
With the content model, the child elements are contained in a list after the ELEMENT keyword, as in the following example:

```
<!ELEMENT prev (setvar)*>
```

The entire content model is surrounded by parentheses. We will look at what the asterisk (*) means a little bit later.
If the element contains only PCDATA, its format would be as follows:

```
<!ELEMENT name (#PCDATA)>
```

With multiple child elements it would like this:

```
<!ELEMENT name (child_element1, child_element2)>
```

The sequence of these child elements is strictly delineated. Therefore, there must be a *child_element1* before a *child_element2* can appear.
With the mixed-content model, the markup becomes something like this:

```
<!ELEMENT name (#PCDATA, child_element1, child_element2).
```

The problem with model is that the order of the elements is no longer strictly delineated and also that you cannot specify choices or cardinality.
The content models can contain a comma between elements to control the order in which elements can be contained within their parent. Furthermore, you can use a vertical bar or pipe (|)to provide a choice among multiple child elements:

```
<!ELEMENT head (access|meta)+>
```

The preceding example gives the user a choice between the access and meta elements inside a head element. The content models can also include the cardinality operators shown in Table 3-5.

Table 3-5 CARDINALITY SYMBOLS

Symbol	Cardinality Meaning
None	Indicates that only one instance of the child is legal.
?	Indicates zero or one child element.
*	Indicates zero or more child elements.
+	Indicates one or more child elements.

And you can use nested parentheses for even more complex markup code. Here is an example of the cardinality operators in action:

```
<!ELEMENT wml (head?, template?, card+)>
```

This example shows how the `wml` element can contain a head, template, and card element in that order. However, `head` is an optional element — you can skip it or include one. The same goes for the template element. But one or more cards can be packaged inside a `wml` element.

ATTRIBUTES IN MARKUP

Attributes are specified in DTD markup code using the ATTLIST keyword, as follows:

```
<!ATTLIST element_name attr_name attr_type attr_default default_value>
```

The element and attribute names must be legal XML names. The attribute names are one of those listed in Table 3-6.

TABLE 3-6 ATTRIBUTE TYPES

Attribute Type	Description
CDATA	Simple text string.
Enumerated list	One of a set of explicitly defined values from a list.
ID	A unique identifier for every instance; must be a text string that conforms to the XML rules.
IDREF	A reference to an ID value and has the same value as the ID.
IDREFS	A list of IDREFs separated by spaces.
NMTOKEN	A text string that conforms to XML name rules except that the first character of the name can be any valid name character.
NMTOKENS	A list of NMTOKENs.
ENTITY	A name for a predefined entity.
ENTITIES	A list of ENTITY names separated by white space.
NOTATION	A notation type declared elsewhere in the DTD.

The following example is a typical WAP element definition done in XML DTD markup.

```
<!ATTLIST go
...
method (post|get)     "get"
...
>
```

This example shows a method attribute for the go element. The attribute has a choice of either POST or GET with GET being the default. Here is another example:

```
<!ATTLIST card
...
id ID #IMPLIED
...
>
```

The ID attribute is a unique identifier for the card element but must follow XML naming rules. This is why cards cannot have an ID of 123, which I will discuss later.

> **NOTE:** A short word about NMTOKEN and NMTOKENs. You have seen CDATA, which places no restrictions on the text within it, and PCDATA, which places some restrictions on XML-sensitive characters. NMTOKEN is a middle ground between the two, and allows everything but punctuation characters and spaces. In most cases, CDATA will do the job fine.

Entities in markup can be general, which means that they can be used in any XML document, or they can be used only within the DTD. General entities are referenced by the ampersand and semicolon symbols (& and ;) as the beginning and ending delimiters. For example, the following code:

```
&name;
```

can refer to the name entity in a document.

Parameter entities can only be referred to inside DTD markup and are referenced by the percent and semicolon symbols (% and ;), as in the following example:

```
%name;
```

General entities are created in markup with the following syntax:

```
<!ENTITY name "some replacement text">
```

These entities cannot be recursive. Here is an example of a general entity definition:

```
<!ENTITY quot "&#34;">
```

The entity is defined by its decimal value. This entity can now be used anywhere in markup with the following syntax:

```
&quot;
```

A double quotation mark will be substituted wherever it appears.

Parameter entities are defined with the following syntax:

```
<!ENTITY % name "some replacement text">
```

Parameter entities are only used in markup to enable you to avoid having to type the same text again and again. The entity could be as simple as this:

```
<!ENTITY % layout "br">
```

or as complex as this:

```
<!ENTITY % task "go | prev | noop | refresh">
```

One last item is attribute defaults. Table 3-7 lists the attribute defaults and their descriptions.

Table 3-7 Attribute Defaults

Attribute	Default Description
#REQUIRED	The attribute must appear in every instance of the element.
#IMPLIED	The attribute is optional.
#FIXED (plus specific value)	The attribute is optional, but if it appears it must use the value specified.
Default values	The attribute is optional, but if it does appear it must match the ATTLIST declaration.

An example of these attributes from the WML DTD is as follows:

```
<!ATTLIST do
type    CDATA     #REQUIRED
label   %vdata;   #IMPLIED
name    NMTOKEN   #IMPLIED
...
>
```

The `type` attribute is mandatory and must be included with every instance of the `do` element. The `label` attribute is not required and the application may replace it with a suitable substitute.

MIME

The last of the technologies you need to look at in order to understand WAP is Multipurpose Internet Mail Extensions (MIME). RFC 822 defines a protocol for how messages and their headers can be written in US-ASCII, but the message body is left as plain-text US-ASCII. In order to extend the system later, when larger character sets became available, Borenstein and Freed added a set of extensions. The extensions were meant to address the problem of adding non-ASCII text in messages, different formats for non-textual messages, multipart messages, and headers that use character sets other than ASCII. RFC 2046 contains details about the media types and is one of a set of five documents from RFC 2045-2049 that detail the mail extensions and solve problems that RFC 822 does not address.

RFC 2046 contains an explanation of the multipart extension to RFC 822. This multipart extension allows for multiple entities to be packaged into a single e-mail or HTTP response. These entities do not have to be of the same type. Consider the case in HTTP of a .gif file on the index.html page. Using standard techniques, the Web browser makes a request for the index.html page. Then it makes another request for the .gif file.

By packaging multiple entities a Web server can send a browser a single message that contains both the HTML data and the .gif file in a single response. The standard responses set their content-type header to the type that is returned. For example, if HTML is returned the following header is used:

```
Content-type: text/html
```

In the case of multipart messages, the content-type header will look like this:

```
Content-type: multipart/mixed; boundary="***"
```

This specifies that the content contained in the entity is actually composed of several pieces that may have disparate properties. The boundary does not have to be three stars; it can be any arbitrary string. Although arbitrary, the boundary defines the delimiter between the different entities of the multipart. The software that builds the MIME content usually programmatically chooses the boundary string such that it is not a subset of any text in any of the entities.

Each individual entity then has its own content-type and other content headers.

Here is an example of a multipart HTTP response that contains an HTML file and a .gif image:

```
HTTP/1.1 200 OK
Server: Apache/1.3.6
Date: Thu, 02 Nov 2000 23:50:10 GMT
Connection: close
Content-Type: multipart/mixed;boundary="***"

--***
Content-type: text/html

<HTML>
<h1> test page </h1>
<img src="test.gif">
```

```
</HTML>
--***
Content-type: image/gif
Content-location: test.gif

<GIF DATA>
--***--
```

The multipart example shows how each different entity gets its own section in the multipart file. The boundary is always precluded by two dashes. Moreover, the last boundary affixes two more dashes to the end of the message. This is the format for the multipart. The content headers within the entity parts must be separated from the entities by a blank line, just as in standard HTTP syntax.

One last thing about multipart messages. The actual order in which the files are placed in the multipart packages is the order in which the browser processes the files. Therefore, in this example the HTML would be displayed first, followed by the .gif file. This rule only results in a few seconds of difference, but in a later chapter, I show how the processing order has a great effect on WAP media types such as Openwave cache operations.

The main content type shown in this section is multipart/mixed. Multipart is considered a main media type by MIME; mixed is a special subtype with properties I described in the description of MIME and in the previous example. Other subtypes, such as alternative, digest, and parallel, exist as defined in RFC 2046, each with its particulars regarding the packaging of disparate content. The alternative subtype is the same as the mixed type except that the entities are just different versions of some main document, the digest subtype is used for e-mail compatibility, and the parallel subtype is used when the order in which the multipart is processed is not significant.

A new multipart subtype was created after the original MIME to handle cases wherein the different parts of the multipart message only have meaning when examined in the aggregate. In other aspects, multipart/related has mostly the same properties as multipart/mixed. Details of the subtype are now specified in RFC 2387. Keep this multipart subtype in mind as you read, as it is used to construct WAP push messages.

Summary

In this chapter I covered some of the basic Internet technologies. Understanding the TCP protocol, for example, is fundamental to discovering why the protocol was found unsuitable for transmission over the wireless network. I then discussed stacks and how they can help you solve specific communication problems. This information will become important when you are faced with advanced WAP stacks that throw in nonstandard layers.

Next I examined XML, both the well-formed and validated forms, and how these forms are parsed and written. Media types define large sections of WAP, and there is no end in sight to new DTDs enabling ever-newer media types to solve problems such as over-the-air provisioning and location-based services-information transfer.

Finally, I mentioned some important MIME extensions that will be necessary to the understanding of some of the advanced wireless-client control operations, such as cache operations and push operations.

In the next chapter, I discuss how these issues apply to WAP.

Chapter 4

Introduction to WAP

IN THIS CHAPTER

- Introduction to WAP
- Examples of WAP services
- Inside the WAP architecture
- Examining the WAP layers

MANY EONS AGO, it seems, within the wireless industry, regardless of which country you went to, there were not many carriers in the marketplace. A few key players who sold only voice services dominated the market. The customers who paid for these services bought them for the one key feature that was useful to them: the fact that calls could be made wirelessly from any location in their area. Coverage was not an issue, voice quality was not an issue, how large the phone was and many other factors were irrelevant to the customer base. However, this type of service never achieved any real penetration into other marketplaces.

In order to attract other customers, the carriers improved their coverage, billing operations, and customer service, and moved to better their technologies. Over time they realized that the technologies deployed throughout the world had limitations in their design. The limitations were largely the results of the technological state of the art at the time, but regardless, carriers concluded that if the wireless market was going to expand it needed to solve some problems with the technologies it was using. The first step was to license the new spectrum, which was done in most countries; in the US new spectrum was purchased in the PCS auctions. The next was to mandate that the new spectrum use newer digital technologies. Unfortunately, there was a bitter commercial and political struggle over the exact digital technology to be used, and no absolute decision was made in the US and some other countries. The market fragmented, and the auctions brought on more chaos as the coverage areas became scattered over the map.

With the new licensing, more competitors entered the marketplace. These new competitors did not have the coverage areas, branding strength, or strong customer service operations of the incumbents and therefore attempted to attract a new class of customer. Some (such as VoiceStream) focused on small businesses, some (such as Nextel) on service businesses, some (such as Omnipoint) only on urban users, and so on.

Over time the operations of these new carriers became as strong as those of the incumbents and they could now compete with the older carriers in terms of coverage, branding, and quality of service. This competition started to bring prices and revenues down. The increasing downturn for voice services meant that carriers had to look elsewhere for ways to increase their value; they had to offer services that their competitors did not have. This search for new value resulted in voicemail, SMS, speakerphone, multiple line phones, and so on. (Yes, voicemail was once considered an advanced feature.) Of course carriers could create service innovation by simply shuffling around how much people paid for existing services. The resulting bucket plans for voice minutes was an interesting twist on customer psychology. The customer now pays regardless of whether the calls are made, and strives to use the allotted minutes, often overshooting and becoming subject to additional fees.

The carrier-manufacturer-consumer triumvirate largely managed these innovations in services. The manufacturers came up with the ideas, the consumers validated them through focus groups, and the carriers then implemented them. However, only a few innovators could continue to keep up with the dizzying pace of the industry and eventually a lot of them quit largely because they had failed to properly have customers validate their solution (Cincinnati Microwave), or because their margin of operations was too small (PCSI). The carriers also struggled to find the cash to pay for the new product innovations and justifications for new services became less inflated.

Some of the innovations were for data services, both the packet and circuit-switched types. The sale of the new data services was based on the possibly flawed assumption that the wireless telephony market and the landline market have the same customers. Carriers therefore concluded that, because the ratio of data to voice traffic on landline was tilted far in favor of the data, wireless telephony was also eventually going to share the same usage profile. The data services were poor sellers and finally settled into niche markets. The data services gave rise to new breed of developers, individuals other than the original triumvirate who created consumer-grade applications. But taking the poor, non-standard, complex data services and creating consumer-grade applications was a challenge, one that often created a conflict of interest between developer and carrier.

A few enterprising people at Unwired Planet out of Redwood City, many of them from the failed Go enterprise with BellSouth, decided to decrease the complexity of data services by creating a simple platform for their creation. The service would solve the carrier's and manufacturer's problems by allowing an unlimited number of services to be created without expensive innovation and deployment cycles. The service would also give the carriers and developers of applications a happy medium from which to deploy stable applications.

The idea behind the service was to bring the Internet to the mobile phone. The argument ran that the number of applications and uses of the Internet were so numerous that consumers on mobile phones would also find value in them and that this would bring added recognition to carriers. No one knew exactly how the recognition would drive revenue. Because the Internet used HTML and HTTP and was more mature than the mobile Internet protocols, carriers and developers had to decide how to create services.

Other manufacturers, such as Nokia and Ericsson, had also hit at the idea of merging the Internet and the mobile phone at the same time. Ericsson created a new ITTP (Intelligent Text Transfer Protocol) standard and Nokia came up with TTML (Tagged Text Markup Language). These two technologies both had to solve the same problem as Unwired Planet: how to merge the Internet and the limited phone environment.

The phone environment was limited in many ways, but one of the biggest problems was that the phone was just making headway as more than just a 1-cent device. This meant that all parties were reluctant to turn it into a $2,000 computer capable of browsing the Internet, although Nokia did attempt this with their 9000 series (which retailed for $1,000). Also, the wireless data rates were much lower than those achievable on the Internet (at the time around 9.6kbps). These two factors led to many compromises regarding how the Internet and mobile devices were integrated.

Unwired Planet decided that, although most of the Web services of the day were defined using the HTML language, this language contained too many limitations to dynamically translate into some wireless language. Furthermore, they argued that the phone UI, processor, and memory limitations made many HTML features unusable and wasteful of resources. Based on that reasoning, they created a language called Handheld Device Markup Language (HDML) and a protocol called Handheld Device Transfer Protocol (HDTP). Their concept was first implemented by AT&T Wireless Services in the U.S. over the CDPD bearer. The architecture had three main components: a browser in the phone, an UP.Link gateway, and an application server or Web server that stored applications. The UP.Link gateway was responsible for translating HTTP/TCP/IP into HDTP/UDP/IP. Because CDPD was a strong packet-based bearer the trials were quite successful. The HDML language was made very similar to HTML to decrease the learning curve for HTML developers.

Ericsson and Nokia took a different line of reasoning. Their engineers, not having learned from the Go enterprise failure, created a three-component architecture as well. They accepted that bandwidth was limited on the wireless network and established a gateway in the middle to protect it. However, they decided to simply translate the Internet HTML services into their own proprietary languages (TTML, in the case of Nokia). The proprietary language would then be sent to the mobile phone and displayed in a special browser. Nokia and Ericsson did not have the benefit of good bearer in their core research and development market area of Europe and began developing this architecture on SMS. The GSM SMS bearer they used allowed for about 140 bytes of information to be sent. This was much too small for browsing and about 16 SMS messages were assembled/disassembled using a Phase 2 improvement of the GSM network to provide a reasonable bearer. Nokia's TTML browser then allowed a user to initiate a request for service by means of a special keyword in an SMS message. This special keyword would be sent to the gateway, where it would check the Internet or private data network for the service and return it to the TTML browser. The special keyword had to be associated with a service

URL by the gateway administrator. This limited service discovery. Nokia and Ericsson also found out that the SMS bearer was too sensitive to network loading and latency problems and that they needed another bearer. They moved to testing the service on GSM circuit-switched bearers.

Meanwhile, Unwired Planet (renamed Phone.com and merged recently with Software.com to create Openwave) achieved increasing acceptance in the US market as the company that could deliver the confluence of the Internet and wireless telephony market. With further commitments from Sprint and Nextel, its approach was looking good. However, acceptance of the HDML approach was lukewarm in Europe and Asia.

In early 1997, Phone.com, Ericsson, Nokia, and Motorola were encouraged by Omnipoint to get together and resolve their differences, because it was not going to accept a proprietary mobile Internet solution. By June of 1997, the companies had created the WAP Forum for the purpose of providing a unified solution to the industry.

One year after that, in April of 1998, the WAP Forum first made public the specifications for WAP. The new WAP system adopted an approach very similar to the original HDML solution. The three-component architecture was kept, a new language called WML was proposed, and instead of HDTP, a whole suite of protocols with W- acronyms was created for the wireless network. This initial release of WAP 1.0 was quickly retired after consultation with the W3C. The WML language was made all lowercase so as to conform to XHTML, and WAP was re-released in February–July of 1999 as WAP 1.1.

WAP 1.1 formed the basis of any services, gateways, and browsers in the marketplace today. Today, however, we are seeing the introduction of some WAP 1.2 features. I will discuss the differences between WAP 1.2 and WAP 1.2.1 in a later section of this chapter.

Because three of the original founders of WAP were phone manufacturers, WAP 1.1 and even WAP 1.2 retains bias toward phones. Telematics (autos) and PDAs manufacturers have begun to demand some attention but it is difficult to predict what will happen as some of them had already spent large amount of research and development dollars on proprietary solutions when WAP 1.1 was announced.

Examining Some Examples of WAP Services

Before actually developing applications, you should see what is possible in the wireless Internet space. This section shows you examples of WAP applications in popular categories. These were randomly chosen and are not product or service endorsements.

The traditional stock-quote query applies as well to the mobile businessperson as it does to the Internet. The average user, however, maintains a portfolio from which he or she would like to derive his or her net worth. Figure 4-1 demonstrates a WAP stock service.

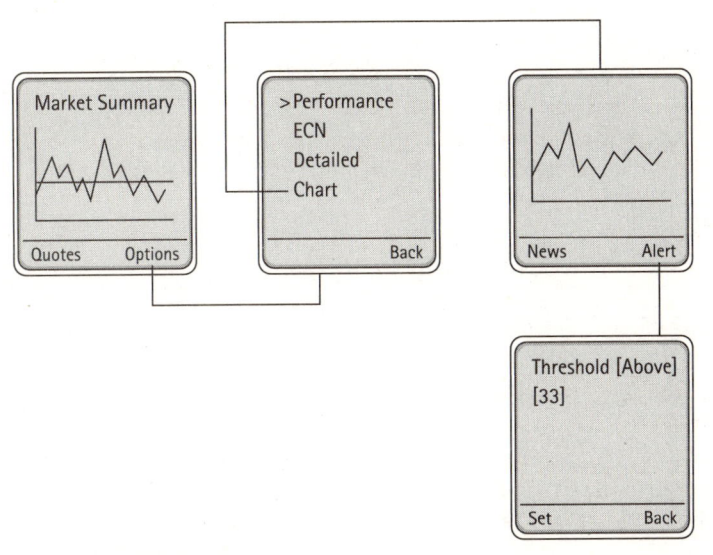

Figure 4-1: Stock service

Another common service is a news service, which gives the user the top stories of the day in a specified region. Nothing complex here; Figure 4-2 shows what the service would look like.

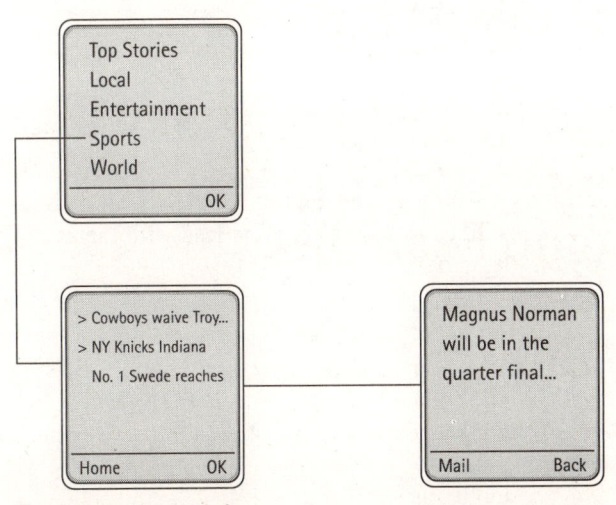

Figure 4-2: News service

Part 1: Foundations

The images in Figure 4-3 show a weather application. In this one, a user enters a city and state, generating radar data and textual weather information to be presented.

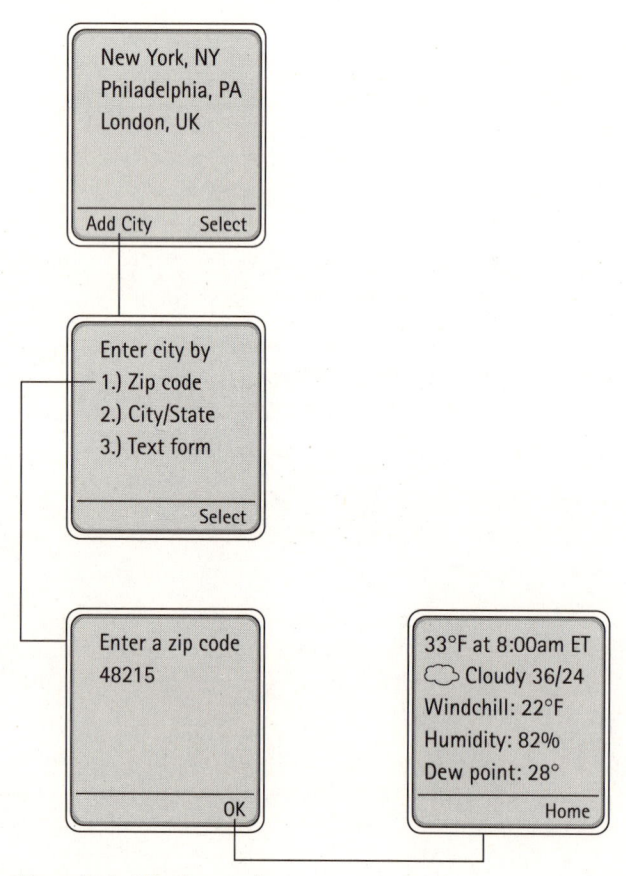

```
┌─────────────────┐
│ New York, NY    │
│ Philadelphia, PA│
│ London, UK      │
│                 │
│                 │
│ Add City  Select│
└─────────────────┘

┌─────────────────┐
│ Enter city by   │
│ 1.) Zip code    │
│ 2.) City/State  │
│ 3.) Text form   │
│                 │
│           Select│
└─────────────────┘

┌─────────────────┐      ┌─────────────────┐
│ Enter a zip code│      │ 33°F at 8:00am ET│
│ 48215           │      │ ☁ Cloudy 36/24  │
│                 │      │ Windchill: 22°F │
│                 │      │ Humidity: 82%   │
│                 │      │ Dew point: 28°  │
│              OK │      │            Home │
└─────────────────┘      └─────────────────┘
```

Figure 4-3: Weather service

Directions are even more useful on a mobile phone. Figure 4-4 shows a location-finder service for WAP. This service would be significantly enhanced with the availability of location information from the carrier.

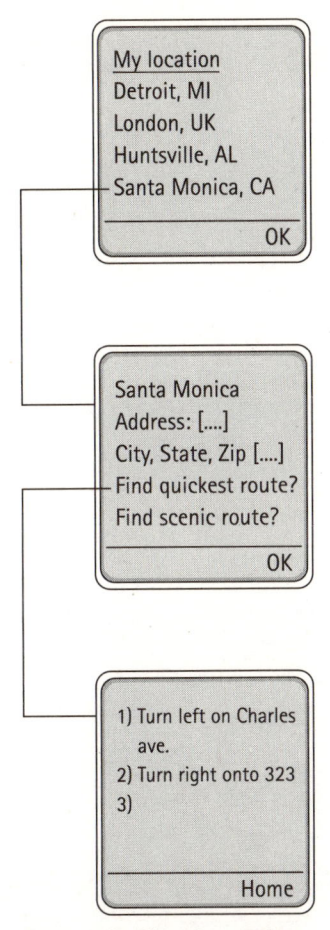

```
┌─────────────────────┐
│ My location         │
│ Detroit, MI         │
│ London, UK          │
│ Huntsville, AL      │
│ Santa Monica, CA    │
│                     │
│                  OK │
└─────────────────────┘

┌─────────────────────┐
│ Santa Monica        │
│ Address: [....]     │
│ City, State, Zip [....] │
│ Find quickest route? │
│ Find scenic route?  │
│                  OK │
└─────────────────────┘

┌─────────────────────┐
│ 1) Turn left on Charles │
│    ave.             │
│ 2) Turn right onto 323 │
│ 3)                  │
│                     │
│                Home │
└─────────────────────┘
```

Figure 4-4: Direction service

Commerce is alive and well on WAP as well as the Internet. The user's limited ability to enter data makes pre-existing profiles important. Figure 4-5 shows a sample WAP application that can be used to purchase books.

```
┌─────────────────────────┐
│      Books R US         │
│   Top Picks of the Day  │
│                         │
│   1) Harry Potter       │
│   2) Pride & Prejudice  │
│   3) Crime & Punishment │
│                         │
│  Search           Back  │
└─────────────────────────┘

┌─────────────────────────┐
│  Search by:             │
│  Author: [....]         │
│  Title: [....]          │
│  ISBN: [....]           │
│                         │
│                   OK    │
└─────────────────────────┘

┌─────────────────────────┐
│   Books matching:       │
│   1) Mommie-Timer       │
│   2) 50 Minute Games    │
│   3) Time Management    │
│                         │
│  OK               Back  │
└─────────────────────────┘
```

Figure 4-5: Purchasing books

The integration of telephony and the Web makes more complex applications available than if you are using just the mobile Web features. For example, incoming calls can be intercepted by an application (such as the one shown in Figure 4-6) that first asks the user what action to take.

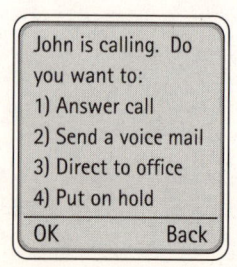

```
┌─────────────────────────┐
│  John is calling. Do    │
│  you want to:           │
│  1) Answer call         │
│  2) Send a voice mail   │
│  3) Direct to office    │
│  4) Put on hold         │
│  OK              Back   │
└─────────────────────────┘
```

Figure 4-6: Intercepting incoming calls

Furthermore, future versions of WAP may offer proximity services, which may signal to the user that a potential dating partner who matches his or her profile is close by.

These applications provide some examples of what you can expect of WAP from a nontechnical perspective. The rest of this chapter delves into the details of the architecture, protocols, and languages of WAP.

Understanding WAP Layers

The WAP suite of protocols is largely only the stack that is used in communication between WAP clients and WAP gateways. Figure 4-7 shows how this layered design is normally presented.

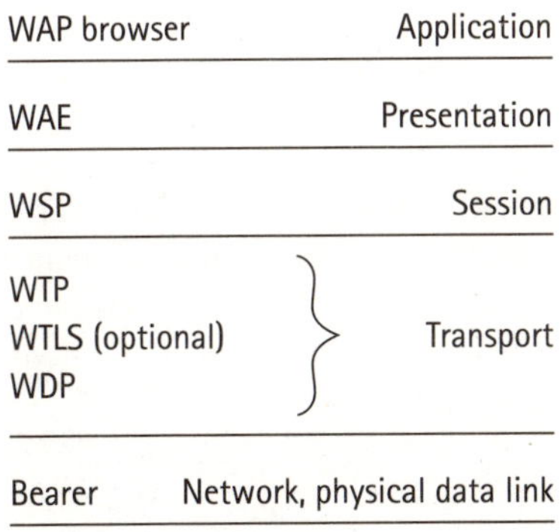

WAP browser	Application
WAE	Presentation
WSP	Session
WTP WTLS (optional) WDP	Transport
Bearer	Network, physical data link

Figure 4-7: WAP layers

The WAP stack shown in Figure 4-7 shows the main layers. These layers are conceptually similar to the layers of the Internet and OSI models I introduced in Chapter 3. However, this WAP stack does not fit neatly into either the OSI or Internet stack models. WAP has only six layers, and they don't correspond well to existing theoretical layers.

Keep in mind, though, that a single-stack diagram does not describe the full picture. Stacks describe how communication is implemented between two devices. Figure 4-8 shows a WAP stack diagram showing the relevance to other items in the architecture and the scope of the WAP protocol suite.

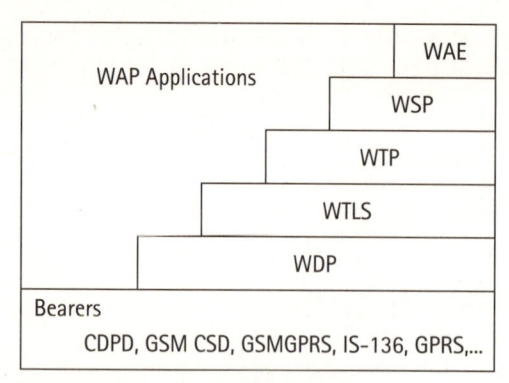

```
                            WAE
WAP Applications
                            WSP
                       WTP
                    WTLS
                WDP
Bearers
CDPD, GSM CSD, GSMGPRS, IS-136, GPRS,...
```

Figure 4-8: WAP and Internet stacks

I describe the layers briefly now and in more detail in the subsequent sections. The topmost layer of the WAP stack is the WAE (Wireless Application Environment), which defines the application environment and contains definitions for the presentation languages, mechanisms and any media types required to convey information to WAP-capable mobile devices.

Below that is the WSP, or Wireless Session Protocol, which creates a WAP session over which data can be transferred. The WSP has the same methods and headers as HTTP/1.1.

Below the WSP layer is the WTP layer. It is a reliable transport layer component that improves the capability of the lower datagram service.

The WTLS (Wireless Transport Layer Security) layer is inserted in the middle of the two transport layers and adds security to the transactions. It has mechanisms that address authentication, integrity, and confidentiality in communications.

The last layer of the WAP stack is the WDP (Wireless Datagram Protocol) layer, which on all IP-capable networks is simply UDP (User Datagram Protocol), unless it is a datagram service.

The WAE layer

This WAP application layer is a general application and presentation area meant to handle the confluence of mobile telephony and the Web. The objective of this layer is to create a stable platform that allows for the efficient building of applications and services. The WAE layer contains details about the presentation of various mobile-aware formats, but it stops short of specifying how these types should be presented.

The main parts of WAE deal with the microbrowser environment and how it should support the following:

- WML – A language markup that shares elements and attributes with HTML4 and HDML3.2.

- WMLScript – A light scripting language that shares semantics with JavaScript.

- **WTA/WTAI** – An environment that allows browser applications to use telephony components.

- **Content formats** – Sets of data formats or content types that define how data are moved over the other layers of the WAP stack.

The following sections offer a detailed introduction to WML and WMLScript.

WML

WML is a markup language very similar to HTML that specifies how content is to be displayed on mobile devices. Developers write the bulk of their WAP services using this language. WML can be thought of as a presentation-layer language. It does not guarantee that the browser will display the code in a certain way.

WML was designed specifically for mobile devices. The narrow-bandwidth connections do not allow for the rich content types of the World Wide Web. The small displays and limited user-input facilities of the mobile devices mean that control of the user interface is very different from control of the user interface of the Web. This distinctly affects how developers applications in WML. Furthermore, the limited computational resources and memory affect how the data is sent to the phone, and so developers must be aware of the management of any semi-persistent or persistent content by the mobile device.

> **Note:** WML shares a lot of functionality with an older markup language created by Openwave called HDML 2.0. Although it has different elements and attributes, it implements a similar organization.

WML defines the concept of a deck, which is packaged as an XML document type. Inside this deck are several cards. The resources for WAP/WML are stored on the application server as WAP decks. When a URL is requested a deck is returned to the mobile device, out of which only a single card is displayed. A user then presses keys and buttons on the mobile device to move around the application. The decks are stored on standard Web servers and can either be static or dynamically generated. Remember that because WML is a presentation format only, the code can be interpreted in different ways depending on the browser being used.

The main features of WML are as follows:

- **Text and image support:** These provide content authors with the ability to specify text and images to be displayed on the mobile device. WML defines textual elements, various presentation screens and complex presentation elements such as tables. A content author has to give up a lot of control in terms of how content is displayed on the mobile-device screen.

A new WBMP format is defined in the Application Environment specifications, which allow for simple black and white images to be supported on the mobile devices.

- **Support for user input:** WML defines a text-entry and option-selection mechanism in order to obtain data from users. Task invocation techniques also fit into this category. Their implementation varies from mobile device to mobile device. WML allows for the navigation to be either activated by the user or automatically based on special events.

- **Navigation and history stack:** The natural choice for Web navigation, URLs are used in WML as well. History and inter-card navigation elements are also specified.

- **International support:** All WML elements are written in Unicode 2.0. Any character set that is a subset of Unicode will work, so the full UCS-4 encoding does not have to be used. Therefore UTF-8, US-ASCII, and ISO-8859-1 are all acceptable.

- **Hardware independence:** The WML language is not tied to any specific mobile device. No features of any device are included in the language definition. The content author writes content independently of the device.

- **Narrow bandwidth optimization:** WML has been specified to optimize communication between the mobile device and the WAP gateway. Variables in WML cards are grouped in order to optimize single transactions and client-side validation of data done with WMLScript.

- **State and context management:** WML uses a single context for the browser environment. The context is uniform and linear. Variables introduced into the context are persistent to the context and can be shared by multiple applications.

WMLSCRIPT

WMLScript is a lightweight scripting language based on ECMAScript, which in turn is based on JavaScript. The scripting language adds procedural logic right into the device and thus improves the network utilization. WMLScript refines the JavaScript for a small footprint, provides integration with WML, and allows for future hooks with other mobile-device services for external hardware.

All of these capabilities allow for WMLScript to do the following:

- Check user-input delivery to an application server
- Access external devices
- Interact with the user without roundtrips to the application server

Chapter 4: Introduction to WAP

- Access internal phone capabilities
- Display error messages without returning to the server

One of the differences between JavaScript and WMLScript is that WMLScript is not inlined code. Although WMLScript can be called from WML, they are not stored in the same file. This means that the first time the WMLScript is called, a request is made for the WMLScript file, which then runs on the mobile device after it has been retrieved. Figure 4-9 shows an example WMLScript in use and how it is used to validate some user input right on the mobile device.

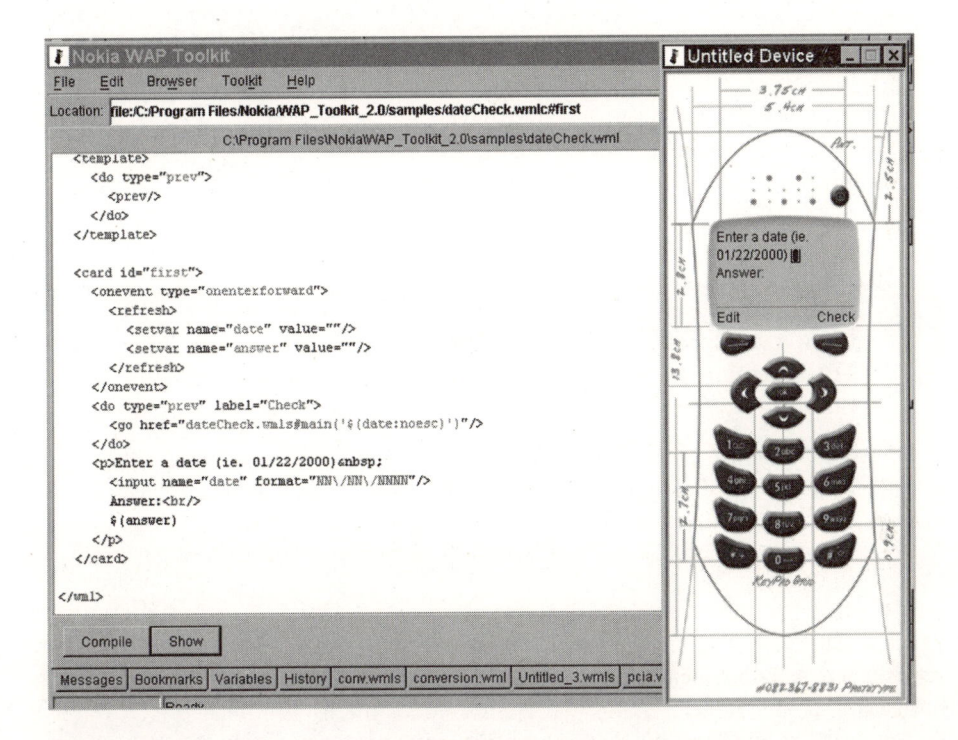

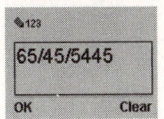

Figure 4-9: WMLScript sample code

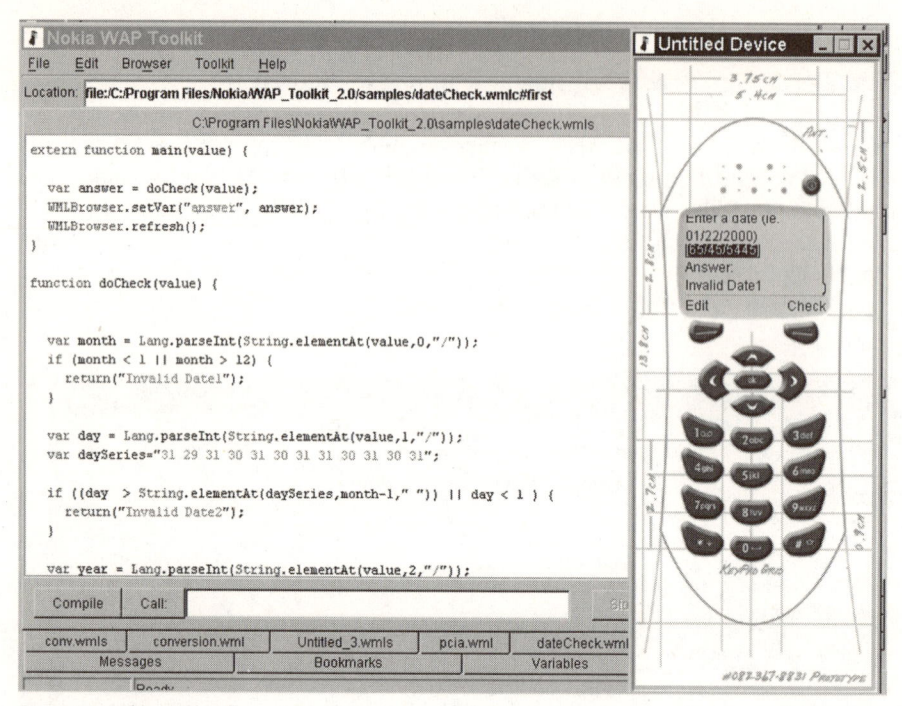

Figure 4-9 (Continued)

The WMLScript file cannot be called on its own; it must be associated with some WML in order to run. The WMLScript files contain functions, which are specified to run within the WML files via URLs.

WSP

Because HTTP/1.1 sessions also exchange additional information in the format of request and response headers, the encoded forms of those headers are also supported in WSP.

The WSP protocol was further extended to support push capability. Not only is WSP used to request data from external URLs, it can also be used with the push architecture to deliver unsynchronized data to the mobile client.

The protocol includes a feature for negotiating support among multiple connections and resources. For example, a deck may contain multiple images. Those requests could be piggybacked on the same open session. This feature is given the technical term *pipelining*; however, it operates the same way the connection: keep-alive and connection: close header statements operate in HTTP/1.1.

The WSP layer and everything beneath it in the WAP stack is defined in the specifications through the use of primitives, specially defined messages that clients and servers use to communicate. An example is the S-connect primitive, which requests that a connection be created with the server. This primitive is a request primitive that requests a service from the layer beneath it, which is the WTP layer or WDP layer. This lower layer then executes further primitives. The whole primitive concept borrows heavily from ISO 10731 and ISO 7498.

The protocol on the whole matches the HTTP/1.1 protocol very closely. It is a session protocol that controls how data are transferred from the WAP client to the WAP gateway and vice versa.

The WSP protocol itself defines two sub-protocols. These are:

- Connection-mode session, which runs over the transaction layer
- Connectionless-mode session, which runs over the datagram service layer

In Chapter 3, "WAP Foundations," you saw examples of session services such as SMTP, DNS, and HTTP. WSP is a similar protocol, but it is binary and more of an effort has been made to optimize traffic over the wireless media.

Because WSP is based on HTTP, it covers the same type of upper-layer services, which are browsing applications. The protocol is responsible for:

- Establishing a reliable session from client to server and then releasing it in an orderly fashion
- Agreeing on a common protocol using capability negotiation
- Exchanging content using a compact encoding
- Suspending and resuming sessions as necessary

Much more specifically, WSP establishes a reliable session between the client and the server by duplicating the methods of HTTP/1.1 and extending those on a session-by-session basis by allowing for extensible request/reply methods. The extended features of WSP also allow it to support composite objects, the ability to send multiple media objects and initiate content-type negotiation, and the ability to recognize certain content types and to exact certain processes on them, the most obvious being binary conversion.

The WSP protocol is a binary HTTP protocol, the architecture of which is shown in Figure 4-10.

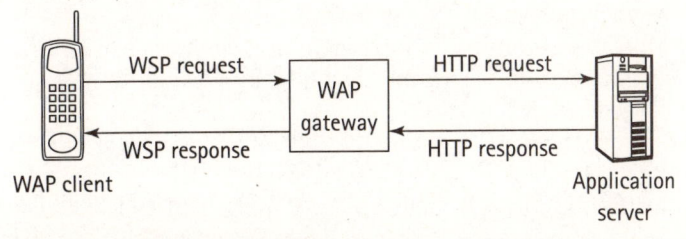

Figure 4-10: WSP protocol architecture

In WSP, the request and response are in a binary form. The GET, POST, and other methods I mentioned in Chapter 3 are used here in WSP. Figure 4-11 gives an example of the WSP binary form.

Figure 4-11 shows how a WSP GET request is structured. The similarities between WSP and HTTP make the WAP gateway translation a relatively seamless operation. The WSP protocol supports all the HTTP/1.1 methods and adds a compact binary encoding format and a compact data format equivalent to the MIME multipart/mixed type.

> **NOTE:** WSP sessions have the added advantage that they can be suspended and resumed even over different bearers at any time. The ability to suspend sessions allows for savings on battery life and freedom to use the mobile device for other activities.

The WSP facility does not simply use the lower-layer protocol service in all cases. The actual lower layer used is dependent on the WSP functionality required. Table 4-1 lists the different WSP facilities and WTP transaction classes used.

TABLE 4-1 WSP FACILITIES AND WTP TRANSACTION CLASSES

WSP Facility	WTP Transaction Class(es)
Session Management	Class 0 and Class 2
Session Resume	Class 0 and Class 2
Method Invocation	Class 2
Push	Class 0
Confirmed Push	Class 1

I describe the WTP protocol and push derivatives in greater detail in the following sections.

Developers of WAP services really don't need to be concerned with the details of the WSP protocol, as there is very little direct developer interaction with WSP. However, familiarity with the concept and terms introduced can help in debugging services.

Chapter 4: Introduction to WAP 85

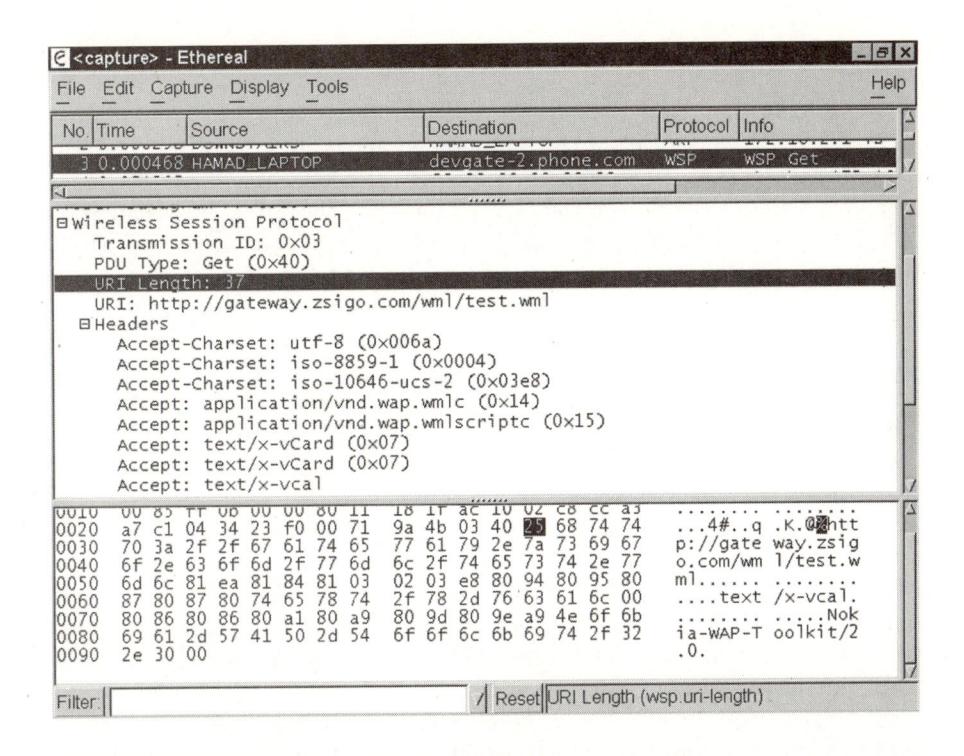

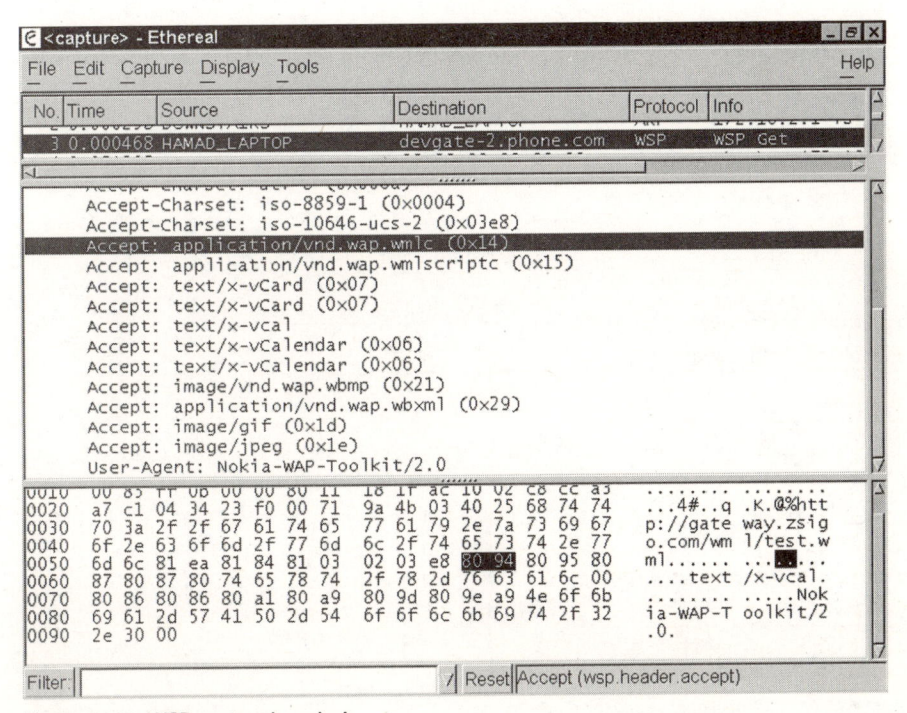

Figure 4-11: WSP protocol analysis

WTP

The wireless transaction protocol establishes a reliable layer over the WDP layer. Both the WTP and WDP layers are part of the transport portion of the WAP stack. The WDP portion or lower layer of the transport is either UDP or a UDP-like service. The WTP portion then defines a transaction class service on top of the lower datagrams. WTP divides the transaction class service into three subclasses of service, each of which has a different reliability level. The subclasses are divided up as in the following list.

- Class 0 – Unreliable message with no result message
- Class 1 – Reliable message with no result message
- Class 2 – Reliable message with exactly one reliable result message

WTP runs over a datagram service, so it has to improve the quality of service in order for reliable sessions to be created by the WSP layer above it. In order to improve the WTP protocol to enable this, the WTP protocol performs retransmissions of lost data, sends acknowledgments, uses unique transaction identifiers, and implements duplicate removal. WTP can also concatenate multiple smaller messages in cases where only one transport unit is required. Unlike with TCP, the basic transaction unit is a message rather than a stream of bytes. The WTP protocol has no explicit beginning or end the way TCP does. The connection's beginning is implied by the first message that is sent, and the connection closes if no messages are received for a set amount of time.

Also, the WTP protocol sends acknowledgements with application data, not separately as in TCP. This helps to reduce WTP protocol overhead.

Figure 4-12 shows a WTP and TCP session side by side.

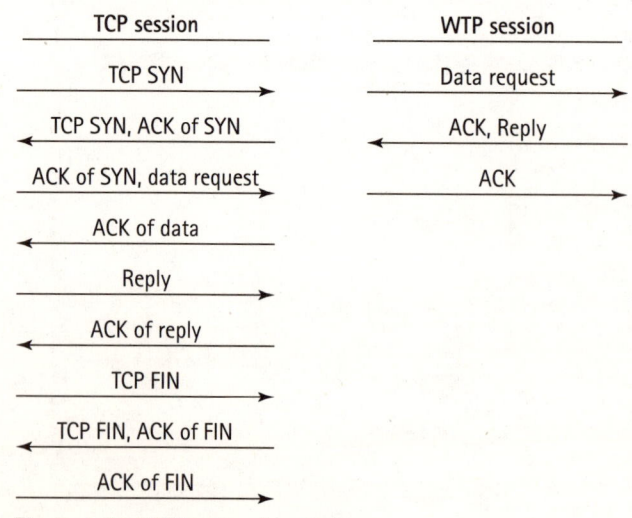

TCP session	WTP session
TCP SYN →	Data request →
← TCP SYN, ACK of SYN	← ACK, Reply
ACK of SYN, data request →	ACK →
← ACK of data	
Reply →	
← ACK of reply	
TCP FIN →	
← TCP FIN, ACK of FIN	
ACK of FIN →	

Figure 4-12: WSP protocol analysis

WTP CLASS 0 SERVICE

In the case of the WTP protocol, any side can initiate a message: the creator of the message is known as the initiator and the intended recipient of the message is known as the responder. In the case of a class 0 service, an initiator sends a request to a responder. Neither the initiator nor the responder is then required to take any more action. The packets of this service look very much like a standard UDP message. The diagram in Figure 4-13 represents how the transaction would look.

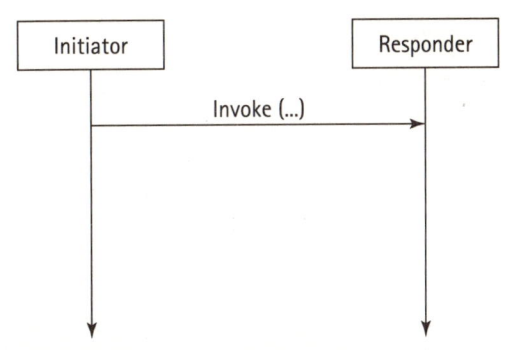

Figure 4-13: WTP Class 0 transaction

WTP CLASS 1 SERVICE

The Class 1 transaction begins with the initiator sending a request to a responder. The responder then sends an acknowledgement of receipt. The responder maintains state information for some time after the transaction ends, just in case it needs to retransmit the acknowledgement message if the initiator requests it again. Figure 4-14 shows a class 1 service sequence diagram.

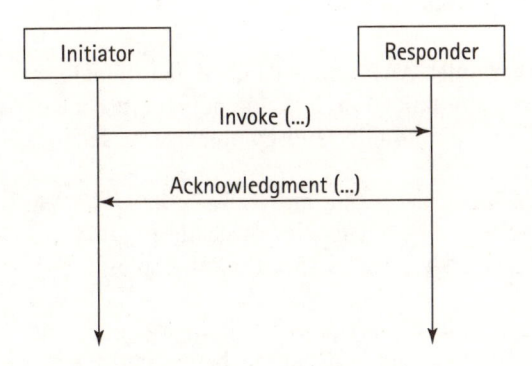

Figure 4-14: WTP Class 1 transaction

WTP CLASS 2 SERVICE

The Class 2 transaction as shown in Figure 4-15 provides a basic invoke/response transaction. A single WSP session may use multiple Class 2 transactions.

The transaction starts out with an initiator sending a message to a responder, which sends a single response to the initiator. The initiator keeps the initial message as a reference in memory for some time in case the responder never sends anything back. The transaction ends when the initiator sends an acknowledgement message to the ACK received from the responder.

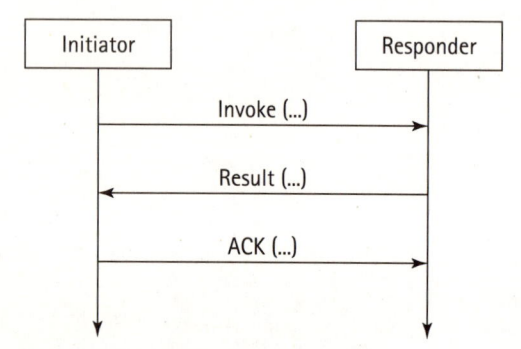

Figure 4-15: WTP Class 2 transaction

WTLS

WTLS is an optional layer of the WAP stack that appears at a lower layer than SSL/TLS on the Internet. It builds a security protocol into the WAP stack. WTLS is based on TLS v1.0, the RFC version of the SSL (Secure Sockets Layer) v.3.0. Both SSL and TLS count on the lower-layer reliability of TCP for proper operation. Unlike them, WTLS sits on top of WDP, a datagram-like service. This results in some problems, which are unique to WTLS.

WTLS addresses all the concerns that other WAP protocols have had to address. Any of the limitations of narrowband communication, high latency, limited memory, and limited processing power affect the number and complexity of security algorithms supported.

WTLS addresses the same security concerns as SSL and TLS, as well as some additional wireless-specific inadequacies. The inadequacies of dealing with wireless issues, for example, created the need for a WTLS-specific anti-replay attack capability.

The WTLS protocol provides services that protect privacy, authentication, and data integrity. Privacy means ensuring that data transmitted between the WAP client and the WAP gateway cannot be intercepted and understood by other parties. Authentication means ensuring for the server that the WAP client is a real client. Reverse authentication is also done, allowing the WAP gateway to authenticate itself to the client.

Data integrity means ensuring that data sent between the WAP client and WAP gateway are not changed or corrupted by intermediate parties.

Figure 4-16 shows the WTLS architecture diagram.

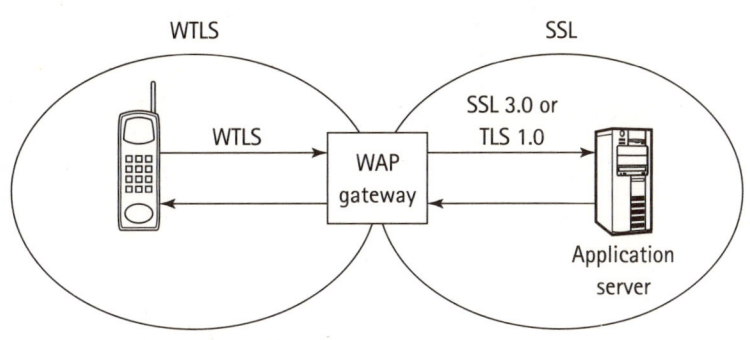

Figure 4-16: The WTLS architecture

The WTLS solution may sit on top of some already secure solution implemented by the carrier. For example, the AT&T CDPD network in the U.S. implements the authentication, privacy, and integrity mechanisms already, as shown in Figure 4-17. However, such protection is usually constrained to a limited portion of the network, whereas WTLS gives protection from the WAP client to the WAP gateway.

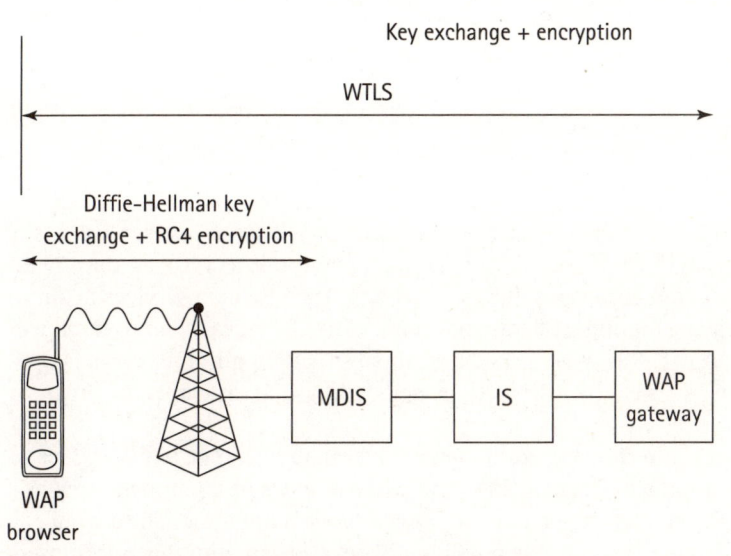

Figure 4-17: WTLS and CDPD integrated security solution

WTLS is divided into three classes of service, which break the protocol into separate feature sets. The higher classes of service have not been deployed as of yet. Table 4-2 shows the distribution of the feature sets.

TABLE 4-2 WTLS CLASSES

Feature	Class 1	Class 2	Class 3
Public-key exchange	Mandatory	Mandatory	Mandatory
Server certificates	Optional	Mandatory	Mandatory
Client certificates	Optional	Optional	Mandatory
MAC	Mandatory	Mandatory	Mandatory
Encryption	Mandatory	Mandatory	Mandatory
Smart card interface		Optional	Optional
Compression		Optional	Optional

> I discuss the individual features of these feature sets in Chapter 16.

WDP

WDP is the lowest layer of the WAP stack and consists of a datagram service. It sits on top of the raw service of the carrier/service operator. The WDP is the lowest layer that offers a common service. Below this point, the raw data services begin to differ in their implementation of data and architecture. In cases wherein the lower data bearers support IP, the WDP protocol is simply UDP. In all other cases, a special adaptation is defined by the WAP specification that attempts to create a UDP/IP-like service.

The WAP protocols were designed to operate over many bearers, but the scope of WAP ends at this interface. The bearers offer different levels of quality with regards to latency, throughput, and errors, but the WAP protocols are designed to compensate for those differences as much as possible. However, even with this effort, users will notice differences among the services. For example, it will easy to tell whether you are browsing using SMS, circuit-switched SMS, or packet-based networks: there are clear differences among these services in terms of delays and throughput.

Summary

Although a mess of protocols is involved, developers have to worry only about writing applications using WML and its associated media types. The applications at the beginning of the chapter showcase some of the possibilities when working with the WAP language.

The acronym WAP refers to a single protocol; however, as shown in this chapter, it is a complex series of intertwined protocols referred to as the WAP stack. Although application heavy, the stack contains many layers, beginning with the datagram service WDP. The layered protocols build above this to provide for the browsing services that reside at the very top. In between are the following: WTP, for improving the datagram service; WTLS, for optional security between WDP and WTP; WSP, for creating reliable sessions between browser and gateway; and WML and other presentation media types, for carrying WAP information.

This WAP stack is relevant only for the communication between the browser and the WAP gateway; the communication between the WAP gateway and the Internet Web server takes place using standard HTTP and therefore is outside the scope of WAP. However, WAP services residing on Internet Web servers have to be coded in WML and the WAP media types, making the presentation layer a critical piece that travels over the entire communication stream from Web server to WAP gateway to WAP client. The next chapter examines how to begin creating rudimentary WML services.

Chapter 5

Introducing WML

IN THIS CHAPTER

- An overview of XML
- Introducing WML structure
- Understanding text display
- Navigating between cards
- Displaying text with tables
- Displaying images

THE MAIN LANGUAGE USED FOR DEVELOPMENT in the WAP environment is Wireless Markup Language (WML). WML sits in the presentation layer of the seven-layer OSI stack model and is important to WAP because it affects how the layers below it are designed. It is very similar to HTML and other markup languages that you may have encountered.

This chapter focuses on getting you started learning this language. There is much more to WAP than just WML, although the other areas are sometimes poorly defined or not defined at all in the early WAP specifications, or simply forgotten by manufacturers. Examples of neglected areas are Wireless Telephony Applications (WTA; see Chapter 11), Push (Chapter 10), and WMLScript (Chapter 7).

This chapter provides a foundation for understanding WML elements and syntax. I divide these up by main functionality within the language. First I provide a summary of the XML language; then I show a simple WML example followed by a look at navigation and display elements. When you finish this chapter, you should be able to write basic WAP sites.

Images of Openwave products in this chapter courtesy of Openwave Systems Inc.

A Brief Overview of XML

Before you can understand WML, you must understand the nuances of XML, because WML is based on XML. A more detailed description of XML is given in Chapter 3, but briefly, XML is a language system used for storing documents for later retrieval and distribution. This purpose differs slightly from that of a language such as HTML, which is a language system that allows documents to be stored *and* that contains information about how they should be displayed. XML focuses on data storage, not display. It leaves the display component to other, complementary technologies such as XSL, or to the definition of displayable components, as in WML.

> **NOTE** XML is a breakaway language defined by the W3C to solve problems with SGML, which is yet another document storage language. SGML was too bulky, and its implementations used too much memory, for the language to be useful for any but the most specialized applications.

XML enables the user to structure data within the document in such a way that they are easily understood by databases and are human-readable. The XML user achieves this structure using metadata. This metadata varies among XML-based languages.

XML metadata is defined by the creators of the specific XML application. Listing 5-1 shows an example of an XML document. It stores information related to a chess game.

Listing 5-1: Chess Game in XML

```
<?xml version="1.0"?>
<!-- A chess game example -->
<chess>
<game total="2" title="Beginner vs. Pro">
        <move number="1" player="white">
            g4!?
        </move>
        <move number="1" player="black">
            e5
        </move>
        <move number="2" player="white">
            f4??
        </move>
        <move number="2" player="black">
            Qh4++
```

```
        </move>
</game>

</chess>
```

In this document, the items in angle brackets are called tags, which you may be familiar with from HTML. Two types of tags exist: those that begin a section and those that end a section. The entire section between the beginning and ending tag is known as an element.

> **TIP:** When an element does not contain anything it can be written in a shorthand form. For example, `<game/>` is a short form of `<game></game>`. The XML specification declares both to be acceptable, but XML programs have been known to make their own interpretations.

Several elements are in use in Listing 5-1. These are the `chess`, `game`, and `move` elements. The `game` element has what is known as an attribute. An attribute is a property of an element that better defines that element. In this document, for example, the attribute `total` stores the number of moves associated with a game. The attribute `title` stores a description of the game.

The second line of code in Listing 5-1 is a comment. Comments are added to XML code by beginning the element with `<!--` and ending it with `-->`. The comment consists of text, to be ignored by XML processors, in an XML document. The comment syntax for XML is the same for WML.

XML parsing

An XML parser is an application that reads the information contained in an XML document and then passes it along to other programs for action. This XML reader checks the document to make sure that it conforms to XML element and attribute syntax. If the document passes all the tests, it is called a well-formed document. The main rules for well-formed documents are the following:

- Internal tags are not allowed to cross. For example, in the chess example, the following code would not be legal:

  ```
  <game>
      <move number="2">
  </game>
      </move>
  ```

- XML parsers are case-sensitive. `game` is not the same as `Game` or `GAme`.

◆ XML must have only one root element. A root element is the main element within which all of the other elements are contained. In the chess example, the root element is chess.

See Chapter 3 for additional information on XML.

All these requirements make XML a much stricter language syntactically than HTML and cause WML to be a strict language as well. All the phones in the marketplace are very strict about how they interpret WAP sites written in WML. Any deviation from the XML rules causes errors to appear on the mobile device.

Element definitions

A modification to the earlier chess example is shown in Listing 5-2.

Listing 5-2: Modified Game Example

```
<?xml version="1.0"?>
<!-- A chess game example -->
<chess>
<game total="1" title="Beginner vs. Pro">
        <move number="1" player="white">
            g4!?
            <chess something="1">
                content
            </chess>
        </move>
</game>
</chess>
```

Now the code contains a chess element inside a game element. How can you prevent the incorrect usage of elements or check for it if it happens accidentally?

If the two sides are using the same version of the XML reader program, they can be assured that the reader on both ends is making the right choices about which elements should go where. However, when hundreds or thousands of users are involved, ensuring that every single user has the same exact version of the software becomes difficult. To deal with this problem, XML uses something called a

Document Type Definition (DTD). The DTD contains rules about where the elements can be stored, what types of attributes they can have, what elements can be containers for others, and other features of the special XML application. If an XML document not only passes the well-formed test but also passes a DTD check, it is said to be valid.

> See the section "Validated XML" in Chapter 3 for a detailed description of DTDs.

WML uses a DTD to define its elements and attributes. The WML 1.3 DTD has been included as an appendix as part of the WML reference. In later versions of the WML specifications, new elements and attributes were added. If the proper DTD is not referred to in the XML document, an XML parser can return the document as invalid. It is also important to understand that validation using the proper DTD does not guarantee that the document will display correctly; it is only an indication that the stored document has passed the rules defined in the DTD.

> If you are not familiar with DTDs, you need to read the XML section in Chapter 3 to understand the element definition statements I discuss in the following sections.

Working with WML Structure

As I mentioned in the previous section, WML is a markup language based on Extensible Markup Language (XML). Like most public languages based on XML, WML has a Document Type Definition (DTD) that contains rules for how the language is formatted.

WML can be divided into four main components:

- Text presentation and layout
- Deck/card organizational metaphor
- Intercard navigation and linking
- String parameterization and state management

This chapter covers the first three components and leaves the fourth for advanced discussion in the next chapter. WML includes elements that indicate how text and images are stored for formatting and layout. It defines collections of information, such as decks and subcollections of cards for storing units of user interaction. It also defines a way of explicitly managing the navigation between cards and decks, and makes provisions for event handling. And WML includes a state model, variable definition capability and parameterization which all allow for a more efficient use of bandwidth. The WML language addresses these four problem areas by defining elements and attributes that specify the relevant components. A WML browser displays information by interpreting these components. The primary component displayed by the browser is a card. This card can contain multiple elements and can be thought of as the equivalent of an HTML page for navigational purposes. However, unlike pages in HTML, all cards must be sent to the mobile device packaged inside one or more decks. The deck is the smallest unit of WML code that can be sent to the mobile device. For almost all WAP devices, it is the also the largest unit that can be sent to the mobile device. But some devices do support digests, composite objects, or multiparts, which are all multiple MIME parts as defined in Chapter 4. In most cases, such deviations from the specification would require little explanation, except for the fact that such pre-WAP devices represent a large percentage of the current U.S. market. Figures 5-1 through 5-3 show the basic units of WML navigation.

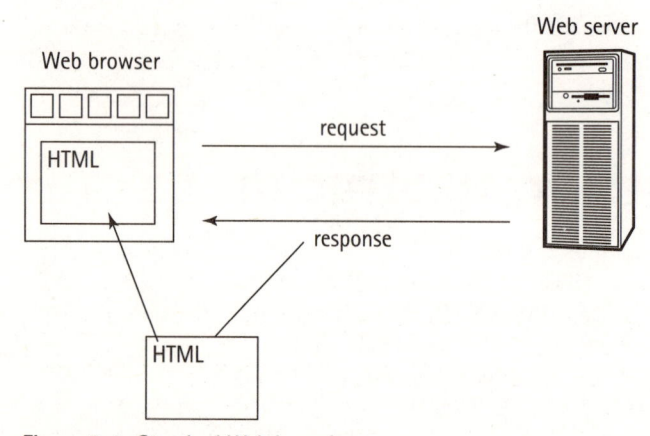

Figure 5-1: Standard Web browsing

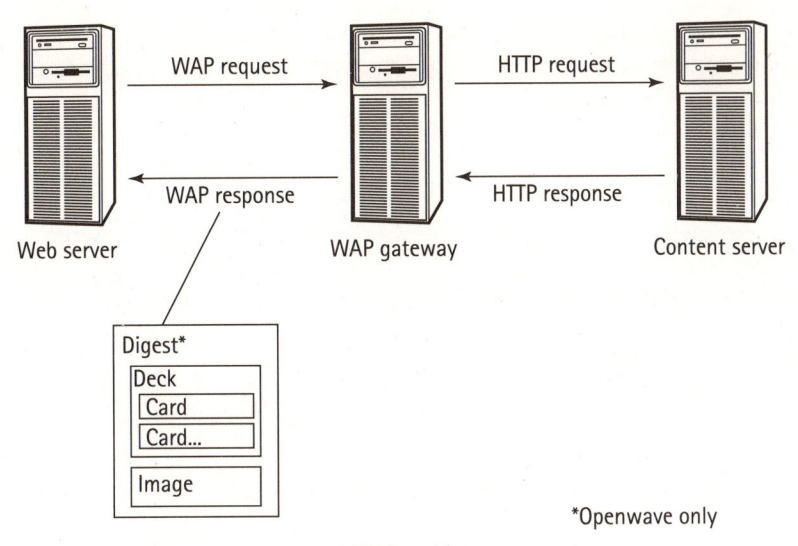

Figure 5-2: WML components and WAP architecture

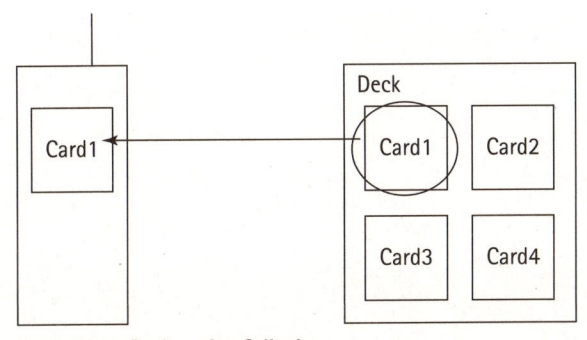

Figure 5-3: Basic unit of display

Each card constructed by the developer contains content and navigational control information. Although a deck containing multiple cards is sent to the device, only a single card is displayed at any one time. This design is intended to improve the performance of this language on narrow-band devices – devices with slow connections to the network. Because applications that reside on a Web server do not have their entire content available locally, the user makes decisions based on what information he or she wants to see. You as a developer can improve the user's interaction with your service by going one step further and predicting what the user is likely to ask for. You then can package this information in a deck.

Figure 5-4 illustrates the classic stock-quote request. The request example shows how a stock quote query can use predictive screen packaging to minimize wireless request/response transactions.

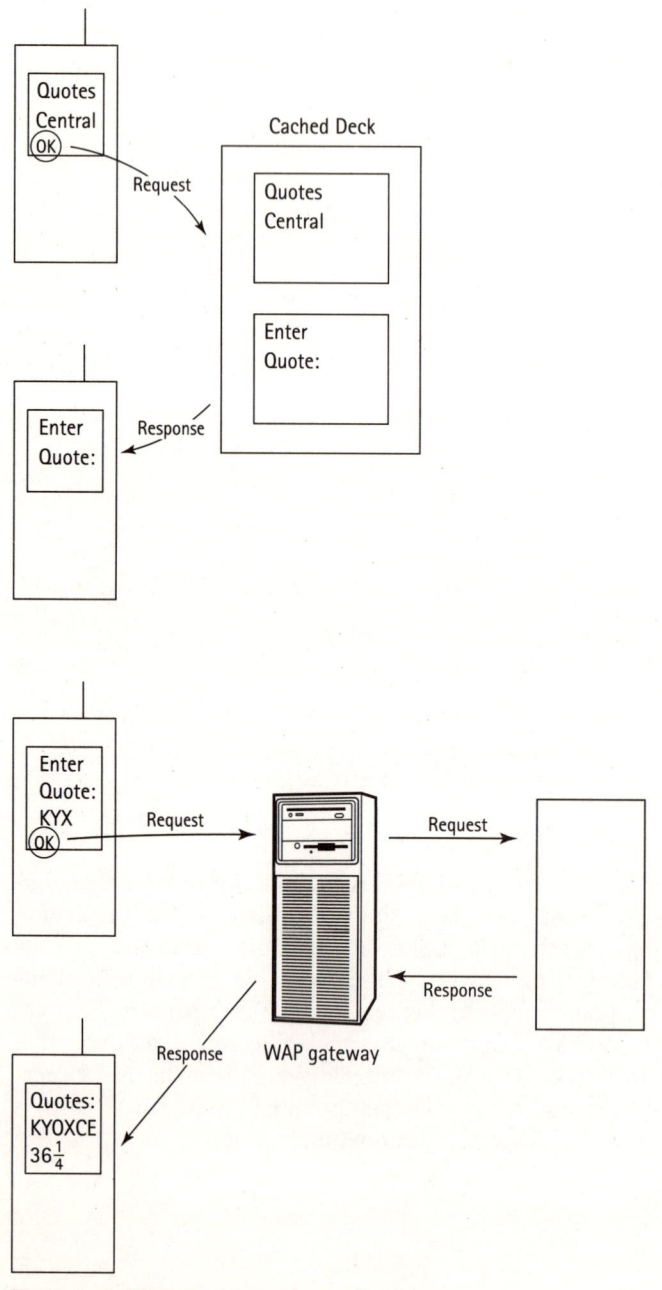

Figure 5-4: Stock-quote request application

A simple example of a WML deck

Now it's time to look at an example of a WML deck. This WML deck contains only one card. Unfortunately, at this time, WML deck presentations are highly dependent on a number of factors, the main one being browser manufacturer, as I discuss in Chapter 14. Therefore, the code in this chapter and others is shown in emulators manufactured by three main browser manufacturers: Nokia, Openwave, and Ericsson. Shown in Listing 5-3 is a WML deck example.

Listing 5-3: Simple WML Example

```
<?xml version="1.0"?>
<!DOCTYPE wml PUBLIC "-//WAPFORUM//DTD WML 1.1//EN"
 "http://www.wapforum.org/DTD/wml_1.1.xml">

<wml>
    <card id="new" title="First Card">
        <p>
            Hello There!
        </p>
    </card>
</wml>
```

The first part of the WML deck in the previous example is the XML version:

```
<?xml version="1.0"?>
```

Version 1.0 is the only XML version right now. Nonetheless, the version number should be included at the beginning of an XML document to indicate the version number of XML in use. It does not have to be there, but is a good way of indicating that your code is compliant to that version, should a new version of XML appear.

The next two lines of the WML deck in the code example indicate the Document Type Definition (DTD):

```
<!DOCTYPE wml PUBLIC "-//WAPFORUM//DTD WML 1.1//EN"
 "http://www.wapforum.org/DTD/wml_1.1.xml">
```

The DTD contains rules about how the WML parser determines that the elements contained within the deck are valid. The DTD displayed here shows the root of the XML document.

```
<!DOCTYPE wml
```

This means that all WML decks must begin with the `<wml>` tag and end with the `</wml>` tag. The next word, PUBLIC, declares the DTD to be publicly accessible from the Internet and other data networks. DTDs can be SYSTEM or PUBLIC. When SYSTEM is used, only one more parameter is needed, a URL. However, systems that do not want to force users to be dependent on the availability of a URL location can use the PUBLIC keyword instead.

Two locations follow a PUBLIC DTD. The first location is an internal Uniform Resource Indicator (URI), which is a more generic form of URL. This first location allows the validating WML reader to determine how to obtain a copy of the DTD. (Most applications would use a cached copy here.) In case the application-specific location results in no DTD being found, a second location is also used in the declaration.

The PUBLIC identifier for WML 1.1 is as follows:

```
"-//WAPFORUM//DTD WML 1.1//EN".
```

The next line gives the second location:

```
"http://www.wapforum.org/DTD/wml_1.1.xml">
```

In XML theory, the second location is technically a SYSTEM location; however, the SYSTEM keyword is not used when the PUBLIC keyword is shown.

For differing major WML specifications, the declaration changes for every version of the language. So the DTD for a WML 1.2 document is as follows:

```
<!DOCTYPE wml PUBLIC "-//WAPFORUM//DTD WML 1.2//EN" "http://www.wapforum.org/DTD/wml12.dtd">
```

The body of the code

The rest of the code is enclosed in a `<wml>` `</wml>` pair as was indicated by the document root property. This pair defines the WML deck and includes all the cards enclosed in `<card>` `</card>` pairs. Any tags in this language may have attributes that better define how they function.

For example, in the following line,

```
<card id="new" title="First Card">
```

one of the attributes of `card` is `id`, and its attribute value is `new`. That attribute programmatically identifies this card for navigation purposes. This way, if I want to navigate to this card, I can reference it using the word `new`.

The other attribute is `title`, which has a text value. The title may be displayed by browsers to give users a description of what they are viewing.

A card may have other attributes, but `id` and `title` are the only ones used here. The rules governing which attributes are allowed, what their values can be, and what is mandatory versus what is optional are all found in the DTD. Listing 5-4 provides an example cut out from the DTD regarding the `card` element.

Listing 5-4: card Element DTD Listing

```
<!ENTITY % coreattrs   "id      ID      #IMPLIED
                        class CDATA  #IMPLIED">

<!ENTITY % cardev
 "onenterforward    %HREF;         #IMPLIED
  onenterbackward  %HREF;         #IMPLIED
  ontimer          %HREF;         #IMPLIED"
 >

<!ELEMENT card (onevent*, timer?, (do | p)*)>
<!ATTLIST card
   title          %vdata;      #IMPLIED
   newcontext     %boolean;    "false"
   ordered        %boolean;    "true"
   xml:lang       NMTOKEN      #IMPLIED
   %cardev;
   %coreattrs;
 >
```

> **XREF:** I examine the other attributes later in this chapter and in the next chapter. The full WML 1.3 DTD is included in Appendix F.

You will see an ATTLIST in the DTD code that shows the full set of attributes available for the `card` element. I have used only `title` and `id` in this example.

Now, going back to the WML code and looking at the lines after the `card` element begins you'll see the following section:

```
<p>
    Hello There!
</p>
```

This code displays text in the browser. The `p` is short for paragraph. A `card` element requires the `p` element to display text. It would be an error to have only the following:

```
<card id="new" title="test">
    Hello There!
</card>
```

Paragraphs of text also have attributes that better define their behavior. I discuss these paragraph attributes in the section on formatting. Figure 5-5 shows how this code would appear in several common browsers.

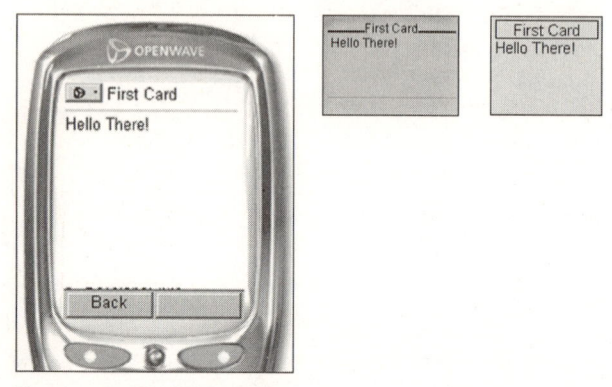

Figure 5-5: First WML code

The simple code here already shows the differences you may encounter when developing WML decks. A major difference between the Nokia/Ericsson browsers and the Openwave browser is that the title is not used in the Openwave simulation.

Common WML attributes

Two WML attributes are common to all WML elements. These are the `id` and `class` attributes. These two core attributes can be used for WAP gateway and Web server-side transformations. The `id` attribute provides any element that contains it with a unique name within the entire deck, and the `class` attribute affiliates an element with one or more classes. Multiple elements can belong to the same class. WML browsers do nothing with the `class` attribute.

Also included in almost every element is the `xml:lang` attribute, which is used to indicate a formal language associated with an element. The attribute indicates the best way to present the user with the language in the element content. Nested elements take the `xml:lang` attribute of their nearest parent if none is defined for them. An example of `xml:lang` in use is as follows:

```
<card id="premiere" xml:lang="fr">
...
</card>
```

```
<card id="deuxieme" xml:lang="fr>
    <p xml:lang="en">
        Hello
    </p>
</card>
```

The example shows how the card attributes are declared in French although the text inside the paragraphs is in English. Legal values for the `xml:lang` attribute are language codes as shown in RFC 1766, "Tags for the Identification of Languages".

> **Note:** You can find these RFCs (Requests for Comments) at `http://www.ietf.org`. If an RFC, which can be submitted by anyone, gains acceptance, it can eventually become an Internet standard. Each RFC is given a number that doesn't change. Updates to the RFC appear in new documents and are assigned a new number.

Understanding Text Display

In Listing 5-3, the phrase `"Hello There!"` appeared inside a `p` element. The `p` stands for paragraph and is used to indicate how text should be displayed on the screen. Following are the `p` element attributes:

- `align=(left|right|center)`: The attribute specifies how the text is aligned. Text can be left aligned, right aligned, or center aligned. Left alignment is the default mode. If this attribute is not specified, then the text alignment is set to "left" as the default.

- `mode=(wrap|nowrap)`: This attribute specifies the line-wrapping mode for the paragraph. `wrap` mode specifies that the text be broken up at word boundaries or at browser-determined locations. `nowrap` mode specifies that the text in the paragraph remain on a single line. If this attribute is not specified, it remains the same as in the previous paragraph element. The first paragraph element, if undefined, is set to `wrap`.

The attributes are good pointers as to what the `p` element is capable of, and the DTD is a good document to examine for answers to questions about where the element can be placed and what other elements can be located inside the `p` element.
Listing 5-5 shows the sections of the DTD that pertain to the `p` element.

Listing 5-5: p Element DTD Listing

```
<!ENTITY % coreattrs    "id       ID      #IMPLIED
                         class CDATA #IMPLIED">

<!ELEMENT card (onevent*, timer?, (do | p)*)>

<!ENTITY % fields    "%flow; | input | select | fieldset">

<!ENTITY % TAlign "(left|right|center)">

<!ENTITY % WrapMode "(wrap|nowrap)" >

<!ELEMENT p (%fields; | do)*>
<!ATTLIST p
  align        %TAlign;       "left"
  mode         %WrapMode;     #IMPLIED
  xml:lang     NMTOKEN        #IMPLIED
  %coreattrs;
  >
```

Listing 5-6 shows that the p element must be contained in a card. This is the only place the element can appear. Also, the listing shows that the element can contain other elements, such as do, input, and select. I discuss all these elements and their behavior in this chapter and the next.

Listing 5-6 shows the p element in use.

Listing 5-6: p Element Code Example

```
<?xml version="1.0"?>
<!DOCTYPE wml PUBLIC "-//WAPFORUM//DTD WML 1.1//EN"
"http://www.wapforum.org/DTD/wml_1.1.xml">

<wml>
    <card id="new" title="First Card">
        <p align="center">
            Hello There!
        </p>
        <p mode="nowrap">
            Another set of comments!
        </p>
    </card>
</wml>
```

Figure 5-6 shows how the code in the example would look in several browsers.

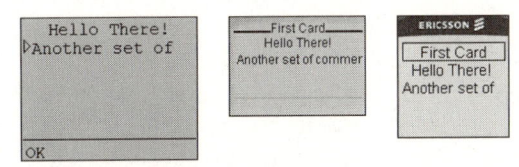

Figure 5-6: p element example

The alignment of the text in the example varies with the use of the `align` attribute. In the previous example, the code `align="center"` sets the statement `"Hello There!"` to be displayed in the center of the browser display. The `mode` attribute then set the way in which the text is handled by the browser. By default, the mode is set to `wrap`, which means that the browser automatically determines whether it should break on the spaces between words. The browsers shown break the text using their own internal rules. If the mode is set to `nowrap`, the entire text is set on a single line. (In this case you would need to use a line-break element to start additional text on a new line.) Openwave and Ericsson browsers (see Chapter 14 for a discussion on interoperability) display the `nowrap` text in Marquee display. Others, like the Nokia browser, let the text scroll to the end of the screen.

The DTD shows that other elements can be included in the p element. Text-formatting elements are the other elements that can be included in the p element and are indicated in the DTD by `%flow`. Table 5-1 lists the different `flow` elements and how to use them.

TABLE 5-1 P ELEMENT FORMATTING

Element	Displayed Style	Description
`<b>Bold</b>`	**Bold**	Displays the text between the tags in boldface.
`<i>Italics</i>`	*Italics*	Displays the text between the tags in italics.
`<u>Underline</u>`	Underline	Underlines the text between the tags.
`<em>Emphasis</em>`	**Emphasis**	Emphasizes the text between the tags to indicate that it is significant. Its applicability is browser dependent.

Continued

TABLE 5-1 P ELEMENT FORMATTING *(Continued)*

Element	Displayed Style	Description
`<strong>`**Strong**`</strong>`	**Strong**	Indicates in some way that the text between the tags is more significant than surrounding text, its applicability is browser dependent.
`<big>`Bigger`</big>`	**Bigger**	Increases the font size of the text between the tags.
`<small>`Smaller`</small>`	Smaller	Decreases the font size of the text between the tags.

Listing 5-7 shows an example of some of the styles indicated in the table. You will notice in Figure 5-7 that there are considerable variations in the ways these elements are supported.

Listing 5-7: p Element Formatting Example

```
<?xml version="1.0"?>
<!DOCTYPE wml PUBLIC "-//WAPFORUM//DTD WML 1.1//EN"
"http://www.wapforum.org/DTD/wml_1.1.xml">

<wml>
    <card id="new" title="24 Hr Weather">
        <p align="center">
            <i><big>Weather Today</big></i>
        </p>
        <p align="left" mode="wrap">
            <br/>
            <u>Ann Arbor</u><br/>
            <i>Sunday </i>11/18<br/>
            Cloudy and windy<br/>
            <i>Monday </i>35/20<br/>
            Partly cloudy
        </p>
        <p>
            <small>Data provided by Weather
Broadcasting Corp. Inc.</small>
```

```
        </p>
    </card>
</wml>
```

Figure 5-7 shows how these elements would appear on various browsers.

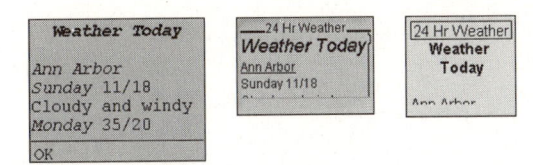

Figure 5-7: p element formatting elements

The example contains another element that is useful in text formatting, the `br` element. It is placed where a new line is required in the text. The browser positions any text that follows the `br` element on its own line. This element does not have any content and therefore it uses the shorthand form of element notation that I introduced earlier in this chapter — in this case, it appears as `<br/>`. The `br` element can appear in paragraphs, as shown in the preceding example, and also in tables.

Certain characters need special formats in order to display properly in the browser. For example, because the angle brackets have special meaning in WML, they cannot be used as such in the text. To get those characters to display, you have to enter the character using either its ISO-10646 number or its named equivalent, if one exists. I discuss both methods in the following sections.

Using the ISO-10646 method for character display

ISO-10646 is a character-set specification currently equivalent to the Unicode 2.0 character set. It assigns each character a numerical equivalent for the purposes of storage on computers. The lowest seven bits of the ISO-10646 standard are equivalent to ASCII. So, for example, the character < can be represented by 60 in decimal notation, 0111100 in binary notation, or 3C in hexadecimal notation. Therefore, either of the following syntaxes represent the symbol equally well: `&#60;` in decimal or `&#x3C;` in hexadecimal. An important point to note is that the document character set (in this case, Unicode) is distinct from the current document encoding. Don't be concerned if you are confused about this point; I discuss encoding and character sets in Chapter 17.

> **NOTE:** ISO-10646 is used by WML because that is the default document encoding for all XML documents.

Part 1: Foundations

Listing 5-8 presents a code sample with a reserved character specified in different ways.

Listing 5-8: Character-Set Example

```
<?xml version="1.0"?>
<!DOCTYPE wml PUBLIC "-//WAPFORUM//DTD WML 1.1//EN"
"http://www.wapforum.org/DTD/wml_1.1.xml">

<wml>
     <card id="new" title="Character test">
          <p>
               Reserved characters<br/>
               &#60; or &#x3C; or &lt;<br/>
               gar&#231;on
          </p>
     </card>
</wml>
```

The displays shown in the sample browsers (see Figure 5-8) indicate that all the methods used for displaying the less-than symbol (<) are syntactically equivalent.

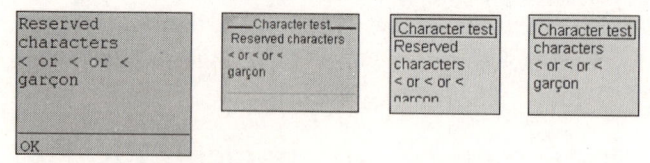

Figure 5-8: Character entities

Using the named-equivalent method for character display

The second way to display reserved characters is by using their named-equivalent, or named-entity, form. The use of an entity is XML's way of pointing to a variable inside the DTD that has been previously defined and can be used in any valid document. These entities are referenced in WML code by the & symbol followed by an XML variable name and the semicolon terminator (;).

The DTD contains definitions for some reserved character entities. You can make use of these by referring to them using the character entity reference.

Listing 5-9 presents the DTD code that shows the named entities.

Listing 5-9: Named Character Entities

```
<!ENTITY quot   "&#34;">         <!-- quotation mark -->
<!ENTITY amp    "&#38;#38;">     <!-- ampersand -->
<!ENTITY apos   "&#39;">         <!-- apostrophe -->
<!ENTITY lt     "&#38;#60;">     <!-- less than -->
<!ENTITY gt     "&#62;">         <!-- greater than -->
<!ENTITY nbsp   " ">        <!-- non-breaking space -->
<!ENTITY shy    "&#173;">        <!-- soft hyphen(discretionary hyphen)-->
```

So, by typing > or ' you would get the equivalent entity shown in the preceding DTD listing. Notice that the DTD ends up defining the entities using the character set form anyway.

The preceding named character entities are the only ones defined in the DTD. If you need to display some other special character you must specify it using the character-set format described in the previous section, "Using the ISO-10646 method for character display."

Another character exists that you should be aware of, one that does not neatly fit into the aforementioned rules. This is the $ character. To display this character on the screen, you need to type $$. This character is reserved because, as I discuss later in this chapter, it is used to identify variables in WML code.

Listing 5-10 provides an example of the $ symbol in use.

Listing 5-10: The $ Symbol

```
<?xml version="1.0"?>
<!DOCTYPE wml PUBLIC "-//WAPFORUM//DTD WML 1.1//EN"
"http://www.wapforum.org/DTD/wml_1.1.xml">

<wml>
    <card id="new" title="Character test">
        <p>
            Price of fruit in &quot;Tulivia&quot;<br/>
            Apples $$4<br/>
            Another fruit can  be 
displayed here 
        </p>
    </card>
</wml>
```

You cannot use $ to print a $ symbol because the symbol has special meaning when standing alone. Using two together is the only way to circumvent the problem. Also included in the example are the " entity and the   entity. The latter, which is the non-breaking space entity, indicates to the browser that it should try not to break the line at that location. Figure 5-9 shows how the code looks in some example browsers.

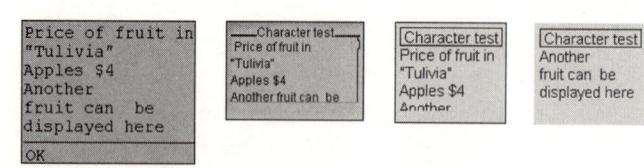

Figure 5-9: The $ symbol

Navigating between Cards in WML

Now that you understand how to display data, the next important concept for you to grasp is how a user can navigate between cards in WML. Three main ways exist to achieve this navigation:

- Selecting a link
- Pressing a soft key
- Using an intrinsic event

I cover the first two here; intrinsic events are described in the next chapter.

In standard HTML coding, the only mechanism used is the linking by reference. A user selects links to navigate among different pages stored on the Web server. In WML, however, the links are not easily selectable because a mouse is not connected to the phone. On mobile devices, soft keys and arrow keys take the place of the mouse. The soft keys are hardware keys on the mobile device whose labeling and functionality the WML programmer specifies. Also possible in the mobile-device scenario are events that may launch a card to be loaded without any user intervention.

Figures 5-10 and 5-11 illustrate the methods of navigation I mentioned earlier and show how they compare to standard Web browsing.

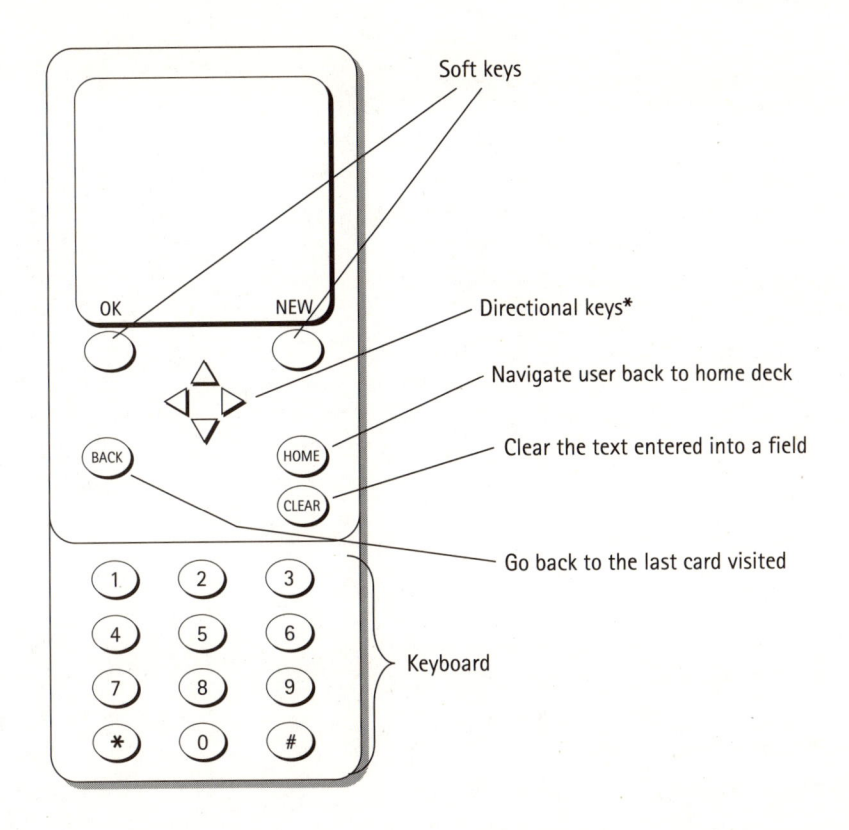

Figure 5-10: Navigational methods

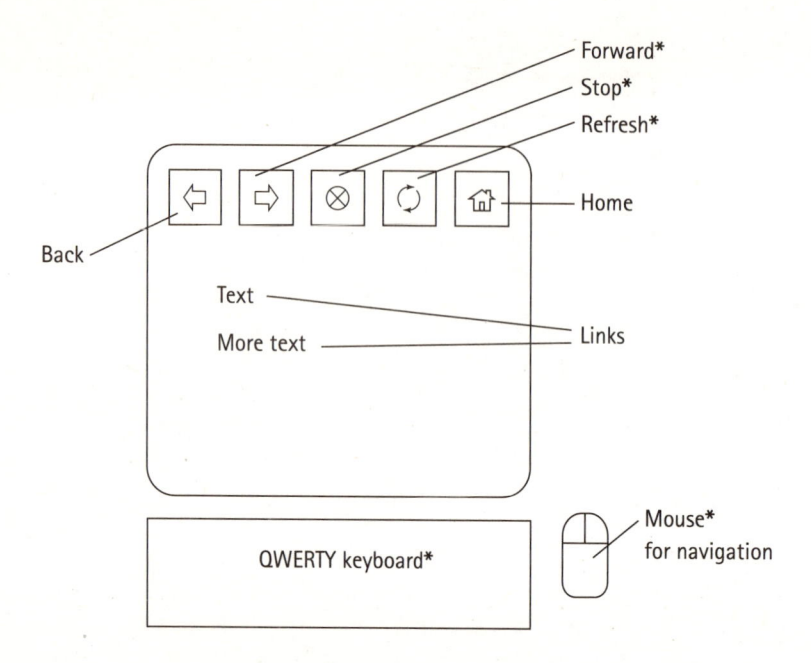

[Figure: diagram of a web browser interface with labeled elements: Back, Forward*, Stop*, Refresh*, Home, Text, More text, Links, QWERTY keyboard*, Mouse* for navigation]

*These are not available on wireless phones.
Other clients such as PDAs may support additional features.

Figure 5-11: Comparison to standard Web browsing

Navigation principles

Navigating by selecting links is common on the World Wide Web (WWW). But before I describe how this type of navigation takes place, you need to see what these links actually look like.

All resources on the WWW are identified using Uniform Resource Locators (URLs). These URLs have the following form:

protocol://host.domain/file/path/filename.ext#fragment?var1=value&var2=value

For navigation of Web sites, the protocol used is the Hyper Text Transfer Protocol (HTTP). Other protocols that browsers support include Simple Mail Transfer Protocol (SMTP) and File Transfer Protocol (FTP).

Although technically a WAP session uses the Wireless Session Protocol to communicate with the WAP gateway, the text `http://` begins the name of any absolute WML reference. The next pieces of the URL are the host and domain name. An example of a host and domain name is `www.domain.com`, in which the host is `www` and the domain is `domain.com`. For WAP sites, the URL could be `wap.domain.com` or `www.domain.com`, at which point for the latter the site would have to use auto-detection of the browser to distinguish between the WAP users and regular browser users. Because all Internet hosts also have IP addresses, an IP address could also be used for the *host.domain* portion; doing so, however, is not considered good practice. Listing 5-11 provides some examples of URLs for WML data.

Listing 5-11: URL Examples

```
http://wap.domain.com/wireless/index.wml
http://wap.domain.com/wireless/index.wml#first
http://207.57.65.101/wireless/index.wml#first
wireless/more/another_index.wml#second
http://wap.domain.com/scripts/calculate.asp?zone=4&amp;country=9
#second
wireless.asp
calculate.asp?zone=4&amp;daylight=0
?zone=5&amp;daylight=1
```

URLs for resources can be both absolute and relative. Lines 1–3 and line 5 show URL examples with absolute references. They indicate the protocol, *domain.host*, and the full path to the resource. The rest of the lines represent relative URLs. Relative URLs do not specify the full path, protocol, or *domain.host*. All those parameters are implied by previous communication. The browser automatically generates the full URL based on parameters stored from previous communication. For example, I could enter http://www.domain.com/news/sports.wml and then place a link on that page to another page called editorials.wml. This second link would be a relative link to a file in the same directory as sports.wml. The relative reference to editorials.wml is still using the same protocol; it is at the same host and domain name and in the same directory as before.

As I point out earlier in the chapter, cards form the basic unit of display. A card, however, is packaged inside a deck and then sent to the mobile device. The deck can contain multiple cards. When a deck is referenced in a URL, as in line 1 of Listing 5-11, the URL example listing, the first card in the deck is loaded by default. To point to a specific card, you add a pound or hash symbol to the deck name, followed by the card id, as shown in line 2 of the URL example listing.

Lines 6–9 of Listing 5-11 show dynamic scripts being referenced in URLs. In these cases the dynamic scripts are responsible for generating WML decks in real time. These dynamic scripts can take input parameters, which may affect the decks that are outputted. For example, a script could be written to calculate the time in a certain world region. Inputs could be the time zone and an indicator showing whether the country or region supports daylight savings time. Now, if the script needed to be re-executed with different parameters, an extremely terse form of URL could be used. An example of doing so appears in line 9 of Listing 5-11. (Attaching variables manually, as shown in the example, is not common practice, and is shown here only to contrast with the recommended technique. Also, for some phones this is the only technique possible.) The variables are placed in a `postfield` element, which I discuss in the next chapter.

Navigation using anchors

Now that we've covered URL details you can see how to write code for navigation using links. In WML, you use the `anchor` element. The element has two forms: one long and the other short. The short form is best because it allows for more efficient conversion of the elements into their binary form. The long form has the following attribute:

> `title=vdata`: A brief text string that identifies the link. This characteristic may be ignored or truncated by the browser.

The `anchor` elements can appear in any text flow, excluding the text in `option` elements, and cannot be nested. See Chapter 6 for more on `option` elements.
Listing 5-12 shows the DTD snippet for the `anchor` element.

Listing 5-12: anchor Element DTD Sections

```
<!ELEMENT anchor ( #PCDATA | br | img | go | prev | refresh )*>

<!ATTLIST anchor
   title        %vdata;     #IMPLIED
   xml:lang     NMTOKEN     #IMPLIED
   %coreattrs;
>
```

The DTD listing shows the different data types that you can place inside an `anchor` element. The URL for the navigation is stored in a `go` element `href` attribute contained within an anchor. (Table 5-3, later in this chapter, shows the `go` element and other tasks.) Only one of these tasks may appear in a single `anchor` element.

You can place the `anchor` element tags around the text that is to be visually highlighted to the user. The visual highlighting varies from browser to browser. An example of such anchoring follows:

```
<anchor>Test Site
<go href="http://www.domain.com/test.wml"/>
</anchor><br/>
```

You can also place `anchor` tags using a short form. You do so with the `a` element. The `a` element has the following attributes:

- `href=HREF`: Specifies the destination as a URL.

- `title=vdata`: Identifies the link. This characteristic may be ignored or truncated by the browser.

The a element can also appear in all text flow, excluding option elements, and cannot be nested. Listing 5-13 shows the relevant section from the DTD.

Listing 5-13: an Element DTD Listing

```
<!ELEMENT a ( #PCDATA | br | img )*>
<!ATTLIST a
    href        %HREF;      #REQUIRED
    title       %vdata;     #IMPLIED
    xml:lang    NMTOKEN     #IMPLIE
    %coreattrs;
>
```

The DTD listing shows that the a element can contain text, a line-break element, or an image reference. The * indicates that multiple 0-n elements can be contained within the a element.

Following are three examples of a element usage:

```
<a href="http://www.domain.com/test.wml">Test Site</a><br/>

<a href="../files/more.wml">More</a><br/>

<a href="#second">Second Card</a><br/>
```

Typically, the short form <a> is used to save time and space. The long form is necessary, however, if a complex go task is being initiated. The anchors in these examples are around text, but the same rules apply for anchors around images.

Following is another code example showing how anchors can be used to navigate between two cards in a deck.

```
<?xml version="1.0"?>
<!DOCTYPE wml PUBLIC "-//WAPFORUM//DTD WML 1.1//EN"
"http://www.wapforum.org/DTD/wml_1.1.xml">

<wml>
    <card id="new" title="Navigation test #1">
        <p>
            Test card #1<br/>
            <a href="#new_two">Go</a>
            <a href="another_deck.wml#new_three">Next</a>
        </p>
    </card>
    <card id="new_two" title="Navigation test #2">
        <p>
            Test card #2
```

```
            </p>
        </card>
</wml>
```

Figure 5-12 shows how the example would look in three common browsers.

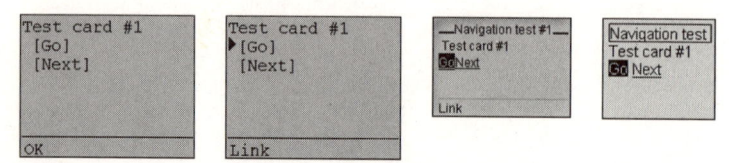

Figure 5-12: Anchor navigation between cards

The figures show how the anchors are visible to users and how navigation between different anchors takes place. Each anchor highlighted has a "halo" around it. Because the first deck has more than one anchor, the user must press the down-arrow key to move the "halo" around the selectable anchor. This "halo" differs among implementations.

For example, see the Openwave browser, which appears in the first two images. The display does not allow the anchors to be selected until the user has scrolled down by pressing the down-arrow key. Then a link soft key appears that, when selected, follows the programmed URL. The existence of links is also indicated by an arrow symbol at the left of the text line.

The example in the Nokia browser shows how the first anchor is automatically selected. A `<br/>` element will be necessary here to force the link to appear on its own line for clarity.

The Ericsson browser uses the same type of link hint as the Nokia browser, but this time the underlining disappears when the item is selected. A `<br/>` element will be necessary again to add some clarity to the links.

Navigation using soft keys

The second method available for navigation is the use of soft keys. Every card presented to the user has a number of soft keys associated with it. These soft keys are actually hardware keys to which WML programmers can map functionality. So, for example, if you want to give the user the option of totaling the entries in a table, you can map that action to a soft key. The number of soft keys and their orientation vary with the browser; some general rules, however, can be applied across the board. Figure 5-13 shows the soft keys as they would appear in some phone displays.

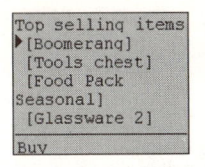

Figure 5-13: Soft keys

First, all soft keys have programmatic references. Each of these references indicates what the user will be most likely to perceive as the key's functionality. Table 5-2 presents the types available.

TABLE 5-2 HARDWARE KEY TYPES

Key Type	Description of Key
accept	Indicates positive acknowledgment or acceptance.
prev	Used for backward history navigation.
help	Sends a request for help; can be context sensitive depending on the browser.
reset	Clears or resets the state.
options	Context-sensitive request for options or additional operations.
delete	Deletes an item or choice.
unknown	A generic do element; is equivalent to an empty string in a type value.
X-*, x-*	Experimental types.
vnd.*, VND.* or other case variation of vnd	Vendor- or browser-specific types.

The key types in the table only define the hardware key mapping. The actual action bound to the key is defined by various other action mappings. Table 5-3 lists the action mappings.

Table 5-3 Action Types

Action Type	Description
go	Goes forward.
prev	Goes backward using the history stack.
refresh	Refreshes the screen after updating variable values.
noop	Indicates that no action should be taken.

To assign actions to soft keys using these key and task mappings, you use the do element. The representation of the do element is dependent on the browser, and the developer can't assume that it will show up in the same place on every phone.

Table 5-4 presents the do element attributes.

Table 5-4 Do Element Attributes

Attribute	Description
type=cdata	This attribute provides a hint to the browser about how it should be displayed. The browser must accept any type; however, if it does not recognize the type, it treats the type as an unknown. Predefined do types are shown in Table 5-2.
label=vdata	If the browser is able to dynamically label the hardware key, this attribute specifies the string used for the label. If the hardware key cannot be labeled, the attribute is ignored.
name=nmtoken	This attribute specifies a programmatic name for the do element binding. This is useful when multiple do elements are bound to the same card. In this case, the do elements must have different names. The name is also used in deck-level binding versus card-level binding determinations. (See the section on templates in this chapter.) If a do element name is not defined, the value defaults to the type attribute.
optional=Boolean	The browser uses this attribute to determine whether the do element may be ignored.

do elements can appear only in card or template elements. Listing 5-14 shows which elements can appear inside a do element.

Listing 5-14: do Element DTD Listing

```
<!ENTITY % task    "go | prev | noop | refresh">

<!ELEMENT do (%task;)>
<!ATTLIST do
    type         CDATA       #REQUIRED
    label        %vdata;     #IMPLIED
    name         NMTOKEN     #IMPLIED
    optional     %boolean;   "false"
    xml:lang     NMTOKEN     #IMPLIED
    %coreattrs;
>
```

Any one of the tasks shown in Table 5-3 can be placed inside a do element.

In the upcoming examples you will see the many combinations that the action types and attributes in Tables 5-3 and 5-4 enable you to create. Listing 5-15 shows a simple forward navigation that achieves the same functionality as an anchor but instead uses the accept soft key.

Listing 5-15: accept Key Example

```
<?xml version="1.0"?>
<!DOCTYPE wml PUBLIC "-//WAPFORUM//DTD WML 1.1//EN"
"http://www.wapforum.org/DTD/wml_1.1.xml">

<wml>
    <card id="new" title="Navigation test #1">
        <do type="accept">
            <go href="#new_two"/>
        </do>

        <p>
            Test card #1<br/>
        </p>
    </card>

    <card id="new_two" title="Navigation test #2">
        <p>
            Test card #2
        </p>
    </card>
</wml>
```

In this example, the navigation is accomplished by the `do` element:

```
<do type="accept">
    <go href="#new_two"/>
</do>
```

A `do` element is inserted into the card `new` to indicate that an action is to be mapped to a key. The `do` element has a `type` attribute. The `type` attribute's value is one of the key types described in Table 5-4. Remember that this `type` attribute points to a potential soft key on the phone. Inside the `do` element is a `go` element. The `go` element contains an `href` attribute that has a URL as its value. The `href` attribute points to another card in the deck in this example. You can think of the `go` action as being mapped to the `accept` soft key.

Figure 5-14 shows how the code looks when displayed by different browsers.

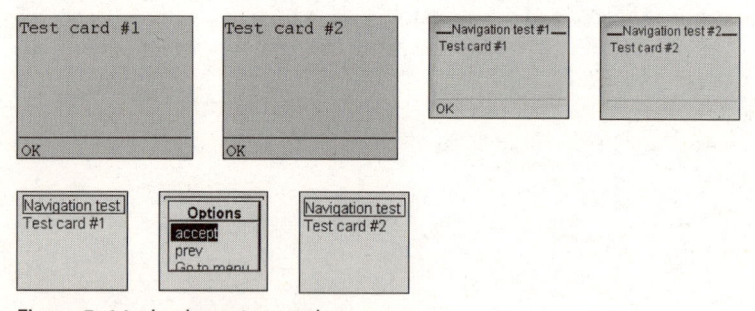

Figure 5-14: do element example

The first two screens show how navigation takes place in the Openwave browser. The user presses the OK key to navigate to the second screen.

The next two screens show the Nokia browser. A notable difference between the Nokia and Openwave browsers is found in the fact that the OK soft key does not appear on the second screen. This is because the Nokia browser does not have a default mapping for the `accept` soft key. Every mapping has to be done explicitly for the Nokia browser.

In the Ericsson browser, no soft key mappings appear; they have to selected from an action menu, which appears when the YES key is pressed.

Backward navigation

On the Web, browsers commonly feature a forward button, which enables users to navigate forward to a page stored in something called the history stack. The history stack is a set of references to URLs that have been visited in the past. On WAP devices, WAP designing engineers decided that the forward navigation would simply be disallowed. WAP software engineers believed that having both forward and backward navigation on the current mobile phones could result in circular navigation. In these cases, the user would simply be navigating backward and forward through the same set of cards.

To allow only backward navigation, WAP browsers carefully massage the history stack. Every time the user goes backward, all subsequent items that reside in the history stack are purged. Figure 5-15 should clarify this point.

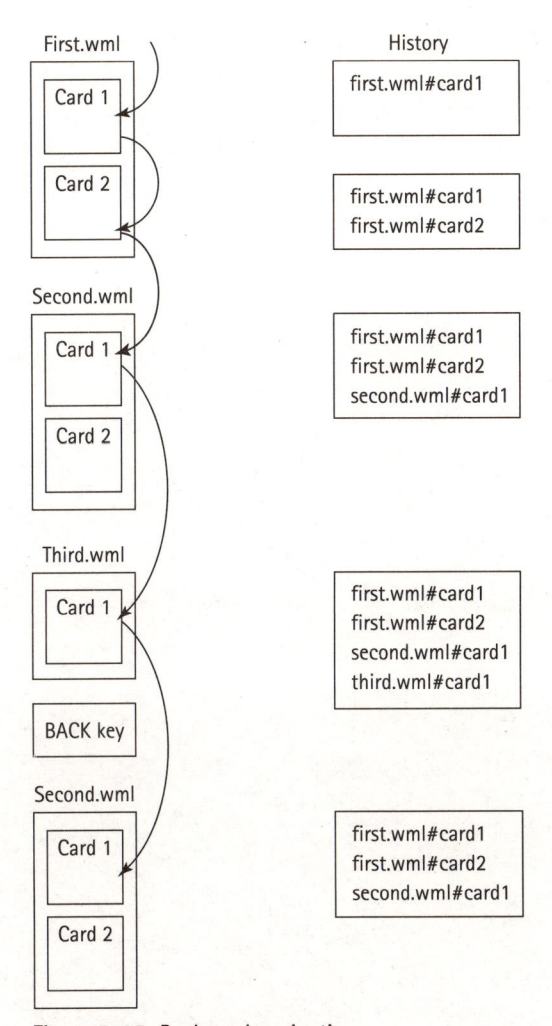

Figure 5-15: Backward navigation

Part 1: Foundations

You can use the two techniques of navigation presented so far to navigate backward on the history stack. Listing 5-16 and Figure 5-16 show both techniques in action as well as a display of the history stack at all points during navigation.

Listing 5-16: Backward-Navigation Example

```
<?xml version="1.0"?>
<!DOCTYPE wml PUBLIC "-//WAPFORUM//DTD WML 1.1//EN"
"http://www.wapforum.org/DTD/wml_1.1.xml">

<wml>

    <card id="new_one" title="Navigation test #1">
        <do type="accept">
            <go href="#new_two"/>
        </do>

        <p>
            Test card #1<br/>
        </p>
    </card>

    <card id="new_two" title="Navigation test #2">
        <do type="accept">
            <go href="#new_three"/>
        </do>
        <do type="prev">
            <prev/>
        </do>
        <p>
            Test card #2
        </p>
    </card>

    <card id="new_three" title="Navigation test #3">
        <p>
```

```
                Test card #3<br/>
                <anchor>Go Back
                    <prev/>
                </anchor>
            </p>
        </card>

</wml>
```

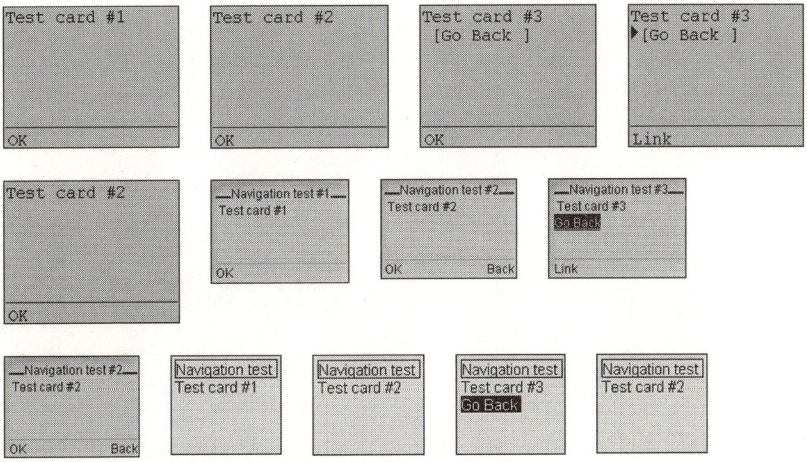

Figure 5-16: Backward navigation in multiple browsers

The long set of examples in Figure 5-16 shows how backward navigation is done with the soft keys. The examples in Figure 5-17 also show the differences between backward navigation using a soft key and backward navigation using an anchor.

You can see in the history stack listings of Figure 5-17 how going backward affects the history-stack listing. The browser simply deletes the reference indicating where you have been if you navigate backward. There is no such thing as forward navigation using the WML history.

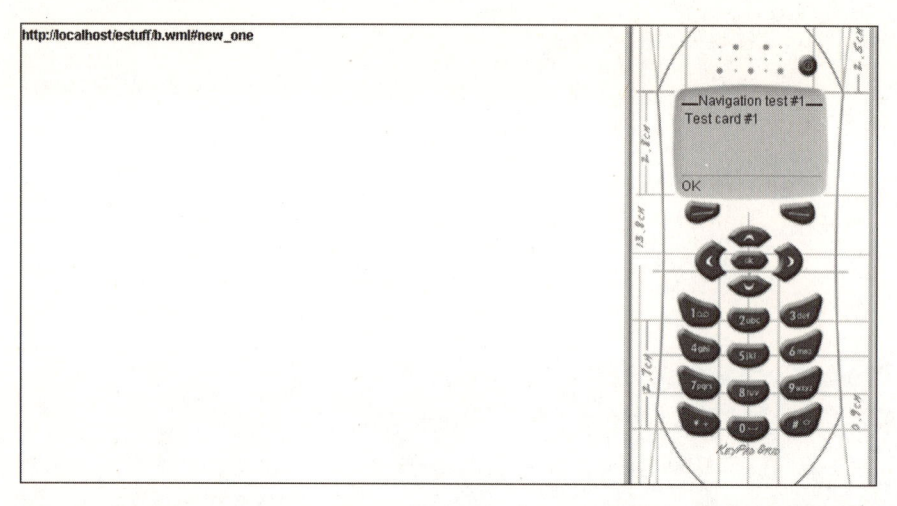

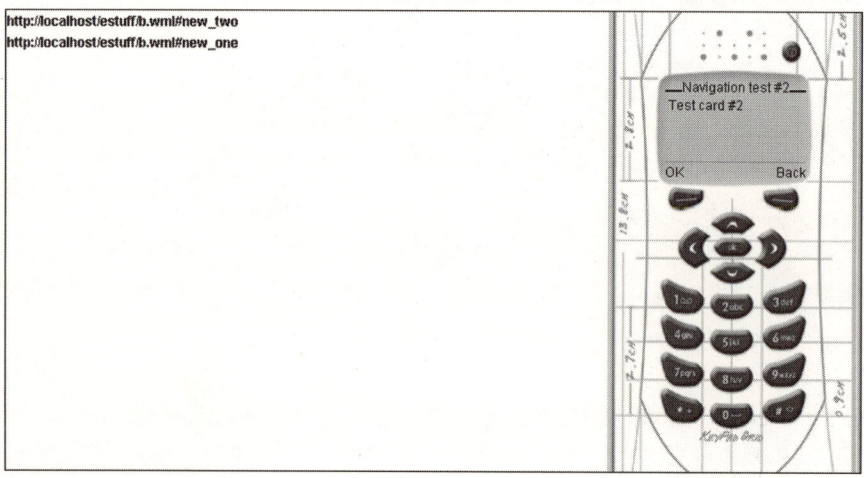

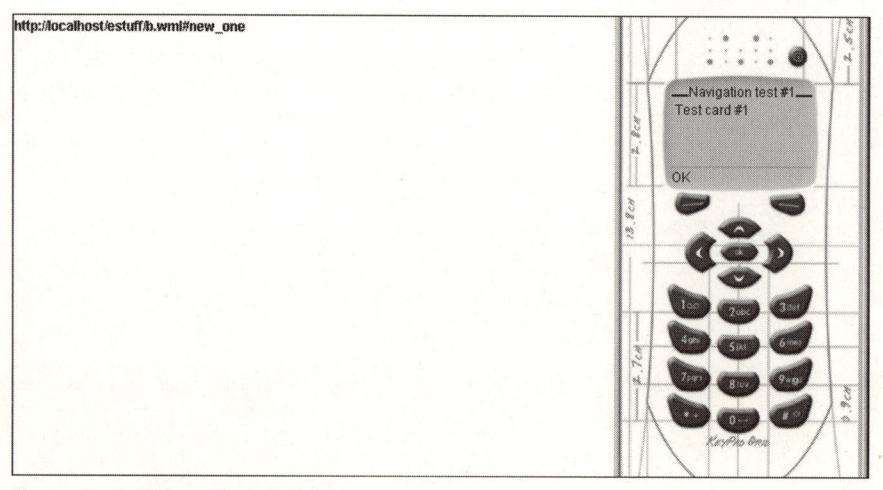

Figure 5-17: History-stack listings

Labeling and other attributes

The previous section entitled "Navigation using soft keys" shows how you can map a task to a key. The section also shows how a programmer can indicate a key's functionality to the user. In the preceding examples I do not specify a label, so the browser automatically determines the locale-specific variant. In English-speaking countries, the browser maps the `accept` key type to the displayed word OK. Browsers vary in the way this auto-mapping takes place.

Labeling is controlled by the `label` attribute of the `do` type, as follows:

```
<do type="accept" label="Next">
...
</do>
```

The other important `do` attribute is the `name`, listed earlier in Table 5-4. This attribute is used when multiple actions are bound to the same soft key. The natural question, then, is where would the additional bindings appear? The answer is that the browser would create a generic label indicating that multiple options exist; then, if the menu option or its equivalent is selected by the user, the browser will open an additional menu that lists all the multiple bindings.

If you wanted to create a card with multiple tasks being bound to a single key, you would create the `do` elements as before, but this time you would distinguish between two `do` elements bound to the same soft key using a `name` attribute.

Listing 5-17 shows an example of `do`-element labeling, multiple bindings, and multiple `do` elements defined for a card.

Listing 5-17: Multiple-Binding Example

```
<?xml version="1.0"?>
<!DOCTYPE wml PUBLIC "-//WAPFORUM//DTD WML 1.1//EN"
 "http://www.wapforum.org/DTD/wml_1.1.xml">

<wml>
    <card id="one" title="Do elements">
        <do type="accept" name="do_one"  label="Next">
            <go href="#two"/>
        </do>
        <do type="accept" name="do_two"  label="Beyond">
            <go href="#three"/>
        </do>

        <p>Test card #1<br/>
        </p>
    </card>
```

Continued

Listing 5-17 *(Continued)*

```
        <card id="two" title="Do test #2">
            <do type="accept" name="do_one"  label="Next">
                <go href="#three"/>
            </do>
            <do type="accept" name="do_two"  label="Way Back">
                <go href="#one"/>
            </do>
            <do type="prev" label="Back">
                <prev/>
            </do>
            <p>Test card #2
            </p>
        </card>

        <card id="three" title="Do test #3">
            <do type="accept" label="Go to Start">
                <go href="#one"/>
            </do>
            <do type="prev">
                <prev/>
            </do>
            <p>Test card #3<br/>
                This is an extremely long news story about
                something occurring somewhere involving somebody
                <anchor>Go Back
                    <prev/>
                </anchor>
            </p>
        </card>
</wml>
```

Figure 5-18 shows how this code appears in some common browsers.

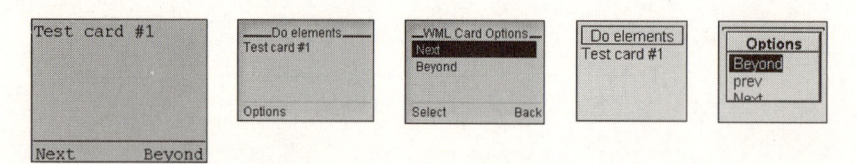

Figure 5-18: Multiple do-element binding

In the first card of the deck in the preceding example, I bound multiple do bindings to the accept soft key. The name token is required in some browsers to distinguish between the two different tasks of the same key. The tasks are generally displayed in their own action menu, which is visible in different ways on different browsers, as shown in Figure 5-18. You can find a more detailed description of the differences among browsers in Chapter 14.

The second card of the deck features multiple bindings to the `accept` soft key, but this time there is a binding to the `prev` soft key as well. Once again, when programming, keep in mind the differences between phones in the way the `prev` key is implemented.

The convention I have used so far is to put the `do` elements immediately under the `card` element. The WML specification does not restrict the `do` elements to appearing first; they can also appear just before the `card` element ends. However, they must appear somewhere in the `card` element. Listing 5-18 shows alternative locations for `do` elements.

Listing 5-18: Alternative do Locations

```
<card id="one" title="Do elements">
    <p>Test card #1<br/>
    </p>
    <do type="accept" name="do_one" label="Next">
        <go href="#two"/>
    </do>
    <do type="accept" name="do_two" label="Beyond">
        <go href="#three"/>
    </do>
</card>
```

Although not commonly used this way, the `do` element can also appear inside the paragraph element in any portion of the paragraph. Listing 5-19 shows a possible implementation.

Listing 5-19: do Element Inside a p Element

```
<p>
<do type="prev">
<prev/>
</do>
Some text here
</p>
```

In the third card of the multiple binding example deck, the `accept` and `prev` keys are bound to the hardware key separately and each appears with its own distinct soft-key labels. The `accept` key label usually has a size limit on phones; the smallest phone implementations are now about six characters. You may find older models with five-character limitations. The browser images shown previously in Figure 5-18 show you the differences among the displays.

The template element

In real-world applications you may need to create decks requiring a soft key mapping on every single card within a deck. One example is an application that needs to make a help key available to its users at all times. This help key may be mapped to a soft key for the duration of the deck. You enable this feature using the `template` element.

The `template` element is specially placed inside a deck near the beginning. The DTD section in Listing 5-20 shows how the WML deck is structured.

Listing 5-20: WML DTD Section

```
<!ELEMENT wml ( head?, template?, card+ )>
<!ATTLIST wml
  xml:lang       NMTOKEN        #IMPLIED
  %coreattrs;
>
```

The DTD section shows that all WML decks must contain one or more cards. Optional components are marked with a ? and must be stored in the WML file in the order shown in the ELEMENT definition. If head, template, and card elements are present, the head appears first, followed by the template and then one or more cards.

> I discuss the head element in Chapter 6.

The `template` element is therefore contained in the WML deck before any cards are defined. The `template` element can contain intrinsic events or `do` elements. (I discuss intrinsic events in Chapter 6.) Listing 5-21 shows the relevant DTD portions concerning the `template` element.

Listing 5-21: Template Element DTD Section

```
<!ENTITY % coreattrs  "id     ID      #IMPLIED
                       class  CDATA   #IMPLIED">

<!ENTITY % navelmts "do | onevent">

<!ENTITY % cardev
 "onenterforward   %HREF;         #IMPLIED
```

```
  onenterbackward %HREF;        #IMPLIED
  ontimer         %HREF;        #IMPLIED"
  >

<!ELEMENT template (%navelmts;)*>
<!ATTLIST template
  %cardev;
  %coreattrs;
  >
```

Next, you can see the `template` element in action. Taking the help discussion further, Listing 5-22 shows a deck with a `help` label mapped to the `options` key type. This mapping makes the `help` option available for all cards in the deck.

Listing 5-22: Help Binding in Template

```
<?xml version="1.0"?>
<!DOCTYPE wml PUBLIC "-//WAPFORUM//DTD WML 1.1//EN"
"http://www.wapforum.org/DTD/wml_1.1.xml">

<wml>
    <template>
        <do type="options" label="Help">
            <go href="#help"/>
        </do>
    </template>

    <card id="one" title="Template test">
        <do type="accept" label="Next">
            <go href="#two"/>
        </do>
        <p>Test card #1<br/>
        </p>
    </card>

    <card id="two" title="Template test #2">
        <do type="prev" label="Back">
            <prev/>
        </do>
        <p>Test card #2
        </p>
    </card>

    <card id="help" title="Help">
        <do type="prev">
```

Continued

Listing 5-22 *(Continued)*

```
            <prev/>
        </do>
        <p>Test card #3<br/>
            Here is some helpful information
        </p>
    </card>
</wml>
```

Figure 5-19 shows how this element is displayed in various browsers.

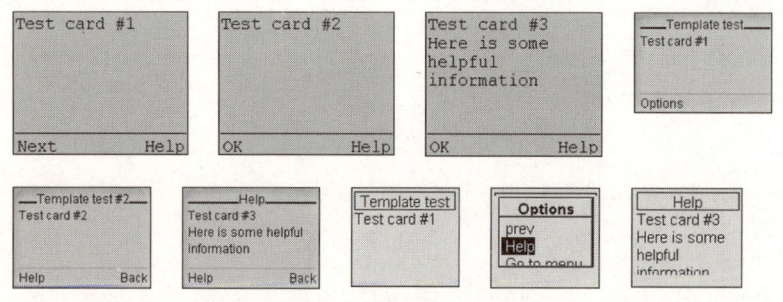

Figure 5-19: Help binding in the template element

The `template` element at the beginning of the deck binds the help navigation to the `options` soft key. The help option is available on all cards, even the help card itself. Notice also how the help option is mapped differently depending on the number of other options available, and the different ways the hardware key is selected from browser model to browser model.

One significant problem with this example is that the help option is available even in the help card itself, which can be confusing to a user. You can remove this option using an action described in Table 5-3: the `noop` element. There are two important concepts here: First, any action mapping done at the template or deck level can be overridden by an action mapping at the card level. This means that I could get the `options` key to do something else if I wanted to in any of the cards in the deck. Second, a `noop` element can be used to map an action to a key to do nothing at all. Both of these concepts can be combined to solve the problem of the help option showing up on the help card. Listing 5-23 shows the modified help card code.

Listing 5-23: Help-Card Modification

```
<card id="help" title="Help">
    <do type="prev">
        <prev/>
    </do>
```

```
        <do type="options">
            <noop/>
        </do>
        <p>Test card #3<br/>
                Here is some helpful information
        </p>
    </card>
```

Now the help card appears properly in some of the simulators, with no additional reference to help. Figure 5-20 shows how the modification works in different browsers.

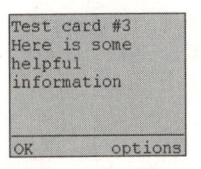

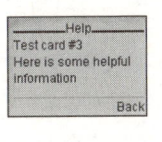

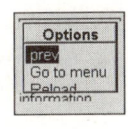

Figure 5-20: Help-card modification

Although an optional soft key label appears for the Openwave browser, this key does not work. A bug in the UP.SDK means that the noop element does not work correctly there. On phones that support the UP.Browser the noop element is also a gamble, and various hacks exist to create a screen without a template mapping.

Displaying Text with Tables

Another feature that enables WML programmers to effectively display information on the screen is the table element. The table element has many fewer features than its counterpart in HTML. In WML, the table element is used with the tr and td elements to create columns of text and images on the mobile-device display. Nesting these table elements is not allowed.

Table 5-5 describes the table element attributes.

TABLE 5-5 TABLE ELEMENT ATTRIBUTES

Attribute	Description
title=vdata	Specifies the title for the table element, which may be used in presenting the table.

Continued

Part 1: Foundations

TABLE 5-5 TABLE ELEMENT ATTRIBUTES *(Continued)*

Attribute	Description
`align=cdata`	Specifies how text and images are shown within the columns of a row. A column's contents can be left aligned, right aligned, or center aligned. Left alignment is indicated by a value of L, right alignment by a value of R, and center alignment by a value of C.
`columns=number`	Specifies the number of columns within a row. The browser must create a row with exactly the number of columns specified by this attribute. If the number of columns is set to 0, an error will result.

The `table` element can appear only inside a `p` element. What can appear inside a `table` element is shown in Listing 5-24.

Listing 5-24: Table Element DTD Section

```
<!ENTITY % emph     "em | strong | b | i | u | big | small">

<!ENTITY % layout   "br">

<!ENTITY % text     "#PCDATA | %emph;">

<!ENTITY % coreattrs "id    ID      #IMPLIED
                      class CDATA   #IMPLIED">

<!ELEMENT table (tr)+>
<!ATTLIST table
  title     %vdata;    #IMPLIED
  align     CDATA      #IMPLIED
  columns   %number;   #REQUIRED
  xml:lang  NMTOKEN    #IMPLIED
  %coreattrs;
>

<!ELEMENT tr (td)+>
<!ATTLIST tr
  %coreattrs;
>

<!ELEMENT td ( %text; | %layout; | img | anchor | a )*>
```

```
<!ATTLIST td
  xml:lang       NMTOKEN       #IMPLIED
  %coreattrs;
>
```

Listing 5-25 is an example of a table displaying the weather forecast for a group of cities.

Listing 5-25: Table Example

```
<?xml version="1.0"?>
<!DOCTYPE wml PUBLIC "-//WAPFORUM//DTD WML 1.1//EN"
"http://www.wapforum.org/DTD/wml_1.1.xml">

<wml>
    <card id="table" title="Weather Today">
        <p>World Weather
            <table columns="2">
                <tr>
                    <td><big>City</big></td>
                    <td><big>Temp.</big></td>
                </tr>
                <tr>
                    <td>London </td>
                    <td>45&#186;F</td>
                </tr>
                <tr>
                    <td>New York </td>
                    <td>43&#186;F</td>
                </tr>
                <tr>
                    <td>Berlin </td>
                    <td>39&#186;F</td>
                </tr>
                <tr>
                    <td>Paris </td>
                    <td>50&#186;F</td>
                </tr>
            </table>
        </p>
    </card>
</wml>
```

Figure 5-21 shows how the weather table looks in several browsers.

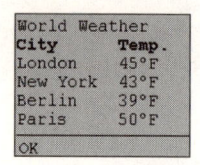

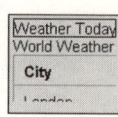

Figure 5-21: Weather-table Images

Note how the table support is quite varied. Some browsers today, such as that of the Nokia 7110 phone, do not support it at all. Each row of the table is contained inside the `tr` element, and each column of the table is contained in the `td` element. The same number of table-data pairs exists inside the table row as specified in the `columns` attribute of the `table` element. The preceding example contains only two columns, so only two table-data pairs appear in the table rows. Some mobile devices have a hard time with anything more than two columns, so tables should be used carefully in all instances.

You can modify the code in the example to make the data inside the cells align in a particular fashion. You do this using the `align` attribute of the `table` element. The attribute is structured to allow for a string that indicates the alignment of the columns in the table. Therefore, `align="LR"` in a two-column table formats the table so that the first column is aligned to the left and the second column is aligned to the right. Making this modification results in Listing 5-26.

Listing 5-26: Table-Alignment Modification Example

```
<?xml version="1.0"?>
<!DOCTYPE wml PUBLIC "-//WAPFORUM//DTD WML 1.1//EN"
"http://www.wapforum.org/DTD/wml_1.1.xml">

<wml>
    <card id="table" title="Weather Today">
        <p>World Weather
            <table columns="2" align="LR">
                <tr>
                    <td><big>City</big></td>
                    <td><big>Temp.</big></td>
                </tr>
                <tr>
                    <td>London </td>
                    <td>45&#186;F</td>
                </tr>
                <tr>
                    <td>New York </td>
                    <td>43&#186;F</td>
```

```
                </tr>
                <tr>
                    <td>Berlin </td>
                    <td>39&#186;F</td>
                </tr>
                <tr>
                    <td>Paris </td>
                    <td>50&#186;F</td>
                </tr>
            </table>
        </p>
    </card>
</wml>
```

Figure 5-22 shows the difference in the browsers' displays.

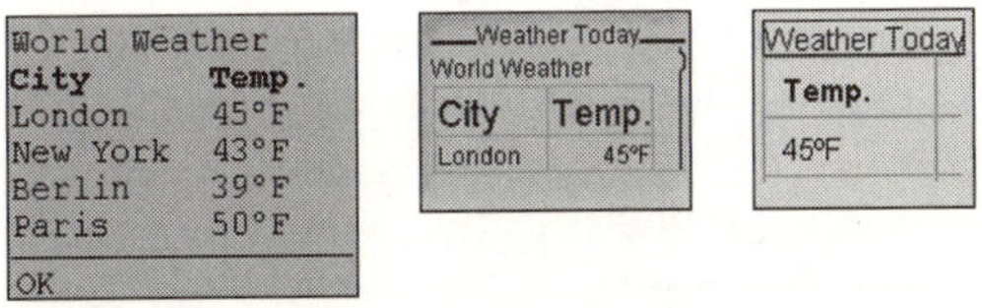

Figure 5-22: Weather-table modification

The `align` attribute supports three types of alignment designation: align to the center, which is represented by a `C`; align to the right, represented by an `R`; and align to the left, represented by an `L`. If you have a four-column table that needs center-left alignment on the first column and center alignment on the rest of the columns, the syntax for that table attribute would be as follows:

```
<table columns="4" align="LCCC">
...
</table>
```

Displaying Images

Graphics are supported by WML and have almost the same syntax as HTML. Mobile devices today have predominantly black-and-white interfaces, limiting the images. Also, the only image format supported officially by the WAP Forum is the Wireless BitMaP (.wbmp) format. This is a one-bit/pixel black-and-white format that all WAP site images must be stored in. The wbmp format does not support compression; developers determined that the routines required for compression were too processor-intensive. A description of the image format can be found in Appendix E. Other image types may be supported by the browser but are dependent on the manufacturer. You can find what image types are supported by the browser by examining the `accepts` header on a GET request. Such a header may look like this:

```
Accepts: image/bmp, image/vnd.wap.wbmp
```

> You may wish to review GET requests in Chapter 3.

The previous code snippet shows a browser that accepts both .bmp and .wbmp images.

You can add images to WML cards by using the `img` element. You can insert them in a paragraph element and its children, anchors, or table data elements.

Table 5-6 lists the `img` element attributes.

TABLE 5-6 IMG ELEMENT ATTRIBUTES

Attribute	Description
alt=vdata	Specifies some alternative text for the browser to use in case the image cannot be displayed.
src=HREF	Specifies the location of the image data in the form of a URL. If the browser supports images, it downloads the image referenced in the `src`; otherwise, it shows the alternative representation.
localsrc=vdata	Specifies an image stored internally by the browser. This attribute takes precedence over the `src` attribute. If an image is not returned by `localsrc`, it defaults to the `src`.
vspace=length, hspace=length	Specifies the amount of white space to be inserted to the left and right of the image using `hspace`, and to the top and bottom of the image using `vspace`. If the `length` attribute is specified using percentages, the resulting size is based on available horizontal and vertical space, not on the natural size of the image. The default length is set to a small, nonzero length.

Attribute	Description
align=(top|middle|bottom)	Specifies how the image is aligned within the text with respect to where it is to be inserted. The default alignment setting is bottom and specifies that the image should be vertically aligned with the current point as its base. The middle setting specifies that the current text point should be at the center of the image. The top setting specifies that the image should be vertically aligned with the top of the current text point.
height=length, width=length	Give the browser an idea of the size of an image. They can use the values by reserving the stated space while waiting for the image content to be retrieved from the server. If percentage values are used for the length, the resulting size is based on the available space.

Listing 5-27 shows a DTD section of the img element that shows the detail surrounding its definition.

Listing 5-27: img DTD

```
<!ENTITY % IAlign "(top|middle|bottom)" >

<!ELEMENT img EMPTY>
<!ATTLIST img
    alt         %vdata;     #REQUIRED
    src         %HREF;      #REQUIRED
    localsrc    %vdata;     #IMPLIED
    vspace      %length;    "0"
    hspace      %length;    "0"
    align       %IAlign;    "bottom"
    height      %length;    #IMPLIED
    width       %length;    #IMPLIED
    xml:lang    NMTOKEN     #IMPLIED
    %coreattrs;
    >
```

The `img` element has an `src` attribute that identifies the location of the image file using URL notation. Also, the `alt` attribute is used to identify a textual description of the data for browsers that cannot display the image data. It is also used in practice as a placeholder until the image data arrive at the mobile device.

Listing 5-28 is an example of the `img` element in use.

Listing 5-28: Image-Code Example

```
<?xml version="1.0"?>
<!DOCTYPE wml PUBLIC "-//WAPFORUM//DTD WML 1.1//EN"
"http://www.wapforum.org/DTD/wml_1.1.xml">

<wml>
<card id="new" title="Traffic Watch">
    <p>
        <img alt="Traffic to Smyrna" src="traffic4.wbmp"/>
    </p>
</card>
</wml>
```

Figure 5-23 shows how the code in Listing 5-28 looks on several browsers.

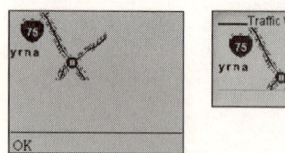

Figure 5-23: Traffic-congestion image

The image shows the congestion on the Atlanta, Georgia I-285 loop near the I-75 junction to Smyrna and is a good example of how images can provide a lot of value to users of mobile devices. A user may be able to change his or her morning commute based on information obtained on the mobile device regarding congestion on the roads. Conveying this information with text alone is often difficult, and the user can perceive the traffic conditions faster with a specific map.

You can include images in anchor links as indicated by the DTD; the code for that is as follows:

```
<a href="forward.wml">
    <img src="rainy.wbmp" alt="Go"/>
</a>
```

Figure 5-24 shows a display of how this code may look.

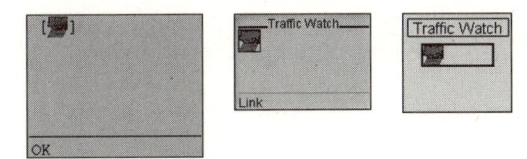

Figure 5-24: Image in anchor

All the browsers support this feature; however, the way it is presented on the screen will change the way it is perceived by users, especially in cases in which the phone anchors depart from standard WWW underlines.

Summary

In this chapter you learned how to write some basic WML decks. These decks are divided into cards, which are used by mobile devices for user navigation. Also, I showed you how to display information using elements inside a card. I then examined how navigation information can be added to the cards to assist the user in moving around the application. Finally, I looked at some advanced display features, tables, and images. You can find a detailed summary of all WML elements introduced in this chapter in Appendix A.

After reading this chapter, you should be able to write some basic WAP/WML sites. In the next chapter, I examine how to get input from the user, show the workings of some advanced navigation concepts, and revisit in greater detail some of the elements I introduced in this chapter. After the next chapter, you should be able to write even more compelling sites for WML-capable mobile devices.

Part II

Development of Services

CHAPTER 6
Doing More with WML

CHAPTER 7
Programming with WMLScript

CHAPTER 8
Using the WMLScript Libraries

CHAPTER 9
Dynamic WAP Services

Chapter 6

Doing More with WML

IN THIS CHAPTER

- Understanding intrinsic events
- Working with variables
- Using the setvar element
- Obtaining user input
- Using input elements
- Making use of timers

BUILDING YOUR FIRST APPLICATION using the steps outlined in the last chapter probably seemed quite simple. The real difference between the experts and the beginners is how usable a site is. Will the user return to your site because you have constructed it in a compelling way? Does your site provide easy access to important information? Too many sites fall by the wayside because they do not meet these requirements. There are two reasons that they don't: the developer was unaware either of usability concerns (which are addressed further in Chapter 15, "Designing User-Friendly Interfaces"); or of the advanced elements that can make a difference in the site. In this chapter I discuss those elements.

This chapter builds upon your knowledge by introducing you to some WML techniques that increase efficiency. The techniques I explain in this chapter show you how to build more efficient navigation links, construct variables for optimized data transfer, collect user input for personalized sites, and use timers to enhance the dynamics of a site.

Understanding Intrinsic Events

In the previous chapter, I discussed how navigation can be programmed in two ways: by using anchored links or by mapping tasks to soft keys. In this section, I introduce the third method of navigation, the intrinsic event.

Images of Openwave products in this chapter courtesy of Openwave Systems Inc.

Intrinsic events are special WML elements capable of generating events when the user interacts with them. The intrinsic events signal to the browser that some special state transition has occurred. The events that send such signals will change depending on the element you're using. Table 6-1 lists the intrinsic events defined by WML.

TABLE 6-1 WML INTRINSIC EVENTS

Intrinsic Event	Element in Which the Event Is Allowed	Description
ontimer	card, template	Occurs when a timer expires. The timers are specified using a special timer element. (I cover timers in a later section of this chapter.)
onenterforward	card, template	Occurs when the user navigates to a new card using the go element or any other element with an href to a new card. Navigating to a new card could also mean forward navigation using the WMLScript library components. (See Chapter 8, "Using the WMLScript Libraries," for more information on WMLScript libraries.)
		You can specify the onenterforward event at the card or deck level using a template element.
onenterbackward	card, template	Occurs when the user navigates to a card using the prev element, or navigates backwards using the WMLScript library components. This means that this event fires when a URL from the history stack is used to display a card. (See Chapter 8 for more information on WMLScript libraries.)
		You can specify the onenterbackward event at the card or deck level using a template element.
onpick	option	Occurs when a user selects an item from an option list. (I'll discuss the option element in the "Obtaining User Input" section.)

Chapter 6: Doing More with WML

Intrinsic events can be specified in two ways: in a short form or in a long form. The short form simply states the event type and a URL pointing to navigation. This form is the equivalent of a `go` task. The following is an example of a short form:

```
<card onenterforward="http://www.domain.com/first.wml#entry">
...
</card>
```

If you needed to set up a more complex task, such as sending variables, or do another task, such as a `prev`, you need to use the long form. With the long form, you must use an element called the `onevent`. Any `onevent`s you set up must be placed at the beginning of a card. The following example shows how the previous example would look using an `onevent`.

```
<card>
<onevent type="onenterforward">
    <go href="http://www.domain.com/first.wml#entry"/>
    </onevent>
...
</card>
```

As Table 6-1 shows, you can declare the intrinsic events at both the card and deck level. As noted in the discussion of scoping rules in Chapter 5, event binding at a card level takes precedence over event binding at the deck level.

The long form of the `onevent` enables you to use any of the tasks I discussed in Chapter 5, "Introducing WML" — `go`, `prev`, `noop` and `refresh` — within it.

The first two intrinsic events described in Table 6-1 enable the user to navigate the site without having to press any key or interact with the phone in any way. You can use `onenterbackward` to initiate a task when the user uses the Back key to go back to a page, or to initiate a task when the user navigates to that card using a `do` element, anchoring, or by entering in the URL directly. When any of these events fire, they run the code associated with the event.

You might use the `onenterbackward` event for a site that displays a splash page before the user navigates forward to the application display. I'll use a fictional "LampsRUs" site as an example. The first item that users see on this site is the LampsRUs logo. Navigating forward, users arrive at the page on which they decide which lamps, if any, they want to buy. After making their purchases, users may not appreciate having to go through the splash page again to exit the site. Listing 6-1 shows how you can use `onenterbackward` to avoid making the user encounter the splash screen.

Listing 6-1: The onenterbackward Method

```
<?xml version="1.0"?>
<!DOCTYPE wml PUBLIC "-//WAPFORUM//DTD WML 1.1//EN"
"http://www.wapforum.org/DTD/wml_1.1.xml">
```

Continued

Listing 6-1 *(Continued)*

```wml
<wml>
    <card id="test" title="Cool deals!">
        <p>
            Index of cool deals!<br/>
            <a href="#splash" title="Lamps">LampsRus </a> and other retailers represented here
        </p>
    </card>

    <card id="splash">
        <onevent type="onenterbackward">
            <prev/>
        </onevent>
        <do type="accept" label="Next">
            <go href="#products"/>
        </do>
        <do type="prev">
            <prev/>
        </do>
        <p align="center">
            <big>LampsRus</big><br/>
        </p>
        <p align="center">The ONLY! place for industrial Lamps<br>
        </p>
        <p>
            <small>&#169; 2000 by LRS</small>
        </p>
    </card>

    <card id="products" title="Products">
        <do type="prev">
            <prev/>
        </do>
        <p>
          <a href="sodium.wml" title="Select">Sodium Lamps</a><br/>
          <a href="metal.wml" title="Select">Metal Halide Lamps</a><br/>
          <a href="fluorescent.wml" title="Select">Fluorescent Lamps</a><br/>
          <a href="used.wml" title="Select">Used Lamps</a>
        </p>
    </card>
</wml>
```

Chapter 6: Doing More with WML 149

In this example, users see the "Cool deals" card first, and if they decide to enter the site they first see the splash screen and then can continue moving forward on the site. When they are navigating backwards, after they are done making their lamp purchases, the splash screen does not appear. This is because the `onenterbackward` event fires and executes the `prev` element. The example exploits an important property of intrinsic events: they can execute before any data is shown on the screen. In this way, many `onenterbackward` events can continuously cascade users backwards to a top-level card. You can also create invisible cards using intrinsic events.

Figure 6-1 shows how the example appears in several browsers.

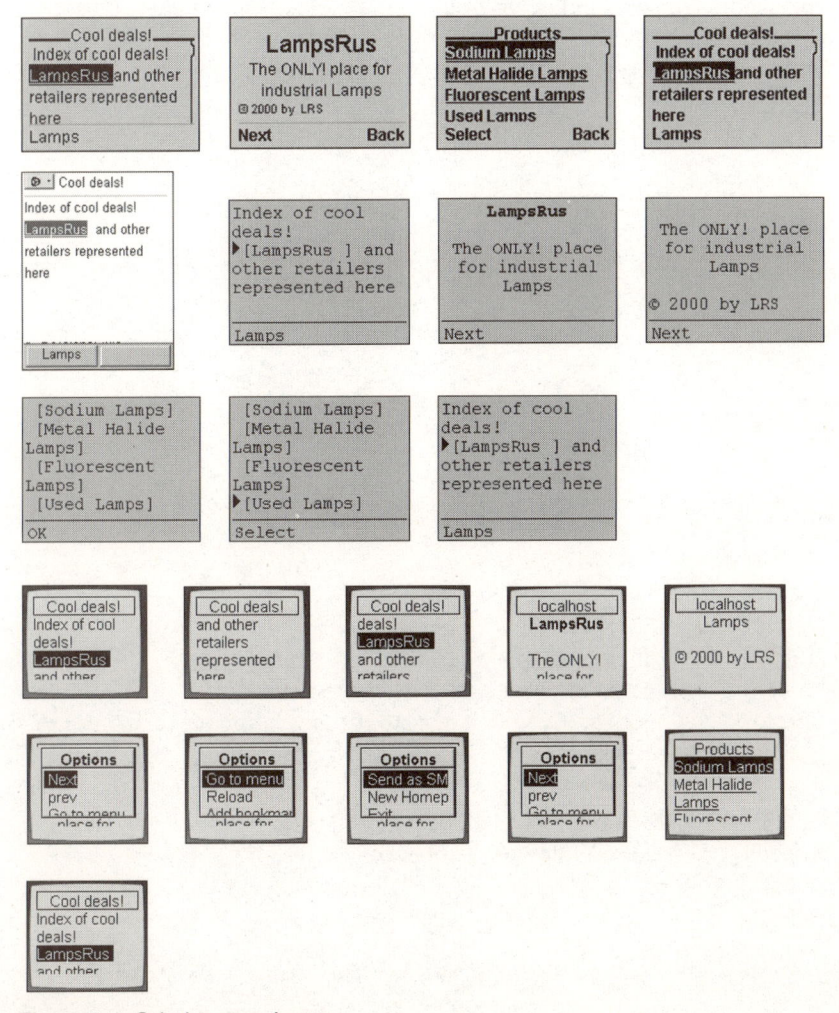

Figure 6-1: Splash-screen bypass

WML deck sizes have hard limits that vary depending on the browser you are working with. The Nokia browser limit is 1488 compiled bytes and the Phone.com browser limit is 1492 compiled bytes. I discuss other compiled byte limits in Chapter 14. Aside from these hard limits is the latency period that users are willing to tolerate; taking this period into account reduces the recommended size of the typical deck even further to about 1000 bytes for the largest deck.

If a long news story must be delivered to mobile device users, it may need to be split up into several pieces. Users don't want to arrive at the last card of the news story and have to press the Back button multiple times to navigate through every card of that story. A better interface would use `onevent` elements with `onenterbackward`, which would simply take users back to where they started. The code for this method appears in Listing 6-2.

Listing 6-2: News-Story Example

```
<?xml version="1.0"?>
<!DOCTYPE wml PUBLIC "-//WAPFORUM//DTD WML 1.1//EN"
"http://www.wapforum.org/DTD/wml_1.1.xml">

<wml>
    <template>
        <onevent type="onenterforward">
            <noop/>
        </onevent>
<do type="prev">
            <prev/>
        </do>
    </template>


    <card id="test" title="Today's Top Stories">
        <p>
            <big>Top stories of the day</big><br/>
            <a href="#story"
title="Elections">Elections</a> results still on hold as Palm Beach recount resumes<br/>
            <a href="#story2"
title="Flooding">England</a> brings in the army to combat flooding around the River Ouse
        </p>
    </card>

    <card id="story" title="Elections...">
        <onevent type="onenterbackward">
            <prev/>
```

```wml
            </onevent>
            <do type="accept" label="Next">
                <go href="#part2"/>
            </do>
            <do type="prev">
                <prev/>
            </do>
            <p>
                The election results were still being disputed...
            </p>
    </card>

    <card id="part2" title="Elections...">
            <onevent type="onenterbackward">
                <prev/>
            </onevent>
            <do type="accept" label="Next">
                <go href="#part3"/>
            </do>
            <p>
                After hours of deliberation...
            </p>
    </card>

    <card id="part3" title="Elections...">
            <onevent type="onenterbackward">
                <prev/>
            </onevent>
            <do type="accept" label="Next">
                <go href="#part4"/>
            </do>
            <p>
                And the Florida Supreme Court today dealt both the candidates a blow by...
            </p>
    </card>

    <card id="part4" title="Elections...">
            <p>
                In a recent twist, military votes without a postmark are now being counted...
            </p>
    </card>
</wml>
```

Figure 6-2 shows the events as they occur in several browsers.

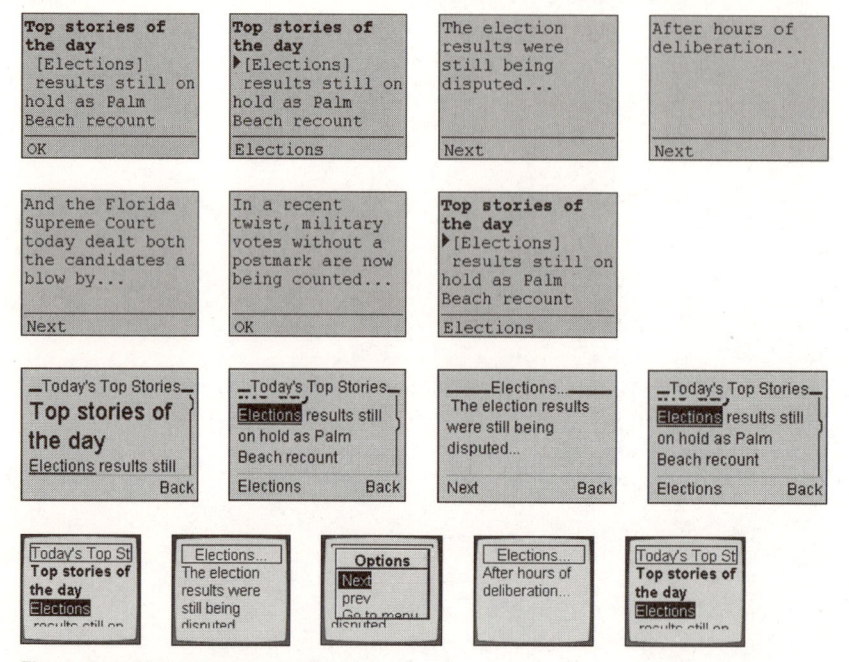

Figure 6-2: News-story example

Because of a series of cascading `onenterbackward` events, a user never sees the news story on the when navigating backwards using the history. Also, this example shows how you can define `onevent`s at the deck level using the `template` element, with the same syntax as defining tasks at the card level. These `onevent`s can be overridden by an event defined at the card level just as tasks defined at the deck level can be overridden at the card level.

An abbreviated form of the event format is available that allows for shorter calling URLs and permits only simple URL navigation. Listing 6-3 shows this short form, as well as the `onenterfoward` and `onenterbackward` events.

Listing 6-3: Short Form of Intrinsic Events Example

```
<?xml version="1.0"?>
<!DOCTYPE wml PUBLIC "-//WAPFORUM//DTD WML 1.1//EN"
 "http://www.wapforum.org/DTD/wml_1.1.xml">

<wml>

    <card id="start" title="Shopping at iWorld">
```

```
            <p>Top selling items<br/>
                <a href="#toys" title="Buy">Boomerang</a><br/>
                <a href="more.wml#tools" title="Buy">Tools chest</a><br/>
                <a href="more.wml#food" title="Buy">Food Pack Seasonal</a><br/>
                <a href="more.wml#housewares" title="Buy">Glassware 2</a><br/>
            </p>
    </card>

    <card id="toys" title="Are you sure?" onenterforward="#input1">
            <do type="accept" label="Yes">
                <prev/>
            </do>
            <do type="prev" label="No">
                <go href="#input1"/>
            </do>
            <p>
                Are you sure?
            </p>
    </card>

    <card id="input1" title="Get Input">
            <onevent type="onenterbackward">
                <prev/>
            </onevent>
            <do type="accept" label="Next">
                <go href="#final"/>
            </do>
            <do type="prev" label="Cancel">
                <prev/>
            </do>
            <p>
                Enter your name, address, etc.
            </p>
    </card>

    <card id="final" title="Accepted!">
            <do type="accept" label="Main">
                <go href="#start"/>
            </do>
            <p>
                Your order was accepted and will be shipped in 3 days to...
```

Continued

Listing 6-3 *(Continued)*

```
                    </p>
        </card>

</wml>
```

Listing 6-3 shows how a card can have an attribute of the event name that points to a URL. The card "toys" contains the `onenterforward` attribute, which has a URL as its value.

As shown in Listing 6-3, the `onenterbackward` events cascade back through the input stream, avoiding the display of input data. In Figures 6-3 and 6-4, note how the history stack is kept clean with cascading: this happens because forward navigation in the history is not supported, and the relevant cards are popped off the stack. The history stack is a limited resource on the phones, so use of variables and cache space and the phone's memory should be kept to a minimum. Several browsers have been known to display ugly "history stack overflow" errors for sites that create large history streams. Figures 6-3 and 6-4 show how the history stack is manipulated using the intrinsic events to minimize the stack overflow problem.

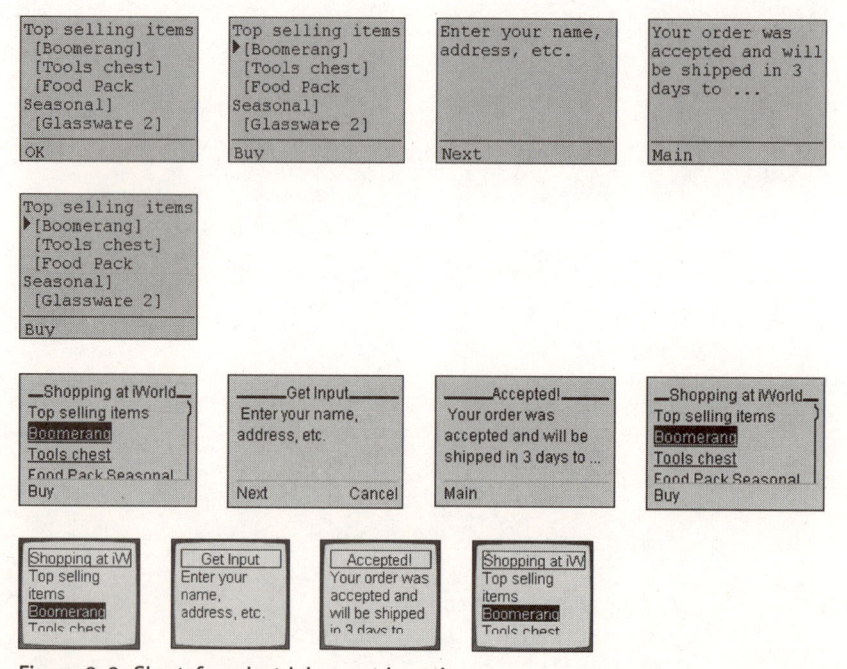

Figure 6-3: Short-form instrinic event in action

Chapter 6: Doing More with WML   155

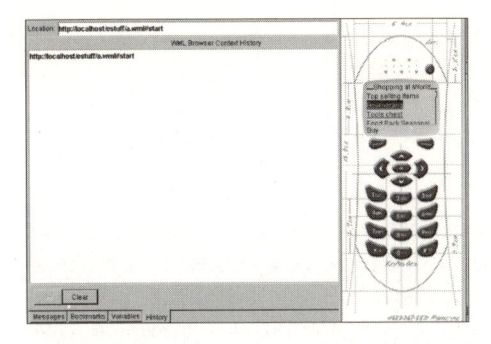

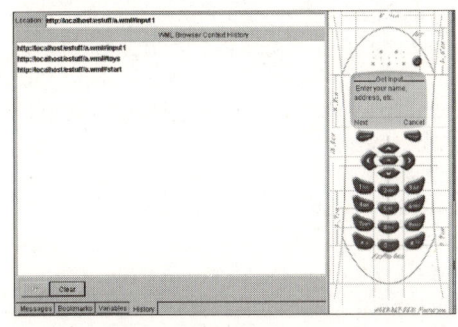

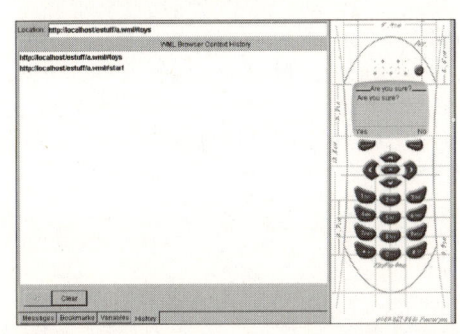

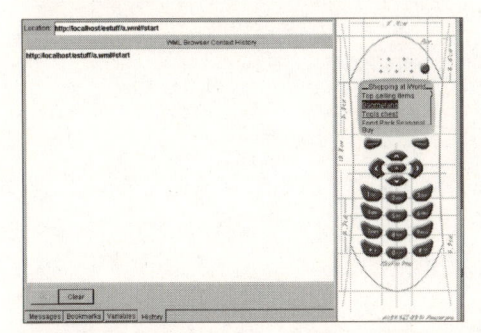

Figure 6-4: History dumps for short-form example

Working with Variables

Before I discuss other WML features, I need to examine variables. This is because much of the power of advanced navigation makes use of variables. In HTML environments, in which bandwidth is not as much of a concern as in wireless communication, variables are quickly sent back to the Web server and managed there. Every fresh page is loaded with no memory of the variables that existed in previous pages. For example, if I order a book on the Internet by entering my selection, my payment information, and my address, the selection, payment parameters, and address information are all passed to the Web server, which usually stores them in a database. If the values are needed in subsequent pages, the Web server retrieves the data from the database and displays the dynamically built page.

The WAP architecture engineers realized that in WML, sending parameters to the backend server on *every* card was too cumbersome for the wireless network. Therefore, they decided to try creating variables on the mobile device that stick around for a long time. This concept automatically raises two questions. How long do the variables stick around? Can someone else read them?

The answer to the first question is that the variables are stored on the mobile device until some event occurs that cleans them out. This event can be as simple as you setting the variable to `null`, or as complex as you issuing a `newcontext`. `newcontext` is an attribute of the `card` element that enables you to erase *all* the variables stored on the mobile device *and* clear out the history stack. Remember that clearing out the history stack renders the `prev` element navigation meaningless: a `prev` task cannot find a card to go back to because the history stack is blank. Listing 6-4 and Figure 6-5 show what occurs when a `newcontext` is issued.

Listing 6-4: newcontext Example

```
<?xml version="1.0"?>
<!DOCTYPE wml PUBLIC "-//WAPFORUM//DTD WML 1.1//EN"
 "http://www.wapforum.org/DTD/wml_1.1.xml">
<wml>
<card id="first">
    <do type="accept">
        <go href="#second"/>
    </do>
    <p>
    Some data
    </p>
</card>
<card id="second" newcontext="true">
<p>
Some more data
</p>
</card>
</wml>
```

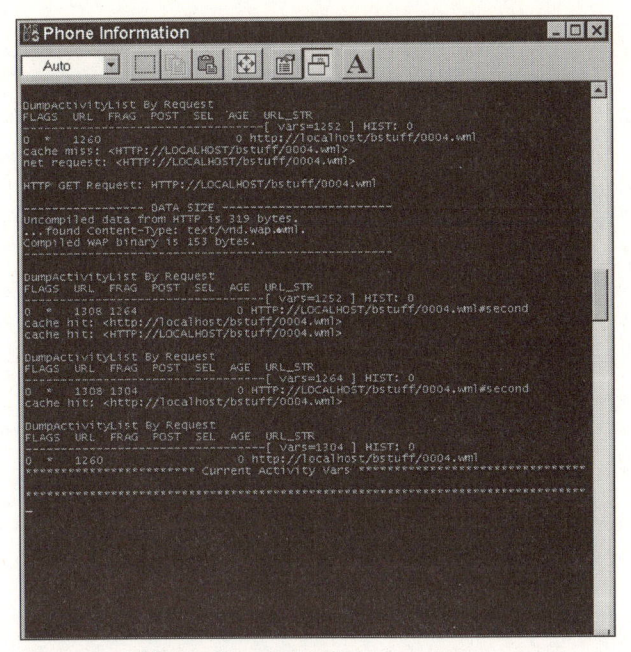

Figure 6-5: Effects of newcontext

The next important question about variables is their security. All variables created on the mobile device using WML are global variables, meaning that other applications can potentially read your variables, or even use them accidentally in their applications. Consider the nightmarish case in which both your application and somebody else's use cc as a variable name for a credit-card number. This case illustrates why you should always clear the variable values before releasing the user from your application.

To ensure that nothing like the aforementioned scenario compromises your site, for security reasons I recommend that you clear your variables and issue newcontext attributes wherever appropriate in your application.

> You can find examples of these and other scenarios in Chapter 16, "Implementing WAP Security."

In WML, the state that manages the variable names is called the browser context. Besides managing the variables, the browser context manages browser history and other implementation-specific information. Because there can be only one context at a time, the contexts contain global values.

Variable values in WML do not have types. Many languages distinguish among integers, Booleans, and so on, but in WML, all variables are strings. So it is the responsibility of the Web programmer to manage the type of the variable using some other referential source such as a backend database.

If you refer to a variable that has not been set, the value will be the empty string. The existence of variables does not imply any logical WML behavior; in fact, all that is done with WML variables is that their values are substituted inside a text stream by the WML browser.

Legal variable names consist of a ASCII letter or an underscore, followed by zero or more letters, digits, or underscores. The use of any other characters is an error in the WML deck. Variable names are also case-sensitive. Some legal variable names are as follows:

- `animal`
- `AnImAl`
- `ANIMal`
- `cat_giraffe`
- `_cat`
- `cat1`
- `_cat2`
- `_`

Following are some illegal variable names:

- `1`
- `4cat`
- `cat/giraffe`

Before you can use a variable in a WML deck, you must first define it. For example, to define the variable `animal` to be `cat`, you use:

```
animal="cat"
```

Note that variables in WML are string values. The syntax that enables you to make use of the variable `animal` in the WML deck consists of the dollar sign ($) followed by the variable, as in

```
$animal
```

For example, in the following line:

```
My $animal is called Pebbles.
```

the browser parsing this would first substitute the variable (`$animal`) for its value (`cat`) and then display the information. The user would see the following:

```
My cat is called Pebbles.
```

If the variable `animal` had a value of `dog`, the user would see this:

```
My dog is called Pebbles.
```

This substitution is useful, but there are many other places in WML where substitution is theoretically possible. Consider the following:

```
<$animal>
<p>
Something goes here
</p>

</$animal>
```

The preceding code would produce an error because it asks for variables to be substituted in the element name. This is illegal. Variables can be substituted in the following three places only:

- Inside PCDATA
- In URLs
- In vdata

These terms might sound a bit foreign right now, but a detailed discussion will help. The first term, PCDATA, refers to any numeric or named characters that appear inside an element. By reading the DTD you will find where PCDATA appears. Anything inside the `p` element is one example of PCDATA.

I have described URLs before, and will shortly give an example showing variables.

The last term is *vdata*, which stands for variable data. It is used in attribute values. You have to look at the WML DTD to determine where vdata can reside; no particular rule of thumb exists. If you study the DTD closely, you will see that URLs are also vdata. Some areas where variables can be substituted are `postfields`, URLs, `setvars`, `do` labels, anchor titles, element titles, select `ivalue`, select `value`, and certain image attributes. These elements are covered more completely later in this chapter. If you are ever in doubt about where variables can be substituted, please examine the DTD you are using in your WML deck for vdata attribute values.

Listing 6-5 shows an example of a deck with variables in legal positions.

Listing 6-5: Legal Variable Positions Example

```
<wml>
<card id="testing" title="All about $animal">
<do type="accept">
          <go href="check.asp?animal=$animal"/>
</do>
<p>
          The $animal is in the bag
</p>
</card>
</wml>
```

As you can see from this example, variables can appear in card titles, URLs, and as part of the text stream in a paragraph element. Everywhere the variable name appears with the $ symbol before it, it is substituted for its value. So if the variable `animal` is equal to "cats", for example, the title of the card will appear as "All about cats".

Using the setvar Element

Now that I've explained the general syntax of variables and how they are substituted in flow text, you can see how they are set. Variables are set using three techniques:

- Using a `setvar` element
- Using an `input` element
- Using an `option` element inside a `select` element

The simplest to explain at this moment is the first technique. A `setvar` element has the following syntax:

```
<setvar name="location" value="variable's value"/>
```

The `setvar` element can appear in the following task elements: `go`, `prev`, and `refresh`. Using this mechanism sets a variable's value as a side effect of executing a task. Listing 6-6 shows an example that sets a variable's value while navigating forward.

Listing 6-6: setvar Example

```
<?xml version="1.0"?>
<!DOCTYPE wml PUBLIC "-//WAPFORUM//DTD WML 1.1//EN"
"http://www.wapforum.org/DTD/wml_1.1.xml">

<wml>

    <card id="first" title="Set Zone">
        <do type="accept" label="Next">
            <go href="#next">
                <setvar name="zone" value="GMT-5"/>
            </go>
        </do>
        <p>
            Press Next to continue...
        </p>
    </card>

    <card id="next" title="Value">
        <p>
            The current time zone is $zone
        </p>
    </card>

</wml>
```

Listing 6-5 shows that you can use the `setvar` element to set a variable's value. The next case creates a variable called `zone` whose value is set to the string `"GMT-5"`. This value is then used in a subsequent card. The problem with the example shown in Listing 6-6 is that the user has to navigate through a dummy card that does nothing but set the variable's value. One workaround is presented in Listing 6-7.

Listing 6-7: Better setvar Example

```
<?xml version="1.0"?>
<!DOCTYPE wml PUBLIC "-//WAPFORUM//DTD WML 1.1//EN"
"http://www.wapforum.org/DTD/wml_1.1.xml">

<wml>

    <card id="first" title="Set Zone">
        <onevent type="onenterforward">
            <go href="#next">
                <setvar name="zone" value="GMT-5"/>
```

Continued

Listing 6-7 *(Continued)*

```
                        </go>
            </onevent>
            <p>
                    Press ok to continue...
            </p>
    </card>

    <card id="next" title="Value">
            <p>
                    The current time zone is $zone
            </p>
    </card>
</wml>
```

Now when navigating forward the user simply sees the final card displaying the time zone that has been selected. The intrinsic event `onenterforward` prevents users from seeing the dummy card. This example works, but it has two side effects that may not be useful, depending on the application. First, you must also map the intrinsic events in the backward direction so that the dummy card is not presented in that direction. (Maybe you can set the zone variable to an empty string on the way back.) Second, the history stack is affected by this example because two cards are entered on it, while one of the cards is never visible. Figure 6-6 shows how the `setvar`/instrinic event combination would display on several browsers.

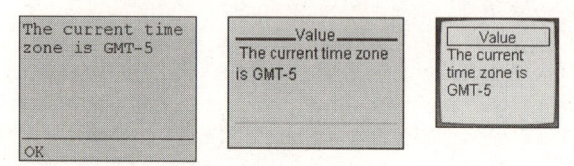

Figure 6-6: Better setvar example

Refreshing the display

Now that I have shown a common technique for setting variables, you can look at the `refresh` task, a tool you can use for refreshing the display with a new set of variable values. This task can appear in `do` elements, `onevents`, and `anchors`.

A `refresh` element can have zero or more `setvar` elements inside it. It takes the following steps when it executes:

1. Replaces variables with strings in each `setvar`.

2. Applies variable assignments to the current context.

3. Starts the `timer` element, if the card has a timer.

4. Redisplays the current card using current variable states.

I have not discussed timers yet, but the other steps should make sense at this point. The `refresh` task makes variable assignments pertaining to `setvar` or other mechanisms (such as the WMLScript) and then displays the current card with those updated variable substitutions.

Listing 6-7, which appeared previously, shows a time zone setting that can now be optimized to a to a single card, as shown in Listing 6-8.

Listing 6-8: Optimized Time Zone Using Refresh Example

```
<?xml version="1.0"?>
<!DOCTYPE wml PUBLIC "-//WAPFORUM//DTD WML 1.1//EN"
"http://www.wapforum.org/DTD/wml_1.1.xml">

<wml>

    <card id="first" title="Time Zone">
        <onevent type="onenterforward">
            <refresh>
                <setvar name="zone" value="GMT-5"/>
            </refresh>
        </onevent>
        <p>
            The current time zone is $zone
        </p>
    </card>

</wml>
```

This example solves the excess screen problem by reducing the variable assignment to one card, but the true power of `refresh` is shown in Listing 6-9, which is a modification of the code in Listing 6-8.

Listing 6-9: Modified Refresh Example

```
<?xml version="1.0"?>
<!DOCTYPE wml PUBLIC "-//WAPFORUM//DTD WML 1.1//EN"
"http://www.wapforum.org/DTD/wml_1.1.xml">

<wml>

    <card id="first" title="Time Zone">
        <do type="accept" label="GMT-4">
            <refresh>
```

Continued

Listing 6-9 *(Continued)*

```
                    <setvar name="zone" value="GMT-4"/>
                </refresh>
            </do>
            <do type="options" label="GMT-5">
                <refresh>
                    <setvar name="zone" value="GMT-5"/>
                </refresh>
            </do>
            <p>
                The current time zone is $zone
            </p>
        </card>
</wml>
```

The code in Listing 6-9 shows how the `setvar` element is executed on the spot because of its position inside the `refresh` task, and how the associated variable values are updated immediately in the display. Figure 6-7 shows how the example displays on several browsers.

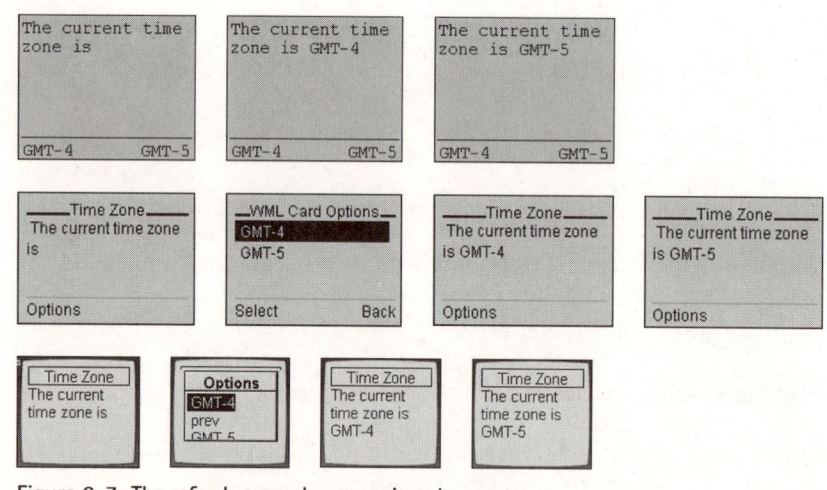

Figure 6-7: The refresh examples on various browsers

Escaping variables

Variables that are not clearly separated from the surrounding text do not substitute correctly. For example, with the following section of code:

```
The $animal's food is in the bag, but where did the $animals go?
```

the variable `$animal="hyena"` will not substitute correctly.

The problem with the first substitution is that the browser thinks that `$animal's` is the variable name and the WML parser in the WAP gateway marks it as an error because the apostrophe (`'`) is not a legal character in a variable name. The next variable substitution is not distinct enough, so the browser looks for a variable called `$animals`. Because all variables are set to the empty string if they are not defined, an empty string would be given to the browser to display in that second substitution.

To clear up the problem, the WML specification allows the use of parentheses around the variable to definitively indicate where the variable begins and ends. The previous lines of code could then be rewritten as:

```
The $(animal)'s food is in the bag, but where did the $(animal)s go?
```

With `$animal="hyena"`, the browser now knows that the variable is only the `$animal` portion of the text.

When typing URLs into a browser you must escape the URLs properly, meaning that you must make sure that the characters that form the URL fall within a fixed set. (The set of valid characters is defined in RFC 2396.) Anything outside this fixed set of valid characters must be escaped before it can be part of the URL. In the process of escaping, the problematic character is replaced with a % symbol followed by the hex number for its computer representation in the Unicode character set. A quick rule of thumb is that if the character is not alphanumeric, it probably needs escaping if it is to appear inside a URL.

> **NOTE** To avoid the escaping problem when sending variable values in a URL, the WML parser in the WAP gateway automatically escapes all variables that appear in any `href` or link.

When a variable is substituted, it is converted into a format appropriate for the location in which the substitution occurs. If the variable substitution occurs in a location where a URL is expected, the variable is automatically escaped. (This occurs in `onenterbackward`, `onenterforward`, `href`, and `src`, for example.) If the variable substitution occurs in any other location, the variable is not escaped before execution.

You do have some control over the situation and can override the escaping. If you do not want the browser to automatically determine whether it should escape or not, you can attach a character or statement after the variable to make it so.

If you want to URL-escape a variable, you also have that option. And if you want to unescape — that is, convert the % hex numbers into real characters, you have that option as well. Table 6-2 summarizes the possibilities for variable conversion.

Table 6-2 Variable Conversion Codes

Conversion Code	Effect
noesc or n or N	Makes no change to the variable on substitution
escape or e or E	URL-escapes the value of the variable before substitution
unesc or u or U	URL-unescapes the value of the variable before substitution

Use of these conversions does not affect the value of the variable, just how it is substituted.

The following variable substitution examples show some syntactically equivalent settings:

```
$(variable:noesc)
$(variable:n)
$(variable:N)
```

Here is an example of some escaping in action:

```
<go href="calendar.wmls#check($(date:unesc))"/>
```

In this case, imagine that the user has entered a date in DD/MM/YYYY format. The / characters that have meaning in standard URLs are escaped in the example. In this case, you do not want to do this. Instead, you want to pass the DD/MM/YYYY format to the WMLScript exactly as the user entered it so that it can parse the date data using the / characters as a delimiter. So, to ensure that the / appears as required, the date variable value is unescaped.

Obtaining User Input

Using setvar is not the only way to set variables in WML. You can also define and give values to variables when obtaining input from the user. The user input can be entered by the user in the form of an input screen or in the form of a selection from a list of items. In this section I discuss the select element first.

Selection on the phone is controlled by using a select element, which presents a choice to the user in the form of list of selectable items. (How the actual selection is displayed on the mobile device depends on the device.) The process of selection is controlled by the attributes of the `select` element; these attributes are shown in Table 6-3.

TABLE 6-3 SELECT ATTRIBUTES

Attribute	Description
`multiple=`*true*/*false*	Specifies whether the selection list allows multiple selections. If this attribute is not set, it defaults to `false`, which does not allow multiple selections from the list.
`name=`*nmtoken*, `value=`*vdata*	Sets when the user picks an item from the list. The variable's value is set to a string value indicated by the `option` element.
	The value of the `name` variable is used to set the default selection if the variable is not set already. This means that if the `name` variable is already set to a value, the `value` attribute will be ignored.
	If multiple choices are allowed from the selection, then the variable's value is a semicolon-delimited set of data.
`iname=`*nmtoken*, `ivalue=`*vdata*	Shows the name of the variable to be set by the index result of the selection. This means that the first item on the list will result in an `ivalue` of 1, the second with an `ivalue` of 2, and so on. If the `iname` is set to 0 no option is selected and other elements are reviewed to determine automatic selection.
	The `ivalue` indicates the default option index. If the `iname` variable name already contains a value, the `ivalue` is ignored.
	If multiple choices are allowed from the selection, the `iname` variable is set to a semicolon-delimited list of indices selected.
`title=`*vdata*	Specifies a title for the `select` element; whether it is presented to the user or not is left up to the browser.

The `select` element can only appear inside a `p` element and it can contain only `optgroup` or `option` elements. The `optgroup` is not well supported by phone browsers but you can use it to group `option` elements into categories that help the user understand how to make the best selection.

The main element inside the `select` element is the `option` element. This element specifies what each selection looks like to the user and what happens programmatically when the user makes a selection. Listing 6-10 shows a DTD showing the relevant section for the `select` element. As you can see, both the `optgroup` and `option` elements can appear inside the `select` element. At least one of each item must appear to make the code valid.

Listing 6-10: select Element DTD Listing

```
<!ELEMENT select (optgroup|option)+>
<!ATTLIST select
    title       %vdata;         #IMPLIED
    name        NMTOKEN         #IMPLIED
    value       %vdata;         #IMPLIED
    iname       NMTOKEN         #IMPLIED
    ivalue      %vdata;         #IMPLIED
    multiple    %boolean;       "false"
    tabindex    %number;        #IMPLIED
    xml:lang    NMTOKEN         #IMPLIED
    %coreattrs;
>
```

As I mentioned earlier, the actual definition of each selection is defined in the `option` element. Series of `option` elements can be organized into option groups. The `option` element attributes are shown in Table 6-4.

TABLE 6-4 OPTION ATTRIBUTES

Attribute	Description
value=vdata	Specifies the value of the variable defined in the `select` element.
title=vdata	Sets up a title for the `option` element; may or may not be used, depending on the browser.
onpick=HREF	Generates an intrinsic event that occurs whenever the selection is chosen on single-choice `select` elements and whenever the item is selected or deselected on multiple-choice `select` elements.
	The intrinsic event here simply enables the user to navigate forward to the `href` indicated by the `onpick` attribute value.

Chapter 6: Doing More with WML

The `option` element can appear only inside a `select` element, as shown in Table 6-4. Listing 6-11 shows the `option` element in use.

Listing 6-11: option Element DTD Listing

```
<!ELEMENT option (#PCDATA | onevent)*>
<!ATTLIST option
  value     %vdata;    #IMPLIED
  title     %vdata;    #IMPLIED
  onpick    %HREF;     #IMPLIED
  xml:lang  NMTOKEN    #IMPLIED
  %coreattrs;
>
```

Listing 6-11 shows that the `option` element tags surround either text data or a more complex `onevent`. Typically the `option` elements contain text data, which is highlighted to the user. Listing 6-12 shows an example of the `select` and `option` elements in use.

Listing 6-12: select Element Usage

```
<?xml version="1.0"?>
<!DOCTYPE wml PUBLIC "-//WAPFORUM//DTD WML 1.1//EN"
 "http://www.wapforum.org/DTD/wml_1.1.xml">

<wml>

    <card id="first" title="Job Codes">
        <p>
            Please select the job you are looking for:
            <select name="job">
                <option value="arch">Architect</option>
                <option value="nrse">Nurse</option>
                <option value="tpst">Therapist</option>
                <option value="lwyr">Lawyer</option>
                <option value="slor">Sailor</option>
            </select>
        </p>
        <p>
            You selected $(job)
        </p>
    </card>

</wml>
```

In the preceding example, the user is presented with a set of job options to select from. The job selection the user makes assigns the corresponding value to the variable name indicated in the `select` element `name` attribute. The variable called `job` is set to `"tpst"` if the user selects `Therapist` from the list.

Note that the variable assignment for the first `option` element is the default assignment. So the user does not have to select any option and the variable value `arch` is assigned to `job`. Note also that the variable value can be used right away; in the example in Listing 6-12, the information is simply presented on a separate paragraph element.

Figure 6-8 shows how the code appears in several browsers.

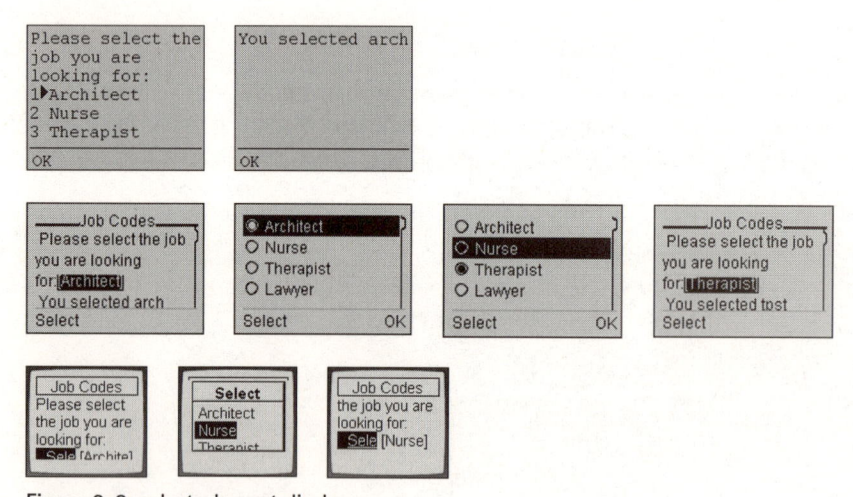

Figure 6-8: select-element display

Listing 6-12 is your first encounter with a browser breaking up a deck into multiple cards based on the browser's inability to display all the elements in one display. In the Nokia browsers, the `select` element is presented on the screen at the same time as the subsequent paragraph element. However, in v3.x and v4.x Openwave browsers, the screens are split up. The important point here is that even though I specified that the `select` element and the subsequent paragraph information should appear on one card, they were separated.

An even more complicated example of a browser choosing how to break up elements is shown in Listing 6-13, which is a rewrite of Listing 6-12.

Listing 6-13: select Element Example Rewritten

```
<?xml version="1.0"?>
<!DOCTYPE wml PUBLIC "-//WAPFORUM//DTD WML 1.1//EN"
 "http://www.wapforum.org/DTD/wml_1.1.xml">

<wml>
```

```
        <card id="first" title="Job Codes">
            <p>
                Please select the job you are looking for:
                <select name="job">
                    <option value="arch">Architect</option>
                    <option value="nrse">Nurse</option>
                    <option value="tpst">Therapist</option>
                    <option value="lwyr">Lawyer</option>
                    <option value="slor">Sailor</option>
                </select>
                You selected $(job)
            </p>
        </card>

</wml>
```

In this case, no separate paragraph element for the text appears near the end after the `select` element. Even though a separate paragraph element is not there, the `select` element is given its own card on the Openwave browser. Look at Listing 6-13, shown previously, and Figure 6-9 to see how the browser decided which components appear on the screen.

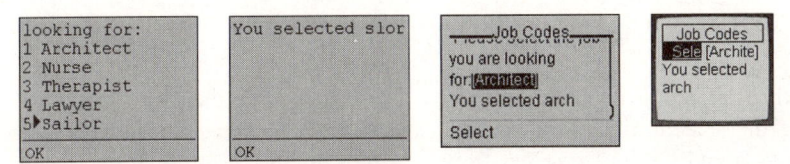

Figure 6-9: The select element revisited

Adding `optgroups` to the `select` example will show you how this element is used. As I mentioned earlier, these groupings are not well supported by all browsers.

Imagine that the worker categories in Listing 6-13 were divided into alphabetical categories from A–L and M–Z in order to improve the selection. In this scenario, users do not see every category when they go to make a selection, but rather just those that start with the letters they select. Listing 6-14 shows how the `optgroup` element can help you arrange lists into categories.

Listing 6-14: optgroup Element Example

```
<?xml version="1.0"?>
<!DOCTYPE wml PUBLIC "-//WAPFORUM//DTD WML 1.1//EN"
"http://www.wapforum.org/DTD/wml_1.1.xml">
```

Continued

Listing 6-14 *(Continued)*

```
<wml>
    <card id="first" title="Job Codes">
        <p>
            Please select the job you are looking for:
            <select name="job">
                <optgroup title="A-L">
                    <option value="arch">Architect</option>
                    <option value="bsdr">Bus Driver</option>
                    <option value="jugg">Juggler</option>
                    <option value="lwyr">Lawyer</option>
                </optgroup>
                <optgroup title="M-Z">
                    <option value="minr">Miner</option>
                    <option value="nrse">Nurse</option>
                    <option value="slor">Sailor</option>
                    <option value="tpst">Therapist</option>
                </optgroup>
            </select>
        </p>
        <p>
            You selected $(job)
        </p>
    </card>
</wml>
```

The default item is still the one defined by the first `option` element, but when users change the selection the choices are grouped in a hierarchical pattern that may help users avoid having to select from a large number of irrelevant options. Figure 6-10 shows how the previous example displays on various browsers.

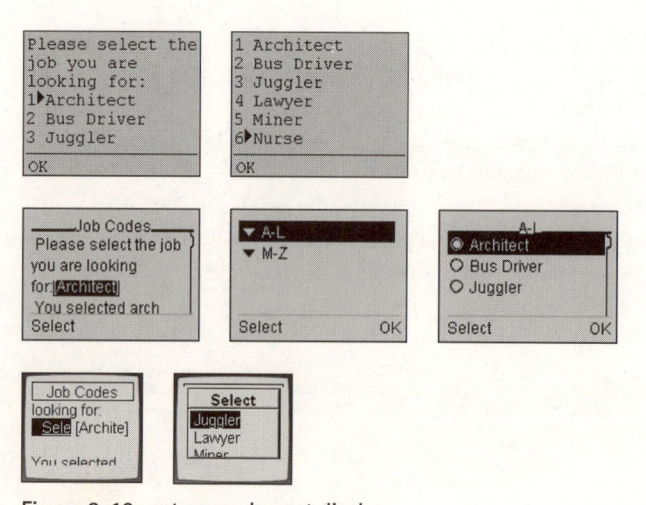

Figure 6-10: optgroup element displays

In the previous examples the first option was selected by default. To change this, you could specify another option by using the `value` attribute of the `select` element. Listing 6-15 shows how this would look.

Listing 6-15: value Attribute in select Element

```
<?xml version="1.0"?>
<!DOCTYPE wml PUBLIC "-//WAPFORUM//DTD WML 1.1//EN"
"http://www.wapforum.org/DTD/wml_1.1.xml>

<wml>
    <card id="first" title="Job Codes">
        <p>
            Please select the job you are looking for:
            <select name="job" value="lwyr">
                <option value="arch">Architect</option>
                <option value="nrse">Nurse</option>
                <option value="tpst">Therapist</option>
                <option value="lwyr">Lawyer</option>
                <option value="slor">Sailor</option>
            </select>
            You selected $(job)
        </p>
    </card>
</wml>
```

The `select` statement now simply uses a `value` assignment to determine which default selection to display.

Another attribute of the `select` element is `multiple`, which you use when multiple values can be selected from the list in question. For example, say that the user needs to choose breakfast items for an airline trip. Among the choices of yogurt, muffin, eggs, fruit, and cereal, the user can pick one or more. Listing 6-16 shows how this multiple-selection possibility appears in code.

Listing 6-16: Multiple-Choice Example

```
<?xml version="1.0"?>
<!DOCTYPE wml PUBLIC "-//WAPFORUM//DTD WML 1.1//EN"
"http://www.wapforum.org/DTD/wml_1.1.xml">

<wml>
    <card id="test" title="Breakfast Items">
        <p>
            Please select your breakfast items:<br/>
            <select name="breakfast" value="mu;fr"
```

Continued

Listing 6-16 *(Continued)*

```
multiple="true">
                    <option value="yo">Yogurt</option>
                    <option value="mu">Muffin</option>
                    <option value="eg">Eggs</option>
                    <option value="fr">Fruit</option>
                    <option value="ce">Cereal</option>
                </select>
                You selected $(breakfast)
            </p>
    </card>
</wml>
```

Figure 6-11 shows how this code and several variable settings look on several browsers.

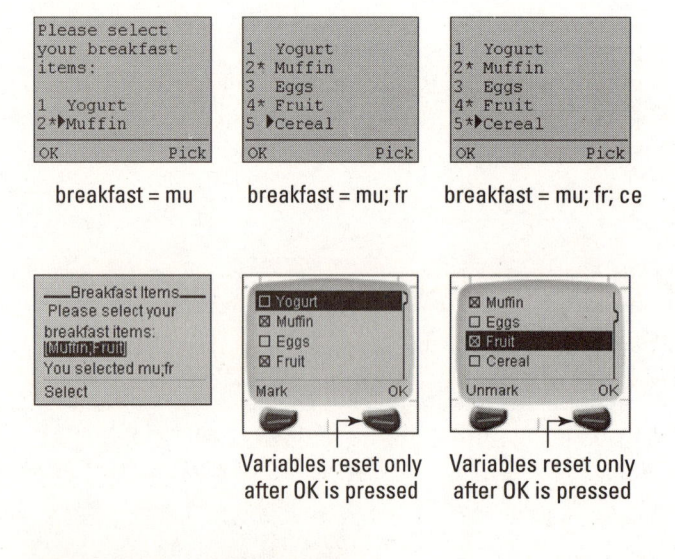

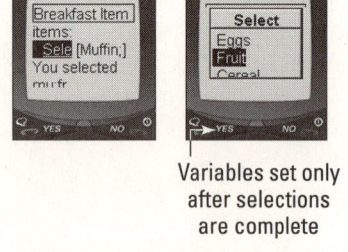

Figure 6-11: Multiple-choice displays

The code sample shows how you can allow multiple options by setting the `multiple` attribute to `true`. (It is set to `false` by default.) Also, notice how, when multiple options are selected, the variable's value is represented by a semicolon-delimited list of each of the selected option's values. Similarly, when setting the default value, you will have to use a semicolon-delimited list to identify the value.

Two other attributes of the `select` element can help you select the default choice value: `ivalue` and `iname`. The `ivalue` attribute takes a number as its value. If the number corresponds to the index value of one of the options, that option is set to the default value. Consider the example shown in Listing 6-17.

Listing 6-17: ivalue Example

```
<?xml version="1.0"?>
<!DOCTYPE wml PUBLIC "-//WAPFORUM//DTD WML 1.1//EN"
"http://www.wapforum.org/DTD/wml_1.1.xml">

<wml>
    <card id="test" title="Example of Items">
        <p>
            Select an item:<br/>
            <select name="placement" ivalue="2">
                <option value="first">First</option>
                <option value="second">Second</option>
                <option value="third">Third</option>
                <option value="fourth">Fourth</option>
                <option value="fifth">Fifth</option>
            </select>
            You selected the $(placement) option.
        </p>
    </card>
</wml>
```

In this case, because the `ivalue` is set to 2, the second option is selected from the list as the default item. The `ivalue` determines how far down the list you go, starting with the value of 1 representing the first option. An `ivalue` of 3, for example, selects the third option by default. Also, if a variable's value is set to an invalid index, say -1 or 200, then the first option in the list is selected; and if the variable value is already defined in the browser context, then the `ivalue` is not used.

Another way to set the default value of a `select` element, as I mentioned earlier, is to use the `iname` attribute. The `iname` attribute value contains a variable name. The value associated with the variable name is used to define the default selection. Listing 6-18 shows an example of how this is done.

Listing 6-18: iname Example

```
<?xml version="1.0"?>
<!DOCTYPE wml PUBLIC "-//WAPFORUM//DTD WML 1.1//EN"
```

Continued

Listing 6-18 *(Continued)*

```
"http://www.wapforum.org/DTD/wml_1.1.xml">

<wml>
    <card id="test" title="Rate our site?">
        <do type="accept" label="Next">
            <go href="#test2"/>
        </do>
        <p>Rate this site:<br/>
            * being the lowest<br/>
            <select name="index" ivalue="1">
                <option value="1">*</option>
                <option value="2">**</option>
                <option value="3">***</option>
                <option value="4">****</option>
                <option value="5">*****</option>
            </select>
        </p>
    </card>
    <card id="test2" title="Selecting a sum">
        <do type="accept" label="Continue">
            <go href="#test3"/>
        </do>
        <p>And your favorite shape?<br/>
            <select name="shape" iname="index">
                <option value="circle">Circle</option>
                <option value="pentagon">Pentagon</option>
                <option value="oval">Oval</option>
                <option value="rectangle">Rectangle</option>
                <option value="triangle">Triangle</option>
            </select>
        </p>
    </card>
    <card id="test3" title="Statement">
        <p>
            You gave the site $(index) star(s) and selected the $(shape) shape.
        </p>
    </card>
</wml>
```

Listing 6-18 shows how the `iname` attribute of the second `select` element is set to `index`, a variable that has been set in the previous card. The value in `index` is used to select a default index for the shape. Figure 6-12 shows how the navigation looks in several browsers.

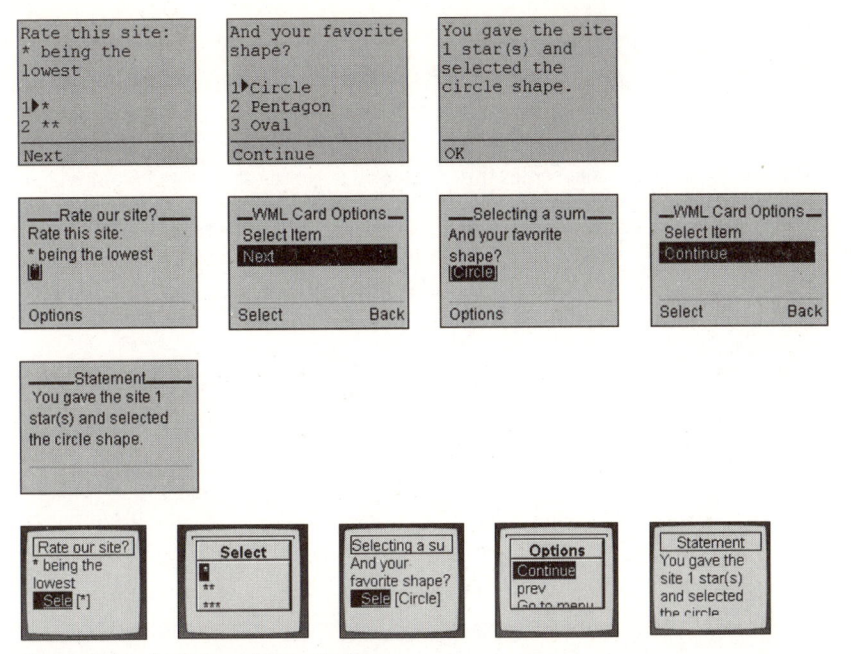

Figure 6-12: An iname demonstration

Using the input Element to Obtain User Input and Set Variables

So far, you have seen how user input can be obtained by using the `select` element. The second way to obtain user input is to use the `input` element. This element gives the user the option of freeform entry of text into the display, whereupon the input from the user is set in a variable defined by an `input` element attribute. This method is less restrictive than the `select` element outlined in the previous section; however, it also allows more room for bad data entry. The `input` element has a number of attributes that control how it gets data from the user. These attributes are shown in Table 6-5.

TABLE 6-5 INPUT ELEMENT ATTRIBUTES

Attribute	Description
`name=`*nmtoken*	Specifies the variable being set by the user's text input.
`value=`*vdata*	Contains a default value used to set the `name` attribute. If the named variable already contains a value, this value is ignored. If the variable does not correspond to the input mask, the value is ignored.
`text=(`*text*`|`*password*`)`	Specifies the type of input, the default being the `text` type. For `text`: The browser echoes the user's input and sets the variable unaltered in the browser context. For `password`: The browser echoes the characters in an obscured form. (`*`s, for example.) This setting does not imply that the variable is secure, just that it is not visible to the user. The browser sets the variable unaltered in the browser context.
`format=`*cdata*	Specifies an input mask for user entries. Only specific format codes are recognized in the `format` attribute value. See Table 6-6 for the `format` codes.
`emptyok=`*Boolean*	Indicates whether the `input` element supports empty input or not; typically set to `true` for optional input fields.
`size=`*number*	Specifies the width that the input entry field should be set to. The browser is not required to implement this feature.
`maxlength=`*number*	Specifies the maximum number of characters that can be entered. The default value is `unlimited`.
`title=`*vdata*	Specifies a title for the element, and *may* be used by the browser in presenting the element.

The `input` element appears inside paragraph elements and never has any content, just the attributes listed in Table 6-5. Listing 6-19 shows an example of the `input` element in use.

Listing 6-19: input Element Example

```
<?xml version="1.0"?>
<!DOCTYPE wml PUBLIC "-//WAPFORUM//DTD WML 1.1//EN"
"http://www.wapforum.org/DTD/wml_1.1.xml">

<wml>
    <card id="test" title="First Name">
        <do type="accept" label="Next">
            <go href="#test2"/>
        </do>
        <p>What is your first name?
            <input name="fname"/>
        </p>
    </card>

    <card id="test2">
        <p>
            You entered $(fname)
        </p>
    </card>
</wml>
```

Figure 6-13 shows how this code looks in several browsers.

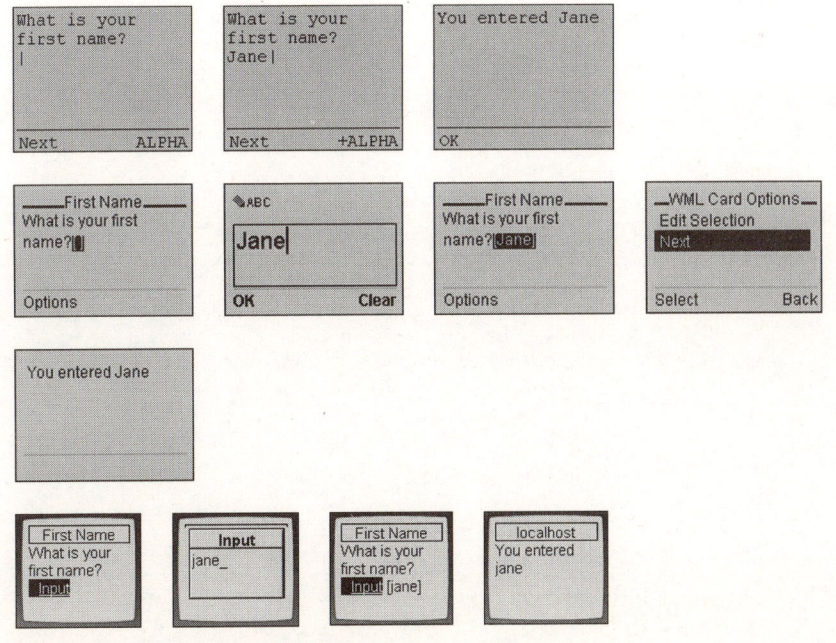

Figure 6-13: input-element displays

Listing 6-19 introduced the syntax of the `input` element. The element in the example had an attribute called `name`, which functions just like the `name` attribute of the `select` element. It creates a variable called `fname` and assigns it a value equivalent to what the user enters. `input` elements can appear only inside paragraph elements, as shown in the example. `input` elements do not contain any content, so they appear with a forward slash (/) ending.

Following are a few more examples of `input` element usage. First, take a look at the default value. To give the user a strong hint about what to input, you can set a default value. You can also offer a default option for a variable that is not often changed: for example, a product being sold via a WAP site that expected the bulk of its sales to occur in the U.S. may have an option allowing for the country of origin to be changed, but a default of U.S. would be set. Listing 6-20 shows an example of both of these uses of the default option.

Listing 6-20: Default Value Example

```
<?xml version="1.0"?>
<!DOCTYPE wml PUBLIC "-//WAPFORUM//DTD WML 1.1//EN"
"http://www.wapforum.org/DTD/wml_1.1.xml">

<wml>
    <card id="test" title="First Name">
        <do type="accept" label="Next">
            <go href="#test2"/>
        </do>
        <p>Enter the year of your birth?
            <input name="birth" value="1860"/>
        </p>
    </card>

    <card id="test2" title="First Name">
        <do type="accept" label="Next">
            <go href="#test3"/>
        </do>
        <p>Enter your title?
            <input name="title" value="Mr."/>
        </p>
    </card>

    <card id="test3">
        <p>
            Hey, $(title), you were born in $(birth).
        </p>
    </card>
</wml>
```

Figure 6-14 shows how this code looks in various browsers.

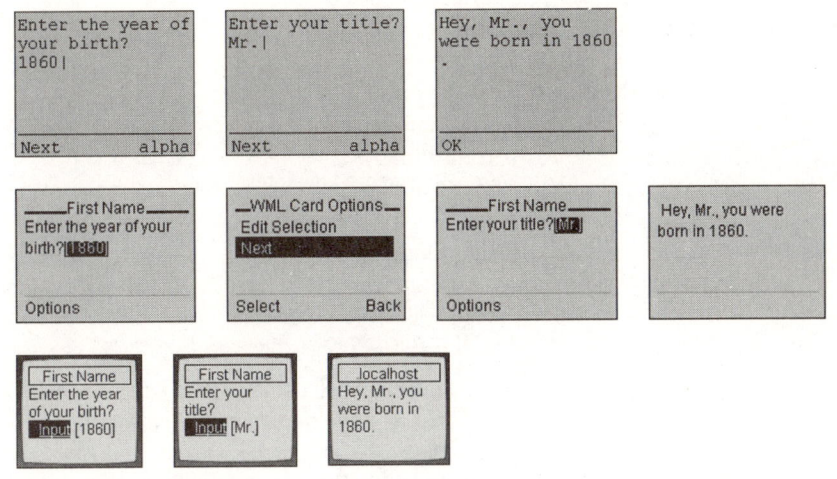

Figure 6-14: Default value in an input element

Giving users hints about what to enter in the `input` element is one way of leading them to enter valid data. However, constraining the allowable characters of the input is a better way to do it. Several solutions are available; two of them are scripting-related. The data that is input can either be parsed by the Web server, or parsed locally on the client using WMLScript.

Setting an input mask

Another solution is available in WML via the input mask. An input mask enables you to constrain `input` elements to a set of characters and also allows forced characters in the text stream. You set input masks in the `format` attribute of the `input` element; if unspecified, they are set to `*M` by default. Table 6-6 shows the legal format characters.

TABLE 6-6 FORMAT ATTRIBUTE CODES

Format Control Character	Description
A	Entry of any uppercase character or punctuation character.
a	Entry of any lowercase character or punctuation character.

Continued

Table 6-6 FORMAT ATTRIBUTE CODES *(Continued)*

Format Control Character	Description
N	Entry of any numeric character.
X	Entry of any uppercase character.
x	Entry of any lowercase character.
M	Entry of any character (the browser may assume the character is uppercase to begin with).
m	Entry of any character (the browser may assume the character is lowercase to begin with).
*f	Entry of any number of characters specified by f, where f is one of the preceding format codes; this format may be only specified once and can appear only at the end of the format string.
nf	Entry of n characters where n is a number from 1 to 9 and f is any of the preceding codes (except for *f); this format may be only specified once and can appear only at the end of the format string.
\c	Displays the character indicated by the c in a forced manner in the text-entry area.
	These are often referred to as "escaped characters" and must be preserved in a variables value. A mask takes precedence over the `value` attribute. If a value does not conform to the mask it is disregarded.

Table 6-7 shows several possible input requirements and their corresponding `format` attributes.

Table 6-7 FORMAT ATTRIBUTE EXAMPLES

Input Requirement	Format Attribute Value
Four-digit year	*NNNN*
Six-character Michigan light truck license plate	*AA\ NNNN*
U.S. social security number	*NNN\-NN\-NNNN*

Input Requirement	Format Attribute Value
Two-character U.S. state postal abbreviation	*AA*
Month, day and year (MM/DD/YYYY format)	*NN\/NN\/NNNN*
U.S. postal ID	*NNNNN\-4N*
Postal ID for island of Guernsey (England)	*\G\YN\ NAA*
New German postal code for Berlin	*\D\-\1NNNN*
License plate issued to the Dutch Royal Family	*\A\A\-NN*
Post-1980 U.S.-origin VIN Number	*\1MMAMMMNMMNNNNN*

Listing 6-21 shows the `format` attribute in a more complete example specifying a height in feet and inches.

Listing 6-21: format Attribute Example

```
<?xml version="1.0"?>
<!DOCTYPE wml PUBLIC "-//WAPFORUM//DTD WML 1.1//EN"
"http://www.wapforum.org/DTD/wml_1.1.xml">

<wml>
    <card id="test" title="Height">
        <do type="accept" label="Next">
            <go href="#test2"/>
        </do>
        <p>Enter your height in feet and inches? <br/>( ie. 5' 06")
            <input name="height"
format="N\&apos;\ NN\&quot;"/>
        </p>
    </card>
    <card id="test2">
        <p>
            Your height is $(height)
        </p>
    </card>
</wml>
```

Figure 6-15 shows how this code displays in several browsers.

184 Part II: Development of Services

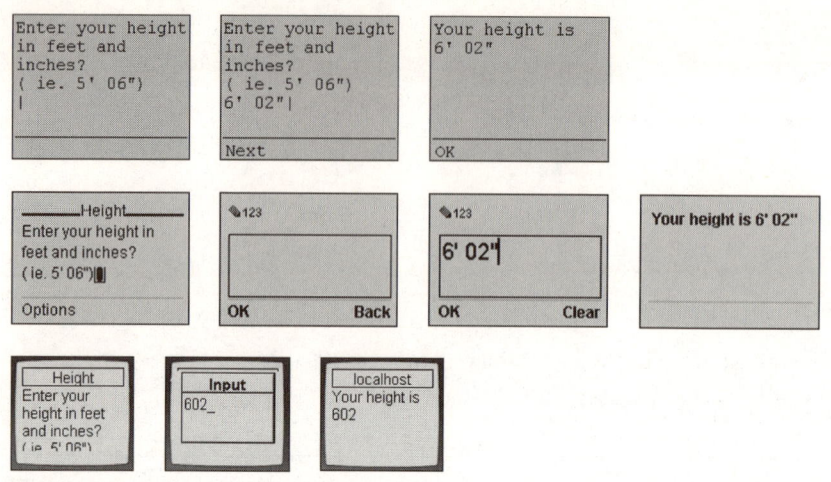

Figure 6-15: format attribute displays

As you can see, the restrictive input masks help you with more than just formatting. They also provide the browser with hints as to what type of mode the keypad is in.

The user can still get away with a ridiculous height like 5' 34". Unfortunately, the only recourse in situations like that is to use client- or server-side scripting for value validation.

You can use other `input` element attributes to limit the amount of data a user enters; for example, the `maxlength` attribute is commonly used to ensure that the `input` field synchronizes well with back-end database limitations. Say you need to gather the first names of a group of people and one of those names was longer than 20 characters. You have to determine how many characters your back-end database supports for the first name and then truncate the input silently. WML enables you to create such a character-limited value using the `maxlength` attribute.

For example, the following code would limit first names to 20 characters:

```
<input name="fname" maxlength="20"/>
```

Some browsers use the `title` attribute to better label the input field. Following is another example using the `title` attribute; Figure 6-16 shows how various browsers render it.

```
<?xml version="1.0"?>
<!DOCTYPE wml PUBLIC "-//WAPFORUM//DTD WML 1.1//EN"
 "http://www.wapforum.org/DTD/wml_1.1.xml">

<wml>
    <card id="test" title="Height">
        <do type="accept" label="Next">
```

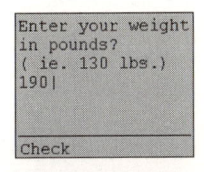

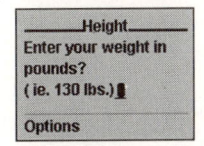

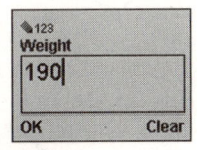

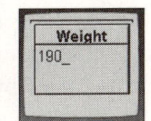

```
                <go href="#test2"/>
        </do>
        <p>Enter your weight in pounds? <br/>( ie. 130 lbs.)
                <input name="weight" format="3N" title="Weight"/>
        </p>
    </card>
    <card id="test2">
        <p>
                Your weight is $(weight) lbs.
        </p>
    </card>
</wml>
```

Figure 6-16: A title attribute example

Figure 6-16 shows how the input window has changed in some browsers to show the new input-window title.

Posting input data

In all the examples I have presented so far the focus has been on getting the data from the user. We haven't done anything useful with the data except to store them on the mobile device. In the real world, the information is sent back to the server and parsed for storage or processing. The programs that parse and store the data after the information is sent to the server are known as server-side scripts, or dynamic scripts. All the standard dynamic scripting languages are acceptable for use with WML. You simply rip out HTML and replace it with WML. I provide specific examples of this kind of substitution in Chapter 9, "Developing Dynamic WAP Services."

Because we know that dynamic scripts on the Web server are going to receive the variable values, one of the most common problems we'll encounter is the problem of sending the data that have been input from the mobile device to the Web server.

Two methods are available. One is the GET method; the other the POST method. Both are HTTP methods. I discuss the HTTP protocol and its methods in Chapter 3, "WAP Foundations."

The GET method is the most common. With this method the variable values are packaged in the URL. Contrast this with the POST method, in which the variables are packaged in the body of the request. You may be familiar with the POST method on the regular Web because it is used in HTML forms.

With the GET method, the variables are appended to the actual URL in a known format. This known format contains the names of the variables and their values separated by ampersands. In WML you have to go one step further by using the character-entity code (&amp) for the ampersand symbol.

Listing 6-22 shows an example of how the ampersand symbol is written as &.

Listing 6-22: Simple go Example

```
<do type="accept" label="Go">
<go href="calculate.asp?fname=Jane&amp;lname=Doe"/>
</do>
```

In Listing 6-22, the mobile device issues a GET request for the URL indicated in the `href` attribute value. Notice that the URL contains a resource location, the calculate.asp script on the server, followed by a question mark. The question mark indicates that the script is being passed some variables. The variables are being passed in paired statements that contain the variable name and variable value separated by an equals sign (=), such as `fname=Jane`. The difference between this format and the regular HTML forms is that the ampersand symbol that separates these variable pairs must be substituted with its special character-entity code to be escaped properly in the URL.

Listing 6-23 issues the same request to the server, but notice the differences in syntax from the code shown in Listing 6-22.

Listing 6-23: go Example Using postfield Syntax

```
<do type="accept" label="Go">
    <go href="calculate.asp" method="get">
        <postfield name="fname" value="Jane"/>
        <postfield name="lname" value="Doe"/>
    </go>
</do>
```

Listing 6-23 is an improvement over Listing 6-22 because the mobile device is what builds the URL for you. This way, there is less of a chance for errors in constructing the URL strings, and the browser takes care of any special escaping. The `postfield` elements inside the `go` element handle all the escaping rules for you. These `postfield` elements contain two attributes, a `name` attribute for a variable name and a `value` attribute for a variable value. Both of these are used to construct the name/value pairs in the URL request string.

With the POST method, the long string of concatenated variable names and values are now inserted in the body of the URL request, as opposed to being contained in a URL.

To issue a POST request rather than a GET request, you change the method attribute in the previous example to `post`. Listing 6-24 shows the new code sample.

Listing 6-24: POST Method Example

```
<do type="accept" label="Go">
    <go href="calculate.asp" method="post">
        <postfield name="fname" value="Jane"/>
        <postfield name="lname" value="Doe"/>
    </go>
</do>
```

When the method attribute is set to `post`, a few different things occur. The string `fname="Jane"&amp;lname="Doe"` is built as before, but now the mobile device creates a content type called `application/x-www-form-urlencoded` and places `fname="Jane"&lname="Doe"` in that content type. So in this scenario, the question mark is not needed and the ampersand need not be escaped. The other major difference is that the entire request is issued to the Web server using a POST method rather than a GET.

Listing 6-25 shows how this method actually looks on its way to the Web server. Keep in mind that the examples presented so far are contrived: no real data are being sent. Listing 6-25 also shows how data gathered from the user are sent back to the server in the `href` attribute. The fact that this can be done is because the particular XML DTD type of this attribute is of a `vdata` type, which enables variable substitutions. If that last bit was confusing, look again at Chapter 4, which examines the DTD structure.

Listing 6-25: POST Example Using Variables

```
<?xml version="1.0"?>
<!DOCTYPE wml PUBLIC "-//WAPFORUM//DTD WML 1.1//EN"
"http://www.wapforum.org/DTD/wml_1.1.xml">

<wml>
```

Continued

Listing 6-25 *(Continued)*

```
        <card id="test" title="Height">
            <do type="accept" label="Check">
                <go href="bodyfat.asp" method="post">
                    <postfield name="weight" value="$(weight)"/>
                </go>
            </do>
            <p>Enter your weight in pounds? <br/>( ie. 130 lbs.)
                <input name="weight" format="3N" title="Weight"/>
            </p>
        </card>
</wml>
```

In this example a person's weight is requested in order to initiate a calculation of the recommended body fat. The data are sent to the Web server using a POST method. The `postfield` element contains the name and value of the data to be built automatically and included in the content type of `x-www-form-urlencoded` in the request. Following is one possible interpretation of the HTTP request data if a snapshot was taken as the WML browser made the request from the WAP gateway.

```
POST /bodyfat.asp HTTP/1.1

Date: Thu, 23 Nov 2000 08:27:13 GMT
Content-Length: 10
Content-Type: application/x-www-form-urlencoded
Accept: text/vnd.wap.wml, text/vnd.wap.wmlscript,
application/vnd.wap.wmlc, application/vnd.wap.wmlscriptc, text/x-
vCard, text/x-vcard, text/x-vcal,text/x-vCalendar, text/x-vcalendar,
image/vnd.wap.wbmp, application/vnd.wap.wbxml, image/gif, image/jpeg
Accept-Charset: UTF-8
Host: www.domain.com
User-Agent: Nokia-WAP-Toolkit/2.0

weight=123
```

This code shows how the HTTP request for data would look and how the actual POST variable data are packaged in the body of the message.

When evaluating which method to use, consider the relative trade-offs of GET and POST, as shown in Table 6-8. You will find that POST is generally the better alternative.

Table 6-8 GET VERSUS POST

GET Advantage/Disadvantage	POST Advantage/Disadvantage
Easy to view and debug errors	Not so easy to view and debug errors
Data are easily visible	Data are hidden from casual view
Data limited to 127 bytes in many browser/gateway combinations	Data not encumbered by 127-byte limit
Data requires proper encoding	Data in body does not require encoding
Data are not automatically handled by character-set translators	Data are automatically handled by character-set translators

After the data are sent to the Web server, a server-side script must parse them out and handle them in some way. Details on how the data sent to the server in either a GET or POST request can be extracted is covered in Chapter 9.

Making Use of Timers

One of the other intrinsic events I mentioned at the beginning of this chapter was ontimer. This event allows navigation or some task to occur without any user intervention. For example, it can enable you to create applications (such as a WML clock) that maintain fresh content on the mobile device. In addition to the intrinsic event ontimer, you must also create a timer separately using a timer element. The DTD definition of this element is shown in Listing 6-26.

Listing 6-26: timer Element DTD Listing

```
<!ELEMENT timer EMPTY>
<!ATTLIST timer
  name       NMTOKEN        #IMPLIED
  value      %vdata;        #REQUIRED
  %coreattrs;
>

<!ELEMENT card (onevent*, timer?, (do | p)*)>
```

The `timer` element can appear only inside a `card` element. The `timer` must be defined as the second element in a card, as shown in Listing 6-26.

The main attributes of this element are shown in Table 6-9.

TABLE 6-9 TIMER ELEMENT ATTRIBUTES

Attribute	Description
name=nmtoken	Specifies the name of the variable to be set with the value of the timer. The value is decremented when `ontimer` fires on card entry and set to 0 when the timer expires.
value=vdata	Indicates the default value of the variable defined by the `name` attribute.
	If the `name` variable already contains a value, this value attribute is ignored. It is only if the name variable is un-initialized that this value is honored.

A timer element is fired upon card entry and decremented as time passes to 0. The value of the timer is defined in tenths of a second, so `timer="60"` is a timer set for six seconds. When the time hits 0, the `ontimer` event fires and executes any associated tasks.

The `timer` element simply declares a card timer; the actual action that occurs is defined elsewhere in an intrinsic event of the `ontimer` type. As shown previously in Listing 6-3, the intrinsic event can be in the short form in a `card` attribute or in the long form in an `onevent`.

Listing 6-27 shows an example that should clear things up. It is based on an example that I introduced in Listing 6-1 of this chapter. In that example, `onenterbackward` was used to bypass the splash screen in any backward navigation. You can also improve the application's ability to navigate forward by adding a timer that sends the user to the main application screen.

Listing 6-27: Simple Timer Example

```
<?xml version="1.0"?>
<!DOCTYPE wml PUBLIC "-//WAPFORUM//DTD WML 1.1//EN"
 "http://www.wapforum.org/DTD/wml_1.1.xml">

<wml>
    <card id="test" title="Cool deals!">
        <p>
            Index of cool deals!<br/>
```

```
                    <a href="#splash" title="Lamps">LampsRus </a> and
other retailers represented here
            </p>
    </card>

    <card id="splash">
                <onevent type="ontimer">
                    <go href="#products"/>
                </onevent>
                <onevent type="onenterbackward">
                    <prev/>
                </onevent>
                <timer value="40"/>
                <do type="accept" label="Next">
                    <go href="#products"/>
                </do>
                <do type="prev">
                    <prev/>
                </do>
                <p align="center">
                    <big>LampsRus</big><br/>
                </p>
                <p align="center">The ONLY! place for industrial
Lamps<br/>
                </p>
                <p>
                    <small>&#169; 2000 by LRS</small>
                </p>
    </card>

    <card id="products" title="Products">
          <do type="prev">
                <prev/>
          </do>
          <p>
           <a href="sodium.wml" title="Select">Sodium Lamps</a><br/>
           <a href="metal.wml" title="Select">Metal Halide
Lamps</a><br/>
           <a href="fluorescent.wml" title="Select">Fluorescent
Lamps</a><br/>
           <a href="used.wml" title="Select">Used Lamps</a>
          </p>
    </card>
</wml>
```

192   Part II: Development of Services

Listing 6-27 shows a typical case in which you can use a timer. Many applications in WML use the `timer` element and `ontimer` event to build a splash-screen timeout. In this example, the timeout is set to four seconds. When the timer expires, the splash screen goes away and is replaced with the main products screen of the application. Figures 6-17 and 6-18 show how the timer element is used to control splash screen displays.

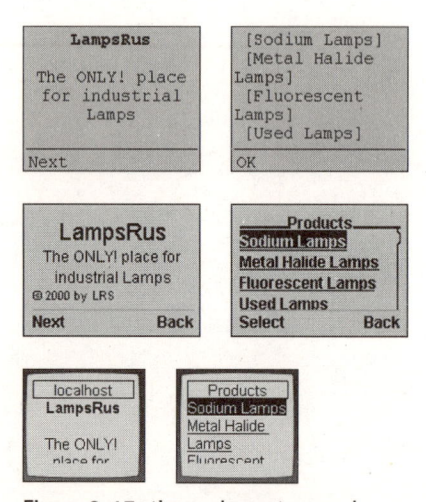

Figure 6-17: timer-element example

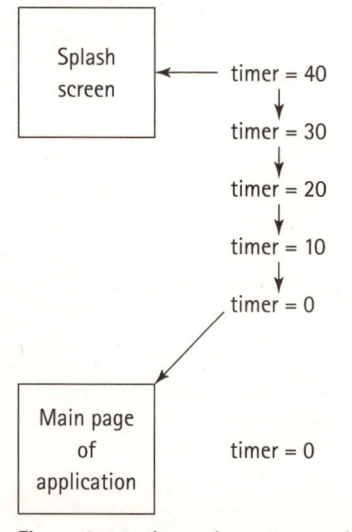

Figure 6-18: timer-element countdown

You can find more complex examples of timers in Chapter 8, in which a timer is used for creating animation. Also, Chapter 12, "Caching and Cache Operations," presents an example wherein a timer is used to create a clock; and Chapter 16 includes an example wherein a timer is used to clear variables for security reasons.

Summary

In this chapter, I discussed intrinsic events and how you can use them to aid in efficient site navigation and history management. Any of these navigational techniques greatly improve the user's perception of your application and are one of the required catalysts toward improving site performance.

I also showed you how to create variables in WML. I presented three methods: the `setvar` element, the `select` element, and the `input` element. Besides being able to create variables, the `select` element and `input` element serve as important ways in which you can gather user input for use by your application. Finally, I returned to a more advanced intrinsic event, the `ontimer`, and demonstrated its use in a simple application.

With this chapter you should be able to create more advanced WAP/WML sites. In several upcoming chapters, I show how you can supplement this knowledge with a thorough understanding of other WAP protocols, an understanding of differences among browsers, and some usability best practices.

In the next chapter, I look at a client-side scripting language called WMLScript that is available to sites written in WML.

Chapter 7

Programming with WMLScript

IN THIS CHAPTER

- Understanding the need for WMLScript
- Getting started with WMLScript
- WMLScript language basics
- Building a Sine function

DEVELOPING WEB SITES ON THE INTERNET has quickly progressed from a static endeavor to a highly interactive one. Dynamic sites are tailored to the unique needs of each user who enters the site. This tailoring usually takes place by the use of scripts on the Web servers. These scripts are stored on the Web servers and represent one way to tackle the problem of adding dynamic behavior. Another approach is to use scripts client-side with the browser as a point of dynamic code generation. This approach becomes critical in the wireless world because transactions are more expensive here than in the wired world.

Both the browser-generated and Web-server generated techniques can be used in the WAP world. The dynamic generation of content on Web servers remains the same as in the Internet world, but on the mobile browser, because of memory constraints, the JavaScript language is not used. A more compact language was created as a substitute — WMLScript.

The syntax of WMLScript is very similar to the syntax of JavaScript and ECMAScript, which were used as reference points in the creation of the new language. However, you do not need to be an expert in any of the regular browser languages to understand WMLScript. In this chapter, I explain some of the motivations for using WMLScript, provide a simple example to get you started quickly, and look at the WMLScript programming-language concepts in detail. I end with an advanced example of WMLScript usage.

Images of Openwave products in this chapter courtesy of Openwave Systems Inc.

Why WMLScript?

One of the important premises of the WAP architecture is that all applications reside on a Web server, and it is the responsibility of server-side scripts to provide the logical control of an application. Every time this logical control or some complex action is required, a request is sent from the micro-browser client to the Web server, which sends back a response in the form of content.

These multiple requests and responses cause two problems. First, they can add to the cost of running your application, because data traffic over the wireless network costs money and usually a lot more than landline data traffic. So every additional roundtrip request and response costs the user of your application more. Second, existing wireless bandwidth is limited and multiple requests and responses result in delays represented by unresponsive applications. To mitigate these problems, a minimal scripting language that enables you to execute certain operations on the client was devised for WAP appliances.

This mobile device-based language complements the WML protocol by checking the validity of user input, generating local messages and dialogs, and parsing information local to the mobile device. WMLScript is also capable of accessing device functionality directly: for example, by placing a phone call, adding contacts to the address book, or reading data from the SIM (Software Identity Module) card. These types of WMLScript functions are known as WTA functions and I will discuss them in Chapter 11. Today, most actual WMLScript-capable mobile devices are limited to localized scripting and the use of standard libraries. Figure 7-1 shows the WMLScript virtual machine and important surrounding components for its operation.

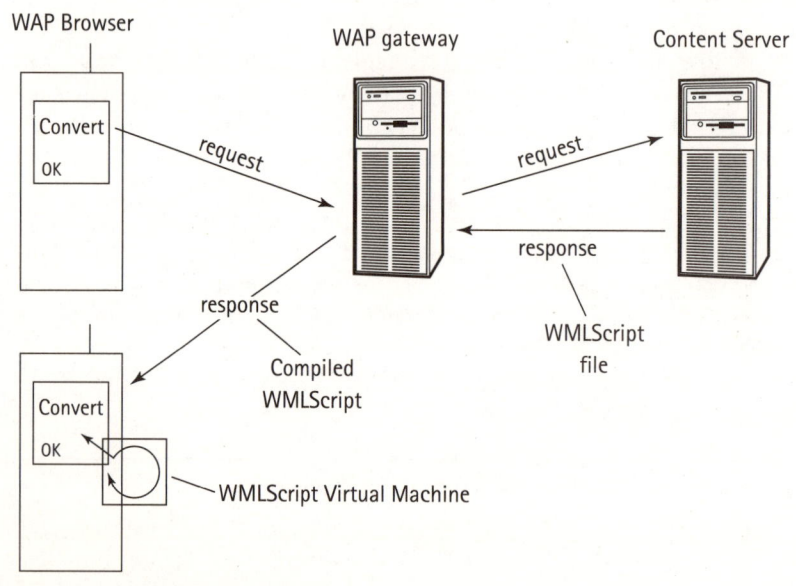

Figure 7-1: WMLScript operation

Storing and Calling WMLScript

You may have encountered two major differences between WMLScript and other languages. First, WMLScript is not contained as a preamble to markup language code—it is contained within a separate file and is sent to the client when it is needed. Second, the WMLScript code cannot exist by itself. It must be combined with WML code to create a working application. So an `href` within a WML card must explicitly call the WMLScript file.

WMLScript files are usually stored on a server with a .wmls extension and therefore require the addition of a MIME type for static files. However, they can also be dynamically generated. WMLScript files contain a series of functions and only `extern` functions are callable from within a WML. Listing 7-1 shows an example of a WMLScript call.

Listing 7-1: Sample WML Code with a WMLScript Call

```
<?xml version="1.0"?>
<!DOCTYPE wml PUBLIC "-//WAPFORUM//DTD WML 1.1//EN"
"http://www.wapforum.org/DTD/wml_1.1.xml">
<wml>

    <card id="calc" >
       <do type="accept" label="Yes">
          <go href="calculate.wmls#doMath($number)"/>
       </do>

       <p>
          Find the square root of?
          <input name="number" format="10N"/>
       </p>
    </card>

    <card id="answer">
       <do type="accept" label="Again">
          <go href="#calc">
             <setvar name="number" value=""/>
          </go>
       </do>

       <p>
          The square root of $number is $answer.
       </p>
    </card>

</wml>
```

The WML code in Listing 7-1 implements a simple calculator of square roots. It is composed of two cards, the first of which gets an input value from the user. This input value is fed into a WMLScript function that does the calculation. The second card in the WML deck displays the calculated answer. Note that it was necessary for the variable answer to have been populated by the WMLScript code. (I show you how the WMLScript code assigns a value to a WML variable next.)

Note how the WMLScript file in Listing 7-1 is called and the way in which parameters are passed to it:

```
<go href="calculate.wmls#doMath($number)"/>
```

The file is linked in much the same way as any other resource except that the fragment specifies the function to be called within the WMLScript file. The function here is doMath(...). This function takes a single parameter: an integer.

The following code sample shows the WMLScript code, which is in the file calculate.wmls:

```
extern function doMath(num){
   var ans;
   ans = Float.sqrt(num);
   WMLBrowser.setVar("answer",String.format("%5.4f",ans));
   WMLBrowser.go("#answer");
}
```

In this trivial case, only one function is contained in the file. Multiple functions can be included in the .wmls file. However, only functions with the `extern`keyword are callable from outside the WMLScript file, either from a WML deck or from another WMLScript file.

In the second line of the previous WMLScript code sample, I create a variable called `ans`. All variables in WMLScript must be declared before they are first used. Then the function accesses the `Float` library function called `sqrt`. Besides the standard language grammar, WMLScript libraries are available to assist with common tasks. You call them by referring to the `Library` and the `Function(...)`, as in `Library.Function(...)`. The floating-point function then calculates the square root and assigns it to the variable `ans`. Variables are weakly typed, so the input `num` enters as a string, and the variable `ans` is output as a `float`.

After the answer has been obtained, you can set a variable in the WML browser context by using the function `setVar` from the WMLBrowser library. Because the `ans` variable contains a `float`, it must be formatted properly for generic user display. If it is an application for the scientific or engineering community, this step is not necessary.

Finally, when a script has finished executing it returns to the card on which the script was first instantiated. In this case, it would be the first card in my two-card deck. But I want the answer card to display after execution, so I use the `go(...)` function in the WMLBrowser library to navigate to the card called "answer" in the same deck as the calling deck.

I've tested the previous example using the Openwave Emulator and the Nokia Toolkit. Examples of how it looks in these emulators are shown in Figures 7-2 and 7-3.

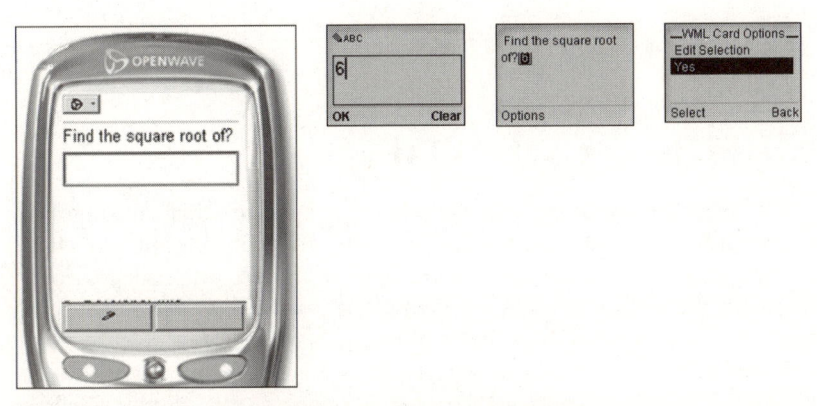

Figure 7-2: Square-root example in the Openwave Emulator

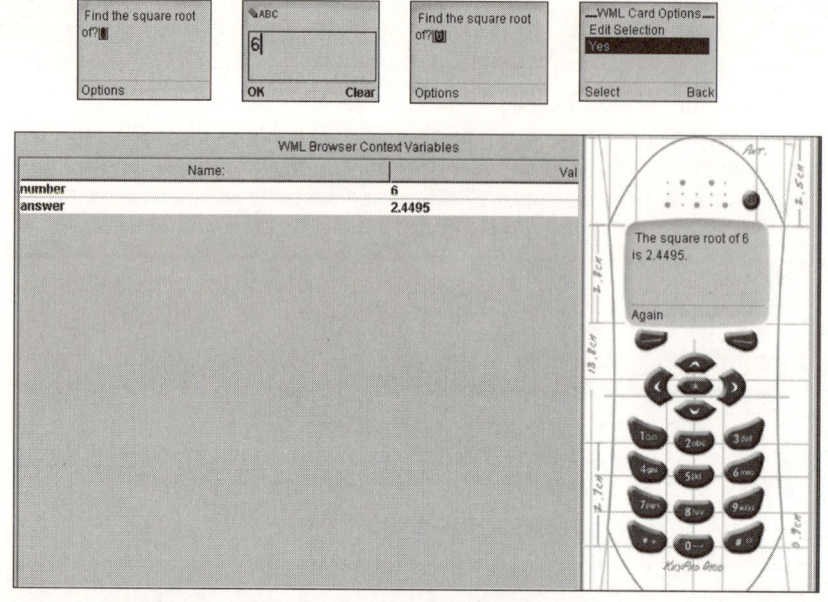

Figure 7-3: Square-root example in the Nokia Toolkit

Introducing WMLScript

One of the best ways to learn WMLScript is by comparing it to other languages in terms of its capabilities. You do not need to be an expert in JavaScript or C++ to understand WMLScript, although general knowledge of object-oriented programming will certainly help. The methods and functions available in WMLScript are object-oriented and require some knowledge of encapsulation.

WML and WMLScript code reside in separate files where the WMLScript file is only fetched after the user requests a URL. Even though the WMLScript file is a separate entity, it cannot be requested by itself. The WMLScript code must be called from a WML file and returned to the WML code after execution.

As with most WAP content types, the WAP gateway modifies WMLScript code before it is sent over the air. However, unlike other content types, which are simply tokenized according to tables, WMLScript is converted into byte codes that are then interpreted by the WMLScript virtual machine at the wireless device.

Variables and data types

Variables in WMLScript are weakly typed and stored internally as the same type. You can declare different types of variables, but they can be easily converted to other types using type conversion functions. A variable can contain a value of any type, and functions can return values of all types. The data obtained from the WML browser context are given to you as a string, and you have to type-convert them if, for example, you want to do calculations. Also, functions that combine data of different types are implicitly typecast. For example, if a floating-point function is given an integer type, it is converted to a `float` before the function is executed. The type of result is dependent on the input. For example, 4 + 4 is 8 but, "4" + "hire" is "4hire." What about 2 + 2 + "hire"?

When an expression contains mixed data types, the expression is evaluated in terms of whether the data types can be converted into a valid type. For the + operation, for example, `strings`, `integers`, and `floats` are accepted. Five main data types exist in WMLScript: integers, Booleans, floats, strings, and invalids. Table 7-1 lists the values that these data types can take on.

TABLE 7-1 WMLSCRIPT DATA TYPES AND VALUES

Data Type	Possible Values
Boolean	True or false
Integer	-2147483648 to 2147483648 (32-bit signed)
Float	3.40282347E+38 to 1.17549435E-38 (IEEE single precision)
String	Any character data, such as "diatribe" (arbitrary length of characters limited by memory restrictions on a WML browser)
Invalid	A type that is not any of the other data types; usually the result of operations that did not go well, as a result of which the return type is set to invalid to let you know for debugging.

The last data type in the table is `invalid`, which is set when an assignment evaluates to an error or when an expression could not be evaluated to a valid data type. In the first case, `var value = 1/0` is going to set the data type for `value` to `invalid`, because the expression 1/0 results in a number that cannot be represented.

In the following example, a is set to 36:

`a = Float.pow(6,2) // a = 36`

In the next example, the number 0 to the -1 power results in an `invalid` data type:

`a = Float.pow(0,-1) //a is invalid`

The script interpreter attempts to convert one data type to another based on the calculation being attempted. If the conversion fails for some reason, the assignment becomes invalid. This occurs most often when mixed types are used in a single operation, as in the following example:

```
a = 5 + 5.0
```

The first input is converted to a `float` and added to the second `float` and the result is a `float` with a value of `10.0`. An unsuccessful conversion example is as follows:

```
a = 6.0 / "hello"
```

Here, a string cannot divide the float `6.0`, so the variable `a` is set to `invalid`.

You should keep three important rules in mind when evaluating whether expressions result in invalid data types and what occurs when mixing data types:

- An order of precedence exists for type conversion
- Automatic type conversion only makes sense for certain operations
- Tables exist that list how the type conversions take place

The order of precedence for type conversion is as follows from highest to lowest:

- `invalid`
- `string`
- `float`
- `integer`
- `Boolean`

So, the result of `"3222"` + `32` would be the string `"322232"` because `32` would be converted to a string.

The next important factor to note is that all operations accept a constrained set of data types. A `+` or `++` operation works on `strings`, `floats`, and `integers`. The `-`, `*`, and `/` work only with `integers` and `floats`. The full list of operations and what type of input they take and the possible outputs are listed in Appendix B, "WMLScript Language Reference." If the data types being used are outside the accepted set for an operation, the expression will evaluate to `invalid`.

The last thing to note is that automatic conversion rules exist for the different data types. If a Boolean `true` must be converted into an integer, it is converted into a `1`. Table 7-2 lists the conversion rules.

Table 7-2 Data-Type Conversion Rules

Input as	Boolean	Integer	Floating-point	String
Boolean `true`	-	1	1.0	`"true"`
Boolean `false`	-	0	0.0	`"false"`
Integer 0	`false`	-	0.0	`"0"`
Other integers	`true`	-	Floating value of the number	String representation of the integer
Floating-point 0.0	`false`	Illegal	-	String representation of floating-point value; can be implementation-dependent
Any other floating-point number	`true`	Illegal	-	String representation of floating-point value; can be implementation-dependent
Empty string	`false`	Illegal	Illegal	-
Non-empty string	`true`	Integer value of the string or illegal	Floating-point value of the string or illegal	-
`invalid`	Illegal	Illegal	Illegal	Illegal

With these rules in mind, take a look at a complex example. What happens if the following function is evaluated?

```
function test(){
   var d;
   var bool = true;
   var a = 6;
   var b = 1e2;
   var c = 2.0;
   d = a + b + c + bool;
   return d;
}
```

First, the variable `d` is declared. It will be used to store the final answer. Then a variable of type Boolean, called `bool`, is declared and initialized to `true`. After that, an integer is declared and initialized to 6. Then a `float` called b is declared and initialized to 1e2. And another `float` called c is initialized and set to 2.0. Then all the types are added.

The addition operations start from left and move right. When a is added to b, the integer is auto-converted into a `float` of 6.0, and the result is 106.0 so far. Then that is added to 2.0, which is also a `float`. The result so far is 108.0. Finally, the result is added to the Boolean `true`, which has the lowest precedence according to the order of the precedence list shown previously. The Boolean is auto-converted into the `float` 1.0 and then added to 108.0. The function then returns the `float` d with a value of 109.0.

Variable declaration, initialization, and scope

WMLScript variables are case-sensitive, so `myVar` is different from `MyVar`. The length of variables should not affect the size of a single WMLScript file, as all variables are represented by reference tokens after compilation.

Variables must be declared before they are used for the first time, but they do not have to be initialized. You declare a variable simply by using the `var` keyword. For example, the uninitialized keyword `var mammal;` assigns the empty string "" to the variable `mammal`. The variable `mammal` could be initialized on the same line like this:

```
var mammal = "zebra";
```

You can declare multiple variables on the same line like this:

```
var mammal, insect, reptile;
```

or declare and initialize them on the same line like this:

```
var mammal = "giraffe", insect = "ant", reptile = "crocodile";
```

When you declare a variable you can reference it within the function in which you declared it by using its identifier. The following code shows an example of variable-referencing:

```
function one(){
   var a = 1;
   var b = 2;
   var c = a + b;
   var counter = 0;
   while (counter < 3)
   {
      // adding this here would be an error
      // var a = 10;
```

```
        counter = counter + a;
   };
   return counter + c;
}
```

Note the different declarations. A variable's lifetime exists only as long as the end of the function within which it is scoped. Block statements do not provide new scope within a function and variable names within functions must be unique. This means that redeclaring the variable a within the `while` block in the previous example is an error.

> **NOTE**: Note that you can declare variables anywhere in the code but you can only use them in the function following their declaration. Another function within the same WMLScript file could reuse the variables a, b, and c. If you truly need a global variable, you can set and unset WML context variables using WMLBrowser library calls.

The diagram in Figure 7-4 presents the various scoping possibilities.

```
                function test(a)  {

Scope           var one;
 of
variable        var two;                Scope           Scope
 a                                       of              of
                                        variable        variable
                }                        two             one

                function another( )  {

                   ...

                }
```

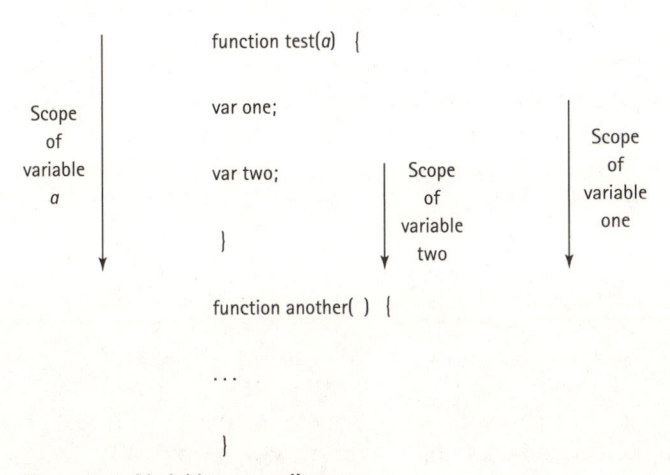

Figure 7-4: Variable-scope diagram

Emulated array support

No array support exists within WMLScript; however, the creators of WMLScript included the concept of string arrays. These arrays are defined by a sequence of strings of varying lengths delimited by a known character. The entire sequence is itself a string. The functions with which to manipulate these string sequences are contained within the `String` library.

The following code sample provides an example of how to use the library:

```
function array_test() {
   var sentence = "The quick brown fox jumped over the lazy pig, the gate and the horse!";
   var fourth_word = String.elementAt(sentence,3," ");
   return fourth_word;
}
```

Note that indexing begins at 0, so the fourth element in the sequence is referred to as the index number 3. These arrays can be only a one-dimensional sequence of variable strings.

> **XREF** For a more thorough investigation of these arrays, see the section "String library" in Chapter 8, "Using the WML Script Libraries."

Operators and built-in functions

WMLScript supports all the normal arithmetic, bitwise, comparison, conditional, and logical operators also available in JavaScript.

The simplest of these operators is the assignment operator, which simply assigns a value to a variable. A variable is assigned a value with an equals (=) symbol. For example, z = 25 is an example of an assignment. All variables must be declared before they are used, so the usage is `var z = 25;` or something like the following:

```
var z;
z=25;
//more examples
z=26;
var y = z;
```

The second assignment of z removes the variable's original value and the line after that declares and initializes a new variable y to the new value of z. WMLScript also supports basic arithmetic operations, as shown in Table 7-3.

TABLE 7-3 SIMPLE WMLSCRIPT OPERATIONS

Operator	Function
+=	Adds numbers/combines strings and assigns
-=	Subtracts and assigns

Operator	Function
*=	Multiplies and assigns
/=	Divides and assigns

Examples of these simple WMLScript operations are included in the following code:

```
function operators(){
   var a = 100;
   var b = 100;
   var c = 100;
   var counter = 0;
   while (counter < 1)
   {
      a /= 2;
      b *= 2;
      c -= 50;
      counter++;
   };
   return a+b+c;
}

// the answer is 50 + 200 + 50 = 300
```

In the previous code sample the loop executes once and modifies the values of variables using assignment operators. These are a shortcut for writing the full expression: in the case of /= 2, the long form would be = a / 2. The two statements are functionally equivalent.

Other assignment operators, shown in Table 7-4, are available.

TABLE 7-4 WMLSCRIPT ASSIGNMENT OPERATORS

Operator	Function
div=	Integer divide and assign
%=	Find remainder and assign
<<=	Bitwise left shift and assign

Continued

TABLE 7-4 WMLSCRIPT ASSIGNMENT OPERATORS *(Continued)*

>>=	Bitwise right shift and assign
>>>=	Bitwise right shift zero fill and assign
&=	Bitwise AND and assign
^=	Bitwise XOR and assign
|=	Bitwise OR and assign

The following code provides an example of the assignment operators in use:

```
function operators(){
   var a = 100;
   var b = 33;
   var c = a;
   var counter = 0;

   while (counter < 1)
   {
      a div= b;
      c %= b;
      counter++;
   };

   WMLBrowser.setVar("a",a);
   WMLBrowser.setVar("c",c);

   return a + c;
}
```

The code should return values of 3 and 1 for a and c, respectively.

Besides these operators, standard arithmetic operators exist that support basic binary operations on variables and literals. Table 7-5 lists the full set of these operators.

Table 7-5 WMLSCRIPT BASIC OPERATIONS

Operator	Function
+	Adds numbers/combines strings
-	Subtracts one number from another
*	Multiplies two numbers
/	Divides one number by another
div	Divides an integer
%	Finds a remainder
<<	Returns a bitwise left shift
>>	Returns a bitwise right shift
>>>	Returns a bitwise right shift zero fill
&	Returns a bitwise AND
^	Returns a bitwise XOR
|	Returns a bitwise OR

The use of the WMLScript operations in the previous table is quite simple; the following code provides an example:

```
function more_operators(){
   var a = 100;
   var b = 250;
   var c = 500;

   var d = c - a; // d = 400
   var e = c + a; // e = 600
   var f = c / b; // f = 2
   var g = b * a; // g = 25000

   var h = b div a; // h = 2
   var i = b % a; // i = 50

   return d+e+f+g+h+i;
}
```

There is also a set of unary operators that can act on just one value. The unary operators are listed in Table 7-6.

Table 7-6 WMLSCRIPT UNARY OPERATORS

Operator	Function
+	Plus
-	Minus
--	Pre-or-post decrement
++	Pre-or-post increment
~	Bitwise NOT

The following code shows the unary operators in action:

```
function unary_operators(){

    var a = 100;
    var b = 600;
    var c = 500;

    var d = -c + a;     // d = -400
    var e = ++b;        // b = 601, e = 601
    var f = b++;        // b = 602, f = 601
    var g = b--;        // b = 601, g = 602
    var h = --b;        // b = 600, h = 600

    return e+f+g+h;
}
```

And even more operators exist in WMLScript; these are the logical operators that evaluate inputs and test different results for their Boolean values (true or false). These operators are used extensively to give the local WMLScript its intelligence. Table 7-7 lists the logical operators supported in WMLScript.

Table 7-7 WMLSCRIPT LOGICAL OPERATORS

Operator	Function
&&	Logical AND
||	Logical OR
!	Logical NOT

The logical AND operator evaluates the first input and tests the result. If the result is `false` the result of the entire operation is `false` and the second input is not evaluated. If the first input is evaluated to `true` the result of the operation is the combination of that input and the logical value of the second input. If the first input is `invalid`, the second input is not evaluated and the whole operation results in an `invalid`.

In very much the same way, the OR returns `true` if either input is `true`, and only returns `false` if both are `false`. The NOT operator returns the logical opposite of the input Boolean. It is conceivable for an OR operation to contain an `invalid` element as the second item and still return a real response. (See the fourth test in the Listing 7-2.) Because the NOT operation is unary, if the input is invalid, the output will also be invalid.

Listing 7-2 provides an example of the Boolean operators with comments indicating how the operators assign values.

Listing 7-2: Boolean Operators Example

```
function boolean_operators(){

    var a = false;
    var b = true;
    var c = 1/0;

    var d = b && b;     // d = true
    var e = a || b;     // b = true
    var f = a || a;     // f = false
    var g = b || c;     // g = true
    //Some SDKs do not honor the next statement
    //as invalid
    var h = c || a;     // h is invalid

}
```

Comparisons, commas, and typeof

Comparison operators perform comparisons that produce Boolean results (`true` or `false`). WMLScript supports all the basic comparison operations. Table 7-8 lists the comparison operators available in WMLScript.

Table 7-8 WMLScript Comparison Operators

Operator	Function
<	Less than
<=	Less than or equal to
==	Equal to
>=	Greater than or equal to
>	Greater than
!=	Not equal to

Comparison operators apply to Booleans, integers, floating points, and strings. Following are some of the rules to use when evaluated expressions that compare items:

- Boolean: true is larger than false.
- Integer: Comparison is based simply on the value of the integer.
- Floating-point: Comparison is based simply on the value of the floating-point.
- String: Comparison is based on the order of character codes in the input strings.

For example: "x" > "X" is true, and "x" > "?" is true.

Comparisons of any invalid inputs result in an invalid type. Listing 7-3 shows the comparison operators in use.

Listing 7-3: Comparison Operators Example

```
function comparison_operators(){

    var a = false;
    var b = true;
    var c = 20, d = 40, e = 20;
    var f = "x", g = "X", h = "?";
    var i = "2.0", j = "2.0001", k = "2.00";
    var l = 1/0;

    var m = a > b;          // m = false
    var n = c <= d;         // n = true
    var o = c == e;         // o = true
```

```
    var p = f == g;        // p is false
    var q = f < h;         // h is false
    var r = a != b;        // r is true
    var s = i <= j;        // s is true
    var t = i == k;        // t is false
    var u = k > l;         // u is invalid

}
```

You can use a comma operator at any time to combine multiple statements onto one line so that multiple evaluations are performed at the same time. In the most trivial case, you have already seen multiple assignments occurring together like this:

```
var a = 4, b = 5
```

In much the same way you can place multiple elements in a control construct that I examine in the next section. An example of this is the following code:

```
for (a=2, b=10; a < 20; a++, b++) { ...
```

The situation gets especially tricky when you use the comma operator as in the following code:

```
function test_comma_operator(){
    var a = 4, b = 5, c = 6;
    var d = a + b, b + c;    // d is b+c or 11
}
```

It is also useful to test the type of a variable, especially with the possibility of expressions resulting in `invalid`. Two operators can help here: `typeof` and `isvalid`. Table 7-9 lists the values returned by the `typeof` operation.

TABLE 7-9 TYPEOF RETURN VALUES

Type	Code Returned
Integer	0
Floating-point	1
String	2
Boolean	3
Invalid	4

The `isvalid` operator simply determines whether a variable is valid or invalid. If the variable is valid, it returns `true`; if not, it returns `false`.

The following example shows the `typeof` operator and `isvalid` in action.

```
function type_operators() {
    var a = 1;
    var b = 0;
    var c = isvalid(a);     // c is true
    var d = isvalid(a/b);   // d is false
    var e = "time";
    var f = 12.02;
    var g = true;

    var h = typeof e;       // h is 2
    var i = typeof f;       // i is 1
    var j = typeof g;       // j is 3
    var k = typeof (a/b);   // k is 4
    var m = typeof b;       // m is 0
}
```

Operator precedence

Now that you have seen all the operators, you should know that it is conceivable for an expression to contain a combination of these operators, and that operator precedence sets the rules that determine the order in which operators are executed. You can override operator precedence using parentheses. WMLScript follows the standard mathematical rules for its precedence rules.

Another aspect of precedence to be on the lookout for is associativity, which defines the rules that determine the side from which the operations are performed. For example, 6 + 6 * 3 will evaluate from the left as 6 + 18 and then 24. But for !true || ! false || !true, Because ! has higher precedence, the expression evaluates to `false || true || false` starting from the right side. Then the logical ORs are evaluated from the left side as `true || false` and then `true`. The first expression could be evaluated differently, if you use parentheses, to (6 + 6) * 3. In this case the + evaluates first and then the *, both from the left-hand side. And this time the answer is 36. The full list of operator precedences can be found in Appendix B.

Control statements

Control statements add the most power to the WMLScript language compared to other WMLScript keywords, because they add the core of the dynamic features that bring the language past WML. The program uses these statements to make decisions and branch code based on the value of a decision indicator.

The most basic control statement is the `if` statement. Its syntax looks like this:

```
if (expression) statement else statement
OR
if (expression) statement
```

If the expression evaluates to `true`, the first statement is executed and the command after the `if` section is executed. If the expression evaluates to `false` or `invalid`, the statement after the `else` (optional) is executed and the code after the `if` statement is executed. Note that the second statement can be a nested `if`, in which case the `else` is tied to the closest `if` statement.

> **TIP** If multiple statements must be executed as the result of an `if` statement you can combine them in a single block, which is a series of statements surrounded by braces (`{ }`).

There is no `elseif` statement or any type of switch statement as there is in other languages, but nothing prevents you from chaining multiple `if-else` statements together to achieve the same effect, as shown in the following example:

```
if (a == 1) {
   ...
} else if (a == 2) {
   ...
} else if (a == 3) {
   ...
} else {
   ...
}
```

Listing 7-4 shows several examples of the control statements in use.

Listing 7-4: Control Statements Example

```
function sqrt(input) {
   //Get the square root of the input

   var answer;

   if (input == 0) {
      return 0.0;
   }

   if (input > 0) {
      // do some calculation
```

Continued

Listing 7-4 *(Continued)*

```
      answer = Float.sqrt(input);
   } else
   {
      answer = Float.sqrt(Lang.abs(input));
   }

   return answer;
}
```

WMLScript also has looping capabilities. You can use a `while` or `for` loop. These are the standard looping statements available in most languages. The syntax for the `while` statement is:

`while (`*expression*`) `*statement*

The `while` expression can be any WMLScript expression that evaluates to a Boolean, either directly or indirectly through the conversion rules listed in Table 7-2. The condition is evaluated before the execution of every loop. If the expression evaluates to `true`, the statement is executed. Otherwise, on an `invalid` or `false` expression, the execution continues with the statement following the `while` statement. The `while` statement is executed as long as the `while` expression is `true`, which can potentially result in infinite loops. Once again, the `while` statement can be a series of statements contained in a block.

Listing 7-5 shows how the `while` loop works in WMLScript.

Listing 7-5: while Loop Example

```
function fill_diagonal_array() {

   // Create a 3 x 3 matrix in 1-D format
   // and fill with diagonal 3's

   var m = 1;
   var n = 1;
   var array;   // this will be an empty string
   var index = 0;

   while (m < 4) {

      while (n < 4) {

         if (m == n) {
            Console.println("3 at " + m + "," + n);
            array = String.insertAt(array,3,index++,",");
         } else
```

```
            {
                Console.println("0 at " + m + "," + n);
                array = String.insertAt(array,0,index++,",");
            }

            n++;
        }

        n=1;
        m++;
    }

    Console.println(array);
    return array;
}
```

The output of this code example in the Phone.com SDK window is as follows:

```
3 at 1,1
0 at 1,2
0 at 1,3
0 at 2,1
3 at 2,2
0 at 2,3
0 at 3,1
0 at 3,2
3 at 3,3
3,0,0,0,3,0,0,0,3
```

The code in Listing 7-5 creates a three-by-three diagonal matrix and stores it in the nine element one-dimensional array shown in the output. This is proof that you can create multidimensional arrays using this rudimentary syntax.

Another way to set up loops is to use the `for` statement, as in the following example:

```
for (expression1 ; expression2 ; expression3) statement
OR
for (var variable list ; expression2 ; expression3) statement
```

All the expressions in parentheses are optional but typically include counter initializing, counter checking, and counter incrementing. The first expression or variable list is used to initialize a counter or set of counters. The second expression is evaluated to a Boolean that is checked on each pass through the loop. If omitted, it evaluates to `true` on every pass of the loop. The third expression can be used to update or increment the counter variable. The `for` statement or block of statements is executed as long as the conditional expressions evaluate to `true`. Listing 7-6 provides an example of `for`-loop usage.

Listing 7-6: for Loop Example

```
function add_array() {

   // Add two 2 x 2 arrays

   var array1 = "2,0,0,2";
   var array2 = "5,6,7,8";
   var array3;
   var add_val;
   var element1;
   var element2;

   if (String.elements(array1,",") !=
String.elements(array2,",")) {
      return "Arrays can not be added";
   } else
   {
      for (var i = 0; i < 4; i++) {
         element1 =
Lang.parseInt(String.elementAt(array1,i,","));
         element2 =
Lang.parseInt(String.elementAt(array2,i,","));
         add_val = element1 + element2;
         array3 = String.insertAt(array3,add_val,i,",");
      }
   }
   Console.println(array3);
   return array3;
}
// output is 7,6,7,10
```

Listing 7-6 adds two two-by-two matrices. The matrices are defined by a sequence of comma-delimited elements in one-dimensional arrays. First, the length of the arrays is checked to see whether they can be added. If the dimensions are equivalent, the elements from the same row and column are extracted and converted into integers. These integers are then added and assigned to the final array.

Note that the keyword `break` can be used to break out of a `while` or `for` loop. It is an error to use it outside of a `while` or `for` statement. A `continue` statement is also available that terminates execution of the current iteration and goes on to the next iteration but does not end the loop. The following code example shows these language statements in action:

```
function continue_break() {

   var sum = 0;

   // add all the numbers from 1 to 5 except for 3

   for (var index = 1; true; index++) {
      if (index == 3) continue;
      if (index == 6) break;
      sum += index;
   }

   Console.println(index);
   return sum;

   // the result is 12
}
```

Functions and passing parameters

By this point you have seen many examples of functions, but no formal explanation of what they are. As mentioned in the introduction of this chapter, all code units within WMLScript are contained inside functions. Your code cannot exist outside of a function. Each function contains a set of modular code that relates to your application. The syntax for functions looks like this:

```
[extern] function(parameter1, parameter2, ...) {
    var value;
    return(value);
}
```

The `extern` keyword is required only when you want your function to be accessible from within the WML browser space. A function is accessible by any other function contained within the same WMLScript file. There is no special significance attached to the order in which the functions are contained in a WMLScript file. These functions always pass back a return value, either using the `return` statement if it is included or passing back the default empty string. The `return` statements can be included anywhere in the function and break execution immediately by returning context to the calling function.

Standard library functions are special types of functions that come preloaded on a mobile device that supports WMLScript. You call these functions using the following format:

Library.functionThatDoesSomething(...)

I discuss these functions in detail in Chapter 8, "Using WML Script Libraries." For a quick reference containing the functions refer to Appendix C, "WMLScript Libraries." Library names begin with a capital letter. Function names begin with a lowercase letter and are a combination of words, all but the first of which beginning with uppercase letters.

> **Caution:** Any of the parameters passed into a function can be used by the function without any declaration. The parameter definition in the function statement *is* the declaration. A calling function must call the function with the required parameters; otherwise it is an error.

It is common for functions internal to a WMLScript file and between WMLScript files to use parameter passing, but WML variables in the browser context can be set from within WMLScript code with code like the following:

```
WMLBrowser.setVar("variable",variable_value);
```

This is the only technique possible when your main WMLScript function returns a value or a set of values to the WML browser. I discuss many examples of these techniques elsewhere in this chapter; here is another one:

```
extern function multiply(a,b) {

    var c = example(a,b);
    WMLBrowser.setVar("c",c);
    WMLBrowser.go("#somecard");
}

function example(a2,b2) {

    var c = a2 * b2;
    return c;
}
```

Only the first function can be called by the WML code. The second function is called by the WMLScript interpreter to multiply two parameters and return a result. This result is then set to the WML browser context using the first function. The first function in the code then instructs the browser to navigate to a card other than the one that originated the WMLScript call.

Building a Sine Function

Now that you have an understanding of the basics of WMLScript it is time to look at a more engaging example. One of the functions not included with the standard libraries is a `Sine` function, which you can build using the simple multiplication and addition operations you've learned about. You can find a formula for calculating the sine from a simple Taylor series in most calculus textbooks:

Sine(x) = $x-x^3/3!+x^5/5!-x^7/7!+x^9/9!-x^{11}/11!+$ ...

where x is the angle in radians.

The conversion from degrees to radians can be found from this equivalence:

▼/2 = 90º

The series converges to the value of Sine(x) over a large number of elements in the series. However, normally the series is calculated to the level of precision needed for the calculation. (Note that the value of the series converges faster around 0 radians, because that is how the Taylor series was calculated.) However, to determine the Sine(x) up to about four decimal places you have to evaluate each of the terms after the first one and decide whether it is less than 10^-4 (less than four digits after the decimal place). If it is, the calculation stops and the final value of Sine(x) is present in the sum of the terms that have been calculated up to that point.

When you input an angle, you must first convert it from degrees to radians before the formula is applicable. Because the conversion requires an estimate of pi there is a slight loss of precision at that point. After the conversion from degrees to radians, the value is used repeatedly in the formula. Each time it is used in a power format there is a loss of precision equivalent to the inaccuracy in the estimate of pi. So if pi is estimated to be 3.14 and then a calculation is made of pi^3 the result will be 30.959144. This value has accumulated three times the inaccuracy of the first estimate. So if the first value is inaccurate by the third decimal place or 10^-3, the calculation of pi^3 is inaccurate by 3*10^-3. In the previous sine calculation, you need to account for the fact that there may be at the most one hundred of these power calculations. This means that if you estimate the value of pi to 10^-6, the final calculation may yield a precision of 10^-4. Because I only need my function to be good to four decimal places, it will be acceptable to estimate pi to at least six places.

Furthermore, no factorial function is included in the standard libraries or the language, so you will have to build one from the basic operations. To summarize, the top-level pseudocode looks like this:

```
WML:
1: Ask input for sine calculation in degrees
2: Display answer from calculation
WMLScript:
1: Convert value to radians
2: Calculate the value of sine by assembling the series
```

The first step is to build the WML code, as shown in Listing 7-7.

Listing 7-7: WML Code for Sine Calculation

```
<?xml version="1.0"?>
<!DOCTYPE wml PUBLIC "-//WAPFORUM//DTD WML 1.1//EN"
"http://www.wapforum.org/DTD/wml_1.1.xml">

<wml>

    <card id="sine" >

        <do type="accept" label="Yes">
           <go href="sine.wmls#doCalc($number)"/>
        </do>

        <p>Find the sine of what angle? (degrees)
           <input name="number" format="*N"/>
        </p>

    </card>

    <card id="answer">

       <do type="accept" label="Again">
           <go href="#sine">
           <setvar name="number" value=""/></go>
       </do>

       <p>The sine of $number is $answer.
       </p>

    </card>

</wml>
```

The WML code listing for the sine calculation builds the framework for the WMLScript functionality. Two cards have been created, the first to take the input and the second to display the output of the WMLScript calculation.

Here is the factorial function code:

```
function doFactorial(num) {

    var factorial = 1;

    while (num > 1) {
        factorial = factorial * num;
        num--;
    }
```

```
    return factorial;

}
```

The factorial is calculated by slowly decrementing the value of the input and multiplying it by the previous product. This is an internal function and since it is not exposed, the inputs are not checked very stringently. The Sine function will not require a factorial for 1, for example.

Listing 7-8 shows an eSine function that will accept the input value only in radians.

Listing 7-8: doSine Function

```
function doSine(rads) {

    //set the counter to one
    var n = 3;

    //set the calculated current value to 0
    var current = 0;


    //set the summation to the input; see formula
    var final = rads;

    //initialize the sign
    var sign = -1;

    //initialize the next in series value
    var next;

    //start a loop that ends when we have 4 decimal
    //places of accuracy
    while (next < 1e-4) {

        current = sign * Float.pow(rads,n)/doFactorial(n);
        next = Lang.abs(Float.pow(rads,n+2)/doFactorial(n+2));
        final += current;
        n += 2;
        sign *= -1;

    }
    return final;
}
```

Part II: Development of Services

Now that the `Sine` function is done, you have to create a function that converts from degrees to radians. You can do this using the following formula:

```
radians = degrees*pi/180
```

Here is the code for the `doConvert` function:

```
function doConvert(degrees) {
   var pi = 3.1415926;
   var radians = degrees * pi / 180;
   return radians;
}
```

The value of pi is estimated to seven decimal places and the conversion to radians is done. Next, the main function is constructed and the output is formatted correctly, as shown in this example:

```
extern function doCalc(num) {

   //convert the input into radians
   var rads = doConvert(num);

   //calculate the sine
   var answer = doSine(rads);

   WMLBrowser.setVar("answer",
                    String.format("%2.4f",answer));
   WMLBrowser.go("#answer");

}
```

And very quickly, checking some values, the WMLScript gives the results listed in Table 7-10.

Table 7-10 Sine Program Results

Angle (Degrees)	My Sine Function (Four Digits)	Calculator (Six Digits)
20	0.3420	0.342020
30	0.4997	0.500000
90	0.9248	1.000000

This Taylor series works best close to the point from which the series was derived, around 0 degrees/0 radians. However, you can change the WMLScript to provide greater precision for larger values. Simply change the `doSine(...)` function to stop the `while` loop at a higher precision. Several SDKs I tested did not change the values for `Sine(90)` even after increasing the number of precision by increasing the iteration number, which means that the values of the floating points are not really stored in IEEE single precision. Figures 7-5 and 7-6 show how the `Sine` function displays in the Openwave and Nokia emulators, respectively.

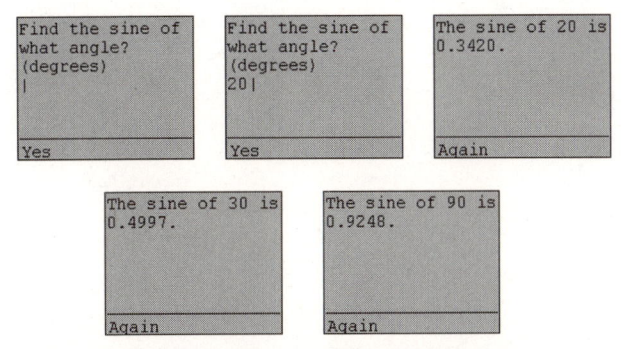

Figure 7-5: Sine example in the Openwave Emulator

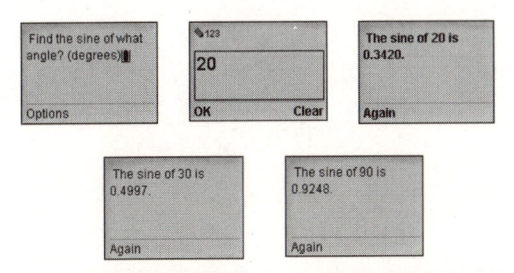

Figure 7-6: Sine example in the Nokia WAP Toolkit

Summary

In this chapter, I discussed the capabilities of the WMLScript language included in WAP. The important things to remember are the following:

- ◆ WMLScript is an application-layer, client-side scripting language based on ECMAScript and JavaScript that you can use to add procedural logic to your WAP applications.

- ◆ WMLScript has a set of libraries that adds to its core language capabilities.

◆ WMLScript has a large number of small operations that you can use to build complex functionality.

In the next chapter, I discuss some advanced features of the WMLScript language and also look in detail at the WMLScript standard libraries.

Chapter 8

Using the WMLScript Libraries

IN THIS CHAPTER

- Understanding advanced WMLScript concepts
- Using WMLScript libraries
- Using proprietary functions (Nokia and Openwave)
- Building a WMLScript credit-card verifier

CLIENT-SIDE CODE DOES NOT TRULY COME ALIVE until the WMLScript libraries are used. This chapter provides an in-depth look at the libraries and the functions you can use in WMLScript. It builds upon your previous WMLScript knowledge by showing you some advanced WMLScript techniques — some of which you must understand before attempting to understand the WMLScript library functionality. The techniques I explain in this chapter show you how to use all of the WMLScript libraries.

Introducing Advanced WMLScript Concepts

This section covers the advanced WMLScript topics, including using functions, using pragmas, and understanding the WMLScript virtual machine.

Using functions

An entire WMLScript file can be thought of as a single compilation unit, because the WAP gateway compiles the WMLScript file before sending the optimized form to the mobile device. A function declaration inside this compilation unit identifies a single function. This function can have optional parameters and a block statement that is associated with the function. All functions have the following characteristics:

Images of Openwave products in this chapter courtesy of Openwave Systems Inc.

227

- Function declarations cannot be nested.
- Function names must be unique within the WMLScript file.
- Function parameters are passed by value.
- The number of function call arguments must match when a function is called when compared to its declaration.
- Function parameters are treated as variables that have been initialized before the function block.
- A function *always* returns a value. This is an empty string by default; otherwise the return statement is used to specify other values.

The syntax of functions is as follows, where the WMLScript keywords are shown in bold:

extern function *Identifier(Parameter_List) Block;*

> The `extern`, `Parameter_List`, and `Block;` elements are optional. Functions do not need to have the `extern` keyword; that keyword is used only when the function is called from within WML. The identifier is a name for the function and complies with the syntax for variable names. The parameter list is a comma-delimited list of parameters the function takes in. The block is the main part of the function and is executed when the function is called with its parameters.

The following code shows some examples of functions:

```
extern function findVolumeCylinder(radius, height) {
   var squareRadius = radius * radius;
   var pi = 3.14;
   var answer = findVolume(pi, squareRadius, height);
};
function findVolume(pi, squareRadius, height) {
   doNothing();
   var returnedValue = doNothingAgain();
     return pi * squareRadius * height;
};
function doNothing() {
}
function doNothingAgain() {
}
```

The first function in the listing is the external function that can be called from WML. It has two parameters, the radius and the height, which are initialized and declared before `findVolumeCylinder(...)` is executed. Two variables are declared and initialized, and then the variable `answer` is declared and initialized to the value returned from calling the `findVolume(...)` function. The `findVolume(...)` function uses three parameters and calls the `doNothing()` function. The `doNothing()` function takes no parameters and does not return any variables. Although it returns an empty string, this string is ignored. It is possible for function calls to ignore the returned value.

Then the function `doNothingAgain()` is called, which does nothing and returns the default empty string. After that, the `findVolume(...)` function returns the volume of the cylinder to the main function. (Notice that the last two functions do not end in a semicolon. The semicolon is an optional end to the function. It is legal to omit it at the end of a function-block definition.)

The way in which a function is called depends on what type of function it is. In general, functions are categorized as either internal or external. Internal functions can be defined inside a single WMLScript file and can be called from within that same WMLScript file. This type of function call is seen in the preceding example, with `doNothing()` being called from within `findVolume(...)`. You can use these types of functions even before the actual function has been defined.

In this case of external functions, the functions reside in an external file. In this case, the WMLScript file containing the function must be declared before any function within it can be called. Here is an example of an external function call:

```
use url areaFunctions "http://www.domain.com/scripts/areas.wmls";
function areaSquare(inputList) {
   return areaFunctions#square(inputList);
};
```

The file with the external functions is declared at the beginning using the `use url` pragma. (See the next section for more information on pragmas.) The function is then called by referring to its declared mapping, concatenating a hash or pound symbol, and then using the function identifier and any parameters.

The third and last way a function can be called applies to standard WMLScript library functions. A library function is called by prefixing the function name with the library name and a period (.), as in the following example:

```
function square(number) {
   return Float.pow(number,2);
};
```

The `pow` function is called from the `Float` standard library to square a number.

Using pragmas

The WMLScript language supports some very special programming elements, called *pragmas*, which begin the entire WMLScript file. Pragmas must be included before any functions in the file and must include the keyword use. WMLScript defines only three pragmas, one for allowing access to external functions (use url), one for security and access control (use access), and one for passing meta-information between browsers and servers (use meta).

USE URL

This use url function is useful when a large library of pre-built functions is available in a self-contained file. The pre-built functions can be included again and again without having to rewrite a new routine every time.

The external function pragma (use url) enables you to call functions external to the current file from within the file. In the following example, the use url pragma is used to access a WMLScript file called test.wmls located on a Web server at domain.com. This WMLScript function contained within the file can be referenced by using the prefix defined in the use url pragma.

```
use url otherFile "http://www.domain.com/test.wmls";

function first(var1) {
    var var2 = otherFile#test(var1);
    return var2 + 1;
}
```

USE ACCESS

The access pragma serves as security protection that WMLScript files can include. The security measure prevents individuals from accessing your WMLScript file through unauthorized entry paths – specifically, unknown URLs.

The access control pragma performs a check on the calling file to determine whether it has access to the WMLScript file. Either path or domain attributes of this pragma determine how the access control is handled. The domain and path matching is done based on exact element rules. So www.domain.com will match domain.com but not main.com. /first/second will match /first but not /firsta. The sets of code show examples in which the executions of a WMLScript file are restricted using the access pragma. The first one here shows that the WMLScript file can be executed only if the caller is in the auto.de domain and has a URL path ending in /auto.

```
use access domain "auto.de" path="/auto";
```

The following caller would not be allowed access to a file with the use url pragma, as shown in the last line.

```
http://www.zucker.de/auto/start.jsp
```

The following caller would be allowed access to a file with the `use url` pragma, as shown in the `access` pragma introduced in the first line of this example.

```
http://www.auto.de/auto/finance.jsp
```

USE META
The `use meta` pragma specifies meta-information or name-value pairs that can be used by the browser. A browser is not required to act on the meta-information. The meta-information comes in three parts: property name, property value, and an optional scheme that specifies how the property value should be interpreted. There are three schemes: `name`, `http equiv`, and `user agent`. The `name` attribute of this meta pragma sends information to the Web server to interpret. Browsers do not interpret the `name` meta-pragma. In the following example, the meta-information consists of an author's name:

```
use meta name "Author" "Max Sorenson";
```

The `http equiv` meta-pragma provides information that is interpreted as an HTTP header. This information is converted into a WSP or HTTP header as soon as the WMLScript file hits the WAP gateway. In the following code snippet, the meta-pragma is being used to set up an assignment with the meta-name of `Search` that has the values of `deer` and `headlights`.

```
use meta http equiv "Search" "deer,headlights";
```

The `user agent` meta-pragma provides information that is sent to the Web server to interpret. The name-value pair is delivered to the browser on the phone in an HTTP response. How the meta variables are handled is up to the specific browser. In the following example, the variable `Keys` is assigned a value of `Experimental`. This value is passed to the browser and used almost exactly like an HTTP header if the browser is capable.

```
use meta user agent "Keys" "Experimental";
```

Using the WMLScript virtual machine

A WMLScript virtual machine is a self-contained environment that behaves as though it makes up the entire operating system. This is important for system independence of the code written that uses it. In this case, the diverse OS environment of cell phones is not forced onto programmers; they can write an application regardless of phone hardware or operating system. The virtual machine also protects the phone from any spurious code written for it. The code has no direct contact with the operating system.

It is important to note that the browser code logic in the phone does not understand the textual form of WMLScript in which your code is written. The WAP gateway takes the .wmls file code and compiles it into a binary format. This binary format is then sent by the WAP gateway in a .wmlsc file to the browser. The browser uses a virtual machine to interpret the codes in the binary file to run the WMLScript when it is called.

Although the entire WMLScript file is converted to binary, only the specific function or functions are called from the binary code. This binary code is in fact a set of special WMLScript bytecodes, which are used by the WMLScript interpreter or virtual machine to maintain the following state information:

- *IP (Instruction Set Pointer)* – Instructions in bytecode that are interpreted. These bytecodes are a compact binary representation of the compiled WMLScript functions. The bytecode file consists of a header followed by instructions, which are assembly-level functions that must be used to encode all WMLScript language constructs and operations. The way the bytecodes are designed makes them easily compatible with interpreters that need to move from phone to phone.

- *Variables* – Function parameters and variables

- *Operand Stack* – Used for passing arguments to called functions and returning them to the caller

- *Function call stack* – Maintains information about functions and their return addresses

Figure 8-1 depicts the virtual machine.

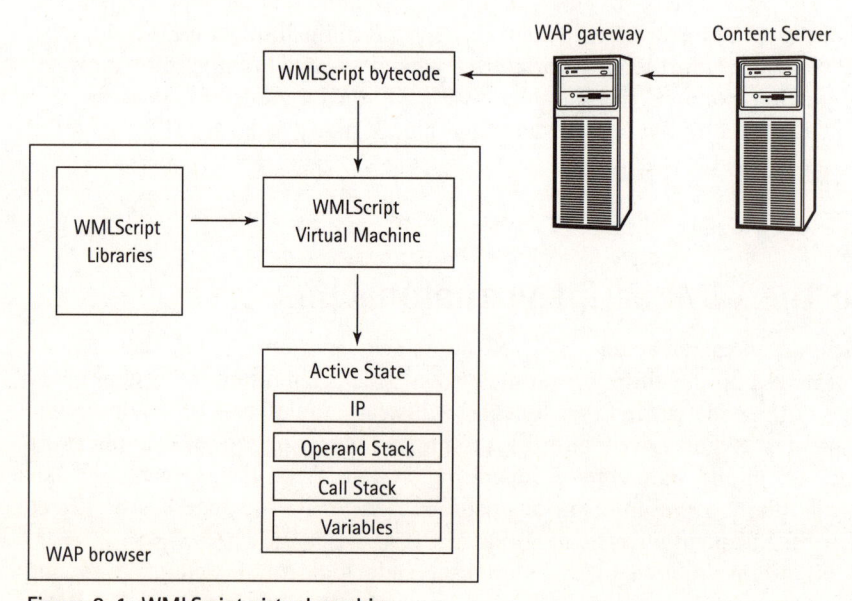

Figure 8-1: WMLScript virtual machine

> The full instruction set and semantics of the virtual machine are not important to the development of services, so I do not discuss them further in this book. You can find more information at the WAP Forum Web site at `www.wapforum.org`. The main point of this discussion is to underscore how WMLScript code is treated differently from WML code that is sent to the browser.

Standard WMLScript Libraries

Standard libraries provide a way for the WMLScript language to be enhanced and follow all the rules for WMLScript that I have discussed so far. Table 8-1 provides an at-a-glance overview of the standard libraries.

The keywords of the WMLScript language are very limited and not much can be done in WMLScript without some use of libraries. The libraries are much smaller and limited when compared with the libraries available on desktop systems, but then this is because of the limited memory for storage and execution of programs on cellular phones. The limited nature of the environment forced the designers of WAP to carefully pick just the most useful of a wider set of possibilities. The following sections detail how to use these standard WMLScript libraries.

TABLE 8-1 WMLSCRIPT LIBRARIES

Library Name	Description
Lang	Contains functions closely related to the language.
Float	Contains functions for typical arithmetic floating-point operations. If floating-point operations are not supported by the hardware, all functions must return `invalid`.
String	Contains functions that manipulate strings in WMLScript.
URL	Contains functions that extract information from URLs, build URLs, and load textual content types.
WMLBrowser	Contains functions by which the WML browser context can be accessed. Some of the functions it contains allow WMLScript coders to navigate to cards or to set variables in the WML browser context.
Dialogs	Contains functions to build typical user-interface displays.
Crypto (WAP 1.2)	Contains a single function that enables the user to sign a document.

Lang library

Table 8-2 lists the Lang library functions.

TABLE 8-2 LANG LIBRARY FUNCTIONS

Lang Library Function	Description

abs(value)	Returns the absolute value of a number. Example:
	
	var m = -4;
	
	var n = Lang.abs(m); // n = 4

min(value1, value2)	Returns the minimum value of the two given numbers. The value and type returned are the same as for the selected number. Example:
	
	var m = -4, n = 7.6;
	
	var p = Lang.min(m,n); // p = -4

max(value1, value2)	Returns the maximum value of the two given numbers. The value and type returned are the same as for the selected number. Example:
	
	var m = -4, n = 7.6;
	
	var p = Lang.max(m,n); // p = 7.6

parseInt(value)	Returns an integer value defined by the string-input value. Example:
	
	var m = "7658";
	
	var n = "16 km";
	
	var p = "15% of 600";
	
	var q = Lang.parseInt(m); // q = 7658
	
	var r = Lang.parseInt(n); // n = 16
	
	var s = Lang.parseInt(p); // s = 15

Lang Library Function	Description

parseFloat(*value*)	Returns a floating-point value defined by the string-input value. The parsing ends when the first character is encountered that cannot be parsed. Example:
	
	var m = "7.7";
	
	var n = "16.1 Gauss";
	
	var p = "15 e-2";
	
	var q = "+45.7 miles";
	
	var r = "Here is 7.7";
	
	var s = Lang.parseFloat(m); // s = 7.7
	
	var t = Lang.parseFloat(n); // t = 16.1
	
	var u = Lang.parseFloat(p); // u = 15e-2
	
	var v = Lang.parseFloat(q); // v = 45.7
	
	var w = Lang.parseFloat(r); // w = invalid

isInt(*value*)	Returns a Boolean value that is true if the given value can be converted into an integer using parseInt, false if it cannot. Example:
	
	var m = "-7;"
	
	var n = "16.1";
	
	var p = "Name";
	
	var q = false;
	
	var r = "Here is 7.7";
	
	var s = Lang.isInt(m); // s = true
	
	var t = Lang.isInt(n); // t = true
	
	var u = Lang.isInt(p); // u = false
	
	var v = Lang.isInt(q); // v = false
	
	var w = Lang.isInt(r); // w = false

Continued

TABLE 8-2 LANG LIBRARY FUNCTIONS *(Continued)*

Lang Library Function	Description

isFloat(*value*)	Returns a Boolean value that is true if the given value can be converted into an integer using parseFloat, false if it cannot. Example:
	
	var m = "-7";
	var n = "16.1";
	var p = "Name";
	var q = false;
	var r = "Here is 7.7";
	var s = Lang.isFloat(m); // s = true
	var t = Lang.isFloat(n); // t = true
	var u = Lang.isFloat(p); // u = false
	var v = Lang.isFloat(q); // v = false
	var w = Lang.isFloat(r); // w = false

maxInt()	Returns the maximum integer value supported by the WMLScript interpreter. Example: var m = Lang.maxInt(); // m = 2147483647
minInt()	Returns the minimum integer value supported by the WMLScript interpreter. Example: var m = Lang.minInt(); // m = -2147483648
float()	Returns true if floating-points are supported, false if they are not. Example: var m = Lang.float(); // m = true or false

exit(*value*)	Ends the WMLScript interpretation and returns control to the caller (the WML interpreter) with the given return value. Example:
	
	Lang.exit("End"); // return string "End"
	Lang.exit(64); // return integer 64

Lang Library Function	Description

abort(*errorDescription*)	Aborts the WMLScript interpretation and returns control to the caller (the WML interpreter) with the error-description string. Example:
	
	`Lang.abort("Execution error");`
	
	`// return error string "Execution error"`

random(*value*)	Returns an integer value with positive sign that is greater than or equal to 0 but less than or equal to the given value. If the input is a floating point, it is converted to integer first using `Float.int(...)`. Example: `var m = Lang.random(10.3);   // m= 0...10`
seed(*value*)	Initializes the pseudo-random number sequence and returns an empty string. The function call affects the random numbers generated by random(*value*). Example: `var m = Lang.seed(25);   // m= ""`

characterSet()	Returns the character set supported by WMLScript. The return value is an integer that denotes an enumerated value (`MIBEnum`) assigned by IANA for all character sets. Example:
	
	`var m = Lang.characterSet();`
	
	`// ie. character set is set to 1000 for`
	
	`// iso-10646-ucs-2`

Listing 8-1 shows a more detailed view of the Abs function. The absolute value function takes a given number and finds its absolute value. The function attempts to convert the input into an integer or floating-point number. If the result is successful, the same type is returned; otherwise, invalid is returned. Listing 8-1 shows the code for this function.

Listing 8-1: Abs Value Example

```
<?xml version="1.0"?>
<!DOCTYPE wml PUBLIC "-//WAPFORUM//DTD WML 1.1//EN"
"http://www.wapforum.org/DTD/wml_1.1.xml">
```

Continued

Listing 8-1 *(Continued)*

```
<wml>
<card id="abs">
    <onevent type="onenterforward">
        <refresh>
            <setvar name="input" value=""/>
            <setvar name="answer" value=""/>
        </refresh>
    </onevent>
    <p>Input value<br/>
        <do type="accept" label="Abs">
            <go href="langTest.wmls#doAbs()"/>
        </do>
        <select name="input">
            <option value="-5">-5</option>
            <option value="5">5</option>
            <option value="3e7">3e7</option>
            <option value="re34">re34</option>
            <option value="true">true</option>
        </select>
    </p>
</card>

<card id="abs2">
    <p>
        Answer:<br/>
        $(answer)
    </p>
</card>

</wml>
```

The following code shows the relevant WMLScript for the absolute value example:

```
extern function doAbs() {
    var in_value = WMLBrowser.getVar("input");
    var answer = Lang.abs(Lang.parseFloat(in_value));
    if (typeof answer == 4) {
        WMLBrowser.setVar("answer", "Invalid");
    }
    else {
        WMLBrowser.setVar("answer", answer);
    }
    WMLBrowser.go("#abs2");
}
```

In the absolute value example, the Nokia browser takes the word `true` and converts it from its assumed Boolean form into an integer. The Openwave browser does not do the conversion and refuses to accept `"re34"` as a parameter. These differences make testing your code thoroughly in the target browser important. Figure 8-2 shows some test shots from the Nokia and Openwave browsers.

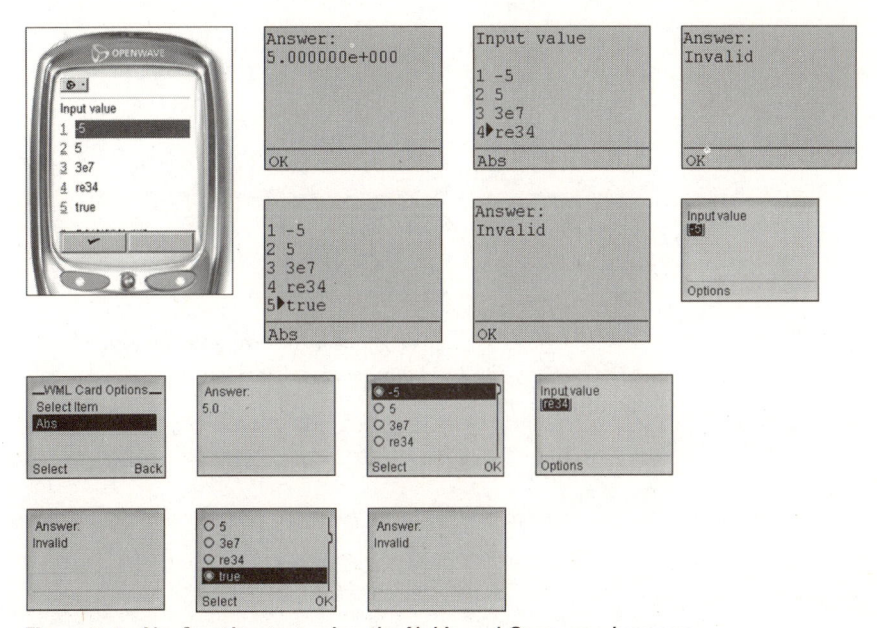

Figure 8-2: Abs function test using the Nokia and Openwave browsers

String library

The string library contains a set of functions that manipulate strings. Every string defined in WMLScript can be thought of as an array of characters with each character position being an index. The first character is set to an index of 0. The number of characters in the array defines the length of the string.

You can also add a special separator to strings so they can be separated into elements. These elements are extracted by specifying the index number and the separator. Once again, the first item in the element list has an index of 0.

Table 8-3 provides an overview of the string library functions.

Table 8-3 STRING LIBRARY FUNCTIONS

String Library Function	Description

length(*string*)	Returns the number of characters in a given string. Example:
	
	var m = "Test";
	
	var n = "";
	
	var p = 60000;
	
	var q = String.length(m); // q = 4
	
	var r = String.length(n); // r = 0
	
	var s = String.length(p); // s = 5

isEmpty(*string*)	Returns Boolean true if the string length is zero and Boolean false otherwise. Example:
	
	var m = "Test";
	
	var n = "";
	
	var p = true;
	
	var q = String.isEmpty(m); // q = false
	
	var r = String.isEmpty(n); // r = true
	
	var s = String.isEmpty(p); // s = false

charAt(*string*,index)	Returns a single character representing the specified index in the string. Example:
	
	var m = "How was your day?";
	
	var q = String.charAt(m,0); // q = "H"
	
	var r = String.charAt(m,2); // r = "w"
	
	var s = String.charAt(m,3); // s = " "
	
	var t = String.charAt(m,300); // t = ""

String Library Function	Description

subString (string, startIndex, length)	Returns a new string that is a substring of the inputted string. The substring begins at the startIndex and continues for the length specified. If the number of remaining characters is smaller than the length, the length is replaced with the number of remaining characters. The first character of a string is at index position 0, the second character at 1, and so on. Example:
	
	var m = "Where did they go?";
	
	var q = *String.subString*(m,1,5);
	
	// q = "here "
	
	var r = *String.subString*(m,0,1);
	
	// r = "W"
	
	var s = *String.subString*(m,10,3);
	
	// s = "the"

find(*string, subString*)	Returns the index of the first character in the string that matches the *subString*. If no match is found the returned value is an integer set to -1. The characters in the strings should match exactly, including characters with multiple representations. Example:
	
	var m = "I believe they walked over to the funny car under the over pass.";
	
	var q = String.find(m,"over");
	
	// q = 22
	
	var r = String.find(m,"strafe");
	
	// r = -1
	
	var s = String.find(m,"I");
	
	// s = 0

Continued

TABLE 8-3 STRING LIBRARY FUNCTIONS *(Continued)*

String Library Function	Description

`replace(`*string*`,` *oldSubString*`,` *newSubString*`)`	Returns a new string resulting from replacing all the instances of *oldSubString* with *newSubString*. The characters in the strings should match exactly, including characters with multiple representations. Example:
	
	`var m = "That's funny.  I don't see a funny car under there.";`
	
	`var q = String.replace(m,"funny","weird");`
	
	`// q = That's weird.  I don't see a weird car under there.";`

`elements(`*string*`,` *separator*`)`	Returns the number of elements in the given string separated by the indicated separator. The empty string is a valid element, so the function will never return a value less than or equal to 0. Example:
	
	`var m = "Yes, you are right.  Where did the car go?";`
	
	`var q = String.elements(m," ");`
	
	`// q = 9`

`elementAt(`*string*`,` *index*`,` *separator*`)`	Returns a string value of the *index*'th element inside the given string using the indicated separator. An index of less than 0 forces the first element to be selected. If the index is larger than the number of elements, the last element is returned. If the string is empty then the empty string is returned. Example:
	
	`var m = "Oh, look!  The car just disappeared into that tunnel.";`
	
	`var q = String.elementAt(m,0," ");`
	
	`// q = "Oh,"`
	
	`var r = String.elementAt(m,200," ");`
	
	`// r = ""`
	
	`var s = String.elementAt(m,4," ");`
	
	`// s = "car"`

String Library Function	Description

removeAt(*string*, *index*, *separator*)	Returns a new string where an element from the string has been removed using the index and separator specified. If the index is less than 0, the first element is removed; if the index is larger than the number of elements, the last element is removed. Example:
	
	var m = "Well, that sure is surprising, considering the tunnel was not there a minute ago."
	
	var q = String.removeAt(m,3," ");
	
	// q = "Well, that is surprising,
	
	// considering the tunnel was not there a // minute ago."
	
	var r = String.removeAt(m,200,",");
	
	// r = "Well, that sure is surprising"

replaceAt(*string*, *element*, *index*, *separator*)	Returns a new string wherein an element from the string is replaced using the index and separator specified. If the index is less than 0, the first element is replaced; if the index is larger than the number of elements, the last element is replaced. Example:
	
	var m = "Now what? They are going North on the road to Tuscany.";
	
	var q = String.replaceAt(m,"South",6," ");
	
	// q = "Now what? They are going South on
	
	// the road to Tuscany.";

insertAt(*string*, *element*, *index*, *separator*)	Returns a new string with the element and a separator (if needed). If the index is less than 0, the element is inserted in the first position; if the index is larger than the number of elements, the element is placed in the last position. Example: var m = "Now what? They are going North on the road to Tuscany.";

Continued

TABLE 8-3 STRING LIBRARY FUNCTIONS *(Continued)*

String Library Function	Description

	`var q = String.insertAt(m, "Stazione",10," ");`
	`// q = "Now what? They are going South on`
	`// the road to Stazione Tuscany.";`

squeeze(*string*)	Returns a string wherein any consecutive white spaces within a string have been reduced to single white space. Example:
	`var m = " apple orange   banana  ;  pear"`
	`var q = String.squeeze(m);`
	`// q =  " apple orange banana ; pear"`

trim(*string*)	Returns a string wherein all the leading or trailing white spaces have been removed. Example:
	`var m = " apple orange   banana  ;  pear"`
	`var q = String.trim(m);`
	`// q =  "apple orange banana   ;  pear"`

compare(*string1*, *string2*)	Returns a value that indicates the relationship between *string1* and *string2* based on the character codes of the native character set. The return value is -1 if *string1* is less than *string2*, 0 if *string1* is the same as *string2*, and 1 if *string1* is greater than *string2*. Example:
	`var m = "apple";`
	`var n = "pear";`
	`var q = String.compare(m,n);`
	`// q =  -1`
	`var r = String.compare("apple","Apple");`
	`// r = 1`

String Library Function	Description

toString(*value*)	Returns a string representation of the given value. This is exactly the same conversion that occurs when the WMLScript language attempts to type convert to string. Example:
	
	`var m = 25;`
	
	`var n = false;`
	
	`var p = 34.0;`
	
	`var q = String.toString(m);   // q = "25"`
	
	`var r = String.toString(n);`
	`// r = "false"`
	
	`var s = String.toString(p);`
	`// s = "34.0"`

format(format, *value*)	Returns a string that converts the value into a string using the formatting provided in the format string. For more details, see Table 8-4 and the section on formatting output. Example:
	
	`var m = String.format("giraffes: %6d",24);`
	
	`m = "giraffes:     24"`

Listings 8-2 and 8-3 and Listings 8-4 and 8-5 provide two examples that show how you can use the String functions and other library functions to create useful input verifiers that can process data locally on the mobile device. The examples check the validity of an e-mail address and verify a calendar date.

VERIFYING AN E-MAIL ADDRESS

One of the ways to verify an e-mail address is to look for the @ symbol and then check for a reasonably valid hostname, one that has at least a domain name and proper hostname format.

Listing 8-2 shows the WML code that you can use to obtain an e-mail address.

Listing 8-2: WML Code for E-mail Address Check

```
<?xml version="1.0"?>
<!DOCTYPE wml PUBLIC "-//WAPFORUM//DTD WML 1.1//EN"
"http://www.wapforum.org/DTD/wml_1.1.xml">
```

Continued

Listing 8-2 *(Continued)*

```
<wml>

  <template>
      <do type="prev">
          <prev/>
      </do>
  </template>

  <card id="first">
      <onevent type="onenterforward">
          <refresh>
              <setvar name="email" value=""/>
              <setvar name="answer" value=""/>
          </refresh>
      </onevent>
      <do type="prev" label="Check">
          <go href="stringTest.wmls#checkEmailAddress('$(email:noesc)')"/>
      </do>
      <p>Enter an email address...
          <input name="email"/>
          Answer:<br/>
          $(answer)
      </p>
  </card>
</wml>
```

Listing 8-3 shows the WMLScript code that you can use to perform the actual check:

Listing 8-3: WMLScript Code for E-mail Address Check

```
extern function checkEmailAddress(value) {

    var numberOfAddressParts = String.elements(value,"@");
    var emailName = String.elementAt(value,0,"@");
    var host = String.elementAt(value,1,"@");
    var numberOfHostParts = String.elements(host,".");

    if (emailName == "" || host == "" || numberOfAddressParts != 2 || numberOfHostParts < 2) {
            WMLBrowser.setVar("answer", "Invalid Email address");
    }
    else {
            WMLBrowser.setVar("answer", "Good Email address");
    }
    WMLBrowser.refresh();
}
```

The WMLScript code splits the e-mail address into two pieces using `String.elementAt` and then checks the number of elements in the address. It also checks the number of host pieces. In the two split pieces of the address, neither the name portion nor the host portion can be blank. Furthermore, the host portion has to contain at least two parts, and after splitting the entire address, there can only be two parts, the name and the domain. These checks are made and the appropriate value returned to the WML space.

Listing 8-3 represents the simplest level of address checking. I recommend more involved methods — such as base domain matching or MX domain matching or even absolute validation by sending the user an e-mail — to augment this solution. Figure 8-3 shows how the listing appears in a WAP browser.

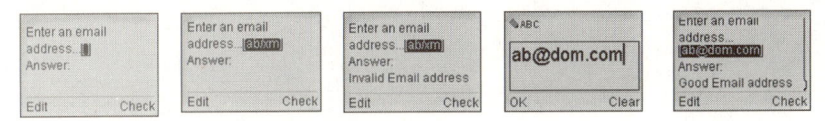

Figure 8-3: E-mail-address checker

VERIFYING A CALENDAR DATE

As I discussed in Chapter 6, you can use many different format types with the input statement. However, at times, the input cannot be fully checked for accuracy — such as in the case of the entry of dates.

If a date must be entered in WML in the format MM/DD/YYYY, where MM is a two-digit month, DD a two-digit day, and YYYY a four-digit year, you can get many bad values. In the WML format, you can partially solve the problem by putting in forced characters, and also making sure the entire string is just numbers, with a format like this:

```
format="NN\/NN\/NNNN"
```

However, this format does not preclude the entry 22/23/2000, with 22 being an invalid month. Nor does it prevent 09/31/2000, although September has only 30 days. Therefore, let's look at the checks that have to be done:

- Only numbers between 01 and 12 are valid months, and only numbers between 01 and 31 are valid day numbers.

- The month must have the correct number of days.

- February can have either 28 or 29 days, depending on whether the year it's in is a leap year.

Listing 8-4 shows the WML deck that obtains the preliminary date information.

Listing 8-4: WML Deck for Date Input

```
<?xml version="1.0"?>
<!DOCTYPE wml PUBLIC "-//WAPFORUM//DTD WML 1.1//EN"
"http://www.wapforum.org/DTD/wml_1.1.xml">

<wml>
    <template>
        <do type="prev">
            <prev/>
        </do>
    </template>

    <card id="first">
        <onevent type="onenterforward">
            <refresh>
                <setvar name="date" value=""/>
                <setvar name="answer" value=""/>
            </refresh>
        </onevent>
        <do type="prev" label="Check">
            <go href="dateCheck.wmls#main('$(date:noesc)')"/>
        </do>
        <p>Enter a date (ie. 01/22/2000) 
            <input name="date" format="NN\/NN\/NNNN"/>
            Answer:<br/>
            $(answer)
        </p>
    </card>
</wml>
```

Listing 8-5 shows the associated WMLScript code to check the date.

Listing 8-5: WMLScript Data Checker

```
extern function main(value) {

    var answer = doCheck(value);
    WMLBrowser.setVar("answer", answer);
    WMLBrowser.refresh();
}


function doCheck(value) {


    var month = Lang.parseInt(String.elementAt(value,0,"/"));
```

```
    if (month < 1 || month > 12) {
            return("Invalid Date1");
    }

    var day = Lang.parseInt(String.elementAt(value,1,"/"));
    var daySeries="31 29 31 30 31 30 31 31 30 31 30 31";

    if ((day  > String.elementAt(daySeries,month-1," ")) || day < 1)
{
            return("Invalid Date2");
    }

    var year = Lang.parseInt(String.elementAt(value,2,"/"));

    if (day == 29 && !checkLeapYear(year)) {
            return("Invalid Date3");
    }

    return("Valid Date");
}


function checkLeapYear(year) {

if ((year % 400) == 0) {
    return true;
} else if ((year % 100) == 0) {
    return false;
} else if ((year % 4) == 0) {
    return true;
} else {
    return false;
}

}
```

All the variables passed in from WML are strings, so in order to use the day, month, and year in calculations, you must convert them. You can rely on the automatic type conversion or do it yourself. I use type conversion in this example to avoid debugging errors.

The main functionality of this example is in the doCheck(...) function, which parses out the month, day, and year using the string library functions. After those are extracted, the values are compared to acceptable numbers and the date format is checked, starting with the easiest checks first and then moving on to the more involved checks.

The day given is compared to the indexed value in an array using the string library. At that point, a determination is made as to whether the year is a leap year. The leap year determinant is compared to the number of days entered for February, which concludes the WMLScript date validation.

Figure 8-4 shows what date-checking looks like in the Nokia browser.

Figure 8-4: Date-checking in the Nokia browser

FORMATTING OUTPUT

When you're working with strings or numbers, you might find it necessary to present data in a precise format. For example, rather than display 3e2, you might want to display 300. Or instead of 34.45452, you might want to display 34.45. To achieve this precision, the string library contains a `format` function.

This `format` function takes an input value, which can be any valid WMLScript type, and converts it into a string. While converting the input value into a string, it applies a formatting rule specified in a format string. The formatting rule takes the following form:

`%[width][.precision]type`

Other text is allowed around the formatting rule, but there can be only *one* formatting rule in the string. Here are some examples of formatting rules:

```
"This value: %11f"
"Answer is %4s"
"That converts to %4.2d dollars"
```

> **NOTE** The formatting rule can be situated anywhere within the string. After a formatting rule is applied to your input, it effectively becomes a string that looks like the formatting rule with your value stuck in there.

The formatting rule consists of three parts:

- *Width* — Indicates the total minimum length of the format. For example, if you want the number 300 to be represented by a string of 10 characters, the formatting rule would begin with %10 and appear as "   300".

- *Precision* — Controls the precision with which the data are presented. How the precision is interpreted depends on the format code type that follows it.

- *Format code type* — Controls how the final data are output into the string. Only three format code types exist. Table 8-4 shows how the definition of the precision changes depending on the format code type.

TABLE 8-4 FORMAT CODES AND CORRESPONDING PRECISION AND OUTPUT VALUES

Format Code	Precision Value	Output Value
d	Identifies the total number of digits in the number. The output value is padded on the left with zeros. The value is not truncated when it exceeds the precision.	Has the form [-]ddd, where ddd is one or more digits.
f	Identifies the total number of digits after the decimal point. If a decimal point appears, at least one digit appears. The default precision is 6, and a precision of 0 means that no decimal point appears.	Has the form [-]ddd where ddd is one or more digits. The number of digits before the decimal depends on the number, and the number of digits after the decimal depends on the precision.
s	Specifies the maximum number of characters to be printed. By default, all characters are printed.	Characters are printed up to the precision value. If the width is larger than the precision, the width is ignored.

The following examples show the format code types in use:

```
var m = 20;
var p = "Hello";
var q = "2.7183";
var r = String.format("Value: %3d",m);   // r = "Value:  20"
var s = String.format("%s there!",p);    // s = "Hello there!"
var t = String.format("%7.8",q);         // t = "2.7183000"
```

Remember that the width only specifies the minimum length, and that the string can end up longer than specified.

URL library

The main purpose of the functions in the URL library is to operate on a URL and extract the pieces of interest to the developer. The functions handle both absolute and relative URLs. The following URL syntax is supported:

scheme://<host>:<port>/<path>;<params>?<query>#<fragment>

Some of the parts identified here can be extracted. The library also contains other functions that handle URL escaping and loading content from URLs. Table 8-5 explains the functions supported by this library.

TABLE 8-5 URL LIBRARY FUNCTIONS

URL Library Function	Description

isValid(*URL*)	Returns true if the input URL has the right syntax; otherwise it returns false. Supports both absolute and relative URLs. Example:
	
	var m = URL.isValid("http://www.domain.com");
	
	// m = true

getScheme(*URL*)	Returns the scheme used in the input URL. Supports both absolute and relative URLs. Example:
	
	var m = URL.getScheme("http://www.domain.com");
	
	// m = "http"
	
	var n = URL.getScheme("path/to/directory");
	
	// n = ""

getHost(*URL*)	Returns the host used in the input URL. Supports both absolute and relative URLs. Example:
	
	var m = URL.getHost("http://www.domain.com");
	
	// m = "www.domain.com"

URL Library Function	Description
	`var n = URL.getHost("path/to/directory");`
	`// n = ""`
getPort (URL)	Returns the port number specified in the input URL. Supports both absolute and relative URLs. Example:
	`var m = URL.getPort("http://www.domain.com");`
	`// m = ""`
	`var n = URL.getPort("http://www.domain.com:80");`
	`// n = "80"`
getPath(URL)	Returns the path specified in the input URL. Supports both absolute and relative URLs. Example:
	`var m = URL.getPath("http://www.domain.com");`
	`// m = ""`
	`var n = URL.getPath("path/to/directory");`
	`// n = "path/to/directory"`
getParameters(URL)	Returns the parameters used in the input URL. If the URL contains no parameters an empty string is returned. Supports both absolute and relative URLs. Example:
	`var m = URL.getParameters("http://www.domain.com/code;12;24;36");`
	`// m = "12;24;36"`
getQuery(URL)	Returns the query part of the URL in the input. If there is no query part an empty string is returned. Supports both absolute and relative URLs. Example:
	`var m = URL.getQuery("http://www.domain.com/code.jsp?fname=Jane&lname=Doe");`
	`// m = "fname=Jane&lname=Doe"`

Continued

TABLE 8-5 URL LIBRARY FUNCTIONS *(Continued)*

URL Library Function	Description

getFragment(*URL*)	Returns the fragment part of the URL in the input. If there is no fragment an empty string is returned. Both absolute and relative URLs are supported by this function. Example:
	
	`var m = URL.getFragment("http://www.domain.com/main#fifth");`
	
	`// m = "fifth"`

GetBase()	Returns an absolute URL (uppercase or lowercase) without its fragment of the current WMLScript file. Example:
	
	`var m = URL.getBase();`
	
	`// m = "http://www.domain.com/a.wmls");`

getReferer()	Returns the smallest relative URL of the resource that called the current WMLScript file. If there is no referrer an empty string is returned. Example:
	
	`var m = URL.getReferer();`
	
	`// m = "first.wml";`

resolve(*baseURL, embeddedURL*)	Returns an absolute URL from the given input URLs. If the embedded URL is already absolute the returned string is the same. Example:
	
	`var i = "http://www.domain.com";`
	
	`var j = "file.wml";`
	
	`var m = URL.resolve(i,j);`
	
	`// m = "http://www.domain.com/file.wml");`

escapeString(*string*)	Returns a new version of the string in which the special characters have been replaced by their hexadecimal escape sequence (in the form %*xx*). Non-ASCII characters in the string will force an invalid response.

URL Library Function	Description

unescapeString(*string*)	Returns a new version of the string in which escape sequences have been replaced by the special characters they represent. Non-ASCII characters in the string will force an invalid response. Example:
	
	`var i = "http://www.domain.com/%40";`
	
	`var m = URL.unescapeString(i);`
	
	`// m = "http://www.domain.com/@");`

loadString (*URL*, contentType)	Returns the content referenced by the URL as a string. There must be only *one* content type, and it must be of type `text` (it can be of any subtype). If the content type does not match the loaded value, the result is `invalid`.
	
	Loading from URLs may result in scheme-specific error codes such as HTTP 404. In this case the value returned is an integer. Example:
	
	`var i = "http://www.domain.com/security.str";`
	
	`var m = URL.loadString(i,"text/x-str");`

Of all the functions listed in Table 8-5, the `escapeString()` function deserves the closest look because of some complications that may result when dealing with passing strings back and forth from WML and WMLScript. As discussed in Chapter 5, "Introducing WML," strings in URLs can be only in U.S. ASCII. Furthermore, certain special U.S. ASCII characters are not acceptable in a URL. In order for this special group of U.S. ASCII characters to be sent in a URL, they must be escaped.

Escaping the URL string means replacing all the special U.S. ASCII characters with the string %*xx*, where *xx* is the two-digit hexadecimal form of the U.S. ASCII character. The U.S. ASCII character set is a seven-bit character set, meaning that it stores each character using seven bits of data. Even though this is the case, computers work better with data in bytes, so ASCII data is stored in the computer as eight bits, with the most significant bit set to 0. Therefore the smallest U.S. ASCII character is 0000`0000 and the largest is 0111`1111.

An easy way to convert the eight bits into hexadecimal is to take the first four binary digits, find their decimal equivalent, convert the decimal equivalent to hex, and then do the same for the last four digits. Therefore, the largest ASCII character in hexadecimal format is a combination of 7 using 0111, and F using 1111 or 15. If you ever want the ASCII character represented by 7F to show up in your URL, you can replace it with %7F.

Table 8-6 lists the types of characters in a URL that must be replaced by their hexadecimal equivalents.

TABLE 8-6 RESERVED CHARACTERS IN URLS

Reserved Character	Hex or ASCII Representation of Character
Control characters	Hex 00-1F and 7F
Space	Hex 20
Reserved	; / ? : @ & = + $,
Unwise	{ } | \ ^ [ ] `
Delimiters	< > # % "

> **NOTE:** The reserved characters in Table 8-6 actually have some meaning inside a URL. For example, the question mark (?) stands for the beginning of a query string and the forward slashes (/) separate the paths. If the intended meaning of the character in the URL is as defined by such reserved meanings, it need not be escaped.

The escapeString() function takes a string and converts any of the characters in the previous table into their hexadecimal equivalents. Here are some examples:

```
extern function a() {
    var string =
"http://www.domain.com/???/@@@/panel.jsp?filename=psq:#&";
    var escapedString = URL.escapeString(string);
    WMLBrowser.setVar("escapedStuff",escapedString);
    Dialogs.alert(escaped_string);
}
// escaped url now looks like
/*
http%3A%2F%2Fwww.domain.com%2F%3F%3F%3F%2F%40%40%40%2Fstuff.asp%3Ffi
lename%3Dpsq%3A%23%26
*/
```

Even though the HTTP scheme contains colon (:) and forward slash (/) characters in valid positions, they are replaced by their equivalent hexadecimal values.

WMLBrowser library

The functions in this library are important because they provide the only interaction between WML and WMLScript. The most frequently used functions are setVar and getVar. Since the variable spaces for WML are separate from WMLScript, variables needed in WMLScript must be obtained from the WML space. Likewise, variables needed in the WML space must be set in the WML space by the WMLScript code. Other functions exist in this library and many of these give WMLScript functions navigational control over WML displays.

WMLScript cannot be called from anywhere other than a WML browser. If it is called from some other program then all the functions return invalid.

The WMLBrowser library contains the functions shown in Table 8-7.

TABLE 8-7 WMLBROWSER LIBRARY FUNCTIONS

Function	Description

getVar(name)	Returns the value of the named variable in the WML context. This is an empty string if the variable is not defined. Example:
	
	var m = WMLBrowser.getVar("ccno");
	
	// m = 4356 2236 2323 3490

setVar(name, value)	Returns true if the named variable was set successfully in the current WML context; returns false otherwise. The syntax of WML variables should be complied with and the variable's value must be legal XML CDATA. Example:
	
	var m = WMLBrowser.setVar("age","23");
	
	// m = true

go(URL)	Specifies to load the content denoted by the given URL. The functionality here is exactly the same as in a WML go task. Example:
	
	WMLBrowser.go("#second_card");
	
	// this navigates to the second card in the
	
	// calling WML file

Continued

Table 8-7 WMLBROWSER LIBRARY FUNCTIONS (Continued)

Function	Description

prev()	Specifies to load the previous URL as indicated by the navigational history. Both the prev() and go() functions override each other. Only the last prev() or go() function is honored by the WML context. Example:
	
	WMLBrowser.prev();
	
	// this navigates to the the last card in
	// the history

newContext()	Returns an empty string after clearing the WML context; has exactly the same functionality as a WML card newcontext attribute. Example: WMLBrowser.newContext(); // issues a newContext for the WML space

getCurrentCard()	Returns the smallest relative URL used to access the current WMLScript file. Example:
	
	var m = WMLBrowser.getCurrentCard();
	
	// m = "first.wml#second_card"

refresh()	Forces the WML browser context to execute the refresh task, which is equivalent to the WML refresh task. The user interface may be updated as a result of this function call. Example:
	
	WMLBrowser.refresh();
	
	// refreshes the screen in WML space based on
	// variable updates

Listing 8-6 shows an example of the some of the functions in the WMLBrowser library in use. The example uses both WML and WMLScript code.

Listing 8-6: WML Code For WMLBrowser Test

```
<?xml version="1.0"?>
<!DOCTYPE wml PUBLIC "-//WAPFORUM//DTD WML 1.1//EN"
"http://www.wapforum.org/DTD/wml_1.1.xml">
```

```
<wml>

  <template>
    <do type="prev"><prev/></do>
  </template>

  <card id="card1" title="Card #1">

        <do type="unknown" label="Count">
            <go href="WMLBrowserTest.wmls#count()"/>
        </do>

    <p>
            Enter a string...
            <input name="entry"/>
    </p>

  </card>

  <card id="card2" title="Card #2">

    <p align="center">
       The string you entered has $(count) characters in it.
    </p>

  </card>

</wml>
```

And here is the WMLScript code for the `WMLBrowserTest` function:

```
extern function count() {
         var inputString = WMLBrowser.getVar("entry");
         var charsInputString = String.length(inputString);
         WMLBrowser.setVar("count",charsInputString);

         var currentCard = WMLBrowser.getCurrentCard();
         Dialogs.alert(currentCard);
         WMLBrowser.go("#card2");
}
```

Listing 8-6 shows a WML application that simply counts the number of characters in an input string. A WML `input` element functions as an entry mechanism for a string. The WMLScript code can then be activated by the `count` command in the soft key menu. The WMLScript gets the variable entry from the WML space. It counts the number of characters in that string using the string library function `length`. The result is assigned to a variable called `charsInputString`. The next line sets a variable called `count` in the WML space.

The `getCurrentCard()` function from the WMLBrowser library is then invoked to get the card that called the current WMLScript file. The result is shown in both Listing 8-6 and Figure 8-5 by using a function from the Dialogs library. The WMLBrowser function `go` is used to navigate to the second card. This navigation is queued up to execute as soon as the WMLScript code has finished. Only a single navigation action can be queued up, so if multiple navigations are defined in the WMLScript functions, only the very last one is honored.

Figure 8-5 shows what this example looks like in a Nokia browser.

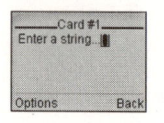

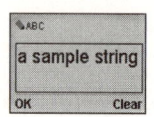

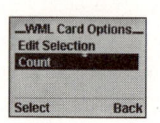

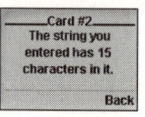

Figure 8-5: WMLBrowser test using the Nokia browser

Dialogs library

The Dialogs library is used in WMLScript to provide very simple interaction with the user. Because an application cannot be written completely in WMLScript, this library exists simply to supplement the WML capability. It is a convenient interaction mechanism because it allows for simple prompts or input without forcing the user to exit into WML and then return to WMLScript. Otherwise multiple key presses would be required.

Table 8-8 shows the functions included in the Dialogs library.

TABLE 8-8 DIALOGS LIBRARY FUNCTIONS

Function	Description
prompt(*message*, *defaultInput*)	Displays the given text message and prompts for user input and returns the user input as a string. Example: var m = "11/22/74"; var n = Dialogs.prompt("DOB ", m);
confirm(*message*, *ok*, *cancel*)	Displays the given text message and prompts for two possible inputs, `ok` and `cancel`. The function then waits for the user to select an option, and returns `true` for `ok` and `false` for `cancel`. Example:

Function	Description
| | ```
var m = Dialogs.confirm
("Is this correct?","Yes","No");
if m == false {
    // set default value
} else
{
    // continue using input value
}
``` |
| alert(*message*) | Displays the given text message to the user and waits for user confirmation. The function returns the empty string (""). Example:

`Dialogs.alert("The date is invalid");` |

Listings 8-7 and 8-8 show the Dialogs library functions in use by a calculator that uses both WML and WMLScript code.

Listing 8-7: Dialogs Library WML Test Code

```
<?xml version="1.0"?>
<!DOCTYPE wml PUBLIC "-//WAPFORUM//DTD WML 1.1//EN"
"http://www.wapforum.org/DTD/wml_1.1.xml">

<wml>
    <template>
        <do type="prev">
        </do>
    </template>
    <card id="calc">
        <do type="accept" label="Start">
            <go href="dialogsTest.wmls#main()"/>
        </do>
        <p>Welcome to the scientific calculator.<br/>
            Click start to begin or try again.
        </p>
    </card>
</wml>
```
```

Part II: Development of Services

Listing 8-8: Dialogs Library WMLScript Code

```
extern function main() {
     var checkResponse = Dialogs.confirm("This function will calculate the square of a number. Would you like to continue?","Yes","No");
       if (checkResponse == false) {
           return;
       } else {
          var input = Dialogs.prompt("Enter no. from 1-10","");
          var valueEntered = Lang.parseInt(input);
            if ((typeof valueEntered) == 4) {
               Dialogs.alert("That wasn't a number");
            } else
            {
              if (valueEntered < 1 || valueEntered > 10) {
              Dialogs.alert("It needs to be between 1 and 10");
              } else
              {
              Dialogs.alert("The square of " +
              input + " is " + valueEntered*valueEntered);
              }
           }
        }
     }
}
```

The WMLScript function in Listing 8-8 uses the `confirm()` function from the Dialogs library to determine whether the user wants to continue. If the user does not want to continue, the function ends and returns the user to WML. If the user does choose to continue, he or she can enter a number from 1 to 10. This input is obtained by using the `input` function from the Dialogs library. After some type checking of the input value, various screens are presented using the `alert()` function of the Dialogs library. In a successful case, the square of the input number is displayed.

Figure 8-6 shows how this example looks in the Nokia and Openwave browsers.

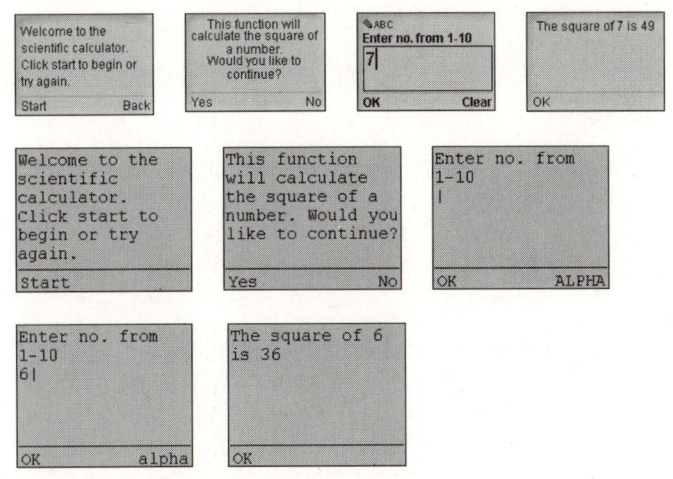

Figure 8-6: Dialogs in the Nokia and Openwave browsers

Float library

The Float library provides a set of functions that can be used to calculate floating-point operations in WMLScript. Not all phones have the necessary hardware to do floating-point operations: if the library is not supported, the entire set of functions returns `invalid`. If you want to determine whether these functions are supported, use the `float` function in the `Lang` library.

Table 8-9 explains the Float library functions.

TABLE 8-9 FLOAT LIBRARY FUNCTIONS

Function	Description

int(*value*)	Returns the integer part of the value. If the value is an integer, then the same value is returned. Example:
	
	`var m = 2.7183;`
	
	`var n = Float.int(m);   // n = 2`

floor(*value*)	Returns the greatest integer that is not *greater* than the value. If the value is an integer, then the same value is returned. Example:
	
	`var m = 2.7183;`
	
	`var n = Float.floor(m);   // n = 2`

Continued

TABLE 8-9 FLOAT LIBRARY FUNCTIONS *(Continued)*

Function	Description

ceil(*value*)	Returns the smallest integer that is not *less* than the value. If the value is an integer, then the same value is returned. Example:
	
	var m = 2.7183;
	
	var n = Float.ceil(m); // n = 3

pow (*value1*, *value2*)	Returns an approximation of the result of raising *value1* to the power of *value2*. If *value1* is a negative number, then *value2* must be an integer.
	
	var m = 2;
	
	var n = 3;
	
	var p = Float.pow(m,n); // p = 8

round(*value*)	Returns the number value that is closest to the value and is mathematically equivalent. If two integers are equally likely to be the closest, the larger value is chosen. If the value is an integer, then the same value is returned. Example:
	
	var m = 2.7183;
	
	var n = Float.round(m); // n = 3
	
	var p = -2.2183;
	
	var q = Float.round(p); // q = -2

sqrt(*value*)	Returns an approximation of the square root of the input value. Example:
	
	var m = 16.0;
	
	var n = Float.sqrt(m); // n = 4.0
	
	var m = 200.0;
	
	var n = Float.sqrt(m); // n = 14.142

maxFloat()	Returns the maximum floating-point value supported by the WMLScript interpreter. This should be the IEEE single-precision maximum, which is 3.40282347E+38. Example:
	
	var m = Float.maxFloat();
	
	// m = 3.40282347E+38

Function	Description

minFloat()	Returns the smallest non-zero floating-point value supported by the WMLScript interpreter. This should be the IEEE single-precision minimum, which is 1.17549435E-38. Example:
	
	var m = Float.minFloat();
	
	// m = 1.17549435E-38

Listings 8-9 and 8-10 provide examples of the use of several functions from this library. Listing 8-10 shows how to use a WMLScript function to calculate a quadratic root. Quadratics are functions that contain an unknown to the second power. All quadratics take the form $y=ax_{-}+bx+c$. When these equations take the form $0 = ax_{-}+bx+c$, the unknown x can be found using various methods, the easiest to program being the quadratic formula. This formula takes the form $(-b \pm \sqrt{b_{-}-4ac})/2a$, which gives the roots where $a \neq 0$.

Listing 8-9 queries for the values a, b, and c of the quadratic equation, and then passes these on to WMLScript, which returns control to WMLScript to present the two quadratic roots.

Listing 8-9: WML Code for a Quadratic Equation

```
<?xml version="1.0"?>
<!DOCTYPE wml PUBLIC "-//WAPFORUM//DTD WML 1.1//EN"
"http://www.wapforum.org/DTD/wml_1.1.xml">

<wml>
    <template>
        <do type="prev">
            <prev/>
        </do>
    </template>
    <card id="calc">
        <onevent type="onenterforward">
            <refresh>
                <setvar name="visit" value="begin"/>
            </refresh>
        </onevent>
        <do type="accept" label="Start">
            <go href="floatTest.wmls#main()"/>
```

Continued

Listing 8-9 *(Continued)*

```
            </do>
            <p>Welcome to a quadratic calculator.<br/>
                Click start to $visit.
            </p>
    </card>

    <card id="second">

            <p>The quadratic you entered has the following
roots:<br/>
                $roots
            </p>

    </card>

</wml>
```

Listing 8-10 shows the WMLScript code for the functions needed to take in user input and calculate the two roots.

Listing 8-10: WMLScript Quadratic-Function Code

```
extern function main() {
    var checkResponse = Dialogs.confirm("This function will calculate the roots of a quadratic. Would you like to continue?","Yes","No");
        if (checkResponse == false) {
            return;
        } else {

            var a, b, c;

            a = getInput("a");
            if (a == "Try Again") return;

            b = getInput("b");
            if (b == "Try Again") return;

            c = getInput("c");
            if (c == "Try Again") return;

            var roots = calcRoots(a,b,c);
            WMLBrowser.setVar("roots",roots);
```

```
            WMLBrowser.go("#second");
    }
}

function getInput(value) {

    var input = Dialogs.prompt("Enter " + value + " of
ax^2+bx+c","");
    var valueEntered = Lang.parseInt(input);

    if (typeof valueEntered != 0) {
            Dialogs.alert("That was not a number.  Try again.");
            WMLBrowser.setVar("visit","try Again");
            WMLBrowser.refresh();
            return "Try Again";
    }
    WMLBrowser.setVar("visit","begin");
    return valueEntered;   // is a number

}

function calcRoots(a,b,c) {

    var answer1 = (-b + Float.sqrt(Float.pow(b,2)-4*a*c))/(2*a);
    var answer2 = (-b - Float.sqrt(Float.pow(b,2)-4*a*c))/(2*a);

    return answer1 + "," + answer2;

}
```

Figure 8-7 illustrates how the Quadratic function code calculations look in the Nokia browser.

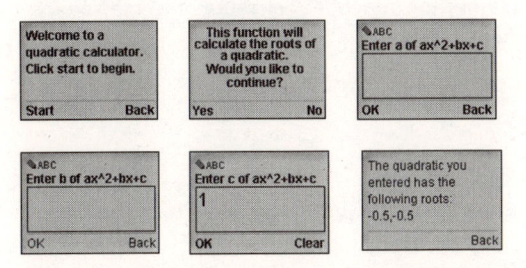

Figure 8-7: Float library test using the Nokia browser

Crypto library

The Crypto library is new in WAP 1.2 and contains only one function, the `signText` function. The syntax for this function is as follows:

signedString = signText (stringToSign, *options*, *keyIdtype*, *keyId*)

where *options* can be (Note: these can be ORed together):

- 0 – No options
- 1 – Include `stringToSign` in the result
- 2 – Include key's hash in the result
- 4 – Include certificate URL in the result

where *keyIdType* can be:

- 0 – No key identifier indicated; use anything available
- 1 – An SHA-1 hash of a user public key is specified in `keyId`
- 2 – An SHA-1 hash of a trusted CA public key is specified in `keyId`

and where *keyed*, which is the last parameter in the list, contains the 20-byte SHA-1 hash if applicable.

The `signText` function returns a base-64 encoded signed string that can be sent to a Web server and stored for accountability purposes. When using this function, be sure to use keys that are different from WTLS keys.

> **Note:** Because the string is presented to the user, the function can be cancelled, in which case it will return the error message `error:userCancel`. The function may not find a valid key to sign the string with. In any case where a valid key is not found for any reason, the function will return the message `error:noCert`. Any other errors will result in an `invalid` type being returned.

The `signText` function was added to WMLScript to compensate for the lack of any application-level nonrepudiation mechanism in WAP. Although the WTLS protocol provides some mechanisms, they are not transaction-specific.

The `signText` function displays the string of text to be signed, asking the user for confirmation. If the user acknowledges, the browser signs the text using a key and sends it to the Web server. A Web server can use this signed document for accountability purposes related to some transaction. For example, if money were to be moved from a Swiss bank account, www.swissbank.com might ask for the transfer transaction to be signed as evidence of the transaction.

The following code provides an example of the `signText` function:

```
var confirmed = Crypto.signText("Transfer $2000 into account no.
2345 3439 0658 0982", 0, 1,
"\x98\x11\xC4\x12\x13\x91\xE8\xB1\xA1\x28\xD9\x12\x39\x51\xE2
\x15\x16\x29\xC1\xE7");
```

The previous string is presented to the user and upon positive acknowledgement the value is signed using the signature whose SHA-1 hash is shown. The signature is found either in the URL or stored in the phone or some other valid source. The algorithm for the signature is either PKCS #1 or X.9.62, depending on the WTLS settings.

> **NOTE:** As of this writing, there are no simulators or actual phones that support this function.

Proprietary Libraries

As it currently stands, the WMLScript definition discusses how new WMLScript libraries can be added by any developer. However, the numbering authority of WAP, WINA (Wireless Internet Numbering Authority), has not identified a process or application by means of which these libraries may be submitted and accepted. This has not stopped manufacturers from adding their own libraries. Both Nokia and Openwave have added new proprietary libraries to their WAP simulators to address the lack of debugging functions.

The Nokia Debug library

I have seen older Nokia toolkits that include a Debug library. Table 8-10 shows what functions are supported.

TABLE 8-10 NOKIA DEBUG LIBRARY FUNCTIONS

Function	Description
closeFile()	Closes an open debugging file. Example: Debug.openFile("c:\testing.txt", "w"); Debug.printLn("Variable value is" + x); Debug.closeFile();
openFile(filename, mode)	Opens a file for debugging purposes. The modes include "a" for appending, "r" for reading only, and "w" for writing or killing an existing file and starting over. Example: Debug.openFile("c:\testing.txt", "a"); Debug.printLn("Variable value is" + x); Debug.closeFile();
printLn(string)	Writes to an open debugging file. Example: Debug.openFile("c:\testing.txt", "a"); Debug.printLn("Variable value is" + x); Debug.closeFile();

Although these functions are useful for debugging, you can supplement them with the Dialogs.alert or WMLBrowser.setVar(" "," ") functions, which might also be useful for debugging.

The Openwave Console library

Table 8-11 lists the debugging functions included in the Openwave library.

TABLE 8-11 OPENWAVE CONSOLE LIBRARY

Function	Description
print(string)	Writes text to a debug window. Example: Console.print("Variable value is" + x);

Function	Description
printLn(*string*)	Writes text to a debug window *and* inserts a newline character after it. Example: `Console.printLn("Variable value is" + x);`

As of this writing, the Openwave SDK and simulator is composed of a simulator window and a debug window. This debug window is a continuously scrolling DOS window that is useful to the developer for dumping variable values, activity history, and many other important parameters. The Console library simply prints out the text string into this debug window. Figure 8-8 shows an example of the Openwave Console library.

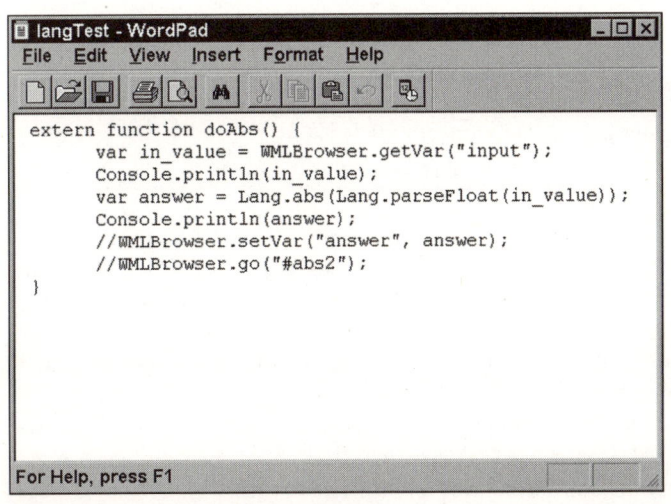

```
extern function doAbs() {
    var in_value = WMLBrowser.getVar("input");
    Console.println(in_value);
    var answer = Lang.abs(Lang.parseFloat(in_value));
    Console.println(answer);
    //WMLBrowser.setVar("answer", answer);
    //WMLBrowser.go("#abs2");
}
```

Figure 8-8: Openwave Console library

Building a WMLScript Credit-Card Verifier

This section provides a complex example using the libraries and functions and keywords that I introduced both in this chapter and in Chapter 7, "Programming with WMLScript." In this example, I show you how to build a credit-card verifier using WMLScript and WML. Although credit-card numbers may appear to be a series of random numbers, actually they all contain a set of check digits that can be verified by known algorithms.

Credit-card numbers vary in numerical size, check algorithm used, and start digits. These variables combined can make a check of a number's potential validity very reliable. Table 8-12 shows the major credit cards and important parameters that can be used to determine whether they are valid.

TABLE 8-12 CREDIT-CARD NUMBER PARAMETERS

Credit Card	Prefix	Length	Algorithm
MasterCard	51-55	16	mod 10
Visa	4	13, 16	mod 10
Amex	34, 37	15	mod 10
Discover	6011	16	mod 10
Carte Blanche	30, 36, 38	14	mod 10
Diners Club	30, 36, 38	14	mod 10
enRoute	2014, 2149	15	Not restricted
JCB	3088, 3096, 3112, 3158, 3337, 3528	16	mod 10

The prefix parameter in Table 8-12 is the first few digits in the credit-card number. Notice how none of the credit-card companies have overlapping prefixes (Carte Blanche and Diners Club are issued by the same credit-card company). The length parameter indicates how long the credit-card number is. The algorithm indicates how the number can be verified.

As an example, let me show you how the mod 10 algorithm would work, if you were given the credit-card number 5412 3456 7890 0119. First, beginning with the right side, multiply every second number by 2. This results in:

(10)4(2)2(6)4(10)6(14)8(18)0(0)1(2)9

Now add the digits of the answers you obtained by multiplying by 2. The result of this operation is:

(1)4(2)2(6)4(1)6(5)8(9)0(0)1(2)9

Next, find the sum of all the digits. This is 60. Since 60 is divisible by 10, the credit-card number supplied passes the mod 10 test. Furthermore, the number begins with 51, which is the prefix for MasterCard, and it has the right number of digits. Therefore, it would be fair to say that it is a potentially valid MasterCard number.

Listing 8-11 provides an example of a simple verifier. Every credit-card entry also includes an expiration date.

Listing 8-11: WML Code for a Credit-Card Verifier

```
<?xml version="1.0"?>
<!DOCTYPE wml PUBLIC "-//WAPFORUM//DTD WML 1.1//EN"
"http://www.wapforum.org/DTD/wml_1.1.xml">

<wml>
    <template>
        <do type="prev">
            <prev/>
        </do>
    </template>
    <card id="entry" title="Credit Card Verifier">
        <onevent type="onenterforward">
            <refresh>
                <setvar name="credit" value=""/>
            </refresh>
        </onevent>

        <do type="prev" label="Check">
            <go href="creditCardTest.wmls#main()"/>
        </do>
        <p>Please enter a credit card number<br/>
            <input name="credit" format="*N" title="Credit Card No."/>
        </p>
    </card>

    <card id="second">

        <p>The credit card number you entered is $(valid)
        </p>

    </card>

</wml>
```

Listing 8-12 provides the WMLScript code for verifying the credit-card numbers. The code is structured to operate like a sieve: it moves through an algorithm of checks, quickly identifying card numbers that do not fit a known scheme.

Listing 8-12: WMLScript Code for Credit-Card Verifier

```
extern function main() {

//get inputted cc number
     var ccno = WMLBrowser.getVar("credit");
//check length
     if (checkLength(ccno) == false) { endFunction(false); }
//check digits
     if (checkDigits(ccno) == false) { endFunction(false); }
//check mod 10
     if (checkAlgorithm(ccno) == false) { endFunction(false); }
//everything went well
     endFunction(true);
}

function checkLength(ccno) {
     var length = String.length(ccno);
     if (length > 16 || length < 13) {
          return false;
     } else {
          WMLBrowser.setVar("cclength",length);
          return true;
     }
}

function checkDigits(ccno) {

     // This is a table that contains the following for each cc,
     // no. of elements, type of card, valid prefixes
     var cc_table =  "2,VISA,4,";
     cc_table += "6,MasterCard,51,52,53,54,55,";
     cc_table += "3,Amex,34,37,";
     cc_table += "4,Diners Club,30,36,38,";
     cc_table += "2,Discover,6011,";
     cc_table += "3,enRoute,2014,2149,";
     cc_table += "7,JCB,3088,3096,3112,3158,3337,3528";

     //pick up first count
     //check prefix and if good get out with true
     var pointer_end =
Lang.parseInt(String.elementAt(cc_table,0,",")) + 1;
     var pointer_start = 0;

     for (var j = 1; j < 8; j++) {
```

```
            for (var i = pointer_start + 2; i < pointer_end; i++) {
                var prefix = String.elementAt(cc_table,i,",");
                var stuff = String.subString(ccno, 0,
String.length(prefix));

                if (String.subString(ccno, 0, String.length(prefix))
== prefix) {
                    WMLBrowser.setVar("cctype",
String.elementAt(cc_table,pointer_start + 1,","));
                    return true;
                }
                //Dialogs.alert(i + "," + prefix + "," +
pointer_start + "," + pointer_end);
            }
            pointer_start = pointer_end;
            pointer_end =
Lang.parseInt(String.elementAt(cc_table,pointer_start,",")) +
pointer_start + 1 ;

    }

    return false;
}

function endFunction(input) {

    var bad = "not valid.";
    var good1 = "a valid ";
    var good2 = " number";

    if (input == false) {

    //clear the cctype variable out
    WMLBrowser.setVar("cctype","");
    WMLBrowser.setVar("valid",bad);

    } else {

    WMLBrowser.setVar("valid",good1 + WMLBrowser.getVar("cctype") +
good2);
    }
    WMLBrowser.go("#second");
    Lang.exit("");
}
```

Continued

Listing 8-12 *(Continued)*

```
extern function checkAlgorithm(input) {

    var reference_table = "0, 2, 4, 6, 8, 1, 3, 5, 7, 9";
    var string_length = String.length(input);
    var sum = 0;

    //cycle thru every second character from the right and replace with character from ref table
    for (var i = string_length-1; i > -1; i--) {
        var character = String.charAt(input,i);
        if ((i % 2) == 1) {
            sum = Lang.parseInt(character) + sum;
        } else
        {
            sum = Lang.parseInt(String.elementAt(reference_table,Lang.parseInt(character),",")) + sum;
        }
    }

    if (sum % 10 == 0) {
        return true;
    } else
    {
        return false;
    }
}
```

The code is structured so that it does the most costly checks near the end. Figure 8-9 shows how the code runs in a Nokia browser.

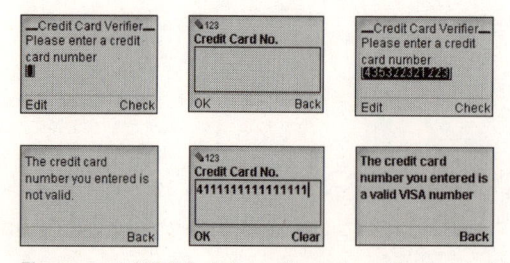

Figure 8-9: WMLScript credit-card verifier in the Nokia browser

Summary

In this chapter I covered some advanced features of the WMLScript language, including a detailed examination of functions, a look at pragmas, and a brief overview of the WMLScript virtual machine. This should round out your knowledge of WMLScript and prepare you for the much more advanced WMLScript functionality to come in Chapter11, "Combining Web and Telephony Using WTA."

- After a look at WMLScript advanced features, I described the set of WMLScript libraries available to your applications. These libraries are critical to WMLScript programs since very little can be done with the standard WMLScript keywords. The most important of the libraries is the WMLBrowser set, which forms the basis for interaction with the WML space.

- I described some proprietary functions and provided a complex example that uses a large number of the library functions introduced in this chapter.

At this point you should be able to write some compelling WMLScript applications that harness the full power of client-side WAP. In Chapter 9, "Dynamic WAP Services," I look at the most popular server-side scripting languages and how you can use them to create WAP applications.

Chapter 9

Dynamic WAP Services

IN THIS CHAPTER

- Creating dynamic services using ASP (Active Server Pages)
- Delivering dynamic content with Java servlets
- Using JSP (Java Server Pages) to deliver content
- Using PHP (Personal Home Page Hypertext) to deliver content
- Writing dynamic code with Perl CGI
- Using CFML (ColdFusion Markup Language)

IN WRITING COMPUTER PROGRAMS FOR PCs, one can quickly generate the most rudimentary form of program construction, assembly, or machine code. This type of code can be abstracted even more to higher-level languages such as C, C++, Java, FORTRAN, COBOL, and so on. Such languages contain many constructs to make logical decisions and the ability to input and output data of many different types.

In the case of the WWW, the argument is that you are constructing a system for allowing users to navigate resources using hyperlinks. This is simply achieved by allowing developers to code straight text pages with hyperlinks in them. Inevitably, these pages have become more complex, such that not only is straight text sent back and forth but additional headers that contain control information are sent as well. This header information assists in forming the user interaction, for example, for controlling stale content, setting up the browser identification, identifying a user's domain, identifying where the user is coming from, and so on.

Next, the content information that is combined with WML tags to produce WML is not always so static in the real world. Consider the case of a stock listing, news feed, or the temperature today, or the exchange rate. These values change at discrete periods depending on the sensors. For example, stocks change continuously during trading hours, but discretely depending on how good your update feed is. Or exchange rates, change continuously, however, most consumers will accept a daily figure. Such content can be pulled from databases and delivered to users. However, the logic required to pull this content requires writing programs very similar to those written using high level languages described in the first paragraph. In the case of the Web, the software vendors have chosen to build more Web-friendly languages that have an even higher level of abstraction, like Perl CGI, Java, JSP, ASP, and CFML. Each of the software vendors has created these languages to assist developers of the Web. For example, Perl CGI is an outgrowth of a language that most system administrators use for UNIX machines, Java and JSP come from those who like its portability, ASP for users of Microsoft Windows IIS, and CFML for those who like ColdFusion's ease of database content extraction.

Dynamic Web sites and applications are the guiding forces on the WWW, in the constant struggle to provide more efficient services in order to get and retain the users attention and to provide effective interfaces. Because developers have to address users in such a way as to add value to their visits, this forces developers to dynamically present the users with a highly personalized path to the data that the users are looking for. The dynamic programming and scripting languages discussed in this chapter are the major languages in use throughout the Web. Therefore, Web developers from all walks of the Web should be able to pick up the sections that interest them and quickly examine the changes they must make in order to serve up WAP applications.

Dynamic services become even more important with WAP as compared to PC browsers because many activities, such as reading headers and responding to headers in different ways, are hard to do statically. Furthermore, WAP users require a greater degree of personalization than Web users. This is mostly because the WAP services are costing the users money and are hard to read because of the limited screen size and because entering information and setting up the services are difficult. So overall, the right information has to be available *above* the fold; otherwise your service will not get used.

Active Server Pages

One of the most popular ways to output dynamic pages from a Web server is to use Active Server Pages (ASP), a dynamic scripting environment available on Microsoft servers. ChiliSoft has created alternative versions for adding this capability to other types of servers, such as Linux, but these versions are not as widely used.

ASP is an embedded language, and like all the languages in this chapter is focused on returning HTML output from the server to the client browser. By embedded, I mean that the language is placed in and around the HTML. The file is then renamed and given an extension of .asp. The server then passes any requests for the ASP file to the ASP engine first, which interprets the code. Then the output, with the ASP code sections executed and the results inserted into the HTML, is sent back to the client browser. Figure 9-1 shows a diagram of the ASP architecture.

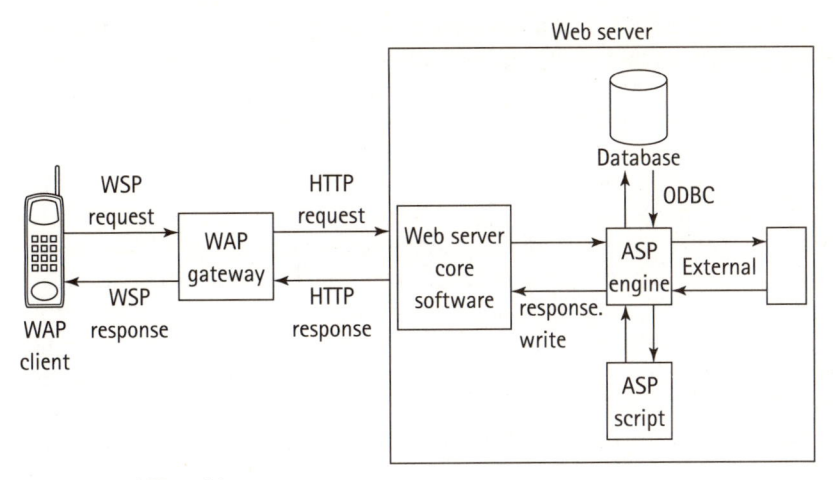

Figure 9-1: ASP architecture

ASP is pretty flexible – it supports development in JScript, PerlScript, and VBScript, the most popular format being VBScript.

Although ASP and the other programming languages in this chapter were designed to output HTML code, you can make a slight modification to the header output to send WML instead. In order to do this, add the following line to the top of the ASP file:

```
<% Response.ContentType = "text/vnd.wap.wml" %>
```

The following example illustrates how you can use ASP to output some WML code. In this example, a date is presented to the user:

```
<%
Response.ContentType = "text/vnd.wap.wml"
%>

<?xml version="1.0"?>
<!DOCTYPE wml PUBLIC "-//WAPFORUM//DTD WML 1.1//EN"
 "http://www.wapforum.org/DTD/wml_1.1.xml">

<wml>
<card id="time">
    <p>
    <% =Now() %>
    </p>
</card>
</wml>
```

The ASP code is everything contained between the tags <% and %>; the rest of the code is standard WML. Some of the code outputs items to the WML response. Other parts are directives to the ASP engine to execute some logic. You can use all of the ASP-supported functions when outputting WML code.

ASP request object

ASP is much simpler to use than other dynamic scripting languages. You do not have to understand many of the lower-level protocol functionalities, of either HTTP or any operating-system features you may be accessing. This decreases the learning curve at the beginning, but when you reach the stage where you need to debug effectively or optimize sites, the learning curve is quite steep with the ASP/IIS or ASP/PWS combination.

ASP enables programmers to access HTTP functionality and write complex applications using objects. Special objects are available with ASP that you do not need to declare before use. These special objects are part of the ASP object model. These objects hide many of the low-level details surrounding the HTTP protocol and Web server. The objects are presented in a manner familiar to programmers who understand the Component Object Model (COM). The objects have methods, properties, collections, and events like any standard Microsoft COM object. The HTTP protocol is a request/response protocol. And so, in the spirit of simplification, one of these special objects, the Request object, extracts useful information from requests. Table 9-1 shows the request objects collections.

The only Request object property is TotalBytes, which specifies the total number of bytes the client is sending in the body of the request. Note that this property is read-only.

The only Request object method is BinaryRead, which retrieves data sent to the server from the client as part of a POST request.

TABLE 9-1 REQUEST COLLECTIONS

Collection	Description
ClientCertificate	The values of fields stored in the client certificate that is sent in the HTTP request.
Cookies	The values of cookies sent in the HTTP request.
Form	The values of form elements in the HTTP request body.
QueryString	The values of variables in the HTTP query string.
ServerVariables	The values of predetermined environment variables.

As you can see, the `Request` object enables developers to obtain most of the HTTP request data. Consider a case wherein the following is the URL for a GET request:

```
query.asp?user="test"&password="jxyqz"
```

The username and password can be parsed out of the `querystring` collection as follows:

```
<% =request.querystring("user") %> and <% =request.querystring("password") %>
```

The preceding code would output the values to the HTML page to be returned to the client browser.

Response object

The second important object is the `Response` object, which is used to create the headers and content that comprise the data sent to the browser. The script builds the response mostly using this object. The data in the response can be sent all at once or in pieces.

Tables 9-2 and 9-3 show the `Response` object properties and methods. The only `Response` collection is `Cookies`, which enables you to set cookie values.

TABLE 9-2 RESPONSE PROPERTIES

Property	Description
Buffer	Indicates whether page output is buffered.
CacheControl	Determines whether proxy servers can cache the output generated by ASP.
Charset	Appends the name of the character set to the content-type header.
ContentType	Specifies the HTTP content type for the response.
Expires	Specifies the length of time before a page cached on a browser expires.
ExpiresAbsolute	Specifies the date and time on which a page cached on a browser expires.

Continued

TABLE 9-2 RESPONSE PROPERTIES *(Continued)*

Property	Description
IsClientConnected	Indicates whether the client has disconnected from the server.
Pics	Adds the value of a PICS label to the pics-label field of the response header.
Status	Indicates the value of the status line returned by the server.

TABLE 9-3 RESPONSE METHODS

Method	Description
AddHeader	Allows you to add your own HTTP response header and corresponding custom value.
AppendToLog	Adds a string to the end of the Web-server log entry for this request.
BinaryWrite	Writes the given information to the current HTTP output without any character-set conversion.
Clear	Erases any buffered HTML output.
End	Stops all storage of information in the response buffer and sends the current contents of the buffer to the client.
Flush	Sends buffered output immediately.
Redirect	Sends a redirect message to the browser, causing it to attempt to connect to a different URL.
Write	Writes a variable to the current HTTP output as a string.

THE RESPONSE.WRITE() METHOD

One of the important methods here is the `response.write()` method, which has the shortcut "=". This method is used in ASP to construct part of the response. Remember, though, that you could construct part of the response simply by placing text outside the <% %> symbols. The technique used depends on the ASP programmer and the performance characteristics of mixing `response.write` with plain text. For example,

```
<p> <% =request.servervariables("stuff") %>
```

is equivalent to:

```
response.write "<p>" & request.servervariables("stuff") & "</p>"
```

A NOTE ON BUFFERS

As I mentioned earlier, it is possible to send all the response data at one time, or to send them in pieces. Holding onto data and sending them to the browser in pieces is known as *buffering*, and it is used to improve server performance at the cost of user-perceived delay. Programmatically, this means that you can store output in the buffer until you either reach the end of the ASP file (in which case the buffer is sent automatically), or a program condition is met. If the program condition requires that the page be abandoned for whatever reason, the buffer is simply discarded and the user is none the wiser.

Buffering is off in the default configuration of IIS 3.0 but turned on in IIS 4.0 and later. If buffering is off, each line is sent to the browser as soon as it is written to the response stream. You can also control buffering from within an ASP page by using the following syntax:

```
<% response.buffer = true|false %>
```

The remaining special objects deal with Microsoft Web server additions to the HTTP protocol. They are the `Session` object, `Application` object, `Server` object, and `ror` object.

The Session object is used to either store information about the current session with the user or to store specific variables that the developer would like to track in association with a specific user. All the session information is casually presented in this object but the object is actually using cookies to keep track of these variables. Unfortunately, the use of cookies is limited at this time to the Openwave platform where they are actually maintained at the server instead of the client browser as on PCs. If you're using another platform, for example, Nokia, you will have to use different solutions until the WAP standard defines how cookies will work in the WAP framework.

The Application object stores variables at the server, and these special objects not only have persistence for the duration that the application is running on the server but also are global in scope. If any code in any module changes the contents of an Application object, that change is instantly visible to all other users of the application. Application objects should therefore be used with due caution. Application objects are usually used to store information that is relatively static, such as the file path to a particular database, which can be initialized with a value when the application is started and then simply referred to (read only) from the remaining decks in the application.

The Server object allows you access to the server itself. The most important method of the Server object is the `CreateObject` method, which enables you to create instances of server-side components, such as database connections and recordsets (as demonstrated in the next section), and even custom-built Dynamic Link Libraries (DLLs) on the Web server machine.

There is also an `ASPError` object, which traps errors.

Processing user input with ASP

You can obtain user data in ASP by using the `Request` object. It can gather data from both the GET and POST methods from the clients. Listing 9-1 shows an application a customer is using to find out when a flight is due in.

Listing 9-1: ASPCode to POST Data

```
<%
Response.ContentType = "text/vnd.wap.wml"
%>

<?xml version="1.0"?>
<!DOCTYPE wml PUBLIC "-//WAPFORUM//DTD WML 1.1//EN"
"http://www.wapforum.org/DTD/wml_1.1.xml">

<wml>

    <card id="first" title="Airlines">
    <do type="accept" label="Next">
        <go href="#second"/>
    </do>

        <p>
            Please select the airline:
            <select name="airline">
                <option value="Delta">Delta</option>
                <option value="Northwest">Northwest</option>
                <option value="American">American</option>
                <option value="United">United</option>
                <option value="TWA">TWA</option>
            </select>
        </p>
    </card>

    <card id="second">
        <do type="accept" label="Find">
            <go href="find_flight.asp" method="post">
                <postfield name="airline" value="$airline"/>
                <postfield name="flight" value="$flight"/>
            </go>
```

```
        </do>
        <p>What is the flight number?
            <input name="flight" format="*N"/>
        </p>
    </card>
</wml>
```

The user will need to input the airline and the flight number in this sample application. In a real application you may want to give your users many more options for finding flights, depending on the extent of your database.

In this case, the flight number and airline are input and parsed and returned as a WML file using the ASP `Response` object. The `postfield` elements inside the `go` element build the required POST request and entity. The variables `flight` and `airline` are sent inside this entity.

By pressing the Accept key the user sends the flight number and airline name to the server, and the server-side code will simply return them to the user and show them in the WML browser via the code shown in Listing 9-2.

Listing 9-2: Return POSTed Data to Browser

```
<%
Response.ContentType = "text/vnd.wap.wml"
%>

<?xml version="1.0"?>
<!DOCTYPE wml PUBLIC "-//WAPFORUM//DTD WML 1.1//EN"
    "http://www.wapforum.org/DTD/wml_1.1.xml">

<wml>

    <card id="first" title="Airlines and Flight Response">
        <p>
            You entered <%=Request.Form("airline")%> flight
No. <%
            =Request.Form("flight")%>
        </p>
    </card>

</wml>
```

The POST data are extracted from the request entity with the `response.form` collection. The data can be stored either in variables or in a database, or simply returned to the user, as is the case in the previous example.

The previous example could have been modified such that the data were sent in the URL as part of the GET request. The `go` element would look like this:

```
<go href="find_flight.asp" method="get">
  <postfield name="airline" value="$airline"/>
  <postfield name="flight" value="$flight"/>
</go>
```

You could leave the `method="get"` out of the code if you want to build the string yourself, like so:

```
<go href="find_flight.asp?airline=$airline&amp;flight=$flight"/>
```

This works if the default method issued is a GET. Variables are then obtained by using the `request.querystring` collection.

Listing 9-3 shows the retrieval of variables set by a URL string.

Listing 9-3: Collecting and Displaying Data from GET Method

```
<%
Response.ContentType = "text/vnd.wap.wml"
%>

<?xml version="1.0"?>
<!DOCTYPE wml PUBLIC "-//WAPFORUM//DTD WML 1.1//EN"
"http://www.wapforum.org/DTD/wml_1.1.xml">

<wml>

    <card id="first" title="Airlines and Flight Response">
        <p>
            You entered <%=Request.Querystring("airline")%>
flight No. <%
            =Request.QueryString("flight")%>
        </p>
    </card>

</wml>
```

Using the variables to initiate a query

The ASP example shown in Listing 9-1 simply picked up the variables and sent them back to the browser in a response. What would be really useful is searching a database that contains the flights and airline numbers and returning an estimated arrival time.

Table 9-4 shows an example of possible search results.

Table 9-4 FLIGHT-INFO TABLE

Flight	Airline	Arrival Time	Gate No.
7991	Delta	4:01 pm	A11
2	Northwest	2:37 pm	B23
76	TWA	1:34 pm	C32
324	United	2:15 pm	F15
987	United	3:10 pm	G19
8117	Delta	5:19 pm	A1
423	Northwest	3:22 pm	E9
778	American Airlines	3:45 pm	A4
4707	Delta	1:20 pm	A2

Listing 9-4 shows the ASP code that searches through the database and finds the requested information.

Listing 9-4: ASP Code to Search Flight Database

```
<%@ Language=VBScript %>

<%
Response.ContentType = "text/vnd.wap.wml"
%>

<?xml version="1.0"?><!DOCTYPE wml PUBLIC "-//WAPFORUM//DTD WML
1.1//EN" "http://www.wapforum.org/DTD/wml_1.1.xml">
<wml>

<%
    Dim conn, rs
    Set conn = Server.CreateObject("ADODB.Connection")
    Set rs   = Server.CreateObject("ADODB.Recordset")
    conn.open "DRIVER={Microsoft Access Driver (*.mdb)};DBQ=" &
Server.MapPath("flights.mdb") & ";"
%>
```

Continued

Listing 9-4 *(Continued)*

```
<card id="check" title="Flight Results">
    <p>
    <%
        Dim sqlQuery
        sqlQuery = "SELECT * FROM Flights WHERE flight='" &
Request.Form("flight") & "' AND airline='" & Request.Form("airline")
& "'"
        Set rs = conn.Execute(sqlQuery)

        if not rs.EOF then
            Session("flight") = Request.Form("flight")
            Session("airline") = Request.Form("airline")
            Response.Write "<strong>That flight is due in at " &
rs("arrival") & " at gate no." & rs("gate") & "</strong>"
        else
                Response.Write "The flight information you entered could
not be found in our database"
            Response.Write "<do type='accept' label='Retry'>"
            Response.Write "    <go href='flight.asp'/>"
            Response.Write "</do>"
        end if
        rs.Close
    %>
    </p>
</card>
</wml>

<%
    conn.Close
%>
```

Adding additional headers and cookies

Adding other headers in ASP is the same as writing any other output to the client. You insert them by identifying the proper string, as shown in the following example:

```
Response.AddHeader("Set-cookie: name=John");
```

You can add any header to the response output this way. Remember that if the actual WML has been sent to the browser, additional headers cannot be added. Typically, data is buffered at the server until all the headers have been set.

Java Servlets

Java servlets are another popular means of delivering dynamic content to browsers. *Servlets* are small modules written in the Java programming language and compiled into Java byte codes. The servlet architecture is different from others in that the Web server requires special engines in order to understand where to send the servlet file for interpretation. Some advanced eCommerce Web servers support servlets natively; others need an engine installed. The portability of the Java servlet code is a big advantage of this dynamic scripting format. Figure 9-2 illustrates the Java servlets architecture.

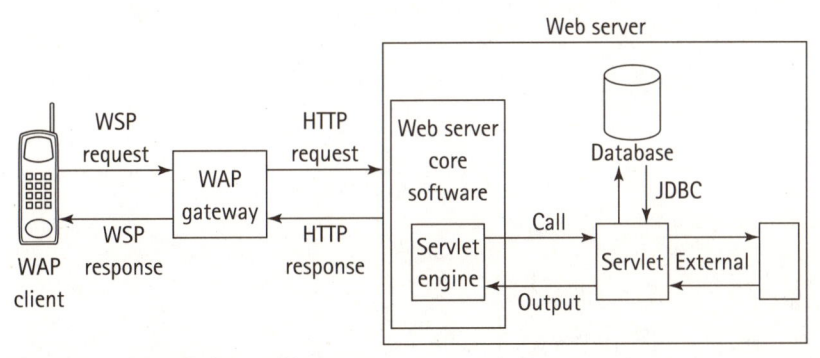

Figure 9-2: Java servlets architecture

The relevant classes and interfaces for servlets are contained in the `javax.servlet` and the `javax.servlet.http` packages. The main methods used are contained in the Java servlet API in the generic servlet interface in the `javax.servlet` package. When the servlet interface is implemented, the `HttpServlet` class then inherits from the `javax.servlet.http` package. `HttpServlet` inherits methods and attributes from the Java servlet class so all of the methods and attributes of the superclasses are also available.

When a browser calls a Java servlet, the servlet is given two objects: the request and the response, `ServletRequest` and `ServletResponse`. As I explained previously, the `ServletRequest` deals with parameters the browser sends to the server, and the `ServletResponse` builds a response that is sent back to the browser.

Listing 9-5 provides an example of a servlet that shows the current date and time in a WML deck.

Listing 9-5: Java Servlet Code to Display Time

```java
import java.io.*;
import javax.servlet.*;
import javax.servlet.http.*;
import java.util.*;

public class DateServlet extends HttpServlet {

    public void doGet(HttpServletRequest request, HttpServletResponse response)

throws ServletException, IOException
{

PrintWriter out;

response.setContentType("text/vnd.wap.wml");

out = response.getWriter();

out.println("<?xml version=\"1.0\"?>");

out.println("<!DOCTYPE wml PUBLIC \"-//WAPFORUM//DTD WML 1.1//EN\"");
out.println("\"http://www.wapforum.org/DTD/wml_1.1.xml\">");

out.println("<wml>");
out.println("<card id=\"time\">");
out.println("<p>");

now = new Date();

out.println(now);
out.println("</p>");
out.println("</card>");
out.println("</wml>");

out.close();

}

}
```

The servlet shown in Listing 9-5 inherits from `HttpServlet`. It then implements the `HttpServlet` interface method `doGet` and handles the possible exceptions. The `doGet` method is presented with both a `Request` and `Response` object. The `Request` contains the details of the query. The `Response` is then built to be sent to the WAP client. One of the first important elements of the code is that the content type of the WML code is set. You do this by using the following line:

```
response.setContentType("text/vnd.wap.wml");
```

Then the regular `print` and `println` methods of the `PrintWriter` object are used to send the response to standard output. The `PrintWriter` object comes from the java.io package. In the code, the `getWriter` method creates a reference to an object that can be used to output the response. The `close` method of this object is used to send the data to the WAP browser.

Processing user input

Servlets support reading of input from the user in both the GET and POST formats. I describe the POST scenario first. In the sample application in Listing 9-6, a user must select from a set of options the type of vehicle he or she would like to buy. The service responds with the dealer price for those vehicles. The input is a selection from a list of vehicle types and then a selection of specific models. A ZIP code is normally required because dealer prices vary by area. Also, my table will be skipping trim lines. For example, the Volkswagen Jetta can be GL, GLS, or GLX, with Turbo, TDI and V6 trims. For the sake of simplicity, the code also disregards the difference between two-door and four-door models. I will assume these are the prices for new cars. Listing 9-6 shows the code that captures the user input.

Listing 9-6: Code to Get Vehicle Information

```
import java.io.*;
import javax.servlet.*;
import javax.servlet.http.*;
import java.util.*;

public class VehicleServlet extends HttpServlet {

    public void doGet(HttpServletRequest request,
HttpServletResponse response)

throws ServletException, IOException
{
```

Continued

Listing 9-6 *(Continued)*

```
PrintWriter out;

response.setContentType("text/vnd.wap.wml");

out = response.getWriter();

out.println("<?xml version=\"1.0\"?>");
out.println("<!DOCTYPE wml PUBLIC \"-//WAPFORUM//DTD WML 1.1//EN\"");
out.println("http://www.wapforum.org/DTD/wml_1.1.xml>");
out.println("<wml>");
out.println("<template>");
out.println("<do type=\"accept\" label=\"Find\">");
out.println("<go href=\"FindVehicleServlet\" method=\"post\">");
out.println("<postfield name=\"vehicle\" value=\"$vehicle\"/>");
out.println("<postfield name=\"type\" value=\"$type\"/>");
out.println("</go>");
out.println("</do>");
out.println("</template>");
out.println("<card id=\"first\" title=\"Vehicles\">");
out.println("<do type=\"accept\">");
out.println("<noop/>");
out.println("</do>");
out.println("<p>");
out.println("Please select your vehicle:");
out.println("<select name=\"vehicle\">");
out.println("<option value=\"Buick\" onpick=\"#bu\">Buick</option>");
out.println("<option value=\"Cadillac\" onpick=\"#ca\">Cadillac</option>");
out.println("<option value=\"Daewoo\" onpick=\"#da\">Daewoo</option>");
out.println("<option value=\"Lincoln\" onpick=\"#li\">Lincoln</option>");
out.println("</select>");
out.println("</p>");
out.println("</card>");
out.println("// although this data could be dynamically loaded with database access%>");
out.println("// it is hardcoded here to prevent another round trip%>");
out.println("<card id=\"bu\" title=\"Vehicle Type\">");
out.println("<p>");
out.println("And the $(vehicle) type:");
```

```
out.println("<select name=\"type\">");
out.println("<option value=\"Century\">Century</option>");
out.println("<option value=\"Regal\">Regal</option>");
out.println("<option value=\"LeSabre\">LeSabre</option>");
out.println("<option value=\"ParkAve\">Park Avenue</option>");
out.println("</select>");
out.println("</p>");
out.println("</card>");
out.println("<card id=\"ca\" title=\"Vehicle Type\">");
out.println("<p>");
out.println("And the $(vehicle) type:");
out.println("<select name=\"type\">");
out.println("<option value=\"Catera\">Catera</option>");
out.println("<option value=\"DeVille\">DeVille</option>");
out.println("<option value=\"Eldorado\">Eldorado</option>");
out.println("<option value=\"Seville\">Seville</option>");
out.println("</select>");
out.println("</p>");
out.println("</card>");
out.println("<card id=\"da\" title=\"Vehicle Type\">");
out.println("<p>");
out.println("And the $(vehicle) type:");
out.println("<select name=\"type\">");
out.println("<option value=\"Lanos\">Lanos</option>");
out.println("<option value=\"Nubira\">Nubira</option>");
out.println("<option value=\"Leganza\">Leganza</option>");
out.println("<option value=\"NubiraWg\">Nubira Wagon</option>");
out.println("</select>");
out.println("</p>");
out.println("</card>");
out.println("<card id=\"li\" title=\"Vehicle Type\">");
out.println("<p>");
out.println("And the $(vehicle) type:");
out.println("<select name=\"type\">");
out.println("<option value=\"LS\">LS</option>");
out.println("<option value=\"Continental\">Continental</option>");
out.println("<option value=\"TownCar\">TownCar</option>");
out.println("<option value=\"Navigator\">Navigator</option>");
out.println("</select>");
out.println("</p>");
out.println("</card>");
out.println("</wml>");
```

Continued

Listing 9-6 *(Continued)*

```
out.close();

}

}
```

The code asks the user for a type of vehicle and puts together a WML file, which is sent to WAP client. The code on the client uses `postfield` elements inside the `go` element to automatically generate the required POST request and entity. The variable `vehicle_id` is sent inside this entity.

By pressing the Accept key the user sends the `vehicle_id` as POST data to the Web server, where it will be parsed by another Java servlet file. In this trivial case, the file simply acknowledges the variable and sends it back in the response, as shown in Listing 9-7.

Listing 9-7: Simple Acknowledgement of POST Data

```
import java.io.*;
import javax.servlet.*;
import javax.servlet.http.*;
import java.util.*;

public class FindVehicleServlet extends HttpServlet {

     public void doPost(HttpServletRequest request,
HttpServletResponse response)

throws ServletException, IOException
{

PrintWriter out;

response.setContentType("text/vnd.wap.wml");

out = response.getWriter();

out.println("<?xml version=\"1.0\"?>");
out.println("<!DOCTYPE wml PUBLIC \"-//WAPFORUM//DTD WML 1.1//EN\"");


out.println("<wml>");
out.println("<card id=\"first\" title=\"Vehicle Response\">");
out.println("<p>");
```

```
    String vehicle = request.getParameter("vehicle");
    String type = request.getParameter("type");

out.println("You selected a " + vehicle + " " + type);

out.println("</p>");
out.println("</card>");
out.println("</wml>");

out.close();

}

}
```

These client requests are handled in Java by the `service` method. The `service` method sends the request to the appropriate method, such as a `doGet` or a `doPost`. The common programming solution is to implement the `doGet` or the `doPost` method directly, while inheriting from the `HttpServlet` class.

The `HttpServletRequest` object contains any form details that the user may have entered. This object has a `getParameter` method, which is used to get the actual parameters sent by the client.

Listing 9-7 could have been modified such that the data is sent in the URL as part of GET request. The `go` element would look like this:

```
<go href="check_vehicle.cgi?vehicle=$(vehicle)&amp;type=$(type)"/>
```

where the default method issued is a GET. Variables are then obtained in the servlet by implementing the `doGet` method instead of `doPost`. There is really no other difference between the `doGet` and `doPost` methods, except that things become a little bit more complicated because you must use the `StringTokenizer` class to parse the values out of the URL, as shown in Listing 9-8.

Listing 9-8: Simple Acknowledgement of GET Data

```
import java.io.*;
import javax.servlet.*;
import javax.servlet.http.*;
import java.util.*;

public class FindVehicleServlet extends HttpServlet {
```

Continued

Listing 9-8 *(Continued)*

```
    public void doGet(HttpServletRequest request,
HttpServletResponse response)

throws ServletException, IOException
{

PrintWriter out;

response.setContentType("text/vnd.wap.wml");

out = response.getWriter();

out.println("<?xml version=\"1.0\"?>");
out.println("<!DOCTYPE wml PUBLIC \"-//WAPFORUM//DTD WML 1.1//EN\"");


out.println("<wml>");
out.println("<card id=\"first\" title=\"Vehicle Response\">");
out.println("<p>");

   String url_data = request.getQueryString();
   String printout = "";

   if (data != null) {
      StringTokenizer tmp = new StringTokenizer(url_data, &);
      while (tmp.hasMoreTokens()) {
         String tmp_more = tmp.nextToken();
         String name = tmp_more.substring(0,
tmp_more.indexOf('='));
         String value = tmp_more.substring(tmp_more.indexOf('=' +
1, tmp_more.length));
         printout += value + " ";
      }
   }


out.println("You selected a " + printout);

out.println("</p>");
out.println("</card>");
out.println("</wml>");

out.close();
```

}

}

You may need to get more variables from the user, such as an accessory request for the vehicle. Maybe the user wants a vehicle with a sunroof as opposed to the standard-issue vehicle on the lot. Then he or she would be presented with two types of selection, one for the vehicle and the second for the sunroof option. In the case of multiple parameters being sent by the client, the form field can fill out multiple values. You can use arrays to fill the variable values and then return the details to the supervisor.

More manual parsing of the data is required with the GET method before the variable pairs can be obtained. The `HttpServletResponse` object sends the variables to your program. Once there they are passed to the `doGet` program. Because this program gives you the lump sum query, you must split it up. One way to do this is by using the `StringTokenizer` class from the `java.util` package to divide the string based on the plus symbol.

Using the variables to initiate a query

In the previous examples, the data gathered was simply returned in a response. More practically, the actual vehicle information can be stored in a database, checked, and sent to the user.

Table 9-5 provides the details of the vehicles and their dealer prices.

TABLE 9-5 DEALER PRICES FOR VEHICLES

Vehicle	Type	Dealer Price
Buick	Century	21,000
Buick	Regal	23,000
Buick	LeSabre	26,000
Buick	ParkAvenue	35,000
Cadillac	Catera	31,000
Cadillac	DeVille	40,000
Cadillac	Eldorado	42,000
Cadillac	Seville	44,000

Continued

TABLE 9-5 DEALER PRICES FOR VEHICLES *(Continued)*

Vehicle	Type	Dealer Price
Daewoo	Lanos	10,000
Daewoo	Nubira	12,000
Daewoo	Leganza	15,000
Daewoo	NubiraWgn	14,500
Lincoln	LS	32,000
Lincoln	Continental	39,000
Lincoln	TownCar	43,000
Lincoln	Navigator	45,000

The Java servlet in this case needs to connect to a database and pull out the relevant price information. Listing 9-9 presents the code that enables this.

Listing 9-9: JDBC Code to Retrieve Vehicle Data

```
import java.io.*;
import javax.servlet.*;
import javax.servlet.http.*;
import java.util.*;
import java.sql.*;

public class FindVehicleServlet extends HttpServlet {

      public void doPost(HttpServletRequest request,
HttpServletResponse response)

throws ServletException, IOException
{

   String vehicle = request.getParameter("vehicle");
   String type = request.getParameter("type");

String url = "jdbc:someProtocol:someDataSource";
Connection conn;
Statement stm;
```

```java
try {

    Class.forName("someDriver.ClassName");
}
 catch(java.lang.ClassNotFoundException e) {
   System.err.print("ClassNotFoundException: ");
   System.err.println(e.getMessage());
}

   try {
       conn = DriverManager.getConnection(url, "someLogin",
"somePassword");
       stm = con.createStatement();
       ResultSet results = stm.executeQuery("SELECT * FROM Vehicles
WHERE vehicle=" + vehicle + " AND type=" + type);

PrintWriter out;

response.setContentType("text/vnd.wap.wml");

out = response.getWriter();

out.println("<?xml version=\"1.0\"?>");
out.println("<!DOCTYPE wml PUBLIC \"-//WAPFORUM//DTD WML
1.1//EN\"");


out.println("<wml>");
out.println("<card id=\"check\" title=\"Vehicle Results\">");
out.println("<p>");

     if (results.next()) {


       out.println("<strong>The dealer price for that vehicle is" +
results.getString("price") + "</strong>")

    }
   else {
out.println("<do type=\"accept\" label=\"Retry\">");
       out.println("<go href=\"vehicles.asp\"/>");
       out.println("</do>");
```

Continued

Listing 9-9 *(Continued)*

```
    out.println("The vehicle information you entered could not be found in our database");

  }

    results.close();
    stm.close();
    conn.close();

  } catch(SQLException exc) {
      // exception print out
        System.err.println("SQLException: " + exc.getMessage());
    }

out.println("</p>");
out.println("</card>");
out.println("</wml>");

out.close();

}

}
```

Creating additional headers and cookies

You can create additional headers in Java servlets by using the `Response` object. In Java servlet development I recommend that you set the response headers using special methods from the Java response library. The following code gives an example of adding a cookie to an outgoing response:

```
response.setHeader("Set-Cookie","name=value");
```

However, this is not recommended. The response library has a specific method for setting the cookie header. Here is a modified version of the preceding line, using that approach:

```
cookie stuff = new Cookie("firstname","John");
response.addCookie(stuff);
```

About the Java servlet process

Java services go through three phases when they are run. The first is the initialization, or `init`, phase. This is the point at which heavy-duty services, such as connecting to databases, take place. This phase is important because no requests can be taken at this point. The `init` phase of a servlet can be called when the server initializes or when the first request is issued, depending on the server and the configuration. For servers on which the servlet initializes on the first call, there can understandably be a delay while that call is finished.

The second phase of the life cycle is the execution phase. In this phase the servlet is doing its program duties. This is the normal state of affairs.

The third and last phase is the destroy phase, during and after which the servlet cannot be called until it has been started up again with another `init`.

Both the `init` and `destroy` methods can be trumped by other references within the code.

Unlike some other dynamic scripting environments, Java servlets can run simultaneously. If you want to ensure that only one servlet executes at a time, you can implement the `SingleThreadModel` class. This class ensures that the servlet remains single-threaded and cannot be delivered simultaneously.

Java Server Pages (JSPs)

You can easily regard JSP as the Java equivalent to Microsoft's Active Server Pages. Because it is a Java version of an embedded scripting language, it has the advantage over other languages that any code written in it is portable to other Java platforms. JSP requires that a server engine (in this case to handle JSP instead of ASP) be installed on the server. One advantage that JSP has over Java servlets is that it gets kind of tiring to keep writing `out.println` lines.

The JSP code is embedded inside `<%` and `%>` delimiters. Standard Java code is supported here, so anything that applied to servlets can also be applied here. The `ServletRequest` and `ServletResponse` objects are used again to handle JSP requests and send back responses. The JSP code is converted into the servlet format the first time it is called. From that point on, the servlet stored in memory is called directly, not the JSP, until the JSP file changes. This becomes a problem when any Java bean that the JSP file refers to changes, requiring that the page be "touched" to force an update.

> **NOTE:** A *Java bean* is a reusable software component written in Java. A reusable software component is a piece of code that provides a well-defined unit of functionality. The functionality is encapsulated in such a way that it can be reused in other larger components or pieces of code. The functionality itself can be something very small and simple, such as a text label on the user interface, or it can be something as large as an entire application.

To send the correct header in the response, use the following code:

```
<%@ page contentType="text/vnd.wap.wml" %>
```

The JSP syntax can be in either XML or non-XML format. If you are coding without a JSP editor the XML format is difficult to type off the top of your head. In the examples in this section I use the non-XML format.

The non-XML format for JSP can be summarized as a set of directives, declarations, expressions, code fragments, and comments, as shown in Table 9-6.

TABLE 9-6 NON-XML JSP CODE SHEET

Element Type	Description

Directives	Meant to be handled by the JSP engine; do not produce any output in a response.
	
	Syntax:
	
	`<%@ directive %>`
	
	Example:
	
	`<%@ include file="/headers.jsp" %>`

Declarations	Set up variables that can be used later on in a script; can also do some type of initialization.
	
	Syntax:
	
	`<%! declarations %>`
	
	Example:
	
	`<%! int k=16; %>`

Expressions	Where the output is actually presented in the response. The code is evaluated, executed, or both and the results are inserted into the WML code at that point.
	
	Syntax:
	
	`<%= expression %>`
	
	Example:
	
	`<%= 65 + Celsius %>`

Element Type	Description

Code fragments	Pieces of code used to make logical decisions within the response statements. The fragments are understood to be part of the combination of JSP code and thus are not expected to be complete on their own.
	
	Syntax:
	
	`<% the code %>`
	
	Example:
	
	`<% while ( I < 0) { %>`

Comments	This style of comment is visible only from the original JSP file. The comment is not processed by the JSP engine and is not passed onto the output stream. You cannot nest comments.
	
	Syntax:
	
	`<%-- comment --%>`
	
	Example:
	
	`<%-- here is a sample comment --%>`

The following code shows a simple example in JSP, which returns the current date and time to a WML browser:

```
<%@ page contentType="text/vnd.wap.wml" %>

<?xml version="1.0"?>
<!DOCTYPE wml PUBLIC "-//WAPFORUM//DTD WML 1.1//EN"
"http://www.wapforum.org/DTD/wml_1.1.xml">

<wml>
<card id="time">
    <p>
    <% = new java.util.Date() %>
    </p>
</card>
</wml>
```

JSP also has something known as action elements. These reference servlets inside the JSP code. You include them in JSP by using the XML style, as follows:

```
<jsp:useBean>
```

Three types of actions exist: `useBean`, `getProperty`, and `setProperty`. A bean is a Java class that has a no-argument constructor, that is serializable, and that follows the `set` and `get` methods. Beans are a good for structuring JSP applications so that they don't look like spaghetti Java code strewn inside the WML. So you can use them to group a set of procedures, scientific functions for example, and quarantine them to a bean. These beans are then easier to maintain than lines of interspersed code in the JSP file itself.

The `useBean` action defines the class name, its scope, and its programmatic name:

```
<jsp:useBean id="newbean" scope="session"
class="scientific.MainDeal" />
```

The ID is a programmatic reference to the bean. The scope can be a page, request, session, or application, depending on how long you want to maintain the references to the bean. And the class is the full name of the class being referred to.

The `setProperty` action can then follow the `useBean` action and set a property name and value for the statement. These are typically values obtained from the user as some type of input. You can also use the `getProperty` action in your JSP code to retrieve these values for use in a later portion of your application.

Processing user input

The JSP engine is quite capable of pulling data out of either the GET or POST methods from the clients. Listing 9-10, which shows the International Postal Calculator, is a POST case wherein a customer is searching through a WAP application looking for international postage rates. The customer is required to select a country for which he or she wants to mail a letter. Listing 9-10 provides the code that allows the customer to select the country and input a weight. (This application applies only to standard letters mailed from the United States to a foreign country.) Table 9-7 maps the country to a U.S. Post Office Letter-Post Rate Group. Table 9-8 gives the grid for the cost of a postal item of a given weight to a Rate Group. Both tables are excerpts from Publication 51, January 2001 from the U.S. Post Office.

Table 9-7 COUNTRY GROUP RATE SCHEDULE

Country	Letter-Post Rate Group
Argentina	5
Australia	4
Canada	1
Denmark	3
Japan	4
Mexico	2

Table 9-8 LETTER-POST RATES

Weight Not Over (oz.)	Rate Group 1	Rate Group 2	Rate Group 3	Rate Group 4	Rate Group 5
1.0	$0.60	$0.60	$0.80	$0.80	$0.80
2.0	$0.85	$0.85	$1.60	$1.70	$1.55
3.0	$1.10	$1.25	$2.40	$2.60	$2.30
4.0	$1.35	$1.65	$3.20	$3.50	$3.05
5.0	$1.60	$2.05	$4.00	$4.40	$3.80
6.0	$2.10	$2.45	$4.80	$5.30	$4.55
7.0	$2.35	$2.85	$5.60	$6.20	$5.30
8.0	$3.10	$3.25	$6.40	$7.10	$6.05
12.0	$3.75	$4.00	$7.55	$8.40	$7.65
16.0	$4.40	$5.15	$8.70	$9.70	$9.25

Listing 9-10: International Postal Calculator Input

```
<%@ page contentType="text/vnd.wap.wml" %>

<?xml version="1.0"?>
<!DOCTYPE wml PUBLIC "-//WAPFORUM//DTD WML 1.1//EN"
"http://www.wapforum.org/DTD/wml_1.1.xml">

<wml>
    <card id="first" title="Country Selection">
        <do type="accept">
            <go href="#second"/>
        </do>
        <p>
            Please select the country to mail a letter to:
            <select name="vehicle">
                <option value="Argentina">Argentina</option>
                <option value="Australia">Australia</option>
                <option value="Canada">Canada</option>
                <option value="Denmark">Denmark</option>
                <option value="Japan">Japan</option>
                <option value="Mexico">Mexico</option>
            </select>
        </p>
    </card>

    <card id="second" title="Letter Weight">
        <do type="accept" label="Find">
            <go href="find_mailrate.jsp" method="post">
                <postfield name="country" value="$country"/>
                <postfield name="weight" value="$weight"/>
            </go>
        </do>

        <p>
            Your letter weighs
            <select name="weight">
                <option value="1">under 1 oz</option>
                <option value="2">under 2 oz</option>
                <option value="3">under 3 oz</option>
                <option value="4">under 4 oz</option>
                <option value="5">under 5 oz</option>
                <option value="6">under 6 oz</option>
                <option value="7">under 7 oz</option>
                <option value="8">under 8 oz</option>
```

```
                    <option value="12">under 12 oz</option>
                    <option value="16">under 16 oz</option>
                </select>
            </p>
        </card>
</wml>
```

In this case, the user enters the country and weight, which are parsed and returned as a WML file using JSP. The `postfield` elements inside the `go` element build the required POST request and entity. The variables `country` and `weight` are sent inside this entity.

When the user presses the Accept soft key, the country and weight variables are sent to the Web server as POST data, which will be parsed by another JSP file (`find_mailrate.jsp`). The code presented in Listing 9-11 accepts the data and simply returns them to the user.

Listing 9-11: JSP Code to Display POSTed DATA

```
<%@ page contentType="text/vnd.wap.wml" %>

<% String type = request.getParameter("type");
   String country = request.getParameter("country");
%>


<?xml version="1.0"?>
<!DOCTYPE wml PUBLIC "-//WAPFORUM//DTD WML 1.1//EN"
"http://www.wapforum.org/DTD/wml_1.1.xml">

<wml>

        <card id="first" title="International Letter Response">
            <p>
                You want to send a letter weighing <%
                =type%> ounces to <%=country%>
            </p>
        </card>
</wml>
```

You can modify the code in Listing 9-11 to handle the data as part of the URL in a GET request. The `go` element would be as follows:

```
<go href="find_mailrate.jsp?country=$(country)&weight=$(weight)"/>
```

where the default method issued is a GET. Variables are then obtained using the JSP code shown in Listing 9-12.

Listing 9-12: JSP Code to Retrieve Variables in GET Method

```
<%@ page contentType="text/vnd.wap.wml" %>

<% String type = request.getParameter("type");
   String country = request.getParameter("country");
%>



<?xml version="1.0"?>
<!DOCTYPE wml PUBLIC "-//WAPFORUM//DTD WML 1.1//EN"
"http://www.wapforum.org/DTD/wml_1.1.xml">

<wml>

       <card id="first" title="International Letter Response">
           <p>
                   You want to send a letter weighing <%
                   =type%> ounces to <%=country%>
           </p>
       </card>
</wml>
```

Using the variables to initiate a query

The example in Listings 9-10 and 9-11 picked up the variables and sent them back to the browser in a response. But what you would really like to do is search a database that contains the mailing rates and return an appropriate response to the client.

The JSP code would then use JDBC to search through this "mailing rate" table and find and print the correct mailing rate, as shown in Listing 9-13.

Listing 9-13: JSP Database Query

```
<%@ page language="java" import="java.sql.*"
contentType="text/vnd.wap.wml" %>

<%! String type = request.getParameter("type");
    String country = request.getParameter("country");
    String url = "jdbc:someProtocol:someDataSource";
%>
```

```
<?xml version="1.0"?>
<!DOCTYPE wml PUBLIC "-//WAPFORUM//DTD WML 1.1//EN"
"http://www.wapforum.org/DTD/wml_1.1.xml">

<wml>
<card id="check" title="Mail Rate Results">
    <p>

<%    Connection conn = DriverManager.getConnection(url,
"someLogin", "somePassword");
        Class.forName("someDriver.ClassName");
        Statement stm = con.createStatement();

        ResultSet results = stm.executeQuery(""SELECT [rate] FROM
Group, Rates WHERE group.country=" + country + " AND rates.weight="
+ weight;

%>

    <%

        if (results.next()) {
            out.print("In order to send that letter out to " +
country + it would cost you " + results.getString("rate") +
"</strong>");

        }
        else
        {
out.print("This should not have happened.");
   out.print("<do type=\"accept\" label=\"Retry\">");
   out.print("<go href=\"mailrate.asp\"/>");
   out.print("</do>");
        }
%>
    </p>
</card>
</wml>

<%
    results.close();
    stm.close();
    conn.close();
%>
```

JDBC is the Java version of a database connectivity framework. A database is specified using its name and a `Connection` object constructor, which handles the details of the connection. Other information that may be needed is a username and password. After having made a connection to the database, a developer can build a SQL string to run against the database using the `executeQuery()` method. Listing 9-13 shows how the string is built and how the method is used to retrieve the data.

The preceding example uses JDBC 1.0. You should consult a JDBC/JSP reference for more details about optimizing database connectivity.

Adding headers and cookies in JSP

Adding other headers in JSP is quite simple. You insert them into the embedded file using the same commands as in Java. The following code examples show headers that set some caching properties and cookies. These headers are set much as they would be in standard Java.

```
<%
response.setHeader("Cache-Control","no-cache");
response.setDateHeader ("Expires", 0); //prevents caching

Cookie samplecookie = new Cookie("fName","Jake");
response.addCookie(samplecookie);
%>
```

You can also put any additional headers anywhere in the JSP code if the request is not set to flush immediately.

Personal Home Page Hypertext Processor

Personal Home Page Hypertext Processor (PHP) is an up-and-coming dynamic scripting environment. It is open source and free of charge, which makes it a popular choice in the home programming community. On top of that, PHP has aligned itself quite well with the home programming community in general, because it's bundled with most if not all versions of Linux. PHP is often used in combination with the "mySQL" database environment to deliver dynamic content.

You program in PHP by inserting special PHP statements inside the WML code. The server interprets these special PHP statements before they are sent to the clients.

PHP is unique among languages in that it has some native image-control formats. This enables PHP programmers to seamlessly add jazzed-up details to the look and feel of a WAP project.

The following example demonstrates how the content type and other aspects of the PHP language are laid out by outputting today's date:

```
<?php
header("Content-type = "text/vnd.wap.wml");

echo "<?xml version=\"1.0\"?>";
echo "<!DOCTYPE wml PUBLIC \"-//WAPFORUM//DTD WML 1.1//EN\"
    \"http://www.wapforum.org/DTD/wml_1.1.xml\">";
?>

<wml>
<card id="time">
  <p>
     <?php
     $time = date("F j, Y, g:i a");
     print $time;
     ?>
  </p>
</card>
</wml>
```

PHP code is embedded inside and around the WML code. The statements that begin with `<?php` and end with `?>` define a PHP code block. The content-type header is added to the response with the following line:

```
header("Content-type: text/vnd.wap.wml");
```

The characters inside the PHP `date()` function are formatting commands, and in the case of the preceding function call would produce the output string in the form of `"August 10, 2001, 11:16 pm"`.

Processing user input

PHP is certainly efficient at pulling user-inputted data out of either the GET or POST methods from the clients. For example, suppose that you want to search a database that contains weight and height measurements to determine how they relate to a Body Mass Index (BMI) value for an individual.

> **NOTE** BMI is an index value that purportedly indicates the relationship between the height and weight of a person. It can be used to assess a person's level of health risk.

314 Part II: Development of Services

To calculate the BMI, you need to know a person's height and weight. For the purposes of this example, I use "feet and inches" for height, and "pounds" for weight, rather than "meters" and "kilos," respectively. You can use Table 9-9 to determine BMI values. This is a subset of a full BMI table given here for the purpose of this example.

TABLE 9-9 BMI TABLE

Weight (lbs.)	110	115	120	125	130	135	140
Height (feet)							
5' 8"	17	17	18	19	20	21	21
5' 9"	16	17	18	18	19	20	21
5' 10"	16	17	17	18	19	19	20
5' 11"	15	16	17	17	18	19	20
6' 0"	15	16	16	17	18	18	19
6' 1"	15	15	16	16	17	18	18
6' 2"	14	15	15	16	17	17	18
6' 3"	14	14	15	16	16	17	17
6' 4"	13	14	15	15	16	16	17

Listing 9-14 shows a POST scenario featuring an application wherein a customer is looking for his or her BMI value from the height and weight inputs in Table 9-9.

Listing 9-14: Height and Weight Input

```
<?php
header("Content-type = "text/vnd.wap.wml");

echo "<?xml version=\"1.0\"?>";
echo "<!DOCTYPE wml PUBLIC \"-//WAPFORUM//DTD WML 1.1//EN\"
     \"http://www.wapforum.org/DTD/wml_1.1.xml\">";
?>

<wml>

      <card id="first" title="Height">
```

```
            <do type="accept">
                <go href="#second"/>
            </do>

            <p>
                Your height (x' xx"):
                    <input name="height" format="N\'\ NN\""/>
            </p>

        </card>

        <card id="second" title="Weight">
            <do type="accept" label="Find">
                <go href="find_BMI.php" method="post">
                    <postfield name="weight" value="$weight"/>
                    <postfield name="height" value="$height"/>
                </go>
            </do>

            <p>
                Your weight (x lbs):
                    <input name="weight" format="*N"/>
            </p>
        </card>

</wml>
```

In this case, the user enters his or her height and weight, which are parsed and returned as a WML file using PHP. The `postfield` elements inside the `go` element build the required POST request and entity. The variables `height` and `weight` are sent inside this entity.

When the user presses the Accept soft key, he or she sends the `height` and `weight` variables as POST data to the Web server where they will be parsed by another PHP file (BMI.php). The file accepts the measurements and sends them back to the user, as shown in the following listing of BMI.php:

```
<?php
header("Content-type = "text/vnd.wap.wml");

echo "<?xml version=\"1.0\"?>";
echo "<!DOCTYPE wml PUBLIC \"-//WAPFORUM//DTD WML 1.1//EN\""
    . " \"http://www.wapforum.org/DTD/wml_1.1.xml\">";
?>

<wml>
```

```
        <card id="first" title="BMI Calculation Response">
            <p>

<?php
print "Your height is " . $height . " and your weight is " . $weight
. " lbs.";
?>

</p>
        </card>

</wml>
```

PHP is very efficient in its use of parameters: any variable sent to the PHP file automatically becomes available as part of the environment.

You could modify the previous example so that the data are sent in the URL as part of the GET request. The go element would look like this:

```
<go href="find_BMI.php?height=$(height)&amp;weight=$(weight))"/>
```

where the default method issued is a GET. Variables are then obtained by the PHP in exactly the same way regardless of whether the method is a GET or a POST.

The following example shows the retrieval of variables set by a URL string:

```
<?php

header("Content-type = "text/vnd.wap.wml");

echo "<?xml version=\"1.0\"?>";
echo "<!DOCTYPE wml PUBLIC \"-//WAPFORUM//DTD WML 1.1//EN\""
    . " \"http://www.wapforum.org/DTD/wml_1.1.xml\">";
?>

<wml>

        <card id="first" title="BMI Calculation Response">
            <p>

            <?php
                print "Your height is " . $height . " and your
weight is " . $weight . " lbs.";
            ?>
```

```
            </p>
        </card>
</wml>
```

Using the variables to initiate a query

The PHP example shown in Listing 9-14 simply picked up the variables and sent them back to the browser in a response. But what you would really like to do is search a database that contains the height, weight, and BMI value tables and return an appropriate response to the client.

The correct weight is first looked up in a general table listing the relationship of weight to BMI. Then the result is used to find the details from another table listing the relationship of height to BMI. Listing 9-15 shows the PHP code required to perform these tasks.

Listing 9-15: PHP Code to Retrieve BMI Information Data

```
<?php

header("Content-type = "text/vnd.wap.wml");

echo "<?xml version=\"1.0\"?>";
echo "<!DOCTYPE wml PUBLIC \"-//WAPFORUM//DTD WML 1.1//EN\""
    . " \"http://www.wapforum.org/DTD/wml_1.1.xml\">";
?>

<wml>
<card id="check" title="BMI Value Results">
    <p>

<?php
    $height_feet = substr(height, 0, 1);
    $height_inches = substr(height, 3, 2);
    $height_total = $height_feet*12 + $height_inches;

    if ($height_total < 68 or $height_total > 76) :
        print "Sorry but that height value is not in our database!";
        print "</p>";
        print "</card>";
        print "</wml>";
        exit;
    endif;
```

Part II: Development of Services

```
        if ($weight < 110 or $weight > 140) :
            print "Sorry but your weight is not in our database!";
            print "</p>";
            print "</card>";
            print "</wml>";
            exit;
        endif;
?>

<?php
        // connect to mysql database
        $bmi_connect = mysql_pconnect("www.test.com");

        // select database
        $db_select = mysql_select_db("bmi");

        // select information from bmi database
        $query = "SELECT bmi_result from weight, height WHERE class='$weight'
AND height.class=$height_total'";

        $bmi_result = @mysql_query($query);

        if (mysql_num_rows($bmi_result) > 0) :

            print "<strong>Your BMI value is $bmi_result </strong>";

            endwhile;

        else:

            print "Not sure how that happened";
            print "<do type='accept' label='Retry'>";
            print "   <go href='bmi.asp'/>";
            print "</do>";

        endif;

        ?>

    </p>
</card>
</wml>
```

Adding headers and cookies in PHP

Adding other headers in PHP is quite simple. You insert them into the embedded file using the `header` command. So a header that sets some cookies would look like this:

```
header("Set-cookie: name=John");
```

You can add any additional headers just by putting a similar line of code in the PHP file.

Perl CGI

Common Gateway Interface (CGI) is another enabler of dynamic coding on Web servers. It has been part of the WWW since at least 1993 when it was created by the NCSA and CERN. The current version of CGI is 1.1. It defines a set of environment variables and parameters that you can access by means of a programming language at the Web server.

CGI programs can output any media format, and you can enable them with any programming language. Because of this flexibility and portability, the language has been quite popular on the Web. Figure 9-3 shows a diagram of the CGI architecture.

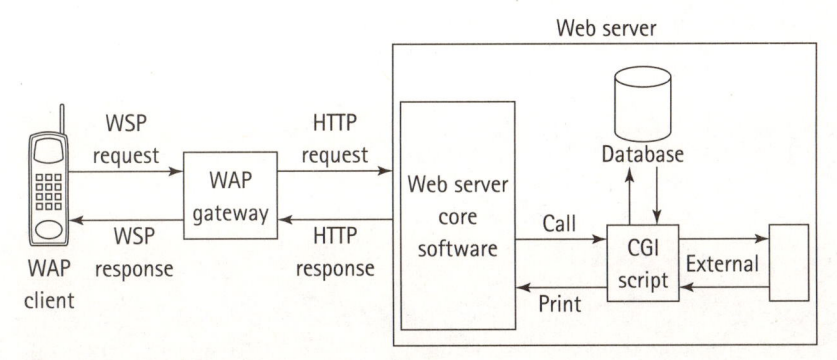

Figure 9-3: The CGI architecture at a glance

The GET and POST methods are used by the HTTP protocol to retrieve and send information to a Web server. CGI programs can obtain these methods using the string `REQUEST_METHOD`. Other data you can obtain are the header information and any entities included in the HTTP request. You can obtain the headers by using their standard CGI names. All the standard HTTP headers have specific names. For example, CONTENT_TYPE specifies the returned or posted media type. Other frequently used header types include CONTENT_LENGTH for posts and QUERY_STRING for the full URL.

The examples in this section use Perl CGI although other CGI formats are possible.

The following piece of code sets the content type of the CGI output so that the response issued by the server contains the right media type:

```
print "Content-Type: text/vnd.wap.wml\n\n;
```

This outputs the correct header, followed by two new line characters.

A test page that prints today's date in Perl CGI would therefore look like this:

```
print "Content-Type: text/vnd.wap.wml\n\n;

print "<?xml version=\"1.0\"?>\n";
print "<!DOCTYPE wml PUBLIC \"-//WAPFORUM//DTD WML 1.1//EN\"
\"http://www.wapforum.org/DTD/wml_1.1.xml\">\n";

$time = localtime;

print "<wml>\n";
print "<card id=\"time\">\n";
print "<p>\n";
print $time . "\n";
print "</p>\n";
print "</card>\n";
print "</wml>\n";
```

Processing user input

Used to create the oldest user input forms on the Web, Perl CGI certainly has the ability to parse any input from the WAP client, either as a GET or as a POST. I'll start with a POST scenario. In this scenario, users of an application can check what year of the Chinese calendar their birth year overlaps with. A user inputs a year and the back-end processor checks that year against a database of numbers.

According to legend, Buddha once invited all the animals to visit him before he departed for heaven. However, only 12 animals came. Buddha then honored these 12 animals as the 12 signs of the Chinese calendar, each representing one year in a 12-year cycle. The 12 animals are, in their correct order, the rat, ox, tiger, rabbit, dragon, snake, horse, goat, monkey, rooster, dog, and pig. For example, people born in 1924 were born in the Year of the Rat.

> **NOTE:** Actually there is a bit of a complication here as the Chinese New Year follows a lunar cycle and falls somewhere in January or February; if you have a birthday then, you will have to do some more digging to get a definitive answer on your Chinese birth year.

So if you know that 1924 is the Year of the Rat, 12 years later, 1936, is also the Year of the Rat, just as 1816, 120 years earlier, was also the Year of the Rat. This means you can calculate the Year of the Rat with the equation $y=12x+1804$: just substitute any number for x and you will get the Year of the Rat. However, if you modify the formula to $y=12x+1804+b$, where $0<b<12$, you can set the value of b to correspond to the Ox, let's say ($b=1$), and use it to calculate the Year of the Ox. So, $x=0$, $b=1$, and the result is 1805, the Year of the Ox. And so on for the corresponding values of b for the rest of the animals.

Now, if someone gives you just a birth date, you will have to reverse the formula to find the right birth animal. You must then change the formula by setting y to `birth_year` so that `birth_year`$-1804-12x$ = Chinese sign. However, x is still an unknown, but you can get around this problem by finding the modulus to 12. The remainder will then be the Chinese sign value b.

Listing 9-16 shows the calculation for the user's birth year in Perl.

Listing 9-16: Birth-Year Query

```
print "Content-Type: text/vnd.wap.wml\n\n;

print "<?xml version=\"1.0\"?>\n";
print "<!DOCTYPE wml PUBLIC \"-//WAPFORUM//DTD WML 1.1//EN\"
\"http://www.wapforum.org/DTD/wml_1.1.xml\">\n";

print <<"EOF";
<wml>
  <card id="first">
  <do type="accept" label="Find">
  <go href="find_sign.cgi" method="get">
     <postfield name="birth_year" value="$birth_year"/>
  </go>
  </do>
     <p>What is the birth year (19XX)?
        <input name="birth_year" format="NNNN"/>
     </p>
  </card>
</wml>
EOF
```

Part II: Development of Services

This code simply asks the user for his or her birth year and parses together a WML file using Perl CGI, located on the Web server. Using `postfield` elements inside the `go` element automatically generates the required POST request and entity. The variable `birth_year` is sent inside this entity. The simple preceding example does not have to be coded in Perl, but is written in Perl in order to keep everything intact during debugging.

By pressing the Accept soft key the user sends his or her birth year as POST data to the Web server, where it will be parsed by another Perl CGI file called `find_sign.cgi`. The file accepts the birth year and simply returns it to the user. In the case of posted data, the input comes in via STDIN and is read by using the `read` function. The `read` function takes as one of its arguments a variable in which all the inputted data are stored. An environment variable called `CONTENT_LENGTH` is used to find out how long the posted data are. This is really just an easy way of pulling an entity-specific HTTP header in the posted response. Listing 9-17 shows how to split the posted response into usable data.

Listing 9-17: Birth-Year Loopback

```
print "Content-Type: text/vnd.wap.wml\n\n;

print "<?xml version=\"1.0\"?>\n";
print "<!DOCTYPE wml PUBLIC \"-//WAPFORUM//DTD WML 1.1//EN\"
\"http://www.wapforum.org/DTD/wml_1.1.xml\">\n";

$data_length = $ENV{'CONTENT_LENGTH'};
read(STDIN, $input_data, $data_length);
# split the data into the name value pairs
@name_value_pairs = split (/&/, $input_data);
my %form_data = ();
foreach $pair (@value_pairs) {
    ($key, $value) = split (/=/, $pair);
    $value =~ tr/+/ /;
    $value =~ s/%([\dA-Fa-f][\dA-Fa-f])/pack ("C", hex ($1))/ge;
    $form_data{$key} = $value;
}
print <<"EOF";
<wml>
   <card id="first" title="Chinese Calendar Response">
      <p>
Your entry for birthdate year was $form_data{birth_year}
      </p>
</card>
</wml>
EOF
```

A little bit more work has to be done in Perl than in other languages, because without a library the form data must be parsed manually and the variables put into an array (or *hash* as it is also known).

You can modify the previous example so that the data are sent in the URL as part of a GET request. The go element would then look like this:

```
<go href="check_sign.cgi?birth_year=$(birth_year)"/>
```

where the default method issued is a GET. The Perl CGI then obtains variables by examining the QUERY_STRING instead of STDIN, as shown in Listing 9-18.

Listing 9-18: Getting the Data from a URL

```perl
print "Content-Type: text/vnd.wap.wml\n\n;

print "<?xml version=\"1.0\"?>\n";
print "<!DOCTYPE wml PUBLIC \"-//WAPFORUM//DTD WML 1.1//EN\"
\"http://www.wapforum.org/DTD/wml_1.1.xml\">\n";

# the following commented code can be used to check what type
# of method was used, a GET or a POST

# my $method = $ENV{'REQUEST_METHOD'};
# if ($method eq "GET") {
#    use the GET technique
# }
# else {
#      use the POST technique
# }

$input_data = $ENV{'QUERY_STRING'};

# split the data into the name value pairs
@name_value_pairs = split (/&/, $input_data);
my %query_string_data = ();
foreach $pair (@value_pairs) {
    ($key, $value) = split (/=/, $pair);
    $value =~ tr/+/ /;
    $value =~ s/%([\dA-Fa-f][\dA-Fa-f])/pack ("C", hex ($1))/ge;
    $query_string_data{$key} = $value;
}
print <<"EOF";
```

Continued

Listing 9-18 *(Continued)*

```
<wml>
    <card id="first" title="Chinese Calendar Response">
       <p>
Your entry for birthdate year was $query_string_data{birth_year}
       </p>
</card>
</wml>
EOF
```

Using the variables to initiate a query

In Listing 9-18, the data gathered were simply returned to the user. In practice it is more likely that the actual Chinese years would be stored in a database or array and the data checked before a valid response is returned.

Here is how the formula for calculating Chinese years might look.

```
mod(birth_year - 1804,12) = Chinese sign index
```

By referring to Table 9-10 you should be able to find the correct animal.

TABLE 9-10 CHINESE CALENDAR SIGNS

Chinese Sign	Formula Result
Rat	0
Ox	1
Tiger	2
Rabbit	3
Dragon	4
Snake	5
Horse	6
Goat	7
Monkey	8
Rooster	9
Dog	10
Pig	11

The Perl CGI will then search through a database, determine what animal corresponds to the year, and send it back to the user, as shown in Listing 9-19.

Listing 9-19: Calculating the Chinese Calendar Year

```perl
use DBI;
print "Content-Type: text/vnd.wap.wml\n\n;

print "<?xml version=\"1.0\"?>\n";
print "<!DOCTYPE wml PUBLIC \"-//WAPFORUM//DTD WML 1.1//EN\"
\"http://www.wapforum.org/DTD/wml_1.1.xml\">\n";

$data_length = $ENV{'CONTENT_LENGTH'};
read(STDIN, $input_data, $data_length);
# split the data into the name value pairs
@name_value_pairs = split (/&/, $input_data);
my %form_data = ();
foreach $pair (@value_pairs) {
    ($key, $value) = split (/=/, $pair);
    $value =~ tr/+/ /;
    $value =~ s/%([\dA-Fa-f][\dA-Fa-f])/pack ("C", hex ($1))/ge;
    $form_data{$key} = $value;
}

$birth_year = $form_data{birth_year};
$year_check = ($birth_year - 1804) % 12;

my $dbc = DBI->connect('DBI:Oracle:calendar') or die "couldn't
connect to database" . DBI->errstr;

my $stc = $dbc->prepare('SELECT * FROM Calendar WHERE year_check=?')
or die "couldn't prepare query: " .
$dbc->errstr;

print <<"EOF";
<wml>
<card id="check" title="Calendar Results">
    <p>
EOF

$stc->execute($year_check) or die "couldn't execute query" .
$stc->errstr;
```

Continued

Listing 9-19 *(Continued)*

```perl
if ($stc->rows == 0) {

    print "Not sure how that happened\n";
    print "<do type=\"accept\" label=\"Retry\">\n";
    print "<go href=\"calendar.asp\"/>\n";
    print "</do>\n";

&closing;

    exit;
}

    my @data;
    @data = $stc->fetchrow_array();

    my $year_sign = $data[2];

print "<strong>birth_year represents the year of the " . $year_sign . "</strong>\n";

&closing;
exit;

sub closing {

print <<"EOF";
    </p>
</card>
</wml>
EOF

$stc->finish;
$dbc->disconnect;

}
```

Adding headers and cookies in Perl

Adding other headers in Perl CGI is quite easy. You can insert them either after or before the `content-type` printout using the same syntax, except that here only one new line is inserted between the headers. The following code provides an example that sets up a cookie as well as the content-type headers:

```
print "Set-Cookie: Name=Jerry\n";
print "Content-type: text/vnd.wap.wml\n";
```

ColdFusion Markup Language

ColdFusion Markup Language (CFML) is another dynamic scripting environment used for programming services. It works in both UNIX and NT environments and is adept at connecting to multiple database environments. Like most of the dynamic scripting environments I discuss in this chapter, CFML was designed to output HTML pages. With some simple modifications, though, you can reconfigure it to output WML decks. Before I look into that, here is an overview of the CFML architecture.

ColdFusion architecture

ColdFusion defines a dynamic language called CFML for writing dynamic code. Normal markup language code is interspersed with CFML tags to add logic and dynamic content to the output of the WML deck. The CFML tags must be interpreted somehow and the ColdFusion server is the component that does this. ColdFusion also supports error handling, state management, and other enterprise-ready features.

Figure 9-4 shows the ColdFusion architecture.

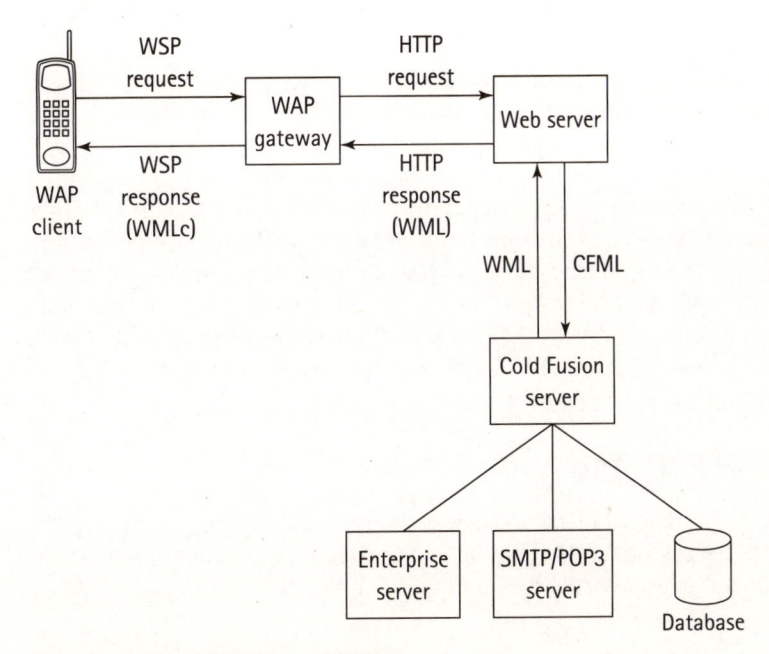

Figure 9-4: The ColdFusion architecture

A mobile user accesses a WAP service with the URL http://www.site.com/index.cfml. The WAP gateway sends this URL as an HTTP request to a Web server. The Web server then finds the resource and sends it off to the ColdFusion server, which interprets the CFML tags in the markup code. The interpreted tags are replaced with WML code or text. The resulting WML page is sent back to the Web server and from there an HTTP response is generated and sent to the WAP gateway.

The ColdFusion server interprets the CFML and outputs WML; therefore standard browsers and Web servers can become part of the architecture. The following code shows how to output a time and date to WML using CFML:

```
<CFCONTENT TYPE="text/vnd.wap.wml">

<?xml version="1.0"?>
<!DOCTYPE wml PUBLIC "-//WAPFORUM//DTD WML 1.1//EN"
"http://www.wapforum.org/DTD/wml_1.1.xml">

<wml>

<card id="time">
    <p>
        <cfoutput>#Dateformat(Now(), "Mmmm dd, yyyy")#</cfoutput>
    </p>
</card>

</wml>
```

The previous example illustrates how CFML tags work alongside WML tags. CFML is a scripting language that supports variables, functions, server-side tags and third-party component tags. The example shows how the CF tags are special functions, which are first interpreted by the ColdFusion server. The example shows how a time and date are dynamically inserted into the WML deck using CFML functions. Like all the dynamic environments built for HTML, the content type must be explicitly set so that the response is sent as WML. You can set it with a CFCONTENT function at the start of the CFML code. This CFCONTENT is juxtaposed with the XML version declaration so as to prevent the first line of the response from being blank.

You can save these CFML files either with the .cfml or. cfm extensions, depending on the operating system environment.

The CFCONTENT tag

As I mentioned earlier, the CFML markup was designed for HTML and an explicit CFCONTENT tag is required at the beginning of the code to set the content type for WML or any other WAP-supported media type. For a WML deck this tag would be set as:

```
<CFCONTENT TYPE="text/vnd.wap.wml">
```

Processing user input

CFML is able to parse any input entered into the WAP client by the user. This input can come as part of a GET request or a POST request. Listing 9-20 provides the code for a POST example. In this scenario, `postfield` tags are used in the WML input deck to send data to a CFML script. What if national lottery players were checking to see whether their tickets held the winning numbers? Listing 9-20 assumes a lottery that has four numbers, each from 1 to 49, and that a single number cannot be used twice on the same ticket.

Listing 9-20: Lottery Input

```
<CFCONTENT TYPE="text/vnd.wap.wml">
<?xml version="1.0"?>
<!DOCTYPE wml PUBLIC "-//WAPFORUM//DTD WML 1.1//EN"
"http://www.wapforum.org/DTD/wml_1.1.xml">

<wml>

        <card id="first" title="First Number">
            <do type="accept">
                <go href="#second"/>
            </do>

            <p>
                First lottery number:
                    <input name="number_one" format="*N"/>
            </p>

        </card>

        <card id="second" title="Second Number">
            <do type="accept">
                <go href="#third"/>
            </do>

            <p>
                Second lottery number:
                    <input name="number_two" format="*N"/>
            </p>
```

Continued

Listing 9-20 *(Continued)*

```
        </card>

        <card id="third" title="Third Number">
            <do type="accept">
                <go href="#fourth"/>
            </do>

            <p>
                First lottery number:
                    <input name="number_three" format="*N"/>
            </p>

        </card>

        <card id="fourth" title="Fourth Number">
            <do type="accept" label="Check">
                <go href="find_lottery.cfm" method="post">
                    <postfield name="number_one" value="$number_one"/>
                    <postfield name="number_two" value="$number_two"/>
                    <postfield name="number_three" value="$number_three"/>
                    <postfield name="number_four" value="$number_four"/>
                </go>
            </do>
            <p>
                Fourth lottery number:
                    <input name="number_four" format="*N"/>
            </p>

        </card>

</wml>
```

The code in Listing 9-20 simply asks the user for his or her lottery number and sends it to the CFML file (lottery.cfm) located on the Web server. Using `postfield` elements inside the `go` element automatically generates the required POST request and entity. At the moment no reason exists for using CFML code in this input-gathering deck; however, it is still advantageous to keep it there because if CFML code is required later, you can simply add it.

By pressing the Accept soft key the user sends the variables `number_one`, `number_two`, `number_three` and `number_four` `lotto_num` as POST data to the

CFML script file. The CFML code then has to extract the numbers and check them against a database of the week's winning numbers. Listing 9-21 shows the CFML code that returns the posted variable to the user.

Listing 9-21: Returning POSTed Data

```
<CFCONTENT TYPE="text/vnd.wap.wml">
<?xml version="1.0"?>
<!DOCTYPE wml PUBLIC "-//WAPFORUM//DTD WML 1.1//EN"
"http://www.wapforum.org/DTD/wml_1.1.xml">

<wml>

    <card id="first" title="Lottery Response">
        <p>
            You numbers entered were
            <Cfoutput>

#Form.number_one#,#Form.number_two#,#Form.number_three#,#Form.number_four#
            </cfoutput>

        </p>
    </card>

</wml>
```

Because most data are inputted in POST entities for forms submitted in HTML, I use the same form syntax here for WML. The form name is the variable prefix, and the actual variable name is the same as the variable name that was posted from the input form. The `form` prefix is actually not required by ColdFusion; you could simply have abbreviated the reference as #number_one#, #number_two# and so on.

You could modify Listing 9-20 so that the data are sent in the URL as part of a GET request. In this case, the `go` element would look like this:

```
<go href="find_lottery.asp" method="get">
    <postfield name="number_one" value="$number_one"/>
    <postfield name="number_two" value="$number_two"/>
    <postfield name="number_three" value="$number_three"/>
    <postfield name="number_four" value="$number_four"/>
</go>
```

where the default method issued is a GET.

Using the variables to initiate a query

In Listings 9-20 and 9-21, the data gathered was simply returned to the user. In practice it is more likely that you would need to check the lottery numbers entered and return a valid response to the user. In that case, you would store the lottery numbers in a database of some kind attached to the ColdFusion server. The database must be properly configured and defined as a data source so that queries can be processed. Table 9-11 shows what a possible winning-number table from such a database may look like.

TABLE 9-11 PAST WINNING LOTTERY NUMBERS

WN1	WN2	WN3	WN4	Date
31	32	4	5	3/27/01
12	24	38	2	3/28/01
6	7	37	42	3/29/01
8	17	32	46	3/30/01
22	32	42	46	4/01/01
1	10	40	49	4/02/01
15	16	41	44	4/03/01
4	22	31	44	4/04/01

Using a database like this, the server can identify whether a user's lottery numbers are on the winning list, as shown in Listing 9-22.

Listing 9-22: Winning-Combination Query

```
<CFCONTENT TYPE="text/vnd.wap.wml">

<?xml version="1.0"?><!DOCTYPE wml PUBLIC "-//WAPFORUM//DTD WML
1.1//EN" "http://www.wapforum.org/DTD/wml_1.1.xml">
<wml>

<card id="check" title="Lottery Results">
   <p>

  <Cfif (Form.number_one lt 0 OR Form.number_one gt 49) OR
```

```
        (Form.number_two lt 0 OR Form.number_two gt 49) OR
        (Form.number_three lt 0 OR Form.number_three gt 49) OR
        (Form.number_four lt 0 OR Form.number_four gt 49)>
            Numbers need to be between 1 and 49!
                </p>
                </card>
                </wml>
                <Cfabort>
</cfif>

        <!--- we are connecting to an ODBC datasource called lottery --->
        <cfquery name="winningnumbers" datasource="lottery" dbtype="ODBC">
        SELECT * FROM Lottery WHERE number_one='#form.number_one#'
        AND number_two='#form.number_two#'
        AND number_three='#form.number_three#'
        AND number_four='#form.number_four#'
        </cfquery>

        <Cfif  winningnumbers.recordcount gt 0>
        <strong>Wow, that number was a winner on
<cfoutput>#DateFormat(winningnumbers.date, "Mm/dd/yyyy")#</cfoutput>
</strong>
         <Cfelse>
             Sorry, that number has not been a winner.
         <do type='accept' label='Retry'>
            <go href='lottery.cfm'/>
         </do>

         </cfif>

         </p>
</card>
</wml>
```

The CFQUERY tag is a special programmatic reference to a query. Once the query has been created and given a specific name, information about, or from, a query can then be used in the rest of the code. The CFQUERY command simply executes the query on the database and stores information about it in a holding area on the ColdFusion server. It is now up to the programmer in the rest of the CFML code to make use of this information. For example, the query returns a set of columns, such as the remaining winning numbers or the date of the last time the winning number appeared in a given position. The main prefix in such a situation is queryname. For example, queryname.recordcount lists the number of records returned from the search.

Using the HomeSite editor

Because CFML code is plain text, you can use any text editor to write it. However, there is a much faster way to write CFML pages than to type in the special functions by hand. The ColdFusion Express Server comes with the Allaire HomeSite HTML editor, which you can also use for WAP development. The features that make it a good editor are tag attribute auto-selection and tag completion. Although you can also use it as a static file WML editor, it leaves a lot to be desired, as the HTML focus of the product results in the need for workarounds. The HomeSite WML and WAP support is biased towards Openwave-specific DTDs. The following sections provide descriptions of some of the best of what HomeSite has to offer.

TAG ATTRIBUTE AUTO-SELECTION

When entering WML tags you can see the attributes for the tags when you need a little help on what the attributes could or should be. If you type in a tag name and then press the spacebar, a list will pop up that enables you select from a list of available attribute options.

If this is not working for you, check Options → Settings → Tag Insight and then adjust the length of the wait before the auto-selection shows up.

The auto-selection not only enables you to select an attribute but also helps you fill out the attribute's value. Both these features will work on tags you have already entered as well as new ones.

This feature does have its problems: HTML and WML tags with the same names cause some incorrect attributes to be shown, attributes may sometimes be added in uppercase, and the choice of attributes is specific to Openwave. Entering or modifying the library of tags in the editor can eliminate some of these problems.

TAG EDITORS

HomeSite has a nifty feature for adding tags, which enables you to enter them by using a dialog box. You create the dialog box by modifying or creating special tag files, which saves you the trouble of typing in attributes by hand.

You can make another type of selection from a categorized list of tags. You can do this by activating the Tag Chooser (Tools/Tag Chooser) and then selecting from the list of WML tags. Very simple tags are inserted into the code immediately.

CREATING HEADERS IN CFML

Often, you will need to add headers to your WML deck for modifying browser behavior. For example, headers may be required to modify caching behavior. To add headers or modify automatically generated headers in ColdFusion code requires that you add CFHEADER tags to the top of the page, as in the following code:

```
<CFHEADER name="Cache-control" value="No-cache">
```

This code will generate the appropriate HTTP response header and send it to the Web server, which will honor the header as is.

Summary

This chapter covered the major dynamic scripting languages used by Web programmers the world over. One of the most common questions I have been asked is what I believe is the most effective editor for writing WML code. Inevitably, the discussion moves to the type of editor the developer currently uses. There is no magic bullet in the form of a new simulator/SDK that allows developers to churn out some type of new code for the wireless Web. The problems faced in writing pages for the wireless Internet are exactly the same ones that plague those writing pages for the wired Internet. First a decision has to be made as to whether pages are coded as static or dynamic. Do the developers write the WML tags around the content and save as a file to store on the Web server, or do they write a dynamic page, one that senses user capabilities and formulates the appropriate WML tags on the fly? In the first case, with static pages, developers can either write code in a text editor or they can use a WYSIWYG editor. With dynamic code, there are no significant WYSIWYG editors mirroring the sophistication of the developers' demands. In this case, then developers pick the language with which they have the most experience on the Web server. If they are Perl CGI developers, they select Perl for WAP development; if they have experience with Java, they select it. The decision is wide open.

Once that decision has been made, the developer's current SDK can be improved to assist in WAP development by the inclusion of object tools to help them more quickly add items to their text editors.

This chapter then to summarize gives the developer insights into various techniques that were either insignificant in traditional Web development or are important specifics that need to be addressed in WAP development.

Take a look at the Web site associated with this book (www.hungryminds.com/extras/) for a reference to code that appears throughout this book. The code at the Web site is recast in all the major scripting environments to give dynamic scripting programmers a clearer idea of how their environments are used to write WAP code.

Part III

Services on Advanced AB Architecture

CHAPTER 10
Building Active Applications Using Push Technology

CHAPTER 11
WTA

CHAPTER 12
Caching and Cache Operations

Chapter 10

Building Active Applications Using Push Technology

IN THIS CHAPTER

- ◆ Introducing Push
- ◆ Working with general push systems
- ◆ Using proprietary push mechanisms
- ◆ Implementing push services using WAP

PUSH SERVICES ARE A VERY POWERFUL ADDITION to the WAP suite. Combined with the mobility of the WAP client, push services let users choose when and where they want to receive information. The push models also do away with the limitation of the request/response architecture of the Web.

In this chapter, I explain why push is a powerful concept. Then I briefly turn your attention to how the push problem has been solved on the Internet. This will lead to a discussion of the proprietary push mechanisms widely used on WAP clients. Finally, in the core of the chapter, I examine in detail the push architecture and the components and protocols that surround it.

Introducing Push

So far, I have covered two-way transactions in which content is requested and a response is sent to a client. A whole class of applications exists for which this model is not suitable, however. For example, whenever a content holder wants a client to view information without a request being made, information not tied to any particular request has to be sent to the client. An example of this is a stock-quote service. Users of the service can register their portfolios with the service; when a user-controlled or service-initiated trigger occurs, a message can be sent to the client.

To initiate one of these "informational" messages, the service must start up a transaction. In this chapter I call these types of messages push messages, which is the WAP Forum's term. Other terms are used by the industry: for example, Openwave calls these messages notifications. Microsoft has a technology called channels that sounds like the same thing, but is not. I discuss all the competing technologies and the WAP push mechanism in this chapter.

The server creates push messages by using certain parameters; no matter what the technology, some basics are required. First of all, the server needs to know the identity of the client. This unique identity differs depending on the underlying technology being used. In the case of Openwave notifications, the identity is unique browser ID; in the case of SMS (Short Message Service), it is the telephone number; and in WAP push, it could be an IPv4 address, a Mobile Identification Number (MIN), an IPv6 address, or a randomly generated number.

The next basic element that is required is the content of the message. This is the information to be pushed to the client. It is what the users see if they view the message on the client. In some cases, it may be only a pointer to what they will see if they follow up on the message.

Beyond the identity and the content, every other parameter or option in a push system is usually an optional component that controls how the message is delivered to the client. However, WAP has two other important parameters that you should know about. These are push type and expiration time.

In WAP push, many types of push exist; they essentially differ in how they deliver information to the client. Some of these push types are purely programmatic commands directing the WAP browser to take some action behind the scenes. I discuss what they are in the WAP push section, but for now remember that the action you specify controls what the required parameters for a push transaction will be.

The other important parameter is the expiration time. This time controls how long a message stays on a carrier server or network trying to deliver a message to the client. If a phone is turned off for 12 days, a carrier is not willing to keep trying to deliver that message for that entire time. Usually the carrier will use a backoff schedule to attempt to deliver messages. This means that the carrier will try to deliver the message in one minute, and, if that doesn't work, wait two minutes, try again; wait four, try again; wait eight, and so on, until the message expires or the carrier decides to drop it.

In the following sections I examine some specific technologies. First, I discuss what is available on the Internet and how WAP push compares to some of the other systems in use.

Understanding Push Systems

Before examining wireless push, you might find it useful to look at the push technologies on the Internet. On a TCP/IP network all the clients are IP addressable and usually also routable, barring the use of private addresses and firewalls. Given the fact that the machines are routable and addressable, if a proprietary client and server are constructed, it is possible to push information to a client, because its IP address is given by the socket connection used to establish the connection. In this scenario, the client IP address is not expected to change.

Things get tricky when the client's IP address is not static and instead is obtained via DHCP or some other dynamic mechanism. Now the server that wants to send you information is unsure whether the IP address it has stored for you is the most accurate. For the purpose of this example, imagine that you as a client are also behind a corporate firewall. Now, if you want to receive a message, the IT department has to open up a port or IP address list in the firewall.

Because IP addresses can change dynamically on the Internet, a big problem with implementing push services is that they require a central authority to manage the association between your current IP address and some other global unique identifier. Push on the Internet is often simply client-scheduled pull, which is essentially a series of specifically timed HTTP requests. This is the case with Microsoft channels and CDF (Channel Definition Format), Marimba's CastaNet, and PointCast and other systems. You set up a content location with which you want to remain up to date. One of the options allows the user to decide how often you want to update, and the client follows this schedule to obtain the information.

The other problem with implementing push services on the Internet concerns dealing with the firewalls, which usually have the HTTP port 80 open. Therefore, that protocol is normally used to pass information back and forth, including client-scheduled pull messages.

In the wireless space, things have developed a little bit differently, owing partly to the control exerted by the carriers and other parties. The first widely used push system was SMS. The system was originally intended to be used only for clients to send short messages to each other. Eventually, multiple hooks were added so that messages could also be delivered to the clients in SMS format although they originated from disparate networks. Eventually, this meant that e-mail gateways, HTTP gateways, and other proprietary mechanisms could be used to deliver an SMS message to a wireless client. These systems were truly push. The client did not initiate any request. The problem with these systems is that you have to be familiar with the addressing format to send a message to the client. Sometimes this information is difficult to obtain for a network. In the case of disparate networks, such as Internet to wireless, very often the gateway is responsible for translating from the network the server is on to the network the client is on. In these cases, in addition to the client address, the gateway address also becomes important.

For privacy reasons, the carriers do not want their customers to be bombarded with messages, and addresses for clients or gateways are not being promoted strongly in the United States. The problem is compounded by the SMS service in all networks in the U.S. being one-way, meaning that a message can be delivered to the client but the client cannot respond using the same protocol. The only exception is PCS-1900 networks, such as VoiceStream nationwide or Verizon's PacBell in California. These networks are based on upbanded GSM technology, in which the established vendors and technology deliver two-way SMS.

Given the poor adoption of SMS technology in the U.S., when Openwave was creating its proprietary browser solution, it developed a system known as notifications, which worked closely with the browser. This system had the advantage of being independent of wireless technology. Disadvantages of the system were that it created a unique ID system and required knowledge of the unique ID as an identification mechanism for delivering messages. Furthermore, the technology set up a central gateway that managed the address mapping and controlled the entry for delivery of the push messages. Beyond that, Openwave instituted a system that used proprietary ports to which content servers had to connect in order to deliver push messages. This system also required proprietary APIs in order to send push messages. As you can see, the system went against what was accepted on comparable Internet systems.

WAP Forum members soon wrote up a specification that addressed some of the problems with the Openwave system. The specification eliminated the proprietary API system by creating an XML-compatible delivery system. It also mandated the use of HTTP port 80 to deliver the information. Then, instead of using a centrally managed mapping system, the WAP Forum members specified a system that distributed the problem among the carriers, allowing each one to come up with its own technology to specify identity. Even today, no implementations of WAP push are deployed, and no inter-gateway roaming is used.

That brings you up to date with the current situation. Now that you have the background, I examine how these different systems work and how the push messages can be sent. Figure 10-1 clarifies the discussion on the different types of Internet push systems introduced so far.

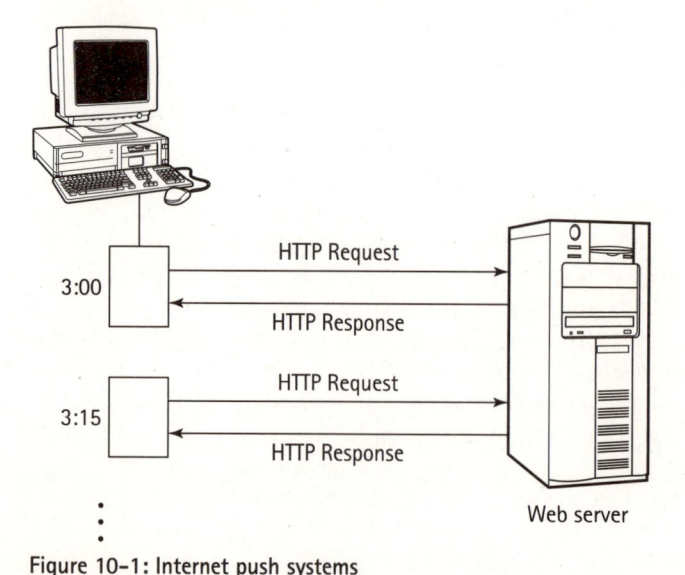

Figure 10-1: Internet push systems

Dealing with Mechanisms Outside WAP: Openwave

I would like to make it clear that this system is not part of WAP. I discuss it here because it is the predominant push system deployed with browsers in the United States. The next generation of these servers are expected to be WAP-compliant. The system sends push messages called notifications from the server.

Figure 10-2 shows the Openwave system architecture, which looks very much like the WAP models discussed in previous chapters.

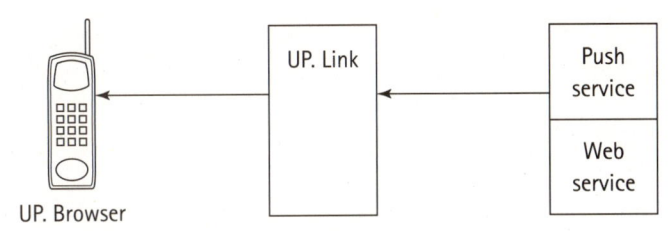

Figure 10-2: General Openwave architecture

Notifications come in three types: push, pull, and cache operation. The purpose of these operations is to send very little information to the client, because wireless bandwidth is limited. The push and pull operations are very similar to one another, so I discuss those first.

Push notification

The push operation simply sends a URL with a brief description to a client. The client then invokes a URL request if the user indicates an interest in the information. The URL request/response session follows the standard browsing mechanism, and therefore only the initial URL delivery can be considered push.

A server must use the proprietary push API provided by Openwave to send information to the client, and the server must deliver this information to the WAP gateway with some basic parameters. The proprietary API used actually generates a multipart MIME message that contains the URL content as one part and the operation and its commands as the other part.

From the user's perspective, this push notification shows up as an alert. When the notification shows up at the client, it notifies the client with a beep or vibration and displays a message informing the user that the notification has arrived. The notification is also added to a notification manager where the most recently received alerts are stored. Although the alert descriptions are visible from the wireless client, only the URLs are stored there in a deck. The actual alert or notification has to be fetched from the UP.Link, the Openwave special WAP gateway that manages the notifications. Figure 10-3 shows a notification as a user would see it.

```
┌─────────────────┐
│ Message from    │
│ ASX.com; View   │
│ it now?         │
│                 │
│                 │
│                 │
│ View      Skip  │
└─────────────────┘
         │
┌─────────────────┐
│ ASX.com         │
│ Great prices on │
│ our new roller  │
│ blades!         │
│                 │
│                 │
│ OK        Next  │
└─────────────────┘
```

Figure 10-3: Consumer view of a notification

After a user selects a push notification, the user client actually navigates to the URL indicated by the push message. This URL request begins a standard request/response transaction to obtain content from information servers.

WAP browsing services are considered data services because they use data bearers in order to carry information back and forth between the client and the content servers. The data bearers can be very diverse, as mentioned in Chapter 2. For technological or business reasons, some data bearers do not allow a wireless client's data service to be up all the time. The user must initiate a connection before the data bearer becomes active. In these cases, push services may not be delivered in a timely manner.

The Openwave UP.Link attempts to deliver a push notification regardless of the bearer type, but notifications may not get through on limited bearers until the user chooses to connect. The Openwave UP.Link attempts to deliver the message periodically, according to a backoff schedule, if the client is not available.

Figure 10-4 shows how the push notifications are sent to the client and the different network components involved in their transmission.

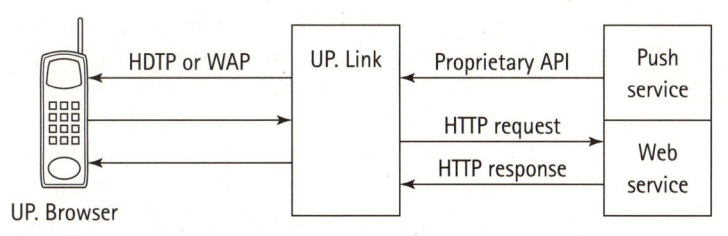

Chapter 10: Building Active Applications Using Push Technology

Figure 10-4: Openwave push architecture — push notifications

The push notifications support only content types that send a URL and a short description.

Pull notifications

The pull notifications are very similar to push notifications except that different information is sent to the client. With push notifications, only the URL and short description are sent to the client. It is then up to the user to request the information in the sent URL.

With push notifications, a URL and short description are also sent to the client. But in this case, the UP.Link obtains the information pointed to by the URL, combines that information with the URL, and sends it to the client.

Figure 10-5 shows how the architecture for pull notifications looks. The pull notification acts different on limited-connectivity bearers. In those cases, the UP.Link requests only the content associated with the URL after the user has connected to the WAP service.

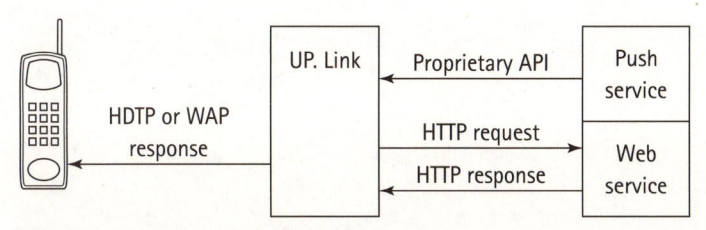

Figure 10-5: Openwave notifications (pull)

Pull notifications allow more content types to be sent to the client. Besides the simple URL and description, you can also send decks, images, and digests.

Cache operations

I cover cache operations only briefly here; Chapter 12, "Caching and Cache Operations," goes much further into this topic. Cache operations are actions, specified by a content server, that invalidate cached elements on a client device. A cache operation can invalidate a single element or multiple elements simultaneously.

When a client visits a site, the client usually caches the content obtained to improve performance. The next time the site and page are visited, the client may use the cached content instead of fetching new content from the server. The algorithms associated with using cached content versus requesting new data are quite complex; I examine them in detail in Chapter 12. However, it may be necessary for some applications, especially those that cannot rely on caching algorithms, to forcibly delete or invalidate the cached content. This is what a caching operation does. By deleting cached content, a server forces the client to request new data.

Cache operations require the use of the push style of notifications and mirror the behavior of that style. For example, they require an active bearer at all times to be a meaningful means of controlling cached content.

Cache operations work silently in the background. A user will not see any indicator that a cache operation has occurred or is occurring. It is possible to indirectly test whether the invalidation has occurred by re-navigating to URLs, which were stored in the cache.

Cache operations do not need to be sent inside push messages; you can package them along with other content types, but only in the Openwave platform. By packaging a cache operation with a home deck, for example, a developer can be sure that no residual stale content resides on a client.

The cache operations come in two types, as shown in Figure 10-6: one that invalidates a single named resource in the cache, and one that invalidates everything under a named directory tree.

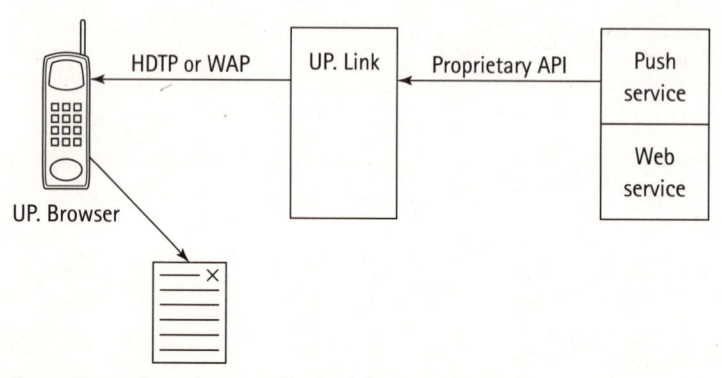

Figure 10-6: Openwave notifications (cache operations)

UP.Link server queuing

To implement this form of pushing, Openwave also instituted a few other features, which it found necessary based on tests with users. Most wireless clients tested were very often out of range, turned off, or simply not available to receive push messages a large percentage of the time. To combat this problem, it was necessary to be very explicit in defining good algorithms for deciding when to discard user push messages. The algorithms were initially tested on packet-switched networks with high client availability.

The first feature that Openwave added was a means of managing a notification queue for each client. The UP.Link uses it to manage a list of pending messages and attempts to deliver them based on their individual schedules. For economic reasons, carriers often do not wish to store data for long periods of time; therefore, the UP.Link server allows content to be removed from the notification queue if it has been there for too long. The carrier can also specify individual schedules for delivery of messages.

Another added feature was a TTL, or time to live, with each push message. The TTL allowed content servers to control how long a message could reside in a notification queue.

Eventually, Openwave found that multiple push messages sometimes originate from a content server, all of which have the same URL. For these cases Openwave added a feature to the UP.Link that allowed the UP.Link to replace the list of messages with matching URLs using the most recent message. This freed up the notification queue for other push messages.

Later on, it became necessary to adapt this technology to limited bearer connections such as circuit-switched-only networks. In those cases, it was a waste of resources to attempt to deliver a message to a client who was obviously disconnected. A feature was added that allowed pull notifications to be sent to the client, but only after the client had connected with the UP.Link. As a result, the UP.Link had to store all the push messages until the client started the service.

> The Openwave system is limited to nine messages in the notification queue. If a tenth message arrives, it simply writes over the ninth message. If an eleventh message arrives, it also writes over the ninth spot. This occurs for all subsequent messages until the notification queue is decremented below eight.

Sending notifications

To send notifications to a client using the Openwave system, you must know the subscriber ID of the browser being sent a message. This ID is delivered to the server in the form of a proprietary HTTP header, HTTP_X_UP_SUBNO. You can locate the ID on the client by viewing its settings.

Next, because the system uses a nonstandard port, you need to ensure that your server can send data out on TCP ports 3356 (nonsecure) and 4445 (secure).

The tools available for sending these notifications are a Windows-based COM Notification Library and a UNIX/Solaris C++ Notification Library. Functions are included with the libraries that enable you to check the status of sent push notifications.

Using the COM Notification Library

The COM Notification Library is a language-independent means of calling functions from the Windows environment. The library contains two classes, `Ntfn3Client` and `Ntfn3Sclient`. An older class, `NtfnClient`, also exists and is used to send messages using older UP.Link servers.

Here is an example that shows how to send a message using ASP and the COM library.

Working with WAP Push

When the push drafting committee within WAP Forum looked at push, the committee built upon the techniques that Openwave had used in sending push notifications in its proprietary format. The committee made several distinct changes to improve the original system by creating a more open standard, one that is more secure, one with more capabilities. Even with this improvement, at the time of this writing there are no deployments of the WAP push system. The WAP push specifications themselves were not among the first release of WAP 1.1; they were added later in WAP 1.2, and the delay ensured they were not included in WAP first-generation products.

Push architecture

The architecture for WAP push has some of the same components located architecturally where we would expect them to be—only the names are different. Figure 10-7 illustrates these components, which are the Push Initiator (PI), the Push Proxy Gateway (PPG), and the Push Client (client). The links between the components are Push Access Protocol (PAP), which links the PI and PPG, and Push Over the Air Protocol (Push OTA), which links the PPG and the client. Although theoretically, it's recommended that the PPG be implemented as a separate software process on an independent machine, in practice it can be implemented as part of the WAP gateway cluster for performance reasons. For example, a push message that generates a subsequent URL request is better performed for transaction latency reasons if both actions are closely coordinated.

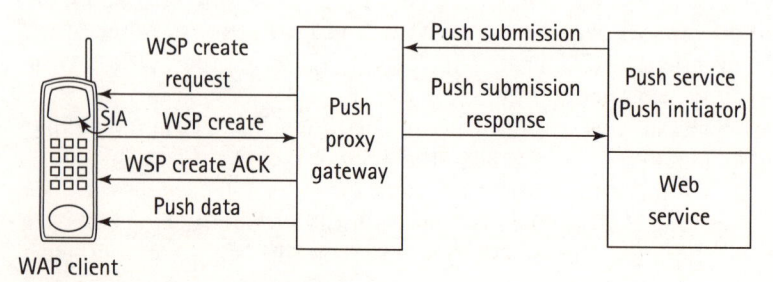

Figure 10-7: WAP push architecture

To send a push message in the system, the server creates a specially formatted PAP message and delivers it to the PPG. The PPG checks it for completeness and accuracy. If the message is okay, the PPG accepts it and attempts to deliver it to the client.

For the most part, early developers will be working to create the PAP message from scratch without the assistance of any tools, so that process will be the focus of my discussion. Other aspects of push, such as the Push OTA, are less significant for developers; however, I will discuss them briefly.

Push access protocol

The push access protocol is the main protocol proposed by the WAP Forum to enable developers to send push messages to wireless clients. It allows Internet-based push initiators on the Internet to send push messages to WAP clients. The protocol has been designed with more care than the proprietary standards discussed earlier in this chapter. The standard will eventually work on more than one bearer, meaning that a message may be pushed using HTTP, SMTP, or possibly even a binary-based session over TCP/IP.

The general structure of a PAP message is in the form of an XML-style entity that may be combined with other media types and components in a multipart/related document. The PAP messages support five operations and one bad-message operation. The five operations all have two components. There is a message submittal and then a message response. These operations are listed in Table 10-1.

TABLE 10-1 PAP OPERATIONS

PAP Operation	Direction	Description	Required to be Supported by PPG?
Push submission	PI → PPG	The initial message sent by the PI to submit some push content	Mandatory
Push submission response	PI ← PPG	The response to the push submission received by the PI	Mandatory
Result notification submission	PI ← PPG	A result notification delivered to the PI when the message is acknowledged by the wireless client	Mandatory
Result notification response	PI → PPG	A response the PI sends to acknowledge receipt of the result notification; the PPG will keep trying until it is sent	Mandatory

Continued

TABLE 10-1 PAP OPERATIONS *(Continued)*

PAP Operation	Direction	Description	Required to be Supported by PPG?
Push cancellation	PI → PPG	Used by a PI to cancel a previously sent push message	Optional
Push cancellation response	PI ← PPG	The response received by the PI indicating receipt of the push cancellation message	Optional
Status query	PI → PPG	Used by the PI to query the status of a previously sent message	Optional
Status query response	PI ← PPG	Indicates the status of the messages indicated in the original query; received right away by the PPG	Optional
Client capabilities query	PI → PPG	Allows the PI to find out the capabilities of the client	Optional
Client capabilities query response	PI ← PPG	A response to the client capabilities query, with the capabilities attached in RDF format, as specified by UAProf	Optional
Bad-message response	PI ← PPG	A response to anything the PPG receives that does not make sense syntactically to the XML parser	Mandatory

Depending on the operation being performed, the push message submitted by the push initiator can contain from one to three entities. The order of the entities is fixed; however, all three entities do not need to appear in all types of operations. The order in which the entities need to be included in the push submission is as follows:

- Control entity
- Content entity
- Capability entity

Chapter 10: Building Active Applications Using Push Technology

The control entity contains delivery instructions destined for the Push Proxy Gateway and is an XML application further constrained by the PAP DTD. This component contains all the control information needed to deliver the push message to the wireless client.

The content entity is the information that is actually delivered to the WAP client. Unlike a standard WAP gateway, the PPG does not have to convert the content into an optimized form if it is not recognized. It can attempt to deliver the content information without modifying it. This feature is useful when delivering encrypting information to the WAP client.

The last potential component is the capability entity, which conforms to the UAProf standard for indicating what the client capabilities are for the client.

PUSH SUBMISSION AND RESPONSE

A push submission is composed of two mandatory parts and, sometimes, another optional part. It must contain a control portion and some content to be pushed. It can also have a client capabilities query attached to the end of it, which allows the PI to indicate to the PPG what the PI thinks the client capabilities are.

PUSH SUBMISSION The PAP DTD specifies the control information for a push submission. Listing 10-1 shows the PAP DTD for the push message submission.

Listing 10-1: PAP DTD

```
<!ELEMENT push-message ( address+, quality-of-service? ) >
<!ATTLIST push-message
push-id CDATA #REQUIRED
deliver-before-timestamp %Datetime; #IMPLIED
deliver-after-timestamp %Datetime; #IMPLIED
source-reference CDATA #IMPLIED
ppg-notify-requested-to CDATA #IMPLIED
progress-notes-requested ( true | false ) "false"
>
```

The DTD shows that the push message may contain one or more addresses and a `quality-of-service` element. The attribute list for the push message includes a `push-id`, `deliver-before-` or `-after` timestamps, a `source-reference`, a `ppg-notify-request-to`, and `progress-notes-requested`. Table 10-2 describes each of the push message attributes.

TABLE 10-2 PUSH MESSAGE ATTRIBUTES

Attribute	Description
push-id	A unique identifier for each message that the PI is responsible for maintaining. I recommend that you that you end the push-id with the PI domain name. *Example*: 3923973249-zsigo.com
deliver-before-timestamp deliver-after-timestamp	These dates and times indicate the requirements for the time constraints regarding the delivery of the push message.
source-reference	An optional component that contains a textual string that identifies the push content source.
ppg-notify-requested-to	Gives information about the address (URL) that should be used by the PPG to notify the PI of any results notifications.
progress-notes-requested	Set to either true or false; indicates whether or not progress notes should be sent to the wireless client on intermediate stages of push delivery — for example, when the message is sent by the PPG but not yet acknowledged by the wireless client.

The most important child element of the push message is the address element. Multiple address elements are allowed and contain information about where the push message is to be delivered. (An address element indicates where the push message is to be delivered. Multiple addresses can be targeted on a single request.)

Listing 10-2 shows how an example PAP message would look.

Listing 10-2: Example PAP Message

```
Content-Type: multipart/related; boundary=this_is_a_test;
type="application/xml"

--this_is_a_test

Content-Type: application/xml
<?xml version="1.0"?>
```

Chapter 10: Building Active Applications Using Push Technology

```xml
<!DOCTYPE pap PUBLIC "-//WAPFORUM//DTD PAP 1.0//EN"
"http://www.wapforum.org/DTD/pap_1.0.dtd">
<pap>
<push-message push-id="39870932802@push_service.com">
<address address-
value="wappush=934702/type=user@push_proxy.carrier.com">
</address>
</push-message>
</pap>

--asdlfkjiurwghasf

Content-Type: text/vnd.wap.wml

<?xml version="1.0"?>
<!DOCTYPE WML PUBLIC "-//WAPFORUM//DTD WML 1.1//EN"
"http://www.wapforum.org/DTD/wml_1.1.xml">
<wml>
<card>
<p>A test WML file</p>
</card>
</wml>

--asdlfkjiurwghasf

Content-Type: application/xml

<?xml version="1.0"?>
<rdf:RDF xmlns:rdf="http://www.w3.org/1999/02/22-rdf-syntax-ns#"
xmlns:prf="http://www.wapforum.org/UAPROF/ccppschema1.0#">

<rdf:Description>
<prf:WapVersion>1.2</prf:WapVersion>
<prf:WmlDeckSize>2000 octets</prf:WmlDeckSize>
<prf:WapDeviceClass>A </prf:WapDeviceClass>
<prf:WapPushMsgSize>2000 octets</prf:WapPushMsgSize>
<prf:WmlVersion>
<rdf:Bag>
<rdf:li>1.2</rdf:li>
</rdf:Bag>
</prf:WmlVersion>
</rdf:Description>
</rdf:RDF>
--asdlfkjiurwghasf--
```

The preceding example shows the three parts of the push submission, as well as the optional client capabilities query.

In an initial push submission, the control portion contains parameters for delivery of the push message. The content contains information intended for the client, and the optional UAProf section contains a listing of client capabilities that the push initiator believes are accurate for the client being sent a message.

PUSH SUBMISSION RESPONSE   The PPG uses the push submission response to tell the PI the immediate status of the push submission. A message can be rejected even in this early phase of the processing cycle. If there is a problem with the push submission the problem is reported in the push submission and not via the HTTP protocol or any other protocol being used. If HTTP is being used, a `202 Accepted` is always returned here.

A push submission response contains only a control entity and therefore does not have to be packaged as a multipart/mixed. The push submission response is defined by the PAP DTD, as shown in Figure 10-8.

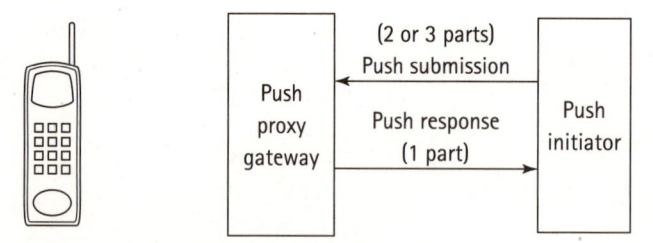

Figure 10-8: Push submission response

The attributes of the push submission response are the `push-id`, `sender-address`, `sender-name`, and `reply-time` attributes, as described in Table 10-3.

TABLE 10-3 PUSH MESSAGE RESPONSE ATTRIBUTES

Attribute	Description
push-id	A unique identifier for each message that the PI is responsible for maintaining. I recommend that the `push-id` value end in the PI domain name so that it does not clash with other push IDs that the PPG is tracking. *Example:* 3923973249-zsigo.com The push message response returns this `push-id` so that the PI can keep track of its message.

Attribute	Description
sender-address	Contains the PPG URL to which the message was originally posted.
sender-name	Contains the textual name of the PPG, which may be useful to some human reading the response.
reply-time	The time and date associated with the creation of the response.

The push submission response can contain progress notes or a single response result. This response result contains a code and a textual description of the code. The codes used by the responses in all the remaining operations are the same. They are very similar to HTTP codes, except that the PAP return codes consist of four digits. The code attribute is in one of five classes, described in Table 10-4.

TABLE 10-4 RETURN CODE CLASSES

Code Range	Description
1xxx	The operation was successfully received and accepted for action.
2xxx	The operation contains bad syntax or the client cannot fulfill it.
3xxx	The operation contains bad syntax or the server cannot fulfill it even though it may be valid according to the syntactical rules.
4xxx	The service could not be performed this time; you can try again later.
5xxx	The wireless client aborted the transaction.

You could generate a push submission using the code shown in Listing 10-3.

Listing 10-3: Push Submission Code

```
<?xml version="1.0"?>
<!DOCTYPE pap PUBLIC "-//WAPFORUM//DTD PAP 1.0//EN"
"http://www.wapforum.org/DTD/pap_1.0.dtd">
<pap>
<push-response push-id="2034209249@push_service.com">
```

Continued

Listing 10-3 *(Continued)*

```
<address address-
value="wappush=40349/type=user@push_proxy.carrier.com"></address>
</push-response>
</pap>
```

RESULT NOTIFICATION AND RESULT NOTIFICATION RESPONSE

The result notification is the only operation initiated by the PPG. You can instruct the PPG to contact the PI whenever a message has reached the final stage of its delivery criteria by setting the appropriate attribute in the original push submission. In the case of two-way devices, the acknowledgement happens when the device acknowledges receipt; in the case of one-way devices, it happens when the message is sent to the device.

Figure 10-9 shows the timing for when the result notification is called. The PPG tells the PI the outcome of previous message using the result notification.

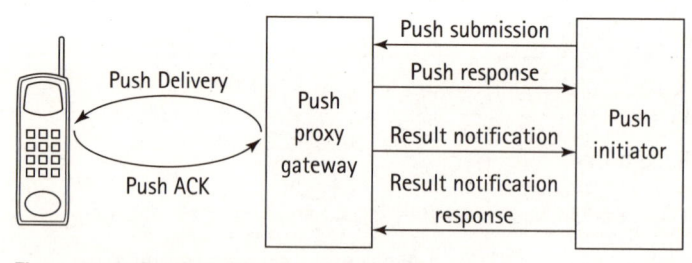

Figure 10-9: Result notification message flow

Note that when the message is initially sent from the PI to the PPG, the response returned for the push submission indicates whether the mobile device received the message successfully. If there is a problem with the message, the PPG is specified to return an error automatically; otherwise, you can assume that the PPG has assumed responsibility for the message and that it will be delivered to the WAP client according to the specified parameters. In that case the error code is received right away and a result notification is never generated.

A result notification contains many of the same attributes we have seen in other push operations, as shown by the following DTD:

```
<!ELEMENT resultnotification-message ( address, quality-of-service?
) >
<!ATTLIST resultnotification-message
push-id CDATA #REQUIRED
sender-address CDATA #IMPLIED
sender-name CDATA #IMPLIED
received-time %Datetime; #IMPLIED
event-time %Datetime; #IMPLIED
```

```
message-state %State; #REQUIRED
code CDATA #REQUIRED
desc CDATA #IMPLIED
>
```

Here is an example of a result notification message:

```
< resultnotification-message push-id="2034209249@push_service.com"
message-state="delivered" code="1000" desc="OK"
>
<address address-
value="wappush=40349/type=user@push_proxy.carrier.com"></address>
</resultnotification-message>
```

The only component not yet discussed is the message state. A push message can have many message states, but the PAP specification defines some standard milestones that a message may progress through before being considered delivered. Table 10-5 shows what they are.

TABLE 10-5 PUSH MESSAGE STATES

Message State	Description
rejected	Message was refused by the PPG.
pending	Message was accepted by the PPG and delivery is pending.
delivered	Message was delivered to the wireless client.
undelivered	Message could not be delivered to the wireless client.
expired	The message exceeded the PPG implementation-specific timeout or the timeout as specified in the push submission.
aborted	The wireless client or its user aborted the message.
timeout	The message timed out according to some internal process.
cancelled	The message was cancelled by the PI using the `cancel` operation.
unknown	The PPG does not know the status of the message.

The PI uses the result notification response to tell the PPG that it has received the result notification response successfully. This result notification response contains a `resultnotification-response` and three attributes, which are the `push-id`, a code, and the code description. Both the PI and the PPG use the `push-id` to keep track of messages. The `push-id` is a passthrough variable. The following sections of code show the Result Notification Response DTD and a typical PI result notification response.

```
<!ELEMENT resultnotification-response ( address ) >
<!ATTLIST resultnotification-response
push-id CDATA #REQUIRED
code CDATA #REQUIRED
desc CDATA #IMPLIED
>
<resultnotification-response push-id="320302498@push_service.com" code="3006" desc="Transformation Failure">
<address address-value="wappush=40349/type=user@push_proxy.carrier.com"></address>
</resultnotification>
```

PUSH CANCELLATION AND PUSH CANCELLATION RESPONSE

A push cancellation is used to cancel a push submission if doing so is still possible — that is, the message has still not gone through because, for example, the mobile device has been switched off. This operation is useful when a message is being sent through multiple channels. If a success condition is achieved through one of the wireless networks, a cancel request is issued to all the others. The push cancellation can also be initiated in cases in which a previously sent push message has become outdated. In this case, if the older message has not yet been received by the wireless client, it can be replaced with new content.

Figure 10-10 shows the push cancellation process.

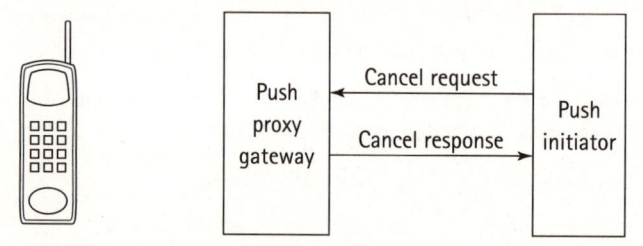

Figure 10-10: Push cancellation architecture

Following is an example of a cancel-message. Very simply, it takes only a `push-id` or reference to the original message.

```
<cancel-message push-id="320302498@push_service.com">
<address address-value="wappush=40349/type=user@push_proxy.carrier.com"></address>
</cancel-message>
```

The PPG then sends the cancel response, indicating whether it (the PPG) was able to cancel the message or not. Following is an example of a typical response.

```
<cancel-response push-id="320302498@push_service.com">
<cancel-result code="3001" desc="Not Implemented"/>
</cancel-response>
```

In this case, 3001 is returned because the PPG does not support the cancel message operation. The only attribute of a cancel response is the `push-id`.

STATUS QUERY AND STATUS QUERY RESPONSE

This operation is another optional XML-style entity, which gives the push initiator the ability to track the status of a previously sent message. The following code shows what the status query and status query response messages look like. The only required attributes of the status query are the `push-id` and the address element.

Here is the status query request:

```
<statusquery-message push-id="320302498@push_service.com">
<address address-value="wappush=40349/type=user@push_proxy.carrier.com"></address>
</statusquery-message>
```

And here is the status query response:

```
<statusquery-response push-id="320302498@push_service.com">
<!ELEMENT statusquery-result ( address*, quality-of-service? ) >
<!ATTLIST statusquery-result message-state="undelivered" code="4000" desc="Service Failure"
>
</statusquery-response>
```

The status query response contains a `statusquery-result` element, which contains the timestamp, message state, code, and description of the queried message. This information should give the PI enough to maintain a status report.

CLIENT CAPABILITIES QUERY AND CLIENT CAPABILITIES QUERY RESPONSE

The last of the possible operations of which a PI is capable is the client capabilities query, which the PI makes by checking on a specific client's capabilities. The PPG responds to the request with a multipart/related message, which contains the result of the request as the first part and the capabilities of a device as the second part. These device capabilities are formatted using the UAProf, which I discuss in Chapter 14, "Targeted Development."

Following is an example of a client capabilities query.

```
<ccq-message query-id="233208032@push_service.com"
app-id="standard">
<address address-
value="wappush=40349/type=user@push_proxy.carrier.com"></address>
</ccq-message>
```

The possible attributes of the `ccq-message` are the `query-id` and the `app-id`. To match multiple responses to their origin, the PI can use both of these attributes. They are unique strings generated by the PI.

The `ccq-response` is a little bit more involved because it is a multipart/related response. The first part of the response is the PAP code I discussed earlier in this chapter. The control code contains only the `ccq-response` element and its code and description attributes along with the original `query-id` or `app-id`, if either is used. Inside the `ccq-response` control element are the various addresses that were part of the original query.

The second part of the `ccq-response` is the RDF-structured capabilities of the wireless client being queried. Following is an example of the `ccq-response`.

```
Content-Type: multipart/related; boundary=this_is_a_test;
type="application/xml"

--this_is_a_test

Content-Type: application/xml

<?xml version="1.0"?>
<!DOCTYPE pap PUBLIC "-//WAPFORUM//DTD PAP 1.0//EN"
"http://www.wapforum.org/DTD/pap_1.0.dtd">
<pap>
<ccq-response query-id="233208032@push_service.com"
code="1000" desc="OK">
<address address-
value="wappush=40349/type=user@push_proxy.carrier.com"></address>
</ccq-reponse>
</pap>

--this_is_a_test

Content-Type: application/xml

<?xml version="1.0"?>
<rdf:RDF xmlns:rdf="http://www.w3.org/1999/02/22-rdf-syntax-ns#"
xmlns:prf="http://www.wapforum.org/UAPROF/ccppschema1.0#">

<rdf:Description>
```

```
<prf:WapVersion>1.2</prf:WapVersion>
<prf:WmlDeckSize>2000 octets</prf:WmlDeckSize>
<prf:WapDeviceClass>A </prf:WapDeviceClass>
<prf:WapPushMsgSize>2000 octets</prf:WapPushMsgSize>
<prf:WmlVersion>
<rdf:Bag>
<rdf:li>1.2</rdf:li>
</rdf:Bag>
</prf:WmlVersion>
</rdf:Description>
</rdf:RDF>
--this_is_a_test--
```

BAD MESSAGE

This message does not fit neatly into any of the previous responses but is used by the PPG when the original request is unrecognizable. A fragment of the original message can be contained in the response to help the developer at the PI.

Following is an example of a bad message response.

```
<badmessage-response bad-message-fragment="lsfkjlsdkjf309282309"/>
```

HTTP TUNNELING

The PI as an Internet host uses the HTTP protocol to establish a session with the PPG. In future versions of the PAP protocol it may possible to tunnel the PAP protocol over something other than HTTP, such as SMTP or a binary session over TCP.

The PI makes requests using an HTTP POST method and, as a result, receives a 202 code, which indicates that the message has been accepted by the PPG for processing. The 202 addresses only the issue of the HTTP transaction, not the PAP protocol itself. Therefore, a PAP message with error information can still be sent to the PI.

Service indications, service loadings, and cache operations

The way the PAP protocol is specified, you can include any media type in the second part of the message as content — even a media type that a PPG or WAP gateway will not comprehend. Rather than reject this content, the PPG is required to send it to the wireless client as is. Encrypted media types can be sent and decrypted by a specific application on the wireless client.

Besides the special cases, all the standard media types such as WML can be packaged into a push content message. However, for the time being, the PPG supports only a limited set of media types: service indication, service loading, and cache operation.

To minimize memory requirements and conserve bandwidth over the air, you should send the wireless client only a URL reference that points to the actual data. This is exactly what the service loading and service indication media types were created to do.

SERVICE INDICATION

Service indications are exactly like the push messages on the Openwave system, which I described in the Openwave push section of this chapter. They enable you to send a URL to the wireless client along with short description of the service associated with the URL. The service indication works as shown in Figure 10-11.

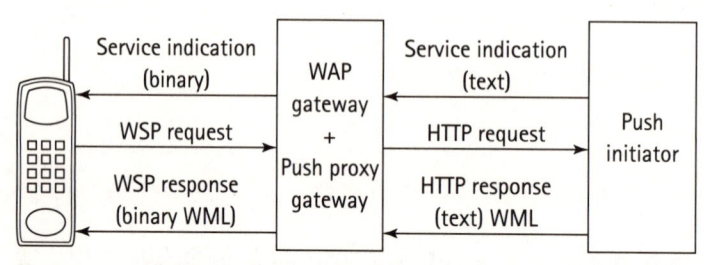

Figure 10-11: Service indication architecture

A new content type called an SI has been created for sending service indications. The SI is an application of XML, and the details can be found in an SI DTD. Here is an example of what an SI could look like:

```
<?xml version="1.0"?>
<!DOCTYPE si PUBLIC "-//WAPFORUM//DTD SI 1.0//EN"
"http://www.wapforum.org/DTD/si.dtd">
<si>
<indication href="http://www.zsigo.com/mailbox.wml"
created="2000-09-02T07:33:00Z"
si-expires="2000-09-02T07:50:00Z"
     action="signal-medium">
         You have 3 new messages.
     </indication>
</si>
```

The SI is an XML application that must be validated. The root element is the `si`. Inside the root element, only the `indication` element and `info` elements are allowed as children. The `info` element is an optional child that specifies additional information about the `indication` element attributes. The `indication` attributes are shown in the following DTD code:

```
<!ELEMENT si(indication,info?)>

<!ELEMENT indication (#PCDATA)>
<!ATTLIST indication
href %URI; #IMPLIED
si-id CDATA #IMPLIED
```

```
created %Datetime; #IMPLIED
si-expires %Datetime; #IMPLIED
action (signal-none|signal-low|
signal-medium|signal-high|delete) "signal-medium"
>

<!ELEMENT info (item+)>
<!ELEMENT item (#PCDATA)>
<!ATTLIST item
class NMTOKEN #REQUIRED
>
```

The first of the `indication` attributes shown is the `href`, which is a reference to some valid content on an Internet server. The `si-id` follows, which may contain a unique ID for the service indication. After that, the `created` and `si-expires` dates appear; these specify when the service indication was created and how long it can take to get the message to the user before the message is automatically discarded by the wireless client.

The last parameter in an `indication` is the `action` signal. This signal indicates how intrusive the push message is when it gets to the WAP client. These range from `signal-none` all the way to `signal-high`. A `delete` is also available, which indicates that the user never sees the `si`; the wireless client discards it as soon as it arrives.

Overall, the `si` is a very simple content type that sends only a reference to the wireless client. The WAP client has to establish a separate WSP/HTTP request of the WAP gateway to actually retrieve the data indicated by the SI.

SERVICE LOADING

With the exception of a few subtleties, the service loading is effectively the same as the service indication. It is yet another mechanism for sending a short reference URL to the phone. This time, however, instead of just receiving the reference to the URL, the phone receives both the short message and the data stored at the URL. Figure 10-12 shows how this works.

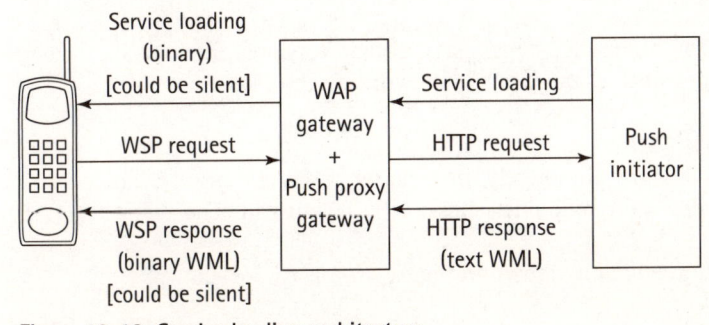

Figure 10-12: Service loading architecture

The wireless client receives the SL and then, without user interaction, proceeds to fetch the URL specified in the SL href attribute. Here is an example SL message:

```
<?xml vesion="1.0"?>
<!DOCTYPE sl PUBLIC "-//WAPFORUM//DTD SL 1.0//EN"
 "http://www.wapforum.org/DTD/sl.dtd">
<sl
href="http://www.zsigo.com/mailbox.wml"
     action="execute-low"
/>
```

The SL DTD is shown in the next snippet of code.

```
<!ENTITY % URI "CDATA"> <!-- URI designating a
hypertext node -->

<!ELEMENT sl EMPTY>
<!ATTLIST sl
href %URI; #REQUIRED
action (execute-low|execute-high|cache) "execute-low"
>
```

The SL message is another application of XML and has its own DTD, against which the message must be validated. The SL message has a root element of sl along with two attributes, one being the URL and another specifying the action the mobile device has to take with the SL message. The SL can be executed with high privilege or low privilege, or the data can be cached on the wireless client without being shown to the user.

> **TIP** I recommend using an SL when the content does not go stale quickly; otherwise, you should use an SI. This is because an SI fetches fresh content from the server every single time.

Both the SI and the SL content types have binary versions, SIc and SLc, which are used when being sent over the wireless network by the PPG.

CACHE OPERATIONS

Caching is discussed more completely in Chapter 12. Very briefly, however, a cache operation is also a possible push message that you can send using the PAP protocol.

The cache operation works as shown in Figure 10-13.

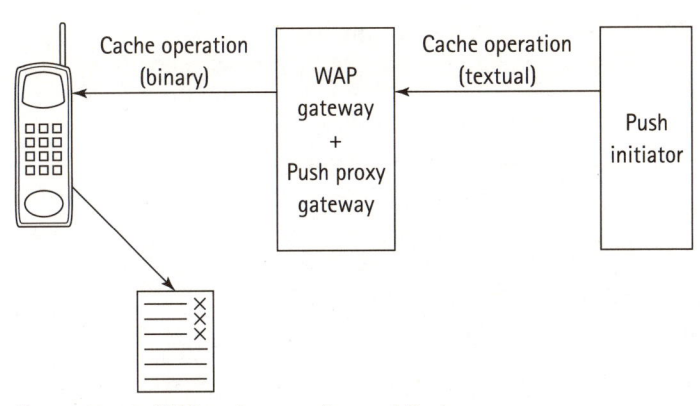

Chapter 10: Building Active Applications Using Push Technology

Figure 10-13: WAP cache operation architecture

Caching operations remove content stored in memory on the wireless client. Caching may be required if stale content can potentially wreak havoc on your application. For example, outdated screens may be presented to the user pointing to broken or stale contents of your WAP site. Imagine someone buying a concert ticket at a special price no longer being offered. Also, you can use caching to synchronize changes between user response and server interaction. For example, if the user deletes an item from a list, the item is expected to go away, and you can make sure it does using cache operations.

Like the other preferred push types, cache operations have their own DTDs and root elements. Following is an example cache operation:

```
<?xml vesion="1.0"?>
<!DOCTYPE co PUBLIC "-//WAPFORUM//DTD CO 1.0//EN"
"http://www.wapforum.org/DTD/co_1.0.dtd">
<co>
<invalidate-object uri="test.gif"></invalidate-object>
<invalidate-service uri="http://www.zsigo.com/wireless">
</invalidate-service>
</co>
```

The cache operation example shows a root element of `co` with two children, `invalidate-object` and `invalid-service`. The `co` element can contain any number of either of these child elements. The `invalidate-object` operation removes the item specified from the cache of the wireless client. The `invalidate-service` operation removes all items that have a URL beginning with the `uri` fragment specified in the operation by the push initiator.

PPG

The Push Proxy Gateway is the core of the push architecture. Its responsibilities are to ensure that content from push initiators on the Internet is delivered to the mobile network clients. The PPG is the main access point for everything associated with the delivery of push messages, including authentication, security, checking where clients are, and maintaining status information. The PPG software process functionality can be included in WAP gateways by vendors. These combined units then enable sessions created for standard WAP requests and responses to be reused for push messages.

The PPG is responsible for several services. In its minimal configuration it is expected to perform the following:

- Identifying and authenticating the PI (access control)
- Detecting errors in control information and then parsing this information
- Discovering the location of clients
- Resolving addresses
- Encoding recognized types
- Managing traffic from WSP to HTTP

A PPG accepts content from Internet hosts called PIs using the PAP protocol. It has to identify the PI and determine whether it is allowed access to the push facilities. In most cases, a prior security relationship should have been established with the PI before it is allowed access to push services. After receiving a push message a PPG has to use its XML parser to make sure the message is well formed and to validate it against the DTD. If the message passes this stage, a response is issued immediately.

A PPG then has to use its wireless network capabilities to resolve the address and determine how best to send the push message to the wireless client. If any recognized content types in the push message can be encoded for more efficient transfer, they are then tokenized and the message is shipped using one of the push modes specified. For example, the encoding for WML, binary WML, is well known and can be implemented for any WML content sent in a push message.

A PPG will have the same management role that a WAP gateway has regarding the relationship between the HTTP traffic on one side and the WSP (Wireless Session Protocol) or WDP (Wireless Datagram Protocol) traffic on the other side.

Push OTA

The push OTA protocol is used between the PPG and the WAP client. The push traffic is carried over the wireless portion of the network. The OTA protocol defines a binary optimized layer that sits on top of the WAP stack. OTA uses WSP methods to push content to the wireless client. Different types of OTA push exist, with different levels of reliability. The types are the following:

- Connectionless push
- Connection-oriented push without confirmation
- Connection-oriented push with confirmation

A connectionless push is the simplest of these mechanisms. The operation requires a simple WTP class-3 message that is essentially WDP. Two WDP ports, one secure and one insecure, are reserved on WAP clients for the connectionless push. The push message is sent to the phone; then, using the application ID header, the WAP client decides which application should receive the push content. Today the WAP browser on the wireless client is considered a single application. In the future, it may be possible to create other applications that need to receive push content independently of each other.

The connection-oriented methods I listed previously require that the push message be sent over a WSP session. However, the WAP gateway cannot begin a WSP session; the session must be client-initiated. Therefore, a WAP gateway actually begins the transaction with a short message to the wireless client with parameters for starting a WSP session. The wireless client starts the WSP session with the WAP gateway and the push content is sent through it.

The services on the client that listen for these special WSP startup messages are called the Session Initiation Application (SIA). This SIA constantly listens for WSP startup messages and, if it encounters them, begins a new WSP session with the PPG specified in the session request and using the parameters in the original session request.

Another important service in the wireless client is the application dispatcher. The application dispatcher is responsible for examining the push message headers for the `X-Wap-Application-Id` line. It delivers this special header to the specification application specified in the header value. The standard application ID is for the WML browser. It is possible for the application ID to refer to the WTA browser or to other applications on the wireless client. If the application specified cannot be found, an error message is sent to the PPG and the PPG in return indicates and error condition to the PI. The application dispatcher is responsible for sending out acknowledgements to the PPG that a message has been delivered successfully. It effectively issues the successful ACK message for push content.

Summary

In this chapter I covered the basics of the push architectures in use now and those that can be expected in the future. Unfortunately, given the late release of the WAP push specifications, most products do not contain the push functionality and the market is fragmented into several implementation camps.

This chapter gave you details on how to code for the varying implementations of push services and also gave you insight into how push services will look in WAP.

In the next chapter, I expand the coverage of advanced services and look at WTA.

Chapter 11

WTA

IN THIS CHAPTER

- ◆ Introducing WTA
- ◆ Understanding WTA architecture
- ◆ Understanding WTA security
- ◆ Using the WTA Interface (WTAI)
- ◆ Considering network common events
- ◆ Considering WTA repository and channels
- ◆ Understanding WTA event handling

IN THIS CHAPTER, I discuss the Wireless Telephony Application (WTA) portion of WAP. First, I provide an overview of the WTA architecture; then I explain how you can develop applications with this new component of WAP.

WTA allows services in WAP to become fully integrated with the telephony device they are housed in. However, with intimate access to the telephony device comes an added security risk. This risk must be taken into account along with the need to develop rich dual-purpose applications in the WAP environment. In this chapter I also discuss the decisions made surrounding the WTA system.

The introduction of quick network events to the programming also raises a number of questions regarding network event handling and being able to deal with these events in a timely manner. Once again, I describe these issues and give examples of how the messages would flow.

I end the chapter by giving developers a methodology for development on the current WTA platform.

> The material in this chapter represents concepts that are in the theoretical stage only. No one has actually implemented any part of the specifications described here except for one public function (the WTA `make call` function) that allows calls to be made from a handset.

A Brief Introduction to WTA

In the past few chapters I described how to create services for display on a wireless client. In the early days of WAP, because the target client was a cellular phone, it was obvious that the capabilities of the phone could, and should, be leveraged to create enhanced services. For example, a restaurant-ranking service would list the restaurants in an area, their cuisine, the cost of an average meal, and a review of each restaurant. If a user decided a restaurant presented by the service was worth visiting, he or she would have to write down the number and then use another phone. Even without call integration on PCs, you can still easily place the call in the desktop environment today - you see a number on a Web site that you want to call, and you dial it on the phone next to your computer.

Figure 11-1 shows how you should be able to place a call directly from your WAP application:

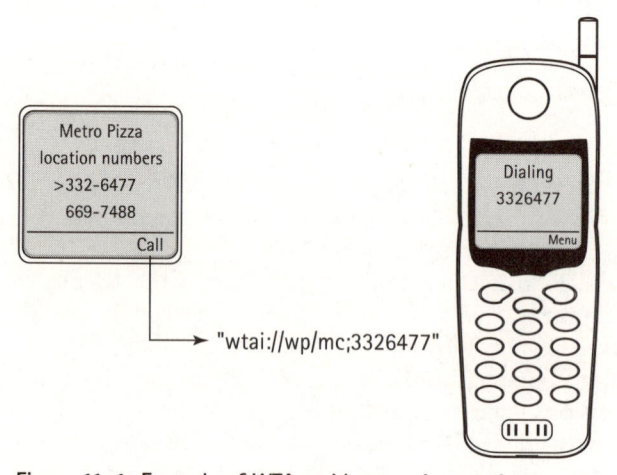

Figure 11-1: Example of WTA and browser integration

The Wireless Telephony Application Interface (WTAI) and its surrounding architecture use the phone as more than just a platform for a browser. The phone has voice capabilities that can be integrated into a specific sites design. Going back to the preceding example, the restaurant-rating service could have been designed so that by pressing a single button on his or her wireless client the user can dial the number associated with a restaurant. WTAI, from a developer's perspective, allows for applications to be written that integrate with capabilities of the wireless client, should that wireless client also happen to be a cellular phone.

The carrier or service operator also has a unique perspective. The growth of WAP services was originally driven by the fierce battle for control of the customer. In the early days of wireless telephony, it was acceptable for carriers to sell only voice services. In those days, the mere fact that a landline call could be made from a wherever the user happened to be was more important than the number of services or even voice quality. After the giddiness subsided, carriers became differentiated on the basis of their coverage. If a call could be placed in more locations on one carrier than on another, then chances were the user would sign with that carrier. Later, the competitive landscape shifted to brand identity, as various wireless carriers collectively created conglomerates to relieve users of roaming charges and multiple bills, and to provide a single service organization. With the move to second-generation services, the battle became one of differentiation through price. When the carriers finally reached a point where stable prices were offered to their respective customers, the focus shifted to providing services. *Services* is a very broad term that covers every conceivable feature that carriers can offer their customers. More and more carriers are recognizing that simply providing voice services is no longer acceptable. Services such as SMS (Short Message Service) or voicemail were added near the beginning of the service battle. A large number of other services, such as distinctive ring, alternative billing, and inbound call routing, are coming into the wireless market. Every service that the carrier provides improves its chances of retaining its existing customer base and getting new customers.

Some services, such as WAP, have become such complex additions to the service portfolio that some carriers have created entirely new organizations to field the problems associated with providing the services. An example of this is the Canadian company Microcell, which created "i5" to deal with service creation, management, and maintenance issues. Others have decided to retain some control. One such company is Sprint in the United States, which has outsourced the management of the WAP portal to Yahoo! Inc., because Yahoo! is the better-known brand for providing Internet services. Yet other companies decided to outsource the entire WAP service problem. BTCellnet in the United Kingdom, for example, contracted third-party firm "Genie" to take care of the entire WAP service problem. With 2.5G and 3G services on the horizon, companies will continue to make these kinds of arrangements.

The high level of competition has consistently driven prices down, as shown in Figure 11-2.

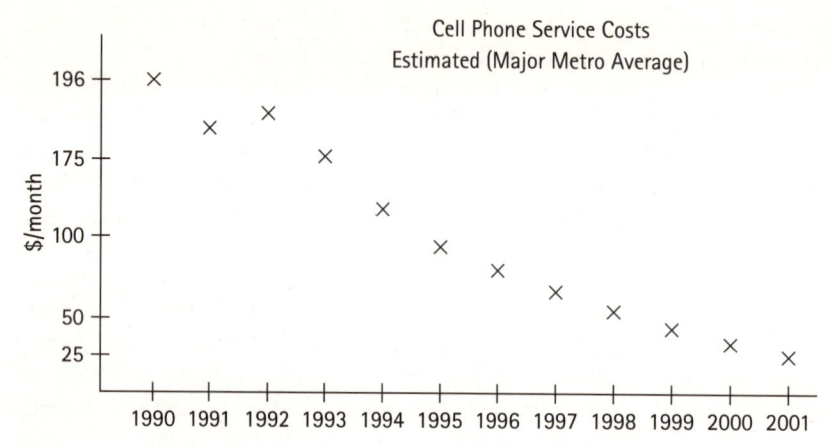

372   Part III: Services on Advanced AB Architecture

Cell Phone Service Costs
Estimated (Major Metro Average)

[Scatter plot showing $/month on y-axis (25, 50, 100, 175, 196) vs years 1990–2001 on x-axis, with points declining from ~196 in 1990 to ~25 in 2001]

Figure 11-2: Carrier value chart

The bottom line is that the value of the carrier organization is constantly under scrutiny and any mechanism that enables the carrier to create new services that will attract new customers while retaining existing customers is investigated.

WTA is such a service-creating mechanism. It intertwines telephony and browser components to allow for more complex and pertinent services that can immediately generate more income for the carrier by allowing the user to instantly place an "impulse" call. WTA also enables you to handle complex differences between the browser and telephony components. For example, the browser request/response transaction is measured in the five- to ten-second range, whereas you would expect a phone call to be placed or cleared in five to ten milliseconds.

An Overview of the WTA Architecture

WTA is a framework for the creation of combined browser/telephony services. Because reliability and security became higher priorities with the involvement of telephony components it was decided that a new user agent be placed in the wireless client. This new WTA user agent is the same as the standard WML browser, except for the addition of certain capabilities, such as being able to access the phonebook. Even though the WTA user agent is simply an extension of the standard user agent, it must still run in its own memory space. Therefore, the WTA user agent and standard user agent are distinct logical entities on the wireless client. The nature of the security is described later in this chapter, in the section entitled "The WTA Security Model."

Even with the separate browser, WTA greatly enhances the usefulness of the regular browser. To enable the additional features available, WTA relies on the WTAI function library to define a set of functions and events, which are divided into security/availability categories.

Figures 11-3 and 11-4 show how this new WTA user agent interacts with other components on the wireless device as well as with components in the mobile network.

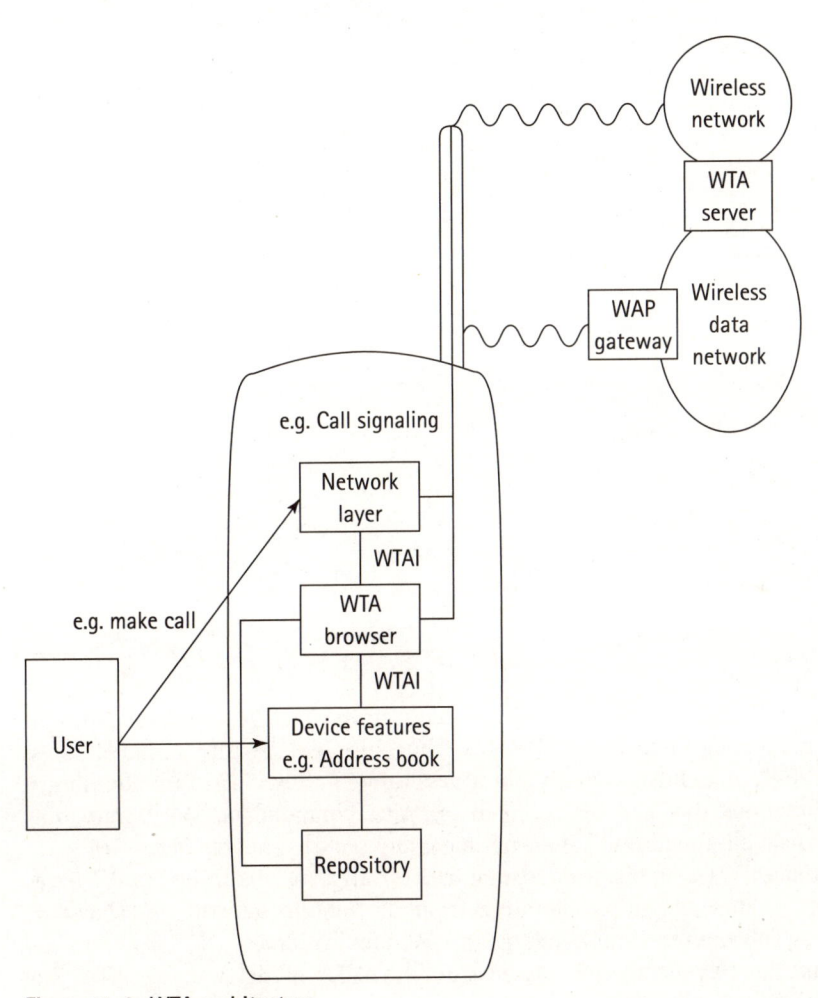

Figure 11-3: WTA architecture

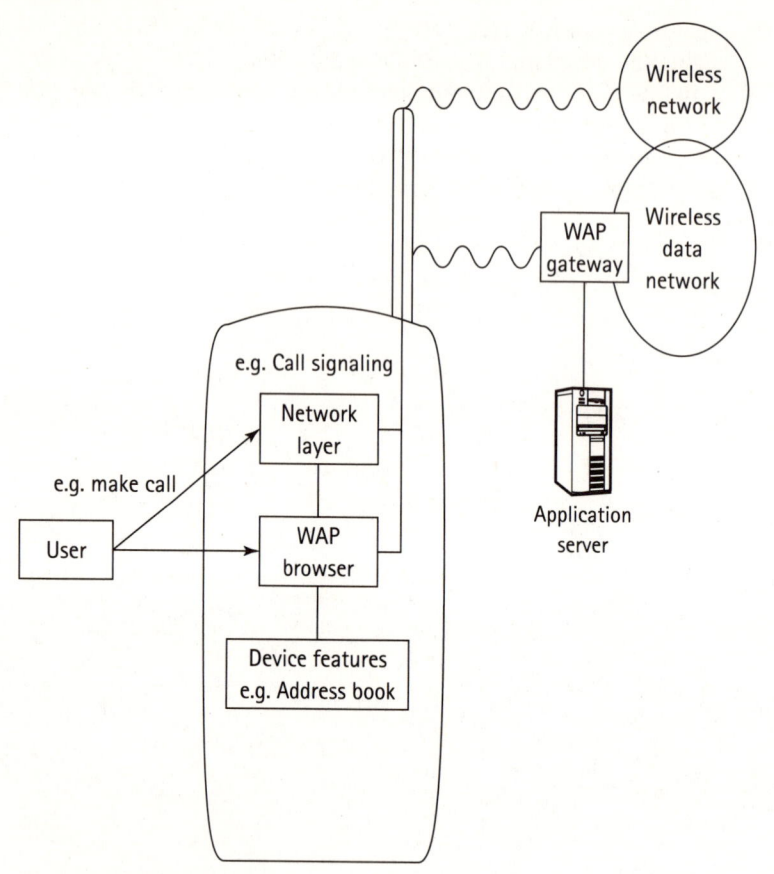

Figure 11-4: WAE architecture

Figures 11-3 and 11-4 show how the architecture of WTA looks and how the Wireless Application Environment (WAE) architecture looks, with its limited access to WTA. The WAE architecture only has access to the public WTAI function library, a set of functions that can be executed on WTA components. The library only implements simple functions that do not have any security-related side effects.

The standard WTA architecture also allows for applications to be started based on network events and other signaling from the mobile network, as shown in Figure 11-3. This option is not available to WAE applications.

The important elements that are new to the WTA model are the WTA user agent, WTA server, repository, device-specific features, and the Network Layer. I describe these elements briefly here and examine them in more detail in their separate sections.

WTA user agent

The WTA user agent is an extension of the standard WTA browser; as such, it is also capable of understanding WML and WMLScript. Only three differences exist between the WTA user agent and the standard WAE user agent. First, the user agent is able to access the repository (persistent storage) and other WTA entities. Second, it has a much stricter context-management mechanism. (WTA contexts have well-defined associations to network events.) Third, the user agent has `endcontext` and `newcontext` functions that enable a developer to control the lifetime of a context, as opposed to standard WAE, which has no such functions.

Device-specific features

WTA enables developers to use the mobile device to access areas of memory that would normally not be considered browser accessible. An example of this is a service that writes an entry to the user's address book.

Repository

The repository is an area of persistent storage on the phone that stores applications for long periods of time. It enables users to use a specific application even when not connected to the network. The main motivation to create the repository was the need for fast access to an application with speeds equivalent to those of network events. I discuss the repository in detail later, in the section called "WTA Repository and Channels."

WTA server

A WTA server is a standard Web server that sits in a secure area of the carrier network. As a Web server, it straddles the line between the telephony network, such as voicemail servers or Intelligent Node (IN) applications, and the HTTP session to the WAP gateway. Because it is a Web server, a WTA server is accessible via URLs on one side and the proprietary interfaces on the other side. For example, you might use the URL `http://www.yourcarrier.com/voicemail.cgi` to access your voicemail service.

WTA services

WTA services are the applications that a user actually uses. A WTA service can be stored in the same way as a standard WAP service. The differences lie in the ways these services can be launched and where they can reside. Figure 11-5 shows the four ways that the WTA service can be initiated.

Part III: Services on Advanced AB Architecture

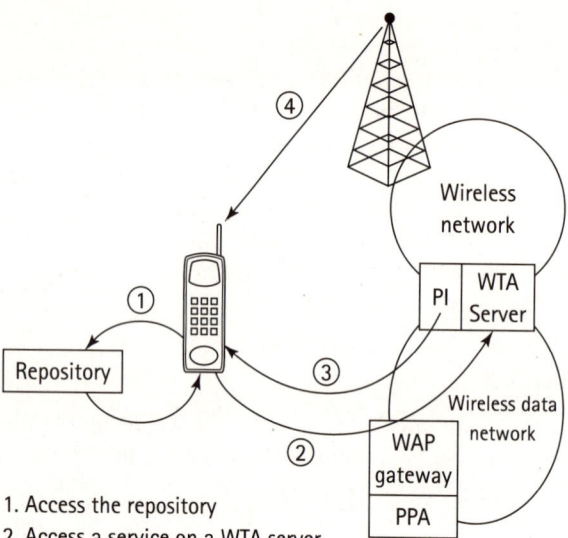

1. Access the repository
2. Access a service on a WTA server
3. Service is pushed by a PI
4. Wireless network activates an event launching a WTA service

Figure 11-5: WTA service initiation

Therefore, the four ways to access a service are as follows:

- *A URL via the repository* — In this case the service is in the persistent storage area and is simply accessed via localized URL.

- *A URL via the WTA server* — In this case, the service resides on a WTA server. Once requested, the relevant service response is sent to the mobile device.

- *A service indication* — In this case a service-related URL is sent to the mobile device. This URL can reference either an entry in the repository or some location on the WTA server.

- *A network event* — In this case, a service is triggered by an event. WTA services are launched when a network event is activated in the mobile device. An example of this is an incoming phone call triggering a phone call-monitoring service.

To summarize, the WTA framework extends the standard WAP architecture by including the following:

- A set of telephony functions that can be called using WML and WMLScript
- The ability of the wireless client to handle incoming mobile-network events

- A repository for quick access to browser services dependent on network events
- A separate model for WTA user agent state and context management
- A security model

The WTA Security Model

WTA was designed with a stronger security model than regular WAE, in part because services in WTA could be quite destructive. For example, consider a service that accesses a user's phonebook and deletes all the entries, or uses location information to spy on his or her activities. Even worse, the service could take a user's phonebook entries and send them to a master database for later telemarketing.

In order to protect the user's security, various features were added to the overall architecture. First, the WTA user agent and the WAE user agent establish sessions with the WAP gateway on completely different ports, and any session data received on one port that were meant for the other are automatically discarded in WTA-WSP to WAE-WSP sessions.

The WAP gateway in WTA is required to use a WTLS Class 2 connection with full server-side authentication as a secure link between itself and the WAP browser. Additionally, users can specify their permissions for the execution of functions. It is not clear at this time how this feature will be implemented in a standard way, but functions and events inside applications are separated into groups that dictate how long their executable lifetimes can be. Table 11-1 shows the security groupings. Executables are applications (composed of WML and/or WMLScript). The executable may either be in the repository or on a WTA or other application server.

TABLE 11-1 SECURITY GROUPINGS FOR FUNCTIONS

Permission Category	Description
Blanket Permission	The user can access the WTAI library function for an indefinite period of time. The original permission granted by the user is good for all subsequent sessions. This is the broadest category of security.
Context Permission	The user gives permission to the WTAI function only for the run-time context. Once the context has ended, the application has to go back to the user and ask for new permission.

Continued

TABLE 11-1 SECURITY GROUPINGS FOR FUNCTIONS *(Continued)*

Permission Category	Description
Single Action Permission	The user gives permission for the function to act only once. For example, a restaurant-locator service is given permission to use location information only for the purpose of locating a restaurant once; it would have to go back to the users for permission to make any other requests.

Beyond these security techniques, the split in architecture between functions that can be called from WTA and those that can be called from WAE limits the amount of access that developers have to telephony functions. The next section shows that the telephony functionality available in the public domain is very well monitored and constricted in its usage.

The WTAI Libraries

WTAI is the portion of WTA that covers how developers can access telephony functions and events through the browser. The WTAI defines functions and events that can be accessed from both WML and WMLScript. Many ways exist to divide up the functions and events to show the main types. One of the ways to partition the collections or libraries is by the type of the function and its availability, as shown in Table 11-2.

TABLE 11-2 WTAI LIBRARIES

WTAI Library	Description
Network Common WTAI	The functions and events in this library address features common to all network technologies and that are available in the respective network types. These functions and events are only accessible from within the WTA user agent.

WTAI Library	Description
Network Specific WTAI	The functions and events in these libraries are specific to the type of network technology or network type. Carriers may also create their functions and events if they choose. If the Integrated Digital Enhanced Network (IDEN) group decided to write a function for push to talk that worked only on their network, then that would become part of the IDEN-specific WTAI library. The functions and events are only accessible from within the WTA user agent.
Public WTAI	This is a set of simple functions that developers can use within the standard browser *only*.

The separation between network specific and network common WTAI is simply that different types of networks have different characteristics. For example, a Time Division Multiple Access (TDMA) network may not have the capability to do call-forwarding although Global System for Mobile communications (GSM) networks do. The functions and events in WTAI vary in terms of exactly which component is required to run them. A `makecall` function is activated by the WTA User Agent placing a call with the telephony network, whereas an `update phonebook` function simply accesses an area of local phone memory. The network-specific libraries that are currently part of the specifications are the GSM-, PDC-, and IS-136-specific libraries. Other libraries for IS-95 and TETRA are forthcoming.

The WTAI public library is composed of a set of three functions that were deemed safe enough to be activated from the standard browser. These functions, which are intentionally limited, form a set of basic telephony features that can be integrated with browser applications.

WTAI syntax

You can call WTAI functions in one of two ways: with WML or with WMLScript. Not all functions allow for both types of call. Some may only have a WMLScript function and not a WML URL.

USING WML

The syntax for calling functions in WML uses a URL format, as shown in the following example:

```
wtai://{library}/{function};{parameter1},{parameter2}!{result1},{result2}
```

The URL format begins with `wtai://` scheme and then includes a library. This URL format is a short URL form of the library name. In the case of WTAI public functions, the library name is wp. Next comes a function, which is a standard shorter version of the full function name. In the case of the makeCall function, mc is used for the URL format. Then come parameters that are separated from the function by a semicolon. Multiple parameters within a function are separated by commas. The variables to be populated follow after an exclamation point. The variables are separated from each other by commas.

Here is an example of the WML syntax for the makeCall function:

```
wtai://wp/mc;17145634567
```

In this case the function has no results and only one parameter. Compare this to the WMLScript syntax in the following section.

USING WMLSCRIPT

You can use WMLScript to call functions by identifying the library name followed by the function name. For example, a makeCall function would have the following function syntax:

```
makeCall("8172783287");
```

However, in calling WMLScript functions you must use a library name that identifies the relevant WTAI library. In this example, makeCall resides in the WTAPublic library. Therefore the full syntax for the function would look like this:

```
WTAPublic.makeCall("8172783287");
```

Public WTAI

The public library has three functions:

- Make a call: makeCall
- Send DTMF tones: sendDTMF
- Add entry to phonebook: addPBentry

The makeCall function allows an application to set up a phone call using the telephony component of the wireless client. In the WTAPublic library there is no way for the application to close the call, so the user must do this manually. Once the call has ended, it is expected that the user will return to the deck in the browser that he or she was originally viewing. The only accepted characters for dialing are an unescaped + and the numbers 0–9. The plus sign allows the phone to substitute the country-specific information for accessing international numbers.

The sendDTMF function enables a developer to send a DTMF (Dual Tone Multi-Frequency) sequence to a phone call established by the makeCall function. A user can use the sendDTMF function to dial a phone number and navigate an Interactive Voice Response (IVR) structure using navigation keys. In this way, the user has immediate access to the service associated with the browser application. The accepted characters in the DTMF string are the special characters "*", and "#", the letters A, B, C, and D, and the numbers 0-9. Some banks have call servers that enable you to check your balance, transfer money, and perform similar actions using this mechanism.

The add entry to phonebook function (`addPBentry`) enables a developer to add an entry to the phonebook of the user. The only parameters of this function are the telephone number and the name of the person, which are added to the existing phonebook as a new entry. There are no corresponding functions in the public library to remove, read, or change existing entries in the phonebook. This was done intentionally, in order to limit the damage that public functions could cause. Table 11-3 shows some details about these functions. (A complete description can be found in Appendix D, "WTAI Libraries and Events.")

TABLE 11-3 WTAI PUBLIC LIBRARY FUNCTIONS

Functions	Description

WMLScript:
`makeCall(number)`
WML:
`wtai://wp/mc;number!retVal`
	Begins a voice call using the number specified by the *number* parameter. The WTAI public developer cannot stop the call once it has been initiated. The number must be a valid phone number that can be dialed by the phone interface. The function returns an empty string if successful, `invalid` if unsuccessful, or an error code as here.
	
	Return values:
	
	Empty string, `invalid`, or one of the following error codes:
	
	105 - Called number is busy
	
	106 - Network is unavailable
	
	107 - Called number was not answered
	
	200 - Invocation error (URL form only)
	
	1 - Unknown error
	
	Example:
	
	`var retVal = WTAPublic.makeCall ("18882349876")`
	
	`<go href="wtai://wp/mc; 18882349876!retVal"/>`

Continued

TABLE 11-3 WTAI PUBLIC LIBRARY FUNCTIONS *(Continued)*

Functions	Description
WMLScript: sendDTMF(*dtmfString*) *WML:* wtai://wp/sd;*dtmfString*!retVal	Sends a DTMF string to the device that has answered a call that has been made, while the line is still open. The function returns an empty string if successful, invalid if unsuccessful, and an error code for any other issues. *Return values:* Empty string, invalid, or one of the following error code: -108 no active voice call -200 invocation error (URL form only) -1 unknown error *Example:* var retVal = WTAPublic.sendDTMF ("1113*657") <go href="wtai://wp/sd;1113*657!retVal"/>
WMLScript: addPBEntry(*number,name*) *WML:* wtai://wp/ap;*number;name*!retVal	Adds a new entry to the phone address book. The function returns an empty string if successful, invalid if unsuccessful, and an error code for any other issues. *Return values:* Empty string, invalid, or one of the following error codes: -100 name is too long or cannot be accepted -101 number is not a valid phone number -102 number is too long -103 name and number could not be written -104 phone address book is full -1 unspecified error

Functions	Description
	-200 invocation error (URL form only)
	Example:
	`var retVal = WTAPublic.addPBEntry ("5551212", "Info")`
	`<go href="wtai://wp/ap;5551212; Info!retVal"/>`

Network common WTAI

According to the WAP specifications, the functions I have discussed so far are the only ones to be made available to public developers. WTAI does specify functions and events above and beyond the public set, and developers who have a special trusted relationship with the carrier can access these. The network common WTAI and network-specific WTAI both fall into this special access category. The other distinction between the two categories is that the functions in the special access category are executed in the WTA user agent and not the standard browser.

Both of the network common and network-specific WTAI collections contain more than just WTAI functions. Both sets also have WTAI events, which are triggers from the mobile network that an application can respond to.

The WTAI common collection can be divided into the following five libraries:

- Voice Call library
- Phonebook library
- Network Message library
- Call Log library
- WTA Miscellaneous library

THE VOICE CALL LIBRARY

This library allows for both outgoing and incoming calls to be precisely controlled according to a call model. The functionality is available on all networks and is part of the `vc` library in WML or WTAVoiceCall library in WMLScript. This library contains six functions, which are summarized in Table 11-4. A more detailed description can be found in Appendix D, "WTAI Libraries and Events".

TABLE 11-4 WTAI VOICE CALL LIBRARY FUNCTIONS

Function	Description
setup	Initiates a call from the mobile phone that is nonblocking to subsequent function calls. A mode parameter specifies whether to drop or keep the call if the WTA context terminates.
accept	Accepts an incoming voice call. This is also a non-blocking function and it triggers various events that can be used to check the call progress.
release	Releases a voice call and sends out an event that indicates that the call has been released.
sendDTMF	Sends a DTMF sequence on a previously arranged voice call.
callStatus	Returns information about the call that is useful to the developer, such as name, number, status, duration, and mode.

List	Returns a call handle that can be subsequently applied to finding the call-status information.
	
	The function must be called repeatedly to traverse a history list of previously issued calls available in the current context. For example, imagine that four calls are available: #1, #2, #3, and #4. The list function has a Boolean parameter, which is controlled to specify which call from the list to obtain. So, list(true) returns the oldest call, #1. list(false) returns the next oldest call, #2. To traverse the list you would use the following code:
	
	list(true); // #1
	list(false); // #2
	list(false); // #3
	list(false); // #4

In order to better understand the voice call library I shall examine the call control model, what states a call can be in, and also what events are generated by movements from one state to another. An event is a special WTAI mechanism that application developers can use to monitor the application as it moves from state to state or to trigger other components of an application. For example, if a call-cleared event fired that let you know the call was over while you were waiting for ringing, you could be prompted to restart the call within the application. Figures 11-6 and 11-7 show the call model: there are two models, one for incoming calls and the other for outgoing calls.

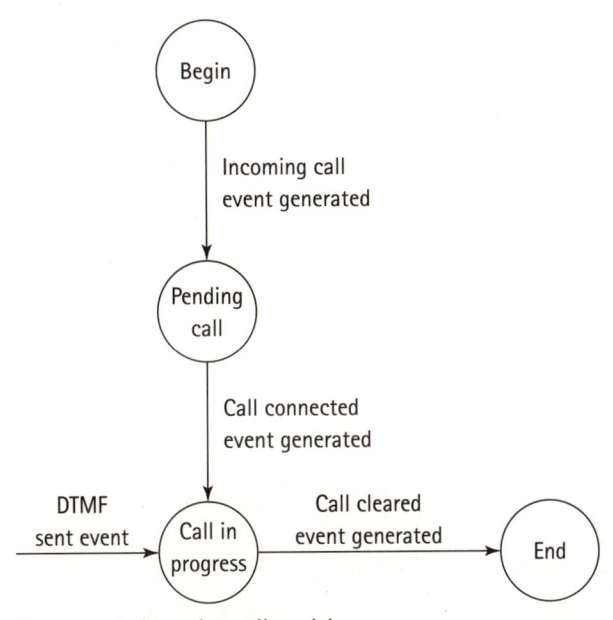

Figure 11-6: Incoming call model

Every call made using the WTAI library is given a handle, which acts as an identifier for the call and which you can use to keep track of calls for later inspection. Developers use these handles to obtain information about the call such as its status, the number being called, and other fields as specified in the `callStatus` function.

CALL-STATE MANAGEMENT

Call-state management implicit in the function libraries defines what happens to a call when it is associated with a single context. If a call has been established by a service in some other context or by the user interface of the mobile device then it will not be affected. Call-state management only affects calls established by one of the call functions in the WTAI libraries. For example, the `setup` or `accept` functions in the network common library have a mode parameter. This mode parameter identifies what happens when the context is destroyed. If the mode is set to 0 the call is very tightly integrated with the context, and will be dropped when the context is destroyed. If the mode is set to 1 the call is not tightly integrated and will continue even when the context is destroyed.

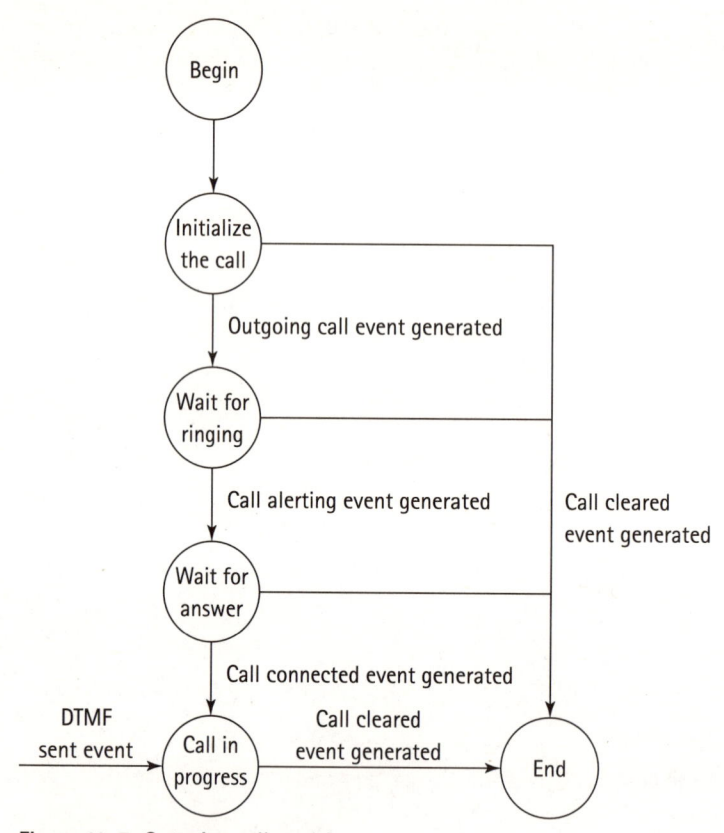

Figure 11-7: Outgoing call model

THE NETWORK MESSAGE LIBRARY

The Network Message library contains functions used to send and receive messages and obtain information about previously sent messages. The library contains five functions, which are summarized in Table 11-5. In the case of the network messages, only the WMLScript form of invocation is available. A more detailed description of the functions is available in Appendix D, "WTAI Libraries and Events."

Table 11-5 WTAI Network Message Library Functions

Function	Description
send	Sends a short text message.
list	Returns a message handle for the existing message.

	The function must be called repeatedly to traverse a history list of previously issued calls available in the current context. For example, imagine that four calls are available: #1, #2, #3, and #4. The list function has a Boolean parameter, which is controlled to specify which call from the list to obtain. So, list(true) returns the oldest call, #1. list(false) returns the next oldest call, #2. To traverse the list, you would use the following code:
	
	list(true); // #1
	
	list(false); // #2
	
	list(false); // #3
	
	list(false); // #4

remove	Removes an incoming or outgoing message from the mobile device.
getFieldValue	Obtains information about a specific field of a message.
markAsRead	Marks a message as having been read.

The Network Message library has a control model very similar to that of the Voice Call libraries. Although simpler than the voice model, it is an important indicator of the states that can occur and the events generated as an application moves through the different functions and states. Figures 11-8 and 11-9 show the models for network messages, one for inbound messages and the other for outbound messages. The models represent individual inbound and outbound messages.

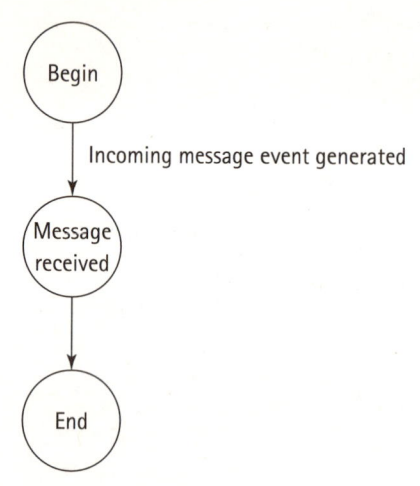

Figure 11-8: Incoming call model

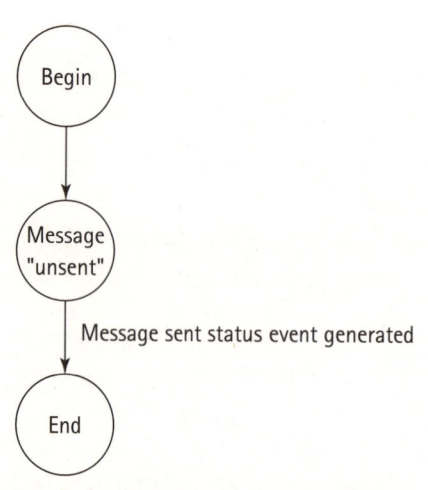

Figure 11-9: Outbound message model

Network messages also have handles very similar to those in the Voice Call library; however, this time the information associated with the handle concerns the status details of a network text message.

THE PHONEBOOK LIBRARY

The Phonebook library contains functions used to search for, retrieve, change, or add new entries into the phonebook. The library contains five functions, which are summarized in Table 11-6. A more detailed description of the functions is available in Appendix D, "WTAI Libraries and Events".

TABLE 11-6 WTAI PHONEBOOK LIBRARY FUNCTIONS

Function	Description
write	Writes an entry to the phonebook, overwriting anything in the phonebook.
read	Searches through the phonebook for an entry matching the given criteria. The index of an empty phonebook is never returned.
remove	Removes an entry from the phonebook.
getFieldValue	Retrieves a field value from a phonebook entry.
change	Stores the given value in the specified field in a phonebook entry, overwriting any existing value.

The Phonebook library is a simple library: no events are associated with any of the functions. The library contains only WMLScript functions; there are no WML versions. The functions shown in Table 11-6 are all common to every implementation of WTA.

THE CALL LOG LIBRARY

The Call Log library contains functions that retrieve information from logs on the phone. It is expected that a phone that implements this feature will have access to the logs of all calls to the phone that were dialed, all that were received, and all that were missed. The library enables users to access the log for each type of call and present fields within those logs to an application. The library contains four functions, which are summarized in Table 11-7. These functions are limited to WMLScript implementations; there is no URL form available. A more detailed description of the functions is available in Appendix D.

TABLE 11-7 WTAI CALL LOGS LIBRARY

Function	Description
dialed	Returns the call-log handle of an entry from the call log. You can call it repeatedly to obtain all such entries.
missed	Returns the call-log handle of an entry from the missed call log. You can call it repeatedly to obtain all such entries.

Continued

TABLE 11-7 WTAI CALL LOGS LIBRARY *(Continued)*

Function	Description
received	Returns the call-log handle of an entry from the received call log. You can call it repeatedly to obtain all such entries.
getFieldValue	Retrieves a field value from a specific call-log entry.

This library contains no events and all functions can be called only via their WMLScript formats.

MISCELLANEOUS LIBRARY

The Miscellaneous library contains miscellaneous functions common to all networks implementing WTA. You can use these functions for context management and to control logical WTA indicators. The library contains four functions, which are summarized in Table 11-8. A more detailed description of these functions is available in Appendix D.

TABLE 11-8 WTAI MISCELLANEOUS LIBRARY FUNCTIONS

Function	Description
setIndicator	Modifies the state of a logical indicator. You can use this indicator for incoming voice calls, data calls, or other messages that the device may be capable of. The mobile device uses the indicators to show the type of the incoming call to the user. You can use this function to set or unset the indicator programmatically.
endContext	Terminates the current WTA user agent context.
getProtection	Retrieves the protection mode of the current WTA context. I discuss protection modes in the section on call state management.
setProtection	Sets the protection mode of the current WTA context. I discuss protection modes in the section on call state management.

The Miscellaneous library simply contains some miscellaneous functions you can use to manipulate contexts and set indicators. Only the endContext function for ending context can be called from WML and WMLScript. All of the other functions can be called only from WMLScript.

Network-specific libraries

The WTAI libraries also include other collection libraries, which are grouped by the specific network technology they are associated with. The current libraries for this group are for GSM, TDMA (also known as ANSI 136), and Personal Digital Cellular (PDC). For example, the GSM network has a shorter text-message feature called Unstructured Supplementary Service Data (USSD) built in. The USSD message must be included in the GSM-specific library, because it is not available on the other networks. More advanced call control is available on GSM networks, which enable call deflection and call-active indications, features that are also available in the network-specific library. The GSM library also contains a location function, which enables a developer to obtain the location of the cell-ID and sector that the mobile device is using, along with the country, network, and location area codes.

TDMA (ANSI 136)-specific libraries add functions and events that provide access to that network technology's ability to send flash codes and alerts through active voice connections.

The PDC-specific libraries add functions and events related to multiparty calls and transferring calls. The PDC library also completely redefines the voice-control model for that network, as it gives the user more precise control over a call than generic networks. In the PDC networks, you can temporarily pause a call and return to an active state.

Additionally, libraries for the IS-95 and TETRA networks are presently being drafted.

A full description of all these library functions and events can be found in Appendix D.

Network Common Events

One of the unique attributes of the WTA architecture is that applications can actually be launched via a network-initiated action called a network event. The mobile device launches the application for some prearranged events by translating a control-channel event into a string that is delivered to the WTA user agent. An example of this procedure is triggered by an incoming phone call. The incoming call is signaled to the mobile device on the paging channel and translated into a string by the mobile-device implementation. You have encountered some common network events already in the call and network models I discussed earlier. These are examples wherein events are generated as the mobile device moves from state to state during a call, or a "message receive" or "message send".

Table 11-9 lists all the network common events. Network-specific events are listed in Appendix D next to the specific technology.

TABLE 11-9 NETWORK COMMON EVENTS

Event	Description
wtaev-cc/ic	Indicates that an incoming call is arriving on the mobile device. An `acceptCall` function can be used to start the call. *Parameters:* *callHandle* — Call handle for the call (used to track the calls) *callerID* — Phone number of the caller
wtaev-cc/cl	Indicates that a voice call has cleared. *Parameters:* *callHandle* — Call handle for the call (used to track the calls) *result* — Contains a description of why the call was cancelled. The return codes are the following: 0 — Normal termination 1 — No details available 2 — Network reason 3 — Call was dropped 4 — Called party was busy 5 — Network is not available 6 — Called party did not answer
wtaev-cc/co	Indicates that a called party has accepted a call. *Parameters:* *callHandle* — Call handle for the call (used to track the calls) *callerID* — Phone number of the caller
wtaev-cc/oc	Indicates that an outgoing call is being initiated. *Parameters:* *callHandle* — Call handle for the call (used to track the calls) *number* — Phone number being called

Event	Description
wtaev-cc/cc	Indicates that a call has been placed to another party and the phone being called is ringing. *Parameters:* *callHandle* — Call handle for the call
wtaev-cc/dtmf	Indicates that a DTMF string is being sent to the called party. *Parameters:* *callHandle* — Call handle for the call *dtmfString* — DTMF sequence that was sent
wtaev-nt/st	Indicates that the status of an outgoing message has changed. *Parameters:* *msgHandle* — Message handle *result* — Description of the change to the outgoing message. The return codes are the following: 0 — Message sent 1 — Message abandoned for unknown reason 2 — Message abandoned for network reasons 3 — Message abandoned because of lack of resources
wtaev-nt/it	Indicates that a message has been received. *Parameters:* *msgHandle* — Message handle *sender* — Identity of the sender as a network-address field (null string if unknown)

Continued

TABLE 11-9 NETWORK COMMON EVENTS *(Continued)*

Event	Description
`wtaev-ms/ns`	Indicates that the value of one or more of the defined network status parameters has changed.

Parameters:

`inService` — Indicates whether the device is capable of placing or receiving calls

0 — Device is not in service

1 — Device is in service

`networkName` — Identifier of the network that the device is using (undefined if the device is not in service)

`explanation` — The reason why the device is not in service (undefined if the device is in service

0 — No explanation given

1 — No networks found

2 — All networks found were forbidden |

WTA Repository and Channels

The WAP architecture defines a structure wherein applications reside completely on back-end servers. If content is required, the architecture enables users to issue requests, which result in a response with the required data. The data are stored temporarily on the mobile device. However, the data are volatile, which prevents them from being reused after a long period of time or if a large amount of data must be stored on the mobile device. The limitation of the existing solutions to volatility such as the cache is that they are too small. They are also shared resources, which means that others can overwrite your entries.

You can use other proprietary solutions to the volatility problem, such as prefetch using the Openwave link element, but developers need to guess as to the user's probable intentions when developing applications using such techniques.

Furthermore, none of these proprietary solutions solves the problems of out-of-coverage usage. What if you were driving between two metropolitan areas with coverage and accessing a WAP site for directions? As soon as you were to enter the area between the metropolitan areas you would lose access to the site.

WTA repository

The solution to the volatility problem is to create some long-term application-storage area on the mobile device that a developer can depend on being available. The effort to create a persistent storage area is being promoted within the WAP Forum today and a final specification is expected in WAP-NG. The WTA team, however, has proposed a long-term storage structure for its immediate needs.

The immediate needs of the WTA team concern the WTA network events, which are typically 100-1000 orders of magnitude faster at execution than WSP request/response transactions. The increased latency demand of these events demands that the relevant WAP applications be available quickly and with some reliability – hence the need for a storage structure.

The team's proposed structure is known as the repository. The repository is divided into smaller units of space called *channels*. These channels can contain resources of any of the valid WAP media types. Figure 11-10 shows the structure of the repository.

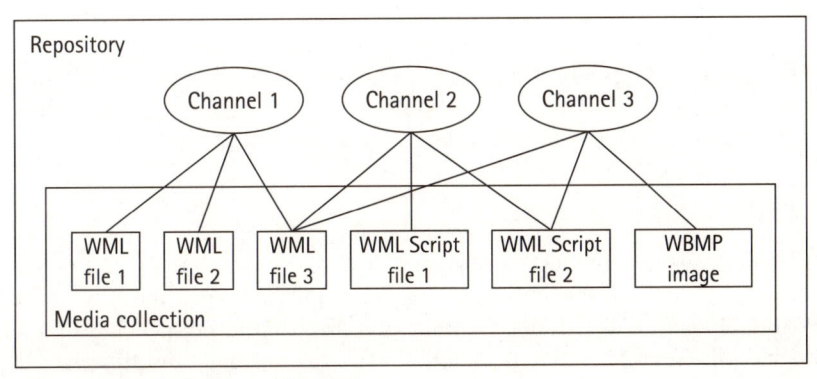

Figure 11-10: Repository architecture

The repository-storage specification, like the draft-persistent storage specification, describes an area on the phone that stores the data in an implementation-specific manner. The actual data can be thought of as being available on your desktop PC and entire Web site for viewing. The resources for such a site are simply stored on your hard drive, and you can bring them up quickly without establishing a connection with the actual Web site. The repository works in the same way, except that because the repository was created for WTA needs, only WTA WAP sites can be stored in the repository. We will have to wait for the full persistent-storage specification before standard sites can be stored in the repository.

An important new concept here is the channel, which is the equivalent of a WAP site that is available for offline viewing.

Key properties of channels are as follows:

- Each is defined by a set of URLs
- Each has a unique identity
- They are atomic

In order to place a site in the repository, the channel designer has to use URLs to indicate where the resources are to be found. The channel is then treated very much like software: it has to be loaded or installed onto the mobile device. During the installation process, the URLs are crawled by the channel installation process and the data collected and stored on the mobile device. Of course, it is possible for network to go down, or the phone to be turned off in the middle of an installation, and so the decision was made that the channels would be valid only if they were completely loaded, or in other words, considered to be "atomic" or indivisible in nature. A half-loaded channel would simply be deleted and hence unavailable.

The channels are also unique. It is not possible for other channels to overwrite them just because they need the space in memory. Channels also have specific lifetimes, very much like cached data. However, these lifetimes are separate to those of ordinary cached data. On expiry, the data for a channel are considered stale and marked for systematic removal by the mobile-device processes. An individual resource can also be considered stale if at least one channel does not point to it.

The channel DTD

A well understood mechanism must be designed to store information about how the channel can be installed into the mobile device. For maximum consistency with the existing WAP architecture, it was decided that channels should be specified by the developer via XML. Therefore, a new channel DTD was created to outline how a channel-content format could be created to initiate a channel installation when sent to the mobile device. In order to initiate an installation, a user can browse through software listings and select a channel, which will make a request for the channel information that is then delivered to the mobile device. A channel can also be pushed to the mobile device by the push server using the push architecture discussed in Chapter 10. When you use this method the channel becomes part of the service indication, which the user can decide to install.

A third option is available for carriers: pre-installing the channel on a set of devices. This way, the channel is available by default on a set of mobile devices.

The channel defined through XML has its own media type, `text/vnd.wap.channel`, and binary form, `application/vnd.wap.channelc`. Listing 11-1 shows an example of a channel; Listing 11-2 provides a description of the elements and attributes of the new XML type.

Listing 11-1 shows a joke application that a user might want access to at later time. Maybe a user wants to make callers laugh with an up-to-date joke: this application gives the user some ideas. The example shows how the `root-element` structure is used, along with some key attributes regarding the definition and use of channels. A title and abstract explain to the user what the service is all about, and are followed by a set of URLs pointing to the resources that are to be loaded onto the mobile device.

Listing 11-1: Joke Channel

```
Content-type: text/vnd.wap.channel

<?xml version="1.0"?>
<!DOCTYPE channel PUBLIC "-//WAPFORUM/DTD CHANNEL 1.2//EN"
channel.dtd>

<channel
    maxspace="1024"
    base="http://wta-apps.carrier.com"
    eventid="wtaev-cc/ic"
    success="good.wml"
    failure="bad.wml"
>

<title>
    The Joke Service
</title>

<abstract>
    This service presents a joke on incoming calls
</abstract>

<resource href="index.wml"/>
<resource href="jokes.wml"/>
<resource href="jokesrus.wbmp"/>
<resource href="joke-randomizer.wmls"/>
<resource href="calls.wml"/>

</channel>
```

Listing 11-1 shows the different attributes in use for the channel to be defined. Listing 11-2 shows the DTD for the channel format.

Listing 11-2: Channel DTD

```
<!--
This DTD is identified by the PUBLIC identifier:
"-//WAPFORUM//DTD CHANNEL 1.2//EN"
```

Continued

Listing 11-2 *(Continued)*

```
-->
<!ENTITY % Boolean "( true | false )">
<!-- a Uniform Resource Identifier -->
<!ENTITY % URI "CDATA" >
<!-- one or more digits (NUMBER) -->
<!ENTITY % Number "CDATA" >
<!-- Channel Events -->
<!ENTITY % ChannelEvent.attribs
"success %URI; #IMPLIED
failure %URI; #IMPLIED"
>
<!ELEMENT channel (title , abstract? , resource* <!ATTLIST channel
maxspace %Number; #REQUIRED
base %URI; #IMPLIED
eventid CDATA #IMPLIED
channelid CDATA #REQUIRED
useraccessible %Boolean; "false"
%ChannelEvent.attribs;
>
<!ELEMENT title (#PCDATA)>
<!ELEMENT abstract (#PCDATA)>
<!ELEMENT resource EMPTY>
<!ATTLIST resource
href %URI; #REQUIRED
lastmod %Number; #IMPLIED
etag NMTOKEN #IMPLIED
md5 NMTOKEN #IMPLIED
>
```

Tables 11-10 and 11-11 list the elements and attributes of the channel element.

TABLE 11-10 CHANNEL ELEMENTS

Channel Element	Description
maxspace=%number	Specifies the maximum memory in bytes that the channel can use. The server must guarantee that this size is not exceeded by the sum (in bytes) of all resources. If the client decides that the maxspace is excessive it may decide to abort the installation.

Chapter 11: WTA   399

Channel Element	Description
`base=%URI`	Specifies the base URL for all resources specified as relative URLs. If this attribute is not defined the resources must be specified using absolute URLs.
`success=%URI`	Points to a deck that is loaded if the installation goes well.
`failure=%URI`	Indicates that the installation doesn't go so well. Because loading a channel is atomic, all the loaded resources up to that point are marked as invalid, or stale.
`channelid=CDATA`	Shows the identity of the channel. Used to load and unload a channel and can be displayed in a menu.
`eventid=CDATA`	Refers to the specific event that if fired will launch the service.
`useraccessible=(true|false)`	Indicates whether the user can access the service through a menu or only through some network-initiation mechanism.

TABLE 11-11 RESOURCE ELEMENT ATTRIBUTES

Attribute	Description
`href=%URI`	Points to the location of the resources needed for the channel to install correctly.
`lastmod=%number`	Shows the time that the resource was last modified, which the user agent uses if it needs to make an if-modified-since calculation on the resource in the repository. These calculations are exactly the same as those for standard HTTP.
`etag=nmtoken`	Available for resources that need a finer granularity of control than `lastmod` offers, `etags` are unique strings associated with a resource to identify a specific version.
`md5=nmtoken`	Contains a fingerprint of the data in a resource that is written using a one-way hash algorithm (as specified in RFC 1321). I discuss md5 and other security algorithms for integrity in Chapter 16.

In the next section I look at how the events are handled by WTA channels, and the distinction between temporary and global event bindings.

WTA Event Handling

WTA events are actually events that come from the mobile network. These network events are translated from their physical channel form into a predefined format for the various WTA events. I mention the syntax for the predefined format in Table 11-9.

You can program WTA user agents to take actions when a specific WTA event is received. The network events are real-time events, so the actions that are associated with them must also take place in real time. Any content associated with them must not be delayed for any reason — network load, for example. This is why these programmed actions are often placed in the repository in the form of a channel.

You can use two separate methods to respond to a WTA event:

- *Global bindings* — In this case a channel is bound to a WTA event and starts up the channel service every time the WTA event occurs. I showed you how this works in the previous Joke channel example.
- *Temporary bindings* — In this case, an application is already loaded into the phones memory and an `onevent` tag in the loaded deck contains a WTA event pointer. A temporary binding to handle incoming calls would look something like this: `<onevent type="wtaev-cc/ic"> <go href="..."><onevent>`.

Example WTA Applications

Now that we have been through a lot of the theory, let's look at the potential of WTA as demonstrated by several sample applications.

WTA incoming-call selection

The first example is a simple service that intercepts an incoming call event and starts another service that gives the user some options, such as the following:

- Accept the call
- Reject the call
- Direct the call to voicemail
- Send a special message to the caller

Figure 11-11 illustrates what this service would look like.

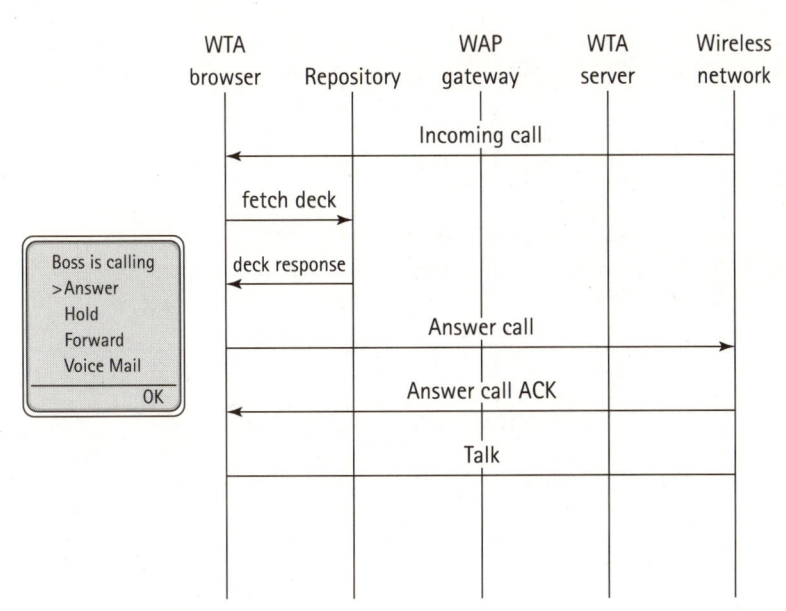

Figure 11-11: WTA incoming call selection

Figure 11-11 shows how an incoming call over the network generates a WTA event of type `wtaev-cc/ic`. The WTA user agent checks the repository to see whether any of the services have dedicated channels. The application data are obtained from the repository and presented to the user for the first listed service. The content is loaded and the user decides which option to select. The relevant WTAI function is then called to communicate with the mobile network. After that, the call uses the existing telephony infrastructure.

WTA voicemail server

This example (see Figure 11-12) illustrates how a user would be notified of new incoming voicemails. The screen displays the list of voicemails once the user signs on. The user can browse through and select various messages from the list and then set up a call with the voicemail server, which accesses the selected message.

Figure 11-12 shows how a voicemail system notifies the WTA server of new voicemails. A list of new voicemails is also sent to the WTA server at the same time and cached for later use. The WTA server then acts as a push initiator and delivers a push message to the WAP gateway/Push Proxy gateway. The gateway then delivers the push message to the phone in the form of a service indication. The user then uses the service indication URL to issue a GET request for the actual resource. Because all the data are cached at the WTA server, the user can browse through them for some time. It is only when a message actually needs to be played that the WTA server sets up a call with the user, so that he or she can hear the message recordings.

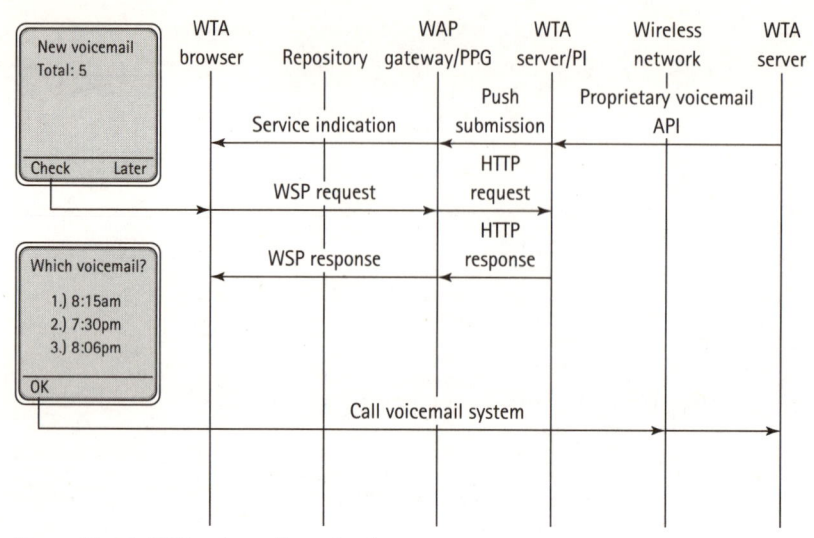

Figure 11-12: WTA voicemail application

Summary

In this chapter I started out by listing some of the motivations for the WTA architecture and how carriers would benefit by implementing it. Then I laid out the architecture and examined the intricacies of developing for this platform and meeting its unique security requirements. The WTA architecture introduces many new components from the telephony space to the picture. I discussed integrating and planning services based on these components.

It should be noted that, with the exception of the WTA `makecall` function, developers cannot use any of the functions or events described in this chapter. No infrastructure deployments of WTA services exists, nor is there any support for them by major handset manufacturers. So even though it is part of WAP, WTA is not well supported by the marketplace. Time will tell if and when it becomes an accepted standard for this kind of development.

In the next chapter, I will examine the role of cache operations in building advanced applications for WAP.

Chapter 12

Caching and Cache Operations

IN THIS CHAPTER

- Understanding HTTP caching behavior
- Differentiating WAP caching features
- Implementing cache operations for synchronization
- Using proprietary techniques for directed development

EVERY TIME YOU BROWSE A SITE ON THE WEB, the HTML code received by the browser is stored in memory on the machine. This area of memory on the desktop is known as the cache. If you browse again later using the same URL, the older page can be loaded without the browser having to issue a new request. Also, when you press the Back button in the browser, the cached content is displayed first. In the desktop world, both the browser and the developer of Web services can control how data are stored in the cache with the user retaining the ultimate control.

As shown in Chapter 3, the HTTP protocol specifies that responses stored in memory on the browser machine must include both the headers and the content. The act of putting this information into memory on the browser machine is known as caching.

Because a portion of the WAP architecture is based on HTTP, and the WSP side inherits some HTTP-like functionality, a decision had to made about the level of caching support in WAP. Earlier phones did not have much memory, nor did the level of the average user sophistication approach the sophistication of average Internet users. This is because in order to actually get to the browsing stage on a computer, a user has to go through a large number of hurdles, such as getting the PC to run correctly, getting a Web browser to run, and then figuring out how to navigate the Web. In contrast, users of phones are accustomed to an appliance that works all the time in a consistent manner. Any minor variation in the normal behavior is thought by the users to indicate a broken appliance. For these reasons, the cache was implemented only in a limited fashion. Even to this day, the WAP standard defines a caching mechanism that is less than what is expected in Internet browsing.

You may wonder why I take caching seriously enough to devote an entire chapter to it. The answer is that caching is much more important to wireless devices than it is to development in the desktop world. This is because of some mitigating factors related to the wireless environment.

These mitigating factors are as follows:

- Wireless-device memory
- Wireless-device bandwidth
- WAP architecture
- Variety of caching-support models
- Caching-model differences between HTTP and WAP
- Limited browser control

Wireless device memory is limited, and as tradeoffs in design were implemented, only a few pieces of data remained that could be stored on the phones (see Chapter 4). The largest piece of data stored on the wireless device is the cache. Because the cache holds the largest percentage of storage, it effectively becomes a storage area on the wireless device that developers can maintain, much like a directory. Until this problem of limited memory is solved with the use of persistent storage, developers will continue to use the cache as a short-term application-resource storage area.

> See Chapter 20, "The Future of WAP," for more information about persistent storage.

Limited bandwidth forces developers to use the cache to improve user response and to pre-load for better response.

WAP architecture uses a proxy that does some caching of its own and disallows some caching features available in HTTP. Technically, no proxy of the HTTP protocol can touch any of the caching headers. However, WAP departs from this practice, and most WAP gateways modify this information.

A number of caching models are supported on phones in the market. I discuss the differences, but some knowledge of all of them can result in better application response.

The WAP caching model is not simply a copy of the HTTP model. Differences exist, and this chapter clears up some misuses of the caching behavior where developers expect HTTP-compliant behavior to occur.

An application may modify its own entries in the browser cache or ignore the browser cache entirely to maintain an application flow. The extensive caching-control headers and augmented WAP cache operations available allow for finely controlled application behavior, letting applications make the necessary modifications to the cache or to ignore it entirely. As some later examples illustrate, sometimes you may want applications to do one or the other.

As mentioned previously, the user can control the caching behavior of a site in the desktop by using option dialog boxes. The Web community requires this level of user control. Strangely, in the wireless world, a user has very little control and in many cases does not have the authority to delete information from the cache.

Because little user control exists, the control that is left belongs to the developers of Web services. The HTTP protocol defines a set of useful caching headers that may be modified to manipulate the caching capability. Furthermore, an explicit push message can be sent to the wireless device in order to send delete commands to the cache. The ability to delete items from the cache may be useful in synchronizing data between the cache and a Web service.

In this chapter I explain how effective use of caching headers can improve your applications and enable better control of user perception of your application than many of the optimizations described in Chapter 6.

Introducing HTTP Caching

First, I discuss caching as it occurs on desktop browsers using HTTP. Then I apply those desktop-browsing concepts to the wireless environment. The HTTP protocol provides some insight into the headers and their function.

Caching and desktop browsers

The overall operation of HTTP allows for communication between the browser and the server to be separated by many intermediary servers. Therefore, a request chain may potentially be established through multiple proxies. Still, the WAP gateway must be on one end of the request chain.

Caching in HTTP was added to improve performance, namely with regard to multiple round trips to servers to retrieve data that may or may not have not changed. On a simple level, the round trips are sometimes simply eliminated because a cached copy exists in browser memory. On another level, the round trips may be made smaller, because only a brief update response is sent to the browser. The first type of problem on a desktop browser that a memory cache addresses is the number of request/response sessions, and the second is the usage of the network bandwidth.

To address both of these issues, a server can issue implicit directives to caches. These directives (`Expires` and `Validation`) are implied by the headers being passed back and forth. Servers can also, using the `Cache-Control` header, issue more explicit directives that force specific behavior on the client cache. The HTTP protocol allows `Cache-Control` headers to be inserted in both client requests and server responses. If you are a third-party WAP developer, only the `Cache-Control` headers in the server responses are useful for your needs. This is because no options exist today on most phones for modifying client-cache behavior. For example, in Internet Explorer, you are able to specify that you do not want any data cached.

SETTING EXPIRATION TIMES

With server-specified expiration (Implicit), the Web server sets an expiration time header on a response. The benefit of this method is that the client does not need to resend a request. It simply checks the expiration date and determines whether a new request is required. If not, the requested resource is obtained from the cache. If a server wants to force fresh responses using this header, you can write the headers such that the `Expires` time is immediately stale. Servers can also specify explicit `Expires` times using the `Expires` header or the `max-age` directive in the `Cache-Control` header.

Web servers do not always provide explicit expiration times, so the Web browser determines the HTTP cache heuristically by using algorithms that use other header values, such as Last-Modified time, to estimate a possible expiration time. You should use explicit expiration times wherever possible.

To accurately establish expiration times, an accurate clock is needed to confirm the relative freshness of resources. The HTTP protocol requires that all hosts, both the client and the server, maintain accurate clocks using NTP or similar timing protocol. Also, servers are required to send `Date` headers, which indicate when a response was generated.

DETERMINING AGE OF RESOURCES

Age headers specify the estimated age of a response message when a resource is obtained from the cache. The `Age` field is the cache's estimate of the time since the Web server generated the response. The browser calculates the `Age` field in WAP by determining the skew between the current time and the `Date` value. An even more complex formula also involves the use of corrected received `Age`.

To calculate whether a resource is fresh, the browser compares the freshness lifetime of the resource (`Expires` header) to its `Age`. The browser calculates the freshness lifetime using the following formulas.

First, if `max-age` is set, then the freshness lifetime is simply equal to `max-age`. If `Expires` is present in the response, the calculation implemented by the browser is as follows:

```
freshness_lifetime = expires_value - date_value
```

If none of these estimators of freshness exists (no `Expires` or `max-age`), a browser can determine the lifetime of the resource using an internal heuristic. As you will see later, most WAP browsers set this value to 30 days.

If a resource has been determined to be stale by the browser, the resource `Date` needs to be checked against the Web server value to see whether the stale value is still usable. Several conditional methods, or validators, are available to render a full round trip to the Web server unnecessary.

When the Web server generates a "full" response, a validator is attached as a header and kept in the browser as part of the cache entry. When the browser makes a "conditional" request, the same validator is sent as part of the request. When the server encounters this validator in such a conditional request, it determines whether a full response is necessary or whether a special `Not Modified` response with no entity body is adequate.

The HTTP protocol defines both positive and negative forms of this validation. This means that the request can state that the method be performed only if the validator matches, or only if no validator matches.

The two validators most commonly used are `Last-Modified` dates and Entity Tags:

- The `Last-Modified` entity header value is used such that a cached entry is considered as valid if the entity has not been modified since the `Last-Modified` value.

- The Entity Tag (Etag) provides an "opaque" cache validator. This is a better solution for conditions in which it is inconvenient to store modification dates, the one-second resolution of date values is not sufficient, or when you wish to avoid certain paradoxes that can result from calculating modification dates; for example, when the clock on the mobile is slow, the device may actually prefer content in the cache over new content on the Web server.

By comparing two validators, a decision is made as to whether the resource has changed; therefore, it makes sense that if the resource changes, its corresponding validator is updated at the same time. This is an example of a strong validator. A weak validator is based on a heuristic of whether some resource has changed; for example, Web browsers may use other header values such as the `Last-Modified` time to estimate a possible expiration time for a document.

> **NOTE:** A key distinction between strong and weak validators is that the strong validator absolutely changes when the document changes; a weak validator, however, may change only when a significant change is made to the document.

HTTP caching and headers

You have seen how caching is involved in the way information in a network transaction is sent as part of a request/response exchange. Caching is done especially to reduce the bandwidth usage. This reduction will actually reduce the overall latency of the connection.

Proxies and/or intermediaries may also maintain their own caches, but they must preserve all `Cache-Control` headers when handling an end-to-end hop.

After data are cached in memory on the browser machine, the browser will need a way to find out when data has changed on the server. HTTP uses special headers to send this information back and forth between the client browsers and the servers.

The main technique involves checking on the some freshness attribute of the knowledge. This can be done in two ways, one by the client and the other by the server.

The client can check the most recent modification of the document, or it can determine whether the Entity Tag associated with the document has changed.

Documents on the server, when set up with the appropriate `Cache-Control` headers, are used to implement this feature. The headers determine the client's caching behavior based on security and volatility criteria. Following are sections that cover some of the most commonly used `Cache-Control` headers and the `If-Modified-Since` process.

THE IF-MODIFIED-SINCE HEADER

Using the `If-Modified-Since` process, a client can use the `If-Modified-Since` header with the GET method to control caching behavior. The client requests the server to send a URL only if the URL has been modified since a specified time. This request can produce two results, either a 200 or 304, with the following four possibilities:

- If the document was modified according to time, the server will give a response code of `200` and return the document in the entity body.

- If the document was *not* modified, the server will give a response code of `304` (not modified).

- If the `304 status` code is returned by the Web server, the document has not been modified since the specified time and a cached version can be used.

- If the document is newer, the standard `200 OK` response code is issued by the Web server along with the new document as an entity. This response may also contain a `Last-Modified` header so that clients know about the last change to the document.

A related header here is `If-Not-Modified-Since`, which is the opposite of `If-Modified Since`. It sends the document only if the document has not been modified since the modified date. An example of how this header is useful is when an HTTP GET of a document is followed by an HTTP PUT. The PUT command, which uploads a document onto a Web server, can use the `If-Modified-Since` header to prevent multiple users from overwriting each other's work.

The `Expires` header tells the client that the document will not change before the time specified in the header. This is less processor intensive than normal operation on the client because no request has to be made until the expiration date.

ENTITY TAGS

The Entity Tag (Etag) feature is new to HTTP 1.1. It gives clients and servers a new way to maintain cache management. Instead of serving to check the URL and last modified headers, the Etags function as "fingerprints" attached as headers to each document. Etags are useful when several copies of a document may exist. The client will be able to tell that this is the case using the Etag only. Also, documents can be changed by Web site automated authoring programs very rapidly — as frequently as twice a second. In those cases, Etags are a better way to keep track of the document changes than the date headers previously mentioned.

An Etag is a unique identifier associated with all copies of the document. If the document changes, the Etag changes. This simple change characteristic allows for only a single variable, the Etag, to be monitored, whereas before with dates, multiple dates were involved and calculations above and beyond that were also required. If the server supports the Etags, they are sent with an Etag header. When Etags need to be checked, the browser can use `If-Match` or `If-None-Match` headers.

The client entity and response entity headers control most of the caching behavior discussed so far. Following are client request headers for caching behavior:

- `If-Modified-Since:` *date*: Indicates that the data pointed to by the URL are to be sent only if they have been modified since the date shown in this header. If the document has not been modified since the date shown, a status code of 304 is returned to the browser.

    Example: `If-Modified-Since: Tue, 10 April 2001 06:23:12 GMT`

- `If-Not-Modified-Since:` *date*: The exact opposite of the `If-Modified-Since` header. This time, the URL data are sent only if they have *not* been modified since the date shown in the header.

    Example: `If-Not-Modified-Since: Tue, 10 April 2001 06:23:12 GMT`

Following is a server response header for caching behavior:

- `Etag:` *entity_tag*: Attaches a unique identifier to a resource and is useful for caching purposes.

    Example: `Etag: 234397`

Following are entity headers for caching behavior:

- Content-Location: *URL*: Points to the entity being sent. *URL* can be either relative or absolute.

  Example: Content-Location: ?a=b

- Expires: *date*: Contains a date after which the entity is no longer valid. The presence of an Expires date does not mean that the document is fixed until that time, but only that it is unlikely to be changed until then.

  Example: Expires: Tue, 10 April 2001 06:23:12 GMT

- Last-Modified: *date*: Contains the time the entity was last updated on the server. If the browser has an older copy, it will need to be refreshed.

  Example: Last-Modfied: Tue, 10 April 2001 06:23:12 GMT

Earlier in this section I discussed the general headers that you can use to control the cache. These general directives are sent by both the clients and the servers to manage information in the cache; they are sent in comma-delimited lists that follow a Cache-Control directive. For example:

Cache-control: max-age=300

Following are the two possible directives. Although the directives can be in either requests or responses, only the response Cache-Control directives are listed here.

- no-cache: Indicates that the browser can keep a cached copy but must always revalidate it when accessing the URL.

  Example: Cache-control: no-cache

- max-age = *seconds*: Indicates that the document/resource is stale after the number of seconds shown.

  Example: Cache-control: max-age=600

The WAP Caching Model

The previous sections outline the HTTP caching model used in desktop browsers. With some slight modifications, the standard caching model is also good for WAP. This section describes those modifications:

- The WAP gateway acts as an intermediary in any caching communication. As such, a computer does not exist in the standard Web architecture; its roles and responsibilities need to be defined by the WAP Forum.

- WAP clients do not have enough memory to support the full HTTP desktop caching capabilities.

- WAP Mobile Client behavior is different from the behavior of the desktop.

WAP caching uses the HTTP/1.1 set as the base set of features. The WAP Forum then made modifications or deletions as required, based on the constraints or differences listed.

One of the main changes to the HTTP/1.1 set is that the interaction between the cache and the WML history is controlled by the `Cache-Control: must-revalidate` header. When a user presses the "back" button (Prev), the browser attempts to use any data in the cache by default.

To do something, the `must-revalidate` header can be set; if the resource is stale, the browser must revalidate the resource when going "back." The original request is then made without any user interaction.

If the cached resource does not have must-revalidate header set, and the cached resource is stale, the browser does not revalidate the entity when going back.

Intra-resource navigation

Navigation within a single cached resource does not require revalidation. For example, when function calls within WMLScript files are called, the entire WMLScript file is not re-fetched from the server. This is also the case for interdeck navigation — navigation between two cards.

WAP gateway responsibilities

WAP gateways must implement HTTP/1.1 with regard to its role as HTTP/1.1 proxy and to caching and cache-header transmission. The gateway must cache its WSP responses to fulfill its role as an HTTP 1.1 proxy.

The specification divides the headers into end-to-end headers and hop-to-hop headers. All the `Cache-Control` headers are defined as end-to-end headers.

Cache control by users on mobile phones is limited. Unlike with standard Web browsers, the user of the wireless device can't change device attributes.

Caching Resources for Periods of Time

The section describing the HTTP desktop browsing caching behavior provided a comprehensive description of the caching headers. Three important caching headers for WAP development that I've discussed thus far are as follows:

```
Cache-control: no-cache
Cache-control: max-age=[seconds]
Expires: [date]
```

The next sections cover these headers in more detail, with specific examples to show how they are useful in WAP development.

The Cache-Control: no-cache header

For information that is changing very frequently, caching should be disabled completely. For example, caching should be off when you're first testing applications. However, later on, the usability of your application is going to depend on the proper sequencing of caching.

The `no-cache` header is very useful when placed at the initial entry page for WAP applications or when used in the early stages of development; otherwise, its use must be carefully monitored because excessive traffic might result on the wireless link. In cases in which it is used at the entry point, it is important that the main application be up-to-date. This will force the correct initializations to occur for the service. The most direct way to achieve the up-to-date behavior is to specify:

```
Cache-control: no-cache
```

You can also use one of the following methods:

```
Cache-control: max-age=0
Expires: Tue, 20 Jan 2001 08:00:00 GMT
```

Listing 12-1 shows how you can set `Cache-Control` to not cache a document using some ASP code.

Listing 12-1: Adding a Cache-Control Header to a Response

```
<%
Response.ContentType = "text/vnd.wap.wml"
Response.AddHeader("Cache-control", "no-cache")
%>

<?xml version="1.0"?>
<!DOCTYPE wml PUBLIC "-//WAPFORUM//DTD WML 1.1//EN"
 "http://www.wapforum.org/DTD/wml_1.1.xml">

<wml>
   <card title="testing">
      <p>test page</p>
   </card>
</wml>
```

The Expires: and max-age headers

A resource can stay in the typical wireless device's cache for a period of up to 30 days if the expiration of the resource is undefined. The 30-day value is on the high side and may vary according to the device. You can extend this period of time for data, such as a splash screen, that need to stay on the mobile device longer. In that case, you can set the Expires header as follows:

Expires: Fri, 08 Jan 2005 00:00:00 GMT

Alternatively, you can use a large max-age value,

Cache-control: max-age=6727324

in which the time can be of a maximum integer value to 2,147,483,647.

You can also cache the resource for a specific period of time. For example, a WAP stock service may get a feed only every 15 minutes. If requests come in to the service more frequently, those requests should retrieve data from the cache. Figure 12-1 shows what this request flow looks like.

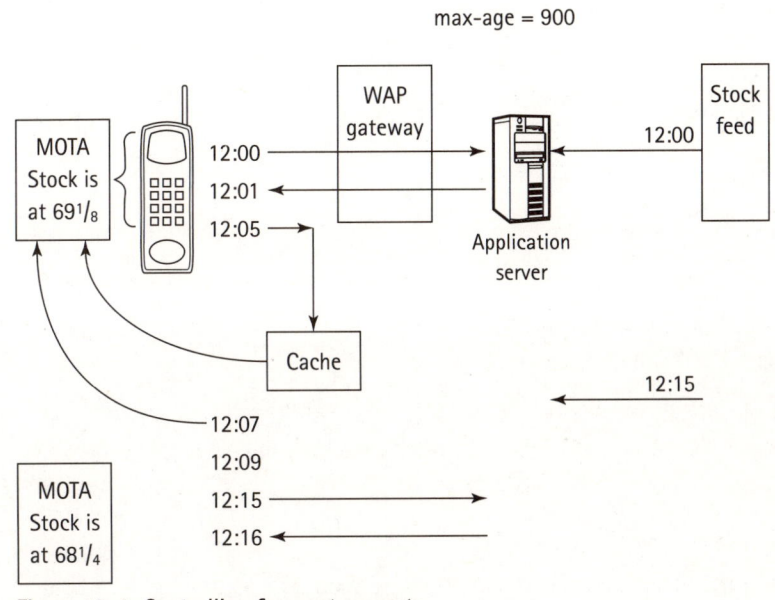

Figure 12-1: Controlling frequent requests

Here are some examples of what the headers look like:

```
Expires: time + 15 min
Cache-control: max-age=900
```

Naturally, when a deck is navigated to for the first time, it is validated whether the resource has expired or not. The history stack directly affects validation in WAP. If the history stack points to a resource, the resource is not validated unless there is a special `must-revalidate` header, as follows:

```
Cache-control: must-revalidate
```

Listing 12-2 presents an example of a clock application that shows why the `must-revalidate` header needs to be used.

Listing 12-2: A Clock Application Using the Same URL

```
<%
Response.ContentType = "text/vnd.wap.wml"
Response.AddHeader("Cache-control", "no-cache, must-revalidate")
%>

<?xml version="1.0"?>
<!DOCTYPE wml PUBLIC "-//WAPFORUM//DTD WML 1.1//EN"
 "http://www.wapforum.org/DTD/wml_1.1.xml">

<wml>
   <card title="time">
      <onevent type="ontimer">
         <go href="clock.asp"/>
      </onevent>
      <timer name="timerVal" value="600"/>
      <do type="options" label="Sync">
         <go href="clock.asp"/>
      </do>
      <p><%=Now()%></p>
   </card>
</wml>
```

In this case, the headers give a combined effect. For example, in `Cache-control: must-revalidate, max-age=900`, the `must-revalidate` is combined with an expiration period for the document.

HTTP Headers and Meta Elements

The WML language includes a meta element that enables you to add any of the HTTP headers I've discussed thus far to the response by the WAP gateway. This is useful when you are somehow limited to writing your applications using only static WML.

The required element in WML is the `meta`. It is also used for other general functionality, and the task of adding headers is a special variation of its overall functionality. Its syntax is as follows:

```
<meta http-equiv="   " content="   ">
```

For example:

```
<meta http-equiv="Cache-control" content="must-revalidate">
```

When the content reaches the WAP gateway, the WAP gateway adds the correct headers to the WSP response sent to the wireless device. The preferred approach to adding these headers is to use the regular HTTP format, because `meta` tags are not supported by all browsers on the market.

WAP Cache Operations

Up to now, you have seen how to use header statements to modify how documents and resources are treated by the caching model. Earlier phone models offered even less control, so an explicit command was made available to enable users to extract specific resources in the browser cache. This is the ultimate way for a service to control the mobile-device cache.

The technique allows any item in the cache to be invalidated by WAP applications as needed. This way, if an item in the cache is requested again, the WAP browser is forced to go to the application server. In the stock feed example description, the caching properties of the data were well known by the application developer and the data's timeout was set to 15 minutes by the application developer. In many cases, the data's volatility is unknown to the developer when it is delivered to the device.

Consider the example of a stock portfolio–management system. Users may want to be able to edit and delete stocks from their lists. This means that any changes they make would affect many screens in the application. The action of deleting a stock from the portfolio is somewhat unpredictable to the application designer because the developer does not know which stock the user will delete from a screen that shows them. If one is deleted, a cache operation is required to prevent the user from seeing cards where the stock would still appear.

The WAP cache operation is specified as an XML document. It indicates items to be deleted from the cache using a given URL.

The two operations supported are the following:

- `invalidate-object`: Invalidate the object in the URL.
- `invalidate-service`: Invalidate objects using a URL prefix.

The cache operation is defined by a `co`, for a content format. A complete DTD (see Listing 12-3) is actually dedicated to the cache operation.

Listing 12-3: DTD for the Cache Operation

```
<!ELEMENT co (invalidate-object | invalidate-service)+>

<!ELEMENT invalidate-object EMPTY>
<!ATTLIST invalidate-object
uri CDATA #REQUIRED
>

<!ELEMENT invalidate-service EMPTY>
<!ATTLIST invalidate-service
uri CDATA #REQUIRED
>
```

The two important possibilities for cache operations therefore are `invalidate-object` and `invalidate-service`. For `invalidate-object`, the URI attribute is used by developers to define the exact URL of the resource in the cache that needs to be deleted. For `invalidate-service`, the URI attribute defines a prefix substring of the URL for the resources to be deleted. All the resources that begin with that prefix are deleted from the cache.

Figure 12-2 provides an example of how a cache operation can be useful in application design. The figure shows a list of stocks. A user can select whether to add, edit, or delete an item on the list.

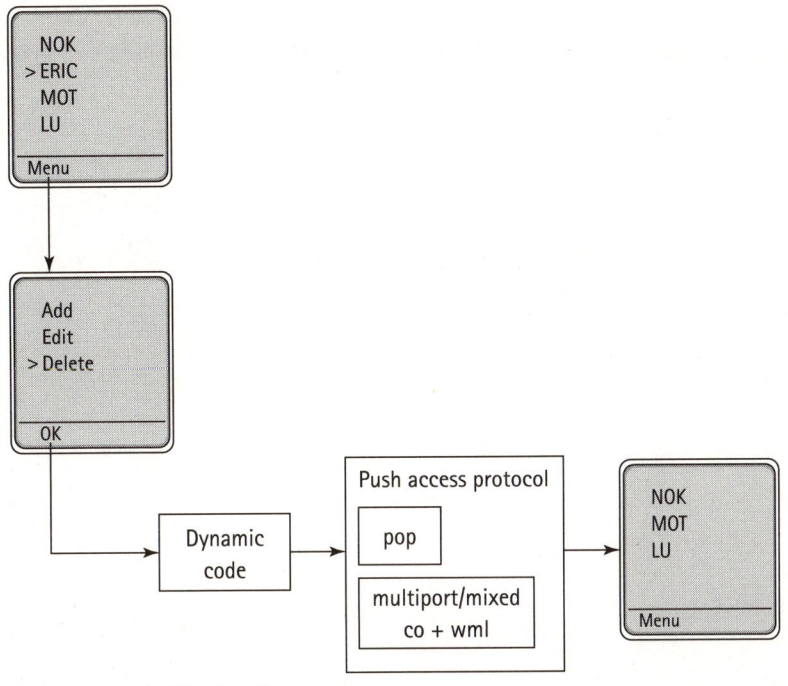

Figure 12-2: Application flow

Proprietary Techniques

Because many phones on the market support the v3 browser by Openwave, I discuss it here. Openwave's v3.*x* browser featured bigger differences between HTTP caching and the implementation than those of standard WAP. In this browser, more responsibility was put on the application server for managing any cached content. The v3.*x* browser did not support If-Modified-Since negotiation. Application developers therefore need to rely more on deck-cache control and cache operation to maintain proper coherency than If-Modified-Since negotiation. The v3.*x* browser also always loads from the cache in the "back" direction, regardless of any must-revalidate header.

To build applications that refer to the same URL as that in the code in v3, the programmer must trick the browser by aliasing the cache ID to some dummy URL. Listing 12-4 shows how to do this trick.

Listing 12-4: A Code v3 Clock using ASP

```
<%
Response.ContentType = "text/vnd.wap.wml"
Response.AddHeader("Content-location", "?foo=bar")
%>

<?xml version="1.0"?>
<!DOCTYPE wml PUBLIC "-//WAPFORUM//DTD WML 1.1//EN"
 "http://www.wapforum.org/DTD/wml_1.1.xml">

<wml>
   <card title="time">
      <onevent type="ontimer">
         <go href="clock.asp"/>
      </onevent>
      <timer name="timerVal" value="600"/>
      <do type="options" label="Sync">
         <go href="clock.asp"/>
      </do>
      <p><%=Now()%></p>
   </card>
</wml>
```

v3.*x* browsers also support the Openwave cache operation. This operation is not sent using XML but rather in a proprietary format using the Openwave notification libraries, currently available only in COM, Solaris C, and Perl. You can find more details in the Openwave reference on invalidating content (www.openwave.com).

v4 browsers support HTTP/1.1 caching models, the WML `meta` element, and more `Cache-Control` headers. Although these browsers are more WAP compliant, you must still use the older cache-operation architecture, which means that developers are still limited by proprietary APIs. True compliance with WAP standards may not appear until v5 for the Openwave browsers.

Summary

Caching is very often overlooked as a means of optimizing Web applications, and in WAP development, it becomes an even more important factor in delivering optimal service.

Developers can make use of the headers, standard caching behavior, and the WAP modifications described in this chapter to create more responsive applications. The implementation of the combined features will give your application the added edge over others.

This chapter covered additional caching manipulation by using cache operations. This little-known technique is the caching equivalent of a well-performed extraction; literally taking out the pages or resources you do not want the wireless client to use.

The chapter finished with a description of proprietary APIs that have been implemented in the North American markets. These proprietary APIs form the only way that cache operations and caching can be done on many of the phones today.

Part IV

Designing Usable WAP Services

CHAPTER 13
Session Management and Identification

CHAPTER 14
Targeted Development

CHAPTER 15
Designing User-Friendly Interfaces

Chapter 13

Session Management and Identification

IN THIS CHAPTER

- ◆ Introducing session management and identification
- ◆ Solving the identification problem
- ◆ Managing sessions
- ◆ Looking toward the future of WAP session management and identification

IN THIS CHAPTER, I explain how content servers can identify a user in order to deliver customized content. Identifying and managing online profiles is even more important to the wireless environment than it is to the regular Web. This is because even the most mundane activities must be managed to increase the speed with which users can navigate. A personalized site is easier to navigate than one that does not cater to your needs.

The techniques that I go over in this chapter are a combination of techniques from the regular Web and some new techniques for identification management. You can expect this area to become better supported as manufacturers learn lessons from existing products and as new identification standards emerge.

I also go over session-handling issues and compare them to existing Web techniques. Finally, I provide you with an overview of what you can expect in the future from the WAP Forum regarding these two areas of WAP development. Many examples in this chapter describe the methods at your disposal for both identification and session management.

As mentioned in Chapter 3, HTTP is a stateless protocol that was not originally designed to allow information to be carried from session to session. This means that if a user navigated to your content server and then came back later there would be no information in the HTTP protocol to let the content server know that the user had been there before. Furthermore, there was also no way to uniquely identify the user.

Images of Openwave products in this chapter courtesy of Openwave Systems Inc.

This situation may have been adequate in a CERN laboratory (the birthplace of the World Wide Web), but when the commercial market started implementing HTTP servers and HTML content, it became necessary to solve the problems of session management and identification. Many schemes have been put forward to solve both problems; each has obtained varying degrees of acceptance given the range of hardware and software in the marketplace. I look briefly at the state of the Web industry today and then proceed to the mechanisms that have been adapted for use in the WAP space.

First let's look at the identification problem, and then at the session-management issues.

Solving the Identification Problem

The original HTTP specifications left out any identification mechanism. HTTP version 0.9 did not require the client to send any headers in an HTTP request. Then HTTP 1.0 and finally HTTP 1.1 began to mandate more headers and some became required; however, very little identity information was passed from the client to the server.

This was mostly because of concerns about privacy. Firms such as DoubleClick.net had begun collecting data on user behavior and were beginning to build large databases that they were using to correlate their online profile collections with actual identities. Such efforts have been abandoned as the result of privacy-group criticisms.

Although some content servers would tend toward the extreme, tying a specific Social Security Number to each HTTP request, the industry has accepted a middle-of-the-road approach. With this approach, some unique identifier may be passed back and forth with HTTP. The content server is then responsible for tying that unique identifier to a back-end identifier and attempting to obtain a profile for the user. The content server is then responsible for maintaining its own customer record and profile.

There are three ways to send unique identifiers in HTTP:

- Cookies
- Manual identification schemes
- Proprietary headers

A cookie is a temporary text string sent from a Web site to a browser. It may be used to track a visitor to a site or maintain personal preferences specific to a particular Web site. I look at cookies in the section "Session Handling," because they also address the session-management problem well. The manual-identification scheme requires a user to register with a site by providing a unique username and password before entering the site. This username can be tied to an online profile that the content server has built up. However, when carried over to WAP, these

Web-based solutions do not port well. First of all, not all WAP gateways support cookies. Secondly, having the user enter any more data than necessary is not considered very good practice, because data entry is difficult on the phone, and the user is not necessarily in a work environment—he or she may be driving, at a restaurant, or in a taxi going to the airport. Luckily, many WAP gateway and phone manufacturers have recognized these problems and provided a new solution by adding new proprietary headers to the HTTP protocol.

Every request that comes from a browser contains client headers. These client headers can contain standard headers but may also contain some optional headers without affecting the operation of HTTP. Several manufacturers have decided to add new proprietary headers, which contain identification information, to the HTTP client requests. Unfortunately the information added to the client requests currently varies significantly from vendor to software vendor. I discuss the main types you may encounter. These types of proprietary headers will require some discussion of proprietary solutions from Ericsson and Openwave. No solution has yet been proposed by WAP Forum to standardize the identification information to be added to client requests across vendors.

Let's look at some actual examples of how you can construct identification mechanisms in WAP. Because I cover cookies in the section "Using cookies," I start with manual identification schemes and then move on to proprietary headers.

Using manual identification schemes

As discussed earlier, you can construct a manual client authentication that checks against a content-server database to determine whether the client is allowed access to the server. This should be a simple procedure, since you are in control of the authentication mechanism. After a user logs in using this technique, an association is created, which, if properly managed, gives you information about which user is browsing your site and where he or she browsing.

Listing 13-1 provides an example of dynamic code that prompts for a username and password. The user then proceeds to the next part of the script, which determines whether the information matches an entry in the database.

Listing 13-1: Username and Password Prompt

```
<%@ Language=VBScript %>

<%
Option Explicit
Response.ContentType = "text/vnd.wap.wml"
%>

<?xml version="1.0"?>
```

Continued

Listing 13-1 *(Continued)*

```wml
<!DOCTYPE wml PUBLIC "-//WAPFORUM//DTD WML 1.1//EN"
 "http://www.wapforum.org/DTD/wml_1.1.xml">

<wml>
    <card id="user" title="User Login">
        <do type="accept" label="Next">
            <go href="#pass"/>
        </do>

        <p>
            Please enter your username:
            <input name="user"/>
        </p>
    </card>

    <card id="pass" title="Password Entry">
        <do type="accept">
            <go method="post" href="nextpass.asp">
                <postfield name="user" value="$user"/>
                <postfield name="pass" value="$pass"/>
            </go>
        </do>
        <p>
            Please enter your password:
            <input name="pass"/>
        </p>
    </card>
</wml>
```

This file simply pulls in a username and password using standard input elements and sends this information to the server by posting the fields in a follow-up request.

This code is saved as a file. Once the user enters a username and password, he or she moves on to the dynamic script shown in Listing 13-2.

Listing 13-2: Authenticating the User

```
<%@ Language=VBScript %>

<%
Option Explicit
Response.ContentType = "text/vnd.wap.wml"
%>

<?xml version="1.0"?><!DOCTYPE wml PUBLIC "-//WAPFORUM//DTD WML
```

```
1.1//EN" "http://www.wapforum.org/DTD/wml_1.1.xml">
<wml>

<%
    Dim conn, rs
    Set conn = Server.CreateObject("ADODB.Connection")
    Set rs   = Server.CreateObject("ADODB.Recordset")
    conn.open "DRIVER={Microsoft Access Driver (*.mdb)};DBQ=" 
            & Server.MapPath("Users.mdb") & ";"
%>

<card id="check" title="Login Check">
   <p>
   <%
     Dim sqlQuery
       sqlQuery = "SELECT * FROM Users WHERE username='" 
           & Request.Form("user") & "' AND password='" &
           Request.Form("pass") & "'"
       Set rs = conn.Execute(sqlQuery)

       if not rs.EOF then
           Session("user") = Request.Form("user")
           Session("pass") = Request.Form("pass")
           Response.Write "<strong>Welcome, " & rs("username") & "!
</strong><br/>"

       else
           Response.Write "Invalid Login"
           Response.Write "<do type='accept' label='Retry'>"
           Response.Write "    <go href='index.asp'/>"
           Response.Write "</do>"
       end if
       rs.Close
%>
   </p>
</card>
</wml>

<%
   conn.Close
%>
```

The dynamic script opens a connection to the database using Microsoft ODBC and then extracts the information from the client request using the request object. The script then constructs an SQL query to determine whether the entered username and password are in the database. If they are not, the script presents the failure WML code. If they are, the script saves the username and password into the session object for subsequent access. Finally, the script closes out the WML, regardless of success or failure.

> **NOTE:** One disadvantage of this procedure is that it does require you to maintain your own password-management system, which results in local management components. Also, it requires an additional burden on users because they have to enter more information. This is always a burden on wireless users, who may not be in their offices; and character entry is difficult on all phones.

Figure 13-1 shows how the example in Listing 13-2 looks in the Nokia and Openwave browsers.

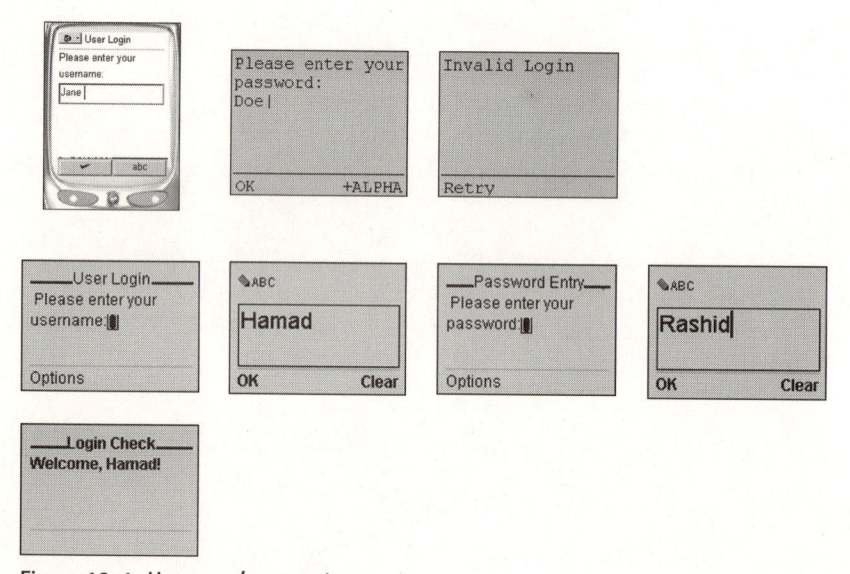

Figure 13-1: Username/password example

Of course, the code in Listings 13-1 and 13-2 would have been much simpler if we had let the Web server manage the user/password pairs by using basic authentication, which is defined by RFC 2617. With basic authentication, the content server must be configured to control the different user-control lists and their associations with the various resources. Essentially, when a user requests a resource that requires a username and password, the content server sends an HTTP 401 (Unauthorized) response with a request for a username and password. The client may then prompt the user for a username and password and package them in a new request to the content server; this time, however, the request contains some authorization information.

With WAP, the authorizing process has to go through a WAP gateway. Therefore, the original request is made in WSP; the WAP gateway issues a request to the content server in HTTP; the 401 response comes back to the WAP gateway; and finally the WAP gateway passes this 401 response back to the wireless client in its WSP form. At this point, the client prompts the user for a username and password. The authorizing feature definitely needs to be tested, because some client and WAP gateway combinations do not support basic authentication.

If, in the previous scenarios, the user does not respond with the correct authorization information, the content server sends back a Forbidden message. In the WAP case, the message is received by the WAP gateway, which then determines how best to inform the client.

> Content-server applications, such as Microsoft IIS, Netscape Enterprise Server, and Apache, vary considerably in terms of basic authentication. Please consult your documentation on how to set up basic authentication for your WAP service.

After authentication has passed, the actual resource requested is sent to the client. The Web server is then aware of the username. Depending on which APIs your Web server has, you may be able to obtain the username information using those APIs. Listing 13-3 provides some password-checking code, written in ASP, that uses the basic authentication scheme I just described. The bulk of the work is actually done by the content server, which contains username and password information and the control files that associate directories and resources with various users. Figure 13-2 shows how this looks in a browser.

Listing 13-3: Identification Using Basic Authentication

```
<%@ Language=VBScript %>

<%
Option Explicit
Response.ContentType = "text/vnd.wap.wml"
%>

<?xml version="1.0"?>

<!DOCTYPE wml PUBLIC "-//WAPFORUM//DTD WML 1.1//EN"
```

Continued

Listing 13-3: *(Continued)*

```
"http://www.wapforum.org/DTD/wml_1.1.xml">

<wml>
   <card id="hello" title="Welcome">
      <p>
         Hello and welcome to our
         site <% =Request("REMOTE_USER") %>
      </p>
   </card>
</wml>
```

> **Note:** When you use the code in Listing 13-3, make sure that the file is located behind a secured area of the site configured with basic authentication. In HTTP, the user information of someone logged in using basic authentication is available in the request headers — which in this case have been extracted by the Microsoft ASP Request object as `REMOTE_USER`. If the authorization is complete, you should see the behavior shown in the following figures.

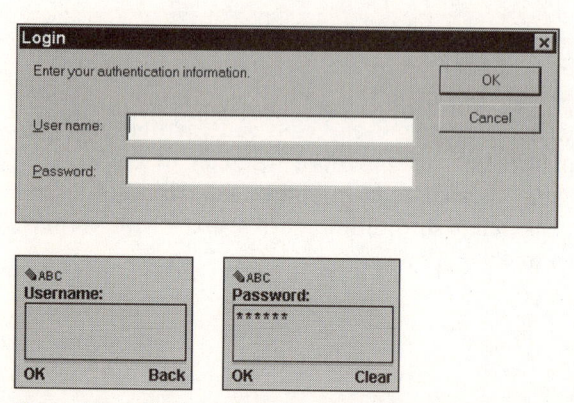

Figure 13-2: Username/password example using basic authentication

The drawback of this approach is that the user is still forced to enter a username and password. This is good authentication information but is not a wireless-sensitive solution if all you want is a user's identity. Also, keep in mind that the username and password in both of the previous examples were sent in the clear.

XREF: Chapter 16, "Implementing WAP Security," discusses how to combine this solution with SSL to improve its privacy capability.

Using proprietary client headers

Another solution for obtaining identity is available in WAP. As you have seen in the architectures, the WAP gateway is responsible for sending requests for resources in the HTTP format to the content server. Typically the carrier or service operator is in control of these machines and can enforce some type of unique identity associated with a browser. In the case of cell phones, the wireless client may already have a phone number or MSISDN, which can be used as a unique identifier for browsing, associated with the phone. The next problem is giving the content server this information.

The most popular method is to attach proprietary portions to the WAP gateway HTTP requests that contain these special headers.

These proprietary headers are just that. They are not specified by any new-generation version of the HTTP protocol; they are hacks to get these identification parameters to the content servers. As discussed earlier, the schemes vary in how they send this information to you. One of the most useful techniques to employ when working with a new implementation is dumping out the request headers arriving at your content server from a new phone/gateway combination. The following code in ASP shows how you implement this technique.

```
<%
Response.ContentType = "text/vnd.wap.wml"
%>

<wml>
<card id="headers>
    <p>
    <% =Request.ServerVariables("ALL_HTTP") %>
    </p>
</card>
</wml>
```

Figure 13-3 illustrates a typical dump done on a real phone and shows you what you can expect if you use this code.

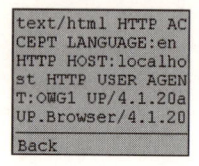

```
text/html HTTP AC
CEPT LANGUAGE:en
HTTP HOST:localho
st HTTP USER AGEN
T:OWG1 UP/4.1.20a
UP.Browser/4.1.20
Back
```

Figure 13-3: HTTP header dump

One of the dominant WAP gateways in use by U.S. carriers or service operators is the Openwave UP.Link.

Openwave gives its carrier customers the ability to uniquely identify each and every browser with a single unique ID. Furthermore, part of this unique ID is the hostname of the carrier WAP gateway, which means that the ID is unique among the Openwave UP.Link community. Carriers are discouraged from reusing IDs once a customer leaves the carrier, and as a result the ID is a very good identifier for a wireless client navigating your site.

These Openwave IDs are known as subscriber IDs. The format for these IDs is as follows:

identifer_WAPgatewayhost

Here is an example for a Nextel phone:

972000001-440001_atlsnup2.adc.nexteldata.net

Openwave recommends to its carrier customers that the identifier be a random number. However, various carriers are known to have chosen a specific format to manage their browsers. For example, in the case of Sprint PCS, the identifier portion of the ID is a phone number.

These special subscriber IDs are sent to the content servers whether they are requested or not. The subscriber IDs are sent to the content servers with an extraneous HTTP header called `HTTP_X_UP_SUBNO`. The `X` indicates that this is an experimental HTTP header tied to the manufacturer Openwave (formerly known as Unwired Planet).

Listing 13-4 shows how you can use the subscriber ID information to identify users and access their wireless profiles in your content service. Remember that you can also implement this code without an UP.Link using any specific proprietary unique ID that you can locate in your WAP client/WAP gateway combination headers. For example, if you are working with carriers for which Ericsson's technology is dominant, then modify the script in Listing 13-4 to use Ericsson's form.

Listing 13-4: Subscriber ID Solution for Openwave

```
<% Response.ContentType = "text/vnd.wap.wml" %>
<?xml version="1.0"?>
```

```
<!DOCTYPE wml PUBLIC "-//WAPFORUM//DTD WML 1.1//EN"
"http://www.wapforum.org/DTD/wml_1.1.xml">
<wml>
<%
    Dim conn, rs
    Set conn = Server.CreateObject("ADODB.Connection")
    Set rs   = Server.CreateObject("ADODB.Recordset")
    conn.open "DRIVER={Microsoft Access Driver (*.mdb)};DBQ=" &
Server.MapPath("Users.mdb") & ";"
%>

<%
sub_id = Request.ServerVariables("HTTP_X_SUBNO")

if sub_id = vbNullString then

    Response.Redirect("other_index.asp")

end if

%>

<card id="check" title="Welcome">
    <p>
    <%
        sqlQuery = "SELECT * FROM Users WHERE id='" & sub_id & "'"
        set rs = conn.Execute(SQLquery)

        if rs.EOF then
            Response.Write "Please register your id at www.site.com
using the following id" & sub_id
        else
            Response.Write "<strong>Welcome, " & rs.Fields("user") & "!
</strong><br/>"
        end if
    %>
    </p>
</card>
</wml>
```

Listing 13-4 shows how to obtain the subscriber ID from the HTTP headers. It is first checked to ensure it is not blank. If it is, the WAP client/WAP gateway combination does not support subscriber IDs. If the subscriber ID is not supported, the application can be routed to another script that implements one of the methods I discussed earlier.

Next the script checks to see whether the ID is in the database. If it is not then the user has to register with the site using the number displayed on his or her phone. It is possible to accept new users dynamically on the phone; whether you should depends on how much information you want to collect before allowing a user access to your service.

If the ID is found in the database, the user is welcomed to the site. This is an academic example; you can use the identity to build more complex services that cater to your users rather than provide a generic set of tools. For example, content services that offer weather information have long been dynamically presenting menus to their users that display the most frequently accessed cities. In order to do this, weather sites must store this information as it relates to unique IDs.

Other WAP gateways use alternative schemes; however, they essentially pass the same type of information to the content server. Here is a list of three other gateways and their chosen schemes:

```
Nokia-> "X-NETWORK-INFO: <bearer>, <ipaddress>, [secured|unsecured]"
Ericsson-> "MSISDN: <number|string>"
Kannel-> uses "X-NETWORK-INFO: <ipaddress>"
```

Next I'll discuss session handling and what mechanisms you can use to establish an HTTP session association.

Session Handling

As I mentioned earlier, HTTP is a stateless protocol that contains little information about an HTTP request pertaining to any previous requests it may have made to the same site. To make up for this lack of information, Netscape engineers created HTTP state-management techniques: their browsers and servers have featured cookie support from the beginning. Much later, others used the same technique to manage state information, and as the mechanism gained momentum it became RFC 2109. The RFC differed slightly in its current implementation, so you will generally find Web clients and servers that conform to both the Netscape and RFC standards.

Both specifications define essentially the same thing, a mechanism whereby a content server can request that a small unit of state be stored on the Web client and then included in subsequent requests to the content server. This small unit of state is called a cookie. The content server can then also control when the cookie will be included in other requests, when the cookie will expire, and other aspects of state management.

The RFC version of cookies makes the Web client responsible for the management of cookies, especially offering users a means by which to control and manage their storage, location, and usage.

Besides cookies, you can lean on some unique identifier within the HTTP headers, such as the subscriber ID, to give state information. Given that this header is unique and constant between multiple requests, you can use it to identify any active session on your content server. However, you cannot use such a mechanism to define a single browser session as you can with cookies.

Two other techniques exist: URL manipulation and hidden postfields.

Using cookies

Regular HTTP cookies can be either permanent or related to a single session. For example, a Web browser can be told to send cookies only until it is closed — or it can be told to keep a cookie for a longer period of time specified by the content server. The main components of a cookie are a name and a value. Something as simple as `username="hamad"` can be a cookie. Another important component of the cookie is its expiration time.

The WAP specifications 1.1 and 1.2 do not require WML browsers to support cookies, which means that you will not always be able to use them the way you will in HTTP. The issue that must still be resolved within the WAP Forum is whether management of the cookie is the job of the WAP gateway or the WAP client. A preliminary draft has proposed a cookie-management proposal wherein both models would be acceptable. I'll discuss this in the next section.

The existing product line from a manufacturer reflects its preferences. For example, Nokia passes the cookie to the client even though Nokia's own phones do not store cookies or enable users to manage them in any way, because of memory constraints. On the other hand, Openwave produces WAP gateways that do not pass cookies to the client. They manage cookies on behalf of the client at the WAP gateway. This means that the cookie is added on the HTTP side of the WAP gateway, and the client technically never receives the cookie.

Listing 13-5 shows a WML cookie example that works with this second set of WAP gateways.

Listing 13-5: Session Handling Using a Cookie

```
<% Option Explicit
   Response.ContentType = "text/vnd.wap.wml"
   Response.Buffer = true
%>

<?xml version="1.0"?>
<!DOCTYPE wml PUBLIC "-//WAPFORUM//DTD WML 1.1//EN"
"http://www.wapforum.org/DTD/wml_1.1.xml">

     <%  dim color, color_pos1, color_pos2
         color_pos1 = Request.Cookies("color")
         color_pos2 = Request.QueryString("color")

         if not color_pos2 = "" then
```

Continued

Listing 13-5 *(Continued)*

```
            color = Request.QueryString("color")
            Response.Cookies("color") = color
%>

            <wml>

            <card id="value1" title="Setting a Cookie">

            <p>
                Your favorite color is set to <% = color %>
            </p>

            </card>

            </wml>

<%
    Response.End
    end if
%>
<%

    if color_pos1 = "" then
    Response.AddHeader "Cache-control", "Must-revalidate"
%>

            <wml>

            <card id="query" title="Value Query">

            <do type="accept" label="Set">
                <go href="cookies.asp" method="get">
                    <postfield name="color" value="$color"/>
                </go>
            </do>

        <p>
            Enter your favorite color?
            <input name="color"/>
        </p>

            </card>
        </wml>


<%
```

```
            Response.End
         end if
%>
<%
      Response.AddHeader "Cache-control", "no-cache"
      Response.AddHeader "Cache-control", "Must-revalidate"
%>
         <wml>

            <card id="value2" title="Setting a Cookie">

                <do type="accept" label="Change">
                    <go href="cookies.asp" method="get">
                       <postfield name="color" value="$color"/>
                    </go>
                </do>

                <p>
                    The color is now set to <% = color_pos1 %>.<br/>
                        Change it to:
                        <input name="color"/>
                </p>

            </card>
         </wml>
```

ASP automatically includes a session object to manage the storage, setting, and unsetting of cookies, as described in Chapter 9, "Dynamic WAP Services." Other dynamic platforms that support cookies include ColdFusion and JSP.

Figure 13-4 shows how the previous example looks in the Openwave browser.

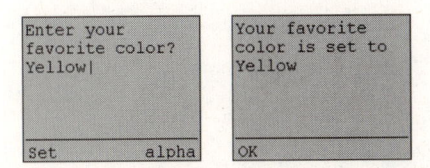

Figure 13-4: Cookie example for WAP cookie proxy

USING SESSION OBJECTS

Some Web servers support a session object natively, which means that you do not need to set and get your own cookies: you can have the Web server software manage them for you. Keep in mind, though, that in the case of WAP gateways that do not support cookies you are just overtaxing your Web server to have it implement the session object.

The session object sets a cookie at the client with a random ID. It then monitors this random ID throughout any communication with the content server. The developer only sees a session object at a high level of abstraction and does not have to code the specific cookie behavior.

> **XREF** For more details on ASP session objects see Chapter 9, "Dynamic WAP Services."

USING WSP IDS

If you happen to be doing development that gives you access to the WAP gateway, for example if you are maintaining it in a corporate setting, you can use WSP IDs to track individual users. You should realize that WSP, the session protocol used between phones and WAP gateways, is not stateless. Every session is uniquely identified with a WSP Session ID. If you have access to this information you can use it to gain session-management information; however, such information is all the WSP Session ID can tell you. It is also very difficult for developers to obtain this level of security proximity to a carrier WAP gateway. Even if you do, other protocols such as Transport Layer WAP Security are required to run your own WAP gateway, which means that these techniques are available only to the select few who can get past the entry costs.

Using hidden postfields

Another technique that you can use for state management allows for information inside postfields that would have meaning only to a program on the content server managing state. Listing 13-6 shows how an example of state management. This example reuses the example in Listing 13-5, wherein you are trying to get a person's first name to stick to a session.

Listing 13-6: Code Example Showing Hidden Postfields

```
<%@ Language=VBScript %>

<%
Option Explicit

Response.ContentType = "text/vnd.wap.wml"

%><?xml version="1.0"?>

<!DOCTYPE wml PUBLIC "-//WAPFORUM//DTD WML 1.1//EN"
```

Chapter 13: Session Management and Identification 439

```
"http://www.wapforum.org/DTD/wml_1.1.xml">

<wml>
    <card id="user" title="User Login">

<%
dim firstname
firstname = Request.QueryString("firstname")

dim options
options = Request.QueryString("options")

if firstname = "" then
    'prompt for a first name
%>
        <do type="accept" label="Go">
            <go href="hidden.asp" method="get">
                <postfield name="options" value="anotherpage1"/>
                <postfield name="firstname" value="$firstname"/>
            </go>
        </do>
        <p>
            Please enter your username:
            <input name="firstname"/>
        </p>
<%
else

    if options = "anotherpage1" then
%>
        <do type="accept" label="Go">
            <go href="hidden.asp" method="get">
              <postfield name="options" value="anotherpage2"/>
              <postfield name="firstname" value="<% =firstname %>"/>
            </go>
        </do>
        <p>
            Yet another page within the application
        </p>
<%
    else
%>
        <do type="accept" label="Go">
            <go href="hidden.asp" method="get">
```

Continued

Listing 13-6 *(Continued)*

```
            <postfield name="options" value="primary"/>
            <postfield name="firstname" value="<% =firstname %>"/>
        </go>
    </do>
    <p>
            Yet another page within the application
            Hit Go to pass the variable somewhere else
    </p>

<%
    end if

end if

%>

    </card>
</wml>
```

In this example, hidden postfields were used to pass the first name between as many pages as was necessary. This technique is quite simple to implement but it can be coding-intensive. You can make the coding-intensive portion easier by using macros in your development environment. In the absence of cookie support, this mechanism is the next best thing.

Figure 13-5 illustrates how the example actually looks when displayed in a Nokia browser.

```
┌──────────────────┐
│ ─── User Login ──│
│  Yet another page│
│ within the       │
│ application      │
│                  │
│ Go               │
└──────────────────┘
```

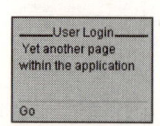

Figure 13-5: Session example using hidden postfields

> **NOTE:** This technique is very susceptible to caching problems. If a deck is improperly stored in a phone, it is possible for a user to retrieve old information. To correct this problem you must pay attention to your `cache-control` headers with hidden postfields. The recommended procedure is to specify a cache timeout for each deck. For more details on caching issues please see Chapter 12, "Caching and Cache Operations."

Manipulating URLs

Much like using hidden postfields allows information about a session to be stored and passed on to subsequent cards, you can also manipulate URLs to do the same. You can store the information somewhere in the body of the URL or in an actual query string. If you want to store the first name inside a URL, you use the following go element:

```
<go href="<% Request.Form("URL") %> ? firstname="<% firstname %>#fragment"/>
```

As you can see, this approach solves the problem, but in practice it is much harder than postfields to maintain — mostly because URLs are difficult to read and debug. Encoding problems may result because of invalid characters in the URL, and old and expired information may result in a real management and debugging problem.

As mentioned previously, another solution is to include the information in the body of the URL, as shown in the following example:

```
<go href="<% Request.Form("URL") %> / firstname="<% firstname %>#fragment"/>
```

This technique may be more beneficial, depending on which specific Web server you have, because it may retrieve the URL paths and parse the directories separately. If not, the breakup may require additional parsing, which is even more difficult to maintain.

The Future of WAP Session Management and Identification

Before ending the chapter, I would like to quickly review some of the latest developments in state management within the WAP Forum. As mentioned in the section on session handling, cookies were not included in earlier specifications of WAP because no one could agree about how they should be handled in the wireless network. Many argued that they should be handled according to a method like that specified in the RFC. Others argued that the WAP gateway should manage cookies on behalf of wireless clients, effectively breaking the Internet RFC.

In order to accommodate both sides, a draft WAP HTTP State Management specification was written that allowed for either approach. The specification allows for standard cookie management by the wireless clients: the same mechanism that sends cookies in HTTP is extended to cover cookie setting, control, and management by WAP protocols. The specification also defines a mechanism that enables intermediate proxies, such as WAP gateways, to store and manage cookies on behalf of WAP clients. As I've stated previously, this second form has advantages such as allowing wireless WAP clients to use their limited memory for activities unrelated to state management. This form of state management also does not transmit cookies over the air with every single request and response transaction. On the other hand, one could also argue that storing cookies on the client gives them more independence from WAP gateways and fits more neatly within a future WAP roaming architecture.

The architecture is designed so that the wireless WAP client can choose which approach to use; therefore, it can select whether to operate in regular cookie mode or in cookie proxy mode.

With regards to cookie proxy operation, the management capability must have capabilities similar to regular cookie functionality. This WAP Forum agreed on how this would be done by creating two new headers to handle the new proxy behavior. These headers are `X-Wap-Proxy-Cookie` and `X-Wap-Proxy-Set-Cookie`, which mirror their standard counterparts, but make cookie management the responsibility of the WAP gateway — not the user, as in RFC 2109.

Standard cookie support, for at least four cookies and 125 bytes total storage space, will be mandatory, but proxy-header support will be optional. The only mandatory proxy support will be supporting the passing of the HTTP headers on behalf of the wireless WAP client.

The specification is still in draft, so things may change on finalization and implementation.

Summary

In this chapter I showed you how to solve problems with identifying users who browse your content server and how to monitor user sessions. I began the chapter with an introduction to the problems at hand. Then I described the current state of the industry with regard to identification. The available techniques are cookies, a manual system, and proprietary headers. I provided examples of manual systems and proprietary headers.

I showed you how to solve the session-management problem by using cookies, and listed some advanced alternatives, including WSP IDs, hidden fields, and URL rewriting. I gave examples of all the alternatives and of the use of cookies.

You should at this point have a good idea of what techniques you will be able to use in the course of your WAP development. In the next chapter, I discuss how browser information from specific users can assist you in developing even more personalized sites.

Chapter 14

Targeted Development

IN THIS CHAPTER

- Learning about targeted development
- Detecting device types
- Building and using device tables
- Examining the possible solution to fragmented clients: UAProf

WHEN APPLICATION DEVELOPMENT REACHES the deployment stage, some very real problems almost always become exposed to the developer for the first time. At this stage, reworking the entire project to bypass these problems results in a large waste of development time and a lot of patched code. To understand some of these problems you need to recognize that even though a lot of devices claim to be WAP-compliant, WAP browsers are not created equal, and neither are WAP gateways.

The development issues surrounding wireless clients can be divided into four areas that often blur together:

- Interoperability problems (for example, does a Nokia phone work with UP.Link 3.1?)
- Problems with a new interface (such as the Openwave input element versus Nokia)
- Content-rendering problems (for example, different screen sizes mean different viewable areas and presentation of text and images for phones versus PDAs versus other similarly sized devices)
- Differences in configurations (such as among different WAP gateway features)

This chapter covers how you can do a little detective work and obtain good information about wireless-client configurations. Doing so will save you a lot of trouble: by the time you hit the deployment stage, the application will require only minor modifications because you made plans to meet the interface, rendering, and configuration challenges.

In this chapter I provide a detailed introduction to targeted development and its implications for wireless-client development. Then I discuss how best to organize the information and how to make decisions regarding different wireless clients.

Finally, I discuss how the WAP Forum intends to solve some of the problem by using the UAProf standard.

What Is Targeted Development?

Like any markup language format, WML does not precisely describe how your WML code will be rendered on a wireless client screen. This is not the fault of WML; it only defines a data-storage mechanism. The actual presentation of the data is left up to the manufacturers of the equipment and their customers. The WAP community is also very innovative — many new ideas and concepts are being tested daily, sometimes in the form of real services. Combine this with the existing spectrum management and new services value-downgrade problems that carriers and service operators contend with and the situation gets worse. What makes the situation a true pressure cooker is the fact that WAP gateways do not interoperate well with other manufacturer phones. The situation has improved somewhat since the outset but is far from ideal.

In this marketplace, applications need to be created that are good sources of content. However, generating content that will appear well in all wireless clients is difficult. Because the initial set of wireless clients for WAP has been phones, many developers have proposed the creation of a generic set of guidelines to address the problem of writing mass-market applications. The WAP Forum and others such as Openwave have begun to create such a set of guidelines, and I discuss the WAP Forum approach in a later section. The approach that I have always advocated is to develop targeted applications that focus on the class or superclass of wireless clients that you expect to be in the hands of users in a specific marketplace. This superclass of wireless clients represents a set of WAP browsers with very similar UI elements and supported feature sets.

The most advantageous development situation is one in which your wireless clients are well known. Consider the case of a wireless-development project at a local hospital that wants to enable its doctors to view patient ECGs using WAP. The hospital can perhaps limit its acquisition to the one or two clients that suit the specific application requirements, such as the processing power to display the ECGs or the screen size to accommodate the graphical display of the ECGs in a manner acceptable to physicians. The WAP gateway and carrier unknowns also become clear, as they will remain static in that marketplace.

On the other end of the spectrum, you could be a developer for a multinational company that has decided that salespeople in 14 countries throughout Europe, the Americas, and the Pacific Rim are to use WAP to access the latest prices on high-volume components for the business. The large number of wireless clients and scenarios is a large problem that is more difficult to solve. A generic solution is doomed to failure and the number of different inter-working components is so high that many points of service incompatibilities exist.

As I proposed previously, the best solution is targeted development. With this approach, you keep your data in a central format and export them on a specific request to any external format you choose. You choose this external format based on the needs of the clients accessing your content server. My proposed technique for WAP is to separate the output form into four types — one for phones with the UP.Browser, another for Nokia browsers, a third for Ericsson browsers, and a fourth for other types. This fourfold division separates the wireless client possibilities into superclass configurations that may be easier to manage.

> **NOTE:** The superclass configurations are important because a phone that uses the UP.Browser, for example, has a particular look and feel, whether it is a Samsung or a Mitsubishi. And don't be too surprised to see Nokia phones that license the UP.Browser for release in the U.S. marketplace. The four types of browsers are the types that have a significant number of deployed units in the field. Others that are gaining popularity are those for PDAs by Neomar and the Mitsubishi GEO phone browser. Any other browser forms have too small a user base to worry about right now, although the ratios should be monitored closely. For example, WAP for Telematics (in automobiles) may result in a user spike if implementations actually occur.

The first step in targeted development is to actually store the content in a core format that is highly accessible and easily manipulated; XML comes to mind but other solutions exist. The next step is to take the content out of core storage format and dump it into the wireless client format. You can do this with a mechanism such as CSS or XSL, which are outside the scope of this book.

> **XREF:** For more information on XML, including discussions of CSS and XSL, see *XML: A Primer, Third Edition*, by Simon St.Laurent (published by M&T Books).

When dumping data into the wireless client format, you have to detect the client and classify it into a known entity whose behavior is previously tabulated if possible. This brings us to detecting devices.

Detecting Device Types

Luckily for us, any HTTP client, including WAP gateways, issues requests to the content server, which contains a user-agent name in the header. The user agent is a standard HTTP header, which contains a string that describes the client in some form. For example, if a Nextel i1000plus phone with the UP.Browser accesses a content server, the user-agent string can be "UP.Browser 3.11 XXXXXXXXXXXXX". Listing 14-1 shows how you can redirect a site based on knowledge of the device-type.

Even though the user-agent string is quite long, you don't have to examine all of it to note the differences. Listing 14-1 is coded in ASP and makes use of the browser type object rather than parsing the `HTTP_USER_AGENT` header manually.

Listing 14-1: HTTP Agent Checker

```
<%
dim wmlCapable
dim browserType

httpAccept = LCase(Request.ServerVariables("HTTP_ACCEPT"))

set bc = Server.CreateObject("MSWC.BrowserType")

if Instr(httpAccept,"wml") then
  wmlCapable = 1
  if bc.browser = "UP.Browser" then
    browserType="Openwave"
  elseif bc.browser = "Nokia" then
    browserType="Nokia"
  elseif bc.browser = "Ericsson" then
    browserType="Ericsson"
  end if
Else
Response.Redirect "/index.html"
End if
Response.End
<%Response.ContentType = "text/vnd.wap.wml"%>
<?xml version="1.0"?>
<!DOCTYPE wml PUBLIC "-//WAPFORUM//DTD WML 1.1//EN"
http"://www.wapforum.org/DTD/wml_1.1.xml">
<wml>
  <card id="firstpage">
    <p>
      <% select case browserType
      case "Openwave"

      Response.Write("You are using a Phone.Com/OpenWave browser"

      case "Nokia"

      Response.Write("You are using a Nokia browser"
```

```
            case "Ericsson"

                Response.Write("You are using an Ericsson browser"
            case else

                Response.Write("I don't know what type of browser you have"
            End select %>
        </p>
    </card>
</wml>
```

The preceding example shows a simple case in which alternative sites are constructed entirely for a specific wireless client. With this approach, the central page acts as a clearinghouse for all formats and routes the client to the right source. It determines whether the browser is HTML capable and, if it is not, goes to other content types, in this case, wireless device types.

Also shown in the preceding example is how the `HTTP_ACCEPT` header can be examined for WAP-specific MIME types. This specific header determines whether the client can even accept any of the WAP formats, or if you will have to route it to some HTML source.

The three main superclasses of devices can be classified simply by pattern-matching UP.Browser, Ericsson, or Nokia in the `HTTP_USER_AGENT` string. Some WAP gateways, such as the Openwave UP.Link, actually add more information to the `USER_AGENT` field about what gateway vendor and version number is being used, as well as adding information about the wireless client. For example, the user-agent field may originally look like this:

```
UP.Browser 3.1
```

but, when modified, becomes

```
UP.Browser 3.1/UP.Link 4.1.1.5
```

Other gateways are passing this extra information as yet another proprietary header called `HTTP_VIA`. The best advice is to examine the headers to see what you are getting.

Building and Using Device Tables

After the wireless-client information is known, the client has to be directed to the content in the format best suited for it. Building the correct format for a client can take a lot of work, and often the work is not easily leveraged across multiple implementations. Consider that the UP.Browser can potentially have bugs in it to the point where, with multiple phones, you must carefully list all the device's unique properties and finally test them when you are done with the application.

Table 14-1 presents an example of typical device tables. These tables should include problems that you have encountered in different WAP implementations in the user space you are focusing on.

TABLE 14-1 BROWSER ANALYSIS TABLE

Phone Feature or Feature Grouping	Property Value
General Phone Data	
Manufacturer	Mitsubishi
Model	T250
Device ID	T250
Security	Proprietary Openwave
Availability	
Availability	Yes
Location	U.S.A.
Network Type	CDPD
Announced Carriers	AT&T
Font Info	
Text style	No
Image Information	
Images	Yes
Alignment	Center
Size in bytes	1492
Size in pixels (*HxW*)	No hard limit
Browser Information	
Browser and version	UP.Browser 3.03
Upgradeable	No
Markup languages	HDML 2.0, HDML 3.0, WML 1.1 (translated)
Screen Size Information	
Rows in display	10

Phone Feature or Feature Grouping	Property Value
Columns in display	23
Width (pixels)	80
Height (pixels)	96
Touch screen	No
Deck Information	
Max deck size	1492 bytes minus 28 bytes for the header
Load sequence	Images, then decks
Softkey Information	
Softkeys	2 soft keys
WAP Compliance Information	
Table support	Yes, Openwave style, only 2-3 columns
Icon buttons	Yes
Calling numbers within WML	Yes, using WTAI
Input elements	Yes
Input formatting	Yes, full support
Image links	Yes
Links formatting	Yes
HTTP Redirect	Yes
Nonstandard Feature Support	
Openwave channels	
Openwave icons	
Openwave contexts	
Openwave cookies with gateway	
Openwave subscriber ID with gateway	

These kinds of tables are hard to put together, considering that even among released products and services, the different services and clients available to users are changing all the time. If you are writing for the horizontal market, you will have to accept that somewhere, someplace, and with some configuration, your site will look broken. Your goal is to limit how broken it looks. Some people have tried to put this kind of device information together. Here are some suggested sites:

- `www.openwave.com`: At the site, click Openwave Developer Site → Resources → Phones.

    This site shows you some of the differences you can expect in developing for phones that have the Openwave browser in them. It also lists differences among the versions of browser and WML element support.

- `www.anywhereyougo.com`: At the site, click WAP → WAP Phones.

    The site has a lot of details about phone models and their different WAP capabilities. It provides information about standards compliance, WAP browser, WAP hardware, screen size, bearer support, availability information, and more.

You can also lift many of the details shown in Table 14-1 out of the header information or at least infer them, but in some cases you just have to buy the phone and configure it on a service before finding out what you want to know.

Making Use of Header Information

As I mentioned previously, you can get plenty of information about devices from proprietary headers, which are included in the HTTP requests from wireless clients. Many times, the code for doing this is not readily available in the language you need, especially because these are proprietary headers. Listings 14-2 and 14-3 show some sample code for ASP, demonstrating how you can read and display all the headers for either an HTML or a WML client. The HTML version of the code is included here only as an example; I strongly recommend that you run the code from a real phone to get the full effect of going through a real service and real WAP phone.

Listing 14-2: Header-Code Dump to HTML

```
<%
Response.ContentType = "text/html"
%>

<html>
    <% =Request.ServerVariables("ALL_HTTP") %>
</html>
```

Listing 14-3: Header-Code Dump to WML

```
<%
```

```
Response.ContentType = "text/vnd.wap.wml"
%>

<wml>
<card id="headers>
    <p>
    <% =Request.ServerVariables("ALL_HTTP") %>
    </p>
</card>
</wml>
```

Introducing UAProf

The WAP Forum recognizes that the existing schemes are using the proprietary headers as a crutch and that the number of WAP devices may reach the point where generating tables for them becomes quite a tedious and expensive task, if it isn't already. To solve the problems of WAP devices with divergent input mechanisms, networking connectivity and level of support languages, WAP Forum proposes the User Agent Profiling Mechanism, or UAProf. The architecture for this mechanism introduces what is called a client capabilities server, which manages the individual wireless client's properties.

The specification defines a user-agent profile, which conveys device-preference information and stores the hardware and software characteristics to a profile on a capabilities server. This content is then made available to content servers, which receive requests from the appropriate client. In order to reuse as much existing work as possible in the area, the WAP Forum chose to leverage the CC/PP (Client Capabilities/Preferences Profile) standard already being used by the W3C.

The CC/PP specifications address both client-capabilities information and preferences profiles. Preferences profiles indicate an application-specific profile that the user has set up for the purpose of selecting information. This feature is not part of UAProf.

The CC/PP standard also defines something called a Resource Decomposition Format (RDF) schema and vocabulary. This format specifies how the client-capabilities information is to be laid out. The UAProf specification then describes a comprehensive list of client capabilities – the big wish list for content developers – and indicates how those capabilities are presented using the definitions and semantics of RDF.

Listing 14-4 presents an example of some RDF code. This is only a portion of the WAP characteristics. Figures 14-1 through 14-5, following the listing, show the full tree and where the WAP characteristics fit in the overall scheme.

Listing 14-4: RDF Code

```
Content-Type: application/xml

<?xml version="1.0"?>
<rdf:RDF xmlns:rdf="http://www.w3.org/1999/02/22-rdf-syntax-ns#"
xmlns:prf="http://www.wapforum.org/UAPROF/ccppschema1.0#">

<rdf:Description>
<prf:WapVersion>1.2</prf:WapVersion>
<prf:WmlDeckSize>2000 octets</prf:WmlDeckSize>
<prf:WapDeviceClass>A </prf:WapDeviceClass>
<prf:WapPushMsgSize>2000 octets</prf:WapPushMsgSize>
<prf:WmlVersion>
<rdf:Bag>
<rdf:li>1.2</rdf:li>
</rdf:Bag>
</prf:WmlVersion>
</rdf:Description>
</rdf:RDF>
```

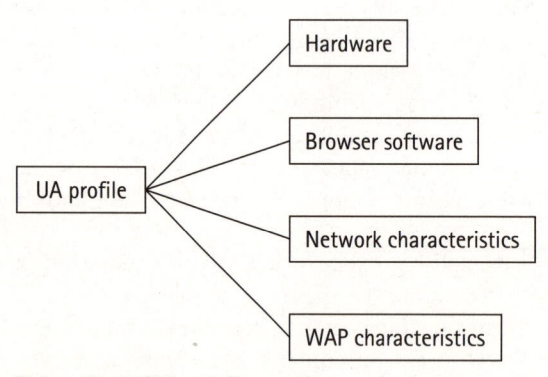

Figure 14-1: Main profile graph

Chapter 14: Targeted Development 453

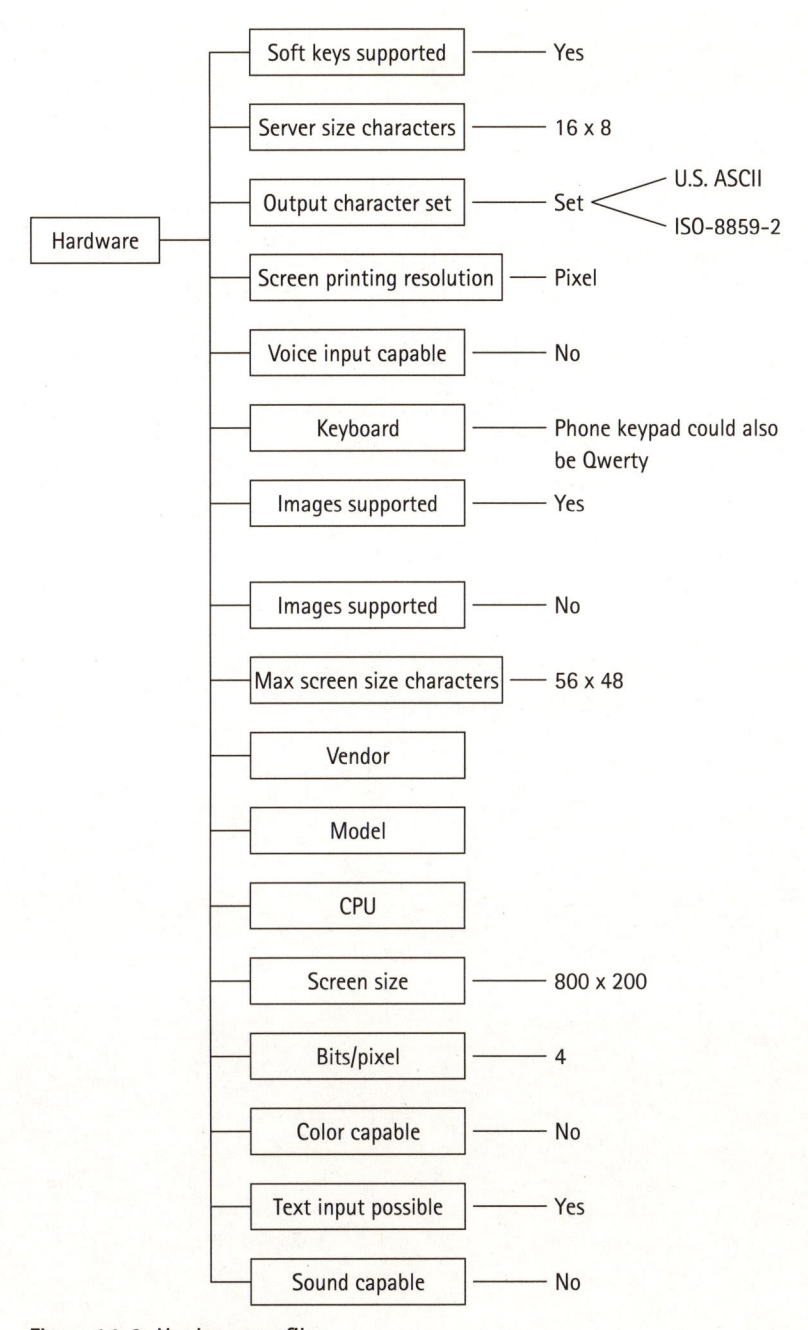

```
                    ┌── Soft keys supported ──── Yes
                    │
                    ├── Server size characters ── 16 x 8
                    │
                    │                                    ┌── U.S. ASCII
                    ├── Output character set ──── Set ──┤
                    │                                    └── ISO-8859-2
                    │
                    ├── Screen printing resolution ── Pixel
                    │
                    ├── Voice input capable ──── No
                    │
                    ├── Keyboard ──── Phone keypad could also
    Hardware ──────┤                  be Qwerty
                    │
                    ├── Images supported ──── Yes
                    │
                    ├── Images supported ──── No
                    │
                    ├── Max screen size characters ── 56 x 48
                    │
                    ├── Vendor
                    │
                    ├── Model
                    │
                    ├── CPU
                    │
                    ├── Screen size ──── 800 x 200
                    │
                    ├── Bits/pixel ──── 4
                    │
                    ├── Color capable ──── No
                    │
                    ├── Text input possible ──── Yes
                    │
                    └── Sound capable ──── No
```

Figure 14-2: Hardware profile

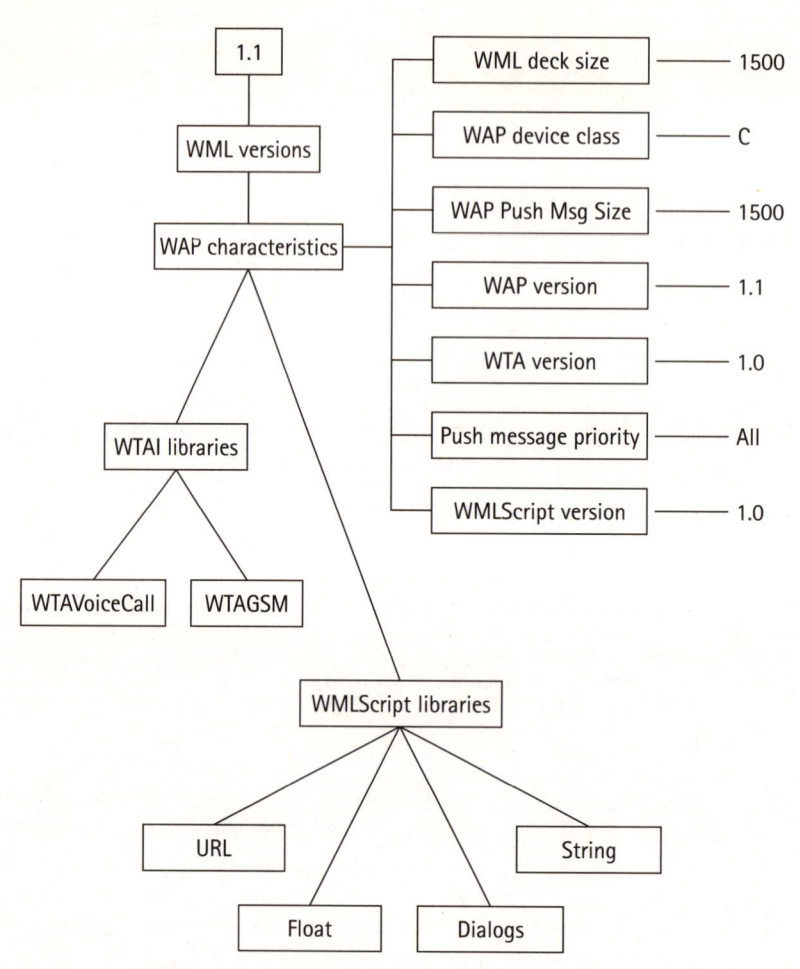

Figure 14-3: WAP characteristics profile

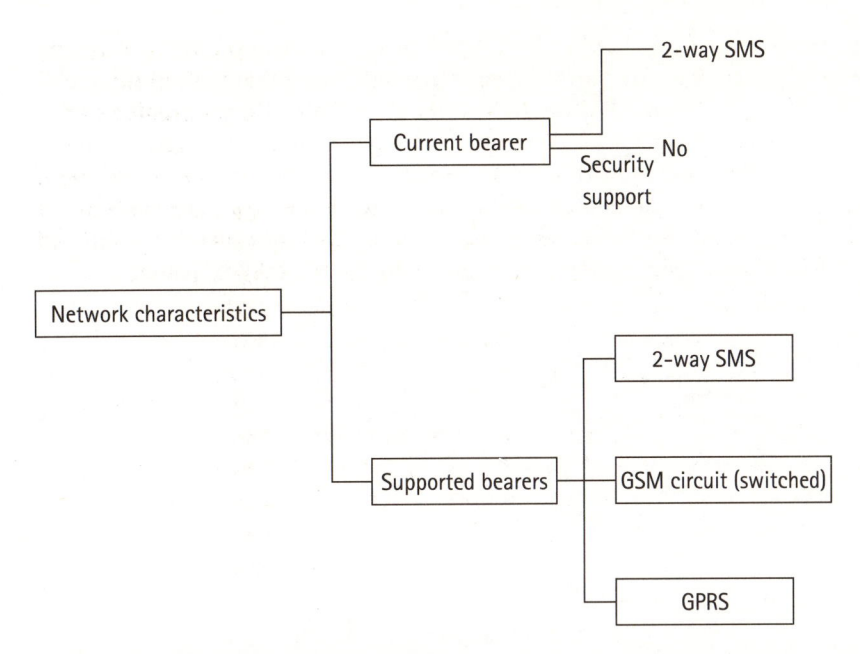

Figure 14-4: Network characteristics profile

    If everything works as specified, the WAP gateway will send out RDF information containing client capabilities. If not, the client capabilities could be requested at any time. In order for content servers to become capable of receiving and understanding this new UAProf information, the existing HTTP 1.1 server will need to be upgraded to be HTTP 1.1 Extension Framework-capable, and also to support CC/PP Exchange Protocol. The content server must then parse the profile, validate the profile syntax, resolve and validate the listed attribute values, and finally customize the content according to the information received.

Although there are many hurdles for UAProf to clear, both **at the WAP client and** at the WAP gateway, they are quickly overcome considering **that both of those elements** are clearly within the WAP-manufacturer community. **Bigger problems exist** at the content server end. Not all Web server products support **user-agent profiles.** Consequently, this information is not expected to be available **to most developers.** Many Web-server vendors are independently working on their **own mechanisms for** content customization, further eroding the value of UAProf. **Therefore, until all** these problems are solved, developers are unable to use the **UAProf features.**

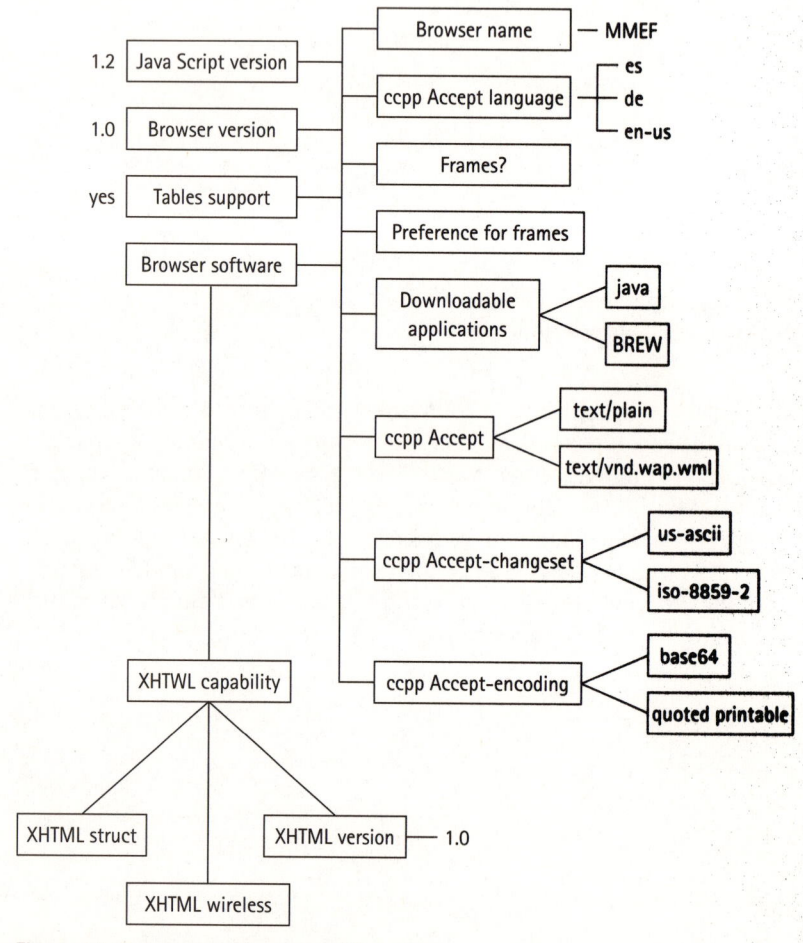

Figure 14-5: Browser software profile

Summary

In this chapter I covered some of the basic techniques you can use to collect information from headers and use this information to render the appropriate content to the wireless device. I also showed how an analysis of your needs and matching them with particular clients can assist you in making development decisions concerning the service. For example, knowing that you will need to develop only in markets with Openwave UP.Links will free you to use specific extensions to enhance the service. If made consciously, these decisions will significantly improve the way your services meet client needs.

The chapter ends with a discussion and demonstration of how the WAP Forum intends to solve the problem of disseminating the information about different devices. In the next chapter, I show you how you can use this information and what specific differences you should be on the lookout for in your development.

Chapter 15

Designing User-Friendly Interfaces

IN THIS CHAPTER

- ◆ Addressing the three main principles of UI design: structure, presentation, and behavior
- ◆ Creating consistent interfaces by proper design and evaluation
- ◆ Building a site structure
- ◆ Structuring behavioral elements for effective WAP sites
- ◆ Living with the differences among browsers
- ◆ Designing with speed in mind

ONE OF THE CASUAL WAYS that I introduce the topic of WAP in elevator speeches is as follows: "Think of the Internet and then imagine you had access to it from your cell phone." This is not a completely accurate description. WAP is not just a mobile version of the Internet. It is a brand new way of accessing content.

The most critical difference between the traditional Web and WAP is the product from which the browsing takes place. The important differences are the form factor (small screen, no keyboard, no mouse) and the way in which users' environments affect the usage of applications (for example, they can be in a car, at a restaurant, and so forth). The differences are often ignored in discussions of UI design; authors often make plain, vapid statement such as, "Try to put a Back button on every screen." Many of these design guidelines exist — Openwave has a few, WAP Forum has one, and several of the carriers/operators have their own.

These documents possess three common failings:

- ◆ They ignore previous usability research.
- ◆ They assemble the usability ideas in a jumbled set of notes.
- ◆ They confuse the parts of the application that are dependent on the markup language and the parts that are dependent on the hardware.

In this chapter, I present a new way of thinking about how the ultimate user interface should be built.

Building a Foundation of UI Design

If you've traced the history of the Web, you know that some researchers at the IBM labs along with some other individuals (such as Tim Berners-Lee, who developed the first model of the Web) needed to collect information research into manageable archives. These obsessive pioneers created the Web, but now it is up to us to create the wireless Web.

Facing the challenges of UI design

Like any printed matter, the wireless Web has a basic conceptual model, which it has inherited from other media. The wireless Web application that is visible on a phone has words. Those words may be organized around pictures on the display, and if the user presses some key, an action may result. This summarizes the main items of concern: words, pictures/display, and background code.

You can think of these concepts according to the OSI model, with terms such as

- **Structure/session:** How is the information organized and stored?
- **Presentation:** How is the information presented to the user?
- **Application/behavior:** How do users interact with the wireless site?

STRUCTURE

WML is a markup language that has inherited a lot from HDML and HTML. HTML's goals of simplicity and forgiveness made it popular. WML is not as forgiving but is still a simple language to work with.

WML follows the same logic as that which went into the creation of other markup languages, its purpose being to increase the dynamics of text to the point where it becomes visually exciting, engaging, and universally readable, and to make the browser able to process the language fast. With a foundation in text and HTML, WML takes you into structured text, files that can be processed by transformation or searching, translated, converted, and so on.

With programming manipulation of the text using dynamic scripts, you can extend WML even further by manipulation based on logic linked to outside applications. You can use further aggregation of external dynamic content to present information to the user.

The tags add structure to the content: some define semantics of the document and others are presentation tags. Application developers need to navigate the thin line between adding rich tags to the data and controlling how the information looks on the screen.

PRESENTATION

WML was never intended to define exactly how the content would display on the screen. And to be honest, HTML wasn't either. HTML programmers have attempted to address things like layout, but most of their efforts have been unsuccessful. Instead, visual layout is becoming the domain of a technology called cascading style sheets. This technology will be built in to WAP 2.0 browsers, moving the wireless industry away from markup languages that mix presentation and content.

BEHAVIOR

There is more to WML than just words and the presentation. This is where print magazines, newspapers, film and all other printed or displayed matter stop. WML adds behavior. Depending on how users look at information on the phone, the content interacts with them. You must never lose sight of this fundamental difference in wireless service design. Where code meets the content and overall structure of information causes the biggest headaches in designing a wireless site. For example, sites would like to present content as fast as possible to the wireless user, yet still maintain their brand. When is the worry about how the site is going to look compromised by the worry about how a user is going to obtain information?

With behavior comes the painful reality that behavior may not appear as you intended because of differences among browsers. This means that you must use redundant coding to weed out all the possible errors. Even then, situations exist wherein you do not know what content is appearing in a browser, and the type of browser may also be unknown.

Solving the UI design problem

Therefore, the design of interfaces is not the domain of a single type of person. The coder doesn't single-handedly create a WML site, the Photoshop graphic artist is not the sole designer of a site, and the information author/editor is not deciding alone how the information will appear. The combination of all these team members' skills is what brings about a successful Web implementation. You can view many sites on the Web or in WML that have been written without thought to one of these three parts, or with the parts out of balance. Many sites have been created in a vacuum, ignoring all three components of successful site design (the code, the content, and the structure of information): for example, in the early days of HDML, the precursor language to WML, many AT&T PocketNet sites were simply straight ports of their HTML counterparts. This meant that the designers ignored WML behavior, and the sites had sub-optimal presentation layouts. Even the words on the site did not make complete sense to a wireless user because they were relevant only to desktop users. Imagine, for example, being asked to download an executable to a phone.

The ideal situation, then, is to have all sides, along with back-end system designers, collaborate on how the interface is to look. This means that there should be three basic teams: software engineers writing the code (back-end and front-end), visual designers deciding on presentation and layout, and information architects writing the text.

The way the data are displayed on a phone can make it painfully obvious to the user if the different parts have not been designed in balance, the synergy of the three components of successful site design is invisible when the items have been carefully thought out.

For those of you without the resources of huge teams for each one of the three components of successful site design, think like a big team. Step back from the wireless-service design and examine the project as if you were on one of those teams. Does the site have the correct behavior? Is the information presented in the most appropriate manner? Is the information written and structured in a digestible form? Does it meet the needs of users navigating to your site?

If you don't address each of the three components, you will just be practicing! Intense collaboration among these disciplines creates the best of what the wireless Web has to offer.

Creating a Consistent User Interface

Imagine how most wireless users get started with the wireless Web. They go to a store and are offered an array of carriers and pricing plans, with access to the Web usually a mere afterthought attached to an existing voice plan. They take the phone home and decide to try out the service, only to face errors that prevent them from getting online because of some IP address problem. They call customer service and fix the problem, and after 40 minutes of working through the problem with customer service, they try it again. This time they see `"connection failed"`! Huh? They try again and this time get connected. Now they go to the browser and enter a URL, but that doesn't work. How about bookmarks? Nothing there. Clicking a hyperlink gets them another error: `Content Type Translation failed`. What's going on here?

The wireless Web is painful. The state-of-the-art WAP site you have may never be seen by anybody, your link is not on the main page, users get confused about where they are, and a lot of them are attempting to justify to themselves why they are paying 30 cents a minute for this nonsense.

Manage the user's expectations by being consistent with other applications on the wireless Web and the intent of wireless manufacturers and carriers! The user who got to your site has been through a lot to get there. Build trust with your users: if they enter your site, it should look like other wireless Web sites that have a similar purpose. And, of course, your site should look consistent with any internal components. Over time we can expect the entire wireless Web to look the same; it is not that way today, and I will explain why in the next section.

Developing and maintaining user trust

When users come to your site, they expect the wireless Web to look a certain way. Because there has been nothing like it before, their first expectation is that it will mirror the way the rest of the phone works in terms of functionality. Many people accept they have to learn how to do something just once – for example, after you learn how to drive a car, you expect to be able to apply that knowledge to every car out there. Using an oven, mailing a letter, ordering a pizza are all examples of activities for which you can identify the basic actions required, regardless of the multiple variations (such as using the oven to cook a chicken or a pie; mailing a letter overseas or to another state; ordering a simple cheese pizza or the Hawaiian with multiple toppings). You don't expect to encounter much variation in activities you have learned how to do already.

Imagine the following changes to how you use the following everyday devices or do the everyday activities.

- Cooking with an oven: Using a trackball to operate the controls
- Mailing a letter: Printing a sticker from the Internet to mail a letter
- Ordering a pizza: Using a computerized auto-attendant that allows no human contact

The same goes for users of phones, who have a consistent image of how a phone should work. Let's not destroy that image by building interfaces that force users into new ways of thinking. For example, the Motorola iDEN i1000plus series of phones enables users to check their minutes and add items to their address books. These activities are critical to using the phone and service effectively, and most users have figured them out. These activities require the user to use the keypad and two keys under the screen to make choices and select and input options. If a WAP site on the phone suddenly requires using hyperlinks as the main method of navigation, that site designer has broken the user's trust and understanding about what the wireless Web should be.

Consistency is easier on the designer as well as the user. Auto engineers don't need to redesign the steering wheel. It's a known item that has to use an analog interface and bear a resemblance to a circle – not a square, a triangle, an oval, or a star. You don't need to reinvent the way that users will navigate through your site; the problem was solved a long time ago. Think about a magazine: you expect it to have an eye-catching front cover, a table of contents, and content that you can access by turning the pages. Although some new designs have come out, most magazines don't question these rules, which form a context in a user's mind. No one expects that a magazine should be scrunched up into a cylinder and read while being rolled on the floor.

WAP is a very young technology, and the only real users are those creating the interfaces. Because of this, WAP is in the middle of a battle among browser vendors, each attempting to determine the consistent interface. Even carriers have entered the battle: on behalf of their users, they would like to see interfaces that can be counted on to do the same things across different applications.

> **NOTE:** One of the most basic things that users of WML expect is to be able to navigate around the application using links or soft keys. Unlike users of the traditional Web, who have grown accustomed to the ubiquitous blue underlined link, users of WAP devices have been bombarded with conflicting navigational techniques. For example, the Openwave browser uses brackets to signify a link. The link should be well defined wherever it appears in the interface. As the context evolves in the WAP space, users should feel more comfortable clicking links to discover an application's use.

Users learn new things in the context of their mental model. They draw from that model to learn about the application (or the WAP site, the toaster, the washing machine, and so on). Consider the example of a city with streets and road signs. You know that you are supposed to drive on the left or right side of the street. The road signs tell you where to stop and how to navigate the roadways to get to your destination. Furthermore, you may have information beyond what the signs provide, such as information about an accident on Highway 96 at D-19, which you should therefore avoid. If you travel to a city in a different country, you will have to get around while you're there. Although your mental model of the area you're visiting may be similar to that of your hometown, you'll encounter some differences; still, you won't have to start from the ground up. You can apply your basic knowledge of cities to learn how the streets and road signs work in the new country.

Have you ever visited a theme park and attempted to navigate without a map? Guess what your brain started doing? It started to build a mental map of the area. You knew that if you turned right at the Shark Escapade, you would end up at the Pearl Diving Demonstration and then the little circle area that led to the Dinosaur Exhibit and the Birds of the World and the walrus show. You would be lost if the reference points you established continually changed. In many applications, you can take some mental models for granted. For example, when Web browsing, you can count on the scrollbar at the side. In WAP, unfortunately, very few of the standard Web hints exist. Everything apart from the keyboard, the size of the screen, and the buttons under the screen is evolving as I write this.

Evaluating the effectiveness of a WAP UI: Three basic questions

You can evaluate the effectiveness of a WAP interface using many different methods, from the complex, with 40 to 50 evaluation points, to the very simple. One of the more simple and effective approaches has been proposed by Keith Instone on his site Usable Web (www.usableweb.com). He applies the model to HTML sites, but I believe it has meaning for WAP sites as well. The model is as follows: pick any page on your WAP site and ask three basic questions:

- Where am I?
- What's here?
- Where can I go?

Pick a WAP site if you don't have one of your own. Can you tell where you are when you enter it? Do you get a sense of where in the site you can go from the current page? Do you get a good sense of what the current page is about? As with the standard Web, you will find many WAP sites that fail these very simple tests.

Often when you enter a WAP site, a splash screen displays and remains there until you press a key. Sometimes the site navigates forward automatically but leaves a scar in the history stack that you must navigate through. So, the answer to the question, "Do users know where they are?" is "Yes — but at what cost?"

FIRST QUESTION: WHERE AM I?

Don't assume that users got to a location on your WAP site by clicking to it from your main deck. The deck may have been pushed to them in the form of a notification, it may be given to them by a friend, or linked from another WAP site or part of the carrier search engine.

Because of this, you must immediately let users know where they are. This is the art of localizing them. You walk out of an airplane in a foreign airport. You would like to know immediately how you can get your bags, so you scan for signs that indicate baggage claim. The same thing applies to users on your WAP site: they are looking for signs.

There is some free localization — some aspects of the WAP browser look the same regardless of the application. In the case of the Nokia WAP browser the title displayed at the top of the deck helps users determine where they are. Then there is the type of localization that ensures that people remember where they are. You can use this kind of localization very simply by stating the brand name in some way. Because WAP is currently black and white and images take extra time to load, you may choose to do something as simple as writing your name on top of the display.

SECOND QUESTION: WHAT'S HERE?

You must quickly tell users what is on the Web page, because they are there looking for information and deciding whether what you have is what they're looking for. Have a very clear description of what is available on your page. If information is presented on the deck, it should be presented in a hierarchy clear enough that the user can quickly find information.

The best way to do this, of course, is to look at other sites that provide similar information. For example, if you are presenting the scores for NCAA basketball games, look at how others are presenting the same sports scores. This gets the users comfortable with the information.

THIRD QUESTION: WHERE CAN I GO?

Once you have established the present location, users will look around to find out where else they can go. With WAP sites, they typically look around by looking at the buttons at the bottom of the screen. Unfortunately, many mobile devices force users to press a button to see where they can go (this is known as multiple task binding).

Building a Site Structure

The Web today is used for searching and researching information. This is very unlike the way in which WAP and the wireless Web will be used. The state of the sites does not allow for a complete picture of any one subject, so one goes back and forth between different sites that address their needs. For example, looking at the weather using WAP is part of the greater picture of planning a trip or vacation. Therefore, planning a trip should also be possible on the site. In this way, the related activities can also be found from the same location. Users frustrated by an inability to find a site that meets a certain need is a common problem on the Web and is one that has become worse on the wireless Web.

This is why portals have become the first place people look for information. Portals have generally provided users with links to services that provide all the necessary related applications that meet possible user needs.

The site structure is quite important because it must defuse the cognitive stress of a user encountering the site. The experience must provide for all possible goals of a typical user, not just a context-specific local sense ("Can I do X?").

WAP, like the Web, is growing and evolving, with a lot of content that is difficult to track. There are two ultimate goals for information architects, who must structure WAP so that either the patterns in complex series of data appear lucidly to outsiders, or the information is mapped in such a way that users can find the information they're looking for.

But as a WAP UI architect, you are supposed to go a little bit beyond simply structuring the information so that it can be presented to the user. You need to make decisions about how best to display the information. This means that you need to show the proper structure, patterns, and relationships in the data in the decks that users see while driving their cars. The general principles are those for structuring the information.

One comparison would be to a cartographer, a person who carefully decides what version of a map he or she wants to create. This depends on who the customer is. Is it an oil driller looking for depths of different types of rocks, or is it a driver who wants to get from one side of the city to another? Different maps would meet those different needs, and the cartographer is responsible for presenting the map and drawing out the items of interest to the viewer.

Presenting the information is a difficult exercise in which you withhold some information, de-emphasized some, and obscure others, but in which the end result is understandable by the target audience. You need to find and expose the patterns in the content to help people reach information.

Consider the case of information about the NCAA standing scores for basketball games. The information architect looks at the "raw" information and the audience goals and combines the two to determine structure. Should he or she display the data chronologically, alphabetically, geographically, or using some other audience-specific mechanism?

Imagine a site that allows a user to find a suitable restaurant. The designers may realize that there are many different audiences for this type of site, and that they all come to the site looking for the same information but with different criteria. Some may come armed with a cuisine of choice, others with a suburb, and still others with a price range. The architecture should be designed to cater to the users' various needs.

Do you think that Johann Gutenberg, inventor of the printing press, understood the mechanics of the press, and the colors, depth, and viscosity of the various inks? He had to in order to practice his workmanship. Technology changed rapidly then to produce better books faster and more cheaply. Today WAP is in the same situation: the code is evolving rapidly. We are moving from a world of complete control to one of not-so-great control. Designing a page no longer means that all users will see the page in exactly the same way.

One of the earlier suggestions by those like WirelessKnowledge (a wireless portal company) was to perfect decks by testing them on every single model of phone in the marketplace. Although it is possible to test a deck on every single model of phone, it's safe to assume that at some point your WAP service will be viewed in an environment you had not thought of testing in.

In many other media the arguments are fixed. We know very well what the limits are for the size of our page, the length of the film for a genre, and so on. There are strong industry standards that have fixed some limits on the allowed variations. In WAP, the limits change depending on the phone, and the gateway and service being provided.

Even the simple stuff is not so simple. Consider the tag <p>. On a Nokia phone this indicates 12 pt. Verdana. On a Openwave display, by contrast, it indicates 10 pt. Times New Roman, bold. One of the bygone phases of the Web was the point at which sites said things like "This site is best viewed with viewer X." Designers of sites like this are yearning for the days when they had control of the medium and are not embracing the new philosophy of the Web, which is where the content's display characteristics are determined by the user's browser application.. The same applies to WAP: your site cannot say "Best viewed with Openwave" – you would be the laughingstock of the WAP world.

Braving the Browser Wars

The browser wars are in progress in the WAP world and there are five, not two, major competitors: Microsoft, Openwave, Ericsson, Nokia, and Mitsubishi. More are hatching, such as Panasonic. Each company's offering has its own bugs and strangeness. For the WAP developer, the world is dark and gray with lots of rain.

Developers have to spend a great deal of time understanding each browser and building interfaces to fit the proper mold. One problem is a general lack of compliance with the standards. This lack of compliance is mostly similar to how HTML has evolved. Rather than conform to a specified standard, the latest versions of the language are simply collections and clarifications of the features that the industry has to offer. If two or three vendors decide to add table support, the forums simply allow all parties to join efforts so that at least the `<table>` tag looks the same for the different phone browsers.

Interoperability and innovation don't necessarily go well together. Developers in the early days spent a lot more time on specifications, defining the entire software before doing any coding. Eventually a group of developers met and hammered out the first prototype. This prototype would be tested and then further refined over subsequent meetings. After the last meeting, the prototype was released to the public as part of a set of an RFC (request for comments). Others would then have a chance to use the RFC for their own versions.

The Web eventually came along and showed everyone how Internet time works. New technologies had to be shipped prematurely so that a vendor could gain market share on its competitors. This happened so much that maintaining any sort of standard has been impossible, and this has resulted in many a WAP browser shipping with bad code because the premature release was forced by market conditions. This speed of development is measured in Internet time, not in terms of creating a reasonable specification.

The shift from poorly planned browser enhancements to ever more stringent controls on feature sets has resulted in development conditions in which the rules are constantly changing. In this type of environment the browser companies decide what is needed in future versions based on their own perceptions of what is better. But the "better standards" that they define on their own may not be better for developers, for users, or for those marketing services using WAP.

> **NOTE:** Because many versions of products that support WAP exist, each with its own bewildering set of bugs, the real question that developers need answered is as follows: What browsers do I support today and how much additional overhead do I have to deal with in releasing a standard WAP site for multiple potential browsers?

In view of all these development issues, should you give up on reining in the technology, or should you take the positive approach and attack the problem head on? I advocate tackling the problem by gaining an understanding of just how broken the WAP browsers are.

You can ask some simple questions to ascertain the answer:

- What browsers are in the phones?
- What tags and technologies are supported in the browsers?
- What percentage of the audience is using each browser?

Then, using this information, a developer should be able to make informed decisions about what development methodology to use and look to the right ways to incorporate new designs into the products.

The Web has become extremely popular owing to the very nature of allowing for multiple browsers. This same strategy can be applied to WAP and increases its viability among diverse sites.

The bottom line is that so much variety exists among the browsers, carriers, gateways, and user preferences, that your site will look broken somewhere, at some time, somehow. And then the kicker is that even though you may be doing everything right, your site doesn't work because a particular version of browser or phone has a bug.

You can give up at this point and build a site according to some generic authoring guide from the WAP Forum. At night, you can be guaranteed that your pager is not going to light up, because your site is rendering perfectly across the entire world. Your site will look and feel about as boring as dishwater. You can build this site, but you may instead strive for a site that takes risks — risks that are properly assessed and managed. If you put new tags into the site design, then put those tags in the appropriate places and present them only to the right user. You will certainly have to figure out who gets what from your site, aside from just maintaining the compatibility among versions.

Hundreds of Web browser variations exist, many with multiple versions, and the situation is fast exploding in WAP as well, with some 30 browser variations available. The best way to deal with the compatibility problem is to divide the browsers into *buckets*. These buckets are special combinations neatly organized so that the right interfaces are presented to them. The actual combination of users using the browsers follows a hyperbolic curve, one in which the largest percentage of users are using a handful of browsers. There may be arcane versions of the browser on older PCSI phones, but very few people are browsing to your WAP site using that phone. Can you ignore those phones? I recommend that you don't, but I get to that in Chapter 14, "Targeted Development." Most users in the United States are using the Openwave series of browsers, a mixture of v.3.1 and v.3.2. In Europe, most are using a Nokia browser.

One of the things about WAP and the Web in general is that if a new browser version is released, all the users in the market do not automatically upgrade to that version. It is rare on desktops; it is even rarer in WAP. There is no easy way to upgrade the browser in your phone except to buy a new phone. The public users retain most phones for at least one to one and a half years, at which point they may upgrade. Corporate customers have even less flexibility, often having to use a phone just because it is the phone given to them.

Okay, so now you have that general understanding of what the stats are. But what you need to do now is discover the versions hitting your site. Is your audience somewhere in Openwave v.2.0? How much does this browser version deviate from a later model, WAP-compliant browser? The server logs should allow developers to find out which user-agent is being used and at least identify the browser being used.

So at some point you get the numbers and you may be pleasantly surprised at the simplicity of it all: only one or two main browser versions are hitting your site. The next thing to do is to figure out which tags and technologies you are going to use given the user base of browsers. You can do this by mapping out the support of each of the tags and technologies against the browsers.

The next thing is to decide how to deal with the differences. The options are the following:

- **Don't ask, don't tell:** This is easy: simply assume that there is no problem and carry on ignoring the differences. This means creating WML 1.1 pages with the generally supported tags. Let's not bother with those advanced Openwave tags. Forget the complexity of WMLScript. The whole point here is to have degradability. The WAP site will work on multiple browsers and multiple servers, but is still able to offer the vanilla services your users require.

- **Browser-specific exploitation:** In this case, you are effectively an early adopter; you have code on your site that may work on only one specific version of the WAP browser. If you enjoy being at the cutting edge this is where your site will be. You can spot these kinds of sites a mile away: they simply don't work in your browser. This strategy is a technical decision, but also a business decision. Turning away your customers is not good business.

- **Conditional responses:** The last possibility is to create multiple sites. This solution presents advanced features to users, but only after determining the details of the user browser. An implementation of this type of conditional response behavior translates into multiple versions of the same site. Each and every page in this strategy is beautifully carved out for the intended version of browser. It is impossible to keep up with the number of browser and gateway combinations. Therefore, the only real way of using this solution is to clump certain versions or vendors together to form a bucket, a collective audience that is then targeted by a specific version of your site. You will have to keep your eye on the ball as far as features in the buckets, as over time they may shift and change.

You can manufacture conditional responses in WAP today only at the application server. These conditional responses can maintain the different architectures using three strategies:

- **Different versions of the page:** In this scenario, a script senses the Web browser type and version and redirects the user to the appropriate version of the page. The code is simple, but multiple versions of the content have to be managed.

- **Single version, multiple switches:** In this scenario, most of the site is written in dynamic code wherein little pieces of the site have portions that are taken out or changed for the appropriate browser. Your code ends up containing large `if...then` statements, which encapsulate the pieces being shifted in or out depending on the browser version and type.

- **Branching:** In this scenario, the site has bigger service-level chunks that change depending on the browser version and type. These bigger chunks may be entire decks that are done differently or a single portion of the system that is managed separately. For example, consider the case wherein the browser may or may not support cookies. You may employ different management systems. For example, if a portion of your dating application allows potential partners to e-mail each other, the e-mail portion may be a separate service that employs cookies. This service requires a lot of planning at the specification stage to get it right.

Designing with Speed in Mind

So, how fast do the decks on your site load on a real phone? Ten seconds? Fifteen seconds? More? Do you know the answer? Maybe you've developed the greatest WAP site with the snazziest features, but if the site does not load fast enough, users will go elsewhere. The problem is exacerbated by the fact that for wireless the links are limited in bandwidth and speed. The issue here is the need to design your WAP site so that they create a perception of speed, even though the decks may take some time to load.

According to WAP developers and carriers alike, the next hot thing to improve WAP will be GPRS (General Packet Radio Service). It will be packet-switched, improve the speeds of the link, and so on. WAP decks will move much faster with GPRS. That is the promised future. In five years' time, when GPRS has been delivered, the complaints will be there: how GPRS is not fast enough and the next greatest thing is needed, maybe 3G or even 4G networks. Until those megabit-per-second rates for wireless appear, there is always the present.

In the present, you optimize your WAP sites, creating the fastest site using the smallest number of bytes possible. When you first enter WAP, cramming a lot of information into small sizes may seem to be an impossible task, but it is possible. Start by looking at the competition. It has definitely been done before. Others have set the standard.

The answers to optimizing sites lie in careful caching and dedication to the speed problem. This dedication often results in sites that are very carefully designed to package as many decks in a single transaction as possible.

Let's take a look at an example of each:

- **Deck packaging:** Consider the case of a WAP application to retrieve stock quotes. The application requires the user to enter a stock symbol. The application then queries the stock symbol against a back-end database to find out what information is available, as shown in Figure 15-1. This software design would be acceptable in most cases, but considering the limited bandwidth and the possibility for multiple pages to be packaged in a single response, it is desirable to guess where the user will most likely navigate before sending the link. In this case, the stock application will probably require that the user enter a quote. This is very likely to be a card to which the user will navigate. You could do a similar analysis for other cards in the application to reach a new application flow, as shown in Figure 15-2.

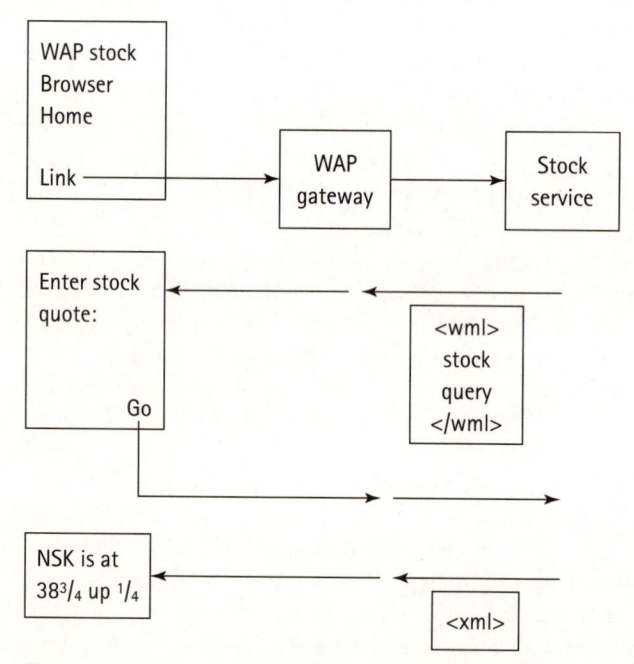

Figure 15-1: Stock-query application (HTML-like design)

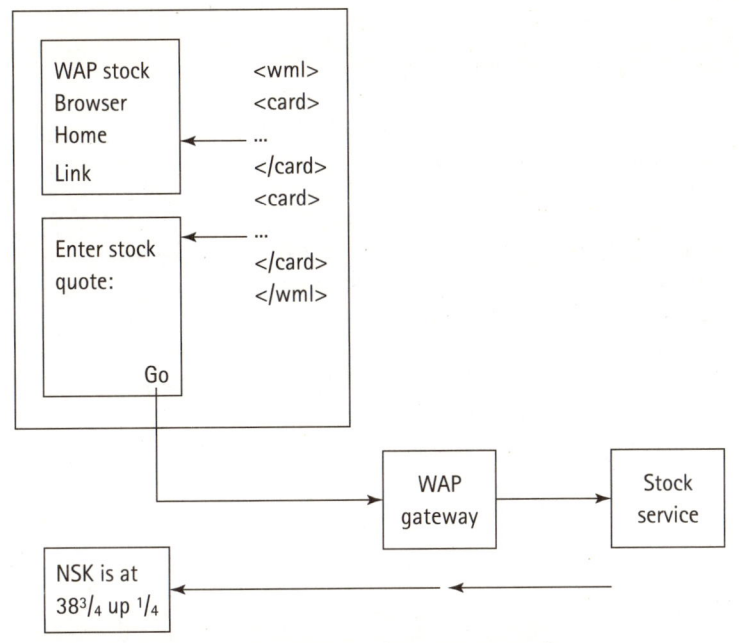

Chapter 15: Designing User-Friendly Interfaces 473

Figure 15-2: Stock-query application (optimized design)

- **Caching:** Again with the stock application you can imagine a scenario wherein a user is fidgeting about a stock quote and requests a quote every minute to monitor its value. However, the news feed on the back end may not be updated for five minutes. Rather than have a new response sent every time, you can structure the caching headers so that the page caches until its expiration. This prevents the application from being perceived as slow. It is able to handle an impatient user.

> **XREF:** You can find other caching optimizations in Chapter 12, "Caching and Cache Operations."

Summary

In this chapter I have deviated from the general approach of UI recommendations by attempting to instill a wireless design philosophy rather then spoon-feeding specific examples. Sites that are designed with proper attention to the issues mentioned in this chapter will avoid problems that plague a large number of WAP services today.

When coding applications, novice programmers to a technology focus too much on the code, ignoring key usability factors mentioned in this chapter, such as speed, UI structure, behavior management, and content optimization.

I hope the chapter has led you in the right direction to create sites that are powerful and enticing enough to make users want to visit them again and again.

Part V

Real-World Issues and WAP

CHAPTER 16
Implementing WAP Security

CHAPTER 17
Localization and Internationalization

CHAPTER 18
Location-Based Services

CHAPTER 19
Deploying WAP Services

CHAPTER 20
The Future of WAP

CHAPTER 21
Future of WAP Competitors

Chapter 16

Implementing WAP Security

IN THIS CHAPTER

- Developing an understanding of security and cryptographic algorithms
- Implementing WAP security into your applications

E-COMMERCE HAS SINGLE-HANDEDLY DRIVEN security solutions on the Internet. As soon as the medium began gaining acceptance, key customers drove Web browser and Web server vendors such as Netscape to create protocols to solve the numerous problems that e-commerce presented, the main ones being identifying buyers and sellers and creating a secure channel between them. Netscape brought forward a solution that attempted to solve a bulk of the e-commerce security problems using a protocol called SSL (Secure Sockets Layer). Although specific to the HTTP protocol, the condensed solution to the problem fueled the industry to create similar protocols in other layers of the Internet stack, each with its own tradeoffs. From the initial SSL to today's TLS and IPSec, a gradual buildup has taken place in the level of sophistication to the security solutions, mostly owing to the enhanced processing power available now.

When the WAP Forum was examining its options regarding security, the two-tiered solution allowed for Internet solutions to exist on one side of the architecture but the other side needed to be designed from scratch. Therefore, this WAP stack is immature in the security sense. For one thing, it has not reached an audience wide enough to truly probe its vulnerabilities. Therefore, any examination of its strengths and weaknesses must resort to observing similarities to the Internet and potentially vulnerable elements of the Internet architecture.

The current WAP security design contains several architectural elements that introduce vulnerabilities of unknown magnitude. Because of the lack of large-scale deployment, the WAP security modifications represent a good-faith attempt at addressing perceived threats. In this chapter, I examine first the standard Internet security protocols and methodologies and then the WAP counterparts.

Understanding Security and Cryptographic Algorithms

Security encompasses all the mechanisms created to protect sensitive data or processes. For example, data in a network setting may become compromised if information is being observed, recorded, or replayed by others during communication. Unauthorized parties may also attack information stored on servers and use it unscrupulously or destroy it. Or an impostor may gain access to sensitive information by signing on to a secure server and pretending to have an actual user's password or other secure token. Attackers may simply decide to destroy or degrade a system so that its original purpose can no longer be fulfilled. And finally, an attacker may sit in the middle of a secure conversation, convincing both sides in the communication that they are indeed talking to each other and not through an attacker.

These types of attacks give rise to the following security philosophies. Any system can be analyzed and its vulnerabilities exposed if you examine it in terms of the following key items:

- Client-side and server-side authentication
- Privacy/confidentiality
- Integrity
- Nonrepudiability/repudiability
- Service availability

Authentication defines the foundations of how systems obtain proof of the identity of the users interacting with services. There is nothing new here; having to provide identification is done daily. For example, when traveling to another country, you are normally required to give proof of your identity. When an officer asks for your passport identification, you may give him the passport to identify yourself. However, how did the officer identify himself? In that case identification may be implicit: you went through an airport barrier and the person on the other end must therefore be the immigration officer.

Authorization refers to the stratification of users who have been authenticated. For example, a CEO of a firm has access to a lot more information about projects than a single project manager does. Authorization techniques have to segregate the two types of users.

Confidentiality ensures that the intended parties are the only readers of messages in communication networks. This area of security has seen the most work, largely because of its necessity in military networks. Even though you may scramble information to protect others from reading it, this does not guarantee their privacy, or the possibility that others may discover your true identity from a message. For example, Alice can send Bob a completely encrypted message, but the e-mail header may contain her address along with her hostname. An attacker can use these bits of information to hack at the encrypted data, or to masquerade as her in some other way, or associate her electronic identity with a real person. For example, Alice=Princess X is sending a message to Bob=her new boyfriend. So, Alice and Bob may be online identities, but if there are leakages of information, onlookers will see that Alice=Princess X and Bob=new boyfriend. These examples show how seemingly trivial disclosures can compromise total system security.

Integrity refers to how a system confirms that a message it has received has not been compromised. For example, if I were remotely administering my oil wells in Texas, I might set up a system that remotely alters the distance of a pressure probe from the bottom of the cavity. If the integrity of my remote messages is compromised, others may be able to alter the remotely managed distances and destroy the probe.

Nonrepudiability has to do with being able to keep some record of identity with a transaction. In this way, if the transaction is ever questioned it can be tied to the identity of either the buyer or seller. There should be no way to deny the transaction. What if a customer called a Swiss bank account and wanted her money transferred to another account? The bank would need some verification of the identity of the caller and some undeniable proof if the transaction order were approved. On the other hand, there are cases in which the capability to deny transactions is considered beneficial: this capability is known as repudiability. It was the whole concept behind the `anon.penet.fi` service, which enabled people to create anonymous addresses and hide their real identities. Any e-mail messages sent to a user's `anon.penet.fi` address would be delivered to the user's actual e-mail address, and outside parties would only know the user's `anon.penet.fi` address.

Service availability refers to keeping systems or services up. The problem of keeping systems up has been known for some time to be a real threat to computing over the Internet. The basic protocols do not have a level of security that prevents spurious threats. The distance of the threats also results in malicious hackers attacking networks from afar without fear of reprisal. This means that threats can be executed masked behind the safety of poor protocol design. Service availability problems were highlighted by the attacks on Yahoo!, Amazon.com, and other service Web sites. The attacks degraded the service usability to the point where legitimate customers could not carry on normal activities.

Security and relativity

Security is enabled to the level required by the information being transmitted. If a compromised transaction could result in a $20,000 loss and the transaction is done 10 times a day for 365 days, 200,000 times 365 or $73,000,000 may be lost. An appropriate percentage of this loss, maybe 10 percent of the total, must be spent on the installation of a security system. Then a percentage of the daily potential loss, perhaps 10 percent or about $20,000, can be allocated to maintaining the system's security.

The previous example shows how an exact cost can be put on a potential loss. This cost determines the relative level of security required. A military-system engineer may spend a lot on developing a system since the attackers will be other governments with similar resources for counterattack. Also, the information traveling over those networks, if discovered, can result in very valuable secrets being compromised.

Even with this concept of relativity in security implementation you must make further compromises because the WAP protocols are carried over mobile networks. In mobile network architectures, the limitations prevent the best cryptographic techniques from being deployed.

Providing security solutions

Now that you have seen the terms in which security systems can be examined, you can build on those concepts and look at how the security systems can be designed to address those specific aspects. Each of the concepts is discussed at in turn, with a detailed description of the available security solutions.

AUTHENTICATION AND AUTHORIZATION

As examined previously, authentication and authorization are security challenges because it must be determined whether a user has security rights to a system and what level of resources they are allowed access to. This problem is commonly solved on public networks by using a token that is a tamper-proof representation of identity. For example, for the car I own I have a key that I can use to open the door and also run the engine. This key is how the car ensures that it is me who drives it. If I chose to give a copy of the key to my wife, she can also use it as an authentication mechanism to drive the car. Now, consider a scenario wherein there are multiple keys: a key for the trunk, another for the engine, a third that allows me to shift the car into high gear, and maybe a fourth for the dash. In this case, very simply, the keys are used for authentication. However, the type of key I have determines the level of access I get. The process of mapping identity to a level of permission is known as *authorization*. With the key system in this example, it is important not only that the car recognize me as the rightful owner, but that I recognize the car. In this way, the key system is two-way authentication. If in the dark I mistake another car for my own, the key will not work. This indicates to me that the car is not mine, because the keys are manufactured in such a way that no two cars have the same keys.

In network communication, a username and password are commonly used to establish secure authentication. A back-end database then links the username to a set of permissions. These permissions encompass the authorization database and determine the level of access.

Another common technique is to have one party show that it knows a secret. In the James Bond movie *From Russia with Love*, an impostor MI-6 operative used a set of special words spoken in the correct order to prove that he was a valid agent to James Bond.

You can use the technique in a network setting by using secret key cryptography, as shown in Figure 16-1.

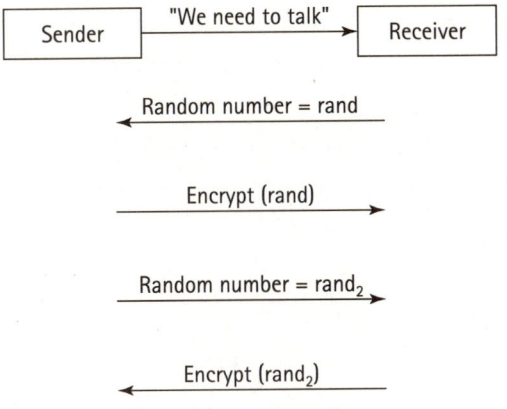

```
Sender  ──"We need to talk"──▶  Receiver

        ◀──Random number = rand──

        ──Encrypt (rand)──▶

        ──Random number = rand_2──▶

        ◀──Encrypt (rand_2)──
```

Figure 16-1: Secret key cryptography

In this scenario the sender and receiver share a secret key. The protocol begins with the sender sending a message to identify him or her. The receiver replies with a message containing some random elements. This is the challenge. The sender sends a response with an encrypted message containing the random elements. The receiver uses the secret key to decrypt and obtain the random elements. If the decrypted elements match the elements sent then the receiver knows he or she is communicating with a known sender. The sender and receiver then repeat the process in the opposite direction so that the sender knows he or she is communicating with a known receiver. For example, in *From Russia with Love*, the conversation was like the diagram shown in Figure 16-2.

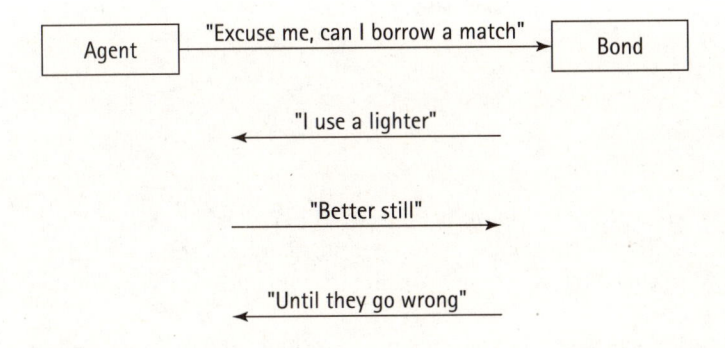

```
Agent  ──"Excuse me, can I borrow a match"──▶  Bond

       ◀──"I use a lighter"──

       ──"Better still"──▶

       ◀──"Until they go wrong"──
```

"From Russia with Love"

Figure 16-2: MI-6 authentication protocol

It is extremely important to the success of this authentication scheme that the random elements be different every time – otherwise an eavesdropper can simply replay the challenges and responses. This is where the term "nonce" or "number once" comes from. It represents a single random element. The disastrous consequences of repeating the authentication scheme were seen in the movie where an imposter was able to use the authentication protocol successfully against James Bond.

INTEGRITY

This is the process whereby data in a transaction are protected from modification in transit. Normally, a "fingerprint" is attached to the data being sent and received. These fingerprints have three special properties:

- They cannot be used to generate the message
- A small change in the message significantly changes the fingerprint
- They should not clash; it should be very difficult to find a message with the same fingerprint

Fingerprints are sometimes called *hashes* or *checksums*.

The size and speed of the hash are also significant because on a wireless network not enough bandwidth is available to send two files of the same size. The processors on mobile devices are also limited, meaning that the algorithms to implement the hash must be chosen carefully.

Figure 16-3 shows how a hash algorithm works.

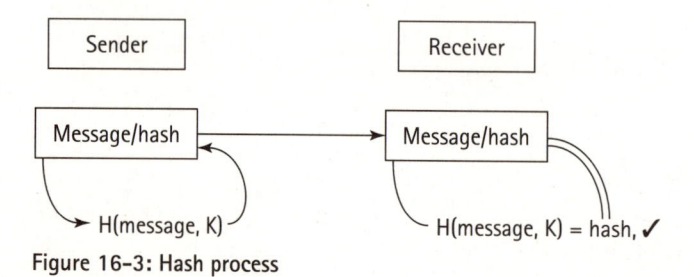

Figure 16-3: Hash process

The sender and receiver first need to agree to a secret key. A sender sends a message with the hash. The receiver takes the message and calculates the hash from it. If it matches what was sent, the receiver can assume that the message was not tampered with in transit.

As I mentioned earlier, checksums are one-way algorithms, and it should be very difficult to find another message with the same checksum. These checksums are also generally shorter than the message. For example, consider a message that is 1500 bytes. The size of a hash could be 150 bytes, about one-tenth the size. In this case, there are 2^1500*8 possible messages, and 2^150*8 possible hashes. So about

$2^{1500*8}/2^{150*8} = 2^{10800}$ messages produce the same checksum. It will also take about 2^{150*8} tries before a message of the checksum is found (assuming statistical averages). If it takes a nanosecond to do checksumming and generation, it will take about 1.72×10^{351} years to produce a message for which the checksum matches.

The MD5 (Message Digest) algorithm is an example of a hash algorithm supported by WAP's WTLS protocol. The algorithm takes a message of any length and divides it into 512-bit sections. A 128-bit buffer is then created to store the hash value. This 128-bit buffer is initialized to some known value. The algorithm goes through each 512-bit section and modifies the 128-bit buffer in a known way after going through the section. When the 512-bit sections are exhausted the buffer contains the hash.

What is more common is to combine the MD5 algorithm with a key. This is the keyed MD5. In this case, the message is padded with zeros and divided into 512-bit sections as before. The secret key is also padded to 512 bits and attached to the back or front of the main message. The MD5 algorithm is then implemented just as before. This type of hash algorithm, which depends on a hash algorithm and a key, is known as a message authentication code (MAC).

You can further improve this MAC by using a hashed message authentication code (HMAC). First the key or shared secret is padded with zeros to 512 bits. The result is XORed with an ipad, 64 repetitions of 00110110. Next, the message is padded to the least possible multiple of 512 bits. MD5 is then applied to the XORed key and the message as it is to the MD5 algorithm and key. This results in a 128-bit hash, which is padded to 512 bits. Then the shared secret key is padded to 512 keys and XORed with opad, 64 repetitions of 01011010. The 128-bit hash and this last opad-XORed key are run through the MD5 algorithm. The result is the final 128-bit hash.

WAP's WTLS supports a more general HMAC, one in which you can adjust the message padding and the hash padding. The WTLS protocol supports two main classes of hash algorithms, MD5, which we have seen, and Secure Hash Algorithm 1 (SHA-1).

SHA-1 is a hash function that produces a 160-bit hash, and many consider it more secure than MD5. Keyed SHA-1 hashes are exactly the same as those for MD5. The SHA-1 HMAC follows a more generalized HMAC, which means that everything is padded into 512 bits as before in the standard HMAC but this time there is a hash size of 160 bits.

WTLS also supports a five-byte XOR checksum. The message is divided into five-byte blocks and padded, if less than or equal to a set of five-byte sections. Then, all the blocks are XORed, one after another. This results in a five-byte hash. It should not be considered very secure.

PRIVACY/CONFIDENTIALITY

Numerous systems have been devised to keep data from prying eyes. Some of the older systems counted on the secrecy of the algorithm to protect the secret. Consider the Caesar cipher, which uses a transposition of letters of the alphabet to maintain privacy. Even the Enigma machine that the Germans used in WWII submarine communication used the secrecy of the algorithm to protect data. Once the algorithm is discovered, attackers can read all encrypted messages.

Modern cryptography techniques separate a secure key from an algorithm. It is the secrecy of the key that keeps the transactions secure. Figure 16-4 shows a basic encryption routine and the terminology used to describe it.

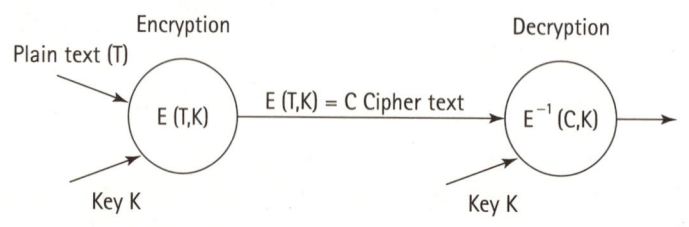

Figure 16-4: Modern encryption

Figure 16-4 shows how unencrypted text (referred to as plain text) is first converted into cipher text and then transmitted over an insecure channel. A secret key or keys are used in the encryption process, along with the algorithm. The receiver needs to use the same secret key or keys to get the original message and must also have the same algorithm on hand. This type of secret-key cryptography is known as symmetric-key cryptography. The most common symmetric algorithms are DES, 3DES, IDEA, and RC5. A discussion of these algorithms is outside the scope of this book.

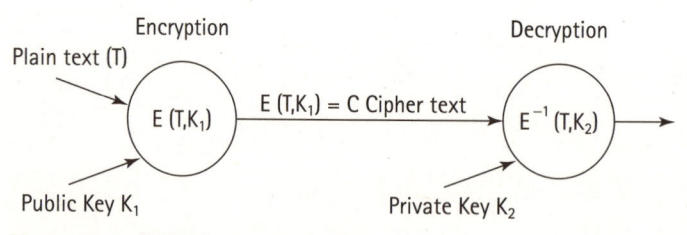

There is also public-key cryptography, in which keys are not shared between the sender and receiver. Two keys exist in a public-key cryptography system, the private key and the public key. Figure 16-5 shows how public-key cryptography works.

Figure 16-5: Public-key cryptography

A receiver generates a public key and private key, and publicly distributes the public key. A sender then uses this public key to encrypt the message. Only the private key of the receiver can decrypt the message. One important requirement of these systems is that one must not be able to derive the private key from the public key. The best example of public-key cryptography is RSA, of which a detailed description is outside the scope of this book. Briefly, RSA is based on the concept of large factorable numbers. If you examine the key structures, the factors and the number form the private key, whereas only the factorable number forms the public key. Therefore, generating the private key becomes a question of finding the factors of a large number. Another example of public-key cryptography is ECC (Elliptic Curve Cryptography), which relies on two vectors in a discretized elliptic curve. Mathematically, the two vectors can be generated that have a factored relationship. However, just knowing the vectors, you would not be able to find out the relationship between them without some intense computing power. Therefore, the public key contains just the two vectors; the private contains the vectors and their relationship.

Public-key cryptography is a very powerful tool: it can be used, not only to ensure privacy, but also for authentication and integrity. One form of authentication, for example, starts when the sender identifies himself or herself. The receiver then picks a random number and sends it to the sender using the public key. The sender then uses his or her private key to decrypt the message and obtain the random number. This random number is then encrypted with the private key and sent back to the receiver. Figure 16-6 shows how this process works.

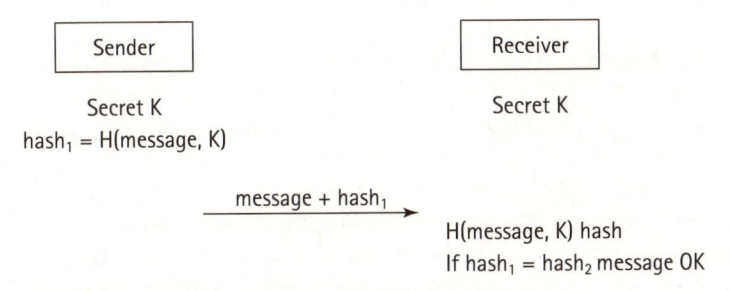

```
    Sender                              Receiver

   Secret K                             Secret K
hash₁ = H(message, K)

              message + hash₁
              ───────────────▶
                                     H(message, K) hash
                                     If hash₁ = hash₂ message OK
```

Figure 16-6: Public-key cryptography for authentication

Public-key cryptography has also been put to work as a nonrepudiation tool. In this scenario, a document is run through a hash algorithm to produce a hash. The hash is then encrypted with the private key of a signator. Because no one has the same private key, the encrypted hash is an effective signature. A receiver can use a public key to decrypt the hash and then check it against the message. If everything is okay, the message could have originated from the sender. Figure 16-7 explains the process.

Although public-key systems are extremely powerful tools, they create a large problem. The public-key cryptography system keys take too long to decrypt and encrypt. For this reason, in most fast-paced communication, public-key cryptography is only used at the beginning of a session to establish a session key. The session key is then used to encrypt the messages using one of the faster symmetric-key algorithms. The session key is also input into the integrity and authentication algorithms I discussed earlier.

```
Pu = Public Key
Pr = Private Key
```

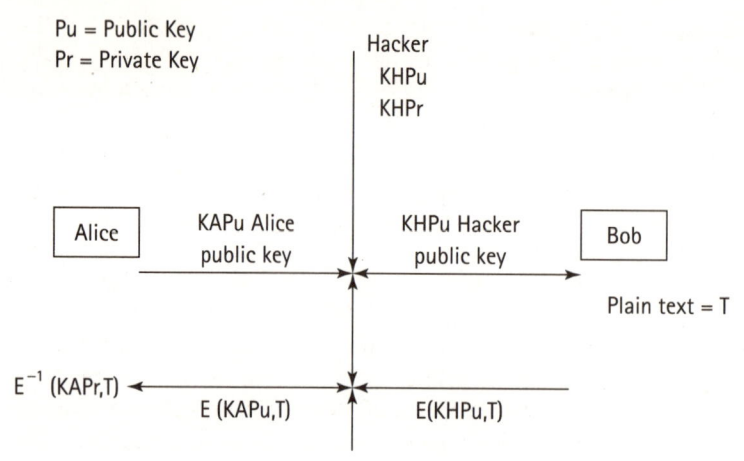

```
                        Hacker
                        KHPu
                        KHPr


   ┌─────┐  KAPu Alice      KHPu Hacker   ┌─────┐
   │Alice│  public key      public key    │ Bob │
   └─────┘                                └─────┘
                                          Plain text = T


   E⁻¹(KAPr,T) ←─────────────
                E (KAPu,T)      E(KHPu,T)
```

Figure 16-7: Public-key cryptography for nonrepudiation

SERVICE GUARANTEE

The original design of the Internet did not make any provisions for ensuring that services would remain up consistently. Taking measures to keep a service up even in the face of attacks is known as a security measure to ensure service guarantee. For example, take the case of a Web service you are using to host a site. In this case, no precautions are taken to monitor service load, and so multiple inbound requests can be repeated and fired to the service. So many illegitimate requests would reach this service that it would be unable to serve the valid ones. There is little that you can do today with the Internet protocol problems in the preceding example, except to add extra software to a system that monitors characteristics that can result in downtime. Internet protocols do not contain any inherent security fields.

Another example of a security attack is recording a valid transaction and then simply replaying it later. This attack can be used to deny service. For example, suppose there is a function that enables developers to delete an entry from the phone book in a mobile phone. An application can issue multiple requests to have entries deleted. This can result in a scenario where a mobile user ends up with no numbers in his or her phone book. This is an example of denial of service.

Other functions may be more damaging, disabling the phones completely. In this case, the phone manufacturers or carriers/service operators may potentially be liable, if the mobile user is unable to dial an emergency service. You could design the function in such a way that the user must confirm any deletions from the address book. Also, the browser must be designed so that an invalid page or other spurious activity does not disable the phone.

No good comprehensive solutions exist to ensure service availability on IP-based protocols today.

NONREPUDIABILITY

With this concept, the sender and/or receiver store information about a transaction so that they can confirm at a later time whether the transaction occurred. Neither side can repudiate the transaction or, in other words, deny that it actually happened.

Consider the example of a bank that enables its customers to move money between checking and savings accounts. If a customer calls on Monday and requests that a sum of money be moved from savings into checking, the bank will usually record the transaction so that it can be confirmed later if necessary. If the same customer calls up Tuesday and insists that they did not make the call, the bank can replay the call to rekindle their memory. Remember that during the call other aspects of security may be used for authentication, authorization, but the fact that the call is recorded and stored is the nonrepudiation mechanism.

Nonrepudiation mechanisms are usually signatures. These signatures, associated with an individual user, uniquely identify that user and when presented at a later time with a recorded action distinguish the individual user from others. In digital communication, nonrepudiation is addressed using digital signatures. These digital signatures uniquely identify an individual user and when stored with a transaction identify that user as having been involved with that event.

Key management

Key management becomes a big problem in today's cryptographic environment. In most systems a key is the only unique component of the transaction. Because the discovery of a key is quite disastrous, keys must be stored carefully and managed so as to avoid publication, which gave rise to the use of key-distribution systems. An example of this is the Kerberos Authentication Service. In this case, every user gets a shared secret key. If user X wants to communicate with user Y, then user X contacts the KDC to get a special key to use with Y. The KDC authenticates X, then selects a special key f(X,Y) and encrypts it using the shared keys of both X and Y. The KDC sends both versions of the key to X. A ticket key f(X,Y) can then be used for secure communication.

Public-key systems require only one key, and its security is less of a headache since knowledge of a public key does not allow you to decrypt encrypted messages. The keys must still be distributed and impostors can step in the middle of communication and generate their own key pairs and a sender and receiver will be none the wiser. Figure 16-8 shows how the attack would look.

488 Part V: Real-World Issues and WAP

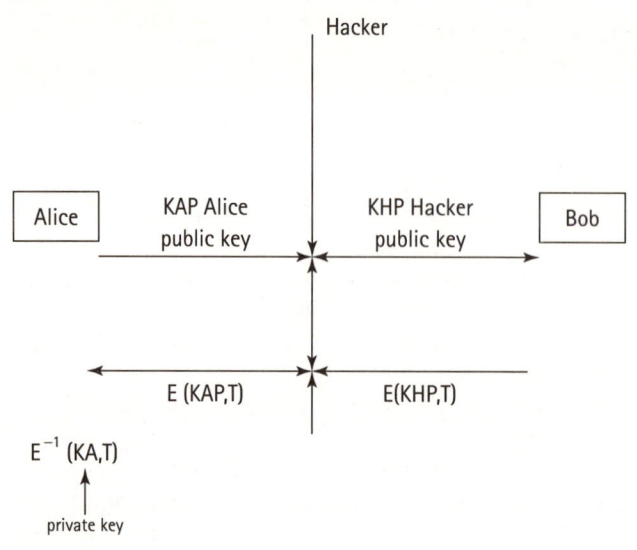

Figure 16-8: Man-in-the-middle attack on public-key cryptography

To combat this type of attack, certificate authorities have been established. These authorities are responsible for taking public keys and issuing certificates. These certificates are signed messages that consist of the username, his or her public key, the serial-number ID for the certificate, and an expiration date. The certificates can then be distributed just like the public keys. If there is any question about the validity of the certificate it can be checked against a directory service run by the CA (Certificate Authority). Given the fast advances in cryptographic technology, key sizes that were good a few years ago are no longer considered good today. To ensure that keys are kept up to date, certificates are only issued for a maximum of two years. Because certificates can expire or become invalid owing to some compromise, CAs actually manage a certificate-revocation list (CRL), which is a list of invalid serial numbers. So to check on a certificate means first checking the validity and then checking for a revocation on the CRL. This entire process (and any computers required to implement it) is known as PKI (Public-Key Infrastructure). This process and architecture are shown in Figure 16-9.

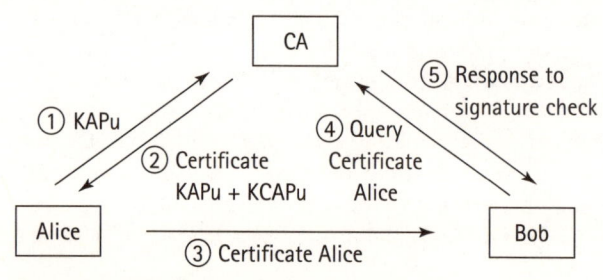

Figure 16-9: Public-key infrastructure (PKI)

The third way to distribute keys does not rely on third-party developers. It is known as the Diffie-Hellman key exchange. It relies on a mathematical property of special modulus numbers. The protocol description is outside the scope of this book.

Understanding the WAP Security Architecture

The WAP architecture can be viewed, like any other system, in terms of its likely shortcomings. The architecture is a combination of wireless architectures and the landline architectures of the Internet component. These networks have different capabilities in terms of bandwidth, latency, and reliability. Therefore, what works on the Internet side does not necessarily port well to the wireless link. Figure 16-10 shows the WAP architecture diagram with the three main components, and the locations where security could be compromised.

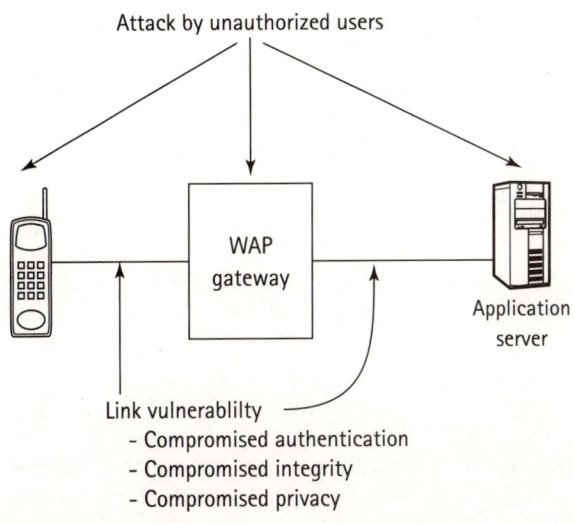

Figure 16-10: WAP architecture vulnerabilities

Designing applications in the wireless space is quite different from doing the same in landline space. The wireless link between the mobile device and the base station is a very easy link to monitor with little hardware. This type of listening can be done surreptitiously, making it difficult to combat. This is a problem unique to wireless, as on a landline system, the electrical properties of the cable change to allow for detection of intruders. The wireless architecture also has the following security problems:

- Low storage
- Lack of bandwidth
- Small computational overhead

Mobile devices like phones are consumer devices and it is uneconomical to add gigabytes to these devices at this time. The likely value of available memory is actually measured in kilobytes. This space requirement affects security needs, because it limits the code space available for cryptography. The low memory affects the sophistication of the algorithms that can be used. Furthermore, many cryptographic routines have become vulnerable and larger key sizes are required with each new processor or mathematical advancement. This means that the larger key size has to be balanced against the requirement that the memory size remain low. Once the keys are transferred to the device, they will also need to be stored efficiently. If any compression can be done, it will alleviate the memory problem. One of the new public-key algorithms called ECC (Elliptic Curve Crypto) has been gaining popularity because its 160-bit key size is much smaller than that of its secure equivalent in RSA, which has a key size of about 1024 bits.

Additionally, the processors in cell phones have limited computing power, only part of which is available for WAP applications. Therefore, security algorithms cannot require much computation.

Lastly, the bandwidth over the air on any wireless link is not unlimited and, in the case of WAP, definitely not free. This means any messages sent over this link must be kept short and any cryptographic details generated from the short message must also be kept short. So MAC algorithms, which generate signatures, must be fine-tuned for the wireless environment. All the characteristics of wireless technologies must be addressed by the choice of proper security algorithm, but furthermore, that choice is a carefully chosen medium between the WAP algorithm requirement and the standard telephony security requirements.

WTLS (Wireless Transport Layer Security)

The WTLS protocol is based on SSL except that it sits on top of UDP/WDP in the WAP environment, which required significant modification to services both above and below the stack. The WTLS protocol is built on top of modifications to SSL based on the bandwidth, latency, and memory requirements of the wireless environment.

WTLS is a client/server protocol in which a client initiates a secure connection. It starts out when a client simply sends out a plain-text hello message, which is simple textual message containing some identification of who the sender is. In the case of a pull transaction, the WTLS-capable browser sends this out on a client request. The server or WAP gateway then has to respond with its server "hello", and optionally a server certificate and client certificate request, and then close with a server "hello done". At this point, the client or WTLS-capable browser can optionally send back a client certificate, client-key exchange and certificate-verification mechanism, or continue with the transaction. After that optional step, the WTLS connection is considered established, and the communication is encrypted using random shared secrets that are agreed upon by both sides. Figure 16-11 shows the full WTLS handshake.

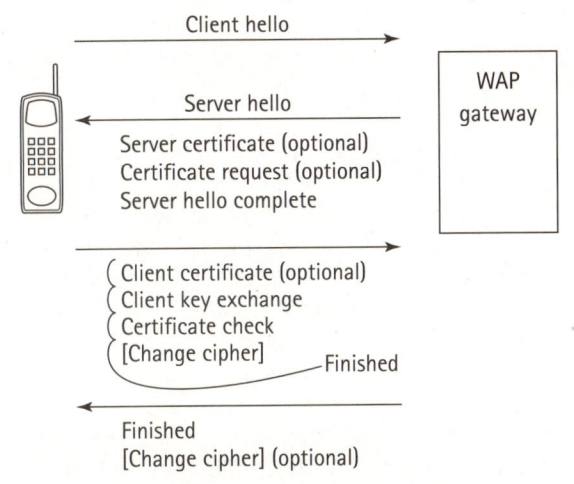

Figure 16-11: WTLS handshake process

The WTLS is itself a layered protocol composed of two separate layers of which the bottom is known as the record layer. This layer is responsible for maintaining the symmetric-key properties and authentication fields. The record layer is also responsible for the rudimentary sending out of data. The record layer is duplicated on both the client and the server. Therefore, a server record layer has the same symmetric-key properties and authentication as the client. Its record layer then receives the data and passes the plain-text version up to the higher layer on the WAP stack.

Because the common state of the record layer is unknown at the beginning of a security transaction it is set to null. If the state of the record layer is set to null, no modification is made to outgoing or incoming data except to add or remove administrative headers. This is why the initial hello message is sent in plain text.

SSL and Internet

From the WAP gateway to the application server any number of accepted security mechanisms can be deployed. The strongest available mechanism is SSL. SSL implementations with both server-side and client certificates are supported by most WAP gateways deployed by U.S. carriers. Developers should use SSL with client-side certificates in cases where Tle2e (Transport Layer End-to-End Security) is not yet available.

WIM (Wireless Identity Module)

The WIM card is a mechanism that enables users to store data on a tamper-proof card on the phone for later retrieval.

The WIM card will be useful when large amounts of data, such as certificates for PKI, need to be stored and managed by mobile devices. In cases in which the network technology supports SIM cards, the WIM is just a logical component of the SIM. In other networks, the WIM can be a special area of memory on the mobile device.

The Crypto library signText function

Although WTLS Class 3 client signatures already provide a form of client authentication, the manner in which they sign information is not persistent. Also, the WTLS layer is implemented at a layer below which applications can interact with it. Furthermore, many types of electronic transactions require proof that the transaction that occurred has been stored for nonrepudiation purposes.

For all these reasons, a `signText` function was created as part of a new WMLScript crypto library. This function allows data presented to the user to be signed by the user's digital signature. The digital signature is either stored in URL form or in WIM persistent storage, both of which have been previously obtained using the PKI architecture. Using the `signText` function, an application server can extract the signed data and store them for later accountability purposes. I strongly recommended that your signature for `signText` be different from the one you use for WTLS.

> **XREF** A description of the `signText` function can be found in Chapter 8, "Using the WMLScript Libraries."

WPKI (Wireless Public-Key Infrastructure)

Because the WAP environment includes a WAP gateway in the architecture, any communication with PKI pieces such as CAs (Certificate Authorities), RAs (Registering Authorities), or OCSP (Online Certificate Status Protocol) responders is done through the use of a PKI portal. This PKI portal sits between the WAP gateway and the PKI server in order to facilitate the following security transactions:

1. CA public-key certificates for WTLS Class 2
2. Client public-key certificates for WTLS Class 3
3. Client public-key certificates for crypto library `signText`

USING CA PUBLIC-KEY CERTIFICATES
In this case, the existing WTLS specifications call for public-key cryptography to be used in the communication between the WAP gateway and the mobile device or in WAP 2.0 between a subordinate proxy and the mobile device. The Class 2 capabilities of the WTLS protocol provide for the client to authenticate the server. Figure 16-12 shows how this is done.

WTLS Class 2 WPKI

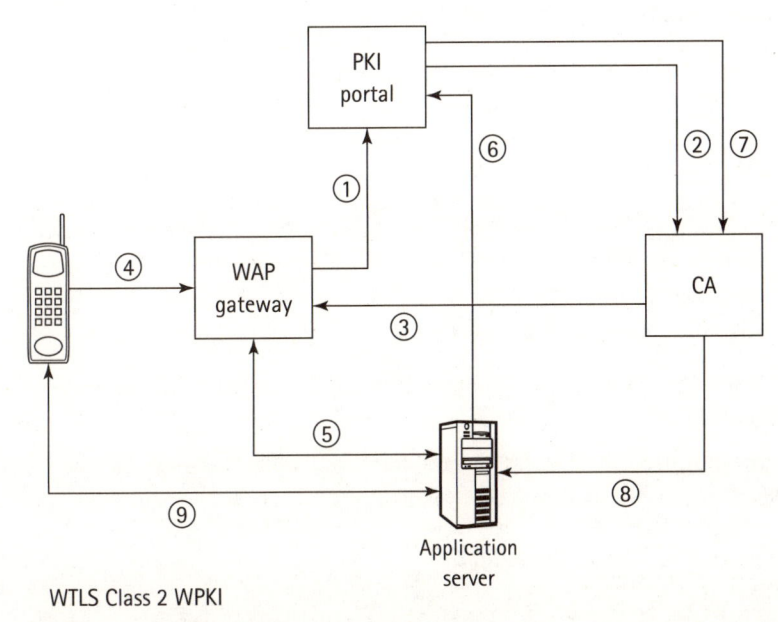

Figure 16-12: WPKI with Class 2 capabilities

The diagram shows both the cases in which an end-to-end security mechanism exists and those in which a mechanism does not exist, as in a two-phase security solution. In the latter case, the WAP gateway sends a certificate request to the portal, which is forwarded on to the CA. The CA then returns the public certificate to the WAP gateway. At this point the mobile client, as shown in the diagram, can invoke a WTLS Class 2 session.

In cases in which end-to-end security is allowed, the application server sends out the certificate request to the PKI portal, which forwards it to the CA. The CA then returns a public certificate directly to the application server. This certificate is then used to establish a direct WTLS connection with the application server.

In Figure 16-12, the handset is provisioned with some CA Root Public Key using the following process. For 1-5, the process is the standard routine of two-phase security. Additionally, with 6-9, you get an end-to-end security model establishment. The steps shown in Figure 16-12 are described as follows:

1. WAP gateway generates a public key/private key pair and sends them to the PKI portal.

2. PKI portal confirms the request and sends the information to the CA.

3. CA sends the signed certificate to the WAP gateway.

4. A WTLS session can now be established between the handset and the WAP gateway.

5. An SSL/TLS session can now be established between the WAP gateway and the application server.

6. In order to establish an end-to-end security model, the application server generates a public key/private key pair and sends a request to the PKI portal.

7. The portal forwards the request to the CA.

8. The CA then sends the response back to the application server, through the PKI portal.

9. Once the public key is forwarded to the handset, a WTLS session can be established from the handset to the application server. The CA finally sends a certificate to the application server, through the portal. This public certificate is then sent to the handset.

USING CLIENT PUBLIC-KEY CERTIFICATES

The other two cases in which client public-key certificates are used are very similar to cases discussed in earlier sections. In these cases, it is now the client that needs to be authenticated and not the server. The architecture for client public-key certificates is shown in Figure 16-13.

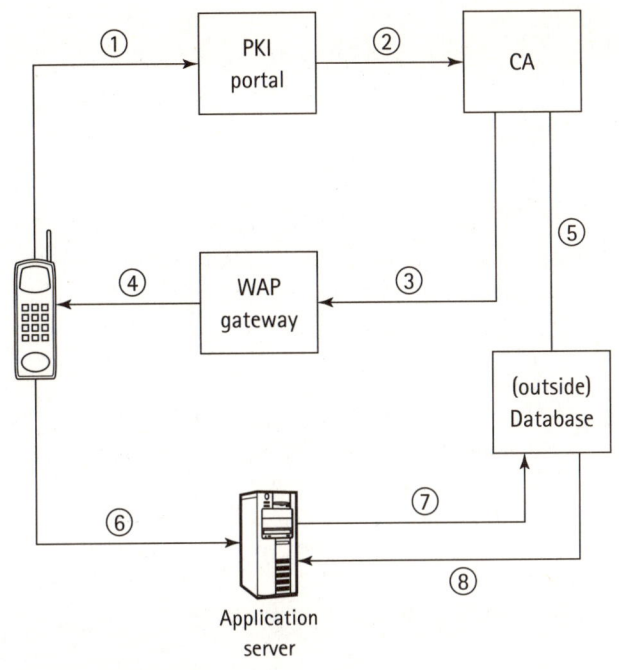

WPKI and Sign text

Figure 16-13: WPKI for client public-key certificates

Figure 16-13 shows how the CA root key must be pre-provisioned on the mobile device. The mobile device requests a certificate through the PKI portal, which passes the request to the CA after confirmation. Then the CA generates a user certificate and sends the URL or the full certificate to the client. The CA also adds an entry to its external database of listed certificates.

The users can now sign any transaction by using their signature, and point to a certificate URL for verification. Therefore, if an application server needs to confirm identity it sends a request to the CA database and receives a response concerning the validity of the signature.

In Figure 16-13, the handset is provisioned with a client private key or a signature that is used to sign challenges from the WTLS server. The steps shown in Figure 16-13 are described as follows:

1. The wireless handset (client) requests a certificate from the PKI portal.

2. PKI portal confirms the request and forwards it to the CA.

3. CA generates a client certificate and sends just the certificate URL to the client (alternatively if the handset has enough space, the full certificate can be sent).

4. The key is given to the handset.

5. A CA establishes an outside interface for certificates to be verified and provided (if only URL is given).

6. A user at the handset signs a document or sends a transaction, signature, and Certificate URL to the application server via the WAP gateway.

7. The application server then uses the Certificate URL to get it from the database if required.

8. The CA database then sends the certificate to the server. Both `signText` and WTLS Class 3 are implemented in the same manner when compared to the standard PKI (Public-Key Infrastructure): they simply require a signed signature to be delivered to the client. This can be done with at least two separate keys on the WAP client, one for `signText` and the other for WTLS. WTLS Class 3 communication can also be implemented end-to-end, as I describe in the next section on end-to-end security.

USING SERVER CERTIFICATES

In the first type of implementation of WPKI, you saw how a CA can sign the server certificates in real time. This is because server authentication in the wireless environment must be much more considerate of bandwidth, roundtrip transactions, memory footprint, and processor demands than in a landline environment. The traditional practice of constantly validating client trust points will not work here.

The servers may use short-lived certificates to alleviate problems in long-term validation. These certificates are typically only good for about 48 hours and are intended for use on a single day, with overlapping period server certificates for subsequent days.

Transport Layer End-to-End Security (TLe2e)

In the existing WAP architecture, the WAP gateway sits at the demarcation point of two different networks. On one side the WAP gateway uses SSL to ensure privacy, integrity, and authenticity in communication with the application server. On the other side, the WAP gateway uses WAP's WTLS protocol to once again ensure privacy, integrity, and authenticity. The main components of the WAP architecture may not be the only ones instituting a security feature. For example, some networks may have over-the-air encryption and/or additional integrity, privacy, and authenticity checks. The WAP architecture described in this paragraph along with potential weaknesses is shown in Figure 16-14.

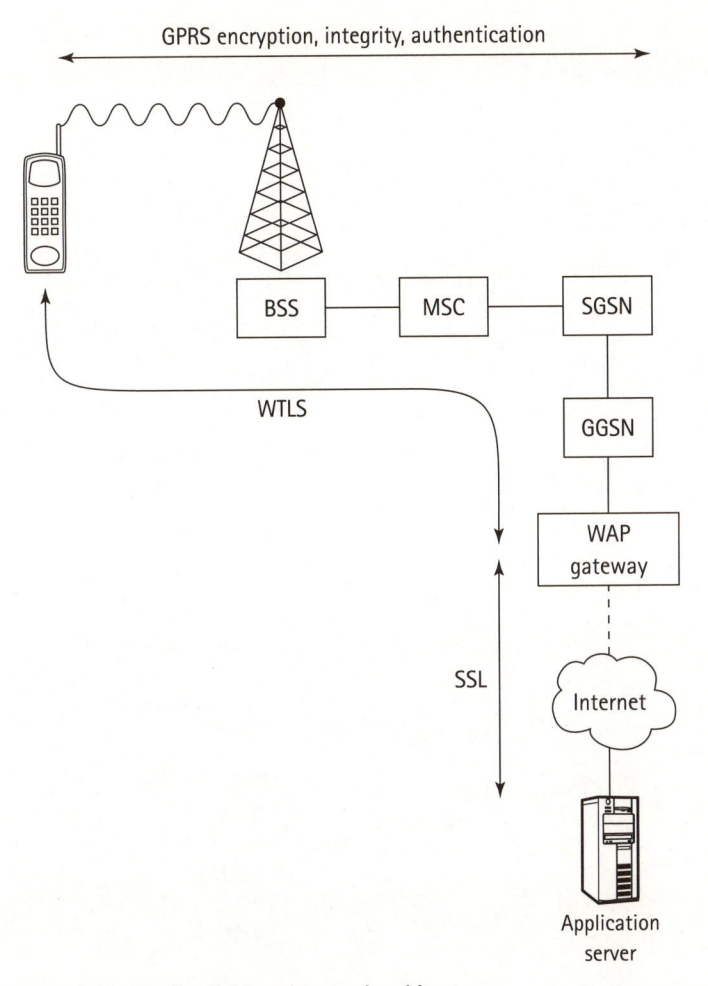

Figure 16-14: The WAP end-to-end architecture

One of the problems with the existing architecture is that messages sent using SSL on one side are then translated into WTLS on the other side and vice versa. The WAP gateway acts as a repository for secure information and has access to the data as it is being translated from one form to another. Because this requires the data to be deencrypted, changing formats, the data are insecure for a short period of time.

Although the transaction takes only milliseconds and may occur in memory on a single machine, the secure connection between a user and the application is broken. Because the WTLS protocol was devised to deal specifically with the limitations in bandwidth, memory, and latency of the wireless environment, it is difficult to argue for an end-to-end SSL solution.

Part V: Real-World Issues and WAP

But you can implement an end-to-end solution using WTLS. Figure 16-15 introduces the new architecture and the terms that describe it.

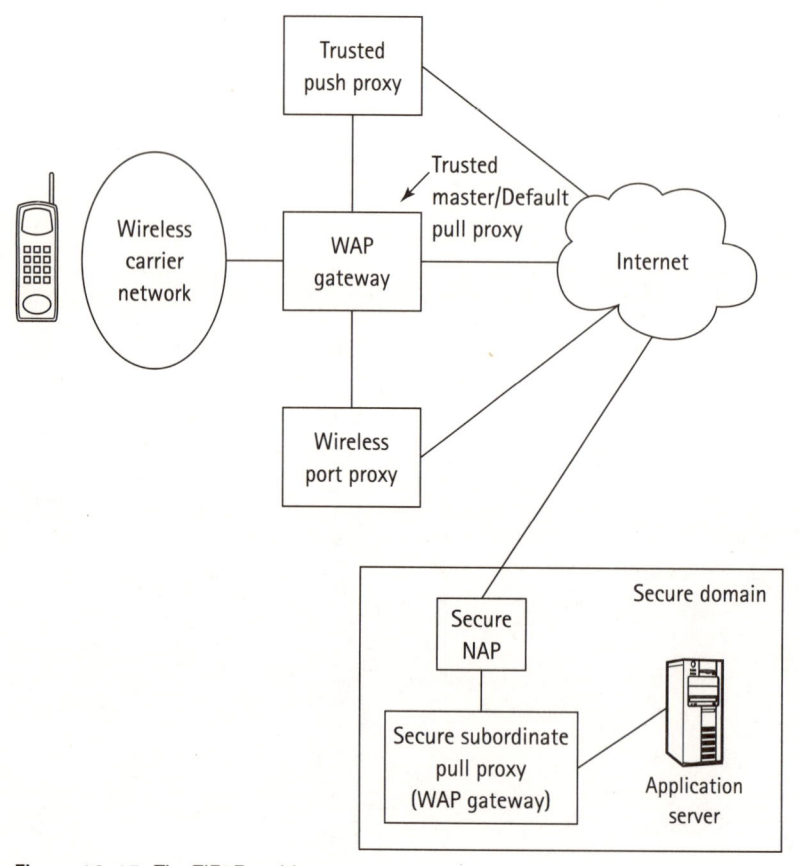

Figure 16-15: The TIE2E architecture

The diagram shows how there are two WAP gateways, one at the wireless network (the master pull proxy) and the other at the secure application server domain (the subordinate pull proxy). These WAP gateways are called proxies because they are intermediaries in a request/response transaction. The main point here is that a separate WAP gateway, which acts as a subordinate, can be purchased by the secure application service to implement end-to-end WTLS security.

With the new architecture, UDP traffic from the mobile device is sent directly to the subordinate pull proxy, bypassing the master pull proxy. WDP traffic has to be carried by a wireless port proxy and circuit traffic has to be established with a secure network-access point in the application-server domain.

Before discussing the nature of the end-to-end security, I'll introduce you to some basic assumptions.

First, because the WTLS connection is directly established between the handset and the subordinate pull proxy, the communication is private and its integrity preserved between those two entities.

Second, WTLS server authentication ensures that the subordinate pull proxy is indeed the intended valid secure party in the communication. Client authentication, however, is performed as needed with existing methodologies such as user-ID/password combinations or WTLS shared secrets.

Third, it is expected with this architecture that the client will handle nonrepudiation on its own.

And last, the architecture covers only end-to-end security for pull transactions. There is no provision for addressing messages that need to be pushed to the mobile device.

Figure 16-16 shows a sequence diagram for the components in the end-to-end architecture.

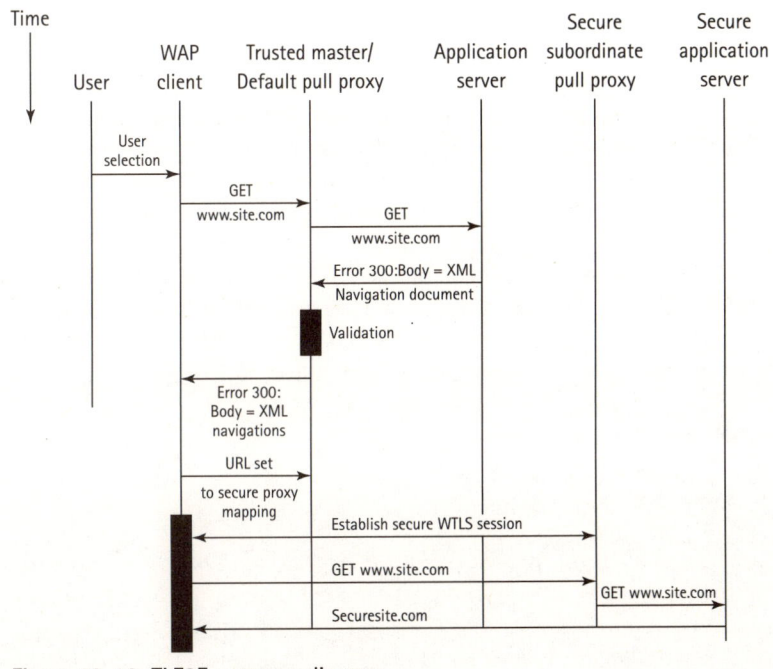

Figure 16-16: TLE2E sequence diagram

In this case, a user decides to navigate to a service that requires end-to-end security. The user is attempting to transfer some funds between accounts at a bank. When the original pull request is made, the master proxy requests the secure data from the Web server, which is refused with a specific XML navigation document and an `Error 300` message. This event is a trigger to the master proxy to send the navigation document back to the mobile device. The mobile device then establishes a secure WTLS session with the subordinate pull proxy and once again attempts to connect to the site. In order to prevent the master pull proxy from simply being bypassed forever, the architecture includes a TTL, which the bypass has to honor. After the time expires, requests to the service go through the master proxy first as before.

Application-level security

When transactions reach the application server or Web server, they are considered to be under the control of the organization. Techniques exist that a WAP developer can use to maintain control over transactional sensitive information. The techniques are just a miscellaneous set of practices that you can use to ensure that your site data or processes are not compromised.

USING WML VARIABLES

As I mentioned in Chapter 5, "Introducing WML," the browser handles WML variables quite differently from their HTML counterparts. WML variables have persistence and are global. This means that if someone enters a password or credit-card number into a WML input field that variable stays around in the memory of the phone. The variable can also be accessed by other applications if they happen to retrieve that variable. For example, if in my application I use the word "password" to designate a user password, another application that retrieved that variable could access that variable. Alternatively, you may access other applications' sensitive data if you use a common enough variable name.

In order to solve the problem of variable permanence, I recommend using a `setvar` element both for initially nulling the variables and then again for posting the data to the application server. In this way you ensure that the variables do not stay in the browser memory. Listing 16-1 shows how to clear these variables.

Listing 16-1: Clearing Out WML Variables

```
<?xml version="1.0"?>
<!DOCTYPE wml PUBLIC "-//WAPFORUM//DTD WML 1.1//EN"
 "http://www.wapforum.org/DTD/wml_1.1.xml">

<wml>

  <template>
    <!-- Template implementation here. -->
    <do type="prev"><prev/></do>
  </template>

  <card id="card1" title="CC Input Card">
    <!-- Clear out variables on application entry -->
```

```wml
        <onevent type="onenterforward">
            <refresh>
                <setvar name="cc" value=""/>
            </refresh>
        </onevent>

    <do type="unknown" label="Next">
        <go href="process_card.cgi">
            <postfield name="cc" value="$(cc)"/>
              <!-- Clear out variables on moving to another deck -->
            <setvar name="cc" value=""/>
        </go>
    </do>

        <p>Enter your credit card number:<br/>
            <input name="cc" format="*N"/>
    </p>
 </card>

</wml>
```

The first `setvar` element is placed in an `onevent` of type `onenterforward` so that when the deck is first presented any previous variables are cleared. The next `setvar` element is placed in the `go` element. While the data are being delivered to the back-end server, the statement clears out the `cc` variable. You should perform this process for any sensitive variables in your application.

USING THE WML SENDREFERER ATTRIBUTE

The `sendreferer` is an attribute of the `go` element, which causes the WML browser to attach a header to the request that contains the URL of the calling deck. The application server can then decide whether it wants to accept applications from that calling URL. The WAP gateway sets the HTTP request header named `HTTP_REFERER` to the calling URL. The `sendreferer` attribute takes a Boolean value of either `false` or `true` and because it is not a required attribute it is set to `false` if it is not being used. Here is an example wherein it is explicitly set:

```
<go href="http://www.wd-site.com/scripts/calc.asp"
sendreferer="true"/>
```

And then on the back end you could use something like this:

```
<%
dim URL_Source
URL_Source =Request.ServerVariables("HTTP_REFERER")
```

```
if Left(URL_Source,22) = "http://www.badsite.com" then
    'reject navigation
end
%>
```

One of the security problems presented by this routine is that it relies on the browser generating a proper `HTTP_REFERER`. This may not always happen, especially if on a compromised network a malicious middleman generates the headers. It is better to use the WML access element (discussed in the following section) because the headers can be manufactured.

USING THE WML ACCESS ELEMENT

Applications can use the `access` element to control which applications are allowed access to the current URL. By default all WML decks are public, which means that any other deck can access them. An application can add access control to the WML deck code, which limits access to the deck using heuristics specified by `access` element attributes. Here is the definition of the WML `access` element:

```
<!ELEMENT access EMPTY>
<!ATTLIST access
domain CDATA #IMPLIED
path CDATA #IMPLIED
%coreattrs;
>
```

The `access` element appears in the `head` element at the very start of the deck. As I mentioned earlier, if the `access` is missing the deck is assumed to be public. The `access` element has two important attributes, the domain and the path, which are described in Table 16-1.

TABLE 16-1 ACCESS ELEMENT ATTRIBUTES

Attribute	Description
domain=cdata	Specifies all domains that are allowed access to the current deck. The referring deck's domain must match the domain-name portion of the attribute value for it to be allowed access. The domain attribute is suffix-matched according to the full element of each component of the hostname. For example, `jelly.zs.com` matches domain `zs.com` but not domain `s.com`.

Attribute	Description
path=cdata	Specifies all paths that are allowed access to the current deck. The referring deck's URI must match the value of the attribute in order for navigation to be successful. The referring deck's path must match the path of the URI in a prefix-matching scheme according to the full element of each element in the path. For example, http://www.zs.com/a/b will match http://www.zs.com/a but not http://www.zs.com/and.

It is not necessary for both elements to exist in the code; if, for example, only domain matching is required, the domain can be the only attribute for the element. It is then assumed that any path is acceptable.

The other important point about this element is that the user agent controls the access. So even if this element is set, the compiled deck is delivered all the way to the mobile device. It is at that point that the browser compares the deck's access-element settings with those of the calling URL.

Figure 16-17 shows examples of the access element in action.

http://www.site.com/a/b/ca.wml

```
<wml>

</wml>
```

Deck #1

OK

http://www.site.com/a/b/c.wml

```
<wml>
<access path = "a/b"/>
</access>
</wml>
```

Deck #2

OK

```
<wml>
<access path = "a/b/d"/>
</access>
</wml>
```

Application error

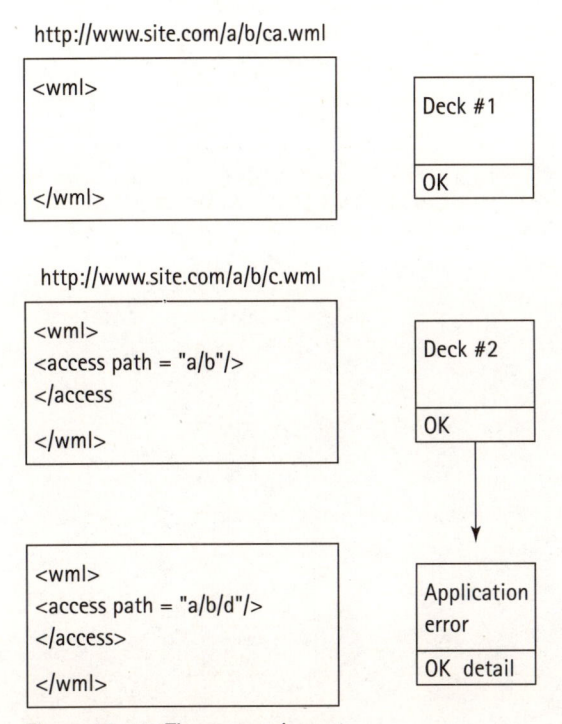

OK detail

Figure 16-17: The access element

You should note that the `domain` attribute is taken literally — any aliases it may have are not followed. So the domain `23.234.21.1` may point to `www.zs.com`, but even if `www.zs2.com` is aliased to the same IP address, its value will not be resolved by the browser. Instead, the value of the `domain` attribute will be taken literally.

> **XREF:** I discuss the issue of basic authentication by applications in Chapter 13, "Session Management and Identification," where you'll find examples of some implementations.

Summary

In this chapter, I introduced many of the basic security concepts you need to understand before designing a system, service, or network. Then I used the concepts to show how WAP security is similar to and different from Internet security.

I analyzed WAP architecture in detail, examining each component and its security attributes and techniques separately. Finally, I discussed how developers can use some security techniques in their application designs.

Next, I discuss some issues to watch for when tackling international WAP applications.

Chapter 17

Localization and Internationalization

IN THIS CHAPTER

- ◆ Understanding character sets and transfer encoding formats
- ◆ Building language level detection into WAP services
- ◆ Sidestepping tricky transcoding issues in International Applications

WAP IS AN INTERNATIONAL STANDARD, intended to work throughout the world with little modification. Any standard with such a purpose needs to solve two problems that application developers have when porting their applications to different regions of the world. The first problem is that of localization. In the process of localization, a program is modified so that people in a specific region can use it. For example, the metric system is the standard in continental Europe; it would therefore be a mistake to expect people there to understand American units. The second problem that international standards must solve is that of internationalization. In the process of internationalization, a content location is adapted to meet the needs of many regions simultaneously.

Making WAP Services Usable Internationally

The WAP standard is designed to support multiple languages and character sets. Most of the system is actually borrowed from existing Internet standards. The standard does not contain any specific attributes to aid in localization, other than allowing the content server to discover the region in which the querying client is located. This regional information can be used to provide localized information.

Images of Openwave products in this chapter courtesy of Openwave Systems Inc.

WAP in its early definition, specifically WAP 1.1, is invariably a request/response architecture, with the bulk of its content emanating from content servers. In this regard, the content server is largely responsible for properly structuring the data so that it is localized and enough hints are sent in its responses that data are properly displayable on the international wireless device. Playing a minimal role, the client wireless device has capabilities that it needs to advertise to the content server. Finally, a WAP gateway acts as a proxy in the channel, transcoding data for receipt by either the content server or the wireless device.

The problem of writing applications for a particular region of the world then can be simplified into two basic problems: the problem of localization and the problem of internationalization.

What is localization?

As I mentioned previously, localization is the modification of a program to make it usable for people in a specific region. For example, a WAP site may need to provide its users with output formatted in Celsius rather than in Fahrenheit. A localized version of the site would use the country or region querying for the information as an indicator of which version to present.

The goal of internationalization

The purpose of internationalization is to make a program independent of locale and fluid enough to support changes to its language or region without requiring a wholesale redesign of the entire software. This means that users in France can expect to see *oui* and *non* appear instead of *yes* and *no* without developers having to recode hundreds of hard-coded strings in the application.

The guidelines for internationalization are as follows:

- ◆ Abstract the locale dependencies and create one version of the application for all the languages and regions you have. This means putting items such as screen elements and messages in string files, not hard-coding them in the source code.

- ◆ Let the user dynamically switch among different locales. Although this capability is not a serious concern in the U.S., it is important in Europe, which contains many different countries within a small area.

- ◆ Make the UI layout allow for word expansion and contraction. A developer should be aware that longer or shorter words may be required to express the same ideas in a different language. For example, Japanese is a contracting language and German an expanding language when compared with English. In WAP, word choice in the soft-key labels becomes a critical factor, because it is by means of these labels that the users find out how to navigate the application.

Chapter 17: Localization and Internationalization 507

- Recognize that one character does not equal one byte for string sizes. Character sets around the world are not equal to ASCII. Different alphabets mean that new characters are introduced into the character sets, and that sometimes too many characters exist to be encapsulated in a single byte. Therefore, multibyte character sets, such as Big5 for China, need more storage space.

Before jumping into how to tackle the internationalization issues, I first go through a basic description of various elements that need to be understood. These elements are attributes of HTTP behavior and sometimes general computer architecture help define how computers and the WWW deal with the differences in languages, character sets, and local features. The basic attributes are character sets, transfer systems, rendering issues, and languages.

Character sets

A character set is a mapping for a relationship between a language character and a binary format in a computer. It provides absolutely no detail about how the information is to be shown on a screen; that information comes from the fonts. The most basic character set that developers are familiar with is the US-ASCII set, which maps seven bits of data to a character representation. The set includes the lowercase letters of the English alphabet, which are represented by the integers 74–108. The integers are represented in binary format by the computer. The most significant bit of this character set is always zero.

Other character sets are used although some have been deprecated. US-ASCII does not contain characters for some special German, Scandinavian, and romance languages in Europe, and definitely does not support the character sets of Japanese and Chinese languages. To compensate for this lack, the international standards organization created some other sets. The most popular of these other sets is the ISO series. These character sets range from ISO-8859-1 to ISO-8859-9. In these sets, the first seven bits are the same as those in US-ASCII. The most significant bit, if additionally used, represents a further 128 characters. Each of the nine sets has a different bunch of 128 characters.

Table 17-1 shows the different ISO-8859-x character sets and the languages they represent.

TABLE 17-1 ISO CHARACTER SETS AND LANGUAGES ADDRESSED

ISO Character Set	Languages Represented
ISO 8859-1	Covers most West European languages including but not limited to French, Spanish, Italian, English, German, and others

Continued

TABLE 17-1 ISO CHARACTER SETS AND LANGUAGES ADDRESSED *(Continued)*

ISO Character Set	Languages Represented
ISO 8859-2	Covers the languages of Central and Eastern Europe including Czech, Polish, Hungarian, Romanian, Croatian, Slovenian, Slovak, and Sorbian
ISO 8859-3	Covers Esperanto and Maltese; was used for Turkish before ISO 8859-9 came about
ISO 8859-4	Covers Estonian, Latvian, and Lithuanian, Greenlandic, and Lappish
ISO 8859-5	Introduces Cyrillic letters important for Bulgarian, Belyorussian, Russian, Serbian, Macedonian, and Ukranian (pre-1990)
ISO 8859-6	Cover letters for the basic Arabic alphabet but doesn't contain the four extra letters for Persian and the eight extra letters for Pakistani Urdu
ISO 8859-7	Covers letters required for modern Greek
ISO 8859-8	Covers letters required for modern Hebrew and Yiddish
ISO 8859-9	Covers letters required for Turkish
ISO 8859-10	Covers letters required for Greenlandic, Eskimo, and Nordic area specific languages such as Skolt Sami (Lappish)

Although the ISO-8859-*x* character sets enable programmers to include other characters used throughout the world, the sets are still not complete enough to handle every single language. A standard known as Unicode, which uses two bytes of memory to store each character, was proposed by the Unicode Consortium to solve the problem. Being able to use two bytes creates room for a total of 65,536 characters. Most software vendors, including Microsoft, Sun, and Oracle, have implemented Unicode into their code. The standard character sets from Unicode are the UCS (Universal Character Sets). Unicode uses the same first 128 characters as ISO-8859-1 and the same first 256 characters as ISO-8859-1. This makes things simpler in terms of backward compatibility.

Transfer systems

Although using the character set is good for representing character information, because in the computer it is an efficient format to map the information to binary format, it may not necessarily be the best way to send information over a network. The network may have limited bandwidth, for example. You can compensate for the limited environment by overloading a character set or by simply not using certain characters from a set.

In some cases, of course, the character set is the same as the transfer system, known as the transfer encoding. Often, however, it is completely different. For example, e-mail in the early days could not contain the nonprintable characters. The system used was base64, which essentially overloaded certain character combinations to create a six-bit transfer encoding. It used six bits to send seven bits of information.

The Unicode standard defines its own set of transfer encodings. There is UTF-16, which says that you must transmit the Unicode exactly as it is stored, using 16 bits or two bytes. However, transmitting two bytes every time is not very efficient, especially in cases in which many bits are not transmitting any useful characters. In order to compensate for this inefficiency, the Unicode standard defines an encoding wherein only the most frequently used 256 characters on the Web (beyond ASCII) are collected and combined with ASCII to form UTF-8.

UTF-8 is the default transfer encoding assumed by XML documents, WAP gateways, and a lot of software used for transmitting data on the Internet. If a character not in the smaller set must be sent in UTF-8, the full two-byte representation is used.

Although UTF-8 is the default transfer encoding, you can use others when necessary. For example, ISO-8859-1 provides excellent base romance-language support.

The HTTP protocol defines something known as the `charset` attribute in the headers. Although the name `charset` implies that it is a character set, the header actually defines a transfer encoding.

When you're developing WAP applications, it is important that you send the correct character set to the WAP handset. If the handset does not support the character set you send, displaying data on the device will be difficult. Characters that are not part of the character set appear simply as ? in the UP.Browser.

The issues are often complicated by the fact that the decision of which character set to send to the WAP phone may be being made in the background by your Web server or dynamic scripting language. Developers can either check the preferred encoding of the WAP browser and send the appropriate type, or let the WAP gateway take care of the problem. I'll discuss both techniques later in this chapter.

Rendering issues

Even though I have discussed character sets and encoding formats, one more software process remains that enables you to view different languages on phones or any other computer. A device may know what the character set is, but it actually needs to map that to a particular font on the phone if the data is to display correctly. This is known as rendering the data.

With a computer, getting that Arabic font loaded onto the system is relatively easy, but on phones, you are kind of stuck with what you get. Generally, if a character set is supported by a handset, a font probably exists that can handle the display portion.

Languages

The character sets, transfer encodings, and rendering issues have to do with the way in which different languages can be represented on the mobile display. No one-to-one correspondence necessarily exists; the English language, for example, can be represented by many different character sets. However, special character sets are better suited to certain languages. For example, it is a good idea to use ISO-8859-8 for Hebrew.

Language choice affects the type of terms used, the words, and even sometimes the way the text is written. For example, Arabic text is read from the right side of the page to the left side. Arabic also has complex rules related to how the characters look when next to each other. Sometimes the characters roll together and other times they just stand on their own. This is very unlike English, in which every character is standalone.

The language that the mobile handset prefers is found in the HTTP request header (`Accept-Language`) in a two-character primary-language abbreviation. This language tag may be followed by another two characters separated by a dash. These additional two characters specify the specific dialect of the language. For example, *it* represents Italian, and *it-va* represents Vatican Italian. *en* represents English, and *en-us* and *en-br* represent U.S. English and British English, respectively. The HTTP header typically contains a comma-delimited list of languages. Here is an example:

```
Accept-Language: en, en-br, fr
```

The preceding header shows that the preferred language is English, followed by British English and French, indicating that French is acceptable if that is all that is available on the application server.

Application Server Language Detection

When dealing with multiple languages, there are two important headers to consider: `Accept-Language` and `Content-Language`. The WAP application server can use the `Accept-Language` header to decide what type of language to serve up to the WAP browser.

In most cases this decision will be quite simple, because the WAP browser will support only one language that is put into this header. In other cases, the user may have ordered the supported languages by preference from the device.

Although WAP site designers can make a set of static files tied to language headers, it is easier to configure for a set of dynamic files, because in that case the request can be directed with real-time decision-making.

Chapter 17: Localization and Internationalization

The following is some ASP code showing the differences in how a deck is served up to a browser upon request, depending on whether the browser prefers German or English.

```
<%
dim language
language = Request.ServerVariables("HTTP_ACCEPT_LANGUAGE")
response.Buffer = true
%>

<?xml version="1.0"?>
<!DOCTYPE wml PUBLIC "-//PHONE.COM//DTD WML 1.1//EN"
                    "http://www.phone.com/dtd/wml11.dtd" >

<wml>
<card id="test">
<p>
<%
   if language ="de" then
     Response.ContentType = "text/vnd.wap.wml; charset=ISO-8859-1"
     response.AddHeader "Content-Language", language
     Response.Write("Wilkommen")
   else
     Response.ContentType = "text/vnd.wap.wml"
             response.AddHeader "Content-Language", "en"
     Response.Write("Welcome")
   end if
%>
</p>
</card>
</wml>
```

The language definition can be a little more precise: You can say that you want only a certain element to use the language definition. Each of the attributes language definition can be configured by using the xml:lang attribute. So one form of the preceding example could be written as:

```
<wml>
<card id="test" xml:lang="de">
<p>
Wilkommen
</p>
</card>
</wml>
```

The `xml:lang` attribute is a precise indicator of language preference that has higher precedence than the `Content-Language` header.

Transcoding

When the WAP gateway sends documents to the WAP browser, it uses a default character set, for other cases, it is important that you send to the WAP gateway a character set that has a chance of being rendered. Also, if the WAP browser sends some content to the Web server through the WAP gateway, it is best if it sends that content in a character set that your application server understands.

The default encoding format for the WAP browsers is UTF-8. You can determine this from the `Accept-Charset` request headers sent to your application server. An example of an `Accept-Charset` header is as follows:

```
Accept-charset: ISO-8859-2, *
```

Once again, the character sets are ranked by preference. The asterisk (*) at the end just means that any type can be sent if the first two are not available.

Say that you are writing an application for the Romanian market. You would need to change the `Content-Type` header to the following:

```
Content-type: text/vnd.wap.wml; charset=ISO-8859-2
```

The document could still be outputted in UTF-16 format: the WAP gateway would be responsible for converting the text from UTF-16 to ISO-8859-2. You will need to confirm that the WAP gateway supports the conversions you need. The WAP gateway process that takes care of this conversion is known as transcoding.

Here is an example of character-set manipulation. If you want to send the Spanish question *¿Que pasa?* to the phone, you need to ensure that the character set is correctly set to ISO-8859-1 so that the correct question marks will appear. Figure 17-1 shows a normal-text display of the data, and Figure 17-2 shows the correct version with the correct character-set representation.

The WML code is as follows:

```
<?xml version="1.0"?>
<!DOCTYPE wml PUBLIC "-//WAPFORUM//DTD WML 1.1//EN"
          "http://www.wapforum.org/DTD/wml_1.1.xml">

<wml>

    <card id="test">

        <p>
```

```
            &#191;Que Pasa?
        </p>
    </card>

</wml>
```

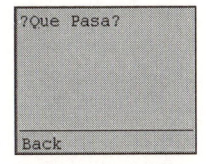

Figure 17-1: Spanish question with improper charset attribute

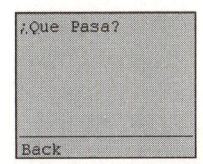

Figure 17-2: Spanish question with correct charset attribute

Charsets and postfields

It is important to note that when a WAP browser sends data inside HTTP GET requests, you must send it in US-ASCII. The HTTP specification declares that all the headers and command syntax must be sent in US-ASCII. To send data in another transfer encoding, I recommend that you use postfields to deliver the content to your application server. You can then modify the `Accept-Charset` attribute of the `go` element to get the proper effect. Here is an example:

```
<card id="example">
<do type="accept">
<go href="http://service.com/nav.asp" method="post"
        accept-charset="ISO-8859-1">
<postfield name="first" value="$(first)"/>
</go>
</do>
<p>
hit nav to go forward
</p>
</card>
```

With this set of code, the post data is sent with the following `Content-Type`:

`Content-type: application/x-www-form-urlencoded; charset=ISO-8859-1`

The data are packaged in the right transfer-encoding/character set.

Summary

In this chapter I have shown the three main issues that surround developing content for International WAP audiences. The first has to do with character support specifically in transfer encoding, the second with language-level detection, and the third with transcoding.

Character support and its associated issues in transfer encoding are important because they determine whether the WAP device is capable of showing the proper characters intended and whether the WAP gateway is able to send the appropriate characters to the WAP browser. I have shown how the character sets and encoding formats are to be defined in order to minimize problems.

Language-level detection is an important capability to include in WAP sites that serve audiences from different countries or language groups. The sample code in the chapter shows which headers are important to making the language distinctions and how the values can be used to make decisions on what WAP deck to return as a response.

The last issue discussed in the chapter is transcoding. This automatic feature of WAP gateways, which allows for translation of character sets on the fly, is explained. It is shown how services can modify the transcoding behavior in WML to obtain a desired effect.

Chapter 18

Location-Based Services

IN THIS CHAPTER

- ◆ Understanding location issues
- ◆ Obtaining the location
- ◆ Looking at location-based technologies
- ◆ Determining when services will be available
- ◆ Understanding the Openwave/SignalSoft system
- ◆ Looking at WAP location-based services

CELLULAR PHONES AND OTHER HANDHELD DEVICES are quickly becoming part of our everyday lives. You could argue that watches are the epitome of the personal appliance. They have an extremely simple user interface: pull the stem out all the way and rotate to set the time, and pull it out halfway and rotate to the set the date. The face of the watch shows the current time. These devices are simple to use, you can generally count on them to be accurate, and they are wearable. It is not surprising to see people wearing watches. Has society adjusted to people wearing phones on their belts? How about larger personal digital assistants (PDAs) on their belts or in their wallets? These devices are quickly becoming accepted as part of our personal space—something we carry around with us all the time. The FCC and other worldwide regulatory bodies have been instrumental in the movement to make devices such as cellular phones more prevalent. These bodies have been successful to the point that cellular-phone users rely on these devices for their safety and security.

An important part of ensuring safety and security involves calling an emergency service if there is trouble. Calls to emergency numbers have increased with the number of cellular subscribers, and as coverage is extended to more remote areas the chances that a user will not be familiar with his or her surroundings increase. Furthermore, it is difficult for emergency services to handle cases in which the user is only strong enough to press a button. The logical thing to do is to create a way to locate a cellular phone so that emergency services can quickly find the user.

In the United States, the FCC has mandated that cellular providers are to solve this problem. The legalese is laid out in the "e911 mandates." This stands for "Enhanced 911," where 911 is the North American emergency services telephone number. These wireless 911 rules seek both to improve the reliability of the North

American wireless 911 services and to provide enhanced features generally available for standard "wired" calls. You can see a full copy of these rules at `http://www.fcc.gov/e911/`. In Europe, Asia, South America, and Africa emergency services also exist, but cellular providers are not legally required to be able to determine a caller's location.

In the United States, the e911 mandates require cellular providers to build the infrastructure with little compensation. This means that carriers have to recover the costs of installation some other way. The cellular providers are expected to do this through some interfaces that provide location information for users other than the emergency services. It is well known that these interfaces will have to be differentiated so that no one's privacy is compromised. The providers have to solve technical problems as well: They have to decide what transport mechanisms are most effective for communicating with third parties and define how the information will travel over their networks without compromising the security and privacy of the users whose location is being disclosed. The WAP Forum's *Location Based Services Expert Group* has begun work on its definition of how these technologies are to be accommodated in the Group's architecture.

This chapter examines the technologies cellular providers and others use to obtain location information, and then moves on to some specific APIs that developers have access to. Finally, it examines how location-based services fit into the WAP architecture.

Understanding Location Issues

A location-based service can be described as any WAP or other application that relies on information about the physical location of a handset. Depending on which industry you are currently in, you may have different ideas about how the location information should be obtained; however, the culmination of the process results in a coordinate-based attribute that gives the location in the form of an x and a y. These represent latitude (x) and longitude (y). As a bonus, height may also be available to definitively pinpoint a location in our three-dimensional world.

Pinpointing place and time

If your location is known at any given time, that information can be stored for later use or used immediately by any application that can utilize the information. For example, applications incorporating global positioning systems (GPSes) have been designed in order to land planes without a pilot. Such an application needs a constant barrage of location updates if the plane is to land successfully.

This chapter examines the tradeoffs between real-time processing and storage of location data, but I don't think anyone will be landing a plane with a WAP application anytime soon. The closest WAP comes to real time would be a security application, wherein the service could be placed inside an asset, such as a VIP limousine, and be used to track the location of that asset in semi-real time.

Establishing proximity

It is difficult to say whether this constitutes its own category or a very specific type of location knowledge. Proximity refers to how close two entities are. It is easier to establish this information if both entities are controlled by the same authority. If this is the case, a single handset may obtain location information and then process that location information in real time in order to determine whether it is close to another handset. As you can imagine, constantly maintaining the proximity of millions of handsets is a nightmare, and so the criteria by which carriers decide which handsets to monitor are important. For example, two handsets might be subscribed to a dating service. The handsets are then monitored for proximity and an alarm goes off when they are within a certain distance of each other.

You can also extrapolate or apply a logical sequence to the location data being received in real time. For example, processing may reveal the current speed of a target, or whether the target has passed a certain point — for example, whether a rental car is being driven into Mexico.

Determining the uses of the service

A distinction must be drawn between the act of physically obtaining a location, and actually using the information to provide some additional value. An example of providing additional value could be that the location information is stored in a database, allowing queries to be run on it at a later time. The raw information needs to be collected first (I discuss the technologies in this chapter). Then the raw information must be processed.

A location-based service could use location information to:

- Find the nearest business in a given industry (the handset location is compared to another database of businesses, this could be nearest exit, nearest McDonald's, nearest health club, nearest bar, nearest subway station, and so on).

- Determine whether a person or an asset (child, truck, car, limousine) is outside or inside a restricted area (the handset location is constantly compared to a perimeter).

- Find the location of a person or an asset (the handset location must be processed and sent to the requestor in a known format).

- Pass the location information to the nearest emergency facility (the handset location must be processed and sent to the facility in a known format).

Obtaining the Location

To obtain the precise location of something, whether it is a handset, you, a ship, a plane, or a dogsled, you have to be able to know where it is in relation to an already known fixed reference point. This is why in ancient Egypt, where triremes were used to fish and explore, the small ships never strayed far from the coastline. They used known landmarks as a reference. The same techniques were used to traverse the desert: early Bedouins used the marks of previous caravans, invisible to the average person, and known oases to keep themselves oriented.

In Columbus's, Vasco de Gama's, Raleigh's, and Vespucci's days the important guides were the stars and the sextant. The location of constellations in the night sky enabled sailors to determine their location at sea.

The modern equivalent of these ancient navigational systems is the GPS (global positioning system). This is a constellation of satellites in orbit around the earth to help the U.S. military keep track of assets and the delivery of munitions to their targets. A comparable Russian system (GLONASS) does effectively the same thing. The GPS system has been very successfully applied to civilian applications and is in widespread use today. I describe how it works later in the section on GPS assisted methods.

Lastly, it has become feasible with today's electronics to keep track of mobile handsets and their locations using just the cellular or PCS infrastructure. These tracking systems are made possible by the move to newer digital technologies that require better knowledge of the mobile's location in relation to the antenna towers. The towers are at fixed locations and the relative distance from them determines the mobile's location.

Each of these types of reference points has a problem. The most common failing of any of these systems is that it is possible to lose contact with the fixed reference point. For example, a trireme that went too far out to sea, lost sight of the landmarks on the coast. Ships at sea have no contact with fixed towers because none are out there. On a cloudy night, sailors cannot use the constellations to find their way, and a GPS satellite may not be visible to determine one's position in an underground parking garage.

FCC requirements and other market proponents

Although you can discover the location of handsets, doing so has only recently been made a priority for cellular and PCS carriers in the U.S. This is mostly because the FCC, the body that governs the use of the cellular and PCS spectrum, has only recently required that the carriers be able to obtain this location information.

As the years have passed, penetration of cellular and PCS services has become quite high. Today it is at a point where a large percentage of calls to emergency services in North America come from cell phones. Callers sometimes have as poor an idea of their locations as the emergency workers. In extreme scenarios emergency-service workers have worked closely with cellular companies to obtain information on handset location. For example, in one case, a woman was stranded by a snowstorm on a rural route, with no link to the outside world but her cell phone. Her location could not be determined for two days. Eventually, when they found her, it was only through some estimation of her location by means of triangulation with the closest base-station antennae. However, this solution does not scale very well. So a proposed remedy to the problem was that for any call to an emergency service in North America, the carrier must know the location of the handset to within a certain distance. The American FCC made this ruling; handsets must begin to be enabled by October 1, 2001. All handsets should be enabled by 2004 at the very latest.

Although this ruling was a win for the consumer, it was not such a win for the carriers' checkbooks. The FCC did not fund the system in any way. This means that the carriers had to come up with the money for the expensive equipment required to establish location. One of the better ideas they came up with was to sell location information to application developers looking to enhance their applications' effectiveness. The WAP applications could certainly be made more effective because WAP devices are very hard for the user to enter text into. Any automatic action, such as the determination of the user's location, is therefore very desirable.

Other location-services sponsors

In Europe the situation is a little more lax, because there is no deadline for providing location-based information. Emergency services are provided with that information but the government largely funds the emergency services system. The work is not done on speculation. This means that the European operators have some leeway when deciding how accurate the provided location information is. Some may accept that providing the cell area is specific enough.

In those cases in which the carriers can provide location-specific information, this facility is added to the carrier or operator portfolio of services to differentiate themselves from others in the marketplace. In these cases, cellular carriers can also charge users differently based on their habits. For example, if a user stays within a 60-mile radius for the entire month, he or she may pay less than someone who travels a lot.

Furthermore, there may be cases in which location information is given to others to create more valuable services. Imagine an earth moving-equipment rental company that wants to keep track of all its assets. It can form some agreement with the carrier, but the carrier would look to the rental company dollars funding a portion of its investment into providing the services.

Location-Based Technologies

Although some proprietary location-based systems exist, the FCC has pushed for a standardized system to be developed so that their development is not closed and so that the innovation can further galvanize the markets. An example of a proprietary system is *LoJack*, which is used in the U.S. to track stolen vehicles and trailers. It involves a very high frequency transmitter placed inside the vehicle. If a vehicle is reported stolen, a signal is sent to the LoJack unit so that it can begin to transmit a signal. Police equipped with a tracking computer can then find the vehicle by tracking that signal. The tracking computers are all connected nationwide through the LoJack network.

However, it is unlikely that a system requiring such specialized technology will see widespread use outside the law-enforcement market. For that purpose, organizations turn to standards-based systems. Following are a few of those. Because this is a book about WAP, the focus here is on how WAP-enabled handsets determine location.

Because mobile handsets are already on a cellular network, it makes sense to leverage the existing investments in infrastructure as much as possible. Furthermore, the newer digital networks already require the handset to show some relative location information in order for the software to manage handoffs to adjacent cells. Therefore, some techniques proposed by the carriers are network-based, and rely on the relative location of towers and signaling, and others rely on standard technology like GPS.

The FCC in the U.S. keeps the choice of technologies to be used for their regulation "e911" open. The only criterion is the one associated with the difference between network-based determination and handset-based determination, which was meant to distinguish GPS-assisted technologies from their cellular network-based counterparts. The next sections provide a brief description of each type of location-based technology and its inner workings. These types are the following:

- Time Difference of Arrival (TDOA)
- Enhanced Observed Time Difference (EOTD)
- Assisted GPS methods

TDOA (Time Difference of Arrival)

With this method, the network measures the time it takes for signals from the handset to appear at the towers. The time is then measured by three or more of the towers or base stations. This time can then be converted into distance by using the speed-time-distance relationship. Remember from Chapter 2 that the speed of electromagnetic waves is the speed of light. Therefore, if the tower knows how long the signal took to get there, it can determine how far away the mobile handset is. If three or more towers can determine this information, circles of fixed radii can be drawn around the towers. The intersection of these circles will be the location of the handset. This can be done in GSM, for example, because a handset is required to monitor three base stations during a handover. Therefore, if a handover is faked, the information that results determines location. Figure 18-1 shows how TDOA works. This system has the disadvantage that it works only when a call is in progress: hence the need for handover.

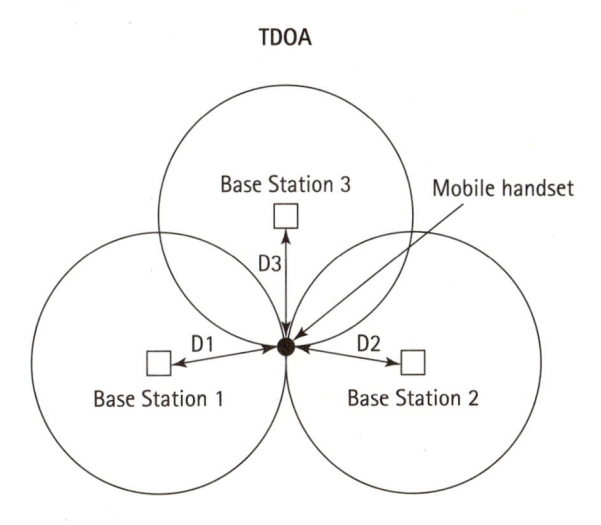

TDOA

Base Station 3
Mobile handset
D3
D1
D2
Base Station 1
Base Station 2

D1 = Distance 1
D2 = Distance 2
D3 = Distance 3

Figure 18-1: TDOA architecture

E-OTD (Enhanced Observed Time Difference)

In this system, the handsets have synchronized clocks. The base station looks at the difference between the time the message was sent, to the time it was delivered to at least two different towers, or antennae. The differences in time determine the proximity of the two handsets. These times are used to plot out lines of constant difference, which can be represented by two hyperbolas. The intersection of the hyperbolas is the location of the mobile handset. Because this method requires an accurate clock in each of the handsets involved, clocks that are also synchronized with the base station, it may require physical changes or upgrades to the network and handsets. Figure 18-2 shows how the technology works.

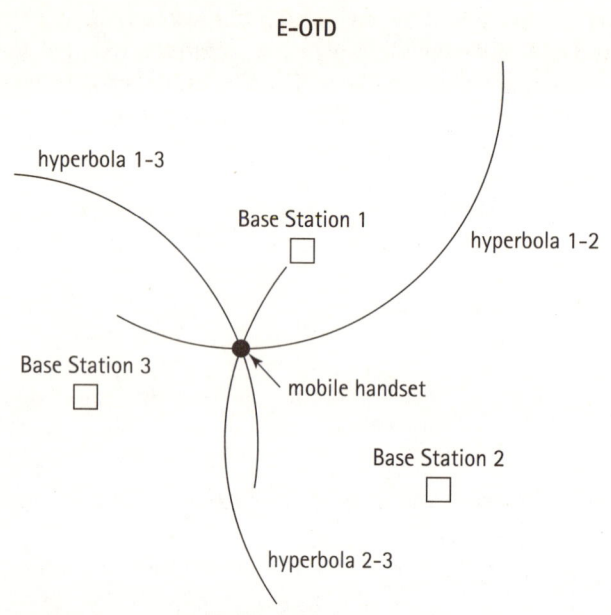

Figure 18-2: E-OTD architecture

Assisted GPS methods

GPS is an example of a technology that uses moving reference points: the satellites in elliptical orbit around the Earth. The nominal GPS Operational Constellation consists of 24 satellites that orbit the earth in 12 hours. There are often more than 24 operational satellites, as new ones are launched to replace older satellites. The orbit altitude is such that the satellites repeat the same track and configuration over any point approximately each 24 hours (four minutes earlier each day). There are six orbital planes (with nominally four satellites in each), equally spaced (60 degrees apart), and inclined at about 55 degrees with respect to the equatorial plane. This constellation provides the user with between five and eight satellites visible from any point on the earth at any moment in time. The GPS receiver uses the time it takes for radio waves to be received from a minimum of four of the satellites. The system relies on a very accurate clock within each satellite to determine the time lag among the different radio paths to the receiver.

Receivers on Earth can triangulate the measurements from three satellites in orbit around the Earth. However, if a fourth satellite is utilized, time corrections can be made with the assistance of some geometric equations. This not only gives a high positional accuracy but also effectively makes each receiver an atomic accuracy clock.

The distances involved are calculated as follows: The satellites transmit what are known as *pseudo-random codes* to Earth. Each satellite has its own unique pseudo-random code. (They are called "pseudo-random" codes because they are intentionally made complex in order to avoid accidental duplication with a signal from any other source.) These codes are sent so that each receiver can synchronize itself with a particular sequence, the time delay between the satellites signal and the receiver's signal giving the exact distance from that satellite to the receiver. After the receiver obtains signals from four satellites, the distances are put in a mathematical equation, which then determines the precise location of the receiver.

Problems exist with GPS signals, however: they may be subject to time delay in the upper atmosphere, or their signals may be delayed intentionally by the military (the purpose being to prevent military use by an enemy against possible targets in the United States), or the clocks on the satellites may be a little off. To counteract these problems, differential GPS is used. With differential GPS, a GPS receiver is attached to a fixed tower. The fixed tower monitors GPS-related signals and stores the corrections for signals reaching it. Any GPS receiver in the vicinity of the tower can receive corrected timing information for each satellite and accurately determine its position to within a couple of yards, or meters. In the mobile world, a system in which a GPS receiver is in the handset, and data is being sent to the cellular network for correction using differential GPS is known as "Assisted GPS."

Other systems

Not all technologies have the limitations of GPS or require such expensive upgrades. It is certainly possible with today's digital systems to ascertain the cell location ID of a handset. This will be a rough area and will certainly not be enough for emergency services purposes, but may be enough for location-based services — for example, for locating nearby businesses.

When Will Services Be Available?

Currently, many factors are restricting the growth of the location-based services market. The situation is the clearest in the United States, where the FCC has pushed carriers to start deploying the services. Even there, the quality of information available to other location-based services may be lower initially than the quality of information available to the emergency services for regulation e911.

In Europe, some uncertainty exists as to how the governments will deal with location services. Some even have suggested that location services present a privacy problem. Laws exist in some European countries that prevent a person's location from being available at all.

European carriers also have to justify additional costs for location services so that the large infrastructure costs can be covered. The additional costs may mean no competitive pressure to actually do anything on location services.

Carriers are upgrading their networks and technologies from 2G to 2.5G and 3G. The addition of location services presents a distraction from adding these high-bandwidth upgrades that may be more justifiable.

Finally, location-services technology is still expensive. It may be cheaper for the carriers to wait a year to make the addition of location services until better and faster technologies come along.

The emergency services-e911-market in the United States is dominated by a single player, SignalSoft. SignalSoft has a gateway product that collects actual location information from multiple technologies and puts it into one database. The information can then be accessed by the e911 services that need it. The system has been extended to provide location-based services and Openwave has teamed up with SignalSoft to provide location information in a WAP-compatible format.

The Openwave/SignalSoft System

As I mention earlier, SignalSoft is the dominant vendor of the "e911" services in the United States market. Openwave has collaborated with SignalSoft to provide WAP compatibility with the SignalSoft Wireless Location Server (WLS).

Figure 18-3 shows the architecture of their system.

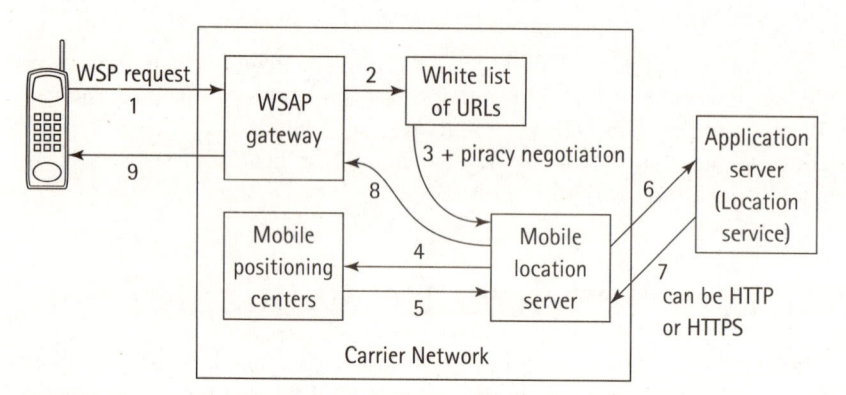

Figure 18-3: Openwave/SignalSoft system architecture

This architecture provides something known as the MLS or Mobile Location Server, which is the same thing as a WLS or Wireless Location Server. It is responsible for collecting location information from multiple sources in the carrier network and storing it. The MLS obtains location information from MPCs or Mobile Positioning Centers, which are spread throughout the carrier network. Position information can be pushed to the MLS and stored there or it MLS can request it. Therefore, if a WAP application needs location information for a handset for which the MLS has no data, a new query has to be executed.

The first step in using the system is to enable the location details. The Openwave architecture supports location information only if your URL has already been registered with the MLS. The URL does not have to be the full URL of the special deck that needs the location information, just a generic URL for the WAP services on your site. When you register your URL you will have to decide what type of information you need. The following options are available to you:

- Latitude
- Longitude
- City
- State/province
- ZIP/Postal code
- Country

You will not be able to change the information you get dynamically; you will only be able to make changes during registration. You can simulate a location information services addition by setting your own URL in the UP.SDK just as a carrier would: go to Location → Set Access List → Add.

Just because you are registered does not necessarily mean that you will get location information. Sometimes the location information is not available, and other times the user may have requested that his or her location not be given out. There are three possibilities at this point:

- The carrier is required by law to give out the location information. This is typically done for emergency services, and it is rare for a developer to get this type of access.
- The user decides that the service can always distribute his or her location.
- With every request for location information, the user is presented with a screen asking for permission to distribute his or her location.

A developer does not have to deal with this privacy issue, but needs to be aware that it exists.

For any URL on the carrier list, the MLS will have determined the privacy policy as one of the previous options. It sends the location information to the WAP service by attaching a GML document to the headers of the request. The Geography Markup Language (GML) is an XML encoding for the transport and storage of geographic information, including both the geometry and properties of geographic features. Information about the GML standard can be found at http://www.opengis.org/techno/specs.htm.

The location information is indicated by one of two headers. They are as follows:

- X-UP-LocDocType: GML
- X-UP-LocDoc: the GML document name

The first header indicates the format type for the location data. (Openwave supports only GML at this point.) The second header contains the document itself. You can actually simulate this second header in the UP.SDK. If you go to Location → Set Location, you will see a dialog box in which you can specify a location. The next tab will enable you to choose as your preferred testing location one of the locations you previously defined.

Listing 18-1 shows an example location from the GML system.

Listing 18-1: Example Location Document Code

```
<?xml version="1.0" encoding="UTF-8"?>
<!DOCTYPE Feature SYSTEM "gmlfeature.dtd">
<Feature typeName="Location">
<property typeName="errorShape">
ellipse
</property>
<property typeName="errorUnit">
meter
</property>
<property typeName="errorMajor">
30
</property>
<property typeName="errorMinor">
20
</property>
<geometricProperty typeName="position">
<Point srsName="EPSG:2233">
<coordinates>
45.110000,49.210000
</coordinates>
</Point>
</geometricProperty>
</Feature>
```

The ASP code in Listing 18-2 shows how the location information could be retrieved from the HTTP headers. This example uses the Microsoft XML parser; however, any other parser you have should be suitable for the task.

Listing 18-2: Code Sample Showing Location Retrieval

```
<%

Sub Main

    Dim entireStr
```

Chapter 18: Location-Based Services 527

```
   Dim GMLDoc, loadStatus
   Dim fullnodeListing, node, pointNode, coordNode
   Dim errShape, errunit, errmajor, errminor
   Dim dumpLoc


   ' Pull the location information from the header and store in a
string

   entireStr = Request.ServerVariables("HTTP_X-UP-LocDoc")

   ' Set up the Microsoft XML parser object

   Set GMLDoc = Server.CreateObject("Microsoft.XMLDOM")
   GMLDoc.async = False

   ' Toss the XML version and DOCTYPE lines

   index = instr(1,entireStr, "<Feature",1)
   rootElement = right(entireStr, len(entireStr) - index +1)

   ' Parse the GML data

   loadStatus = XMLDoc.loadXML(rootElement)

   ' Check if the parsing failed

   If loadStatus = False Then
                    'FAILURE
      Exit Sub
   End If


   ' get all the name and value pairs

   Set fullNodeListing = XMLDoc.getElementsByTagName("property")

   ' Add the name and value pairs to a full data dump for the
property stuff

   For i=0 To (fullNodeListing.length -1)
     Set node = fullNodeListing.item(i)
     dumpLoc = dumpLoc &
node.attributes.getNamedItem("typeName").nodeValue _
```

Continued

Listing 18-2 *(Continued)*

```
      & "=" & node.text & "<br/>" & nl
Next


' Same deal, this time for the <geometricProperty> stuff

Set fullNodeListing =
XMLDoc.getElementsByTagName("geometricProperty")
  If fullNodeListing.length > 0 Then
    Set pointNode = fullNodeListing.item(0)
    Set coordNode = pointNode.childNodes.item(0)
    dumpLoc = dumpLoc & "Coordinates = " & coordNode.text & nl
  End If
```

WAP Location-Based Services

The WAP location-based services standard is currently only in draft format, so the information in this section may soon become outdated. The standard defines four categories, which specify the different ways in which the location information in WAP is passed on to the application server.

Figure 18-4 shows the architecture related to the structure of location based-services.

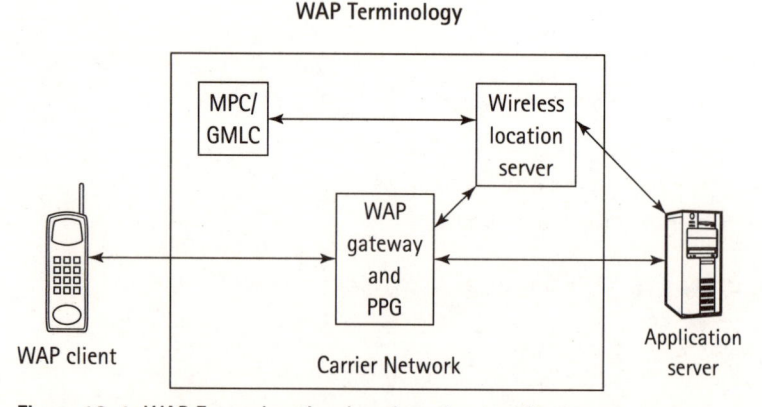

Figure 18-4: WAP Forum location-based services architecture

A Mobile Positioning Center (MPC) refers to a centralized point for collecting a specific location-service technology within the carrier network. However, multiple technologies may be used within a single network and that collective information may be found in a wireless location server (WLS). The WLS is quite likely to have Geographic Information System (GIS) capability as well. The WLS collects location-services information from multiple technologies and multiple points within the carrier network and to integrate it with some GIS system.

The WLS can be either inside or outside the wireless network, depending on how much post-processing work is required. The WAP gateway has to be aware of the fact that the WLS may not be within the carrier's control.

In the most usual case, the WAP client will not have a previous arrangement with the carrier and the request-response flow of the location request will be as shown in Figure 18-5.

WAP Scenario 1

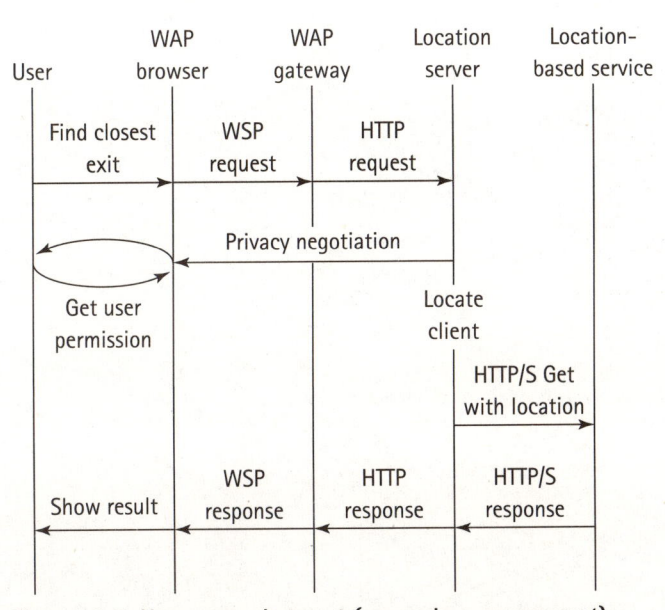

Figure 18-5: Usage scenario type 1 (no previous arrangement)

Another possible scenario, shown in Figure 18-6, is one in which the location service does have a previous arrangement with the carrier.

WAP Scenario 2

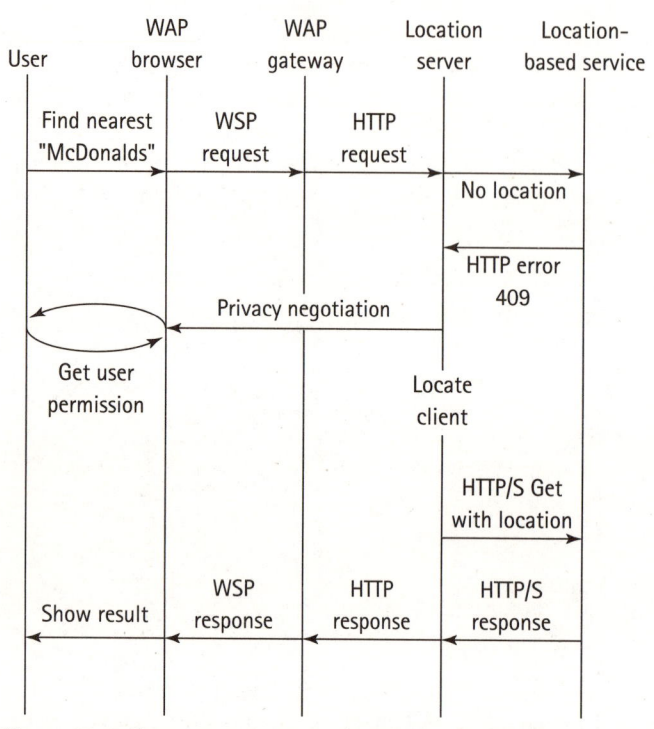

```
User          WAP         WAP         Location    Location-
              browser     gateway     server      based service

Find nearest  WSP         HTTP
"McDonalds"   request     request
                                      No location

                                      HTTP error
                                      409
              Privacy negotiation
Get user
permission                            Locate
                                      client

                                      HTTP/S Get
                                      with location

Show result   WSP         HTTP        HTTP/S
              response    response    response
```

Figure 18-6: Usage scenario type 2 (previous arrangement)

A different type of application that is server-specific may require that the server initiate the application (see Figure 18-7).

WAP Scenario 3

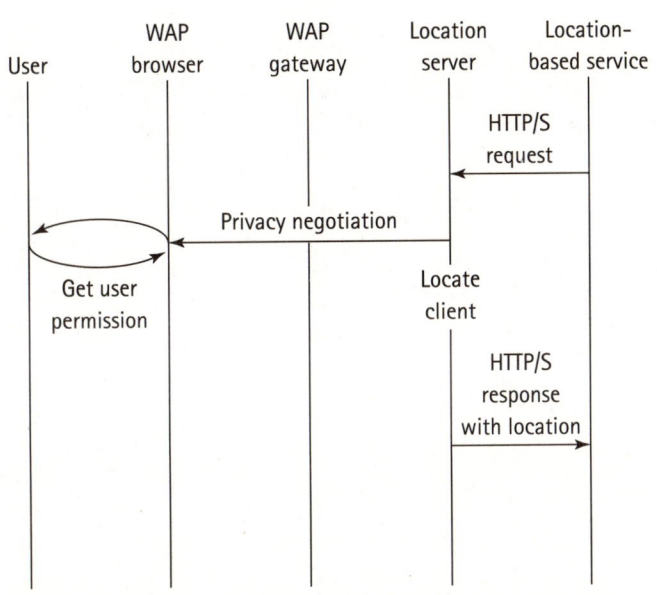

```
User      WAP        WAP       Location    Location-
          browser    gateway   server      based service
  |         |          |         |           |
  |         |          |         |  HTTP/S   |
  |         |          |         |<─request──|
  |         |          |         |           |
  |         |          |<─Privacy negotiation─|
  |         |          |         |           |
  |<─Get user          |       Locate        |
  |  permission        |       client        |
  |         |          |         |           |
  |         |          |         |  HTTP/S   |
  |         |          |         |  response |
  |         |          |         |──with─────>|
  |         |          |         |  location |
```

Figure 18-7: Usage scenario type 3 (application-server initiated)

In the final case, shown in Figure 18-8, an application may be originated completely from the client. In this scenario, the back-end application server is never even contacted.

WAP Scenario 4

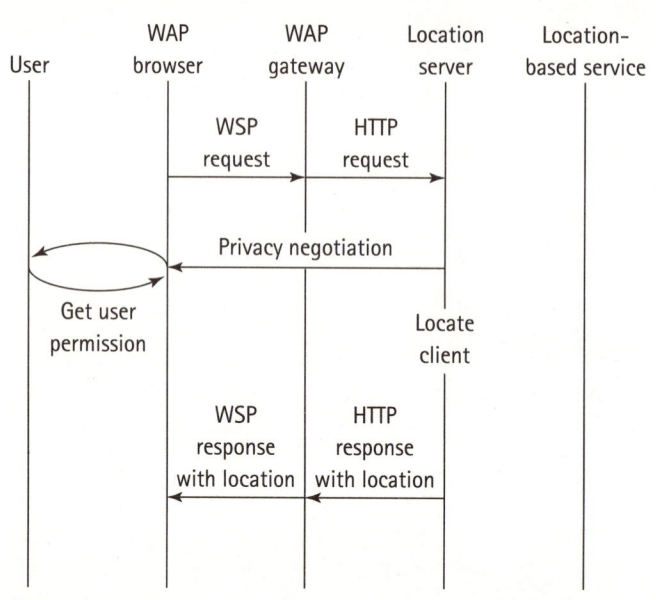

```
User      WAP        WAP       Location    Location-
          browser    gateway   server      based service
           |          |          |           |
           |  WSP     |  HTTP    |           |
           | request  | request  |           |
           |--------->|--------->|           |
           |          |          |           |
           |    Privacy negotiation          |
           |<------------------->|           |
  ⟲ Get user                     |           |
    permission                   | Locate    |
                                 | client    |
                                 |           |
           |  WSP     |  HTTP    |           |
           | response | response |           |
           | with     | with     |           |
           | location | location |           |
           |<---------|<---------|           |
```

Figure 18-8: Usage scenario type 4 (application not on server)

Summary

This chapter introduced you to the different technologies used to determine position information. It described their operation and discussed when they will become available in the U.S. marketplace. Then the chapter described how the technologies are applied to WAP, first in a proprietary system from Openwave and then in the methodology intended by WAP. Any discussion of WAP systems was purely speculative; no approved specification for location-based services is yet available from the WAP Forum.

Chapter 19

Deploying WAP Services

IN THIS CHAPTER

- Choosing a WAP SDK, WAP browser, WAP gateway, and WAP architecture
- Understanding conversion, compiling, and encoding/decoding overheads
- Dealing with latency issues
- Working with WAP application servers
- Controlling a Web server

IN THIS CHAPTER I ADDRESS some issues you will have when you start to deploy your applications onto real Web servers, run them through real WAP gateways, and see how they look on real mobile devices. It is important to test your service as soon as possible on real devices because this enables you to make corrections early in your development cycle.

However, transporting the service is not nearly as simple as it may look in an Internet-based browser. You must watch out for many problems, and handle the architectural issues almost on a case-by-case basis. In this chapter, I provide a systematic methodology for addressing deployment issues for services entering the carrier or service space.

Understanding Deployment Issues

At the time of writing, the WAP browsers found in mobile devices are still under development. A classic case in point is the Nokia 7110 mobile phone. Although the phone itself has physically remained the same in appearance, the micro-browser incorporated in this model has been upgraded as time has gone by. At last count, 22 versions of the Nokia WAP browser were released in this one model of mobile phone alone.

If you take into consideration the total number of models of mobile phones and PDAs that have now been released, each with their own individual characteristics and versions of WAP browsers, you will see the scope of the problem that you as a developer have to face when tackling deployment of your service or application.

Choosing your tool: WAP software development kits (SDKs)

The main SDKs for WAP development are the Nokia WAP Toolkit, the WAP Ericsson IDE, and Openwave's SDK. There are also Motorola's "MobileADK" for the Motorola mobile devices, and Speedware's "MobileDev," which is not manufacturer specific and can be used to develop services across multiple browser platforms. The term SDK encompasses a broad range of products, and some manufacturers produce relatively simple device simulators. Others build advanced IDEs and yet others provide only a set of APIs. The only SDKs I discuss here are those that are in relatively wide use and for which the vendor is actually making a good-faith effort to create a simulation of how its code would perform on a real device.

In many cases a developer does not have access to real devices and real service. This may be because the development cycle is only in the early prototype stage, because of lack of proper initial funding, or simply because the phone or service has not been released. In these cases it is necessary to test the application in desktop-based WAP browsers. Although many WAP browsers, with varying levels of creator commitment, are available in the marketplace, it is recommended that you test your application on the simulator made by the software vendor whose browser is in the real WAP phone. I have identified five main browsers that you should test your application on. These five (see Table 19-1) correspond to the phone browsers with the largest market share. It is especially important to test on simulators for these high-market-share, or "superclass" devices when building for the mass market.

TABLE 19-1 SUPERCLASS SIMULATORS

SDK	Browser	Vendor	URL
UP.SDK 4.1	UP.Browser	Openwave	http://www.openwave.com
Nokia WAP Toolkit 2.1	Nokia	Nokia	http://www.nokia.com
Ericsson WAP IDE	Ericsson	Ericsson	http://www.ericsson.com
Microsoft Mobile Emulator	MME	Microsoft	http://www.benefon.com
Neomar	Neomar	Neomar	http://neomar.com

Choosing your browser

You will recall from the earlier chapter on WAP architecture that the WAP browser itself is a piece of software that resides on the phone. It implements the features of the WAP stack, which allows the mobile device to communicate with the WAP gateway. A browser is built into the phone, PDA, or other mobile device.

The introduction of the browser is a phone-design decision with implications for the memory, screen size, and the physical keys of the device. A phone may also be manufactured by licensing a third-party browser. For some examples, the Ericsson 280 LX in the U.S. market uses an Openwave browser, and the Nokia 7160, which in Europe carries the proprietary Nokia browser, was released in the U.S. with an Openwave browser. None of the different browsers is required to conform to a single standard with regard to how the presentation format is displayed. This is very similar to the disparity with which an HTML Web page is interpreted between Netscape and Microsoft Internet browsers for PCs.

Choosing your gateway

As I discuss in Chapter 4, "Introduction to WAP," a WAP gateway sits in the middle of the request/response transactions of a WAP client and an application server. It manipulates traffic between the mobile and Internet domains. So do you need a WAP gateway? Not to run a WAP service, because the common scenario is one in which the carrier or service operator does this.

WAP gateways vary widely in terms of the functionality they support, but three main grades of WAP gateway have emerged in the marketplace. These are the following:

- Development-type
- Enterprise
- Carrier-grade

These different gateways have diverse properties regarding their

- Deployment
- Cost
- WAP-bearer support
- Non-WAP–bearer support
- WAP standards compliance
- Hardware
- Billing
- Applications

THE DEVELOPMENT GATEWAY

The development gateway is generally the weakest category. These gateways support only IP as a bearer and are not constructed to handle a large volume of traffic as a "live" service to the general public. The gateways in this category are cheap.

Developers should purchase these gateways only if they, during their testing, would like to have access to WAP gateway logs, need a guaranteed uptime schedule, and want a carefully controlled gateway environment with known bandwidth and processor-resource levels.

THE ENTERPRISE GATEWAY

The second category of gateways is the enterprise grade. These gateways are meant for enterprises with the resources to run their own 24x7 gateways. Although the enterprises may need to be online 24 hours a day, 7 days a week, this type of gateway does not support as many bearers — once again, usually only IP. They do not necessarily come with a built-in billing engine and the cost is in the medium range. Because they are considered production-grade, their scalability, the ability to administer them remotely, and the ease of configuration and maintenance are better than with the developer grade.

THE CARRIER GATEWAY

The third category of WAP gateways is the carrier/operator grade. These gateways are the most expensive and require the most robust software, because many customers are dependent on their uptime. The gateways in this category support many bearers, and have interfaces for carrier/operator networks, such as integrated billing-interface APIs.

WAP makes the best sense only for mobile devices and the carrier/operators controlling the mobile network, so it does not help developers if they acquire a carrier-grade gateway. The gateway will have mobile carrier-aware features that the developer will not need. On top of that, the WAP protocol does not define a gateway-to-gateway protocol: therefore, only one gateway can be in the configuration. This does not mean that developers cannot acquire a developer-grade gateway for testing. However, carrier-grade gateways are overpriced for most developers.

Because the selection and use of a particular gateway will in most cases be outside of the developer's control, there are some issues that a developer needs to be aware of. These include:

- Architectural issues and carrier control
- Conversion, compiling, and decoding
- Latency
- Bandwidth
- Security, which is covered in detail in Chapter 16, "Implementing WAP Security"

Choosing your architecture

Architectural-level considerations can affect many other parts of the deployment equation. The architectures for WAP can be divided into the following two main categories:

- Packet-based:
  - v1 service provider control
  - v2 carrier control
  - v3 carrier control with partner
- Circuit-based:
  - v1 content provider control
  - v2 carrier control
  - v3 ISP

For example, consider the scenario in which the architecture is a packet-based network. Figure 19-1 demonstrates three packet-based possibilities.

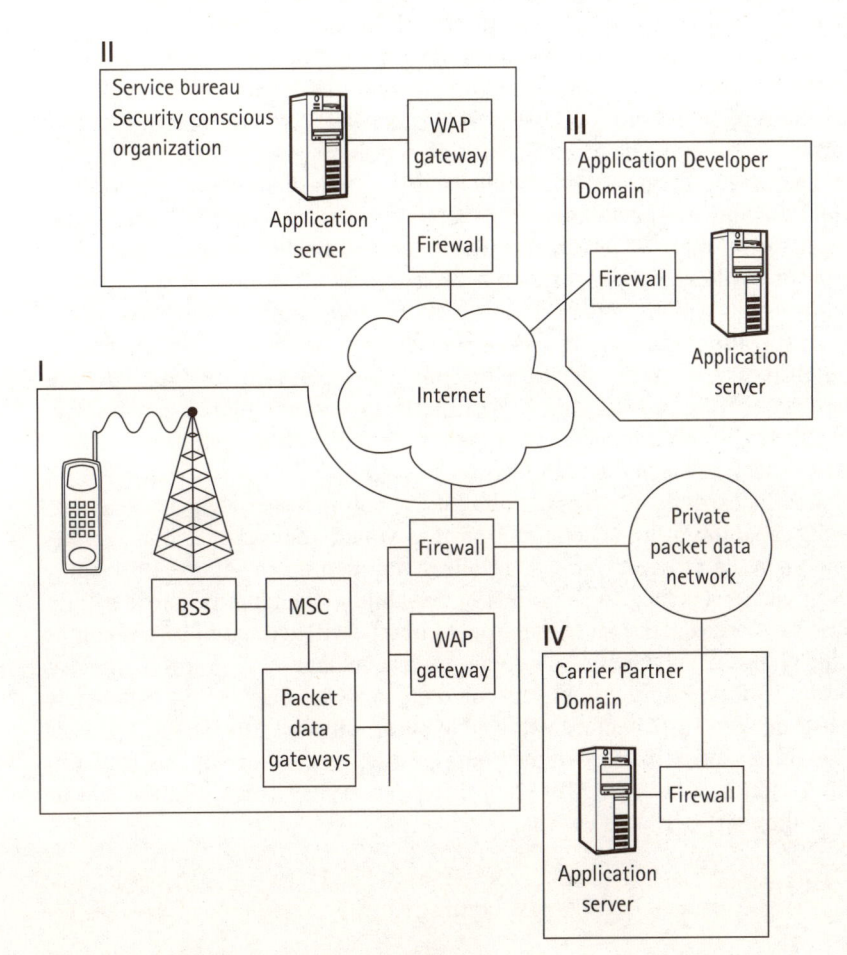

Figure 19-1: Packet-based network architecture

In the second scenario in Figure 19-1, the carrier controls the WAP gateway and the application developer simply puts sites up on a Web server. If the carrier has opened its firewall so that mobile users can access all sites on the Internet, this configuration will work. One problem that exists is that mobile users are unwilling to discover or explore the application because of user-interface limitations. As yet, no comprehensive portal or consistent set of portals across multiple carriers exists. Carriers also know that poorly designed or poorly built applications may give users the perception that the carrier or phone quality is poor. To overcome this perception of the service, the carrier can use the third scenario, as shown in Figure 19-1.

In this scenario, the carrier creates a set of organization(s) or works with a select few partners to create applications that meet the carriers' and users' perceived mobile application requirements. In case III or IV, shown in Figure 19-1, the application developer is at the mercy of a WAP gateway or the carrier infrastructure. The lack of control over the gateway software comes to a head in cases in which upgrades to WAP gateway software may inadvertently break existing applications. The partners and/or developer community need to be kept abreast of changes and/or updates so that users continue to think well of the carrier's services.

In scenario II in Figure 19-1, the service bureau uses the packet-data network of the carrier to send packets through. This approach requires considerable expense on the part of the service bureau, because a WAP gateway purchase is required. But smaller carriers, who don't have the luxury of acquiring a WAP gateway partner with a service bureau, sometimes have to make this purchase. In other scenarios, an organization may be willing to make the purchase, betting that the value of the portal will offset its cost. However, the risk is large considering that the packet-based carrier firewall can simply turn off access.

Another possibility with scenario II is that a large bank or other security-conscious organization will acquire a WAP gateway and work with carrier/service-operator engineers to create a network in which a direct security association is established between the organization's WAP gateway and the mobile device. This solution is called Tle2e and I discuss it in greater detail in Chapter 16.

Figure 19-2 demonstrates the architecture for circuit-switched carriers.

In this case, the carrier can either acquire ISP capability or simply acquire a partner with ISP capability. The special ISP partner would then expose the services using a packet-based structure and the choices represented in Figure 19-1 apply again. If the carrier decides to acquire ISP capability, then many carriers have offered circuit-switched services. If the proper circuit-switched data profiles can be set up on the phone, users may be able to access a developer WAP gateway directly. This scenario is fast losing popularity among carriers, because it completely bypasses their network-architecture value added proposition. If the user does decide to set up his or her own circuit-switched data profile, then he or she has to maintain a unique circuit-data profile for each different service. This option would be unwieldy for the user.

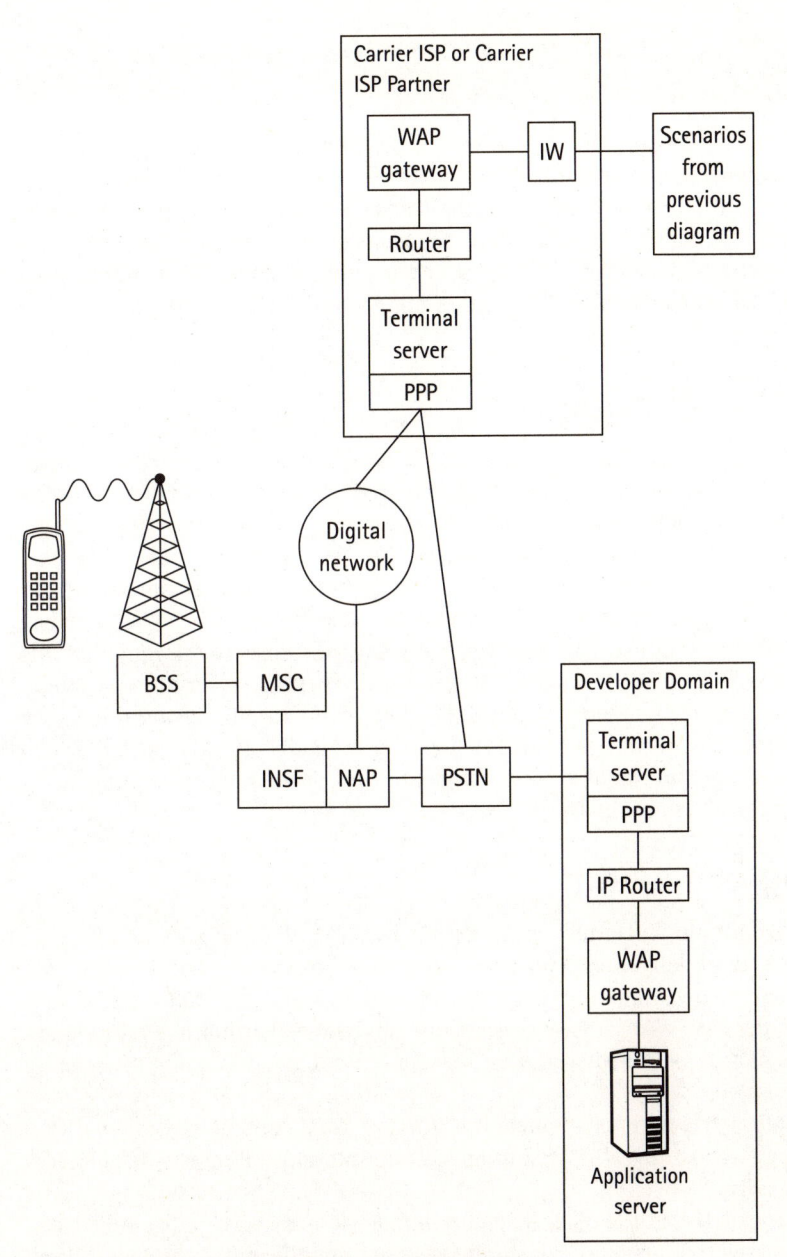

Figure 19-2: Circuit-switched network architecture

Conversion, compiling, and encoding/decoding overheads

The gateway is responsible for converting the WML application code on a developer site into an optimized form for transfer on the wireless network. The gateway must also convert WMLScript into a compiled binary form of bytecodes. It was once considered beneficial to pre-compile the codes so that the gateway would not have to do any work. However, the time saved is negligible and it has been found that different gateways produce different compiled code, which makes delivery to the mobile device problematic.

Latency considerations

When a request is issued from a mobile user, the delays in processing are very much tied to the service bearer. The circuit-switched networks that deploy WAP services are susceptible to the long connect times of the service, somewhere around 10 seconds. Packets networks around the world also have an acquisition time as the data service is accessed. The acquisition time is variable – around three seconds – and will be there as long as the carrier voice and data networks are treated separately.

Two-way SMS is also listed as a bearer, but I know of no network in which it is deployed as a WAP bearer. This is because this type of service is very susceptible to loading and therefore a sudden spike in SMS usage will cause browsing to become unbearably slow. The SMS packet size is usually very small – 100–150 bytes, which is one order of magnitude smaller than a typical response – which makes managing the sequencing of data problematic.

Choosing bandwidth

Although the multiple levels of concatenation by WAP gateways allow for compounding the size of deliverable content, each phone/browser version combination has established its own maximum on the amount of data that can be sent in a response. For the first WAP mobile phones this limit started at around 1,100 bytes. Exact figures can be obtained from the browser vendor or by reading proprietary HTTP headers.

This limitation has serious implications for the way content is designed. For example, a long news story will need to be split up into multiple pieces for delivery to a mobile device.

The memory of the initial WAP-capable mobile devices was quite limited and given the space requirements of cached data it was thought that a bandwidth limit as discussed here would give the WAP phone manufacturers a firm design goal.

Although bandwidth is constrained by a maximum, the recommended size will be based on the actual latency of the network. For example, if you are using a CDPD bearer you will discover that the maximum byte size of 1,100 takes six seconds to deliver to the phone. You may want to reduce the size of the data, say to 60% of its original size, to achieve better delivery characteristics.

Security issues

In almost all of the architectures today, the security implemented by the carrier's is under the covers. A developer does not necessarily know whether WTLS is being implemented. Additionally, WTLS is applied only on the network portion from the wireless handset to the WAP gateway. From the gateway to the application server, SSL security has to be implemented. This is the situation for deployment today. Future scenarios are discussed in Chapter 16.

Additionally, other aspects of security such as WPKI, WMLScript Crypto, and WIM are not implemented on carrier networks.

Therefore, turning the attention back to WTLS, most deployments have only Class 1 implemented or no WAP security, counting instead on lower layer data link security of the wireless airlink.

And then on the application server/Web server side, the SSL security uses a public key/private key pair that is generated by the carrier WAP gateway. The public key of the gateway is sent to the developer and used for encryption. Although this sounds complicated, the gateway and the application server simply communicate using the HTTPS protocol instead of standard HTTP. A standard GET request is redirected to include more security information and to use a different port number.

Different levels of security can be chosen by combining HTTPS usage with basic authentication. A combination of the two provides the highest level of security.

Working with WAP Application Servers

Almost all applications are hosted on a HTTP-capable server. This server does not need to be modified to any great extent to be able to support applications. It should, however, output the correct content type for the XML data being sent to the WAP gateway. For static content, adding MIME types into a table will cause the correct output to be sent. Table 19-2 presents the MIME types that you will need.

TABLE 19-2 APPLICATION-SERVER CONTENT TYPES

Content	Content Type	File Extension
wml	text/vnd.wap.wml	.wml
wmlc	application/vnd.wap.wmlc	.wmlc

Continued

TABLE 19-2 APPLICATION-SERVER CONTENT TYPES *(Continued)*

Content	Content Type	File Extension
wmls	text/vnd.wap.wmlscript	.wmls
wmlsc	application/vnd.wap.wmlscriptc	.wmlsc
wbmp	image/vnd.wap.wbmp	.wbmp

Without the proper content-type setting on HTTP responses, the WAP gateway acts dumb and does not know how to compile the information and simply rejects it. It does this to keep spurious content types from the Internet and in the WAP-mandated set only.

Please consult your Web-server documentation for more information about how to add these MIME types. Most recent builds of the major Web servers include them already. For example, Apache 1.3.16 includes all the major WAP types and other types for push services, which I discuss in Chapter 10, "Building Active Applications Using Push Technology."

For dynamic content, the MIME types table is not examined. You will have to ensure that the dynamic script contains the correct code for the type you want to send. You can find examples of code for PHP, Java, JSP, ASP, CFML, and Perl in Chapter 14, "Targeted Development."

Using a phased development approach

Although development options for WAP feature a variety of browsers, simulators, gateways, and dynamic-scripting environments, you must establish a careful development methodology; otherwise, you will waste time debugging problems.

Developers will not always have access to the latest hardware with which to test their development efforts. Although access is limited and expensive, using the right hardware does give you the advantage of seeing your applications exactly as users will see them. No simulator on the market can give you the real performance characteristics of an actual WAP phone or mobile device. Figure 19-3 shows how the workflow would look in the development methodology process.

For novice developers, I recommend beginning at level 1 in Figure 19-3. At this level, a static WML deck and WMLScript are stored locally and then accessed via the simulator. In this case, the simulator acts as a browser, gateway, and Web server all in one. The best thing to do at this level is to use a simulator of one of the super-class devices mentioned in Table 19-1. Try out new UI elements and see how they affect the service application. Once you are doing well at this level, it is time to move on to controlling a Web server.

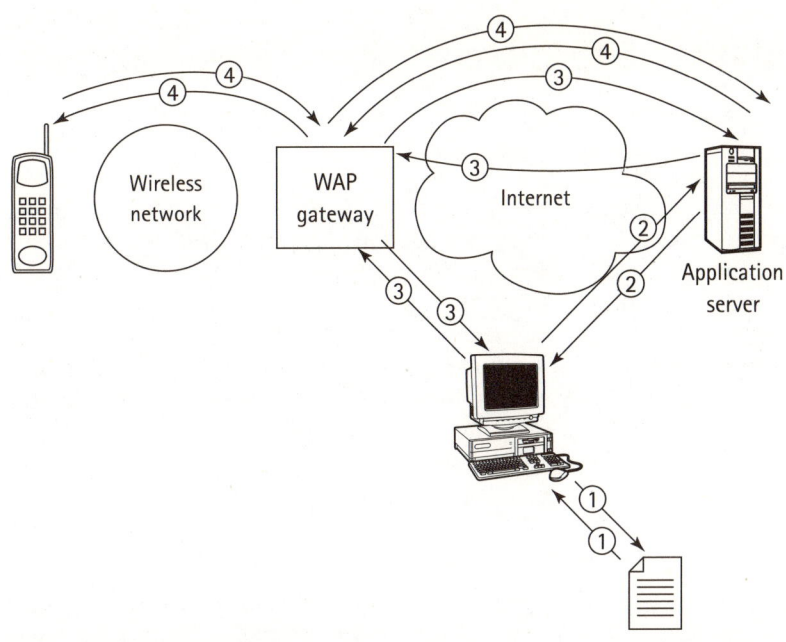

Figure 19-3: Development phases

Controlling a Web server

To gain mastery over the content being sent to the mobile device, you need to have some experience in dealing with WAP from the server. To begin, install a Web server, either locally on your development machine or elsewhere, and configure its MIME types (adding at least the ones I mention in Table 19-2). Upload the content to the server and browse to it from the simulator. Setting the simulator to HTTP Direct mode or HTTP server mode activates of the correct development environment. The WAP simulator is acting as the WAP gateway because it accesses the HTTP server directly. Access to an HTTP server gives you the ability to see real headers and test most HTTP-specific functionality, such as caching behavior. Working directly with the server also enables you to create more dynamic applications.

Working with a gateway

At the next level of development, level 3, I recommend that the developer move up to testing in WAP gateway mode. In this case, the WAP simulator accesses the application server through a specified WAP gateway. Besides being a nice way to exercise the full architecture, this mode enables developers to see real headers as they would emanate from a WAP gateway. (Remember that gateways today add their own proprietary entries to the standard WAP headers.) Also, this mode enables developers to access the developer APIs of a specific gateway. For example, the TimeZone APIof the Openwave UP.Link is only accessible by using the actual gateway itself.

Moving to a Mobile Device

The final level of development, or level 4 as shown in Figure 19-3, simply confirms what is shown in level 3, or in the simulator at the last level. The behavior of the actual physical device does not always match the behavior of the simulated device, so this level is an important part of the process.

The development levels I outline here do not imply any timeline. I recommend that you create prototypes for real phones as soon as you can, because it is only then that you will truly appreciate the limited input, limited bandwidth, limited processor, and other restrictions of the mobile environment.

Summary

In this chapter I looked at the issues that will affect your application development in WAP when you decide to put your application on a server and run it on a real phone or mobile device. I discussed how your choice of tool, browser, gateway, application server, and architecture greatly affects your service performance.

First I listed the major classes of tools that I recommend you use in your development. (I examine the installation of the tools, as well as their relative advantages and disadvantages, in Appendix G.) I addressed the first important issue of deployment, how to choose the appropriate WAP gateway.

Next I presented architectural diagrams that clearly described the different approaches that may affect both the design of your service and the tools you choose. Finally, I showed you how to set up application servers and presented a methodology for developing applications by taking them gradually from the static environment all the way to the WAP client in a mobile device.

In the next chapter I discuss the future of WAP and the major changes from the WAP Forum that will have an impact on development in the next generation of WAP protocols and languages.

Chapter 20

The Future of WAP

IN THIS CHAPTER

- Using past predictors for forecasting WAP's outlook
- Predicting the future of WAP by watching network improvements
- Predicting the future of WAP by looking at wireless device improvements

As was the intention of the FCC in introducing its digital PCS tenders, wireless is fast becoming a part of our lives. Voice services are no longer just the domain of a select few. However, it will be some time before the WAP services become as widespread. WAP and data products are very much attracting only early adopters at this point, and for valid reasons. Currently, the product has performance characteristics that make its uses very specific. WAP-like services have replaced direct voice communication in most dispatch applications that used to support cellular phones. Such a random rate of adoption may discourage many, but it follows a model of stages at which innovations are adopted, as shown in Figure 20-1.

Adoption Curve

| Innovators | Early adopters | Early majority | Late majority | Laggards |

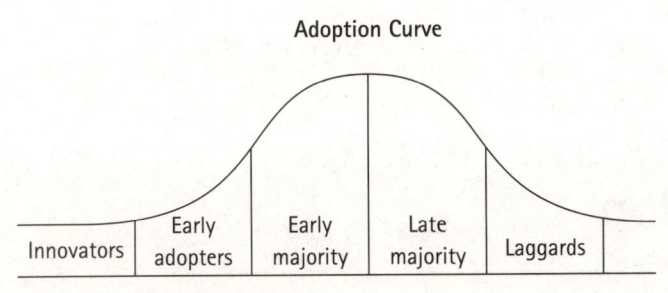

Figure 20-1: Adoption chart

All innovations undergo several stages of adoption by a user base, before and after they enter the so-called mainstream. The first stage of adoption is by the innovators. This group needs very little in the way of motivation — they use the technology because it is there. They are risk takers. The second-stage group is called the early adopters. They pick up new technologies because they have a respect for innovations and the benefits that they offer. This group is attracted to the innovation because it has the potential to help solve some problem. They feel they owe it to themselves to make the best of every minute of their day and they feel that the innovation can help them to do that.

The next stage is the early majority. This group understands the benefits of a technology but thinks hard about the costs and the benefits. This group adopts an innovation when the benefits of doing so are clear. The technology must be clear, practical, safe, and certain before the group adopts the innovation. Then comes the late majority. This group is very skeptical of change. The people in this group only change their old habits when given substantial benefits and/or incentives to do so. The final group is the laggards. They are not at all willing to try new innovations and will stick to the old way of doing things for as long as they can. However, this group cannot be ignored, as it may include the best customers of older products.

WAP is currently somewhere between innovators and early adopters in its life cycle. Things can only get better for the technology, so where is it headed?

As I discussed in Chapter 1, technological change and innovation in an industry come from drivers. These drivers vary according to the technology. For example, the need for a communication system the public could use drove out Morse code and replaced it with the common telephone.

So what drivers are going to shape WAP's future? The key ones I see are the following two:

- The implementation of 3G networks
- The evolution of handsets

The cellular market brings interactive services to the consumer market using two enablers: the mobile device itself and the backend architecture. In the next section, I discuss how changes to these components act as drivers for WAP.

The Network as a Source of Innovation

The implementation of 3G networks improves one of the two main components that enable wireless services, the network. 3G networks will finally bring a packet-based infrastructure to cellular. This introduction of 3G implies that both voice and data services will be carried over the same packets. Packets are much more efficient than existing circuit-switched services and, combined with technical enhancements to the air link, will result in greater rates of access.

Furthermore, the move to a packet-based network is largely based on the success of the Internet. This means that future cellular networks will converge with Internet protocols and mirror trends in those Internet protocols. Then WAP will also follow some of those trends, especially because its creators' inspiration from the beginning has been the World Wide Web.

Therefore, the 3G networks will bring three major improvements to the status quo:

- Higher data rates
- Packet-based communication integrated with voice
- Internet-based protocols

These improvements are reflected in what you can expect in the future of WAP. New enhancements expected in future versions of the WAP protocol mirror the changes envisioned with the move to 3G networks.

Here are the changes and a brief description:

- *Wireless Profiled TCP* — This allows WAP gateways and mobile devices to communicate with each other over a special wireless TCP protocol with standard HTTP as the session layer. Contrast this with today's scenario, WSP over a WAP-specific WTP and WDP. Originally, those technologies were conceived because of the WAP Forum's belief that TCP was too chatty over the limited-bandwidth wireless links. But the move to higher data rates, packet-based communication, and Internet-based protocols combine to make Wireless Profiled HTTP a better solution than WTP/WDP for the future. The wireless TCP does away with fears of a TCP connection hogging the wireless link. I describe the technology in more detail in the following section.

- *XHTML* — The current WML language is very static. There is no clear way within the specification to create dynamic functionality or interact with dynamic services. To counteract this problem, a move is being made by the WAP Forum to enhance WML greatly in future releases. The first change is that WML will be replaced with wireless profiled XHTML. This will put WML on the same revision path as the proposed future standard Internet world markup language framework from the W3C.

Wireless profiled TCP

The standard architecture has three main pieces: the WAP browser, the WAP gateway, and the application or Web server. The WAP stack operates between the WAP browser and the WAP gateway. An Internet stack operates between the WAP gateway and the application server. This disjointed stack model is implemented today. The disjointed model was a good solution when bandwidth constraints on the wireless network demanded it. Now, with the advent of 2.5G and 3G networks, the bandwidth concern is less.

One advantage of the wireless profiled TCP approach is that the TCP is a well-known solution for large-data transfer. The WDP and WTP combination was limited to $2^{15}*$[*packet-size* (that is, 1492 bytes)] bytes of data. This prevented large data-transfer applications such as MP3 or larger media from being transferred. The other advantage of wireless profiled TCP is that it is easier to provide for end-to-end security. Because the link is end-to-end, a single-standard security protocol such as TLS could be used over the entire link. This is opposed to the current solution discussed in Chapter 14, where the wireless link uses WTLS and the landline link uses TLS or other Internet accepted security mechanism.

TCP as it is implemented on the Internet today is defined in RFC 793. There are additional definitions for TCP congestion control and recovery in RFC 2581. Wireless profiled TCP uses RFC 2581 as the base set and suggests optimizations to that set. These optimizations may affect header compression, which requires the use of headers that would otherwise have been discarded by intermediate routers.

The TCP base set has problems with wireless links because of high bit-error rates, long delays, variable bandwidth, and variable delays. These factors combine to create the following TCP problems:

- TCP packet loss and corruption of data
- Sticky low TCP-window sizes — low window sizes are hard to recover from
- Exponential backup that results in long periods of inactivity
- Long periods of disconnection when mobile is in coverage darkness
- Redundant transmissions that may be created by spurious client or server timers

Wireless profiled TCP adds headers to address these problems. Table 20-1 summarizes the features of wireless profiled TCP.

TABLE 20-1 WIRELESS PROFILED TCP SUMMARY

Optimization	Description	Conditions	Required?
Support the Large Window Size based on Bandwidth Delay Product (RFC 1323)	The minimum window size in TCP is calculated by multiplying the available bandwidth by the round-trip time. This BDP (Bandwidth Delay Product), as it is called, allows you to select the appropriate window size based on bandwidth and delay.		Recommended
Support the Window Scale Option (RFC 1323)	An expanded version of the TCP window field.	Window size>=64K	Mandatory

Optimization	Description	Conditions	Required?
Support the Window Scale Option (RFC 1323)	An expanded version of the TCP window field.	Window size<=64K	Optional
Support the TimeStamps Option (RFC 1323) for RTTM	Timestamps give a more accurate representation of response-delay times than standard TCP implementations, which base a round-trip time measurement on one packet per window.	Window size>=64K	Mandatory
Support the TimeStamps Option (RFC 1323) for RTTM	Timestamps give a more accurate representation of response-delay times than standard TCP implementations, which base a round-trip time measurement on one packet per window.	Window size<=64K	Optional
Support Large Initial Windows (windows<=2) (RFC 2581)	A slow start typically reduces the initial window to two segments. You can change this number to around three or four segments when restarting from a congestion condition.	Windows<=2	Mandatory
Support Large Initial Windows (windows>2) (RFC 2414)	A slow start typically reduces the initial window to two segments. You can change this number to around three or four segments when restarting from a congestion condition.	Windows>=2	Optional
SACK, Selective Acknowledgment Option (RFC 2018)	Normally, large windows will result in burst errors and congestion losses on wireless network. SACK adds headers specifying which segments need to be retransmitted.		Mandatory

Continued

TABLE 20-1 WIRELESS PROFILED TCP SUMMARY *(Continued)*

Optimization	Description	Conditions	Required?
Path MTU Discovery (RFC 1191 RFC 1981)	Allows the sender in the communication path to discover the maximum end-to-end transmission-unit size.		Recommended
MTU larger than default IP MTU	You can select an MTU larger than the default in cases where Path MTU Discovery is not supported; however setting MTUs above 1500 is not recommended.	Path MTU Discovery not supported	Optional
Explicit Congestion Notification (RFC 2481)	A receiver of TCP data can return to the sender an ECN-Echo flag that indicates the level of congestion on the network. The user can maintain that flag to control the congestion window. (Requires intermediate IP router ECN support.)		Optional

You can implement wireless profiled TCP in the old WAP proxy architecture or simply as a passthrough, as shown in Figure 20-2. A future WAP implementation will be required to support both approaches.

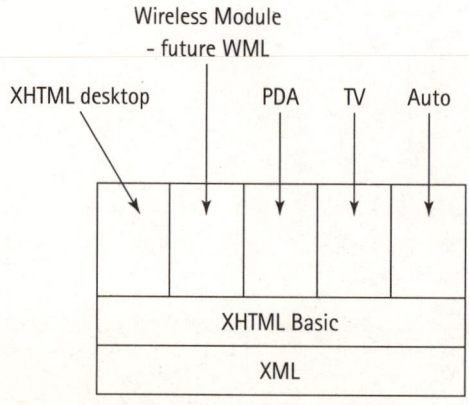

Figure 20-2: Wireless profiled TCP stacks

Convergence with Internet protocols

The WAP Forum intends to make any future markup language compliant with the future Internet W3C Consortium thinking. The W3C HTML group is redoing the standard so that HTML will become an XML language called XHTML. This new language will be devised so that other variants of XHTML can be created by people interested in developing those variations for their product lines. The different variants will all have the same base core, but different additional modules useful to their needs. Figure 20-3 shows how the intended structure will look.

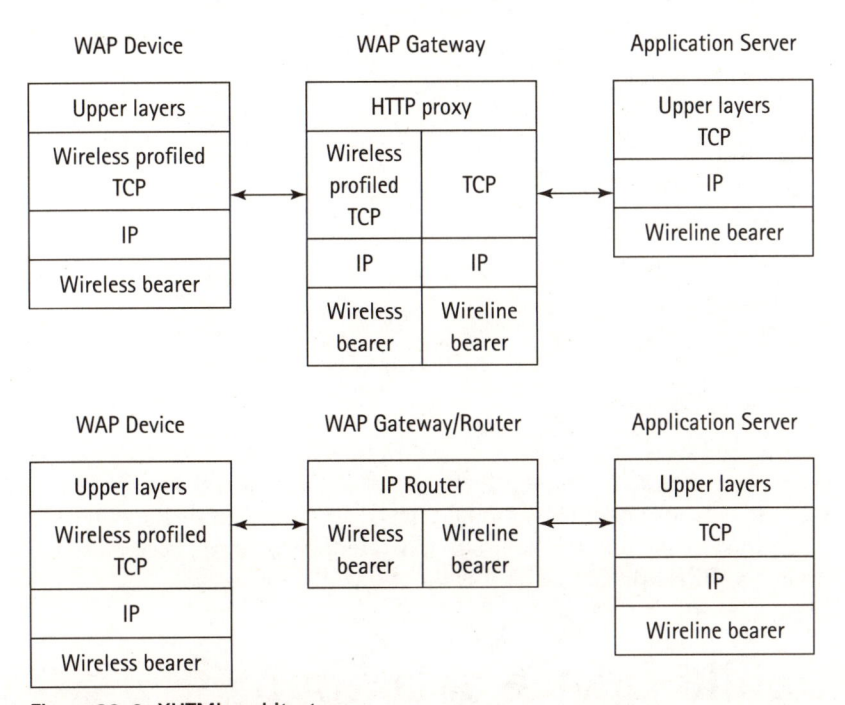

Figure 20-3: XHTML architecture

Listing 20-1 shows a hypothetical example of the mechanics of the language and how it will interact with XHTML.

Listing 20-1: XHTML Code Sample

```
<?xml version="1.0" ?>
<!DOCTYPE html PUBLIC "-//WAPFORUM//DTD Wireless HTML//EN">
<html>
<xmlns:wml="http://wapforum.org/wml11" >
<head><title>Wireless Module and Regular XHTML</title></head>
```

Continued

Listing 20-1 *(Continued)*

```
<body>
<wml:card id="first_card">

<wml:timer value="50" />

<img src="splash.gif" alt="Company" wml:localsrc="our_logo" />

<wml:onevent type="ontimer">
   <wml:go href="#second"/>
<wml:onevent>
</wml:card>

<wml:card id="second_card">
<a href="1.xml">Horoscope</a>
<a href="2.xml">Palm Reading</a>
<wml:do type="accept" name="Find">
   <wml:go href="found.xml" />
</wml:do>
</wml:card>
</body>
</html>
```

Listing 20-1 shows how the elements and attributes have been split into two groups. There are elements and attributes that are part of the standard specification, and those that are part of the wireless module. Those that are part of the wireless module are identified as such by the namespace before their names. Those that are part of the base set of XHTML can be used without this namespace.

The Mobile Device as a Source of Innovation

The future of how the cellular phone will look is even harder to predict. There may be multiple types of phones, each with its specific niche market.

However, some things are clear. With advancements in electronics and the constant desire by consumers for miniaturization of technologies working in the desktop and other personal appliances, manufacturers are forced to make the phones much more capable than devices in the past. The cellular phone, the watch, and possibly the PDA are examples of devices that enter our personal spaces continuously. The constant addition of such devices creates the need for a device that does it all in the palm of our hands. Today, that need is juxtaposed harshly with the complexities of such a device, and the lack of electronics to make it happen.

But some time in the future this need will be met. The most basic enhancements to the mobile device are sustaining innovations that extend current measurable capabilities. These are the size and capability (color, touch, lighting) of the screen, the input/control mechanism (keyboard, keypad, or roller ball). Other sustaining changes are not as obvious. Cell phones today do not have fast processors or large memory-storage areas. With the glut of processing power from the computer industry entering the market cost of electronics is expected to come down to the level affordable for mass-market devices.

Therefore, consumers are still deciding what the device that enters their personal space is going to look like. Today's devices are being extended such that their screens and input capabilities are enhanced. Here is a list of improvements to future phones and what their capabilities are going to be:

- *Attachment of external devices through external functional interface (EFI)* – An external functional interface is being devised to enable users to attach multiple devices to a phone whenever they want. These devices can be many different things, from a thermometer to a video camera to automotive components. Its functionality will be negotiated with the browser. The browser will then be able to externalize this functionality to the user, allowing the user to see what the device's capabilities are. See the section called "External Function Interface" for more details.

- *Access to external devices through Bluetooth* – With the possibility of so many interfaces, there has to be a seamless way of making connections. Bluetooth is a short-range wireless technology that will allow devices to communicate with each other just by being close. The Bluetooth technology is not something being developed by the WAP Forum but is expected to act as an enabler for EFI.

- *Addition of persistent storage areas for large data storage* – Because more memory will be available on the mobile device of the future, using it to enhance services makes sense. One way to use this memory is to create a directory and file structure like that of most operating systems. This will be unlike anything that WAP has seen so far, because all of today's WAP applications formulate a request/response transaction with the application server.

- *Addition of SyncML due to increased data storage* – The potential for more memory in future devices is inspiring new solutions to common problems with wireless devices. One such problem has to do with management of data stored in the back-end office. Such data have a volatility that must be duplicated seamlessly on a wireless device if the data are to be accessed reliably there. The SyncML system may be a way to solve this problem because it is a proposed protocol that defines how data between a wireless device and home base is made the same.

- *Enhancement of the device screen, input capability, output capability, and control* — These enhancements will result in many complex innovations, such as MMS (Multimedia Messaging Service), a new version of WML, and color images.

- *Enhanced processor with MMS capability* — This will enable the device to act more like a computer in terms of its computing capability, especially with regard to its capability to parse together multimedia and render them in the display or through the speaker in real time.

- *Enhanced processor and enhanced storage* — These enhancements to the mobile device will result in its being more capable of handling stronger security algorithms and better systems for keeping data stored on the device away from unintended parties than today's phones.

For more details on future WAP security systems, refer to Chapter 16, "Implementing WAP Security."

External Functional Interface (EFI)

This is collectively the unit of software in the mobile device that handles any external functionality. External means anything that is not part of WAE (the standard WAP browser) or WTA (the Wireless Telephony browser). At a very high level, the architecture becomes as shown in Figure 20-4. EFI gives both the WAE and the WTA the capability to call external functionalities. Any memory, processor, or hardware issues are the responsibility of the implementation.

Figure 20-4 shows the EFI conceptual architecture and how the EFI components will be structured.

The EFE (EF Entity) will be used to implement the bulk of the external functionality even if it may exist outside the mobile device. This EFE may be a top-of-the-line VCR, but it is not expected that the full functionality of the VCR be available to the WAP phone. Only a portion of the functionality is given out to the WAP phone as needed. Examples of EFEs are VCRs, navigation systems, GPS receivers, physical sensors such as temperature sensors and cameras, and automobile equipment.

Chapter 20: The Future of WAP

Then there is an EF Unit. The EF Unit is the actual portion of EFI exposed to WAP applications. One EF Unit may access the functionality contained in many EFEs. For example, a car may have sensors to check the tire pressure, the oil level, and the fuel level. Those are three EFEs. An EF Unit could combine all those readings in a single form and expose it to the WAP browser in a single class.

The EF Class Agent is the part of the class responsible for managing the association with the WAP components. These Class Agents can also be thought of as EF servers. There is then yet another component, called the EF Broker, which is responsible for collecting information from the Class servers and combining it into a form that the WAP browsers understand. The list of services that the EF Broker comes up with is stored in the EF Registry.

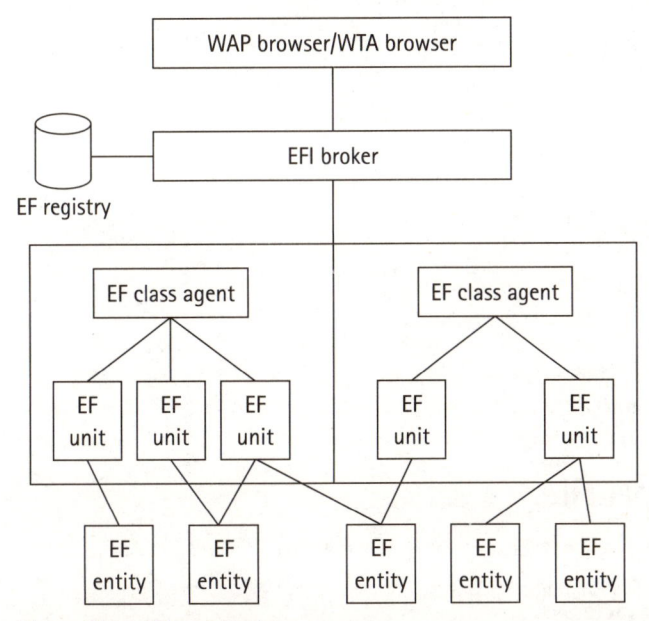

Figure 20-4: EFI architecture

Figure 20-5 shows a real-life example using an automobile and some auxiliary systems to illustrate the EFI concept architecture.

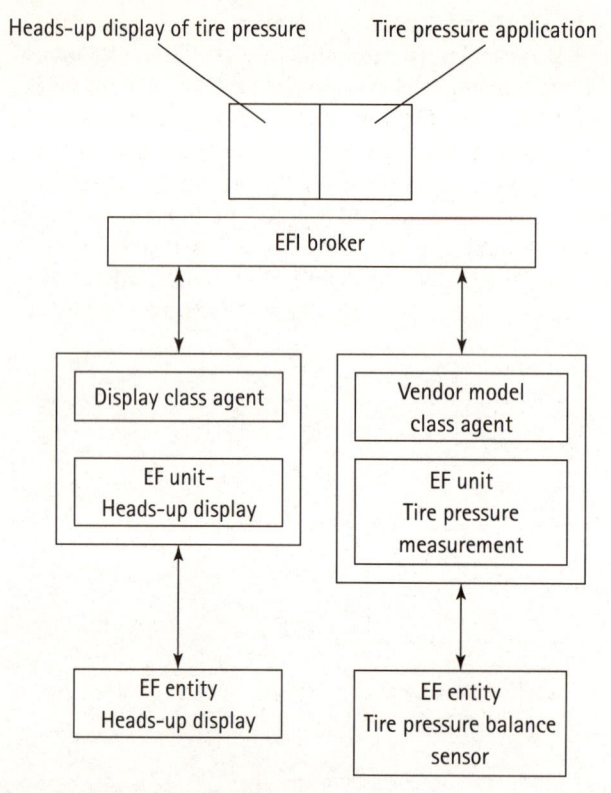

Figure 20-5: A real-life EFI example

Bluetooth WAP profile

Bluetooth is a short-range wireless technology that works in the 2.4GHz frequency in most countries. The weak power signals of about one milliwatt limit the range of the technology to about 10 meters or so.

Bluetooth gives devices at least three advantages. First, it enables them to connect to each other without using cables. And it even works without line of sight because of the high frequency. This is an advantage over both infrared and cables.

Second, it allows you to create ad-hoc networks between devices. Such ad-hoc networks enable automatic information exchange and synchronization. For example, if a refrigerator registers that there is no milk, and the car drives into the garage, those two devices can communicate. In this way, the car has the knowledge about whether more milk is required the next time you are near the grocery store. Better yet, it can contact the store remotely and have the item ordered and delivered.

Lastly, with today's devices, connectivity to a network is an issue. PCs can be connected to the Internet. What if you also wanted your TV connected to the Internet? How about the oven, refrigerator, and dishwasher? You could connect them individually at a large expense. Bluetooth enables a single device to maintain the network connection and all the other devices to share that signal.

So, where does WAP fit in? It certainly has the second and third advantages in creating networks. WAP needs connectivity to a back-end application server and WAP gateway. However, information downloaded over a WAP connection can be used with local devices. In this way, a WAP application can download and purchase tickets to the game Saturday and then print them wirelessly on the local house printer. WAP obtains the information and Bluetooth prints it.

Persistent storage

In the future, WAP clients will have more memory available for WAP usage. One way to use this space is as some type of storage system for WAP data. The mechanics and management of the storage system will be implementation-dependent. However, the WAP Forum will standardize the interface that allows WAP developers to access the data.

Draft specifications hint at something called a storage object. This storage object will be the smallest data element that can be managed by a storage system. These storage objects will then be collected into volumes. Volumes will then be collected into a storage medium such as ROM, EPROM, SRAM, SIM, and so on.

Volumes will be used to group data associated with applications into separate compartments for WAP applications. Much as a file is assigned to a single directory, storage objects can be assigned to a single volume only. The main storage medium contains a single default volume, which is created by the device root system. The only container element for volumes is storage objects. There can be no child volumes.

Storage objects store an object and its related attributes. You can refer to these objects using an URL-like syntax. The current proposed format looks like this:

```
wps://magneticdisk/Somedata/AddressBook
```

The previous URL has a prefix of `wps`, for wireless persistent storage; `magneticdisk` is the name of the storage medium; `Somedata` is the name of a volume; and `AddressBook` is the storage object.

Table 20-2 summarizes the common functions and libraries that enable manipulation of the persistent storage data by applications.

TABLE 20-2 PERSISTENT STORAGE PRIMITIVES

Library.Function	Description
`Pstor.enum`	Enumerates some element types under a specific parent
`Pstor.create`	Creates the named volume or storage object
`Pstor.remove`	Removes the named volume or storage object
`Pstor.getAttribute`	Gets an attribute of a storage object, volume, or medium
	Valid attributes for a medium are: `AvailableSize`, `CreationDate`, `LastModifiedDate`, `Lifetime`, `StorageType`, `SupportsCreateVolume`, `WriteLocked`
	Valid attributes for a volume include: `CreationDate`, `LastModifiedDate`
	Valid attributes for a storage object are: `ContentType`, `CreationDate`, `LastModifiedDate`
`Pstor.setAttribute`	Sets an attribute of a storage object
`Pstor.getDataSize`	Returns the total size of the data object
`Pstor.getData`	Gets the value(s) of the data object name value pair(s)
`Pstor.setData`	Set the value(s) of the data object to some name/value pair(s)
`Pstor.setDataSize`	Truncates or extends the size of the data space

SyncML

SyncML is an initiative being driven by a group of software vendors, headed by Ericsson, IBM, Lotus, Motorola, Nokia, Palm, Psion, and Starfish Software. It addresses the problem of data access. Information that needs to be accessed between two devices is commonly captured using a proprietary format and protocol between them, and very often the format is very specific to a certain type of data, such as calendar or task lists for a Personal Information Manager.

It is SyncML's purpose to change all that by creating a single synchronization format that works across all devices. It is expected that with WAP phones, data may be entered on the phone or at the network or both while the connection between the phone and network is broken. Therefore, to remain up to date, one of the two sides will have to reconnect to update the changes. The synchronization process then makes sure that both sides have the same data.

> **NOTE:** The WAP Forum has sanctioned the SyncML standard as a valid synchronization protocol that may be used in future WAP browser specifications. The protocol was chosen over others mostly because of its effectiveness over both wireless and landline networks.

Table 20-3 shows the type of synchronizations that the protocol supports.

TABLE 20-3 SYNCML SYNC-TYPE SUMMARY

Sync Type	Description
Two-way sync	A basic synchronization wherein both the client and the server in a communication send information about modified data. First the client sends its data modifications, and then the server responds with its changes.
Slow sync	A specialized form of two-way sync wherein the items in the list of changes are compared on a field-by-field level. The client sends all the data to the server, and the server then compares this data to the original.
One-way sync	A form of sync wherein the client sends any changes that have occurred but the server does not send any changes from its end.
Refresh sync from client only	A form of sync that enables the client to send all the data from the database to the server. The server then refreshes all the data by replacing the original database.
One-way sync from server only	A form of sync wherein the client gets all the changes from the server but the server does not see any server-side changes.
Refresh sync from server only	A form of sync wherein a server sends all the data from the database to the client. The client is supposed to delete all its contents and replace them with the data sent by the server.
Server-alerted Sync	A form of sync wherein the server tells the client to begin the sync process, also indicating which of the other syncs the client needs to create.

Summary

Developers can certainly expect that WAP as a standard will change. As evidenced by early experiments in writing standards, a closed-room approach to creating specifications is doomed to failure. An open forum allowing an exchange between vendors of the best ideas is the ideal place for the kindling of WAP and is exactly how the standard was born.

This open forum is guided by key drivers, the same drivers that are pushing the industry forward. These are advances in network technology and advances in electronics on the wireless handset.

The first driver, improvements in network technology, will affect how the wireless link is treated. Already, the future standards are moving toward embracing standard Internet protocols that only five years ago were anathema to the carriers. But now with the faster data rates, such ideas are welcome because they bring with them a closer-knit, single Internet as opposed to two Internets consisting of wireless and landline.

The second driver, improvements in the miniaturization of electronics on the handset, is resulting in more functionality being included in the wireless handset. These devices are one day going to have the same features as today's desktop computer in a far smaller space. Therefore, looking at the future, WAP features are beginning to include aspects that are describing how the extra functionality of handsets will be used. The next chapter gives you a glimpse into the newest generation of WAP browser from Openwave with the GUI and supported by the GSM Association as Mobile Services Initiative or M-Services. It shows the giant leaps in usability occurring in WAP browsers as the industry learns lessons from previous deployments and i-Mode.

Chapter 21

Future of WAP Competitors

IN THIS CHAPTER

- Understanding WAP's competitors
- Looking at M-Services GUI improvements
- Understanding M-Services GUI download protocol

AS I DISCUSSED EXTENSIVELY IN CHAPTER 3, the WAP solution allows carriers to extend their services in a more cost-effective manner when compared to the alternative of modifying hardware in the network and at the wireless handset. In recent years, many proposals have been made for alternatives that take a similar approach to WAP, in that the services are expanded based on software changes at the handset and in a network-based server. Some of those proposals have been quite successful, such as the i-Mode service in Japan, and others are gaining momentum, such as the wireless Java Technology using the KVM (Kilobyte Virtual Machine).

With the many publicized problems of WAP acceptance in the marketplace, including the following, there has been a push for improvement in the overall usability of WAP:

- Lack of a colorful display
- Poor handset availability
- Expensive pricing to consumers
- Problems with slow bearers
- Interoperability among carriers

Images of Openwave products in this chapter courtesy of Openwave Systems Inc.

The listed problems together have so far presented a hindrance to WAP's acceptance in the marketplace, both among carriers and consumers. In Japan, the i-Mode service has been gaining users everyday; it has larger displays and an excellent graphical display available from the start. Also, that particular technology supports music and picture downloads, which are not possible on the WAP handsets available today. The Japanese i-Mode service from NTT DoCoMo also has the advantage of a strong bearer, which is the packet-switched radio network based on its digital wireless technology (PDC-P).

The European and US operators have now decided to correct WAP's shortcomings; there are new technologies being introduced to assist them. First of all, the bearer problems are now well understood and the next generation of WAP services will use GPRS (General Packet Radio Service). This packet-switched protocol is much better suited for carrying WAP packets and is better able to deal with the bursty nature of the traffic and the larger instantaneous bandwidth requirements.

With regards to development considerations, WAP 2.0 handsets will support a basic XHTML protocol, which is the standard to which all markup languages are going to converge per the W3C.

So overall it has been accepted that i-Mode does not have a better technical standard, its service is just much more structured than WAP's is. Although most GSM communities are waiting for WAP 2.0, the standard will probably be commercially available in 2002 and even then it will not be as exhaustive as the demands of consumers, nor does it explain how implementation is to occur. The WAP 2.0 specifications are now released and available at `www.wapforum.org`.

So the speed of the roadmap implementation for WAP 2.0 and its induction into the flow of development (acceptance among handset manufacturers, acceptance among carriers, acceptance among the developer community, and then finally acceptance among consumers) has been quite slow. In order to accelerate the progress and to address the market concerns related to WAP, the GSM Association in June of 2001 introduced a new Mobile Service Initiative (called M-Services). This initiative publishes a set of guidelines with which wireless handsets have to comply to be accepted by the carriers and the mobile Internet community.

The initiative was created with a large amount of input from Openwave, which is the key proponent of this new proposal. The M-Services guidelines require that any handset sold that complies with the standard must support a Graphical User Interface (GUI). This is the largest change to the requirements for WAP handsets. Additionally, the guidelines call for the addition of some download capability that allows users to save files to the wireless handset. This service is meant to increase the functionality of WAP protocols by adding download capabilities very similar to i-Mode's ringing tone and icon downloads.

In addition to the new GUI and support for downloads, the M-Services initiative requires the following to be supported by handsets:

- Animated images and support for standard image formats such as GIF, PNG, and JPEG
- Synchable Personal Information Manager (PIM) Database requirements
- Additional conformance with WAP release June 2000 and 2.0 standards

The chapter looks in detail at the improved GUI and also takes a brief look at the proprietary download protocol from Openwave, which is one of two download solutions recommended by M-Services.

M-Services GUI Improvements

The GUI improvements can be summarized in two parts. The first is that the WAP 1.2 (WML 1.3) is used as a base supporting point. That means M-Services handsets will have to comply with that release of WAP. Although this WML version could be supported using the traditional text based screens, M-Services goes one step further by requiring that the new handsets be GUI capable. What does that mean?

Standard GUI improvements

The following is a summary of the set of improvements to the GUI:

- Title bars
- Softkey icons and labels
- Hyperlinks
- Selection lists
- Push buttons
- Forms
- Back key override behavior

The list includes improvements to the display only when no new developer code is required. The developers do need to be aware that the new features are available in the new handsets so that they can better judge what the users are seeing. The following sections cover each one of these improvements in detail and include examples of how they look in the new GUI browser.

TITLE BAR
The M-Services-compliant handsets have to be capable of displaying a title bar. The title bar was not supported by the previous UP.Browser or by the Nokia and

Ericsson browsers shown in Chapter 5. M-Services requires that the handsets display the title bar at the top of the screen. The title bar must scroll with the data to increase the overall available space. Figures 21-1 and 21-2 show how the title bar looks in the new GUI browser.

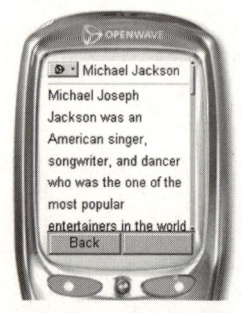

Figure 21-1: Title bar display

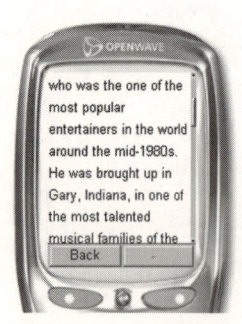

Figure 21-2: Title bar display scrolled down

SOFTKEY ICONS AND LABELS

Softkeys in the new GUI browser appear as buttons at the bottom of the screen. Each of the buttons can also support the use of icons within it, which allows developers to make clear the purpose of the buttons.

In the new browser, the primary softkey concept remains, but this time, the user can use this key to select and deselect interface items. So, I recommend adding a link or button to the end of a card to allow the user to complete the main action. And as before, if no behavior is specified by using `type="accept"` the back task is assigned to the primary softkey.

Additionally, softkey labels appear out of the text flow and close to the physical key to which they are related. Therefore, the paragraph text flow that constitutes what is displayed on the screen is very clearly separated from the on-screen softkey labels.

Figure 21-3 shows the new softkey setup with some different icons.

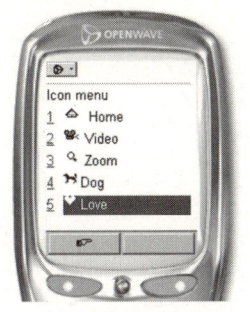

Figure 21-3: Softkey icons

HYPERLINKS

The new mobile browser uses a more common way to display hyperlinks; it shows them as blue underlines, the accepted form on the Internet. In this way, the users do not have to switch their way of thinking to learn any new interface. Additionally, the underline form allows hyperlinks to more easily appear inside a flow of text. In some interface guidelines and in many WAP applications, it has become acceptable to use brackets around a hyperlink. This form is not acceptable in the new GUI browser. It detracts from the user's ability to distinguish the hyperlinks. Figure 21-4 shows hyperlinks as they would look in the new browser.

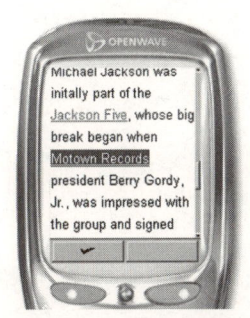

Figure 21-4: Hyperlinks

SELECTION LISTS

The selection lists in the new mobile browser are shown as single line items with the numbers on the side of the display. This is similar to many of the standard WAP browsers, but M-Services requires that the selection list appear in this manner. Some selection lists, such as the ones on Nokia phones, have been known to look different. Examples of the Nokia approach can be found in Chapter 5. Figure 21-5 shows the new selection list in action.

Figure 21-5: Selection list

PUSH BUTTONS

New to the mobile browser and M-Services is the push button. These buttons appear at the bottom of the screen and throughout the forms and must show the text inside of them. The buttons appear on the screen alone and should be very different from input elements or any other form element.

Figure 21-6 shows a push button. Refer also to the new button type section later in this chapter, which shows how buttons can be added to forms on a deck.

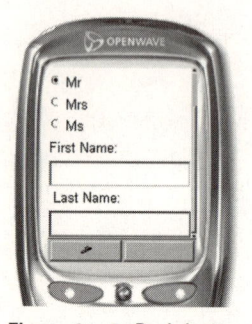

Figure 21-6: Push buttons

FORMS

One of the distinct problems with WAP browsers is their weak attempt at standardizing something like obtaining user input. In all previous WAP browsers, the process of gathering both free-form input and item selections was split up into multiple screens. This meant that to enter five pieces of information, you had to scroll through at least five screens, sometimes even more.

Early developers discovered many problems with usability when they ported applications without regard to the additional screens required. For example, when entering data to determine a destination from a starting point, the number, street, city, and state had to be entered for both locations. If that input process is separated into individual cards, the users may see eight cards before getting the valued information. This can be very time consuming and certainly not the way the rest of the Web works.

In the new GUI browsers, the multiple inputs can be combined into a single form and the information collected together and sent from a single display card. The timesavings are tremendous when measured against the previous approach.

Figure 21-7 shows how the new forms look. In this case, an e-mail message is being generated using a form.

Figure 21-7: Forms

BACK KEY OVERRIDE BEHAVIOR

In some application scenarios, it is necessary to recode the standard backward navigation behavior. This is typically done when the backward navigation can actually result in a loss of data or loss of the transaction. For example, consider balance transfer input variables that require the user to input bank account details along with the balance amount. If the user reaches a form into which all these details have been entered and then proceeds to press the Back button, a developer might wisely choose to override that behavior so that the user does not lose any information.

In the new GUI setup, when the developer redefines the backward navigation button (by programmatically reassigning the Prev key), the developer must redefine the button that implements the back functionality.

GUI Improvements that require additional code

The GUI improvements that require developers to add code need a little bit more explanation. Many of the advanced developers among you are already familiar with the series of extensions that Openwave made to enhance applications intended for handsets with the previous UP.Browser. For the next generation of handsets, Openwave split the development of the browsers into two forks, one is called the Openwave Mobile Browser and the other is the Openwave Universal Browser. I have also seen the terms with "Edition" after them.

The Openwave Mobile Browser effectively replaces the standard UP.Browser; it seems that the last major release of the UP.Browser will be the 4.*x* series. The

Openwave Mobile Browser is compliant with WAP 1.2 (WML 1.3) and includes support for the WML extensions from Openwave. For those of you familiar with WML 1.3 (check out Appendix F if you're not), there are not a whole lot of differences between it and WML 1.1. So the real differences in the mobile browser are the GUI interface and the extensions that improve usability on these handsets. This browser is expected to be available and shipping in handsets in Europe now and 2002 elsewhere.

The other track is the Openwave Universal Browser, which supports the WAP 2.0 standard. It calls for XHTML as the base language; WML 2.0 is used only as the wireless handset extension (see Chapter 20 for a discussion about this modularization). Additionally, this browser supports the older WML 1.x, HDML, cHTML, and most of the Openwave extensions. There is quite a lot in there. However, this browser will be available in Japan in 2001 and 2002 elsewhere.

The supported extensions discussed here will be available in both browsers, but it makes sense to code for them if you expect the introduction of the mobile browser in your market.

NEW BUTTON TYPE

The first of the enhancements is a new button type. The code to insert this new button is as follows:

```
<do type="button" label="some text">
...
</do>
```

This snippet of code causes a button to appear on the screen with the label "some text". You can create more than one button as long as they are contained within a single p element. This means that a paragraph can have its own set of buttons. Also, all buttons within a deck are shown as they appear in the deck. This is unlike how softkeys are defined. The softkey appears based on how its position is hinted by the type field. A button on the other hand will appear after or before other buttons defined in a deck. The following example code and Figure 21-8 show how this new feature looks in the browser.

```
<do type="button" label="Find">
   <go href="findcity.wml"/>
</do>
```

Figure 21-8: New button

SELECT LIST

Originally, the `select` element simply displayed a list. With the new browser specifications, an additional attribute of `select` called `type` determines how the list is displayed. When the `type` attribute is set to `list`, it displays the options in a similar manner to earlier browsers, which is in numerical order with numbers or indices for each item in the list.

Here is a code example; Figure 21-9 shows how this code appears.

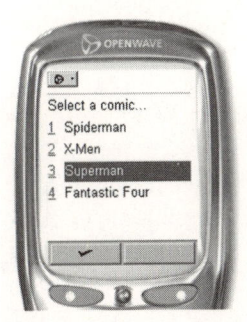

```
<select type="list" name="comic" ivalue="3">
    <option onpick="spiderman.wml">Spiderman</option>
    <option onpick="xmen.wml">X-Men</option>
    <option onpick="superman.wml">Superman</option>
    <option onpick="fanfour.wml">Fantastic Four</option>
</select>
```

Figure 21-9: The select list option

SELECT POPUP

When the `select` type is set to `popup`, a single option is presented in the display until the element is activated and then a pop-up list appears on the screen. The users can then use the up and down arrow keys to select the appropriate option. When user press the accept key, the pop-up goes away and is replaced by the selected option.

This type of selection is quite common and is often represented as a drop-down box. Because a mouse is not available on the handsets, the selection is made on the screen using arrow keys.

Here is an example set of code; Figure 21-10 shows how it appears.

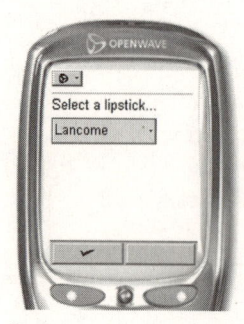

```
<select type="popup" name="lipstick" ivalue="2">
    <option value="clinique">Clinique</option>
    <option value="lancome">Lancome</option>
    <option value="mac">Mac Cosmetics</option>
    <option value="bobbi">Bobbi Brown</option>
    <option value="estee">Estee Lauder</option>
</select>
```

Figure 21-10: The select popup option

SELECT RADIO

The `type` attribute for `select` can also be set to `radio`. This allows the options to show up as radio buttons on the screen. With this particular type, multiple options are not allowed; only one option shows up at a time.

Here is an example set of code; Figure 21-11 shows how it displays.

```
<select type="radio" name="size" ivalue="1">
    <option value="6">Size 6</option>
    <option value="7">Size 7</option>
    <option value="8">Size 8</option>
    <option value="9">Size 9</option>
    <option value="10">Size 10</option>
</select>
```

Figure 21-11: The select radio option

INPUT FIELD

This option has really changed since the older WAP browsers, in which each input field had its own screen. The input field now appears along with the rest of the form display. The users navigate to the input field and then press the accept key to actually insert user data. This will place the users into an input mode that allows them to enter the details required on the form. Users then press the accept key to finalize the transaction and to confirm the input. An options key is also available; it's used to cycle through input-related options.

Because the input field now appears as part of the form, the size of the field is adjustable by using a new `size` attribute. If the `size` attribute is not specified, the size then grows to accommodate the field size. Upon navigating to another component of the deck, only the beginning of the field shows up. Also, if the size is 0 the `input` element appears on a single line.

Here is an example set of code; Figure 21-12 shows how it displays.

```
<p>
Contact Info:
<input name="fname" size="20"/>
<input name="notes"/>
<input name="number" size="0"/>
</p>
```

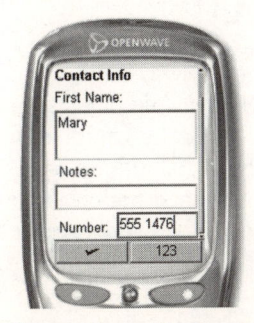

Figure 21-12: The input field option

HORIZONTAL RULE

With the new possibility for multiple elements on a single form, it becomes necessary to split up the screen more efficiently in order to show the different elements. Therefore, a new `hr` element is available that draws a horizontal line across the screen. Using `size` and `width` attributes, you can control the size of the line. The `size` attribute is an integer, where 1 represents a one pixel wide line. The width controls how long the line is beginning on the left side of the screen. The value of `width` can also be a percentage of the screen size, so a value of 50% sets the horizontal line to 50% of the screen width.

Here is the code for some horizontal lines; their associated presentation is shown in Figure 21-13.

```
<p>
Contact Info:
<input name="fname" size="20"/>
<hr/>
<input name="notes"/>
<hr size="5" width="50%"/>
<input name="number" size="0"/>
</p>
```

Figure 21-13: The use of hr lines

M-Services Download Protocol

The June 2000 release of WAP, essentially WAP 1.2, does not define a mechanism for downloading wallpaper, graphics files, ringing tones, or other media objects to the wireless handset. The first option mentioned in M-Services is the use of the standard WAP protocols (WSP) and HTTP GET, but with Segmentation and Reassembly turned on to achieve downloads of large files. The second option is to use the proprietary download fun protocol and then use the download server from Openwave.

The download specification is a three-element architecture very similar to WAP. There is a download client, which is part of the WAP browser, a download server, which resides on the carrier network, and a content server, where all the media objects are stored.

The download architecture goes above and beyond simply allowing downloads to occur; it performs the following additional activities:

- Allows a handset to advertise the types of content it supports
- Allows the server to determine whether there is enough room on the handset prior to the download
- Generates billing records upon successful completion of a download
- Controls the user application flow scenarios for failed and successful downloads

In order to set up the download, the WML file needs to use an URL that begins with `proxy:download` instead of `http`. The browser and client have to be provisioned to get this to work, but when the user selects a link like this, the browser substitutes the download server URL and off you go downloading the media object.

The `proxy:download` URL needs to be composed of the following variables.

- Object type to download (examples are ringtones, images, and music)
- Source URL of the object
- Size of the object
- Optional object title
- Optional object icon
- URL to show after download completes

Here is an example:

```
proxy:download
source=http://www.a.com/pictures/brunette8.jpg&
size=48555&
object=phone:picture&
title_source=http://www.a.com/pictures/index8.txt&
icon_source=http://www.a.com/pictures/icon8.bmp&
status-uri=http://www.a.com/status/success.cgi
```

The download client will then use the previous source code to check for enough space, download the object, download the title if it's there, download the icon if it's there, store the objects in memory, and finally report the success to the server. Files supported by the download server include ringtone, wallpaper, picture, game, java, screensaver, audio, skin, and video.

Some of the benefits of a special download protocol are cleaner billing records, a better application flow that handles failures gracefully, and more flexibility provided by the carrier when deciding how the content is purchased.

Summary

This chapter provided insight into some of the changes that you can expect to see in the new GUI browsers. The many figures and detailed code show how much more usable the new GUI will be. The enhancements will bring WAP on par with what i-Mode offers in Japan.

The chapter explained how developers can utilize the new features of the GUI, including the new button type, `select list`, `select popup`, `select radio`, `input field`, and the use of horizontal rules.

Lastly, the chapter explained what M-Services mandates with regard to downloadable content to the wireless handset, and how developers might be able to use the download fun protocol from Openwave.

As this space is constantly evolving, it will remain to be seen how effective these enhancements will be in sustaining WAP in the future and the level of widespread acceptance the feature sets will retain in the coming months.

Appendix A

WML Elements and Attributes

THIS APPENDIX CONTAINS the full list of the WML elements and their attributes listed alphabetically.

Almost all the elements have core attributes that have been omitted in the tables. These core attributes are the following:

- xml:lang: Specifies the language of the elements and any of its contents (Openwave, Nokia, or Ericsson)
- id: Specifies the programmatic name of the element (Openwave, Nokia, or Ericsson)
- class: Specifies a class name for the element (Supported only by Nokia)

Each of the elements and attributes is shown with the superclass of browsers they are supported in.

The mobile device models don't support all the versions of WML. For this information, you need to check with the manufacturer or obtain the information from request headers.

If the mobile device does indeed support a certain version, make sure that your DTD matches it or is higher than that required.

Following are the DOCTYPE declarations for WML 1.1, 1.2, and 1.3.

WML 1.1:

```
<!DOCTYPE wml PUBLIC "-//WAPFORUM//DTD WML 1.1//EN"
"http://www.wapforum.org/DTD/wml_1.1.xml">
```

WML 1.2:

```
<!DOCTYPE wml PUBLIC "-//WAPFORUM//DTD WML 1.2//EN"
"http://www.wapforum.org/DTD/wml12.dtd">
```

WML 1.3:

```
<!DOCTYPE wml PUBLIC "-//WAPFORUM//DTD WML 1.3//EN"
"http://www.wapforum.org/DTD/wml13.dtd">
```

<a>

This is the short form of specifying an anchor to another resource.

- Element versions: 1.1, 1.2, 1.3
- Supported by: Openwave, Ericsson, and Nokia

> **NOTE:** The tables throughout this appendix represent the manufacturer by the first letter in its name, as follows: O = Openwave, E = Ericsson, N = Nokia.

Attribute	Description	Required?	Versions	Supported by
href	Specifies the URI for the resource location	Yes	1.1, 1.2, 1.3	O, E, N
title	The title that is used by the browser to indicate to the user what the resource is	No	1.1, 1.2, 1.3	O, E, N
accesskey	Defines a single character to allow the user to select the link using a single key press	No	1.2, 1.3	O

<access>

Prevents access of the resource from any URL except those that match either the domain or path indicated in the attributes.

- Element versions: 1.1, 1.2, 1.3
- Supported by: Openwave, Ericsson, and Nokia

Attribute	Description	Required?	Versions	Supported by
domain	The domain in dotted notation that is used to limit access to the deck	No	1.1, 1.2, 1.3	O, E, N
path	The path with slashes that is used to limit access to the deck	No	1.1, 1.2, 1.3	O, E, N

<anchor>

The long form for specifying a link action to a resource. This form is recommended for cases in which the navigation is not limited to the forward direction. For example, both the prev and refresh tags are supported within the anchor.

- ◆ Element versions: 1.1, 1.2, 1.3
- ◆ Supported by: Openwave, Ericsson, and Nokia

Attribute	Description	Required?	Versions	Supported by
title	A text string that identifies the link for the anchor	No	1.1, 1.2, 1.3	O, E, N
accesskey	Defines a single character to allow the user to select the link using a single key press	No	1.2, 1.3	O

<b>

Makes text within the opening and closing tags bold.

- ◆ Element versions: 1.1, 1.2, 1.3
- ◆ Supported by: Openwave, Ericsson, and Nokia

<big>

Makes text within the opening and closing tags appear larger in size than surrounding text.

- Element versions: 1.1, 1.2, 1.3
- Supported by: Openwave, Ericsson, and Nokia

Inserts a line break right after the text line where the element appears.

- Element versions: 1.1, 1.2, 1.3
- Supported by: Openwave, Ericsson, and Nokia

<card>

Identifies the basic resource that is displayed inside a deck. It is also considered a basic level of navigation within WML.

- Element versions: 1.1, 1.2, 1.3
- Supported by: Openwave, Ericsson, and Nokia

Attribute	Description	Required?	Versions	Supported by
title	A card's title can be used to identify its purpose to the user (O does not display this)	No	1.1, 1.2, 1.3	E, N
newcontext	Clears any previously set variables and deletes the history stack	No	1.1, 1.2, 1.3	O, E, N
ordered	Used in the card statement to decide whether the input fields used are presented one at a time or simultaneously in a tree hierarchy (This tag has no effect on E and N phones)	No	1.1, 1.2, 1.3	O

<do>

One of the key methods for navigating applications. It binds an action to a specific key on a mobile device.

- ◆ **Element versions:** 1.1, 1.2, 1.3
- ◆ **Supported by:** Openwave, Ericsson, and Nokia

Attribute	Description	Required?	Versions	Supported by
type	Specifies which of the hardware keys to bind an action to: accept: Positive action prev: Backward action help: Help request reset: Reset the browser state options: Additional operations delete: Equivalent to the clear key unknown: Generic key; browser decides "": Generic key; browser decides x-*, X-*: Experimental keys vnd.*, VND.*: Vendor-specific keys	Yes	1.1, 1.2, 1.3	O, E, N
label	Appears as a hint to the user about what the key will do when pressed	No	1.1, 1.2, 1.3	O, E, N
optional	If set to true, the browser can ignore this attribute; otherwise, rendered to the display as normal	No	1.1, 1.2, 1.3	O, E, N
name	Used for the do event binding; need to use different names when binding multiple tasks to a card or template	No	1.1, 1.2, 1.3	O, E, N

<em>

Adds emphasis to the text between the em tags.

- Element versions: 1.1, 1.2, 1.3
- Supported by: Ericsson and Nokia (No effect on Openwave browser)

<fieldset>

Groups related fields and text so that they are laid out in an optimal fashion in the display or navigation. The attribute for this tag is `title`, which is not required and is a string that you can use to display the object. Because the initial phone displays are quite small, there is no need to support this feature today and most manufacturers have opted not to include any support for this element. As the displays increase in size, browser manufacturers may return to implementing this element to assist in text layout on the screen.

- Element versions: 1.1, 1.2, 1.3
- Supported by: Not supported in any browser

<go>

Navigates to a resource in the forward direction.

- Element versions: 1.1, 1.2, 1.3
- Supported by: Openwave, Ericsson, and Nokia

Attribute	Description	Required?	Versions	Supported by
href	Specifies the URI for the resource location.	Yes	1.1, 1.2, 1.3	O, E, N
sendreferer	Sends the HTTP_REFERER header to the application server; the HTTP_REFERER shows which site is linked to the current deck.	No	1.1, 1.2, 1.3	O, E, N
method	Set to either POST or GET, depending on the HTTP method you need for sending data to the application server.	No	1.1, 1.2, 1.3	O, E, N
cache-control	Can be set to no-cache to control whether the request should be allowed to pull data from the cache.	No	1.3	O, E, N

Attribute	Description	Required?	Versions	Supported by
enctype	Defines an encoding type for parameters that are to be submitted to the server. If any content is to be sent to the server that needs to include additional characters, the accept-charset should be set as well. Today, the only supported enctypes are application/x-www-form-urlencoded multipart/form-data.	No	1.2, 1.3	O, E, N
accept-charset	Specifies the character set for parameters sent to the server. These appear as a comma-separated list of recognized character sets per RFC 2045 and RFC 2046. If unspecified, the default is to assume the same charset as the container element (card).	No	1.1, 1.2, 1.3	O, E, N

\<head\>

Appears at the top of a document and can contain the meta or access element, or both.

- **Element versions:** 1.1, 1.2, 1.3
- **Supported by:** Openwave, Ericsson, and Nokia

\<i\>

Italicizes text that appears inside the \<i\> tags.

- **Element versions:** 1.1, 1.2, 1.3
- **Supported by:** Openwave, Ericsson, and Nokia

`<img />`

Displays images.

- **Element versions:** 1.1, 1.2, 1.3
- **Supported by:** Openwave, Ericsson, and Nokia

Attribute	Description	Required?	Versions	Supported by
src	Specifies the URI for the image resource.	Yes	1.1, 1.2, 1.3	O, E, N
alt	This is an alternative text string that is displayed when the image is not available or the `image src` does not point to a valid location.	Yes	1.1, 1.2, 1.3	O, E, N
localsrc	Sets a predetermined icon to appear on the display. These icons are available on the mobile device locally or close by at the WAP gateway. The icons can be specified by either their number or textual identifier.	No	1.1, 1.2, 1.3	O
align	Indicates how the image is aligned against the bottom of the current text line. The three possibilities are `top`, `middle`, or `bottom`.	No	1.1, 1.2, 1.3	O, E
vspace	Indicates the amount of white space to go above and below the image. The default value is 0.	No	1.1, 1.2, 1.3	O, E, N
hspace	Indicates the amount of white space that is to go to the right and left of the image. The default value is 0.	No	1.1, 1.2, 1.3	O, E, N
height	The suggested height of the image; used so that the browser can reserve the appropriate amount of space.	No	1.1, 1.2, 1.3	E, N

Attribute	Description	Required?	Versions	Supported by
width	The suggested width of the image; used so that the browser can reserve the appropriate amount of space.	No	1.1, 1.2, 1.3	E, N

<input>

Specifies a way for users to enter information into the mobile device.

- Element versions: 1.1, 1.2, 1.3
- Supported by: Openwave, Ericsson, and Nokia

Attribute	Description	Required?	Versions	Supported by
name	Defines the name of the variable that the user's value will be stored in.	Yes	1.1, 1.2, 1.3	O, E, N
value	Sets a default value that is displayed on the screen when the user sees the input.	No	1.1, 1.2, 1.3	O, E, N
type	Sets the type of the text entry. The standard entry type is text. The only other type is password, which displays asterisks in place of any inputted data.	No	1.1, 1.2, 1.3	O, E, N
title	Displayed to indicate what the input is about.	No	1.1, 1.2, 1.3	E, N
maxlength	Specifies the maximum length of any text entered.	No	1.1, 1.2, 1.3	O, E, N
format	Sets up a format for entered text. See Chapter 6 for more details on formats.	No	1.1, 1.2, 1.3	O, E, N

Continued

584   Appendixes

Attribute	Description	Required?	Versions	Supported by
emptyok	Allows no text to be entered for an input even with the `format` attribute set.	No	1.1, 1.2, 1.3	O, E, N
tabindex	Sets up a tab index for this element if tabbing between elements is available on the browser.	No	1.1, 1.2, 1.3	O, E, N
size	Determines the maximum width of the input area in characters.	No	1.1, 1.2, 1.3	O, E, N
accesskey	Sets up a one-character accelerator key used to call the element.	No	1.2, 1.3	O

<meta>

Placed in the head element to specify any meta data for the current deck. The tag is ignored if the meta data is not supported by the browser or the gateway.

- **Element versions:** 1.1, 1.2, 1.3
- **Supported by:** Openwave, but only with proprietary functionality, that is, bookmarks

Attribute	Description	Required?	Versions	Supported by
content	The content type value for the meta data.	Yes	1.1, 1.2, 1.3	None
name	The meta data name. Application servers should not send out any data with this same name.	No	1.1, 1.2, 1.3	None
http-equiv	Use `http-equiv` to deliver meta data to the browser in the form of an HTTP header.	No	1.1, 1.2, 1.3	None

Attribute	Description	Required?	Versions	Supported by
forua	Returning a value of false indicates that the meta data is discarded at the gateway; a value of true allows for the meta data to be sent to the browser for parsing.	No	1.1, 1.2, 1.3	None
scheme	Some form or structure used to interpret the meta data.	No	1.1, 1.2, 1.3	None

<noop />

Tells the browser that no action should be taken; commonly used in invalidating actions set up by templates.

- ◆ **Element versions:** 1.1, 1.2, 1.3
- ◆ **Supported by:** Openwave, Ericsson, and Nokia

<onevent>

Specifies that an event is to take place in a card. The onevent tag executes before any of the display tags, so you can create hidden cards using it.

The attribute that this tag uses is type, which is required and which defines one of the three types of onevent to be used:

- ◆ onenterforward: Fires when the card is navigated to in the forward direction, that is, for the first time.
- ◆ onenterbackward: Fires when the card is navigated to by someone pressing the Back button or using the prev action.
- ◆ ontimer: Fires when a timer on the card expires.

- ◆ **Element versions:** 1.1, 1.2, 1.3
- ◆ **Supported by:** Openwave, Ericsson, and Nokia

\<option\>

Used inside the `select` element to define a list of choices from which a user can select.

- Element versions: 1.1, 1.2, 1.3
- Supporte d by: Openwave, Ericsson, and Nokia

Attribute	Description	Required?	Versions	Supported by
`value`	Specifies the URI for the resource location.	No	1.1, 1.2, 1.3	O, E, N
`title`	The title that is used by the browser to indicate to the user what the resource is.	No	1.1, 1.2, 1.3	O, E, N
`index`	Sets up a unique index for the item in a choice list that can be referred to by attributes of the `select` element allowing for default selections.	No	1.1, 1.2, 1.3	O, E, N
`onpick`	Used when a selection of one of the choices needs to go to another card.	No	1.1, 1.2, 1.3	O (E and N do not support these because of their option implementations)

\<optgroup\>

Breaks up the items in a `select` list into multiple groups.

The attribute for this tag is `title`, which is not required and which is used on the display of each submenu. Openwave, Ericsson, and Nokia support the `title` attribute in browsers.

- Element versions: 1.1, 1.2, 1.3
- Supported by: Openwave, Ericsson, and Nokia

\<p\>

The paragraph element is used to display all text in the browser window.

♦ Element versions: 1.1, 1.2, 1.3

♦ Supported by: Openwave, Ericsson, and Nokia

Attribute	Description	Required?	Versions	Supported by
align	Specifies one of the following types of alignment for the text inside the p element: left, center, or right. The default is to the left.	No	1.1, 1.2, 1.3	O, E, N
	(Openwave fixes the alignment for subsequent p elements in the same card)			
mode	Sets up how the text within the p element is broken up when displayed. It can be broken up on word boundaries, using wrap, or not broken up at all, using nowrap.	No	1.1, 1.2, 1.3	O, N
	(Ericsson does not differentiate between wrap and nowrap)			

<postfield>

Specifies parameters that need to be sent to the application server. This tag appears inside a go element. Be aware that some developers have found that some Openwave browser phones do not support this tag.

♦ Element versions: 1.1, 1.2, 1.3

♦ Supported by: Openwave, Ericsson, and Nokia

Attribute	Description	Required?	Versions	Supported by
name	The parameter to be sent to the application server.	Yes	1.1, 1.2, 1.3	O, E, N
value	The value of the variable to be sent to the application server.	Yes	1.1, 1.2, 1.3	O, E, N

\<pre\>

Tells the browser that any enclosed text has been preformatted. This means that, when dealing with this text, the browsers are to make best efforts to:

- Leave white space intact
- Render text with a fixed-pitch font
- Disable automatic word wrap

\<prev /\>

A navigation action that goes back to the last card in the history stack.

- **Element versions:** 1.1, 1.2, 1.3
- **Supported by:** Openwave, Ericsson, and Nokia

\<refresh\>

A navigation action that redisplays the current card while updating any variable assignments using `setvar`.

- **Element versions:** 1.1, 1.2, 1.3
- **Supported by:** Openwave, Ericsson, and Nokia

\<select\>

Defines a list of choices for the user.

- **Element versions:** 1.1, 1.2, 1.3
- **Supported by:** Openwave, Ericsson, and Nokia

Attribute	Description	Required?	Versions	Supported by
name	A variable that is set by a choice of an option on the list.	No	1.1, 1.2, 1.3	O, E, N
iname	Specifies a name for an index variable. Any index selection in the option settings is assigned to this variable.	No	1.1, 1.2, 1.3	O, E, N

Attribute	Description	Required?	Versions	Supported by
value	A default selection that will be made for the user when first displaying the list of choices.	No	1.1, 1.2, 1.3	O, E, N
ivalue	Specifies a default selection from the choice list based on the index number of the option.	No	1.1, 1.2, 1.3	O, E, N
title	Used in the display of the selection on its own screen.	No	1.1, 1.2, 1.3	O, E, N
multiple	Can be set to true, which means that multiple items from the list can be picked, or false, which is the default. Only one item on the list can be picked at a time.	No	1.1, 1.2, 1.3	O, E, N
tabindex	Sets the order in which this element is tabbed to from the set of elements displayed.	No	1.1, 1.2, 1.3	O, E, N

\<setvar\>

Sets a variable name to a value; can appear only inside the refresh and go elements.

- Element versions: 1.1, 1.2, 1.3
- Supported by: Openwave, Ericsson, and Nokia

Attribute	Description	Required?	Versions	Supported by
name	The name of the variable being set	Yes	1.1, 1.2, 1.3	O, E, N
value	The value that the variable is assigned	Yes	1.1, 1.2, 1.3	O, E, N

\<small\>

Displays text in a smaller-sized font than normal.

- ◆ **Element versions:** 1.1, 1.2, 1.3
- ◆ **Supported by:** Ericsson and Nokia

\<strong\>

Displays text in a more emphasized appearance than normal.

- ◆ **Element versions:** 1.1, 1.2, 1.3
- ◆ **Supported by:** Ericsson and Nokia

\<table\>

Defines how rows and columns of data can appear in a tabular format on the display.

- ◆ **Element versions:** 1.1, 1.2, 1.3
- ◆ **Supported by:** Openwave, Ericsson, and Nokia

Attribute	Description	Required?	Versions	Supported by
title	Provides a name or label for the current table.	No	1.1, 1.2, 1.3	E, N
align	Indicates one of the following types of alignment for items in the table columns: left, center, or right (L, C, or R).	No	1.1, 1.2, 1.3	O, E, N
columns	Specifies the number of columns in the table.	Yes	1.1, 1.2, 1.3	O, E, N

\<td\>

Required in a table to delimit the data in a cell.

- ◆ **Element versions:** 1.1, 1.2, 1.3
- ◆ **Supported by:** Openwave, Ericsson, and Nokia

<template>

Appears at the very top of a deck; specifies actions that apply to all the cards in that deck.

- ◆ **Element versions:** 1.1, 1.2, 1.3
- ◆ **Supported by:** Openwave, Ericsson, and Nokia

<timer>

Defines a timer that starts if the relevant `onevent` is in the current card.

- ◆ **Element versions:** 1.1, 1.2, 1.3
- ◆ **Supported by:** Openwave, Ericsson, and Nokia

Attribute	Description	Required?	Versions	Supported by
name	The programmatic name for referring to the timer.	No	1.1, 1.2, 1.3	O, E, N
value	Specifies how long a timer should run before launching the associated event. The granularity for this value is 1/10ths of a second.	Yes	1.1, 1.2, 1.3	O, E, N

<tr>

Delimits a table row.

- ◆ **Element versions:** 1.1, 1.2, 1.3
- ◆ **Supported by:** Openwave, Ericsson, and Nokia

<u>

Underlines any text that appears between this and the `</u>` tag.

- ◆ **Element versions:** 1.1, 1.2, 1.3
- ◆ **Supported by:** Openwave, Ericsson, and Nokia

<wml>

The root element of any deck; contains every other element.

- **Element versions:** 1.1, 1.2, 1.3
- **Supported by:** Openwave, Ericsson, and Nokia

Elements Specific to Openwave

The following elements are specific to Openwave browsers and will work in Openwave browser versions 4.*x* and higher. I recommend looking at the Openwave documentation for more details on how to use these elements (see www.openwave.com).

Openwave supports WML 1.1 in UP.Browser 3.1, but does so only by translating it into HDML before sending it to the phone.

If you need to use these extended elements, your DOCTYPE declaration should be altered as follows to replace the WAP Forum DOCTYPE declaration:

```
<!DOCTYPE wml PUBLIC "-//PHONE.COM//DTD WML 1.1//EN"
"http://www.phone.com/dtd/wml11.dtd" >
```

<catch>

Describes an action that occurs if there is an error. The `receive` element inside the `catch` stores the variables sent with the exception.

Attribute	Description
name	Specifies the URI for the resource location. Not required.
onthrow	The name of the event (navigation) that needs to occur if the exception occurs. Not required.

<exit>

Exits an Openwave browser context.

<link>

Allows for a resource to be fetched in the background while the user is looking at the current resource.

Attribute	Description
href	Specifies the URI for the resource location to be fetched in the background. Required.
sendreferer	Specifies whether the HTTP_REFERER header is to be sent to the application server. This attribute can be true or false. Not required.
rel	Specifies the relationship between the current deck with the link and the card being navigated to. It is usually set to next. Required.

\<receive\>

Receives data from another context.

Attribute	Description
name	The name of the variable whose values are being received. Required.

\<reset\>

Clears all the variables in the current context.

\<send\>

Sends variables to the calling context.

Attribute	Description
value	Specifies the values that are to be sent to the calling context. Required.

\<spawn\>

Creates a child context.

Attribute	Description
href	The pointer to the URI resource that will begin the new context. Required.
sendreferer	Specifies whether the HTTP_REFERER header is to be sent to the application server. This attribute can be true or false. Not required.
accept-charset	Specifies the character set for parameters sent to the server. These parameters appear as a comma-separated list of recognized character sets per RFC 2045 and RFC 2046. If unspecified, the default is to assume the same charset as the container element (card). Not required.
method	Can be set to either POST or GET, depending on the HTTP method you need for sending data to the application server. The default is GET. Not required.
onexit	The onexit event fires when the context ends if this attribute is set. Not required.

<throw>

Specifies a task that throws an exception.

Attribute	Description
name	The name of the exception to throw. Values are then sent using send elements inside the throw. Required.

Appendix B

WMLScript Operators

THE FOLLOWING SET OF TABLES LISTS the WMLScript operators. These operators are actions that can be taken on a single number or multiple numbers and, when combined, can be used to create more complex calculations or expressions.

TABLE B-1 SIMPLE WMLSCRIPT OPERATION LISTING

Operator	Operation
+=	Add numbers/combine strings and assign
-=	Subtract and assign
*=	Multiply and assign
/=	Divide and assign

TABLE B-2 WMLSCRIPT ASSIGNMENT OPERATORS

Operator	Operation
div=	Integer division and assign
%=	Remainder and assign
<<=	Bitwise left shift and assign
>>=	Bitwise right shift and assign
>>>=	Bitwise right shift zero fill and assign
&=	Bitwise AND and assign
^=	Bitwise XOR and assign
|=	Bitwise OR and assign

Table B-3 WMLSCRIPT BASIC OPERATIONS

Operator	Operation
+	Add numbers/combine strings
-	Subtract two numbers
*	Multiply two numbers
/	Divide two numbers
div	Integer division
%	Remainder
<<	Bitwise left shift
>>	Bitwise right shift
>>>	Bitwise right shift zero fill
&	Bitwise AND
^	Bitwise XOR
|	Bitwise OR

Table B-4 WMLSCRIPT UNARY OPERATORS

Operator	Operation
+	Plus
-	Minus
--	Pre- or post-decrement
++	Pre or post-increment
~	Bitwise NOT

Table B-5 WMLScript Logical Operators

Operator	Operation
&&	Logical AND
||	Logical OR
!	Logical NOT

Table B-6 WMLScript Comparison Operators

Operator	Operation
<	Less than
<=	Less than or equal
==	Equal
>=	Greater than or equal
>	Greater than
!=	Not equal to

WMLScript Operator Precedence

In the absence of any brackets or parentheses, Table B-7 shows the precedence order for operations in WMLScript. Many operators are at the same level of precedence and in those cases, if there are no parentheses, the operators are evaluated equally using the associativity rules. This is shown in the associativity column of the table. Precedences are classified using the A, B, and C scheme (and so on), with class A operations having the highest precedence.

TABLE B-7 OPERATOR PRECEDENCE

Operator	Precedence	Associativity	Input Type(s)	Result Type(s)	Operation Description
++	A	From right to left	number	number	pre- or post-increment (unary)
--	A	From right to left	number	number	pre- or post-decrement (unary)
+	A	From right to left	number	number	unary plus
-	A	From right to left	number	number	unary minus (negation)
~	A	From right to left	integer	integer	bitwise NOT (unary)
!	A	From right to left	Boolean	Boolean	logical NOT (unary)
typeof	A	From right to left	any	integer	return internal data type (unary)
isvalid	A	From right to left	any	Boolean	check for validity (unary)
*	B	From left to right	numbers	number	multiplication
/	B	From left to right	numbers	floating-point	division
div	B	From left to right	integers	integer	integer division
%	B	From left to right	integers	integer	remainder
-	C	From left to right	numbers	number	subtraction

Operator	Precedence	Associativity	Input Type(s)	Result Type(s)	Operation Description
+	C	From left to right	numbers or strings	number or string	addition (numbers) or string concatenation
<<	D	From left to right	integers	integer	bitwise left shift
>>	D	From left to right	integers	integer	bitwise right shift with sign
>>>	D	From left to right	integers	integer	bitwise right shift with zero fill
<, <=	E	From left to right	numbers or strings	Boolean	less than, less than or equal
>, >=	E	From left to right	numbers or strings	Boolean	greater than, greater or equal
==	F	From left to right	numbers or strings	Boolean	equal (identical values)
!=	F	From left to right	numbers or strings	Boolean	not equal (different values)
&	G	From left to right	integers	integer	bitwise AND
^	H	From left to right	integers	integer	bitwise XOR
|	I	From left to right	integers	integer	bitwise OR
&&	J	From left to right	Boolean	Boolean	logical AND
||	K	From left to right	Boolean	Boolean	logical OR

Continued

TABLE B-7 OPERATOR PRECEDENCE *(Continued)*

Operator	Precedence	Associativity	Input Type(s)	Result Type(s)	Operation Description
? :	L	From right to left	Boolean, any, any	any	conditional expression
=	M	From right to left	variable, any	any	assignment
*=, -=	M	From right to left	variable, number	number	assignment with numeric operation
/=	M	From right to left	variable, floating-number	point	assignment with numeric operation
%=, div=	M	From right to left	variable, integer	integer	assignment with integer operation
+=	M	From right to left	variable, number or string	number or string	assignment with addition or concatenation
<<=, >>=, >>>=, &=, ^=, |=	M	From right to left	variable, integer	integer	assignment with bitwise operation
,	N	From left to right	any	any	multiple evaluation

WMLScript Statements

The following set of tables contains information about WMLScript statements. These statements are special expressions and keywords that use a specific syntax. They can be on a single line or span multiple lines with multiple statements appearing on a single line. These statements form the core set of keywords for the WMLScript language.

Appendix B: WMLScript Operators 601

Table B-8 PRIMARY DECLARATIONS

Statement	Description
| Function | This is an important statement in WMLScript because every unit is a function. This statement is used to declare a function and its associated parameters. A `return` statement is used to get a value back to the caller. Example:<br><br>```
function square(x) {
    ...
}
``` |
| Var | This is another important statement because all variables that are used in WMLScript have to be declared. Initializing is not required. Example:<br><br>```
var b;
var a = 5;
``` |
| Use | This is the statement used to start a pragma (see Table B-11). Example:

`use url complex_functions "http://www.test.com/someplace/somescript.wmls` |

Table B-9 LOOPING AND LOGICAL CONTROL

WMLScript Statement	Description
| `while` | Used to create a repeating loop if the beginning test returns a `true`. The loop continues to repeat, all the time checking the condition. The loop terminates when the condition returns a `false`. Example:<br><br>```
while (continue <= 0 )
{
    occurrence = last_val;
    continue = occurrence - 10;
}
``` |

Continued
```

Table B-9 LOOPING AND LOGICAL CONTROL *(Continued)*

WMLScript Statement	Description
| for | Used to create loop by defining three statements enclosed in parentheses and separated by semicolons at the beginning of the loop. These three statements are all optional. The first statement of the three initializes the loop counter(s). The second tests the loop condition, and the last increments the counter. Example:<br><br>```
for (var a=20; a<0; a--)
{
    // do an action
    sum = a + sum;
}
``` |
| if/else | Used to execute a block of statements if the condition is `true` and another block if the condition is `false`. The `else` portion of the `if` statement is optional and does not have to be used. Example:<br><br>```
if (x < 100)
{
    output = "not big enough";
}
else
{
    output = "you made it";
}
``` |

Table B-10 CONTROL STATEMENTS

Statement	Description
break	This statement breaks from a `while` loop at a point in the loop. The program then continues execution after the loop. Example: ```\nwhile (x < 100) {\n\nx = x + 1;\n\nderivative = x*x +1;\n\nif (derivative = 201) {\n\nbreak;\n\n}\n\n}\n```
continue	This statement prevents execution of any statements that appear after it in a continuous loop and proceeds with the next iteration. Example: ```\nvar x = 1;\n\nwhile (x<10) {\n\nif (x == 7) {\n\ncontinue;\n\n}\n\nx = sum + x;\n\n} // skips over 7 when summing\n```
return	Use a `return` statement inside the body of a function to specify the function return value. If you do not specify a `return` statement or none of the function `return` statements is executed, the function returns an empty string. Example: ```\nfunction square(x) {\n\nanswer = x*x;\n\nreturn answer;\n\n}\n```

WMLScript Pragmas

WMLScript supports three pragmas, which can be thought of as WMLScript directives that appear near the beginning of WMLScript files. The directives and their capabilities are shown in the following table.

TABLE B-11 WMLSCRIPT PRAGMAS

Pragma	Description
url	Used to store functions that are required by the current WMLScript to be placed in external WMLScript files. Usage: `use url ID "URL";` Example: `use url math_stuff "http://www.test.com/math/stuff/scripts.wmls"`
access	Used to limit the access of the current WMLScript file only to the URL prefixes calculated from the domain and/or path strings. Usage: `use access domain "domain" path "path";` Example: `use access domain "example.com" path "/test/scripts"`

meta	Used to give additional information to the browser.
	
	Usage: `use meta type property content scheme`
	
	Examples:
	
	`use meta name "Created" "05-April-2001";`
	
	`use meta http equiv "KeyProps" "Scripting,Tables";`
	
	`use meta user agent "Version" "1.01";`
	
	The three types supported for meta are `name`, `http-equiv`, and `user-agent`.
	
	None of the browsers supports this meta pragma right now.

WMLScript Comments

Comments in WMLScript can be in either the C style:

```
/*
a=4
b=5;
*/
```

or in the C++ style:

```
// counter = 15;
```

WMLScript Escape Codes

WMLScript allows for escape codes to be used when characters must be represented that cannot be typed. Table B-12 shows the relevant sequences used to insert those special codes.

TABLE B-12 WMLSCRIPT ESCAPE CODES

Sequence	Character Represented	Unicode	Symbol
\'	Apostrophe or single quotation mark	\u0027	'
\"	Double quotation mark	\u0022	"
\\	Backslash	\u005C	\
\/	Slash	\u002F	/
\b	Backspace	\u0008	
\f	Form feed	\u000C	
\n	Newline	\u000A	
\r	Carriage return	\u000D	
\t	Horizontal tab	\u0009	
\xhh	The character with the encoding specified by two hexadecimal digits *hh* (Latin-1 ISO8859-1)		
\ooo	The character with the encoding specified by the three octal digits *ooo* (Latin-1 ISO8859-1)		
\uhhhh	The Unicode character with the encoding specified by the four hexadecimal digits *hhhh*		

WMLScript Reserved Words

WMLScript reserved words cannot be used as identifiers in WMLScript code because they also have a special meaning in the code. So for example, you cannot create a function called `access` or create a variable called `break`, because those identifiers clash with the WMLScript meaning.

access	extern	path
agent	for	return
break	function	typeof
continue	header	use
div	http	user
div=	if	url
equiv	isvalid	var
domain	meta	while
else	name	

WMLScript keywords not already being used

This list of words also cannot be used as identifiers in WMLScript code. However, the difference between this and the earlier list is that these words have not yet been used in the WMLScript language and might never be used.

delete	new	void
in	null	with
lib	this	

Future reserved words

This is the final list of words that cannot be used as identifiers in WMLScript code. These words do not exist in the WMLScript language today but may exist in future versions of the WMLScript language.

case	enum	sizeof
catch	export	struct
class	extends	super
const	finally	switch
debugger	import	throw
default	private	try
do	public	

Appendix C

WMLScript Libraries

THE WMLSCRIPT VIRTUAL MACHINE INCLUDES support for functions above and beyond the base languages. These functions are grouped into libraries because of their common nature. These groupings are used as a structured way of calling functions within the libraries.

The following libraries were in WAP 1.1.

- Lang
- String
- URL
- WMLBrowser
- Dialogs
- Float

The Crypto library was added in WAP 1.2.

Also, some simulator/SDK vendors have added their own set of libraries to aid developers. The two that are shown in this appendix are for the Nokia and Openwave SDKs. These debugging libraries follow the same syntax and calling structure as a standard library; however, they do not work on a real WAP device.

Tables C-1 through C-9 present the full list of the libraries, with examples. For more detailed examples and screenshots, see Chapter 8.

TABLE C-1 LANG LIBRARY FUNCTIONS

Function	Description

abs(*value*)	Returns the absolute value of a number.
	`var m = -4;`
	`var n = Lang.abs(m);   // n = 4`

Continued

TABLE C-1 LANG LIBRARY FUNCTIONS *(Continued)*

Function	Description

min(*value1, value2*)	Returns the minimum value of the two given numbers. The value and type returned are the same as the selected number.
	
	var m = -4, n = 7.6;
	
	var p = Lang.min(m,n); // p = -4

max(*value1,value2*)	Returns the maximum value of the two given numbers. The value and type returned are the same as the selected number.
	
	var m = -4, n = 7.6;
	
	var p = Lang.max(m,n); // p = 7.6

parseInt(*value*)	Returns an integer value defined by the string input value.
	
	var m = "7658";
	
	var n = "16 km";
	
	var p = "15% of 600";
	
	var q = Lang.parseInt(m); // q = 7658
	
	var r = Lang.parseInt(n); // n = 16
	
	var s = Lang.parseInt(p); // s = 15

parseFloat(*value*)	Returns a floating-point value defined by the string input value. The parsing ends when the first character is encountered that cannot be parsed.
	
	var m = "7.7";
	
	var n = "16.1 Gauss";
	
	var p = "15 e-2";
	
	var q = "+45.7 miles";
	
	var r = "Here is 7.7";
	
	var s = Lang.parseFloat(m); // s = 7.7
	
	var t = Lang.parseFloat(n); // t = 16.1
	
	var u = Lang.parseFloat(p); // u = 15e-2
	
	var v = Lang.parseFloat(q); // v = 45.7
	
	var w = Lang.parseFloat(r); // w = invalid

Function	Description
isInt(*value*)	Returns a Boolean value that is true if the given value can be converted into an integer using parseInt; otherwise, false is returned.
	`var m = "-7";`
	`var n = "16.1";`
	`var p = "Name";`
	`var q = false;`
	`var r = "Here is 7.7";`
	`var s = Lang.isInt(m);    // s = true`
	`var t = Lang.isInt(n);    // t = true`
	`var u = Lang.isInt(p);    // u = false`
	`var v = Lang.isInt(q);    // v = false`
	`var w = Lang.isInt(r);    // w = false`
isFloat(value)	Returns a Boolean value that is true if the given value can be converted into an integer using parseFloat; otherwise, false is returned.
	`var m = "-7";`
	`var n = "16.1";`
	`var p = "Name";`
	`var q = false;`
	`var r = "Here is 7.7";`
	`var s = Lang.isFloat(m);  // s = true`
	`var t = Lang.isFloat(n);  // t = true`
	`var u = Lang.isFloat(p);  // u = false`
	`var v = Lang.isFloat(q);  // v = false`
	`var w = Lang.isFloat(r);  // w = false`

Continued

TABLE C-1 LANG LIBRARY FUNCTIONS *(Continued)*

Function	Description
maxInt()	Returns the maximum integer value supported by the WMLScript interpreter. `var m = Lang.maxInt();   // m = 2147483647`
minInt()	Returns the minimum integer value supported by the WMLScript interpreter. `var m = Lang.minInt();   // m = -2147483648`
float()	Returns `true` if floating-points are supported and `false` if they are not. `var m = Lang.float();   // m = true or false`

exit(*value*)	Ends the WMLScript interpretation and returns control back to the caller (WML space) with the given return value.
	
	`Lang.exit("End");   // return string "End"`
	
	`Lang.exit(64);   // return integer 64`

abort(*errorDescription*)	Aborts the WMLScript interpretation and returns control to the caller (WML space) with the error description string.
	
	`Lang.abort("Execution error");`
	
	`// return error string "Execution error"`

random(*value*)	Returns an integer value with a positive sign that is greater than or equal to 0 but less than or equal to the value input into the function. If the input is a floating point, it is converted to an integer first using `Float.int(...)`. The example shows how a random number between 0 and 10 can be generated. `var m = Lang.random(10.3);   // m= 0...10`

Function	Description
seed(*value*)	Initializes the pseudo-random number sequence and returns an empty string. The function call affects the random numbers generated by random(value). var m = Lang.seed(25); // m= ""

characterSet()	Returns the character set supported by WMLScript. The return value is an integer that denotes an enumerated value (MIBEnum) assigned by IANA for all character sets.
	
	var m = Lang.characterSet();
	
	// ie. character set is set to 1000 for
	
	// iso-10646-ucs-2

TABLE C-2 STRING LIBRARY FUNCTIONS

Function	Description

length(*string*)	Returns the number of characters in a given string.
	
	var m = "Test";
	
	var n = "";
	
	var p = 60000;
	
	var q = String.length(m); // q = 4
	
	var r = String.length(n); // r = 0
	
	var s = String.length(p); // s = 5

Continued

TABLE C-2 STRING LIBRARY FUNCTIONS *(Continued)*

Function	Description

isEmpty(*string*)	Returns Boolean `true` if the string length is zero; returns Boolean `false` otherwise.
	
	`var m = "Test";`
	`var n = "";`
	`var p = true;`
	`var q = String.isEmpty(m);   // q = false`
	`var r = String.isEmpty(n);   // r = true`
	`var s = String.isEmpty(p);   // s = false`

charAt(*string*, *index*)	Returns a single character representing the specified index in the string.
	
	`var m = "How was your day?";`
	`var q = String.charAt(m,0);   // q = "H"`
	`var r = String.charAt(m,2);   // r = "w"`
	`var s = String.charAt(m,3);   // s = " "`
	`var t = String.charAt(m,300); // t = ""`

subString (*string*, *startIndex*, *length*)	Returns a new string that is a substring of the inputted string. The substring begins at the `startIndex` and continues for the length specified. If the number of remaining characters is smaller than the length, the length is replaced with the number of remaining characters. The first character of a string is at index position 0; the second character is at 1; and so on.
	
	`var m = "Where did they go?";`
	`var q = String.subString(m,1,5);`
	`// q = "here "`
	`var r = String.subString(m,0,1);`
	`// r = "W"`
	`var s = String.subString(m,10,3);`
	`// s = "the"`

Function	Description

find(*string*, *subString*)	Returns the index of the first character in the string that matches the subString. If no match is found, the returned value is an integer set to –1. The characters in the strings should match exactly, including characters with multiple representations.
	
	var m = "I believe they walked over to the funny car under the over pass.";
	
	var q = String.find(m,"over");
	
	// q = 22
	
	var r = String.find(m,"strafe");
	
	// r = -1
	
	var s = String.find(m,"I");
	
	// s = 0

replace(*string*, *oldSubString*, *newSubString*)	Returns a new string resulting from replacing all the instances of oldSubString with newSubString. The characters in the strings should match exactly, including characters with multiple representations.
	
	var m = "That's funny. I don't see a funny car under there.";
	
	var q = String.replace(m,"funny","weird");
	
	// q = That's weird. I don't see a weird car under there.";

elements(*string*, *separator*)	Returns the number of elements in the given string separated by the indicated separator. The empty string is a valid element, so the function will never return a value less than or equal to zero.
	
	var m = "Yes, you are right. Where did the car go?";
	
	var q = String.elements(m," ");
	
	// q = 9

Continued

TABLE C-2 STRING LIBRARY FUNCTIONS *(Continued)*

Function	Description

`elementAt(string, index, separator)`	Returns a string value of the index element inside the given string using the indicated separator. An index of less than 0 forces the first element to be selected. If the index is larger than the number of elements, the last element is returned. If the string is empty, the empty string is returned. The string value selection uses a zero base for its index.
	
	`var m = "Oh, look!  The car just disappeared into that tunnel.";`
	
	`var q = String.elementAt(m,0," ");`
	
	`// q = "Oh,"`
	
	`var r = String.elementAt(m,200," ");`
	
	`// r = "tunnel."`
	
	`var s = String.elementAt(m,4," ");`
	
	`// s = "just"`

`removeAt(string, index, separator)`	Returns a new string in which an element from the string has been removed using the index and separator specified. If the index is less than 0, the first element is removed, and if the index is larger than the number of elements, the last element is removed.
	
	`var m = "Well, that sure is surprising, considering the tunnel was not there a minute ago."`
	
	`var q = String.removeAt(m,3," ");`
	
	`// q = "Well, that is surprising,`
	`// considering the tunnel was not there a // minute ago."`
	
	`var r = String.removeAt(m,200,",");`
	
	`// r = "Well, that sure is surprising"`

Function	Description

replaceAt(*string, element, index, separator*)	Returns a new string in which an element from the string is replaced using the index and separator specified. If the index is less than 0, the first element is replaced, and if the index is larger than the number of elements, the last element is replaced.
	
	`var m = "Now what? They are going North on the road to Tuscany.";`
	
	`var q = String.replaceAt(m,"South",6," ");`
	
	`// q = "Now what? They are going South on // the road to Tuscany.";`

insertAt(*string, element, index, separator*)	Returns a new string with the element and a separator (if needed). If the index is less than 0, the element is inserted in the first position, and if the index is larger than the number of elements, the element is placed in the last position.
	
	`var m = "Now what? They are going North on the road to Tuscany.";`
	
	`var q = String.insertAt(m,Stazione,10," ");`
	
	`// q = "Now what? They are going South on // the road to Stazione Tuscany.";`

squeeze(*string*)	Returns a string in which any consecutive white spaces within a string have been reduced to a single white space.
	
	`var m = "  apple orange  banana   ;  pear"`
	
	`var q = String.squeeze(m);`
	
	`// q = " apple orange banana ; pear"`

trim(*string*)	Returns a string in which all the leading or trailing white spaces have been removed.
	
	`var m = " apple orange  banana   ;  pear"`
	
	`var q = String.trim(m);`
	
	`// q = "apple orange  banana   ;  pear"`

Continued

TABLE C-2 STRING LIBRARY FUNCTIONS *(Continued)*

Function	Description

compare(*string1*, *string2*)	Returns a value that indicates what the relationship isbetween *string1* and *string2* based on the character codes of the native character set. The return value is -1 if *string1* is less than *string2*, 0 if *string1* is the same as *string2*, or 1 if *string1* is greater than *string2*.
	
	var m = "apple";
	
	var n = "pear";
	
	var q = String.compare(m,n);
	
	// q = -1
	
	var r = String.compare("apple","Apple");
	
	// r = 1

toString(*value*)	Returns a string representation of the given value. This is exactly the same conversion that occurs when the WMLScript language automatically converts Boolean, integer, and floating-point values to strings.
	
	var m = 25;
	
	var n = false;
	
	var p = 34.0;
	
	var q = String.toString(m); // q = "25"
	
	var r = String.toString(n);
	
	// r = "false"
	
	var s = String.toString(p); // s = "34.0"

format(*format*, *value*)	Returns a string that converts the value into a string using the formatting provided in the format string. You can find more details on this in Table C-3. var m = String.format("giraffes: %6d",24); m = "giraffes: 24"

The following table gives a detailed description of how the format codes for the `String.format` function are interpreted by the browser. These format codes have both a precision meaning and a type meaning. The usage of the letter in the format code has two effects on the output of the format. The first is related to how the numbers and decimals in the code are interpreted; this is the precision meaning. The second is how the letter affects the formatted characters and is the type meaning.

TABLE C-3 FORMAT CODES

Code	Description
d	**Precision meaning:** If the format type is d, the precision value identifies the total number of digits in the number. The output value is padded on the left with 0s. The value is not truncated when it exceeds the precision. **Type meaning:** The output value has the form [-]ddd, where ddd is one or more digits.
f	**Precision meaning:** If the format type is f, the precision value identifies the total number of digits after the decimal point. If a decimal point appears, at least one digit appears. The default precision is 6, and a precision of 0 means no point appears. **Type meaning:** The output value has the form [-]ddd.ddd, which is one or more digits. The number of digits before the decimal depends on the number, and the number of digits after the decimal depends on the precision.
s	**Precision meaning:** If the format type is s, the precision specifies the maximum number of characters to be printed. By default, all characters are printed. **Type meaning:** Characters are printed up to the precision value. If the width is larger than the precision, the width is ignored.

TABLE C-4 URL LIBRARY FUNCTIONS

Function	Description

isValid(*URL*)	Returns `true` if the input URL has the right syntax; otherwise, it returns `false`. Both absolute and relative URLs are supported by this function.
	
	`var m = URL.isValid("http://www.domain.com");`
	`// m = true`

Continued

TABLE C-4 URL LIBRARY FUNCTIONS *(Continued)*

Function	Description

getScheme(*URL*)	Returns the scheme used in the input URL. Both absolute and relative URLs are supported by this function.
	
	`var m = URL.getScheme("http://www.domain.com");`
	`// m = "http"`
	`var n = URL.getScheme("path/to/directory");`
	`// n = ""`

getHost(*URL*)	Returns the host used in the input URL. Both absolute and relative URLs are supported by this function.
	
	`var m = URL.getHost("http://www.domain.com");`
	`// m = "www.domain.com"`
	`var n = URL.getHost("path/to/directory");`
	`// n = ""`

getPort(*URL*)	Returns the port number specified in the input URL. Both absolute and relative URLs are supported by this function.
	
	`var m = URL.getPort("http://www.domain.com");`
	`// m = ""`
	`var n = URL.getPort("http://www.domain.com:80");`
	`// n = "80"`

getPath(*URL*)	Returns the path specified in the input URL. Both absolute and relative URLs are supported by this function.
	
	`var m = URL.getPath("http://www.domain.com");`
	`// m = ""`
	`var n = URL.getPath("path/to/directory");`
	`// n = "path/to/directory"`

getParameters(*URL*)	Returns the parameters used in the input URL. If the URL contains no parameters, an empty string is returned. Both absolute and relative URLs are supported by this function
	
	`var m = URL.getParameters("http://www.domain.com/code;12;24;36");`
	`// m = "12;24;36"`

Function	Description

getQuery(*URL*)	Returns the query part of the URL in the input. If there is no query part in the URL, an empty string is returned. Both absolute and relative URLs are supported by this function.
	
	`var m = URL.getQuery("http://www.domain.com/code.jsp?fname=Jane&lname=Doe");`
	
	`// m = "fname=Jane&lname=Doe"`

getFragment(*URL*)	Returns the fragment part of the URL in the input. If there is no fragment in the URL, an empty string is returned. Both absolute and relative URLs are supported by this function.
	
	`var m = URL.getFragment("http://www.domain.com/main#fifth");`
	
	`// m = "fifth"`

GetBase()	Returns an absolute URL (upper- or lowercase) without its fragment of the current WMLScript file.
	
	`var m = URL.getBase();`
	
	`// m = "http://www.domain.com/a.wmls");`

getReferer()	Returns the smallest relative URL of the resource that called the current WMLScript file. If there is no referrer, an empty string is returned.
	
	`var m = URL.getReferer();`
	
	`// m = "first.wml";`

resolve(*baseURL*, *embeddedURL*)	Returns an absolute URL from the given input URLs. If the embedded URL is already absolute, the returned string is the same.
	
	`var i = "http://www.domain.com";`
	
	`var j = "file.wml";`
	
	`var m = URL.resolve(i,j);`
	
	`// m = "http://www.domain.com/file.wml");`

Continued

TABLE C-4 URL LIBRARY FUNCTIONS *(Continued)*

Function	Description

escapeString (*string*)	Returns a new version of the string in which the special characters have been replaced by their hexadecimal escape sequence (of the form %xx). Non-ASCII characters in the string will force an invalid response. Example:
	
	`var a = URL.escapeString("http://w.h.com/dck?x=\u007f#crd");`
	
	`   // a = "http%3a%2f%2fw.h.com%2fdck%3fx%3d%7f%23crd"`

unescapeString (*string*)	Returns a new version of the string in which escape sequences have been replaced with the special characters they represent. Non-ASCII characters in the string will force an invalid response.
	
	`var i = "http://www.domain.com/%40";`
	
	`var m = URL.unescapeString(i);`
	
	`// m = "http://www.domain.com/@");`

loadString (*URL, contentType*)	Returns the content referenced by the URL as a string.
	
	There must only be *one* content type, and it must be of type text but it can be of any subtype. If the content type does not match the loaded value, the result is invalid.
	
	Loading from URLs may result in scheme-specific error codes; for example, HTTP 404. The value returned is then an integer.
	
	`var i = "http://www.domain.com/security.str";`
	
	`var m = URL.loadString(i,"text/x-str");`

Appendix C: WMLScript Libraries

TABLE C-5 WMLBROWSER LIBRARY FUNCTIONS

Function	Description

getVar(*name*)	Returns the value of the named variable in the WML context. This is an empty string if the variable is not defined.
	
	`var m = WMLBrowser.getVar("ccno");`
	
	`// m = "4356 2236 2323 3490"`

setVar(*name*, *value*)	Returns `true` if the named variable was set successfully in the current WML context, `false` otherwise. The syntax of WML variables should be complied with and the variable's value must be legal XML CDATA.
	
	`var m = WMLBrowser.setVar("age","23");`
	
	`// m = true`

go(*URL*)	Specifies to load the content denoted by the given URL. The functionality here is exactly the same as a WML go task.
	
	`WMLBrowser.go("#second_card");`
	
	`// this navigates to the second card in the`
	
	`// calling WML file`

prev()	Specifies to load the previous URL as indicated by the navigational history. Both the `prev` and `go` functions override each other. Only the last `prev` or `go` function is honored by the WML context.
	
	`WMLBrowser.prev();`
	
	`// this navigates to the last card in`
	
	`// the history`

newContext()	Returns an empty string after clearing the WML context. The function has the same functionality as a WML card `newContext` attribute.
	
	`WMLBrowser.newContext();`
	
	`// issues a newContext for the WML space`

getCurrentCard()	«Returns the smallest relative URL that is used to access the current WMLScript file.
	
	`var m = WMLBrowser.getCurrentCard();`
	
	`// m = "first.wml#second_card"`

Continued

TABLE C-5 WMLBROWSER LIBRARY FUNCTIONS *(Continued)*

Function	Description

refresh ()	Forces the WMLBrowser context to execute the refresh task. This is equivalent to the WML refresh task. The user interface may be updated as a result of this function call.
	
	`WMLBrowser.refresh();`
	
	`// refreshes the screen in WML space based on`
	
	`// variable updates

TABLE C-6 DIALOGS LIBRARY FUNCTIONS

Function	Description

prompt(*message, defaultInput*)	Displays the given text message, prompts for user input, and returns the user input as a string.
	
	`var m = "11/22/74";`
	
	`var n = Dialogs.prompt("DOB ", m);`

confirm(*message, ok, cancel*)	Displays the given text message and prompts for two possible inputs: `ok` and `cancel`. The function then waits for the user to select an option, and returns `true` for `ok` and `false` for `cancel`.
	
	`var m = Dialogs.confirm("Is this correct?","Yes","No");`
	
	`if m == false {`
	
	`   // set default value`
	
	`} else`
	
	`{`
	
	`   // continue using input value`
	
	`}`

Function	Description
alert(`message`)	Displays the given text message to the user and waits for user confirmation. The function returns the empty string. `Dialogs.alert("The date is invalid");`

TABLE C-7 FLOAT LIBRARY FUNCTIONS

Function	Description

int(`value`)	Returns the integer part of the value. If the value is an integer, the same value is returned.
	
	`var m = 2.7183;`
	`var n = Float.int(m);   // n = 2`

floor(`value`)	Returns the greatest integer that is not *greater* than the value. If the value is an integer, the same value is returned.
	
	`var m = 2.7183;`
	`var n = Float.floor(m);   // n = 2`

ceil(`value`)	Returns the smallest integer that is not *less* than the value. If the value is an integer, the same value is returned.
	
	`var m = 2.7183;`
	`var n = Float.ceil(m);   // n = 3`

pow(`value1, value2`)	Returns an approximation of the result of raising `value1` to the power of `value2`. If `value1` is a negative number, `value2` must be an integer.
	
	`var m = 2;`
	`var n = 3;`
	`var p = Float.pow(m,n);   // p = 8`

Continued

TABLE C-7 FLOAT LIBRARY FUNCTIONS *(Continued)*

Function	Description

round(*value*)	Returns the number value that is closest to the value and is mathematically equivalent. If two integers are equally likely to be the closest, the larger value is chosen. If the value is an integer, the same value is returned.
	
	`var m = 2.7183;`
	`var n = Float.round(m);   // n = 3`
	`var p = -2.7183;`
	`var q = Float.round(p);   // q = -2`

sqrt(*value*)	Returns an approximation of the square root of the input value.
	
	`var m = 16.0;`
	`var n = Float.sqrt(m);   // n = 4.0`
	`var m = 200.0;`
	`var n = Float.sqrt(m);   // n = 14.142`

maxFloat()	Returns the maximum floating-point value supported by the WMLScript interpreter. This should be the IEEE single-precision maximum, which is 3.40282347E+38.
	
	`var m = Float.maxFloat();`
	`// m = 3.40282347E+38`

minFloat()	Returns the smallest non-zero floating-point value supported by the WMLScript interpreter. This should be the IEEE single-precision minimum, which is 1.17549435E-38.
	
	`var m = Float.minFloat();`
	`// m = 1.17549435E-38`

Table C-8 Nokia Debug Library Functions

Nokia Debug Library Function	Description

closeFile()	Closes an open debugging file.
	`Debug.openFile("c:\testing.txt", "w");`
	`Debug.printLn("Variable value is" + x);`
	`Debug.closeFile();`

openFile (*filename*, *mode*)	Opens a file for debugging purposes, the modes can be "a" for appending, "r" for reading only, or "w" for writing or killing an existing file and starting over.
	`Debug.openFile("c:\testing.txt", "a");`
	`Debug.printLn("Variable value is" + x);`
	`Debug.closeFile();`

printLn(*string*)	Writes to an open debugging file.
	`Debug.openFile("c:\testing.txt", "a");`
	`Debug.printLn("Variable value is" + x);`
	`Debug.closeFile();`

Table C-9 Openwave Console Library

Openwave Debug Library Function	Description
print(*string*)	Writes text to a debug window. `Console.print("Variable value is" + x);`
printLn(*string*)	Writes text to a debug window *and* inserts a new line character after it. `Console.printLn("Variable value is" + x);`

Crypto library function

The Crypto library function is as follows:

```
signedString = signText (stringToSign, options, keyIdType, keyId)
```

This function returns a base-64 encoded signed string that can be sent to a Web server and stored for accountability purposes. The function should use keys that are different from WTLS keys.

OPTIONS
The following options can be ORed together:

- 0: No options
- 1: Include *stringToSign* in the result
- 2: Include key's hash in the result
- 4: Include certificate URL in the result

For the keyIdType:

- 0: No key identifier indicated; use anything available
- 1: An SHA-1 hash of a user public key is specified in *keyId*
- 2: An SHA-1 hash of a trusted CA public key is specified in *keyId*

KEYID
Contains the 20 byte SHA-1 hash if applicable.

Because the string is presented to the user, the function can be cancelled and, in that case, the function will return error:userCancel.

The function may not find a valid key to sign the string with. In all those cases, it will return error:noCert.

Any other errors will result in an invalid type being returned.

Appendix D

WTAI Libraries and Events

THE WTAI LIBRARIES FOLLOW the syntax and format of WML and WMLScript wherever required by their functions and events. The libraries can be put into three groupings:

- ◆ Public Libraries: Libraries that apply to all networks and can be invoked in the standard browser. This is the only library available to outside developers.

- ◆ Network Common Libraries: Libraries that apply to all networks but can be invoked only by the WTA browser.

- ◆ Network Specific Libraries: Libraries that apply to only one specific network and furthermore can be invoked only by the WTA browser. Today network specific libraries exist only for GSM, IS-136, and PDC. WAP 2.0 added a library for IS-95 networks.

For developers, it is important to note that to date the only noticeable implementation of WTA is the fact that Openwave supports the `makeCall` public function in its browser.

TABLE D-1 WTAI PUBLIC LIBRARY FUNCTIONS

Function	Description

WMLScript: `makeCall(number)`
WML: `wtai://wp/mc;number!retVal`
	Begins a voice call using the number specified. The WTAI public developer cannot stop the call once initiated. The number must be a valid phone number, which can be dialed by the phone interface. The function returns an empty string if successful, an invalid if unsuccessful, and an error-code for any other issues.
	
	Return values:
	
	Empty string or invalid or error code, which is one of the following:
	
	-105 called number is busy
	
	-106 network is unavailable
	
	-107 called number was not answered
	
	-200 invocation error (URL form only)
	
	-1 unknown error
	
	Example:
	
	`var retVal = WTAPublic.makeCall("18882349876")`
	
	`<go href="wtai://wp/mc;18882349876!retVal"/>`

Function	Description
WMLScript: sendDTMF (dtmfString) WML: wtai:// wp/sd;dtmfString!retVal	Sends a DTMF string to the device that answers a call that has previously been set up. The function returns an empty string if successful, an invalid ?? if unsuccessful, and an error-code for any other issues. Return values: Empty string or invalid or error code, which is one of the following, -108 no active voice call -200 invocation error (URL form only) -1 unknown error Example: var retVal = WTAPublic.sendDTMF("1113*657") <go href="wtai://wp/sd;1113*657!retVal"/>
WMLScript: addPBEntry (number,name) WML: wtai: //wp/ap;number;name! retVal	Adds a new entry to the phone address book. The function returns an empty string if successful, an invalid ?? if unsuccessful, and an error-code for any other issues. Return values: Empty string or invalid or error code, which is one of the following, -100 name is too long or cannot be accepted -101 number is not a valid phone number -102 number is too long -103 name and number could not be written -104 phone address book is full -1 unspecified error -200 invocation error (URL form only) Example: var retVal = WTAPublic.addPBEntry ("5551212", "Info") <go href="wtai://wp/ap;5551212;Info! retVal"/>

Table D-2 WTAI Voice Call Library

Function	Description
setup	Initiates a call from the mobile that is nonblocking to subsequent function calls. A mode parameter specifies whether to drop or keep the call if the WTA context terminates.
accept	Accepts an incoming voice call. It is also a nonblocking function, and various events are triggered that can be used to check the call progress.
release	Releases a voice call and sends out an event that the call has been released.
sendDTMF	Sends a DTMF sequence on a previously set up voice call.
callStatus	Returns information about the call that can be useful to the developer, such as the name, number, status, duration, and mode of the call.
list	Returns a call handle that can be subsequently applied to finding the call status information.
	The function must be called repeatedly to traverse a list of previously issued calls available to the current context. For example, say that four calls were available in the context of #1, #2, #3, and #4. The list function has a Boolean parameter, which is controlled to specify which call from the list to obtain. So, list(true) returns the oldest call, #1. list(false) returns the next oldest call, #2 in this case. Therefore, to traverse the list, you would use:
	list(true); // #1
	list(false); // #2
	list(false); // #3
	list(false); // #4

Table D-3 WTAI Network Message Library

Function	Description
send	Sends a short text message.
list	Returns a message handle for the existing message and may be called repeatedly to retrieve information about all messages.

Function	Description
remove	Removes an incoming or outgoing message from the mobile device.
getFieldValue	Obtains information about a specific field for a message.
markAsRead	Marks a message as having been read.

TABLE D-4 WTAI PHONEBOOK LIBRARY

Function	Description
write	Writes an entry to the phonebook overwriting anything in the phonebook.
read	Searches through the phonebook for an entry that matches the given criteria. The index of an empty phonebook is never returned.
remove	Removes an entry from the phonebook.
getFieldValue	Retrieves a field value from a phonebook entry.
change	Stores the given value in the specified field in a phonebook entry, overwriting any existing value.

TABLE D-5 WTAI CALL LOGS LIBRARY

Function	Description
dialed	Returns the call log handle of an entry from the call log. It can be called repeatedly to obtain all such entries.
missed	Returns the call log handle of an entry from the missed call log. It can be called repeatedly to obtain all such entries.
received	Returns the call log handle of an entry from the received call log. It can be called repeatedly to obtain all such entries.
getFieldValue	Retrieves a field value from a specific call long entry.

TABLE D-6 WTAI NETWORK MESSAGE LIBRARY

Function	Description
setIndicator	Modifies the state of a logical indicator. This indicator can be for incoming voice calls, data calls, or multiple other messages that the device may be capable of. The mobile device to indicate an incoming type to the user uses the indicators. This state can be changed by programmatically using this function to set or unset this indicator.
endContext	Terminates the current WTA user agent context.
getProtection	Retrieves the protection mode of the current WTA context. Protection modes are discussed in the call state management section of Chapter 11, "WTA."
setProtection	Sets the protection mode of the current WTA context. Protection modes are discussed in the call state management section of Chapter 11.

TABLE D-7 NETWORK COMMON EVENTS

Event	Description
wtaev-cc/ic	Indicates that an incoming call is arriving on the mobile device. An accept call function can be used to start the call. This is also shown in the call model diagram. Parameters: callHandle: Call handle for the call (used to track the calls) callerID: The phone number of the caller

Event	Description
wtaev-cc/cl	Fires when a voice call has cleared.
	Parameters:
	`callHandle`: Call handle for the call (used to track the calls)
	`result`: Contains a description of why the call was cancelled
	0 normal termination
	1 no details available
	2 network reason
	3 call was dropped
	4 called party was busy
	5 network is not available
	6 called party did not answer
wtaev-cc/co	Sent when a called party has accepted a call.
	Parameters:
	`callHandle`: Call handle for the call (used to track the calls)
	`callerID`: The phone number of the caller
wtaev-cc/oc	Indicates that an outgoing call is being initiated.
	Parameters:
	`callHandle`: Call handle for the call (used to track the calls)
	`number`: The phone number being called
wtaev-cc/cc	Fires when a call has been placed to another party and the phone on that end is ringing.
	Parameters:
	`callHandle`: Contains the call handle to the call
wtaev-cc/dtmf	Fires when a DTMF string is sent to the called party.
	Parameters:
	`callHandle`: Contains the call handle of the call
	`dtmfString`: Contains the DTMF sequence that was sent

Continued

TABLE D-7 NETWORK COMMON EVENTS *(Continued)*

Event	Description
wtaev-nt/st	Indicates that the status of an outgoing message has changed. Parameters: msgHandle: Contains the message handle as defined earlier result: Contains a description of the change to the outgoing message 0 message sent 1 message abandoned for unknown reason 2 message abandoned due to network reasons 3 message abandoned due to lack of resources
wtaev-nt/it	Indicates that a message has been received. Parameters: msgHandle: Contains the message handle sender: Contains the identity of the sender as a network address field or null string if unknown
wtaev-ms/ns	Fires to indicate that the value of one or more of the defined network status parameters has changed. Parameters: inService: Indicates whether the device is capable of placing or receiving calls 0 Device is not in service 1 Device is in service networkName: Contains identifier of the network that the device is using or is undefined if the device is not in service explanation: Contains the reason that the device is not in service or is undefined if the device is not in service 0 No explanation given 1 No networks found 2 All networks found were forbidden

GSM Libraries and Events

Up until now, the libraries and events listed have been quite general, applying to all network technologies. Because the existing digital technologies deviate in terms of the services that they offer users, as well as in the way in which some basic behavior is conducted, this results in differences in some of the WTAI libraries and events.

The last section includes those libraries and events that are common to all technologies. This section describes the additional WTAI libraries and events for GSM.

Table D-8 WTA GSM Library Functions

Function	Description
WTAGSM.hold	Puts a call on hold.
WTAGSM.retrieve	Makes a held call active again.
WTAGSM.transfer	Transfers an active call.
WTAGSM.deflect	Deflects an unanswered call.
WTAGSM.multiparty	Joins/creates a multiparty call.
WTAGSM.separate	Retrieves a party from a multiparty call.
WTAGSM.sendUSSD	Sends a USSD message.
WTAGSM.netinfo	Gets network information.

Table D-9 WTA GSM Events

GSM Event	Description
wtaev-gsm/ch	Fires when a GSM voice or multiparty call is put on hold. The call is put back in active mode by using WTAGSM.retrieve and released by using WTAGSM.release.
wtaev-gsm/ca	Fires when a call is moved from the held state to the active state.
wtaev-gsm/ru	Fires when a USSD message is received by the mobile device.

IS-136 (ANSI 136) Libraries and Events

This section lists the IS-136 libraries and events. They include descriptions of functions such as the flash and alert capability and events related to them. These are the only additional capabilities of IS-136.

TABLE D-10 WTA IS-136 LIBRARY FUNCTIONS

Function	Description
WTAANSI136.sendFlash	Sends out a flash code.
WTAANSI136.sendAlert	Sends out an alert code.

TABLE D-11 WTA IS-136 EVENTS

Event	Description
wtaev-ansi136/ia	Indicates that an incoming alert has been received by the mobile device.
wtaev-ansi136/if	Fires when an incoming alert flash has been received by the mobile device.

PDC Libraries and Events

The following tables list the additional libraries and events for the PDC technology, which is used predominantly in Japan. The PDC technology allows for much greater control of voice calls, which translates into many additional functions and events.

Table D-12 WTA PDC LIBRARY FUNCTIONS

Function	Description
WTAPDC.hold	Puts a call on hold.
WTAPDC.retrieve	Makes a held call active again.
WTAPDC.transfer	Transfers an active call.
WTAPDC.deflect	Deflects an unanswered call.
WTAPDC.multiparty	Creates a multiparty call.
WTAPDC.separate	Retrieves a party from a multiparty call.

Table D-13 WTA PDC EVENTS

Event	Description
wtaev-pdc/ch	Fires when a PDC voice call is put on hold. The call is put back in active mode by using WTAPDC.retrieve and released by using WTAPDC.release.
wtaev-pdc/ca	Fires when a call is moved from the held state to the active state.

IS-95 Libraries and Events

This is a new set of functions and events that have been added specifically for the IS-95 network. The IS-95 technology includes better text capabilities and more voice control functionality.

TABLE D-14 WTA IS-95 LIBRARY FUNCTIONS

Function	Description
WTAIS95.sendText	Sends an SMS message and is a non-blocking function. The events in the next table show how the progress can be checked.
WTAIS95.cancelText	Cancels the delivery of a pending SMS message.
WTAIS95.sendAck	Sends a user SMS acknowledgement in response to an incoming SMS message.

TABLE D-15 WTA IS-95 EVENTS

Event	Description
wtaev-is95/da	This fires when an SMS message has been acknowledged by the handset.
wtaev-is95/ua	This fires when the user acknowledges the receipt of an SMS message.

Appendix E

WBMP Image Format

THE WAP STANDARD TODAY supports the display of only a single image format on the devices. This format is known as WBMP. The display of images on devices is imperative for such tiny screens because conveying information using only text is often very difficult. Directions, a corporate logo, or a graph showing the historical stock price are all good examples of cases in which the textual versions fail in giving the WAP user immediate "visualization" of information.

Many of today's mobile devices limit the amount of data that can be transferred. This limitation varies and affects the size of the image that can be displayed in the WAP client, because it is a resource that must be sent to the device.

WBMP

The image format in WAP is WBMP. The WBMP format is not very different from the BMP format in its definition. WBMP is a 1-bit/pixel format today, where only black and white images are supported. The WBMP file contains two parts, a header and the image data. The header fields are shown in Table E-1.

TABLE E-1 WBMP STRUCTURE

Element	Bytes	Description	Typical Values
Type	1	Image type	Set only to 0 today.
Header properties	1		None defined. Set to 0.
Other headers	0	External headers	No such headers supported now.
Width	1–2	Width of image	
Height	1–2	Height of image	
Image	1–n	0 means black 1 means white	

Height and width

Both of these can be one or two bytes depending on the size of the image. The last bit in the first byte is used to indicate whether two bytes are used. So, 127 can be done using one byte as 1111111, but 128 would be represented as 1000001 11111111. This bit is set to 1 in case two bytes are used.

Image definition

Images are described using 0 or 1 to represent 0 = black and 1 = white. No compression is implemented for WBMP. The most significant bit of each byte is the left pixel in the image, and the upper row of the image is the top row in the byte structure.

Figure E-1 shows an example of using an X, done on a 5x5 space. The first two portions of the header are set to 0 because the `type` field and the `header` field are 0. No extended header field is supported at present. Following are the length and width, which in this case are both 05, for five pixels by five pixels. Then comes the actual image data. Each row uses a multiple number of bytes, with five pixels here per row making one byte per row. Remember that this count starts from left to right, so the first row contains 01110000, which is 70 in the hexadecimal representation of the byte. The next row is 10101000, which is A8 in the hexadecimal representation of the byte. The third row follows the same pattern: 11011000, which is represented by D8 in hexadecimal. The fourth row repeats the second and the fifth row repeats the first. This pattern is shown in Figures E-1 and E-2, which display how the figure is built in the WBMP editor of the Nokia WAP Toolkit.

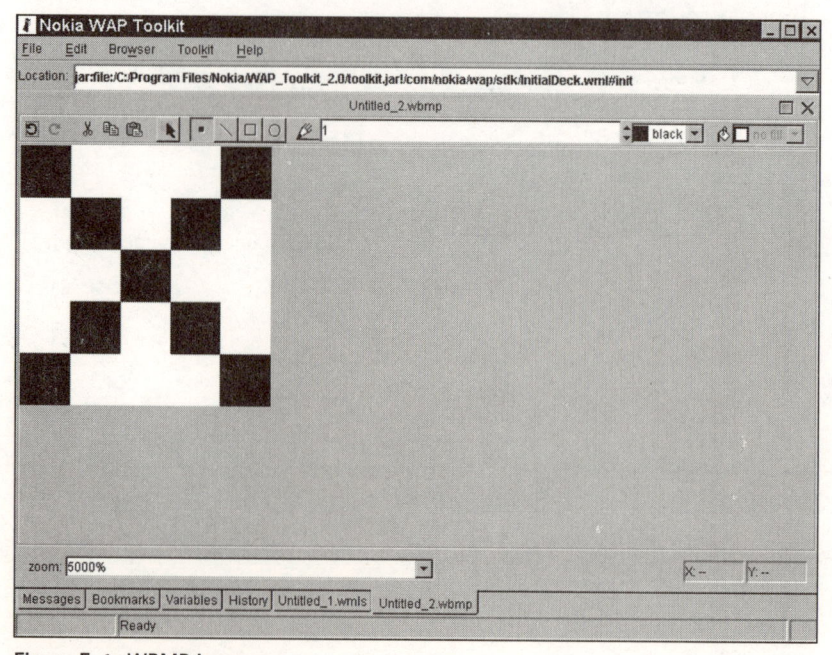

Figure E-1: WBMP image

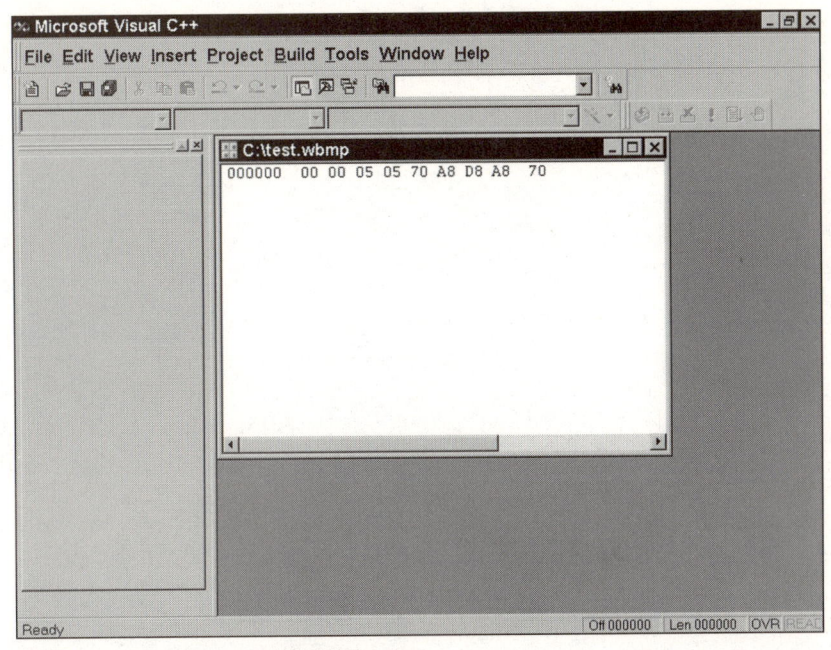

Figure E-2: Binary dump of WBMP image

Appendix F

WML 1.3 DTD Listing

THIS APPENDIX CONTAINS the WML 1.3 DTD, the document type definition for the WML language (see www.wapforum.org for additional information). This is the document that must be referred to at the beginning of any WML document. DTDs exist for WML 1.1 and WML 1.2 but hardly any new attributes or elements were added in the WML 1.3 revision. The exact differences were shown in Appendix A. The main purpose for the inclusion of this document is that it is the definitive reference that you can use if there is any question about the accuracy of WML code. For example, if you are concerned about whether a do element can appear after a p element in a card, the card element definition below will give you the correct answer. For tips on how to read a DTD, refer to Chapter 3.

WML 1.3 DTD Listing

```
<!--
Wireless Markup Language (WML) Document Type Definition.
WML is an XML language. Typical usage:
    <?xml version="1.0"?>
    <!DOCTYPE wml PUBLIC "-//WAPFORUM//DTD WML 1.3//EN"
    "http://www.wapforum.org/DTD/wml13.dtd">
    <wml>
    ...
    </wml>

    Terms and conditions of use are available from the Wireless
Application Protocol Forum
    Ltd. web site at http://www.wapforum.org/docs/copyright.htm.
-->

<!ENTITY % length    "CDATA">         <!-- [0-9]+ for pixels or
[0-9]+"%" for percentage length -->
<!ENTITY % vdata     "CDATA">         <!-- attribute value possibly
containing
                                          variable references -->
<!ENTITY % HREF      "%vdata;">       <!-- URI, URL or URN designating
a hypertext node. May contain variable references -->
<!ENTITY % boolean "(true|false)">
```

Continued

WML 1.3 DTD Listing *(Continued)*

```
<!ENTITY % number    "NMTOKEN">         <!-- a number, with format [0-9]+ -->
<!ENTITY % coreattrs  "id       ID    #IMPLIED
                       class    CDATA #IMPLIED">
<!ENTITY % ContentType "%vdata;">   <!-- media type. May contain variable references -->

<!ENTITY % emph      "em | strong |b |i |u |big |small">
<!ENTITY % layout    "br">

<!ENTITY % text      "#PCDATA | %emph;">

<!-- flow covers "card-level" elements, such as text and images -->
<!ENTITY % flow     "%text; | %layout; | img | anchor |a |table">

<!-- Task types -->
<!ENTITY % task  "go | prev | noop | refresh">

<!-- Navigation and event elements -->
<!ENTITY % navelmts "do | onevent">

<!--================= Decks and Cards =================-->

<!ELEMENT wml ( head?, template?, card+ )>
<!ATTLIST wml
  xml:lang        NMTOKEN     #IMPLIED
  %coreattrs;
>

<!-- card intrinsic events -->
<!ENTITY % cardev
  "onenterforward  %HREF;    #IMPLIED
   onenterbackward %HREF;    #IMPLIED
   ontimer         %HREF;    #IMPLIED"
>

<!-- card field types -->
<!ENTITY % fields "%flow; | input | select | fieldset">
<!ELEMENT card (onevent*, timer?, (do | p | pre)*)>
<!ATTLIST card
  title           %vdata;     #IMPLIED
  newcontext      %boolean;   "false"
  ordered         %boolean;   "true"
  xml:lang        NMTOKEN     #IMPLIED
```

```
  %cardev;
  %coreattrs;
>


<!--================ Event Bindings ================-->

<!ELEMENT do (%task;)>
<!ATTLIST do
  type            CDATA           #REQUIRED
  label           %vdata;         #IMPLIED
  name            NMTOKEN         #IMPLIED
  optional        %boolean;       "false"
  xml:lang        NMTOKEN         #IMPLIED
  %coreattrs;
>

<!ELEMENT onevent (%task;)>
<!ATTLIST onevent
  type            CDATA           #REQUIRED
  %coreattrs;
>


<!--================ Deck-level declarations ================-->

<!ELEMENT head ( access | meta )+>
<!ATTLIST head
  %coreattrs;
>

<!ELEMENT template (%navelmts;)*>
<!ATTLIST template
  %cardev;
  %coreattrs;
>

<!ELEMENT access EMPTY>
<!ATTLIST access
  domain          CDATA           #IMPLIED
  path            CDATA           #IMPLIED
  %coreattrs;
>

<!ELEMENT meta EMPTY>
<!ATTLIST meta
```

Continued

WML 1.3 DTD Listing *(Continued)*

```
    http-equiv       CDATA          #IMPLIED
    name             CDATA          #IMPLIED
    forua            %boolean;      "false"
    content          CDATA          #REQUIRED
    scheme           CDATA          #IMPLIED
    %coreattrs;
>

<!--================ Tasks ================-->

<!ENTITY % cache-control "(no-cache)" >

<!ELEMENT go (postfield | setvar)*>
<!ATTLIST go
    href             %HREF;         #REQUIRED
    sendreferer      %boolean;      "false"
    method           (post|get)     "get"
    enctype          %ContentType;  "application/x-www-form-urlencoded"
    cache-control    %cache-control; #IMPLIED
    accept-charset   CDATA          #IMPLIED
    %coreattrs;
>

<!ELEMENT prev (setvar)*>
<!ATTLIST prev
    %coreattrs;
>

<!ELEMENT refresh (setvar)*>
<!ATTLIST refresh
    %coreattrs;
>

<!ELEMENT noop EMPTY>
<!ATTLIST noop
    %coreattrs;
>

<!--================ postfield ================-->

<!ELEMENT postfield EMPTY>
<!ATTLIST postfield
    name             %vdata;        #REQUIRED
```

```
    value            %vdata;      #REQUIRED
    %coreattrs;
>


<!--================ variables ================-->

<!ELEMENT setvar EMPTY>
<!ATTLIST setvar
    name             %vdata;      #REQUIRED
    value            %vdata;      #REQUIRED
    %coreattrs;
>


<!--================ Card Fields ================-->

<!ELEMENT select (optgroup|option)+>
<!ATTLIST select
    title            %vdata;      #IMPLIED
    name             NMTOKEN      #IMPLIED
    value            %vdata;      #IMPLIED
    iname            NMTOKEN      #IMPLIED
    ivalue           %vdata;      #IMPLIED
    multiple         %boolean;    "false"
    tabindex         %number;     #IMPLIED
    xml:lang         NMTOKEN      #IMPLIED
    %coreattrs;
>

<!ELEMENT optgroup (optgroup|option)+ >
<!ATTLIST optgroup
    title            %vdata;      #IMPLIED
    xml:lang         NMTOKEN      #IMPLIED
    %coreattrs;
>

<!ELEMENT option (#PCDATA | onevent)*>
<!ATTLIST option
    value            %vdata;      #IMPLIED
    title            %vdata;      #IMPLIED
    onpick           %HREF;       #IMPLIED
    xml:lang         NMTOKEN      #IMPLIED
    %coreattrs;
>
```

Continued

WML 1.3 DTD Listing *(Continued)*

```
<!ELEMENT input EMPTY>
<!ATTLIST input
  name            NMTOKEN             #REQUIRED
  type            (text|password)     "text"
  value           %vdata;             #IMPLIED
  format          CDATA               #IMPLIED
  emptyok         %boolean;           #IMPLIED
  size            %number;            #IMPLIED
  maxlength       %number;            #IMPLIED
  tabindex        %number;            #IMPLIED
  title           %vdata;             #IMPLIED
  accesskey       %vdata;             #IMPLIED
  xml:lang        NMTOKEN             #IMPLIED
  %coreattrs;
>

<!ELEMENT fieldset (%fields; | do)* >
<!ATTLIST fieldset
  title           %vdata;             #IMPLIED
  xml:lang        NMTOKEN             #IMPLIED
  %coreattrs;
>

<!ELEMENT timer EMPTY>
<!ATTLIST timer
  name            NMTOKEN             #IMPLIED
  value           %vdata;             #REQUIRED
  %coreattrs;
>

<!--================ Images ================-->

<!ENTITY % IAlign "(top|middle|bottom)" >
<!ELEMENT img EMPTY>
<!ATTLIST img
  alt             %vdata;             #REQUIRED
  src             %HREF;              #REQUIRED
  localsrc        %vdata;             #IMPLIED
  vspace          %length;            "0"
  hspace          %length;            "0"
  align           %IAlign;            "bottom"
  height          %length;            #IMPLIED
  width           %length;            #IMPLIED
  xml:lang        NMTOKEN             #IMPLIED
```

```
    %coreattrs;
>


<!--================ Anchor ================-->

<!ELEMENT anchor ( #PCDATA | br | img | go | prev | refresh )*>
<!ATTLIST anchor
    title           %vdata;         #IMPLIED
    accesskey       %vdata;         #IMPLIED
    xml:lang        NMTOKEN         #IMPLIED
    %coreattrs;
>
<!ELEMENT a ( #PCDATA | br | img )*>
<!ATTLIST a
    href            %HREF;          #REQUIRED
    title           %vdata;         #IMPLIED
    accesskey       %vdata;         #IMPLIED
    xml:lang        NMTOKEN         #IMPLIED
    %coreattrs;
>


<!--================ Tables ================-->

<!ELEMENT table (tr)+>
<!ATTLIST table
    title           %vdata;         #IMPLIED
    align           CDATA           #IMPLIED
    columns         %number;        #REQUIRED
    xml:lang        NMTOKEN         #IMPLIED
    %coreattrs;
>

<!ELEMENT tr (td)+>
<!ATTLIST tr
    %coreattrs;
>
<!ELEMENT td ( %text; | %layout; | img | anchor |a )*>
<!ATTLIST td
    xml:lang        NMTOKEN         #IMPLIED
    %coreattrs;
>

<!--================ Text layout and line breaks ================-->
```

Continued

WML 1.3 DTD Listing *(Continued)*

```
<!ELEMENT em (%flow;)*>
<!ATTLIST em
  xml:lang       NMTOKEN      #IMPLIED
  %coreattrs;
>

<!ELEMENT strong (%flow;)*>
<!ATTLIST strong
  xml:lang       NMTOKEN      #IMPLIED
  %coreattrs;
>

<!ELEMENT b (%flow;)*>
<!ATTLIST b
  xml:lang       NMTOKEN      #IMPLIED
  %coreattrs;
>

<!ELEMENT i (%flow;)*>
<!ATTLIST i
  xml:lang       NMTOKEN      #IMPLIED
  %coreattrs;
>

<!ELEMENT u (%flow;)*>
<!ATTLIST u
  xml:lang       NMTOKEN      #IMPLIED
  %coreattrs;
>

<!ELEMENT big (%flow;)*>
<!ATTLIST big
  xml:lang       NMTOKEN      #IMPLIED
  %coreattrs;
>

<!ELEMENT small (%flow;)*>
<!ATTLIST small
  xml:lang       NMTOKEN      #IMPLIED
  %coreattrs;
>

<!ENTITY % TAlign    "(left|right|center)">
<!ENTITY % WrapMode  "(wrap|nowrap)" >
```

```
<!ELEMENT p (%fields; | do)*>
<!ATTLIST p
  align           %TAlign;      "left"
  mode            %WrapMode;    #IMPLIED
  xml:lang        NMTOKEN       #IMPLIED
  %coreattrs;
>

<!ELEMENT br EMPTY>
<!ATTLIST br
  %coreattrs;
>

<!ELEMENT pre (#PCDATA | a | anchor | do | u | br | i | b | em | strong |
            input | select )*>
<!ATTLIST pre
  xml:space       CDATA         #FIXED      "preserve"
  %coreattrs;
>

<!ENTITY quot  "&#34;">        <!-- quotation mark -->
<!ENTITY amp   "&#38;#38;">    <!-- ampersand -->
<!ENTITY apos  "&#39;">        <!-- apostrophe -->
<!ENTITY lt    "&#38;#60;">    <!-- less than -->
<!ENTITY gt    "&#62;">        <!-- greater than -->
<!ENTITY nbsp  " ">       <!-- non-breaking space -->
<!ENTITY shy   "&#173;">       <!-- soft hyphen (discretionary hyphen) -->
```

Appendix G

Installing, Downloading, and Configuring WAP SDKs

To correctly develop and test your WAP site or application, you must have a Software Development Kit (SDK) installed on your computer. Note that the terms emulator and simulator are used interchangeably.

Several choices are available and completely free for download. The download sites also require you to enable JavaScript and cookies on your browser.

Ericsson WAP IDE

Ericsson's Developer Zone requires a free registration process before you can download its software:

http://www.ericsson.com/mobilityworld/news/content/wapide311_on_site

The WAP IDE includes WapIDE 3.1.1 SDK (for developing WML 1.1 and WMLScript 1.1 sites): Requires Windows 95, 98, Me, NT, and 2000. This version includes a WAP browser that can emulate the Ericsson R320, R380, R520, and T39m phones.

Microsoft Mobile Explorer Emulator

Microsoft's own Mobile Explorer Emulator (MME) is able to display both WAP and HTML content. It also includes a WML compiler and complete documentation. MME is available at:

http://www.microsoft.com/mobile/phones/mme/mmemulator.asp

Microsoft MME requires Windows NT 4.0 (with SP 3) or Windows 2000.

Motorola Mobile Application Development Kit

Motorola's Developer Network requires a free registration process before you can download its software. The Mobile ADK allows you to develop both WAP and VoxMLapplications:

http://developers.motorola.com/developers/wireless/downloads/madk2_download.html

MobileADK (for developing WML 1.1, WMLScript 1.1 and VoxML applications) requires Windows 95, 98, Me, and NT (with SP 3). The Microsoft Agent for speech recognition is required for VoxML.

MobileADK includes a WAP browser that can emulate nine Motorola phones such as the popular i1000plus and v.2287. It also includes a simple application development environment.

Nokia WAP Toolkit

Nokia's WAP Forum site requires a free registration process before you can download its software.

You can choose to download the Nokia WAP Toolkit:

http://forum.nokia.com/wapforum/main/1,6668,1_1_50,00.html

Nokia WAP Toolkit 3.0 (for developing WML 1.1 and WMLScript 1.1 sites) requires Windows 95, 98, Me, NT, and 2000. It also requires the Java Runtime Environment (JRE) 1.3 but will install it for you, if necessary.

Openwave UP.SDK

Openwave's own SDK may be your first stop:

http://developer.openwave.com/download/index.html

Three versions of the UP.SDK are available:

- ◆ UP.SDK 5.0 (for developing WML 1.3 and WMLScript 1.2 sites): Requires Windows 95, 98, Me, NT, and 2000
- ◆ UP.SDK 4.1 (for developing WML 1.1 and WMLScript 1.1 sites): Requires Windows 95, 98, Me, NT, and 2000

- UP.SDK 3.2 (For developing WML 1.1 sites): Requires Windows 95, 98, Me, NT, and 2000, or Sun Solaris

- UP.SDK 3.2 (For developing HDML 3.0 sites): Requires Windows 95, 98, Me, 2000, or Sun Solaris

Besides the UP.Simulator, the UP.SDK also comes with extensive developer documentation, programming examples, and a variety of tools.

The UP.SDK also comes with a few "skins" that enables the SDK to simulate a specific WAP phone. You can download additional skins from Openwave. You will need an unzip program on your computer to extract the files.

Installing a skin is as simple as copying the files into the "configs" folder in your UP.SDK directory. You then launch the UP.Simulator, select File, and then choose Open Configuration. Finally, select the .pho file that represents the phone you want to simulate. For example, the default Openwave skin is named OWG1.pho.

Appendix H

Openwave Icons

TABLE H-1 PRESENTS THE Openwave icons that can be used for development on phones that have the UP.Browser versions 3.*x* and higher. The icons can be used as shown in the following code, either by referring to the number or the name:

```
<img src="" alt="" localsrc="1"/>
```

or

```
<img src="" alt="" localsrc="exclamation1"/>
```

TABLE H-1 OPENWAVE ICONS

Icon Number	Icon Text Identifier
1	exclamation1
2	exclamation2
3	question1
4	question2
5	lefttri1
6	righttri1
7	lefttri2
8	righttri2
9	littlesquare1
10	littlesquare2
11	isymbol
12	wineglass
13	speaker
14	dollarsign

Continued

TABLE H-1 OPENWAVE ICONS *(Continued)*

Icon Number	Icon Text Identifier
15	moon1
16	bolt
17	medsquare1
18	medsquare2
19	littlediamond1
20	littlediamond2
21	bigsquare1
22	bigsquare2
23	littlecircle1
24	littlecircle2
25	wristwatch
26	plus
27	minus
28	star1
29	uparrow1
30	downarrow1
31	circleslash
32	downtri1
33	uptri1
34	downtri1
35	uptri2
36	bigdiamond1
37	bigdiamond2
38	biggetstsquare1
39	biggetstsquare2
40	bigcircle1
41	bigcircle2

Appendix H: Openwave Icons

Icon Number	Icon Text Identifier
42	uparrow2
43	downarrow2
44	sun
45	baseball
46	clock
47	moon2
48	bell
49	pushpin
50	smallface
51	heart
52	martini
53	bud
54	trademark
55	multiply
56	document1
57	hourglass1
58	hourglass2
59	floppy1
60	snowflake
61	cross1
62	cross2
63	rightarrow1
64	leftarrow1
65	mug
66	divide
67	calendar

Continued

TABLE H-1 OPENWAVE ICONS *(Continued)*

Icon Number	Icon Text Identifier
68	smileyface
69	star2
70	rightarrow2
71	leftarrow2
72	gem
73	checkmark1
74	dog
75	star3
76	sparkle
77	lightbulb
78	bird
79	folder1
80	head1
81	copyright
82	registered
83	briefcase
84	folder2
85	phone1
86	voiceballoon
87	creditcard
88	uptri3
89	downtri3
90	usa
91	note3
92	clipboard
93	cup
94	camera1

Appendix H: Openwave Icons

Icon Number	Icon Text Identifier
95	rain
96	football
97	book1
98	stopsign
99	trafficlight
100	book2
101	book3
102	book4
103	document2
104	scissors
105	day
106	ticket
107	cloud
108	envelope1
109	check
110	videocam
111	camcorder
112	house
113	flower
114	knife
115	vidtape
116	glasses
117	roundarrow1
118	roundarrow2
119	magnifyglass
120	key

Continued

TABLE H-1 OPENWAVE ICONS *(Continued)*

Icon Number	Icon Text Identifier
121	note1
122	note2
123	boltnut
124	shoe
125	car
126	floppy2
127	chart
128	graph1
129	mailbox
130	flashlight
131	rolocard
132	check2
133	leaf
134	hound
135	battery
136	scroll
137	thumbtack
138	lockkey
139	dollar
140	lefthand
141	righthand
142	tablet
143	paperclip
144	present
145	tag
146	meal1
147	books

Appendix H: Openwave Icons

Icon Number	Icon Text Identifier
148	truck
149	pencil
150	uplogo
151	envelope2
152	wrench
153	outbox
154	inbox
155	phone2
156	factory
157	ruler1
158	ruler2
159	graph2
160	meal2
161	phone3
162	plug
163	family
164	link
165	package
166	fax
167	partcloudy
168	plane
169	boat
170	dice
171	newspaper
172	train
173	blankfull
174	blankhalf
175	blankquarter

Index

A

`<a>` element, 576
`abort` function, 237, 612
`abs` function, 234, 237–239, 609
`accept-charset` attribute, 581, 594
`accept` function, 384
`Accept-Language` header, 510–511
`accept` soft key, 121–122
`<access>` element, 502–504, 576–577
`accesskey` attribute, 576, 577, 584
action elements, 306
action types, 120
Active Server Pages. *See* ASP
`addPBentry` function, 381, 382–383, 631
Advanced Mobile Phone Service. *See* AMPS
Afuah, Allan, 5–6
age of resources, determining, 406–407
airlink, 32
`alert` function, 261, 625
`align` attribute, 107, 137, 582, 587, 590
`alt` attribute, 140, 582
AM, 16
amplitude, 12
amplitude modulation, 16
AMPS, 19
analog systems
    described, 15
    digital systems compared, 15–16
`<anchor>` element, 577
anchors, 116–118
ANSI-136 events, 638
ANSI-136 libraries, 638
application-level security, 500–504
`Application` object, 285

application server language detection, 510–512
architecture
    CFML, 327–328
    deploying WAP services, 536–539
    Openwave, 343
    WTA, 372–374
array support, 205–206
ASP
    `Application` object, 285
    buffers, 285–286
    cookies, adding, 290
    headers, adding, 290
    overview, 280–282
    queries, using variables to initiate, 288–290
    `Request` object, 282–283
    `Response` object, 283–284, 286–287
    `Response.write ( )` method, 284–285
    `Server` object, 285–286
    `Session` object, 285
    user input, processing, 286–288
assignment operators, 207–208, 595
assisted GPS methods, 522–523
ATTLIST keyword, 60
attribute defaults, 65
attributes
    `accept-charset` attribute, 581, 594
    `accesskey` attribute, 576, 577, 584
    `align` attribute, 107, 137, 582, 587, 590
    `alt` attribute, 140, 582
    attribute defaults, 65
    `cache-control` attribute, 580
    CDATA attribute, 63
    `charset` attribute, 509

continued

667

668 Index

attributes *continued*
   `class` attribute, 104
   `columns` attribute, 590
   common attributes, 104–105
   `content` attribute, 584
   `deliver-after-timestamp` attribute, 352
   `domain` attribute, 577
   `emptyok` attribute, 584
   `enctype` attribute, 581
   ENTITIES attribute, 63
   ENTITY attribute, 63
   enumerated list attribute, 63
   `etag=nmtoken` attribute, 399
   `format` attribute, 182–183, 583
   `forua` attribute, 585
   `height` attribute, 582
   `href` attribute, 576, 580, 593, 594
   `href=%URI` attribute, 399
   `hspace` attribute, 582
   `http-equiv` attribute, 584
   `id` attribute, 63, 104
   IDREF attribute, 63
   IDREFS attribute, 63
   `iname` attribute, 175–176, 588
   `index` attribute, 586
   `ivalue` attribute, 175, 589
   `label` attribute, 127, 579
   `lastmod=%number` attribute, 399
   `localsrc` attribute, 582
   in markup, 62–65
   `maxlength` attribute, 184, 583
   `md5=nmtoken` attribute, 399
   `method` attribute, 580, 594
   `mode` attribute, 107, 587
   `multiple` attribute, 173–174, 589
   `name` attribute, 127, 579, 583, 584, 587, 588, 589, 591, 592, 593, 594
   `newcontext` attribute, 156–157, 578
   NMTOKEN attribute, 63
   NMTOKENS attribute, 63
   NOTATION attribute, 63
   `onexit` attribute, 594
   `onpick` attribute, 586
   `onthrow` attribute, 592
   `optional` attribute, 579
   `ordered` attribute, 578
   `path` attribute, 577
   `ppg-notify-requested-to` attribute, 352
   `progress-notes-requested` attribute, 352
   `push-id` attribute, 352, 354
   `rel` attribute, 593
   `reply-time` attribute, 355
   `scheme` attribute, 585
   `sender-address` attribute, 355
   `sender-name` attribute, 355
   `sendreferer` attribute, 501–502, 580, 593, 594
   `size` attribute, 584
   `source-reference` attribute, 352
   `src` attribute, 140, 582
   `tabindex` attribute, 584, 589
   tag attribute auto-selection, 334
   `title` attribute, 184–185, 576, 577, 578, 583, 586, 589, 590
   `type` attribute, 579, 583
   `value` attribute, 173, 583, 586, 587, 589, 591, 593
   `vspace` attribute, 582
   `width` attribute, 583
   XML, 57–58
   `xml:lang` attribute, 104–105, 511–512
AuC, 33
authentication
   code for authenticating user, 426–427
   described, 478, 480–482
authorization, 480–482

Index

B

\<b\> element, 577
back key override behavior, 567
backward navigation, 122-126
bad message, 361
bandwidth, choosing, 540
`base=%URI` channel element, 399
basic authentication, code for, 429-430
basic DTD markup, 59-62
basic operators, 596
behavior of UI design, 461
Berners-Lee, Tim, 37
\<big\> element, 577-578
blanket permission, 377
block, 228
Bluetooth, 553, 556-557
`Boolean` data type, 201-203
\<br /\> element, 109, 578
branching, 471
browser
    browser-specific code for UI design, 470
    choosing, 534-535
    and HTTP caching, 405-407
    software profile, 456
    UI design, 467-471
BSC, 32
BTS, 32
buckets, 469, 470
buffers, 285-286
buttons, 466

C

CA, 488
CA public-key certificates, 493-494
`cache-control` attribute, 580
Cache-Control headers, 405
caching
    `expires` header, 413-414
    HTTP caching, 405-410
    `max-age` header, 413-414
    meta elements, 415
    `no-cache` header, 412
    Openwave, 345-346, 417-418
    overview, 403-405
    PAP, 364-365
    proprietary techniques, 417-418
    UI design, 472
    WAP caching, 410-411
Cailliau, Robert, 37
calendar date, verifying, 247-250
call logs library, WTAI, 389-390, 633
call-state management, 385
calling, 197-199
`callStatus` function, 384
\<card\> element, 129, 578
cardinality operators, 62
carrier gateway, 536
case sensitivity, 56, 95
\<catch\> element, 592
categories for XML elements, 60-61
CC/PP standard, 451
CDATA attribute, 63
CDMA, 19-20
cdmaOne, 25-26
cdma2000, 30-31
`ceil` function, 264, 625
cellular networks
    airlink, 32
    AMPS, 19
    AuC, 33
    BSC, 32
    BTS, 32
    CDMA, 19-20
    components, 31-33
    DSSS, 20
    EIR, 33
    FDMA, 19
    FHSS, 20
    4G systems, 17-18
    Frequency Division Duplexing (FDD), 18

continued

cellular networks *continued*
   GMSC, 33
   HLR, 32
   MSC, 32
   multiple access, 18-21
   OFDM, 20-21
   1G systems, 17-18
   overview, 17-18
   SDMA, 21
   SMSC, 33
   TDMA, 19
   3G systems. *See* 3G systems
   Time Division Duplexing (TDD), 18
   2G systems. *See* 2G technology
   VLR, 32
Certificate Authority, 488
certificate-revocation list, 488
CFCONTENT tag, 328-329
CFML
   architecture for, 327-328
   CFCONTENT tag, 328-329
   CFQUERY tag, 333
   headers, adding, 334
   HomeSite editor, 334
   overview, 327
   queries, using variables to initiate, 332-333
   tag attribute auto-selection, 334
   tag editors, 334
   tags, adding, 334
   user input, processing, 329-331
CFQUERY tag, 333
CGI
   cookies, adding, 326-327
   headers, adding, 326-327
   overview, 319-320
   queries, using variables to initiate, 324-326
   user input, processing, 320-324
change function, 389
channel DTD, 396-400

channelid=CDATA channel element, 399
channels, 395-396
character sets, 507-508
characterSet function, 237, 613
charAt function, 240, 614
charset attribute, 509
charsets, 513-514
checksums, 482-483
circuit-switched network architecture, 538-539
class 0 service, 87
class 1 service, 87
class 2 service, 88
class attribute, 104
client capabilities query, 359-361
client capabilities query response, 359-361
client public-key certificates, 494-496
closeFile function, 270, 627
Code Division Multiple Access. *See* CDMA
code fragments, JSPs, 305
ColdFusion Markup Language. *See* CFML
columns attribute, 590
COM Notification Library, 348
comma operator, 213
comments
   JSPs, 305
   WMLScript, 604-605
Common Gateway Interface. *See* CGI
compare function, 244, 618
comparison operators, 211-213, 597
competencies, 6
competitors, 561-562
compilation issues, 540
confidentiality, 478-479, 483-485
configuring SDKs, 655-657
confirm function, 260-261, 624
consistent user interface, 462-466

Index 671

content attribute, 584
Content-Language header, 510-512
content models for XML elements, 60-61
context permission, 377
continue statement, 218-219
control statements, 214-219, 603
conversion codes, 166
conversion issues
    data types, rules for, 203
    deploying WAP services, 540
cookies
    adding, 290
    CGI, 326-327
    Java servlets, 302
    JSPs, 312
    PHP, 318
    session handling, 435-438
credit-card verifier, building, 271-276
CRL, 488
Crypto library, 268-269, 628

D

D-AMPS, 24
D-AMPS+, 24-25
data types, 200-204
deck
    example of, 101-102
    packaging, 472
declarations
    described, 57-58
    JSPs, 304
deliver-after-timestamp attribute, 352
denial of service attack, 486
deploying WAP services
    architecture, choosing, 536-539
    bandwidth, choosing, 540
    browser, choosing, 534-535
    carrier gateway, 536
    circuit-switched network architecture, 538-539
    compilation issues, 540
    conversion issues, 540
    development gateway, 535-536
    enterprise gateway, 536
    Ericsson WAP IDE, 534
    gateway, choosing, 535-536
    gateway, using, 543-544
    latency considerations, 540
    Microsoft Mobile Emulator, 534
    mobile device, moving to, 544
    Neomar, 534
    Nokia WAP Toolkit 2.1, 534
    packet-based network architecture, 537-538
    phased development approach, 542
    SDKs, 534
    security issues, 540
    software development kits, 534
    tools, choosing, 534
    UP.SDK 4.1, 534
    WAP application servers, 541-544
    Web server, controlling, 543
destroy phase, Java servlets, 303
development gateway, 535-536
device screen enhancements, 554
device-specific features, 375
device tables, 447-450
device types, detecting, 445-447
dialed function, 389
Dialogs library
    alert function, 261, 625
    confirm function, 260-261, 624
    described, 260
    example of functions in, 261-263
    prompt function, 260, 624
different versions of page in UI design, 471
differential GPS, 523
Diffie-Hellman key exchange, 489

672 Index

Digital Advanced Mobile Phone System, 24
digital signatures, 487
digital systems
    advantages of, 15–16
    analog systems compared, 15–16
    described, 15
Direct Sequence Spread Spectrum, 20
directives, 304
`<do>` element, 120–122, 579
DOCTYPE declarations, 59, 575–576
Document Type Definition, 58–59, 97, 351
documents, requirements for well-formed, 55–58
$ symbol, 111
`domain` attribute, 577
downloading SDKs, 655–657
DSSS, 20
DTDs, 58–59, 97, 351

E

e-mail address, verifying, 245–247
E-OTD, 521–522
ECC, 485
EDGE, 31
effectiveness of UI design, evaluating, 464–466
EFI, 553, 554–555
EIR, 33
electromagnetic spectrum, 12–13
electromagnetic waves
    amplitude, 12
    described, 11–12
    electromagnetic spectrum, 12–13
    frequency, 12
    microwaves, 14
    radio waves, 13–14
    wavelength, 12
ELEMENT keyword, 60
`elementAt` function, 616

elements
    `<a>` element, 576
    `<access>` element, 502–504, 576–577
    action elements, 306
    `<anchor>` element, 577
    `<b>` element, 577
    `base=%URI` channel element, 399
    `<big>` element, 577–578
    `<br />` element, 109, 578
    `<card>` element, 129, 578
    `<catch>` element, 592
    categories for XML elements, 60–61
    `channelid=CDATA` channel element, 399
    content models for XML elements, 60–61
    definitions, 96–97
    `<do>` element, 120–122, 579
    `<em>` element, 579–580
    `eventid=CDATA` channel element, 399
    `<exit>` element, 592
    `failure=%URI` channel element, 399
    `<fieldset>` element, 580
    formatting, 107–109
    `<go>` element, 580–581
    `<head>` element, 581
    `<i>` element, 581
    `<img />` element, 138–141, 582–583
    `<input>` element. *See* `<input>` element
    `<link>` element, 592–593
    `maxspace=%number` channel element, 398
    `<meta>` element, 415, 584–585
    names, 56
    `<noop />` element, 132–133, 585
    `<onevent>` element, 585
    Openwave, elements specific to. *See* Openwave elements
    `<optgroup>` element, 171–172, 586

Index 673

\<option> element, 168–170, 586
\<p> element, 105–107, 586–587
\<postfield> element, 587
\<pre> element, 588
\<prev /> element, 588
\<receive> element, 593
\<refresh> element, 162–164, 588
\<reset> element, 593
root element, 96
\<select> element, 166–176, 588–589
\<send> element, 593
\<setvar> element. *See* \<setvar> element
\<small> element, 590
\<spawn> element, 593–594
\<strong> element, 590
`success=%URI` channel element, 399
\<table> element, 133–137, 590
\<td> element, 590
\<template> element, 130–133, 591
\<throw> element, 594
\<timer> element, 189–193, 591
\<tr> element, 591
\<u> element, 591
`useraccessible=true|false` channel element, 399
\<wml> element, 592
`elements` function, 242, 615
\<em> element, 579–580
emergency services, 518–519
`emptyok` attribute, 584
encryption, 484–485
`enctype` attribute, 581
`endContext` function, 390
endowments, 6
Enhanced Data Rates for GSM Evolution, 31
Enhanced Observed Time Difference, 521–522
e911 mandates, 515–516
enterprise gateway, 536

ENTITIES attribute, 63
ENTITY attribute, 63
ENTITY keyword, 60
entity tags, 409–410
enumerated list attribute, 63
Ericsson WAP IDE, 534, 655
escape codes, 605
`escapeString` function, 254, 255–256, 622
escaping variables, 164–166
`etag=nmtoken` attribute, 399
Etags, 409–410
event handling, 400
`eventid=CDATA` channel element, 399
execution phase, Java servlets, 303
\<exit> element, 592
\<exit> function, 236, 612
expiration times, setting, 406
`expires` header, 413–414
expressions, 304
EXtensible Markup Language. *See* XML
`extern` keyword, 228
external function interface, 553, 554–555

F

`failure=%URI` channel element, 399
FCC requirements, 518–519
FDD, 18
FDMA, 19
FHSS, 20
\<fieldset> element, 580
`find` function, 241, 615
fingerprints, 482–483
fixed reference points, 517–518
`float` data type, 201–203
`float` function, 236, 612
Float library
    `ceil` function, 264, 625
    described, 263

continued

Float library *continued*
    example of use of functions in, 265–267
    `floor` function, 263, 625
    `int` function, 263, 625
    `maxFloat` function, 264, 626
    `minFloat` function, 265, 626
    `pow` function, 264, 625
    `round` function, 264, 626
    `sqrt` function, 264, 626
`floor` function, 263, 625
FM, 16
`for` statement, 217–218
`format` attribute, 182–183, 583
format characters, 181–182
`format` function, 245, 250–252, 618–619
`forua` attribute, 585
4G technology, 17–18
frequency, 12
Frequency Division Duplexing, 18
Frequency Division Multiple Access, 19
Frequency Hopping Spread Spectrum, 20
frequency modulation, 16
function call stack, 232
functions, 219–220, 227–229
future issues
    Bluetooth, 553, 556–557
    device screen enhancements, 554
    EFI, 553, 554–555
    external function interface, 553, 554–555
    identification, 441–442
    Internet protocols, convergence with, 551–552
    mobile device as source of innovation, 552–559
    network as source of innovation, 546–552
    persistent storage, 553, 557–558
    processor enhancements, 554
    session management, 441–442
    storage enhancements, 554
    SyncML, 553, 558–559
    3G networks, 546–547
    wireless profiled TCP, 547–550
    XHTML, 547, 551–552
future reserved words, 606–607

G

gateway
    choosing, 535–536
    using, 543–544
Gaussian Minimum Shift Keying, 17
General Packet Radio Service. *See* GPRS
generally supported tags, using only, 470
Geography Markup Language, 525–526
GET method, 50–51, 186–187, 189
`GetBase` function, 254, 621
`getCurrentCard` function, 258, 623
`getFieldValue` function, 387, 389, 390
`getFragment` function, 254, 621
`getHost` function, 252–253, 620
`getParameters` function, 253, 620
`getPath` function, 253, 620
`getPort` function, 253, 620
`getProtection` function, 390
`getQuery` function, 253, 621
`getReferer` function, 254, 621
`getScheme` function, 252, 620
`getVar` function, 257, 623
global bindings, 400
Global System for Mobile Communication, 22
GML, 525–526
GMSC, 33
`<go>` element, 580–581
`go` function, 257, 623
GPRS
    described, 23
    infrastructure, 33–34
    UI design, 471

Index   675

GPS, 518
GSM, 22
GSM-specific libraries, 391, 637

H

hardware key types, 119
hardware profile, 453
hashed message authentication code, 483
hashes, 482–483
`<head>` element, 581
headers
    adding, 290
    CFML, 334
    CGI, 326–327
    HTTP caching, 407–410
    information, 450–451
    Java servlets, 302
    JSPs, 312
    PHP, 318
`height` attribute, 582
hidden postfields, 438–440
High Speed Circuit Switched Data, 23
history stack overflow, 154–155
HLR, 32
HMAC, 483
HomeSite editor, 334
horizontal rule, 572
`href` attribute, 576, 580, 593, 594
`href=%URI` attribute, 399
HSCSD, 23
`hspace` attribute, 582
HTTP
    analyzed with OSI model, 40
    caching. See HTTP caching
    GET method, 50–51
    methods, list of, 48
    overview, 42–46
    POST method, 51–53
    request-response cycle, 46
    requests. See HTTP requests
    responses. See HTTP responses
    session format, 43
HTTP caching
    age of resources, determining, 406–407
    `Cache-Control` headers, 405
    desktop browsers and, 405–407
    entity tags, 409–410
    Etags, 409–410
    expiration times, setting, 406
    headers and, 407–410
    `If-Modified-Since` header, 408–409
`http-equiv` attribute, 584
HTTP requests
    components, 47
    described, 43–44
    structure of, 47–49
HTTP responses
    components, 50
    described, 45–46
    structure of, 49–50
HTTP tunneling
    PAP, 361
hyperlinks, 565
HyperText Transfer Protocol. See HTTP

I

`<i>` element, 581
Icons, openwave, 659–665
`id` attribute, 63, 104
iDEN, 26
identification issues
    authenticating user, code for, 426–427
    basic authentication, code for, 429–430
    manual identification schemes, 425–430
    overview, 424–425

continued

identification issues *continued*
   proprietary client headers, 431–434
   subscriber IDs, 432–434
   username and password prompt, code for, 425–426
IDREF attribute, 63
IDREFS attribute, 63
`If-Modified-Since` header, 408–409
`if` statement, 214–216
illegal variable names, 158
images, displaying, 137–141, 641–642
`<img />` element, 138–141, 582–583
IMT-2000 upgrade path, 28–29
`iname` attribute, 175–176, 588
incoming-call selection example, 400–401
`index` attribute, 586
information located on page, 465
initialization phase, Java servlets, 302–303
initializing variables, 204–205
innovation, 5–8
Innovation Management (Afuah), 5–6
`<input>` element
   attributes for, 178
   example of, 179
   `format` attributes, 182–183
   format characters, 181–182
   GET method, 186–187, 189
   input mask, 181–185
   `maxlength` attribute, 184
   overview, 177–181, 583–584
   POST method, 187–189
   posting input data, 185–189
   `title` attribute, 184–185
input field, 571
input mask, 181–185
`insertAt` function, 243–244, 617
installing SDKs, 655–657
Instone, Keith, 464
instruction set pointer, 232
`int` function, 263, 625

`integer` data type, 201–203
Integrated Dispatch Enhanced Network, 26
integrity, 479, 482–483
internal tags, 95
internationalization
   `Accept-Language` header, 510–511
   application server language detection, 510–512
   character sets, 507–508
   `charset` attribute, 509
   charsets, 513–514
   `Content-Language` header, 510–512
   defined, 505
   goal of, 506
   guidelines for, 506–507
   ISO-8859-x character sets, 507–508
   language detection, application server, 510–512
   languages, 510
   postfields, 513–514
   rendering issues, 509
   transcoding, 512–514
   transfer systems, 508–509
   US-ASCII, 513
   UTF-8, 509
   UTF-16, 509
   `xml:lang` attribute, 511–512
Internet protocols
   future issues, 551–552
   stack diagrams for, 38
intra-resource navigation, 411
intrinsic events
   history stack overflow, 154–155
   news story example, 150–152
   `onenterbackward` event, 146, 147–148
   `onenterforward` event, 146
   `onpick` event, 146
   `ontimer` event, 146, 189–193
   overview, 145–148
   short form, 147, 152–154

`invalid` data type, 201–203
IS-95 events, 640
IS-95 libraries, 640
IS-136 events, 638
IS-136 libraries, 638
`isEmpty` function, 240, 614
`isFloat` function, 236, 611
`isInt` function, 235, 611
ISO-8859-x character sets, 507–508
ISO-10646 method for character display, 109–110
`isValid` function, 252, 619
`isvalid` operator, 214
`ivalue` attribute, 175, 589

J

Java bean, 303
Java Server Pages. *See* JSPs
Java servlets
   cookies, adding, 302
   described, 291–293
   destroy phase, 303
   example of, 292–293
   execution phase, 303
   headers, adding, 302
   initialization phase, 302–303
   process for, 302–303
   queries, using variables to initiate, 299–302
   `service` method, 297
   user input, processing, 293–299
JDBC, 312
JSPs
   action elements, 306
   code fragments, 305
   comments, 305
   cookies, adding, 312
   declarations, 304
   directives, 304
   expressions, 304
   headers, adding, 312
   JDBC, 312
   non-XML format for, 304–305
   overview, 303–306
   queries, using variables to initiate, 310–312
   user input, processing, 306–310

K

Kerberos Authentication Service, 487
key management, 487–489

L

`label` attribute, 127, 579
labels, 564
`Lang` library, 234–239
`Lang` library functions
   `abort` function, 237, 612
   `abs` function, 234, 237–239, 609
   `characterSet` function, 237, 613
   `exit` function, 236, 612
   `float` function, 236, 612
   `isFloat` function, 236, 611
   `isInt` function, 235, 611
   `max` function, 234, 610
   `maxInt` function, 236, 612
   `min` function, 234, 610
   `minInt` function, 236, 612
   `parseFloat` function, 235, 610
   `parseInt` function, 234, 610
   `random` function, 237, 612
   `seed` function, 237, 613
language detection, application server, 510–512
languages, 510
`lastmod=%number` attribute, 399
latency considerations in deploying WAP services, 540
legal variable names, 158
`length` function, 240, 613

Index

limits on messages in notification queue, 347
<link> element, 592–593
`list` function, 384, 387
`loadString` function, 255, 622
localization
  defined, 505, 506
  UI design, 465
`localsrc` attribute, 582
location-based services
  assisted GPS methods, 522–523
  availability of, 523–524
  differential GPS, 523
  E-OTD, 521–522
  emergency services, 518–519
  Enhanced Observed Time Difference, 521–522
  FCC requirements, 518–519
  fixed reference points, 517–518
  Geography Markup Language, 525–526
  GML, 525–526
  GPS, 518
  obtaining location, 517–519
  Openwave/SignalSoft system, 524–528
  overview, 516–517
  place and time, pinpointing, 516
  proximity, establishing, 517
  pseudo-random codes, 522–523
  SignalSoft, 524–528
  sponsors, 519
  TDOA, 520–521
  Time Difference of Arrival, 520–521
  uses for, 517
  WAP location-based services, 528–532
logical operators, 210–211, 597
looping and logical control statements, 601–602

M

M-Services
  described, 562–563
  download protocol, 572–574
  M-Services GUI improvements, 563–572
M-Services GUI improvements
  back key override behavior, 567
  forms, 566–567
  horizontal rule, 572
  hyperlinks, 565
  input field, 571
  labels, 564
  new button type, 568
  Openwave Mobile Browser, 567–568
  Openwave Universal Browser, 568
  push buttons, 566
  select list, 569
  select popup, 570
  select radio, 570
  selection lists, 565
  softkey icons, 564
  title bar, 563–564
main profile, 452
`makeCall` function, 380, 381, 630
manual identification schemes, 425–430
`markAsRead` function, 387
`max-age` header, 413–414
`max` function, 234, 610
`maxFloat` function, 264, 626
`maxInt` function, 236, 612
`maxlength` attribute, 184, 583
`maxspace=%number` channel element, 398
MD5 algorithm, 483
`md5=nmtoken` attribute, 399
<meta> element, 415, 584–585
`method` attribute, 580, 594
methods, list of, 48
Microsoft Mobile Explorer Emulator, 534, 655

microwaves, 14
MIME, 65-67
min function, 234, 610
minFloat function, 265, 626
minInt function, 236, 612
miscellaneous library, 390-391
missed function, 389
mobile device
    future issues, 552-559
    moving to, 544
mode attribute, 107, 587
Motorola Mobile Application
    Development Kit, 656
MSC, 32
multiple access, 18-21
multiple attribute, 173-174, 589
multiple bindings, 127-129
multiple sites for different browsers, 470
multiple task binding, 466
Multipurpose Internet Mail Extensions, 65-67

N

name attribute, 127, 579, 583, 584, 587, 588, 589, 591, 592, 593, 594
named-equivalent method for character display, 110-111
navigation
    accept soft key, 121-122
    action types, 120
    anchors, 116-118
    backward navigation, 122-126
    card element, 129
    do element, 120-122
    hardware key types, 119
    intrinsic events. *See* intrinsic events
    label attribute, 127
    methods, 112-133
    multiple bindings, 127-129
    name attribute, 127

noop element, 132-133
principles of, 114-116
soft keys, 118-122
template element, 130-133
UI design, 464
URLs, 114-116
Neomar, 534
network as source of innovation, 546-552
network characteristics profile, 455
network common events, 391-394, 634-636
network common WTAI library
    accept function, 384
    call log library, 389-390
    call-state management, 385
    callStatus function, 384
    change function, 389
    described, 383
    dialed function, 389
    endContext function, 390
    getFieldValue function, 387, 389, 390
    getProtection function, 390
    list function, 384, 387
    markAsRead function, 387
    miscellaneous library, 390-391
    missed function, 389
    network message library, 386-388
    phonebook library, 388-389
    read function, 389
    received function, 390
    release function, 384
    remove function, 387, 389
    send function, 387
    sendDTMF function, 384
    setIndicator function, 390
    setProtection function, 390
    setup function, 384
    voice call library, 383-385
    write function, 389

network event, service accessed by, 376
network message library, WTAI,
    386–388, 632–633, 634
network-specific libraries, 391
new button type, 568
`newcontext` attribute, 156–157, 578
`newContext` function, 258, 623
911, wireless, 515–516
NMTOKEN attribute, 63
NMTOKENS attribute, 63
`no-cache` header, 412
Nokia Debug library
    `closeFile` function, 270, 627
    described, 269–270
    `openFile` function, 270, 627
    `printLn` function, 270, 627
Nokia WAP Toolkit, 534, 656
non-validating parsers, 55
non-XML format for JSPs, 304–305
nonrepudiability, 479, 487
<noop /> element, 132–133, 585
NOTATION attribute, 63
NOTATION keyword, 60

O

OFDM, 20–21
1G technology, 17–18
`onenterbackward` event, 146, 147–148
`onenterforward` event, 146
<onevent> element, 585
`onexit` attribute, 594
`onpick` attribute, 586
`onpick` event, 146
`onthrow` attribute, 592
`ontimer` event, 146, 189–193
`openFile` function, 270, 627
Openwave
    architecture of, 343
    cache operations, 345–346
    COM Notification Library, 348
    Console Library. *See* Openwave Console library
    elements specific to. *See* Openwave elements
    icons, 659–665
    limits on messages in notification queue, 347
    pull notifications, 345
    push notification, 343–345
    sending notifications, 347
    UP.Link server queuing, 346–347
Openwave Console library
    `print` function, 270, 627
    `printLn` function, 271, 627
Openwave elements
    <catch> element, 592
    <exit> element, 592
    <link> element, 592–593
    <receive> element, 593
    <reset> element, 593
    <send> element, 593
    <spawn> element, 593–594
    <throw> element, 594
Openwave Mobile Browser, 567–568
Openwave/SignalSoft system, 524–528
Openwave Universal Browser, 568
Openwave UP.SDK, 656–657
operand stack, 232
operator precedence, 214
operators, 206–211
<optgroup> element, 171–172, 586
<option> element, 168–170, 586
`optional` attribute, 579
`ordered` attribute, 578
Orthogonal Division Multiple Access. *See* OFDM
OSI model
    components, 40
    described, 38–40
    HTTP analyzed with, 40
output, formatting, 250–252

P

\<p\> element, 105–107, 586–587
packet-based network architecture, 537–538
packet-data systems, 26–27
PAP
    bad message, 361
    cache operations, 364–365
    client capabilities query, 359–361
    client capabilities query response, 359–361
    `deliver-after-timestamp` attribute, 352
    described, 349–351
    DTD, 351
    example PAP message, 352–353
    HTTP tunneling, 361
    operations, 349–350
    `ppg-notify-requested-to` attribute, 352
    `progress-notes-requested` attribute, 352
    push cancellation, 358–359
    push cancellation response, 358–359
    `push-id` attribute, 352, 354
    push message states, 357
    push submission, 351–354
    push submission response, 354–356
    `reply-time` attribute, 355
    result notification, 356–358
    result notification response, 356–358
    return code classes, 355
    `sender-address` attribute, 355
    `sender-name` attribute, 355
    service indication, 362–363
    service loading, 363–364
    `source-reference` attribute, 352
    status query, 359
    status query response, 359
    WAP push system, 349–361
parameter list, 228
parameter passing, 219–220
`parseFloat` function, 235, 610
`parseInt` function, 234, 610
parsers, 55, 95–96
passwords, 480
`path` attribute, 577
PDC
    described, 24
    events specific to, 639
    libraries specific to, 391, 639
Perl CGI. *See* CGI
persistent storage, 553, 557–558
Personal Digital Cellular. *See* PDC
Personal Home Page HyperText Processor. *See* PHP
phase modulation, 16
phased development approach, 542
phonebook library, WTAI, 388–389, 633
PHP
    cookies, adding, 318
    headers, adding, 318
    overview, 312–313
    queries, using variables to initiate, 317–318
    user input, processing, 313–317
PKI, 488
place and time, pinpointing, 516
PM, 16
polarization, 17
portals, 466
POST method, 51–53, 187–189
\<postfield\> element, 587
postfields, 513–514
posting input data, 185–189
`pow` function, 264, 625
PPG, 365–366
`ppg-notify-requested-to` attribute, 352
pragmas, 230–231, 604
\<pre\> element, 588
precedence, operator, 597–600

presentation and UI design, 461
`<prev />` element, 588
`prev` function, 258, 623
primary declaration statements, 601
`print` function, 270, 627
`printLn` function, 270, 271, 627
privacy, 483–485
processor enhancements, 554
`progress-notes-requested` attribute, 352
`prompt` function, 260, 624
proprietary client headers, 431–434
proprietary libraries, 269–271
proprietary techniques, 417–418
protocol stack, 37
protocols, 37
proximity, establishing, 517
pseudo-random codes, 522–523
public-key cryptography, 484–485
Public-Key Infrastructure, 488
public WTAI library
    `addPBentry` function, 381, 382–383, 631
    described, 380–381
    `makeCall` function, 380, 381, 630
    `sendDTMF` function, 380–381, 382, 631
pull notifications, 345
Push Access Protocol. *See* PAP
push architecture, 348–349
push buttons, 566
push cancellation, 358–359
push cancellation response, 358–359
Push Client, 348
`push-id` attribute, 352, 354
Push Initiator, 348
push message states, 357
push notification, 343–345
push OTA, 348–349, 366–367
Push Proxy Gateway, 348–349
push submission, 351–354
push submission response, 354–356

push systems
    Openwave. *See* Openwave
    overview, 339–342
    WAP push system. *See* WAP push system

Q

queries
    CFML, 332–333
    CGI, 324–326
    described, 288–290
    Java servlets, 299–302
    JSPs, 310–312
    PHP, 317–318

R

radio waves
    amplitude modulation (AM), 16
    described, 13–14
    frequency modulation (FM), 16
    phase modulation (PM), 16
    polarization, 17
    receiving information, 16–17
    transmitting information, 16–17
`random` function, 237, 612
RDF, 451–452
`read` function, 389
`<receive>` element, 593
`received` function, 390
receiving information, 16–17
`<refresh>` element, 162–164, 588
`refresh` function, 258, 624
refreshing the display, 162–164
`rel` attribute, 593
`release` function, 384
`remove` function, 387, 389
`removeAt` function, 243, 616
rendering issues, 509
`replace` function, 242, 615
`replaceAt` function, 243, 617

`reply-time` attribute, 355
repository, 375, 395–396
`Request` object, 282–283
request-response cycle, 46
reserved characters in URLs, 256
reserved words, 606–607
`<reset>` element, 593
`resolve` function, 254, 621
Resource Decomposition Format, 451–452
`Response` object, 283–284, 286–287
`Response.write ( )` method, 284–285
result notification, 356–358
result notification response, 356–358
return code classes, 355
root element, 96
`round` function, 264, 626
RSA, 484–485

S

`scheme` attribute, 585
scope of variables, 205
SDKs
    configuring, 655–657
    deploying WAP services, 534
    downloading, 655–657
    Ericsson WAP IDE, 655
    installing, 655–657
    Microsoft Mobile Explorer Emulator, 655
    Motorola Mobile Application Development Kit, 656
    Nokia WAP Toolkit, 656
    Openwave UP.SDK, 656–657
SDMA, 21
secret key cryptography, 481
security
    authentication, 478, 480–482
    authorization, 480–482
    CA, 488
    Certificate Authority, 488
    certificate-revocation list, 488
    checksums, 482–483
    confidentiality, 478–479, 483–485
    cost issues, 479–480
    CRL, 488
    denial of service attach, 486
    deploying WAP services, 540
    Diffie-Hellman key exchange, 489
    digital signatures, 487
    ECC, 485
    encryption, 484–485
    fingerprints, 482–483
    hashed message authentication code, 483
    hashes, 482–483
    HMAC, 483
    integrity, 479, 482–483
    Kerberos Authentication Service, 487
    key management, 487–489
    MD5 algorithm, 483
    nonrepudiability, 479, 487
    overview, 477–479
    passwords, 480
    PKI, 488
    privacy, 483–485
    public-key cryptography, 484–485
    Public-Key Infrastructure, 488
    RSA, 484–485
    secret key cryptography, 481
    service availability, 479
    service guarantee, 486–487
    session key, 485
    symmetric-key cryptography, 484
    variables, 157
    WAP security architecture, 489–504
    WTLS protocol, 483
security model, 377–378
`seed` function, 237, 613
`<select>` element, 166–176, 588–589
select list, 569
select popup, 570

Index

select radio, 570
selection lists, 565
`<send>` element, 593
`send` function, 387
`sendDTMF` function, 380–381, 382, 384, 631
`sender-address` attribute, 355
`sender-name` attribute, 355
sending notifications, 347
`sendreferer` attribute, 501–502, 580, 593, 594
server, 375
server certificates, 496
`Server` object, 285–286
service availability, 479
service guarantee, 486–487
service indication, 362–363, 376
service initiation, methods of, 376
service loading, 363–364
`service` method, 297
services, 375–376
session format, 43
session handling
    cookies, 435–438
        future issues, 441–442
        hidden postfields, 438–440
        overview, 434–435
        session objects, 437–438
        URLs, manipulating, 441
        WSP IDs, 438
session key, 485
`Session` object, 285
session objects, 437–438
`setIndicator` function, 390
`setProtection` function, 390
`setup` function, 384
`<setvar>` element
    described, 160–162, 589
        `refresh` element, 162–164
    syntax for, 160
    WAP security architecture, 500–501
`setVar` function, 257, 623

short form, intrinsic events, 147, 152–154
SignalSoft, 524–528
`signText` function, 268–269, 492
simple operators, 206–207, 595
`Sine` function, 221–225
single version of page, multiple switches, 471
site structure, building, 466–467
`size` attribute, 584
`<small>` element, 590
SMSC, 33
soft keys, 118–122
softkey icons, 564
software development kits. *See* SDKs
`source-reference` attribute, 352
Space Division Multiple Access, 21
`<spawn>` element, 593–594
speed issues in UI design, 471–473
sponsors, 519
`sqrt` function, 264, 626
`squeeze` function, 244, 617
`src` attribute, 140, 582
SSL, 491
status query, 359
status query response, 359
storage enhancements, 554
storing, 197–199
`string` data type, 201–203
string library
    calendar date, verifying, 247–250
    `charAt` function, 240, 614
    `compare` function, 244, 618
    e-mail address, verifying, 245–247
    `elementAt` function, 616
    `elements` function, 242, 615
    `find` function, 241, 615
    `format` function, 245, 250–252, 618–619
    `insertAt` function, 243–244, 617
    `isEmpty` function, 240, 614
    `length` function, 240, 613

Index 685

output, formatting, 250–252
overview, 239
`removeAt` function, 243, 616
`replace` function, 242, 615
`replaceAt` function, 243, 617
`squeeze` function, 244, 617
`subString` function, 241, 614
`toString` function, 245, 618
`trim` function, 244, 617
`<strong>` element, 590
structure and UI design, 460
subscriber IDs, 432–434
substitution of variables, 158–160
`subString` function, 241, 614
`success=%URI` channel element, 399
symmetric-key cryptography, 484
SyncML, 553, 558–559

T

`tabindex` attribute, 584, 589
`<table>` element, 133–137, 590
tables, displaying text with, 133–137
tag attribute auto-selection, 334
tag editors, 334
tags
    adding, 334
    described, 56
targeted development
    CC/PP standard, 451
    device tables, 447–450
    device types, detecting, 445–447
    header information, 450–451
    overview, 444–445
    RDF, 451–452
    UAProf, 451–456
TCP
    described, 41
    UDP compared, 41
TCP/IP
    historical background, 36–37
    Internet protocols, stack diagrams for, 38

protocol stack, 37
protocols, 37
TCP, 41
transport issues, 41–42
UDP, 41
`<td>` element, 590
TDD, 18
TDMA
    described, 19, 24
    libraries specific to, 391
TDOA, 520–521
technology, innovation, and business, 5–8
technology and society, 4–5
`<template>` element, 130–133, 591
temporary bindings, 400
text display, 105–111
3G networks
    cdma2000, 30–31
    described, 17–18
    EDGE, 31
    future issues, 546–547
    IMT-2000 upgrade path, 28–29
    overview, 27
    W-CDMA, 29–31
`<throw>` element, 594
Time Difference of Arrival, 520–521
Time Division Duplexing, 18
Time Division Multiple Access.
    See TDMA
`<timer>` element, 189–193, 591
`title` attribute, 184–185, 576, 577, 578, 583, 586, 589, 590
title bar, 563–564
TLe2e, 496–500
`toString` function, 245, 618
`<tr>` element, 591
transcoding, 512–514
transfer systems, 508–509
transmitting information, 16–17
Transport Layer End-to-End Security, 496–500

686 Index

`trim` function, 244, 617
trust of user, developing and maintaining, 462–464
2G technology
    cdmaOne, 25–26
    D-AMPS, 24
    D-AMPS+, 24–25
    described, 17–18
    GPRS, 23
    GSM, 22
    HSCSD, 23
    iDEN, 26
    overview, 21–22
    packet-data systems, 26–27
    PDC, 24
    TDMA, 24
    WAP bearers, 21–22
2.5G technology, 27
`type` attribute, 579, 583
`typeof` operator, 213

U

<u> element, 591
UAProf
    browser software profile, 456
    hardware profile, 453
    main profile, 452
    network characteristics profile, 455
    overview, 451–456
    WAP characteristics profile, 454
UDP, TCP compared to, 41
UI design
    behavior, 461
    branching, 471
    browser-specific code, 470
    browsers and, 467–471
    buckets, 469, 470
    buttons, 466
    caching, 472
    challenges of, 460–461
    consistent user interface, 462–466
    deck packaging, 472
    different versions of page, 471
    effectiveness of, evaluating, 464–466
    generally supported tags, using only, 470
    GPRS, 471
    information located on page, 465
    Instone, Keith, 464
    localization, 465
    multiple sites for different browsers, 470
    multiple task binding, 466
    navigation techniques, 464
    overview, 459–462
    portals, 466
    presentation, 461
    single version of page, multiple switches, 471
    site structure, building, 466–467
    solving problem of, 461–462
    speed issues, 471–473
    structure, 460
    trust of user, developing and maintaining, 462–464
    "what's here?", 465
    "where am I?", 465
    "where can I go?", 466
unary operators, 210, 596
`unescapeString` function, 255, 622
UP.Link server queuing, 346–347
UP.SDK 4.1, 534
URL library
    described, 252
    `escapeString` function, 254, 255–256, 622
    `GetBase` function, 254, 621
    `getCurrentCard` function, 623
    `getFragment` function, 254, 621
    `getHost` function, 252–253, 620
    `getParameters` function, 253, 620
    `getPath` function, 253, 620
    `getPort` function, 253, 620

getQuery function, 253, 621
getReferer function, 254, 621
getScheme function, 252, 620
getVar function, 623
go function, 623
isValid function, 252, 619
loadString function, 255, 622
newContext function, 623
prev function, 623
refresh function, 624
reserved characters in URLs, 256
resolve function, 254, 621
setVar function, 623
unescapeString function, 255, 622

URLs
   described, 114–116
   manipulating, 441
   repository, service accessed by URLs via the, 376
   WTA server, service accessed by URLs via, 376

US-ASCII, 513
use access pragma, 230–231
use meta pragma, 231
use url pragma, 230
user agent, 375
User Agent Profiling Mechanism. *See* UAProf

user input
   CFML, 329–331
   CGI, 320–324
   input element used to obtain, 177–189
   Java servlets, 293–299
   JSPs, 306–310
   PHP, 313–317
   processing, 286–288
   select element used to obtain, 166–176

user interface design. *See* UI design
useraccessible=true|false channel element, 399

username and password prompt, code for, 425–426
UTF-8, 509
UTF-16, 509

V

validated XML, 58–65
validating parsers, 55
value attribute, 173, 583, 586, 587, 589, 591, 593
variables
   conversion codes, 166
   declaring, 204–205
   described, 200–205
   escaping, 164–166
   illegal variable names, 158
   iname attribute, 175–176
   input element, 177–189
   ivalue attribute, 175
   legal variable names, 158
   multiple attribute, 173–174
   newcontext attribute, 156–157
   optgroup element, 171–172
   option elements, 168–170
   overview, 156
   refreshing the display, 162–164
   security, 157
   select element, 166–176
   setvar element. *See* <setvar> element
   substitution of, 158–160
   user input, input element used to obtain, 177–189
   user input, select element used to obtain, 166–176
   value attribute, 173
   vdata, 159–160
vdata, 159–160
virtual machine, 231–233
VLR, 32
voice call library, WTAI, 383–385, 632

voicemail server example, 401–402
`vspace` attribute, 582

W

W-CDMA, 29–31
WAE
  architecture, 374
  overview, 78–79
  WML, 79–80
  WMLScript, 80–82
WAP
  application servers, 541–544
  bearers, 21–22
  caching. *See* WAP caching
  commerce example, 75–76
  examples of, 72–77
  gateways, 411
  historical background, 69–72
  incoming calls interception example, 76–77
  layers of, 77–78
  location finder service example, 74–75
  news service example, 73
  obstacles to, 8
  overview, 69–72
  push system. *See* WAP push system
  security architecture. *See* WAP security architecture
  stack diagram, 78
  stock service example, 72–73
  WAE layer. *See* WAE
  WDP layer, 90
  weather application example, 74
  WSP layer, 82–85
  WTLS layer, 88–90
  WTP layer, 86–88
WAP caching
  described, 410–411
  intra-resource navigation, 411
  operations, 415–416
  WAP gateways and, 411

WAP characteristics profile, 454
WAP HTTP State Management specification, 441–442
WAP location-based services, 528–532
WAP push system
  components, 348–349
  overview, 348–349
  PAP, 349–361
  PPG, 365–366
  Push Access Protocol, 348
  push architecture, 348–349
  Push Client, 348
  Push Initiator, 348
  push OTA, 366–367
  Push Over the Air Protocol, 348–349
  Push Proxy Gateway, 348–349
WAP security architecture
  `access` element, 502–504
  application-level security, 500–504
  overview, 489–490
  security, 489–504
  `sendreferer` attribute, 501–502
  `setvar` element, 500–501
  `signText` function, 492
  SSL, 491
  TLe2e, 496–500
  Transport Layer End-to-End Security, 496–500
  WIM, 492
  Wireless Identity Module, 492
  Wireless Public-Key Infrastructure. *See* WPKI
  WML variables, 500–501
  WPKI, 492–496
  WTLS protocol, 490–491
wavelength, 12
WBMP
  described, 641
  height, 642
  image definition, 642
  overview, 137–138
  width, 642
WDP, 90

Index 689

Web server, controlling, 543
"what's here?" question as part of
    UI design, 465
"where am I?" question as part of
    UI design, 465
"where can I go?" question as part of
    UI design, 466
`while` statement, 216–217
white space, 56–57
`width` attribute, 583
WIM, 492
Wireless Identity Module, 492
wireless Internet
    overview, 3–4
    technology and society, 4–5
Wireless Markup Language. *See* WML
wireless profiled TCP, 547–550
Wireless Public-Key Infrastructure.
    See WPKI
Wireless Telephony Application.
    See WTA
Wireless Transport Layer Security.
    See WTLS protocol
WML
    `align` attribute, 107, 137
    `alt` attribute, 140
    attributes, 104–105
    `br` element, 109
    `class` attribute, 104
    code, example of, 101–104
    deck, example of, 101–102
    described, 79–80
    $ symbol, 111
    element formatting, 107–109
    example, 101–104
    functions, used to call, 379–380
    `id` attribute, 104
    images, displaying, 137–141
    `img` element, 138–141
    intrinsic events. *See* intrinsic events
    ISO-10646 method for character
        display, 109–110

    `mode` attribute, 107
    named-equivalent method for
        character display, 110–111
    navigational methods, 112–133
    overview, 97–100
    `p` element, 105–107
    `src` attribute, 140
    `table` element, 133–137
    tables, displaying text with, 133–137
    text display, 105–111
    variables, 500–501
    wbmp format, 137–138
    `xml:lang` attribute, 104–105
WML 1.3 DTD listing, 645–653
`<wml>` element, 592
WMLBrowser library
    described, 257
    example of functions in, 258–260
    `getCurrentCard` function, 258
    `getVar` function, 257
    `go` function, 257
    `newContext` function, 258
    `prev` function, 258
    `refresh` function, 258
    `setVar` function, 257
WMLScript
    advanced concepts, 227–233
    array support, 205–206
    assignment operators, 207–208
    block, 228
    `Boolean` data type, 201–203
    calling, 197–199
    comma operator, 213
    comments, 604–605
    comparison operators, 211–213
    `continue` statement, 218–219
    control statements, 214–219
    conversion rules for data types, 203
    data types, 200–204
    declaring variables, 204–205
    described, 80–82

continued

WMLScript *continued*
   escape codes, 605
   `extern` keyword, 228
   `float` data type, 201-203
   function call stack, 232
   functions, 219-220, 227-229
   future reserved words, 606-607
   `if` statement, 214-216
   initializing variables, 204-205
   instruction set pointer, 232
   `integer` data type, 201-203
   `invalid` data type, 201-203
   `isvalid` operator, 214
   libraries. *See* WMLScript libraries
   logical operators, 210-211
   operand stack, 232
   operator precedence, 214
   operators. *See* WMLScript operators
   overview, 195-196
   parameter list, 228
   parameter passing, 219-220
   pragmas, 230-231, 604
   reserved words, 606-607
   scope of variables, 205
   simple operators, 206-207
   `Sine` function, 221-225
   `for` statement, 217-218
   statements. *See* WMLScript statements
   storing, 197-199
   `string` data type, 201-203
   `typeof` operator, 213
   unary operators, 210
   `use access` pragma, 230-231
   `use meta` pragma, 231
   `use url` pragma, 230
   variables, 200-205
   virtual machine, 231-233
   `while` statement, 216-217
WMLScript libraries
   credit-card verifier, building, 271-276
   Crypto library, 268-269
   Dialogs library, 260-263
   Float library, 263-267
   `Lang` library, 234-239
   Nokia Debug library, 269-270
   Openwave Console library, 270-271
   overview, 233
   proprietary libraries, 269-271
   `signText` function, 268-269
   string library, 239-252
   URL library, 252-257
   WMLBrowser library, 257-260
WMLScript operators
   assignment operators, 595
   basic operators, 596
   comparison operators, 597
   logical operators, 597
   precedence, operator, 597-600
   simple operators, 595
   unary operators, 596
WMLScript statements
   control statements, 603
   described, 600
   looping and logical control statements, 601-602
   primary declaration statements, 601
WPKI
   CA public-key certificates, 493-494
   client public-key certificates, 494-496
   overview, 492-493
   server certificates, 496
   WAP security architecture, 492-496
`write` function, 389
WSP, 82-85
WSP IDs, 438
WTA
   architecture of, 372-374
   `base=%URI` channel element, 399
   blanket permission, 377
   channel DTD, 396-400
   `channelid=CDATA` channel element, 399

Index

channels, 395–396
context permission, 377
device-specific features, 375
`etag=nmtoken` attribute, 399
event handling, 400
`eventid=CDATA` channel element, 399
example WTA applications, 400–402
`failure=%URI` channel element, 399
global bindings, 400
`href=%URI` attribute, 399
incoming-call selection example, 400–401
`lastmod=%number` attribute, 399
`maxspace=%number` channel element, 398
`md5=nmtoken` attribute, 399
network common events, 391–394
network event, service accessed by, 376
overview, 369–374
repository, 375, 395–396
security model, 377–378
server, 375
service indication, service accessed by, 376
service initiation, methods of, 376
services, 375–376
`success=%URI` channel element, 399
temporary bindings, 400
URL via the repository, service accessed by, 376
URL via WTA server, service accessed by, 376
user agent, 375
`useraccessible=true|false` channel element, 399
voicemail server example, 401–402
WAE architecture, 374
`wtaev-cc/cc` event, 393
`wtaev-cc/cl` event, 392
`wtaev-cc/co` event, 392
`wtaev-cc/dtmf` event, 393
`wtaev-cc/ic` event, 392
`wtaev-cc/oc` event, 392
`wtaev-ms/ns` event, 394
`wtaev-nt/it` event, 393
`wtaev-nt/st` event, 393
WTAI libraries. *See* WTAI libraries
`wtaev-cc/cc` event, 393
`wtaev-cc/cl` event, 392
`wtaev-cc/co` event, 392
`wtaev-cc/dtmf` event, 393
`wtaev-cc/ic` event, 392
`wtaev-cc/oc` event, 392
`wtaev-ms/ns` event, 394
`wtaev-nt/it` event, 393
`wtaev-nt/st` event, 393
WTAI libraries
   `accept` function, 384
   `addPBentry` function, 381, 382–383
   call log library, 389–390
   call-state management, 385
   `callStatus` function, 384
   `change` function, 389
   described, 378–379, 380–381, 383
   `dialed` function, 389
   `endContext` function, 390
   `getFieldValue` function, 387, 389, 390
   `getProtection` function, 390
   GSM-specific libraries, 391
   `list` function, 384, 387
   `makeCall` function, 380, 381
   `markAsRead` function, 387
   miscellaneous library, 390–391
   `missed` function, 389
   network common WTAI library, 383–391
   network message library, 386–388
   network-specific libraries, 391
   PDC-specific libraries, 391
   phonebook library, 388–389

continued

WTAI libraries *continued*
  public WTAI library, 380–383
  `read` function, 389
  `received` function, 390
  `release` function, 384
  `remove` function, 387, 389
  `send` function, 387
  `sendDTMF` function, 380–381, 382, 384
  `setIndicator` function, 390
  `setProtection` function, 390
  `setup` function, 384
  TDMA-specific libraries, 391
  voice call library, 383–385
  WML used to call functions, 379–380
  WMLScript used to call functions, 380
  `write` function, 389
  WTAI syntax, 379–380
WTAI syntax, 379–380
WTLS protocol
  described, 88–90
  security, 483
  WAP security architecture, 490–491
WTP
  class 0 service, 87
  class 1 service, 87
  class 2 service, 88
  described, 86

X

XHTML, 547, 551–552
XML
  ATTLIST keyword, 60
  attribute defaults, 65
  attributes, 57–58
  attributes in markup, 62–65
  basic DTD markup, 59–62
  cardinality operators, 62
  case sensitivity, 56, 95
  categories for XML elements, 60–61
  CDATA attribute, 63
  concepts, 55
  content models for XML elements, 60–61
  declarations, 57–58
  DOCTYPE declaration, 59
  documents, requirements for well-formed, 55–58
  DTDs, 58–59, 97
  element definitions, 96–97
  ELEMENT keyword, 60
  element names, 56
  ENTITIES attribute, 63
  ENTITY attribute, 63
  ENTITY keyword, 60
  enumerated list attribute, 63
  ID attribute, 63
  IDREF attribute, 63
  IDREFS attribute, 63
  internal tags, 95
  NMTOKEN attribute, 63
  NMTOKENS attribute, 63
  non-validating parsers, 55
  NOTATION attribute, 63
  NOTATION keyword, 60
  overview, 53–55, 94–95
  parsers, 55, 95–96
  requirements for, 55–58
  root element, 96
  tags, 56
  validated XML, 58–65
  validating parsers, 55
  white space, 56–57
  `xml:lang` attribute, 104–105, 511–512